THE ILIAD

The Greeks believed that *The Iliad* was composed by HOMER. In our ignorance of the man, his life and his work, we are free to believe it or not. Received opinion dates him *c.* 700 BC and places him in Ionia, the Greek-inhabited coast and islands off central western Turkey. The Greeks believed the same man composed *The Odyssey*.

E. V. RIEU, editor of the Penguin Classics from 1944 to 1964, was a scholar of St Paul's School and of Balliol College, Oxford. He joined Methuen in 1923 and was Managing Director from 1933 to 1936, and then Academic and Literary Adviser. He was President of the Virgil Society in 1951 and Vice-President of the Royal Society of Literature in 1958. He was awarded an honorary D.Litt. by Leeds University in 1949 and the CBE in 1953. Among his publications are *The Flattered Flying Fish and Other Poems*, and translations of *The Odyssey*, *The Iliad*, Virgil's *Pastoral Poems*, the *Voyage of Argo* by Apollonius of Rhodes and *The Four Gospels* in the Penguin Classics. He died in 1972.

D. C. H. RIEU, his son, read Classics and English at Queen's College, Oxford. He joined the West Yorkshire Regiment and was wounded at Cheren in 1941, and awarded the Military Cross. He was Headmaster of Simon Langton Grammar School, Canterbury, from 1955 to 1977. He translated the *Acts of the Apostles* in the Penguin Classics, and revised his father's *Odyssey*, in consultation with Dr Peter Jones, and with him has revised his father's translation of *The Iliad*. On retirement he worked for Cruse Bereavement Counselling and for the Samaritans. He has been in Subud for many years, and has written books and articles about it, beginning with *A Life Within a Life* in 1963.

A Cambridge graduate with a London doctorate on Homer, PETER JONES was a schoolteacher and senior lecturer in Classics at the University of Newcastle upon Tyne. He is now a writer, broadcaster and journalist. Appointed MBE in 1983, he is Spokesman for the national Co-ordinating Committtee for Classics and founder with Jeannie Cohen of the charity Friends of Classics. He wrote the *QED* and *Eureka* series for the *Daily Telegraph*, both now published by Duckworth as *Learn Latin* and *Learn Ancient Greek*. Duckworth have also published his *Classics in Translation* (another *Telegraph* series), *Ancient and Modern* (from his weekly column in the *Spectator*) and *An Intelligent Person's Guide to Classics*. He has co-authored the *Reading Greek* and *Reading Latin* series for Cambridge, and published books, articles and commentaries on Homer.

HOMER

The Iliad

Originally translated by E. V. RIEU
Revised and updated by
PETER JONES *with* D. C. H. RIEU
Edited with an Introduction and Notes by
PETER JONES

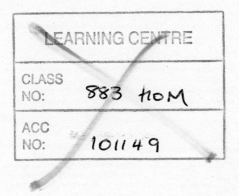
PENGUIN BOOKS

PENGUIN BOOKS

Published by the Penguin Group
Penguin Books Ltd, 80 Strand, London WC2R ORL, England
Penguin Putnam Inc., 375 Hudson Street, New York, New York 10014, USA
Penguin Books Australia Ltd, 250 Camberwell Road, Camberwell, Victoria 3124, Australia
Penguin Books Canada Ltd, 10 Alcorn Avenue, Toronto, Ontario, Canada M4V 3B2
Penguin Books India (P) Ltd, 11, Community Centre, Panchsheel Park, New Delhi – 110 017, India
Penguin Books (NZ) Ltd, Cnr Rosedale and Airborne Roads, Albany, Auckland, New Zealand
Penguin Books (South Africa) (Pty) Ltd, 24 Sturdee Avenue, Rosebank 2196, South Africa

Penguin Books Ltd, Registered Offices: 80 Strand, London WC2R ORL, England

www.penguin.com

E. V. Rieu's translation first published 1950
This revised translation first published 2003

032

Revised translation copyright © the Estate of the late E. V. Rieu, and
Peter Jones, 2003
Introduction to the 1950 Edition copyright © E. V. Rieu, 1950
Introduction, Notes and other editorial matter copyright © Peter V. Jones, 2003
All rights reserved

The moral rights of the translators and editor have been asserted

Set in 10.25/12.25 pt PostScript Adobe Sabon
Typeset by Rowland Phototypesetting Ltd, Bury St Edmunds, Suffolk
Printed in England by Clays Ltd, St Ives plc

www.greenpenguin.co.uk

MIX
Paper from
responsible sources
FSC
www.fsc.org   FSC™ C018179

Penguin Books is committed to a sustainable
future for our business, our readers and our planet.
This book is made from Forest Stewardship
Council™ certified paper.

Contents

The Iliad

Foreword

E. V. Rieu's translations of Homer, *The Odyssey* (1946, the first Penguin Classic) and *The Iliad* (1950), spoke to millions. Never before had this greatest of ancient Greek poets seemed so vivid, so immediate, so approachable to so wide an English-speaking audience.

But popular translations must move with the times. Cultural and linguistic idioms change. Research advances understanding. So in 1988 Penguin invited Dominic Rieu to revise his father's *Odyssey*, and I had the pleasure of acting as consultant. Now the roles have been reversed, and Dominic has acted as consultant for my revision of his father's *Iliad*. He has been an enthusiastic supporter of the project, a wise, perceptive and stimulating critic, restraining and encouraging in equal measure.

This is a revision, not a new translation, but it is a thorough revision, involving more than updating idiom and making technical adjustments in the light of recent scholarship (for which see Notes on this Revision, pp. lxiii–lxv). Consequently, readers can expect to find more changes in Rieu's *Iliad* than in Dominic Rieu's revision of his *Odyssey*. I have also written a new Introduction, added chapter summaries, marginal notes, appendices and an Index, and revised Rieu's list of human and divine characters. The commentaries written by M. M. Willcock and W. Leaf and the commentary series edited by G. S. Kirk have never been far from my elbow (see Further Reading).

My best thanks go to Andrew Morley for the maps and the sketch of the plain of Troy – Ilium, the Greek camp and

surrounding environs (sea, rivers, Mount Ida, etc.) – as Homer
might possibly have envisaged it.

PVJ
Newcastle upon Tyne
April 2002

Introduction

READING HOMER'S *ILIAD*

The *Iliad* is the first work of Western literature, a 15,000-line epic poem composed *c.* 700 BC, so called because it tells of an incident that occurred during the Greek siege of *Ilium*, a town in the region of *Troy* (modern north-west Turkey).*

A reader who wishes to sample it can use the summaries at the start of each book to keep abreast of the plot. Book 1, the quarrel between Agamemnon and Achilles, explains Achilles' anger and withdrawal from battle. The duel between Menelaus and *Hector* and the subsequent *APHRODITE–Paris*–Helen scene in Book 3 introduce the *Trojan* enemy and the reason for the Greek siege. The *Hector–Andromache* scene in Book 6 puts the *Trojan* hero *Hector* in perspective. Book 9 is central, because the *Iliad* hinges on Achilles' rejection here of Agamemnon's offer of reconciliation. The seduction of ZEUS in Book 14 shows Homer's touch at its lightest. At this point the epic becomes more and more centred on Achilles, as his personal tragedy unfolds. Books 16, 18 (the death of Patroclus and Achilles' decision to return to battle) and 22–24 (the death of *Hector*, Patroclus' burial and the return of *Hector*'s body) form the irreducible kernel.

---

* In this Introduction, please note that Trojan names and places are printed in italics (e.g. *Hector*); gods are in capitals (ZEUS), pro-Trojan gods in italic capitals (*APOLLO*). See pp. xli–xlvi for notes to the Introduction.

AN OUTLINE PLOT OF *THE ILIAD*

Trojan Paris seduced Menelaus' wife Helen and took her back to *Ilium*. Menelaus appealed to his brother Agamemnon, and together they raised an expedition to bring her back. The *Iliad* is set in the last year of the Greek siege of *Ilium* and begins with a quarrel.

Agamemnon, leader of the Greek expeditionary force, has been given as booty the daughter of a local priest of *APOLLO*. He is forced to return her and demands a replacement. After a furious quarrel with Achilles, he takes Briseis, Achilles' prize, prompting Achilles and his close companion Patroclus to walk out of the fighting. Achilles' divine mother THETIS wrings a promise out of ZEUS, king of the gods, that the Greeks will start to lose, so that Achilles will be welcomed back and the insult made good. This immediately causes trouble with ZEUS' wife HERA, who supports the Greeks (Book 1).

In Books 2–8, Homer lays the immediate quarrel aside and presents the broader picture – the Greek and *Trojan* combatants on earth, and the gods on Olympus. We see Agamemnon testing the morale of the troops and making a fool of himself (2); *Trojan Paris* defeated in a duel with Menelaus, but saved by his patron goddess *APHRODITE* (3); the gods most hostile to *Troy*, HERA and ATHENE, getting the fighting started again (4); the Greek hero Diomedes routing the *Trojans*, and even wounding *APHRODITE* and the war-god *ARES* (5); *Troy's* greatest fighter *Hector* in moving conversation with his wife *Andromache* and their child (6); *Hector* fighting an inconclusive duel with Ajax, and the Greeks building a defensive wall and ditch (7); and ZEUS tipping the scales in favour of the *Trojans*, who drive the Greeks right back behind their new defences and camp out for the night on the plain (8).

Agamemnon now acknowledges that he was wrong to insult Achilles and agrees to send an embassy to him with massive compensation to beg him to return. Odysseus, Phoenix and Ajax lead the embassy, but to their amazement Achilles rejects them. Achilles' tragedy begins here (Book 9).

In Books 10–15, we see Homer preparing the groundwork for the fatal entry of Patroclus, Achilles' close companion, into battle. Diomedes and Odysseus go on a night expedition into the *Trojan* camp and steal the famous horses of *Rhesus* (10); Agamemnon enjoys a brief solo feat of arms, but the Greeks are driven back. Achilles sends Patroclus to find out what is happening, and wise old Nestor suggests to Patroclus that, if Achilles will not return to the fighting, Patroclus might, dressed in Achilles' armour (11). Meanwhile the *Trojans* force home their attack on the Greek defences. Part of the parapet is torn away; *Hector* smashes down the gate and the *Trojans* pour through (12). ZEUS, assuming the *Trojans* will now win, turns his attention elsewhere, and POSEIDON takes the opportunity to rally the Greeks (13). HERA keeps ZEUS occupied by making love to him. The *Trojans* are routed (14). ZEUS wakes up and, enraged, threatens the gods with violence if they intervene any more. POSEIDON withdraws, *APOLLO* destroys the Greek defences and *Hector* leads the *Trojans* right up to the Greek ships (15).

Patroclus now returns to Achilles and repeats Nestor's suggestion that he go into battle dressed in Achilles' armour. Achilles (fatally) agrees. In a great solo feat of arms Patroclus drives the *Trojans* right back, but is stripped of his armour by *APOLLO* and killed by *Hector* (Book 16). A fierce battle breaks out over Patroclus' body, and *Hector* dons Patroclus' (i.e. Achilles') armour. The Greeks retreat with Patroclus' body (Book 17). Achilles hears about Patroclus' death, acknowledges it is entirely his fault and announces that he will have his revenge on *Hector*. THETIS tells him he will die immediately afterwards, and Achilles accepts the price. Herein lies his tragedy. HEPH-AESTUS makes new armour for Achilles, including the famous shield (Book 18).

Agamemnon and Achilles are reconciled and the gifts delivered to Achilles, who is now urgent for revenge on *Hector* (Book 19). He goes on such a murderous rampage that POSEIDON has to save *Aeneas* from him, and *APOLLO* whisks *Hector* away to safety too (Book 20). The River-god tries to drown Achilles because he has blocked up the River's channels with the dead; even the gods fall to fighting each other (Book 21).

Achilles isolates *Hector* and kills him. Against all custom, he keeps and mutilates the body (Book 22). Patroclus is cremated, and Achilles holds funeral games (Book 23). Still unable to reconcile himself to events, Achilles drags *Hector*'s body futilely round Patroclus' grave-mound. The gods agree Achilles has gone too far and arrange for *Hector*'s father *Priam*, King of Troy, to supplicate Achilles for the return of *Hector*'s body. In the night encounter in Achilles' quarters, old *Priam* succeeds. The *Iliad* ends with laments for *Hector*, and his burial (Book 24).

The *Iliad* ends there, but Homer has still left us with a clear notion of what the immediate future holds – death for Achilles and destruction for *Ilium*.

THE FOCUS OF *THE ILIAD*

As Aristotle saw, Homer decided not to work through the whole Trojan War year by year, but to direct the action of the epic round a single theme – the anger of Achilles announced in the first line of the epic, which brought endless sufferings to his own side (as Homer at once points out) and ultimately himself. As a result, the *Iliad* is distinguished by a tight economy of action. For example, four-fifths of the action occurs on a mere four days and intervening nights (the whole of Books 11–18 takes place over only twenty-four hours). The story centres round the aristocratic heroes, not the general mass of troops. Very many heroes are named, but Homer selects about twenty characters in all from both sides to concentrate on (including *Trojan* women). The human action takes place either in or around the Greek camp on the beach, or in *Ilium*, or on the battlefield, while the divine action takes place on Mount Olympus or one of the mountains around *Troy*, for example *Mount Ida* (see map 1). Nor are the Greeks and *Trojans* significantly differentiated by Homer. For the sake of the story they worship the same gods, speak the same language and share the same assumptions and values. Both armies desire to end the war and live with their families at home, in peace, though the Greeks, as aggressors on a mission, come over as more single-minded than the *Trojans*, defending their homes, for whom there is more to life than battle.

At the same time, however, Homer creates the impression that he is covering the whole war, and even the periods before and after it. In the course of the *Iliad*, for example, and quite outside the time-frame of the story itself, we learn that the goddess THETIS married the mortal Peleus, producing Achilles. Homer gives us a charming picture of Achilles as a baby, an insight into his education, and how his close companion Patroclus – so crucial to the *Iliad* – came to live in his household.

Further, we are told that *Paris*, handsome son of *Priam*, selected *APHRODITE* as the winner of the golden apple – Homer does not mention the apple – and was granted as his reward the most beautiful woman in the world, Helen, wife of Menelaus, ruler of Sparta in Greece. On a visit to Sparta, *Paris* broke all rules of hospitality, seduced Helen and took her back to *Ilium*, much to the disgust of his brother *Hector*, *Troy*'s greatest fighter. Menelaus then appealed to his brother Agamemnon, and together they raised an expedition to retrieve Helen. To judge from Homer's catalogue of ships, it consisted of 29 contingents led by 44 commanders from 175 Greek localities in 1,186 ships containing (one may guess) 100,000 men. The expedition set off with favourable omens.[1]

We are informed that, when the expedition landed in *Troy*, Protesilaus was the first man killed as he leapt ashore; that Menelaus and Odysseus tried to settle the matter by negotiation; that they were rejected – one *Trojan* even thought Menelaus should be murdered then and there – and for nine long years the Greeks laid siege to *Ilium*, without success. Homer looks back to a few incidents from this period, but there was really very little to say about it. He could not construct a convincing epic for a Greek audience about the Greeks' nine-year *inability* to take *Troy*. Nor could any Greek: all other accounts of the Trojan War struggle to fill these years convincingly.

There is, however, one exception. The seeds of Homer's *Iliad* lie in events which took place immediately before the story starts – the Greek raids led by Achilles on neighbouring *Trojan* towns for the purpose of aggrandizement. Two significant towns catch Homer's especial attention: *Thebe*, where Achilles captured the girl *Chryseis* over whose ownership the *Iliad* begins; and *Lyrnessus*, where Achilles captured his favourite woman *Briseis*. Further, Homer lays emphasis on the division of spoils that took place after such raids, and the resentment Achilles felt at its unfairness.[2]

The *Iliad*, in other words, seems to cover much more than a few days during the last year of the Trojan War. In the first work of Western literature, we find an economy and focus combined with a breadth of vision that have informed narrative literature ever since.

THE CENTRAL THEME OF *THE ILIAD*

The purpose of this section is to re-run the *Iliad* and offer some sense of the main issues underlying the narrative. At its heart, the epic raises for Achilles the question 'What is a man's life worth?'. Three preliminary points must be made.

First, battle is sometimes described in Homer as the place 'where men win glory' and, in a trivial sense, the glory of the Homeric hero bears comparison with that of a modern professional sportsman: both perform in the public arena, nothing else counts but winning, and the purpose of the exercise is to gain wealth and respect. So victory and its rewards, material and social, are the Homeric heroes' priorities, the ultimate ambition being *kleos*, fame that stays with you after death; while judgement of success or failure lies in the first place with one's peers, not with any internalized sense of self-worth (which does not mean heroes do not have that sense – Achilles certainly does). Defeat and insult are both taken extremely badly.

Second, heroes are complex and richly characterized humans, not unthinking fighting machines. They would far rather not have to fight at all. *Hector* freely acknowledges that Achilles is

a better fighter than he is. Diomedes can absorb an insult when
it is not deserved, because he knows what he is capable of (but
he does not forget it). But most of all, since in the martial world
of the *Iliad* failure usually means death, fighting is not glorified
for its own sake. *ARES* is the most hateful of gods, and war is
described with a whole range of painful epithets ('with all its
tears', etc.). The heroes do not want to die. Time and again
Homer emphasizes their desire to return home, to the family.
Battle is a means to an end, a way of life that gives them the
chance to win a reputation among their fellows and longed-for
immortal glory, but as the moving *Hector–Andromache* scene
shows, it is set within a larger human framework.[3]

Finally, we must not entertain the idea that the Greek army
is like a modern army, with a clear command structure which
automatically makes disobedience to Agamemnon 'wrong'.
Agamemnon is acknowledged as overall leader of the expedition
by virtue of the number of troops he brought with him, but as
the constant debates make clear, authority is not taken for
granted: it is demonstrated by the ability to win an argument
and to persuade the rest to acquiesce (whence the requirement
for heroes to be effective speakers as well as fighters). Only on
Olympus is there an undisputed master who can command
automatic obedience – ZEUS – and that, in the end, is down to
his sheer physical superiority.

The problem Achilles faces is that he is fated to live only a
short life and therefore knows he has little time in which to earn
eternal fame. So life to him seems peculiarly intense, and when
in Book 1 Agamemnon says that he may well take Achilles' girl
Briseis in place of *Chryseis*, that is serious enough for a man
like Achilles, known for his love of a quarrel, to threaten to
abandon the army. His argument is set out at 1.149–171: (i)
The *Trojans* never did me any harm, (ii) we are fighting for
Menelaus' and Agamemnon's honour, but (iii) while I do all the
fighting, I am given minimal reward, and (iv) now Agamemnon
proposes to take away even what I have been given.

Agamemnon's response precipitates Achilles' exit: he both
urges Achilles to leave the fighting and assures him that he
will certainly take *Briseis*. In other words, Agamemnon is

announcing before the whole army that Achilles, their greatest
fighter, is surplus to his and the expedition's requirements,
and that he (Agamemnon) will do precisely what he likes with
Achilles' hard-won property. It is this violent, public, unjust and
therefore deeply humiliating attack on Achilles' assessment of
his importance to the Greek army, followed by Agamemnon's
seizure of what is his by rights, that drives Achilles to contem-
plate killing Agamemnon, an act from which ATHENE barely
restrains him. It is significant that no Greek objects to Achilles
walking out: Agamemnon is clearly in the wrong and later
admits it.[4]

But in Book 9, when Agamemnon relents and agrees to offer
compensation, Achilles' position has changed. There is now
nothing that will induce him to fight. He repeats to the embassy
the original accusation that he does all the fighting and Agamem-
non gets all the rewards; but now he goes further. No material
compensation can pay him back, because all the compensation
in the world cannot equal the worth of one's life.

The embassy is stunned by this response, and has every right
to be: if Achilles will not accept compensation, offered through
the mediation of those who are his closest friends, what will he
accept? This is simply not the way the material-oriented heroic
world works. The leadership is equally stunned when it hears
of the failure of the mission. Diomedes, however, points
out that the embassy was always going to be a waste of time;
Achilles has never been anything but his own man; he will fight
when he wants to, and there is nothing that can be done about
it. Diomedes is right, as is Achilles' companion Patroclus, who
later points out that, since a hero is supposed to benefit his
people, Achilles' angry absence from battle serves no purpose:
'You and your disastrous greatness – what will future genera-
tions have to thank you for, if *you* do nothing to prevent the
Greeks' humiliating destruction?'

Diomedes sees that Achilles is not dissatisfied with the theory
of material compensation for wrongs suffered. He is just being
Achilles. If Achilles knew what he wanted to induce him back
to the fighting, all he had to do was to say: the embassy would
have promised it at once (and, incidentally, the *Iliad* would have

ended there). But all he knows is that Agamemnon must 'pay back the whole heart-rending insult'. No member of the embassy enquires what he means by this. They are doing all they can, and Achilles is not interested. No wonder Aristotle calls Achilles 'a good man, but a paradigm of obstinacy'.[5]

But if the consequences for the Greeks are bad, they are catastrophic for Achilles. His decision not to rejoin the fighting is the beginning of the end for him. It is the first of a sequence of decisions he now takes in full confidence that he has judged the situation correctly, when in fact he has got it all utterly, and ultimately tragically, wrong. In Book 11, he feels the Greeks really will beg him to return now. But they do not. In Book 16, when *Hector* sets fire to a ship, Achilles agrees that Patroclus should go out to fight in his place to avert the immediate crisis: that, he feels, should solve the problem. He is wrong: *Hector* kills Patroclus. In Book 18 Achilles decides to avenge Patroclus' death. That at least should bring satisfaction. It does not: killing *Hector* achieves nothing for Achilles' state of mind. The burial of Patroclus and the funeral games at least bring some sense of reconciliation with Agamemnon, yet Achilles still cannot sleep and continues to mutilate *Hector*. But over-riding all of these considerations is the grim consequence of his decision to avenge Patroclus' death: it will mean his own death soon after, and he takes the decision in the full knowledge that this is the case. Some tragedies take a man unawares. *Hector* is one such: it is only at the end that *Hector* realizes his time has come, though we have been alert to it well before that. Patroclus is another (though in true tragic fashion Book 16 is full of ironies and markers of his impending doom which none but the audience can see). Achilles looks his tragedy full in the face and does not flinch.[6]

What is a man's life worth? Achilles gives his answer in Book 18 – a man's life is worth revenge on the person who killed his beloved companion. It is in many ways a horrifying decision: Achilles is signing his own death warrant. But it is also in many ways a more than heroic one. The Homeric world of material compensation and heroic status, such critical issues for Achilles back in Book 1, seems far away. Achilles chooses to die not primarily to win everlasting glory (though he hopes his feat of arms will achieve this), but because he holds himself responsible for Patroclus' death.

Nevertheless, even the immediate consequences for Achilles are grim: self-willed lover of conflict he may have been already, but the poet goes out of his way to emphasize how far he plunges off the scale of human normality as he seeks this single-minded revenge. He becomes maddened, almost bestial, in his desire for it, and the gods agree: Achilles is like a lion, destroying pity and knowing no shame.

In his deranged state, it is little wonder that revenge brings Achilles no comfort. This is what makes Book 24 so remarkable. Consumed by his desire for revenge but confronted by its failure to resolve his anguish, Achilles ends his assault on the body of the dead *Hector* and returns it to his father *Priam*. But this is no last-minute conversion, no sudden seeing of the light, even though ZEUS assures THETIS that returning the body will bring Achilles glory. Achilles knows it is ZEUS' will, and that he has no option. Further, his famous speech of consolation to *Priam* is more 'counselling' than consolation. He sees their tragedies jointly intertwined. Life, says Achilles, is at best a mixture of good and ill, as it has been for both *Priam* and Achilles' father Peleus: by Achilles' efforts *Priam*, a father, has lost his son *Hector*; by these same efforts Achilles has lost Patroclus, and his father Peleus will shortly have lost *his* son too. But there is also an extraordinary moment when *Priam* and Achilles gaze on each other in admiration – as if *Priam* sees something of *Hector* in the man who slaughtered his beloved son, and Achilles something of the old, lonely Peleus – soon to be yet more lonely – in the father of his worst enemy. Surely here we sense that there is more to life than revenge, more to manhood than the slaughter of men.

Here, then, in the West's first work of literature, we see the intensive literary exploitation of a great human theme which seems to touch us all, however particular (and alien) the setting. It is not so much about what happens – the action is very limited – as what is going on in the mind of its central figure, Achilles. It will be a model for much future literature.

The *Iliad* is also the world's first tragedy. Two hundred years before the Greek tragic poets invented the medium for the stage, Homer had grasped its essential nature in the figure of Patroclus (see above, and note 6) and even more of Achilles – an initially wronged hero, of divine ancestry, who finds his world inexplicably turning to ashes as a result of the decisions he has freely, if intemperately, taken, whose greatness lies in his refusal to disclaim the responsibility for his actions, even though his own death will be the inevitable consequence.[7]

THE GODS

The ancient Greek historian Herodotus argued that Homer (and Hesiod, a near contemporary epic poet who composed *Theogony*, 'The Birth of the Gods') gave the Greeks their divinities.[8] His point was that, from time immemorial, gods had been worshipped, through ritual, as faceless powers representing almost any aspect of human existence (see 'Personification' in Appendix 1), who needed appeasing in order to stop them acting against humans with all the blind, irresistible force of (say) gravity. But Homer and Hesiod for the first time gave gods an individual, human face and made a community out of them, informing us of their birth, family relationships, character and everyday activities.

This humanness of the gods is evident in the most mundane details. ZEUS is their head, and they quarrel, as all families do. They have a daily life. After a hard day's work they enjoy an evening meal (ambrosia) and drink (nectar), tease each other, listen to the entertainment, and go to bed with their wives in their houses on Olympus. Even more amazing, these immortals do things during the day which frequently bring them nothing but pain, notably battling on behalf of their mortal favourites. The queen of Olympus, HERA, comments on the sweat she expended assembling the Greek army to attack *Troy*; *APHRODITE* complains that the Greek hero Diomedes has wounded her on the wrist (ZEUS smiles and tells her to concentrate on the pleasures of the marriage-bed); *ARES* the war-god complains that Diomedes has stabbed him in the belly (ZEUS tells him to stop whining).[9]

Gods in Homer have their favourites and regularly interact with humans in the *Iliad*, usually without disguise.[10] *APHRO-DITE*, for example, was goddess of the force we associate with sexual desire, and since *Paris* selected her as the winner of the golden apple, she gave him Helen and supported him and the *Trojans* throughout the *Iliad*. Nevertheless, there could be tension in such relationships. Here, for example, *APHRODITE* has instructed Helen to return from the battlements and make love to *Paris*. Helen refuses:

'No, go and sit with him yourself. Forget you are a goddess. Never set foot on Olympus again but go and agonize over Paris, go and pamper him, and one day he may make you his wife – or his concubine. I refuse to go and share that man's bed again – it would be quite wrong. There is not a woman in Troy who would not blame me if I did. I have enough trouble to put up with already.'

This is quite remarkable. Helen is not afraid to argue with a very goddess, and in the most abrasive terms. She speaks as woman to woman. If we associate ancient gods with the mysterious, the numinous, the irrational or the terrifying, Helen's response to *APHRODITE* does not suggest she feels this way about the goddess.[11] But the situation changes abruptly with *APHRODITE*'s reply:

Enraged, celestial Aphrodite spoke to her:
  'Obstinate wretch! Don't get the wrong side of me, or I may desert you in my anger and detest you as vehemently as I have loved you up till now, and provoke Greeks and Trojans alike to such hatred of you that you would come to a dreadful end.'
  So she spoke, and Helen, child of Zeus, was terrified. She wrapped herself up in her shining white robe and went off in silence. (3.406–20)

APHRODITE's reply speaks for itself. No human crosses a god. Gods, in other words, work to extremes. They love you or hate you, support you or disown you, are close or distant.[12] It is part of the magic of Homer that he is so effortlessly able, like Mozart, to reconcile the intimate with the divine.[13]

Whatever their relationship with their favourites, however, Homer's gods are immortal and all-powerful and, ultimately, will brook no effort by mortals to threaten their superiority. They can be utterly ruthless: *APOLLO* mercilessly strips Patroclus so that he can be killed, *HERA* easily barters away her three favourite towns if only *Troy* is destroyed. They can also be kind, like *IRIS* comforting the old king *Priam*; they can be magnificent, like *POSEIDON* racing across the waters on his chariot.

Yet even the gods must acknowledge *ZEUS* as their master: when he nods, Olympus shakes and his will is determined, however much they may try to resist it. So if humans *talk* about, and to, the gods in almost off-hand terms, as if gods were just other, rather more powerful human beings, Homer knows there is more to them than that. When he describes gods in the third-person narrative, they can be majestic beings. For all their occasional triviality, Homer provided the Greeks with a vision that, particularly in the person of *ZEUS*, could eventually translate into a principle of order, and even monotheism.[14]

Nevertheless, one can see why many serious-minded later thinkers (like Plato[15]) took such exception to Homer's treatment of the gods. It is worth quoting here the famous conclusion of an ancient critic we know as Longinus (first century AD?): 'in relating the gods' wounds, quarrels, revenges, tears, imprisonments and manifold misfortunes, Homer, or so it seems to me, has done his best to make the men of the Trojan War gods, and the gods men.'[16] Longinus finds this shocking and explains that the behaviour of the gods must therefore be interpreted allegorically. This was a common response to Homer from as early as the fifth century BC and became even more so in the Christian era when the church acknowledged the primacy of Graeco-Roman education but had to find some way of turning pagan gods into good Christians.

As for destiny, or fate, it is important to remember that, in the absence of sacred scriptures and so of dogma, Greeks were not theologians. For Homer, fate was a purely literary device which he summoned or shelved as he saw fit: it was the will of the poet. By the same token, Homer assigned responsibility for men's actions to both divine will and human impulse at the same time.[17] He could not distinguish between the two (any more than we can): it is as if men and gods were both fully responsible for what happened.

These features generate a sharp sense of human vulnerability and greatness. The epic is being recited by a third-person, omniscient narrator, Homer. He always tells us, his audience, what is happening on Olympus (the comparison with Greek tragedy, where in the absence of the omniscient narrator the world is far more bleak and unknowable, is marked). But his heroes, for the most part, have no idea. This contrast generates pathos, as frail humans battle, without complaint and often with glorious confidence, against these impossible odds. Their deaths in particular can be very moving. Even the gods weep.[18] Perhaps more important, the story is elevated out of the particular and takes on a more general human significance. War between heroes on the battlefield of *Troy* somehow seems to stand for life itself, in all its glory and hopelessness.

POETRY AND HISTORY, FACT AND FICTION: WAS THERE A TROJAN WAR?

Homeric poetry is oral in style (see next section) and its language is of ancient origin. As a result, it is likely that epic poetry was handed down by oral poets from as early as late bronze-age Greece, the so-called 'Mycenaean' age which ended *c.* 1100 BC. That may explain how Homer (*c.* 700 BC) appears to 'know' about bronze armour, for example, and fighting from chariots, unknown in Homer's day, and can describe a city like Mycenae as 'rich in gold' (which indeed it was in the late bronze age, but not in his). It is not, then, impossible, that details of a war between Greeks and *Trojans* round *Ilium* could have been passed down too. This is one of the grounds on which scholars have claimed to find history in Homer.

Unfortunately, we cannot conclude from this that the *Iliad* contains a specific history of a specific Trojan War. First, oral epic poets were not ancient historians, working from historical sources (let alone a text). Homeric epic in fact contains no historical understanding of the Mycenaean world at all: one would never guess from Homer, for example, that writing (Linear B) was used in the bronze age to record the workings of an economically complex, palace-based society.

Second, the end to which oral epic poets worked was the depiction of heroism in action – the winning of glory and fame through warfare and adventure, and the problems this raised. Homer is not unique in this. For example, the Babylonian epic of *Gilgamesh* (far older than Homer) bears some striking general and specific resemblances to the *Iliad*, e.g. Achilles and Gilgamesh are both sons of goddesses; both lose their dearest companions; both are devastated by their loss and take extreme action to try to compensate for it; and so on.[19] Again, it is a universal characteristic of such story-telling to be influenced by the subject-matter and story patterns of folklore and myth. Herodotus already pointed out the folklore nature of the *Iliad* when he argued that no king in real life would ever allow his city to be sacked, his children to be killed and his people to be destroyed because his son had returned home with a foreign female.[20]

Third, the Homers of the Greek world recreated living stories for contemporary audiences by age-old techniques of oral composition common to all heroic poetry, i.e. by stringing together typical sequences of 'themes'. For example, the first book of the *Iliad* contains an introduction, a supplication, a prayer, a divine visitation, summoning and dismissing an assembly, a journey by ship, a sacrifice, meals and entertainment, all entirely common to this type of composition. If one added arming/dressing, various types of battle-scene, messenger-scenes, reception-scenes, omens and sleeping, one would have covered the basic compositional elements of the *Iliad*.[21]

As a result of these sorts of considerations, one could conclude that the whole *Iliad* is invented: the Greeks never did attack

Ilium, and there was no tradition of singing about a Trojan War in bronze-age Greece. But even if there is some truth to a Greek attack on *Ilium*, it is highly likely that four hundred years of oral story-telling obliterated any serious record of it. As for the antique gloss – chariots and bronze armour and so on – poets had an interest in making their poems seem old and authoritative; it may be the gloss was added by the poets themselves. Consequently, many scholars argue that Homer's *Iliad* is much more the creation of contemporary and near-contemporary eighth-century BC culture. It was a response to the demands of a Greek audience of Homer's time who inhabited the region known to Greeks as Ionia, to the south of *Troy* (see map 3: this is why, of course, there are so few *Trojan* place-names in that area). For some reason, now irrecoverable, they wanted an epic about Greek dealings with their neighbours to the north. Homer, drawing on all the resources of oral poetry, gave them one.[22]

Yet this surely cannot be the *whole* story. Even if the *Iliad* is essentially fiction, fiction does not preclude history. After all, novels are fictions but they usually try to evoke a real world, and the real world, at least of Homer's day, looms large throughout the poem. For example, the economic background to the *Iliad* is agricultural, as it was for the whole of the ancient world (and indeed the modern world till the Industrial Revolution). Like the farmers of the ancient Greek poet Hesiod, warriors made their living from the land. Homer does nothing to disguise this world, which constantly emerges even in the heat of battle.[23] Pasturing herds is the real work of the day, and a hero may even come across a nymph while out in the fields, as *Bucolion* did, or some goddesses, as both *Paris*' and *Aeneas*' father *Anchises* did; less fortunately, he may meet a rampant Achilles, as *Andromache*'s brothers did. Diomedes raises horses, *Andromache* personally feeds *Hector*'s, *Pandarus* paints a moving picture of how he looks after his, *Priam* accuses his sons of being sheep- and cattle-thieves and himself rolls in the dung of the courtyard when he hears of *Hector*'s death. 'Shepherd of the people' is a common epithet for these heroes, values are assessed in worth of oxen and the fighting is constantly being likened to farmers defending their livestock against wild animals. The world of the heroes 'back home' is that of the farmer, and it is a proud calling. This is a constant and realistic background to the *Iliad*'s primarily martial, heroic world.[24]

Consider, too, the political implications of Homer's depiction of the Greek army at *Troy*: at one moment it seems to be one united 'people', at another a loose confederation of troops drawn from contingents from all over Greece, whose leaders are in constant conflict with each other to win prestige. If this is a fair description, the army's situation may well reflect Homer's contemporary world, in which old-style, landed aristocrats continued to compete among themselves as a more 'democratic' city-state world began slowly to emerge.

Homer, then, hardly surprisingly, reflects his own world. If therefore one wishes to contend that he also reflects, in some measure, a past world, even one in which a Graeco-*Trojan* conflict did actually take place, one would have to argue that it is surely too much of a coincidence that Homer just happened to guess correctly when he described heroes living in walled palaces, carrying bronze weapons, wearing bronze armour and shin-guards, and fighting from chariots, or that Mycenae was rich in gold (7.180, 11.46). One could then add to the case with reference to his Greek 'catalogue of ships' and list of *Trojan* contingents at the end of Book 2, which do seem to present a picture of a world bearing some resemblance to the bronze-age period (see maps 3 and 5 defining the areas from which the various contingents listed in the catalogues come).

Finally, one could point out that archaeologists have uncovered a flourishing town in the region Homer calls *Troy* (and we call the *Troad*, maps 1, 2). The mound in that area, named Hisarlik in Turkish and excavated by the adventurer and fantasist Heinrich Schliemann from 1870 to 1890,[25] was certainly identified by later Greeks and Romans with Homer's *Ilium*, as one can tell from the monuments they left there. Archaeology shows this town was subject to attack and siege around 1200 BC and also that it was in contact with bronze-age Greeks; and it is interesting that the fifth-century BC Greek historians Herodotus and Thucydides date the Trojan War to round about that same period by counting back generations (some of which are, admittedly, mythical). Nor is Hisarlik too small to have been besieged for ten years, as seemed to be the case till recently. It now appears that Schliemann uncovered merely the citadel. New excavations have been interpreted to mean that the town was ten times larger than first thought: it extended to the south and was defended by a substantial ditch.

All that makes a respectable case for evidence of the deep past in Homer – but again, one has to ask whether it makes a case for a Homeric Trojan war? Opponents of the 'Trojan war' scenario would reply that there is no evidence of any sort that any attack on Hisarlik was ever carried out by Greeks. They would agree that the *Iliad* contains references to the geography of the *Troad* area, suggesting the poet knew it well (e.g. 9.5, 12.10–33), and that *Ilium* as Homer describes it may bear some resemblance to Hisarlik, but they would object that this tells us nothing about the historicity of the epic. Homer needed an ancient site for the battle: Hisarlik may have provided a perfect model for his imagination to work on. Nor does Homer provide us with enough evidence to suggest that he had a late bronze-age view of the area round Hisarlik, whose coastline had altered radically by Homer's time, as core-drilling reveals. Certainly Homer presents a broad mental picture of what he thought the *Trojan* battlefield looked like, which Andrew Morley has made his best guess at representing (map 1), but that is not evidence for a Trojan War. (It is worth pointing out here that there will always be arguments about where the poet mentally envisaged the Greek camp and ships to be. Some place them to the north, along the shore of the Hellespont; others to the west, along the Aegean shore.)

On the balance of evidence at the moment, then, we may conclude that Homer's poetry can be linked with a tradition of oral poetry that existed in the Mycenaean age. But the *Iliad* represents what Homer *thought* the heroic world should have looked like: in other words, he took what the tradition offered him and shaped it into the *Iliad* we have today, in accordance with his own cultural assumptions and narrative priorities as an oral epic poet. To that extent, the question whether there really was a Trojan War is irrelevant to Homer's purposes. If there was one, we must find primary evidence for it outside the *Iliad*. Who knows? Such evidence may indeed emerge, at some time in the future.

But whatever conclusions we wish to draw about the extent to which our *Iliad* might reflect anything that happened around Hisarlik in the thirteenth century BC, we must end by pointing out that Hisarlik itself was an important location at that time in its own right. The core-drilling referred to above has revealed the existence of a bay at that time reaching north from the Dardanelles to Hisarlik (as Morley's representation shows). Since the entrance to the Dardanelles from the Aegean was hampered especially at this point by adverse currents and winds, Hisarlik would have made the perfect harbour in which to shelter. Hisarlik also traded widely in metalwork and textiles, and bred horses (hence those 'horse-taming Trojans'). All this accounts for its great wealth, which can be judged from its fine walls and '*Priam*'s treasure'.[26] Like Constantinople, it was defensible and could have controlled shipping on a major east–west route. So, in the thirteenth century BC, it was a place of strategic importance and certainly did have links with the Greek world.[27]

But, unlike Constantinople, it was unable to maintain its position. The rivers *Scamander* and *Simoïs* slowly silted it up. By Roman times, because of the presumed Homeric connection, it had largely become a tourist attraction.[28]

SOME TECHNICALITIES OF ORAL POETRY

In the 1920s, the American Milman Parry demonstrated that Homeric poetry was oral in style. This meant, first, that it was traditional, developed over hundreds of years of story-telling; indeed, it is clear that much of Homer's language is so ancient that neither he nor we can be certain about the meanings of some of the words he used (see p. lxiv). Second, it meant that it was the sort of poetry that could be composed by professional, trained poets, in performance, without the help of writing.

Since the metre in which Homeric poetry was composed is very complex, the training of poets like Homer must have consisted of listening to and learning from other poets fluent in the medium. To put it rather crudely, the fledgling poet must have somehow got at his fingertips thousands of almost pre-packaged but still flexible phrases, sentences and even whole scenes which fitted the metre and which had, over centuries of story-telling, turned out to be indispensable for the on-the-spot construction of long epic poems.

This accounts for all the verbal repetitions in Homer: everything from 'glorious *Hector*' through 'swift-footed godlike Achilles' to 'he thudded to the ground, and his armour clattered about him'. About a fifth of Homer is, in fact, repeated. It also accounts for the patterns of action that recur again and again, the building-blocks of scene construction that are also part of the oral poet's 'kit'. Scenes of arrival, for example, are structured as follows: A sets off; A arrives; A finds B; B is doing something; others are doing things too; A speaks.[29] Battle-scenes too follow regular patterns, for example (i) A does not kill B, B kills A (B here is always a Greek), (ii) A misses B, B hits but does not penetrate, A kills B (A here is always Greek), (iii) A misses B but kills C.[30]

Again, an oral poet, working without writing, has to learn how to keep a grip on his story-line, and one way Homer does this is by the device known as 'ring-composition'. Here Menelaus protects Patroclus' body:

Warlike Menelaus son of Atreus did not fail to notice that Patroclus had been overcome in battle by the Trojans. He advanced through the front ranks, bronze armour glittering, and stood over Patroclus' body as a mother-cow stands protectively over the first calf she has brought into the world. So auburn-haired Menelaus stood over Patroclus and guarded the body with his spear and round shield, determined to kill anyone who advanced against him. (17.1–9)

Homer describes Menelaus in terms of a mother-cow protecting her calf. But he begins it by saying Menelaus 'stood over Patroclus' body as . . .' and ends it by saying 'So auburn-haired

Menelaus stood over Patroclus . . .'. This is 'ring-composition'
– repeating words or ideas to get the poet back to where he was
when he started. Sometimes there are two or three rings, usually
repeated in reverse order: in the above example, 'bronze armour
glittering' might be picked up by 'with his spear and round
shield'. One might even then argue for a third ring, though it
does involve a change of person – 'Menelaus advanced . . .'
being picked up by 'anyone who advanced against it'. This
would give us three rings – a (advance), b (armour), c (stood) –
picked up in reverse order by (c) stood, (b) armour, (a) advance.

Very many descriptions and similes (i.e. digressions in general)
are structured in this way. So too are speeches.[31]

HOMER'S NARRATIVE STANCE

Our last sight of Achilles is of him asleep in the arms of *Briseis*,
the woman Agamemnon took from him to start the trouble. It
is a poignant farewell to the central figure of the *Iliad*, but it is
typical of Homer that he does no more than describe the
moment: 'But Achilles slept in a corner of his well-made hut;
and fair-cheeked *Briseis* slept beside him' (24.675–6). Generally
speaking, Homer in his role as third-person narrator simply
reports. He does not comment, evaluate or tell us how to
respond. That is why Homer is sometimes called 'restrained' or
even 'objective', as if (to use a modern analogy) he were nothing
but a camera, dispassionately surveying the scene without
making any judgement upon it.

In fact, of course, Homer is as subjective as any camera since
he carefully selects the scenes he wishes to survey and the angle
from which he views them; further, he is free to control in any
way he wishes what his characters do and say to each other, and
how they react and interact. It is in the speeches especially that
moral positions are taken and evaluative language deployed.
But that does not alter the main point: that Homer himself does
not obviously impose his views on us by using his privileged
position as third-person narrator to push us into one response
or another. He lets the characters speak for themselves and

keeps himself in the background. He rarely puts thoughts into people's minds or interprets mental states. Homer's practice can be strongly contrasted with that of the Roman poet Virgil, for example, who is constantly alerting us to the 'correct' view of matters (so Dido, in love with *Aeneas*, 'gave no thought to appearance or her good name and no longer kept her love a secret in her own heart, but called it marriage, using the word to cover her guilt'[32]). The modern novelist, too, can rarely resist the temptation to tell us how to interpret a character or scene.

Nevertheless, Homer is not quite as guileless as all that. Here *Hector* launches his final, fatal attack on Achilles, and Homer decorates the moment with a simile: 'He gathered himself and swooped like a high-flying eagle that drops to earth through black clouds to pounce on a tender lamb or cowering hare' (22.308).

Hector, then, is the eagle and Achilles the tender lamb. We are entitled to wonder how the poet can bring himself to develop such an apparently absurd comparison.

'Focalization' is the technical term for asking of any literary text, 'Through whose eyes is the reader supposed to understand these words'?[33] Clearly Achilles cannot be described as a 'tender lamb' in any objective terms. The simile makes best sense if we 'see' it through *Hector*'s eyes. *Hector* is preparing himself for the ultimate trial. It is as if he is trying to convince himself that he is an eagle, Achilles a lamb, as he charges. The simile is therefore 'focalized' through *Hector*'s eyes, at that moment in time, giving us a subtle narrator's insight into how he is thinking.

It is especially important to bear this technique in mind when we read the speeches. Homeric heroes say what is in their interest to say at the time. It may not be the objective truth. For example, when Achilles sees the Greeks in serious trouble after he has rejected the embassy begging him to return, he exclaims to Patroclus: 'now I think the Greeks will be gathering at my knees in supplication! They are in desperate straits' (11.609). One might object that in Book 9 the Greeks had already gathered at his knees in supplication, and Achilles had rejected them. But that is not the point. This is a mocking cry of triumph – the situation will show the Greeks how much they need Achilles now.

Again, when Achilles rejects that embassy, he informs his audience that he has two life-options:

'My divine mother, silver-footed Thetis, says that destiny has left two courses open to me on my journey to the grave. If I stay here and fight it out round Ilium, there is no home-coming for me, but there will be eternal glory instead. If I go back to the land of my fathers, my heroic glory will be forfeit, but my life will be long and I shall be spared an early death.' (9.410–16)

This is news to us. Up till now, we have been told that Achilles was doomed to a short but glorious life.[34] But this revelation, designed for the moment, is perfectly judged to convince the embassy that it will not succeed. In both these cases Homer is refocalizing the action through the eyes of a specific hero in a specific situation.

The issue of focalization is an important one because it may cause us to rethink our views about the 'objectivity' of Homer's third-person narrative. Can we be quite certain, for example, that when Homer calls Odysseus 'resourceful' or describes war 'with all its tears', he is doing nothing but reporting the facts as he sees them? Might there not still be an element of the evaluative about these descriptions?

SPEECH, ACTION AND CHARACTER

One tends to associate heroic epic with action. But in the *Iliad* there are no fewer than 666 speeches, making up over 40 per cent of the whole work. The most remarkable fact of all is that, though Achilles is absent from more than half the *Iliad*, his voice is heard far more than anyone else's.[35] *Hector* and Agamemnon come next, appropriately enough (though a very long way behind) – they are the leaders of their armies and also the main foils for Achilles. ZEUS as king of the gods has the most to say on the divine side, as one would expect.

These bald statistics reveal the key players and balance of power that prevail on earth and Olympus. But number of speeches is not everything. Intensity of speech is also important. *Hector*'s wife *Andromache* makes only four speeches but they occur at highly emotional moments – when she thinks, and then when she knows, she will never see her husband again. *Briseis*, Achilles' girl taken by Agamemnon, has only one speech, which she delivers when she is handed back to Achilles and finds Patroclus dead. At fourteen lines long, it is an extraordinarily powerful lament.[36]

The speeches carry the psychological weight of the poem. Homer's actors reveal who they are, what makes them tick, primarily in what they say to each other and what they do, especially in how they react to each other. As we have said, there is a strong distinction between speeches, which evaluate and interpret and reveal character, and (third-person) narrative, which seems merely to report (see section above).

Consider, for example, the scene in which Patroclus is sent by Achilles to find out who has been wounded. Patroclus arrives in Nestor's hut, and with exquisite economy Homer uncovers the various relationships. Nestor and Machaon

had quenched their parching thirst and were agreeably engaged in conversation, when Patroclus suddenly appeared in the doorway, a mortal like a god. The old man saw him, got up from his polished chair, took him by the hand, brought him in and told him to sit down. But Patroclus from the other side refused and explained:

'No time for sitting down, my venerable lord; you will not persuade me. That man who sent me to find out the wounded man you just brought in – he commands respect. He is easy to annoy. But, as I can see for myself that it is Machaon, shepherd of the people, I will go back at once and report to Achilles. You know well enough, Olympian-bred sir, what a difficult man he is, quite capable of finding fault without reason.'

Nestor the Gerenian charioteer replied:

'Why is Achilles so concerned about a few Greek casualties, when he knows nothing about the disaster affecting the whole army? (11.642–59)

The moment Patroclus appears, Nestor sees that this is a golden opportunity to get a message across to Achilles through his close companion. No wonder he immediately tries to make Patroclus feel so welcome and at home. Patroclus' reply is just as telling. 'That man', he says, will not like it. He is 'difficult'.

In a few brief, exquisitely suggestive strokes, we know all we need to about the sort of person Achilles is, the hold Achilles has over Patroclus, Patroclus' feelings about Achilles and his (fully justified) unease at getting ensnared by Nestor. But Nestor will not let go. A few Greek casualties? The situation is far worse – and off he goes on a massive 148-line speech to persuade Patroclus that if Achilles will not return to fight, well, perhaps Patroclus should. It is a doom-laden turning-point.

That, incidentally, is why Nestor's speech is so long. This is a critical moment, and such moments are usually expanded by Homer to indicate their importance. For example, in the climactic fight between Achilles and *Hector* in Book 22, the two heroes exchange spear throws, then *Hector* charges and Achilles kills him. But the whole 'moment' takes 340 lines from the moment *Priam* sees Achilles racing across the plain, to *Hector*'s death – the oral poet's expansive art at its finest (22.25–366).

It is also typical of Homer to show character not through direct description but through the reactions of others. For example, when the heralds sent by Agamemnon to fetch *Briseis* arrive at Achilles' quarters:

They came to a halt, too terrified and embarrassed before their lord to address him or ask anything. But [Achilles] realized what was going on and spoke out:

'Heralds, ambassadors of Zeus and men, welcome. Come in. My quarrel is not with you . . .' (1.331–5)

Homer's simple report of the heralds' fear and embarrassment is all that is needed to indicate both how unhappy the heralds are with the task they have been asked to carry out – their role is to deliver messages, yet they stand there tongue-tied and quaking – and the sort of reaction they expected from a man like Achilles who, after all, had only just been prevented from killing Agamemnon. The sense of relief as Achilles absolves them and welcomes them in is almost palpable. This Achilles is capable of human sympathy after all.

Homer keeps himself in the background and lets his characters speak and act for themselves – a fine example of that Homeric 'objectivity', of which the poet is, of course, in total control (see p. xxix). Homer's refusal to interpret scenes for us, but to stand back and merely report what happened and who said what to whom, leaves us room to breathe, to make our own sense of what is going on. So if, for example, we were to ask what is the moral of the *Iliad*, or what Homer really wanted us to think about Achilles, or war, or life, we would struggle to produce a definitive answer.

The novelist, by contrast, goes out of his or her way to leave little to the imagination: the reader is rarely in doubt as to the author's view of the significance of every word and every action, however small or great. To that extent Homer anticipates the theatre. The dramatist cannot shape responses through the authorial third-person narrative: only actors, their words and actions are on display. Interpretation is all. As an oral poet, Homer speaks the parts anyway, like an actor; but although he would be able to impose interpretation through the third-person narrative if he so chose, he tends not to. We make of it what we will.

BATTLES

Of the 15,000 lines in the *Iliad*, battle takes up some 5,500, made up of three hundred encounters.[37] Death, unrealistically, nearly always comes quickly and cleanly after a single blow, though there are some odd or gruesome deaths from particularly nasty blows:

Peneleos struck him under the eyebrow in the socket of the eye. The spear dislodged his eyeball, pierced the eye-socket and came out at the back of his head. He sank back, stretching out both his hands. But Peneleos, drawing his sharp sword, hit him full on the neck and brought head and helmet tumbling down to the ground. The heavy spear was still stuck in the eye as Peneleos raised it aloft, like a poppy-head . . . (14.493-9)

But the field is not littered with moaning, wounded and dying warriors.

Out of the three hundred encounters there are only twenty-eight duels, i.e. where warriors confront each other and agree to fight. Warriors very rarely launch out into an extended sequence of killings (Patroclus and Achilles are among the few exceptions[38]). Hit-and-run is by far the most favoured tactic. The warriors, in other words, tend to look after themselves as best they can. They are not desperate to die. Of the 230 warriors killed in these encounters, 170 are *Trojan*, 50 Greek.[39]

Even though there are many typical sequences and features to the battle-scenes (see p. xxviii), Homer varies them with great ingenuity: general fighting, individual combats, strings of deaths, battle on the ground or from chariots, exhortations, taunts, challenges, routs, counter-attacks, divine interventions, similes, and so on. In particular, he often gives us quite moving individual thumbnail portraits of the dead warriors, evoking personal worlds far from the battlefield:

Then Menelaus son of Atreus caught the brilliant hunter Scamandrius with his sharp spear. Scamandrius was a great man for the chase, who had been taught by the goddess Artemis herself how to bring down any kind of wild game that lives in the mountain forests. But Artemis who delights in arrows was of no help to him now, nor were the long shots that had won him fame. As Scamandrius fled before him, the great spearman Menelaus son of Atreus stabbed him with his spear in the middle of the back between his shoulders and drove it on through his chest. He crashed down on his face, and his armour clattered about him. (5.49-59)

Note the primary information: *Scamandrius*, expert in the chase, is killed by Menelaus. Then comes the development: he was a hunter, taught by ARTEMIS but, ironically, she could not help him now. Finally, the detail of the death: he is stabbed through the back as he fled. This method of describing the death of a warrior is very common.

The contrasting scenes of war and peace add powerfully to the pathos of the *Iliad*. The brief description that accompanies the fall of a warrior often points up the contrast. Here the Greek hero Diomedes cuts down *Xanthus* and *Thoön*:

Then he went after Xanthus and Thoön, sons of Phaenops, both late-born. Phaenops was old now and ailing and had no other son to whom he could leave his wealth. Diomedes killed them both, depriving them of their precious lives and leaving their father only tears and a broken heart. He never welcomed them home alive from the war. Relatives divided up the estate. (5.152–8)

Homer's restraint is typical. The report is enough: he does not have to make efforts to elicit our sympathy with an intrusive emotionalizing comment.

Similes, too, introduce worlds a long way from the battlefield. The natural world, of lions, boars, hunters and farmers, features frequently. This is usually a dangerous world, of defence and attack. Here Idomeneus faces *Aeneas*:

But Idomeneus was not to be scared off like a little boy. He waited for him like some mountain boar, confident in his strength, who faces a crowd of huntsmen advancing on him in a lonely spot: his back bristles, his eyes flame like fire and he sharpens his tusks, eager to take on men and dogs – so the great spearman Idomeneus awaited the onslaught of Aeneas and gave no ground at all. (13.470–78)

Homely similes are equally in evidence. Here the god *APOLLO* smashes through the Greek defences, like a boy on the beach:

Then, with equal ease, the god knocked down the Greek wall, as a boy at the seaside knocks down a sandcastle: he builds it to amuse himself, as children do, and then with his hands and feet wrecks the whole thing for fun – so you, Apollo, wrecked the Greeks' arduous efforts and sowed panic among them. (15.361–6)

Here the poet remembers the pre-war days. As Achilles chases *Hector*, they pass 'the stone washing-places where the wives and lovely daughters of the *Trojans* used to wash their shining clothes in earlier days, when there was peace, before the coming of the Greeks' (22.154–6). This focus on different worlds away from bloodshed and death is one of the *Iliad*'s greatest glories, one source of its rich humanity.

SIMILES

There are over three hundred similes in the *Iliad*, occupying about 1,100 lines (7 per cent of the whole). They are miraculous creations, redirecting the listener's attention in the most unexpected ways and suffusing the poem with vividness, pathos and humour. There are four basic types:

1. Short similes with a single point of comparison, e.g. 'like nightfall' (1.47), 'like fawns' (22.1).
2. An extended short simile, in the form 'like X, which/that . . .', for example 'like fawns that dash across the plain and exhaust themselves and stop, because they have no more will to resist' (4.243–5).
3. The subject is mentioned, and the simile begins in the form 'as when, as, like', and ends 'such was/so X happened' (ring-composition: see p. xxviii). The similes likening Idomeneus to a boar, and *APOLLO* to a boy knocking down a sandcastle, are of this type.
4. The simile introduces the subject *before* the narrative has reached that point – thus 'as when Y happens, so X happened', for example: The spear 'hit Aretus' round shield. This failed to stop it, and the spear pierced it and drove on through his belt into his abdomen. *As* a strong man with a sharp axe strikes a farmyard ox behind the horns and then cuts its throat, and the ox springs forward and then collapses, *so* Aretus sprang forward and then fell on his back' (17.517–23). The point is that *Aretus* had not collapsed when the simile began – the simile describes an ox collapsing and *then* says that was how *Aretus* collapsed.

Similes tend to occur at moments of high emotion, drama and tension, often introducing a change of perspective (e.g. the entrance of a warrior), and they are especially prevalent in battle-scenes. The most common points of comparison with human life and action are lions (used forty times in all), birds, fire, cattle, wind and water, and boars. Thirty-one subjects occur once only: these include mule, ass, worm, rainbow, bean, dew, milk, lead, oil, ivory, trumpet, sandcastle and horse-trainer. As for their function, these similes introduce worlds of peace and plenty into a martial poem; they impose the unchanging world of nature on temporary, fleeting human existence, dignifying and adding significance to it; by using contemporary subject-matter within the experience of all listeners they give contemporary vividness to the world of the heroic past; and they often create deep pathos, for example the dying warrior likened to a poppy heavy with spring rain (8.302). In the similes, perhaps more than elsewhere, Homer speaks most directly to us. Here Achilles addresses Patroclus, who has just been witnessing the *Trojan* onslaught on the Greeks:

'Patroclus, why are you in tears, like a little girl running along beside her mother and begging to be carried, tugging at her skirt to make her stop, although she is in a hurry, and looking tearfully up at her till at last she picks her up? That, Patroclus, is how you look, with the soft tears rolling down your cheeks.' (16.7)

Achilles is likened most frequently to fire (fourteen times), a god and a lion, and nine times in a parent–child image, often involving Patroclus – a significant comparison.

THE AUTHENTICITY AND SURVIVAL
OF HOMER'S TEXT

In his *Prolegomena ad Homerum* (1795), the German scholar F. A. Wolf argued that our *Iliad* and *Odyssey* were the work of more than one man.[40] His reason was that Homer did not know how to write, and that Homer's poems were far too long for oral recitation. He therefore concluded that Homer composed a series of short, connected oral poems *c*. 950 BC; that these were expanded by other poets till writing became available; they were then enlarged even more by ancient literary editors, who used writing; and the result is what we have today. The job of the scholar was therefore to decide what was Homeric, and what was not – the famous Homeric question. So began the long battles between the 'analysts', such as Wolf, and the 'unitarians', who believed there was one composer only of the *Iliad*.

Many competing analytical theories emerged.[41] Some argued that Homer composed only a few songs himself, others that he assembled short songs composed by others into a larger structure. Some thought the *Iliad* was originally a brief poem about Achilles' anger, later expanded either by the addition of episodes, or by enlarging existing episodes. Images of the *Iliad*'s construction abounded: of skins like an onion or layers like a cake, of adding pieces to a puzzle or a superstructure to a house, of dough into which new ingredients were blended, and so on.

But oral theory now holds sway. Most scholars believe that one poet was responsible for our *Iliad*; that its unique size and concentrated focus are indicative of a special poetic effort, generated by whatever cultural and poetic circumstances; that Homer comes at the end of a tradition of oral story-telling going back hundreds of years (so that he has, in a sense, inherited the work of hundreds of earlier oral poets); and that his art consists in the unique way he has reworked these traditional, typical materials devised to enable the oral poet to recite in the first place – from phrase and sentence at one level to 'theme' and story-pattern at larger levels – into the masterpieces we have today. But that leaves the questions – how do they survive to this day, and with what resemblance to any oral 'original' (if, indeed, oral poets had a concept of an 'original')?

All ancient Greek literature was given a definitive form by Greek scholars working in Egypt from the third century BC onwards to produce the best text they could.[42] Their texts form the basis of ours, but it is impossible to tell how far our text

represents any single oral performance: the evidence, by defi-
nition, cannot exist. These ancient Greek scholars, like earlier
ones, felt unhappy about much that they found in Homer,
especially the repetitions (they did not understand how oral
poetry worked – see p. xxviii) and failures of style and logic
(oral poetry is different from written in this respect). They
therefore raised many questions about what was Homeric and
what not, and the idea of 'many Homers' is very old. There is
no doubt that there was interference with the text of Homer
down to the third century BC (at least): the question is, how
much?

There is general scholarly agreement that Book 10 is not by
Homer. It is wholly self-contained, it is never referred to again,
and if it was not there, no one would notice its absence. The
slaughter of sleeping men by night is hardly heroic. There are
many oddities of language, and the speeches are not constructed
as they are in the rest of the epic. Beyond that, there is general
agreement that in conception the *Iliad* is the work of a single
mind, though there continues to be disagreement about detail.[43]
Inconsistencies are generally explained nowadays as the result
of Homer's gradual expansion and development of the story
over a long period of time, or of his incorporation into the
text of material that did not quite fit, rather than because of
interference with the text by others.

That raises another important question: if Homer's epics were
the product of an oral performance *c.* 700 BC, how do they
survive to this day? At some stage they must have been written
down, but we do not know how or when. Some scholars believed
Homer used writing, in which case there is no problem. Written
versions certainly existed by the sixth century BC because we
hear of efforts to produce a standard text of Homer for bards
to recite at competitions. From then on, such was Homer's
influence that his texts were copied and recopied for education
and pleasure throughout the Graeco-Roman periods.

When the Roman empire in the West collapsed in the fifth
century AD, what knowledge of Greek literature there was in
the West disappeared with it.[44] Even the Bible was read for the
next almost thousand years in Jerome's Latin translation (begun

AD 380). But Greek continued to be read and copied in the Roman empire in the East centred round Constantinople (modern Istanbul), an empire inhabited almost entirely by Greek speakers.

However, when Ottoman Turks began to threaten that city from the twelfth century AD onwards, its scholars fled west with their precious manuscripts. This is how Greek literature survives today. Western Europe knew about Homer at this time, of course, because Roman authors mentioned him constantly (Virgil's *Aeneid* was a sort of Roman *Iliad–Odyssey*). So it was a thrilling time for Western scholars in Italy when Greeks began arriving with these great works that they had only heard of but never read. A convenient date to mark Homer's arrival back in the West is 1354, when Petrarch acquired a manuscript of the two epics from Nicolaos Sigeros, a Greek involved in the unification of the Western and Eastern churches. Naturally he could not read them and in a letter he writes: 'Homer is mute to me, or rather I am deaf to him. Still, I enjoy just looking at him and often, embracing him and, sighing, I say, "O great man, how eagerly would I listen to you." '[45]

No one need suffer that fate today.

NOTES

1. Aristotle, *Poetics* 1459a; on the beach the Greeks are said to be living in *klisiai*, literally 'lean-tos', presumably wooden shacks, shelters or huts built next to their ships. Achilles' is surprisingly grand (24.449–56); THETIS' marriage: 24.60–62; Achilles as baby: 9.485–91; his education: 11.831; Patroclus: 23.85–90; *Paris*' looks: 3.39, 54–5, 64–6; *Paris* and *APHRODITE*: 24.27–30; Helen's beauty: 3.156–8; *Paris* abused hospitality: 13.620–27; *Paris*' seduction of Helen: 3.442–6; *Hector*'s attitude: 3.39–66; recruiting mission: 7.127, cf. 11.769 ff.; catalogue of ships: 2.494–779; omens: 2.299–332. It is worth observing that Homer makes no reference to Agamemnon's need to sacrifice his daughter Iphigeneia to raise a favourable wind for Troy, a major theme of ancient Greek tragic poets (e.g. Aeschylus' *Agamemnon*). Note how the past is nearly always 'focalized' (see p. xxx) through the mouths of the characters, not 'objectively' reported by Homer.

2. Protesilaus: 2.701–2; failed negotiation: 3.205–24; proposed murder: 11.141; unsuccessful siege: 2.134–8; past incidents: e.g. 2.721–4, the banishment of Philoctetes to the island of Lemnos; *Chryseis'* capture: 1.366–9; *Briseis*: 2.688–93; division of spoils: e.g. 1.162–8, 9.328–33.

3. Wealth and respect: *timê*, literally 'valuation, worth', shading into 'honour, status, respect', is what Homeric heroes seek from their peers; material rewards: the warriors take extraordinary risks to strip the armour off an opponent, but they need the armour to show they have won, and as their reward (armour is extremely expensive) (see e.g. the severe consequences for Diomedes at 11.370–400); social rewards: e.g. 4.256–63; Achilles' worth: e.g. 9.607; insult: it is worth emphasizing here that expertise at giving good advice is rated as highly as military prowess (see e.g. 2.370–74; 9.440–43; 11.783–91); heroes would rather not fight: 12.322–5; *Hector's* admission: 20.434 (*Aeneas* feels the same at 20.87–100); Diomedes: 4.412–18; 9.34–6; failure and death: see 12.310–28, where *Sarpedon*, a *Trojan* ally, discusses his 'contract' with his community – wealth and an agreeable life-style in exchange for risking his life in battle. Compare Odysseus at 11.404–10; *ARES*: 5.888; painful war: see 13.343 for the horror the battlefield evokes, and cf. 2.401, 3.111–12 and the realism of 17.91–105; family: e.g. 2.292–7 (the deaths of warriors often prompt visions of the families they will never see again, e.g. 5.410–15, 17.300–303); immortal glory: e.g. *Hector* at 22.297–305; *Hector* and *Andromache* scene: 6.390–502.

4. Agamemnon's troops: 1.281, 2.576–80; speakers: 9.439–42 – for debate, see e.g. 9.69–78, 14.83–108; ZEUS' superiority: 8.5–27, 15.105–8; Achilles' short life: 1.352–4 (he offers an alternative prospect at 9.410–16, but the option of a long and tedious life is hardly a convincing one except for the sake of his argument at this stage in the plot); Achilles' threat: 1.169–71; Agamemnon and *Briseis*: 1.172–87; ATHENE and compensation: 1.212–14; Agamemnon's admission: 2.378, 9.115–20, 19.86–138.

5. Agamemnon gets rewards: 9.331–3; no compensation adequate: 9.379–87; value of life: 9.401–9; embassy baffled: e.g. 9.515–23; Diomedes' view: 9.697–703; Patroclus' view: 16.31–2; the insult: 9.387; Aristotle on Achilles: *Poetics* 1454b.

6. Greeks need Achilles to return: 11.608–10; Patroclus should fight: 16.64; avenging Patroclus: 18.90; *Hector's* death pointless: 22.386–90; Agamemnon reconciled: 23.890; *Hector's* mutilation: 24.1–21; Achilles' awareness of fate: 18.94–100; *Hector's* fate: 22.297–305 – we have known of it for certain since 15.68, though 6.486–502 and

8.473–7 hint at it; tragic markers of Patroclus' doom: 16.46–7, 91 ff., 250, 684; tragic irony 16.38 ff., 97, 246; 'now I see': 16.844; cf. ZEUS at 8.470 ff., 15.64 ff.

7. Achilles' feat of arms: 18.121; loves conflict: 1.177; almost bestial: 21.542, 22.346–7, 23.176; like a lion: 24.39–45; revenge achieves nothing: 24.1–21; glory for Achilles: 24.110; will of ZEUS: 24.133–40; Achilles consoles *Priam*: 24.518–51; life both good and ill: 24.525–48; *Priam*'s loss of *Hector*: 24.521, 541–2, 547–8; Achilles' loss: 24.511–12, 540; mutual admiration: 24.629–32.

8. Herodotus, *Histories* 2.53.

9. Gods quarrel: e.g. 1.539, 4.506, 8.5–17, 15.12–33, 21.385–513; go to bed: 1.597–611; HERA's sweat: 4.27–9; APHRODITE's wound: 5.426–30; ARES stabbed: 5.856, 889.

10. The contrast with the *Odyssey* here is notable. There is no need to worry about whether Homer 'really means it' when he introduces a god, i.e. whether it was just another way for Homer to say that something happened naturally. Homer was perfectly capable of saying something happened naturally. When he introduces a god, he introduces a god.

11. It is notable that heroes are hardly ever said to fear the gods. When ZEUS talks to Achilles' mother THETIS about Achilles releasing *Hector*'s body, he adds the condition 'if he will somehow fear me' (24.116)! A veiled threat, of course, but there is a certain truth there.

12. Nor does it detract from the heroes when gods help them. Gods support only winners. Divine help proves the hero is *worthy* of it, and the hero rejoices in it. Look, for example, at Achilles' reaction when ATHENE says she will trick *Hector* into fighting him: he is delighted (22.224).

13. See e.g. Achilles' encounter with ATHENE at 1.197–207.

14. APOLLO strips Patroclus: 16.786–817; HERA barters towns: 4.51–3; IRIS comforts *Priam*: 24.169 ff.; POSEIDON's chariot: 13.17–31; ZEUS nods: 1.528–30.

15. Plato, *Republic* 386b ff.

16. Longinus, *On the Sublime* 9.7, transl. by D. A. Russell, in *Ancient Literary Criticism* (Oxford, 1973).

17. E.g. 9.702, where Diomedes says Achilles will return to the fighting 'when his heart tells him to, and the god moves him'.

18. E.g. ZEUS over the death of *Sarpedon* at 16.459.

19. See M. L. West, *The East Face of Helicon* (Oxford: Clarendon Press, 1997), a brilliant account of near-Eastern influences on early Greek literature.

20. Herodotus, *Histories* 2.120.

21. See C. M. Bowra, *Heroic Poetry* (London, 1952).

22. I do not mean to imply that Homer invented the story of the *Iliad*: I use 'Homer' here to mean 'the oral epic tradition in Ionia'.

23. See H. Strasburger, 'The sociology of the Homeric epics' in Peter Jones and G. M. Wright (eds.), *Homer: German Scholarship in Translation* (Oxford: Clarendon Press, 1997), pp. 47–70. One must stress that the aristocrats of Homer's day did not depend on cattle-raising and raiding quite as much as the Homeric heroes do. Overseas trade and grain-production formed the basis of their wealth.

24. *Bucolion*: 6.25; *Paris* 24.29; *Anchises*: 5.313 – APHRODITE, no less!; *Andromache*'s brothers: 6.423–4; Diomedes' horses: 5.271; *Hector*'s horses: 8.187–9; *Pandarus*' horses: 5.180 ff.; *Priam*'s sons: 24.262; *Priam* rolls in dung: 22.414; value in oxen: e.g. 6.236; farmers and fighting: e.g. 12.299–306; farming a proud calling: 18.556–7.

25. See e.g. David Traill, *Schliemann of Troy: Treasure and Deceit* (Harmondsworth: Penguin, 1995).

26. Cf. 18.288–9.

27. Historically, of course, it is absurd that Homer's inhabitants of *Ilium* do not appear to possess a fleet.

28. On all this, see L. Foxhall and J. K. Davies (eds.), *The Trojan War: Its Historicity and Context* (Bristol: Bristol Classical Press, 1984).

29. E.g. 2.167–72, 19.3–7.

30. E.g. (i) 5.15–9; (ii) 11.231–40 (iii) 8.117–23. See B. Fenik, *Typical Battle Scenes in the 'Iliad'* (Wiesbaden: Franz Steiner Verlag, 1968).

31. See, for example, 6.407–32.

32. Virgil, *Aeneid* 2.170–72, transl. David West (Harmondsworth: Penguin Classics, 1990). Consider, by contrast, how Homer deals with Helen who, full of moving self-reproach as she is, has still been seen by some as a self-serving hypocrite. Penelope in the *Odyssey* is equally difficult to interpret.

33. See I. J. F. de Jong, *Narrators and Focalizers: The Presentation of the Story in the 'Iliad'* (Amsterdam: B. R. Grüner, 1987). See note 1 above for another example.

34. E.g. 1.352, 415–18, 505–6.

35. Speeches are made by 77 characters (28 Greek, 29 Trojan and allies, 19 gods and a horse). Achilles speaks the most (87 speeches, 965 lines in all); then *Hector* (50 speeches, 530 lines), Agamemnon (43 speeches, 445 lines), ZEUS (37 speeches, 337 lines), Nestor (31 speeches, 489 lines), HERA (29 speeches, 238 lines), Diomedes (27 speeches, 239 lines), Odysseus (26 speeches, 342 lines), *Priam* (25 speeches, 213 lines), Menelaus (22 speeches, 152 lines), ATHENE (20 speeches, 159 lines). Statistics from N. J. Lowe, *The Classical*

Plot and the Invention of Western Narrative (Cambridge: Cambridge University Press, 2000), pp. 116–18.

36. 19.287–300. It is worth remarking here that Homer's male and female characters inhabit quite different worlds without generating any sense that one world is inferior and the other superior. The worlds are just different and make their different demands.

37. See Hans van Wees, in A. B. Lloyd (ed.), *Battle in Antiquity* (London: Duckworth, 1996). There are 170 encounters in which we are given some information about the participants and weapons used – the spear is by far the most favoured weapon – and 130 others in which we know only the names or numbers of the dead. Only eighteen encounters involve more than one blow, only six involve more than one exchange of blows. See Introduction to Book 4.

38. E.g. 16.284 ff. and 20.455 ff.

39. In all, 281 *Trojans* are killed, 61 Greeks. There is a continuing debate about the extent to which Homer's pro-Greek bias is simply chauvinism or an essential ingredient of the moral universe of the poem. It has been argued that Homer becomes more sympathetic to the *Trojans* as more are killed.

40. *Prolegomena ad Homerum* has now been translated from its original Latin, with introduction and notes by A. Grafton, G. Most and J. Zetzel (Princeton, 1985).

41. H. W. Clarke, *Homer's Readers: A Historical Introduction to the 'Iliad' and 'Odyssey'* (Associated University Presses, 1981), a brilliant account of the way Homer has engaged readers' imaginations over two millennia, gives analytical detail of the battles in Chapter 4.

42. When Alexander the Great died in 323 BC, the generals he had left in charge of the various regions of his vast, rickety 'empire' soon assumed local control and turned themselves into kings. Ptolemy (*Ptolemaios*) made himself King of Egypt, and decided to turn Alexandria into an intellectual centre to rival Athens. The Alexandrian Library and Museum were the result (we would call them humanities and scientific research centres today), funded in such a way as to attract the very best scholars to work there.

43. The *Iliad*'s relationship to the *Odyssey* is another fascinating question which cannot be explored here.

44. The 'collapse' of the empire in the West meant that Rome was no longer able to tax and control centrally. The result was that the Western empire fragmented into local, autonomous kingdoms, the seeds of modern Europe. But the Roman empire had been effectively divided into western and eastern administrative blocks in the fourth century AD, and the empire in the East (which came to be known as the

Byzantine empire) survived until its capital, Constantinople (ancient Greek Byzantium), fell to Ottoman Turks on 29 May 1453.
45. See Clarke, *Homer's Readers*, p. 57.

Introduction to the 1950 Edition

THE Greeks looked on the *Iliad* as Homer's major work. It was the Story of Achilles, and not the Wanderings of Odysseus as might have been expected, that Alexander the Great took with him as a bedside book on his adventurous campaigns. I myself used not to accept this verdict, and I felt that many modern readers would agree with me. It was therefore with some trepidation that I bade farewell to the *Odyssey* and braced myself for the task of translating the *Iliad*, which I had not read through as a whole for twelve years. I soon began to have very different feelings, and now that I have finished the work I am completely reassured. The Greeks were right.

It is a question, not of any difference in skill, but of artistic levels. The *Odyssey*, with its happy ending, presents the romantic view of life: the *Iliad* is a tragedy.* To paint the Odyssean picture, convincing, just, and beautiful as it is, Homer took his easel to the lower slopes of Mount Olympus, which are pleasant, green, and wooded. It was a good spot, for the Muses certainly come down and play there. But to compose the *Iliad*, he moved higher up the mountain-side, nearer to the eternal snows and to the very homes of the Muses and the other gods. From there he had a different and a clearer view of the same landscape. Some of the mists had dissolved, the sun beat pitilessly on the snow, and a number of new things, many of them very terrible and lovely, came into sight. Homer himself became, if possible, even more human. He had climbed high; he had faced and solved

* I am not implying in what follows that we really know which of them Homer wrote first.

some of the ultimate enigmas; and he could afford to smile both at the ant-like activities of men and the more awe-inspiring pageant of the gods. I am therefore very confident when I assure those who already know the *Odyssey* that they will be brought closer to tears by the death of a single horse in the *Iliad* than by the killing of the whole gang of Suitors; closer too to laughter; and closer, if they follow Homer to the Olympian eminence from which he looks out on the world, to the heights where tears and laughter cease to count.

The plot of the *Iliad* is simple. King Agamemnon the imperial overlord of Greece (or Achaea, as Homer calls it) has, with his brother Menelaus of Sparta, induced the princes who owe him allegiance to join forces with him against King Priam of Troy, because Paris, one of Priam's sons, has run away with Menelaus' wife, the beautiful Helen of Argos. The Achaean forces have for nine years been encamped beside their ships on the shore near Troy, but without bringing the matter to a conclusion, though they have captured and looted a number of towns in Trojan territory, under the dashing leadership of Achilles son of Peleus, Prince of the Myrmidons, the most redoubtable and the most unruly of Agamemnon's royal supporters. The success of these raiding parties leads to a feud between Achilles and his Commander-in-Chief. Agamemnon has been allotted the girl Chryseis as his prize, and he refuses to give her up to her father, a local priest of Apollo, when he comes to the camp with ransom for her release. The priest prays to his god; a plague ensues; and Agamemnon is forced by the strength of public feeling to give up the girl and so propitiate the angry god. But he recoups himself by confiscating one of Achilles' own prizes, a girl named Briseis. Achilles in high dudgeon refuses to fight any more and withdraws the Myrmidon force from the battlefield. After an abortive truce, intended to allow Menelaus and Paris to settle their quarrel by single combat, the two armies meet, and as a result of Achilles' absence from the field the Achaeans, who have hitherto kept the Trojan forces penned up in Troy or close to their own city walls, are slowly but surely put on the defensive. They are even forced to make a trench and a wall round their ships and huts. But these defences are eventually stormed by

Hector the Trojan Commander-in-Chief, who succeeds in setting fire to one of the Achaean ships. At this point Achilles, who has remained obdurate to all entreaties, yields to the extent of permitting his squire and closest friend Patroclus to lead the Myrmidon force to the rescue of the hard-pressed Achaeans. Patroclus brilliantly succeeds in this mission, but he goes too far and is killed under the walls of Troy by Hector. This disaster brings Achilles to life. In an access of rage with Hector and grief for his comrade he reconciles himself with Agamemnon, takes the field once more, hurls the panic-stricken Trojans back into their town, and finally kills Hector. Not content with this revenge, he savagely maltreats the body of his fallen enemy. Hector's father, King Priam, in his grief and horror, is inspired by the gods to visit Achilles in his camp by night, in order to recover his son's body.* Achilles relents; and the *Iliad* ends with an uneasy truce for the funeral of Hector.

Such is the framework of the story. Unlike those who describe the plot of a thriller on its dust-cover, I have disclosed the end. And I have done this, with no fear of spoiling the tale, in order to bring out the fact that the *Iliad* is a fine example of the Greek method of constructing a story or a play. In most cases, since the matter was traditional, the end was already known to the audience when they sat down to the beginning, and the author had to secure his effects by other methods than that of surprise. He could of course show a greater or lesser degree of originality in the details of his composition. In the *Odyssey*, for instance, it was a stroke of dramatic genius to break the narrative by causing Odysseus to recite his own adventures to the Phaeacian nobles in the shadowy hall of King Alcinous. And in the case of the *Iliad*, Homer's first audiences must have been delighted by the daring humour with which he presented the comedy of Olympus; for I believe this to have been one of his major contributions to the old story of the Trojan War. But apart from such innovations, Homer employs two devices, both of which are typical of Greek art. First, like the Attic dramatists, far from

---

* The Achaeans attached even more importance than we do to the proper disposal of their dead. See the ghost of Patroclus on the subject (Book 23).

feeling that his hearers' foreknowledge is a handicap, he makes capital out of it by giving them confidential asides. The ominous remark that follows Hector's promise to Dolon of the horses of Achilles is a case in point. Again, the effect of the magnificent speech in which Achilles repudiates Agamemnon's overtures is heightened by the fact that Achilles really thinks that Destiny leaves him free to go home unscathed, whereas we know that he will be dragged back into the war by the killing of his dearest friend and in the end (or rather beyond it) will himself be killed. Which brings me to a further point. The action of the *Iliad* covers only fifty days in a ten years' war. But by a skilful extension of the device I am discussing, Homer causes two shadows to add their sombre significance to every page, that of the past and that of what is yet to come.

Secondly, Homer employs the device of delayed action. His hearers know what is coming, but not how or when. The sinister figure of Achilles is introduced at the beginning of the poem, but only to be withdrawn into the background till we reach Book 9. We are almost lulled into security – but not quite. There are too many references to the absentee for us to forget him. However, when Achilles does come into the foreground again, he removes himself once more with such a show of indomitable pride that we are left wondering how Homer is going to break this adamantine spirit. And we are not surprised to discover that it takes him nine tremendous Books to do so. The same artifice of suspense is used in the *Odyssey*. There too the chief figure is introduced in the beginning only to vanish and be talked about by other characters till he appears in person in Book 5. Moreover, the parallel in technique extends to the conclusion of both works. In both, Book 22 brings the action to a climax (Hector is killed: the Suitors are disposed of); in Book 23 we have a peaceful interlude (the Funeral Games: Odysseus is recognized by Penelope), and Book 24 provides the resolution of the drama (Achilles obeys the gods and relents: Odysseus is reinstated by divine intervention). This similarity in their composition is one of the many things which incline me to the opinion that one man is the author of both works.

It will astonish people who know nothing of the 'Homeric

question' to learn that these splendidly constructed poems, and especially the *Iliad*, have in the past been picked to pieces by the men who studied them most carefully and should presumably have admired them most. They alleged certain incongruities in the narrative and argued that the *Iliad* is the composite product of a number of poets of varying merit, who had not even the doubtful advantage of sitting in committee, but lived at different times and each patched up his predecessor's work, dropping many stitches in the course of this sartorial process. Now I think it is generally admitted that Homer did not invent the Story of Troy; also that it was the practice of ancient poets to build up their own edifice with the help of bricks taken from existing structures. In fact we should *expect* the *Iliad* to contain quite clear indications that it is the last of a long line of poems. Like Hermes as described by Priam, it bears every sign of good breeding and noble parentage. I have already referred to the evidence of advanced technique which is provided by certain elements in its construction. And I could add other points which in these latter days of literature we are too sophisticated to note with surprise or even to note at all, for instance that in Homer it is already an established convention that the author has been put by his Muse in a position to tell us everything his characters have said or thought, even their last soliloquies. If Homer invented all this technique it would be more than niggardly to deny him originality; but even if we take the likelier view that he inherited a great deal of it from previous poets, we have by no means shown that the *Iliad* was not his own.

We are left, in the end, with one kind of evidence, and that is psychological. To me, the proof of unity afforded by Homer's consistency in character-drawing is the most convincing of many. Note first that he does not describe his characters at length; he makes them disclose themselves by what they say and do in the scenes where they appear. Thetis, for instance, the mother of Achilles, is a sorrowful lady, who always has a grievance: her one obsession is her love for her illustrious but ill-starred son, on whose behalf she is ready to pester any- one from Zeus to Hephaestus. From the moment of her first introduction in Book I, through all the episodes in which she reappears, up to the last Book, Homer presents her with complete consistency – and that in scenes which have all been denied a right to their place in the *Iliad*. I argue that such a high degree of consistency would have proved impossible for more than a single author, particularly without the assistance, in one place or another, of a full-length portrait from the original creator's pen. The same is true if one follows the major figures – Athene, Odysseus, Nestor, or Helen herself – from the *Iliad* into the *Odyssey*. They are always themselves. I feel sure, on general literary grounds, that a fresh author taking them over could not have helped revealing his hand. In fact, any newcomer in the field of Epic poetry who was original enough to have 'contributed' to the *Iliad* or *Odyssey*, could not have failed, indeed would almost certainly have wished, to leave the imprint of his own mind on his characters. The Attic dramatists, who drew so largely on Homer, certainly showed this very human proclivity. It is difficult to recognize the characters of Homer in *their* portraits of Helen, Odysseus, Aias, and the rest.

However, it is inconsistencies in the narrative that were the chief weapons of those who tried to pick the *Iliad* to pieces. I cordially invite new readers to try to find some for themselves, though, unlike Achilles at the sports, I offer no 'splendid prizes' for this event. No marks will be given for the discovery of passages where Homer, after killing a man in battle, brings him back to life – this might happen to any author. One mark (out of ten) is allotted for the detection of minor incongruities in timing. For instance, Odysseus in the course of twenty-four hours, besides eating three dinners, does more things than the most energetic hero of a modern adventure story could have done in three days. But the taking of these little liberties with time is part of a dramatist's privilege, and Homer, particularly in the *Iliad*, is above all things dramatic. Half the poem consists of speeches and all the rest is put before us as though upon a stage – in fact, Homer invented drama before the theatre was invented to receive it. I might allot as much as two marks to the enquiring spirit who asks how it comes about in Book 3 that Priam, who has had the Achaean chieftains knocking at his gates for nine years, has to ask Helen who is who. But full marks will be given only for the detection of a real flaw which cannot be explained away – as can be done, in my opinion, with all the alleged literary crimes for which Homer was dismembered and served up piecemeal to Victorian schoolboys, myself included.

If we have now re-integrated Homer as one person, or at most two (for I believe I am in the minority in attributing the *Iliad* and *Odyssey* to a single author), the next thing that the reader will ask is where the story of the *Iliad* came from. I wish I could tell him. A great deal of scholarly research has been done on the question. It has become fairly certain that there was an earlier *Achilleis* or Story of Achilles, indeed several stories in which the angry young hero who refused to fight till the eleventh hour bore other names than that of Achilles. In fact, Homer himself gives us one of these, in which Meleager figures in the leading role, much as in the *Odyssey* he gives us the 'Wandering Prince' once with Odysseus as hero and once with Menelaus. Stories of the siege and sack of towns are by no means missing from the mythology of other races. And it is my surmise that the stories we read in Homer issued, with an esoteric or at least ritual content, from the mouths of wise men who lived long before him; that in the course of centuries they spread across the world, undergoing many changes of nomenclature and language, and sinking to the folklore level, where, even if they were not fully understood, they were at least enabled to survive by their intrinsic interest and excellence; and that in the age of Homer they were raised to what we recognize as the literary level. That is my impression. It would need a good deal to confirm it; and at this point I will only add my own belief that Homer himself did not realize the esoteric content of his tales, if any. He had his own approach to truth, but that was through art.

Is Homer's narrative in any sense historical? The answer is both yes and no. I do not think that, in telling the story of the Trojan War, he is giving us history, even in its most diluted form. There *was* a place called Troy (or Ilium) and we know that it was more than once destroyed. But even so, this ten years' war, as described by him and thrown back a few generations into the past, did not take place (even without the participation of the gods) either at Troy or, in my opinion, anywhere else. It was a fiction of a very special kind, which had existed long before Homer's time – a fiction that he adorned with the names of people whom his audience believed to be the ancestors of their own ruling princes, and some of whom we ourselves may well accept as having lived. If this view is correct, it enormously enhances the merit of Homer's achievement in building up the tale and the characters who make it. I would rather have the *Iliad* than a whole shelf of Bronze-Age war-reports, however accurate.

Besides, Homer does give us history – the history of his own world. That statement needs but little qualification. We know from the archaeological evidence that Homer attempts to archaeologize, even to take us into the Mycenaean Age. Nestor's cup is a case in point – a comparable vessel, with a couple of doves on top of it, was discovered at Mycenae. Yet in Homer's day there was no science of archaeology, no written history, to assist the historical novelist. Where then did he get these details from the past? I think there is only one answer. He took them from the work of previous poets, in much the same way as he took over from them much of their vocabulary, and even a number of their lines and ways of dealing with recurring situations. Yet in spite of this indebtedness, Homer leaves on our minds the impress of complete originality. It is his own observation of life that he depends on. I am not denying that he invokes the glamour of the mythical past when he confronts Odysseus with the Sirens, or Meleager with the Calydonian Boar. But I feel strongly that in all that matters most, in describing the general structure of society, the relations of men and women to one another, and even the physical circumstances of their existence, he is drawing from contemporary models. I will go even further and say that he could not have done otherwise and at the same time succeeded in holding his audience, who, it must be remembered, did not read him in a printed book with the assistance of learned footnotes, but heard him recite his hexameters to the accompaniment of a lyre, as an after-dinner entertainment, while the wine went round. I maintain that in such circumstances any attempt to describe an alien world must have failed.

Homer, then, appealed to his hearers' minds through what they knew. For instance, every member of his audience would at once recognize the force of the homely simile in which the Myrmidons are likened to a horde of wasps. By the same token they must have known the lion; and for this reason I mistrust the archaeologists who argue that in the period and place in which they wish to locate Homer lions were extinct. Would any narrator today, in his efforts to bring his story to life, present his listeners every few minutes with a dodo in action? If archaeology cannot fit Homer into a period which contains lions and the rest of the things that he refers to in familiar terms, I feel that archaeology must think again. And to be quite frank it does so – every ten or twenty years. At the moment it is fashionable to place Homer as late as 750 BC. I myself would put him in the tenth century before Christ. But the question of his date is extremely difficult, and my only contention here is that Homer gives us a unified picture of the world that he saw with his own eyes, whatever its exact date may have been. In that sense Homer gives us history – and history of a period about which, but for a few broken relics, we should otherwise have known next to nothing.

There is no need for me to describe Homer's world as revealed in the *Iliad*. He does it a great deal better than I could; he looks at it through the eyes of a poet. Hitherto I have discussed him mainly as a constructor of stories; and the problems involved were simple in comparison with the difficulty of assessing him as an imaginative poet. I can make only slanting approaches to this task, and must fall back on some of the new impressions that have crowded in upon me during the many years I have spent in the study of his mind.

I have been struck first by the realism, subtlety and modernity of Homer's character-drawing. When I say 'modernity' I do not mean that we shall meet such characters as Dolon, Paris, Diomedes or Briseis in Piccadilly, but that to Homer they were contemporary and true. He did not summon them from the legendary past: he created them out of his own experience of life. The deep impression of reality which they made upon me entirely banished from my mind (and I hope from my translation) the

idea I had received in my schooldays that Homer was harking
back to the so-called 'heroic age', when 'heroes' were apparently
as common as blackberries. My illusions were shattered by a
single reading of the sordid quarrel between Agamemnon and
Achilles in Book 1. I soon became convinced that human nature
has not materially altered in the three thousand years since
Homer wrote; that his people were a great deal more interesting
than 'heroes'; that his poetic achievement in raising them to the
tragic level was all the more sublime; and, incidentally, that his
whole effect is obscured if one heroizes his men and gods by
describing them and making them talk in a pompous and old-
fashioned style. In other words, I found that Homer is depicting
us in somewhat different circumstances. And I am not at all
shaken in this conclusion when he makes his warriors hurl at
each other lumps of rock 'even to lift which was a feat beyond
the strength of any two men bred to-day.' That is merely a
conventional tribute to the ancient belief that regression rather
than progress is the rule in human affairs.

Another misapprehension that I rapidly corrected was con-
cerned with the humour of Homer. 'Homeric laughter' is an
unfortunate phrase. When the banqueters on Olympus are
doubled up with laughter at the sight of the lame god Hephaestus
bustling about in the hall, it is not Homer that is laughing, but
the gods he had created. Nor is it pertinent to talk, as Dr Leaf
did, of the 'savage humour' of his warriors. If you have just
saved your own life in mortal combat by killing your enemy, it
is ten to one that any joke that may spring to your lips will be
completely lacking in urbanity. Homer is more of a realist than
his critics, most of whom, I dare say, had never seen a battle.
They do not even allow him to relieve a melancholy passage by
a lighter interlude. When a hitch occurs in the cremation of
Patroclus, and Iris hastens to help Achilles by bringing the Winds
to bear on the situation, we are told by Dr Leaf (who does not
fail to detect 'a touch of humour' here) that the whole scene
'falls below the dignity of its surroundings'; indeed, 'an inter-
polator' is blamed for the impropriety.

However, the point I wished to make is that Homer's own
sense of humour is a very different thing from that of his

creatures. It is a subtle, all-pervading essence, like the perfume of Here's imperishable olive-oil, which 'had only to be stirred for the scent to spread through Heaven and earth.' In his treatment of Heaven it is felt from the moment when Zeus comments with sad resignation on the domestic trouble that Thetis has let him in for, and it penetrates every Olympian scene till the last intervention of the gods, when the disguised Hermes compliments Priam on realizing that he comes of not ignoble parentage. What is so remarkable is the fact that Homer leaves us with the feeling not only that he believes in his gods but that they were indeed very worshipful and formidable powers. Moreover, the Greeks accepted him as their first theologian and the creator of the Olympian religion. I know that there have been other faiths whose devotees were not discouraged from laughing at their gods. But I still think that Homer's achievement in this respect is unique for a man of letters. And I cannot explain it.

But there is one fact to which I can point. The comic element is introduced almost solely on occasions when gods are *shown together*, in sympathetic or in hostile action. When dealing with mankind, each in his own capacity, they are far from amusing. Apollo and his Sister Artemis put up a ludicrous show when at war with their Uncle and their Father's Consort, but Apollo acting on his own in the first pages of the *Iliad* is a very serious and unpleasant person; and so is Artemis when King Oeneus has miscounted and she sends him the Calydonian Boar. Even Aphrodite, who cuts such a pathetic figure in a pitched battle, is a power whom Helen herself cannot trifle with when she, the goddess of love, is attending to her own business. This, I think, is how Homer saves the face of his gods – with one exception. He gives the War-god many terrible and bloody attributes, but he takes no pains to make us feel that he is much more than a bully. It is possible that the reason why he persistently degrades and ridicules Areas in a poem which is much concerned with battle, is that the *Iliad* was written not to glorify war (though it admits its fascination) but to emphasize its tragic futility.

Homer then reveres his gods, but rightly feels that it would be untrue to life to make these formidable creatures take one another as seriously as *he* takes each of them. They are members of a family and, as such, are all on much the same level, like the members of a human family, the father of which may be a terror to his office-boy but fulminates with less effect at home. Thus, for a realist like Homer, high comedy in Heaven was artistically inevitable.* And of course it was useful in a tragedy by way of relief or of contrast with the melancholy scene below. But Homer's humour is not confined to Olympus: it pervades the human drama too. Sometimes it comes into this by way of relief, as when Idomeneus and Meriones catch each other taking a rest in the middle of a very terrible battle, or in the brilliant description of the games that follow Patroclus' funeral. But this is not always so. The delightful account of Agamemnon's inspection of his troops, when the tactless Commander-in-Chief succeeds in ruffling the feelings of nearly all his senior officers, is not preceded by a passage where the tension is high. In the end, one is forced to the conclusion that Homer could not help seeing humour both on earth and in Heaven. He found it in the very texture of reality. And I hope that he was right.

Homer's diction is superb and it matches his observation. It is easy to rejoice in these and be content. But some of us are not so quickly satisfied: we wish to know how he achieves nobility. I myself have come to feel that his is the poetry not so much of words but of ideas – if it is possible to separate the two. I approach an understanding through the examination of the epithets which he uses in such abundance. Every manufactured object that he mentions is well and truly made. A ship is always fast, well-benched and seaworthy; a spear is stout, long and sharp, and (we are charmed to note) it is its custom to throw a long shadow on the ground and also to be 'wind-fed' even when resting in a warrior's hand; that is to say, it looks back to the time when its shaft was part of an ash-tree on the windswept mountain-side, or else forward to the moment when it is going to hurtle through the air. Natural phenomena such as the rose-

* But the gods do not retaliate by laughing at mankind. On the contrary, except for some light-hearted backchat with their favourites (e.g. Athene and Diomedes, 5; or Athene and Odysseus, *Od.* 13), they take men seriously and regard them as miserable though fascinating creatures. See Apollo on the subject, 21, or Zeus, 20 and 17.

fingered dawn and the ambrosial and mysterious night are all given adjectives which search out the quintessence of their quality or beauty. Homer's men are all noble, peerless, brave, wise, or characterized by some other excellence; and his women are all lovely, or at least well-dressed and with hair beautifully done. What is the significance of this wholesale use of honorific epithets – epithets which often sound insincere or at least fall in most inappropriate places?* Scholars are inclined to explain them away as the decorative trappings of the Epic style, and as being for the most part a legacy to Homer from his predecessors' work. This does not satisfy me. If Homer did take them over as trappings, his genius put them to a new use, which is a mirror to his own mind. When he calls a warrior brave or great-hearted just at the moment when he is behaving like an arrant coward, I do not think that he is being careless or conventional – he is seeing that warrior as he was, or will be, or indeed as he, in essence, is. When he talks of a beautiful and well-built chariot, he is not labouring under the delusion that all the workmanship of his day (excellent as it no doubt was) attained perfection. He has no use for a shoddy article, and what he sees in his mind's eye is the perfect thing. He does the same with people. Everything I have written earlier in this essay, if it is true, shows what a realist he is. But the reality that he sees has for his eye a certain transparence, through which he sees and records the ideal or higher reality. He puts me in mind of his own picture of Zeus when, sitting on Mount Ida, he wearies of watching the unending battle and turns 'his shining eyes into the distance', where, among other more satisfying things, he can survey 'the Abii, the most law-abiding folk on earth'.

I do not mean by this simile that Homer, when he calls a villain 'great-hearted', is indulging himself in illusion or wishful thinking, but that he is seeing reality at two levels. To which I might add that he sees good as more *real* than evil. It is as though he had anticipated Plato's Theory of Forms, according to which all earthly things are the imperfect and transitory copies of ideal

---

* Like our parliamentary expressions, e.g. 'the noble lord', or 'the honourable and gallant member for X'.

Forms that have a permanent existence in Heaven. I like to fancy that Homer, more privileged than Plato, actually saw these Forms, and even, on one occasion, brought them down to earth. For it is this that he did when he gave immortal horses to Achilles. His attitude to animals in general repays the closest study;* but in these horses of Achilles, if the reader will follow them through their triumphs and their tears, I think he will admit that Homer has given us something unique. And he may also note an interesting point. When the Ideal is manifested in the work-a-day world, it does not put to shame the creatures of a day – it brings them nearer to itself. Thus, when Homer causes Pedasus, a mortal thoroughbred, to be put in as an outrigger with the divine horses of Achilles, he is careful to tell us that Pedasus, though he 'was only an ordinary horse', kept up with the immortal pair, and his subsequent death is one of the most poignant things we have to put up with in all the nightmare battles of the 'lamentable war'.

My theory that Homer's poetry gives us reality and super-reality at the same time does, if it is correct, throw a little light on the central problem of the *Iliad*, the character of Achilles. We have seen in what a sordid light he is presented in the first Book. But this is only the beginning: we are to follow him through every stage of degradation to which the exasperating conditions of a long-drawn-out war can lead a character whose very strength is its weakness. Even his best friend and admirer Patroclus sees him as 'warping a noble nature to ignoble ends'. His pride becomes a monomania, and even his grief at the death of Patroclus, based as it is on injured self-esteem, produces no softening, but leads instead to an outburst of insensate cruelty and rage. Yet all along the gods are honouring Achilles and, with them, Homer somehow makes us feel that, behind all this, true greatness lies concealed. And in the end, in the memorable scene in which Achilles gives up Hector's corpse to his old father, we are allowed one glimpse of what the real Achilles is.

---

* Unlike us, he has no superiority complex in relation to animals. He recognizes not only their essential qualities but their right to display them; he even shows sympathy with the wasp (16) and he is the only writer I know who admires the intrepidity of the fly that keeps settling on one's nose (17).

I say 'is', not 'might have been', for I take it that the function of tragedy is not merely to mourn the wastage of virtue and to cry over spilt milk, but to hint at some ultimate solution, to suggest that if we could only look at things with the Olympian eye of Zeus we should see that, after all, the milk we were crying about is not really spilt.

At the end, I have added a Glossary giving a few facts about the more important characters in the tale. In compiling this I decided to say about these people only what Homer, our chief and earliest authority, permits, while adding in square brackets a little information that we glean from other writers. In the course of the work I hit on some interesting points, for example, the seniority of Paris to Hector, and the normality of Helen's parentage. I was also able to strengthen some of the impressions I had received from the text itself. Homer's main interest lies in the study of human beings and human gods. He is disposed to reject or tone down the grotesque and the supernormal. The beautiful Helen did not emerge from an egg, and, apart from one perfunctory reference to the Judgement of Paris, it was her human frailty and that of her seducer that led to the Trojan War. His handling of the gods and their many interventions and rescues in battle is much on a par with this. When Achilles is fighting the River-god Xanthus, we are left wondering all the time whether a demonic power is at work, or whether Achilles has not merely let himself in for the risk of being drowned by a river in spate. In a word, Homer is inclined to hover on the near side of the line that separates the natural and the supernatural – not that I, for one, object to crossing it now and then with such a guide.

EVR

Highgate,
  September 1949

Note to the 8th Printing

Since the above Introduction was written, Michael Ventris'
decipherment of Linear B has opened a new era in Homeric
studies, and Professor T. B. L. Webster, in *From Mycenae to
Homer*, London (Methuen) 1958 and New York (Praeger),
has taken full advantage of the opportunities now afforded
of achieving greater exactitude in dating Homer's poems and
tracing them to their sources. His brilliant work has convinced
me that I was mistaken in tentatively placing Homer as early as
the tenth century BC; also that some of the earlier poetry to
which I suggested that Homer is indebted was that of the
Mycenaens themselves, whose literary work we still hope to
discover.

EVR

June, 1959

Notes on this Revision

I here draw attention to a number of the conscious decisions I made about the technical and idiomatic updating of E. V. Rieu's text.[1]

1. The oral poet repeats epithets, phrases, sentences, speeches and even whole scenes throughout (see Introduction, p. xxviii), but Rieu did not always use exactly the same words just because Homer did. I have tried to settle on the same form of words for some of the most common repetitions, in most cases by selecting one of Rieu's versions to impose across the board (but see 6 below). The Homeric way of introducing and closing speeches has also been restored; so too has the Homeric way of dealing with similes.

2. The unHomeric language of king, empire and modern warfare has been removed. 'Royal', 'king', 'prince', 'imperial', 'officer', 'battalion', 'fleet', 'squadron', etc., have been replaced by non-specific terms like 'leader', 'contingent', 'ship'. 'Heaven' and 'the heavens', with their Christian connotations, have also gone, and I have tried (not always successfully) to avoid contemporary financial language like 'payment', with its implications of the exchange of coinage.

3. Rieu, a most courteous man, ascribed a similarly courtesy to Greek heroes, making them say 'Please' and 'Would you . . . ?' when the Greek expresses a straight command 'Do X'. The command form has been restored.

4. Rieu took the view that Homer often ascribed to gods what we would ascribe to nature, for example, or chance, and for

that reason sometimes omitted them. But when Homer said the gods did something, he meant it: so in such cases divinities are restored.

5. Rieu used Homer's terms for Greeks, of which there were three – literally, 'men from Achaea' (Achaeans), 'men from Argos' (Argives) and 'descendants of Danaus' (Danaans). These Homeric names have very considerable historical interest, most obviously because Homer does not call Greece or the Greeks by their received ancient and modern names, 'Hellas' and 'Hellenes'. Homer does mention a region called 'Hellas' (e.g. 2.683, see map 4), though no one (to my knowledge) knows why that local name should later have become applied to all Greece.[2] But since Agamemnon's expedition did in fact consist of Greeks from what we know as the central and southern Greek mainland and islands (Mycenaean Greece), Homer's 'Achaeans', 'Argives' and 'Danaans' have all been called 'Greeks' throughout this translation.[3]

6. The meaning of the repeated epithets is often disputed. As ancient commentaries make clear, even Greeks themselves were baffled by many of them. One has to take a position on this. So I differ from Rieu in some of the more common disputed epithets as follows:

> *agkulomêteô* not 'of the crooked counsels' but 'sickle-wielding'
>
> *aigiokhoio* not 'aegis-bearing' but 'who drives the storm-cloud'
>
> *atrugetoio* not 'unharvested' but 'murmuring'
>
> *eriounos* (of HERMES) not 'the luck-bringer' but 'the runner'
>
> *euruopa* not 'far-seeing' but 'far-thundering'
>
> *glaukôpis* not 'of the Flashing Eyes' or 'bright-eyed' but 'grey-eyed'

I have consistently translated *dîogenês* as 'Olympian-born', *dîotrephês* as 'Olympian-bred', *helikôps* as 'dark-eyed', and *hêrôs* as 'warrior'. 'Rosy-fingered Dawn' and 'winged words', of course, stay. I have given up on *mônukhes hippoi*, 'single-hoofed horses', translating simply as 'horses'; likewise *euknêmîdes Akhaioi*, 'Greeks with fine greaves', have usually become 'Greek men-at-arms' (though it is indeed historically very interesting that around 1200 BC Greeks were, apparently, the only soldiers to wear these leather or metal shin-guards).

7. As in Rieu, silent, interpretative glosses have been added to the text where they aid understanding; and names of fathers and epithets have occasionally been omitted, or changed for the sake of clarity (e.g. 'Patroclus' in place of 'the son of Menoetius'). For a list of omitted fathers' names, see Appendix 2.

8. The new chapter summaries and marginal notes will enable readers to keep a firm grip on a plot notorious for its digressions and sheer multiplicity of characters.

9. Line numbers in this revision are from *Homeri opera* I–II (*Iliad*), edited by D. B. Monro and T. W. Allen (Oxford: Oxford University Press, 1920, third edition).

NOTES

1. One obvious example: my warriors do not wear cuirasses or corselets but body-armour. In the Homeric context, no one (I trust) is going to imagine this bears any relation to police uniform. I add here that I have followed the Oxford text of the *Iliad* (ed. D. B. Monro and T. W. Allen, 1920, third edition), except in a few places where I have missed out lines or chosen different readings.

2. The word 'Greek' derives from Latin *Graecus*, which itself derives from the small Greek town Graea (2.498), probably ancient Oropus (by the mouth of the River Asopus, map 4). The Latin name would be explained if Graeans joined the earliest colonization movement to south Italy in the eighth century BC (a tradition suggests they did) and were the first Greek-speakers to have been encountered by Italians.

3. I add here that there are enough proper names in Homer to cope with anyway – *c.* 1,100, of which more than half occur just once.

The Main Characters

GREEKS

Achilles [A-kíll-eez]. Son of the mortal Peleus and the divine Sea-nymph THETIS, from Phthia [F-thée-a] in Thessaly [Théss-a-lee]. Leader of the Myrmidons [Mér-midd-ons]. Patroclus is his dearest friend. Achilles' anger drives the story of the *Iliad* [Íll-ee-ad]. ATHENE is always by his side. Homer foretells his death at the hands of *Paris* and *APOLLO*. Called 'swift-footed' because of his speed at chasing down an enemy in flight.

Agamemnon [A-ga-mém-non]. Son of Atreus and ruler of Mycenae [My-sée-nee] in Argos. He is leader of the expedition to *Troy* because he brings the most ships. He is the elder brother of Menelaus (the pair are referred to together as the 'sons of Atreus'). He was murdered by his wife Clytaemnestra [Kleye-tem-néss-tra] on his return to Greece.

Ajax, son of Oïleus [Áy-jax]. Leader of the Locrians. He is distinguished as the 'lesser' Ajax from his greater namesake.

Ajax, son of Telamon [Áy-jax]. From the island of Salamis [Sáll-a-miss], the 'great' Ajax, defensive bulwark of the Greeks (he never leads an attack), renowned for his huge shield 'like a tower'.

Antilochus [Ant-íll-ock-us]. Son of Nestor; a young warrior prominent in the fighting and also in the games. Has a brother Thrasymedes [Thrass-imm-éed-eez].

Atreus [Áy-tr-yoos]. Father of Agamemnon and Menelaus.

Automedon [Or-tóm-edd-on]. A Myrmidon, and attendant of

Achilles. Serves as attendant and charioteer to Patroclus when he fights without Achilles.

Calchas [Kál-kass]. Son of Thestor; the chief augur and prophet of the Greek expedition.

Diomedes [Die-om-éed-eez]. Son of Tydeus [Tíe-dyoos] and grandson of Oeneus [Óy-nyoos] – a young but brilliant and much-respected warrior. He is always talking about his father, who was killed in the unsuccessful siege of Thebes ('The Seven against Thebes') and had earlier enjoyed a number of athletic victories there, thanks to ATHENE. A great favourite of ATHENE's.

Eurypylus [Eur-ípp-ill-us]. He is wounded by *Paris* and tended by Patroclus.

Helen. Daughter of ZEUS, sister of Castor and Pollux and Clytaemnestra. Married to Menelaus of Sparta, she caused the Trojan War by running away from him with *Paris* to *Troy*.

Heracles [Hérr-a-kleez]. A man who became a god. Involved in a earlier battle against the *Trojans*. He was a son of ZEUS by Alcmene [Alk-mée-nee], so HERA hated him. In his early career he was compelled to carry out twelve labours for Eurystheus [Eur-íss-th-yoos]. He then took revenge on men who had insulted him, including the *Trojan* ruler *Laomedon*, whom he killed. HERA in her rage at this drove him along the coast to the island of *Cos*, and ZEUS punished her by hanging her up with anvils attached to her feet. Attacked even the gods from time to time.

Idomeneus [Eye-dóm-enn-yoos]. Son of Deucalion [Dew-káy-lee-on], from Crete. An older fighter, slow but steady.

Lapiths [Lá-piths]. Race of people from Thessaly who fought the half-horse, half-man Centaurs.

Machaon [Mack-áy-on]. Son of ASCLEPIUS, the famous healer. He tends Menelaus and is later wounded, but saved by Nestor.

Meleager [Mell-ee-áy-ger]. A hero cursed by his mother, Althaea [Al-thée-a], for killing her brother in a dispute. He at once withdrew his services from the battlefield – like Achilles.

Menelaus [Men-ell-áy-us]. Son of Atreus. Ruler of Lacedaemon/

Sparta, and younger brother of Agamemnon. His wife Helen was seduced and abducted to *Troy* by *Paris*.

Menestheus [Men-ésth-yoos]. Leader of the Athenian contingent.

Menoetius [Men-oí-tee-us]. Father of Patroclus.

Meriones [Merr-ée-on-eez]. Son of Molus. Nephew and attendant of Idomeneus, and second-in-command of the Cretan forces.

Nestor [Néss-tor]. Son of Neleus [Née-lyoos]. Ruler of Pylos [Píe-loss]. The oldest of the Greek chieftains fighting at *Troy*, he has the reputation of being a fount of wisdom. Called 'Gerenian' [Gerr-ée-nee-an] – no one knows why.

Odysseus [Odd-íss-yoos]. Son of Laertes [Lay-ért-ees]. Ruler of Ithaca and hero of Homer's *Odyssey*. Known for his quick-thinking. A great favourite of ATHENE's.

Patroclus [Pat-róck-lus]. Son of Menoetius. From Opous; attendant and dearest friend of Achilles.

Peleus [Péel-yoos]. Father of Achilles, a great warrior in his day with his horses, armour and famous ash spear (all given to him by the gods at his wedding to the Sea-nymph THETIS). Now an old man living on his own back home in Phthia.

Phoenix [Fée-nix]. Ruler of the Dolopes and old friend of Achilles. Peleus made him Achilles' tutor.

Sthenelus [Sthén-ell-us]. Son of Capaneus, attendant to Diomedes.

Talthybius [Tal-thíb-ee-us]. Chief herald to Agamemnon.

Telamon [Téll-am-on]. Father of (great) Ajax.

Teucer [T-yóo-sir]. Son of Telamon. Half-brother to the great Ajax. A fine bowman.

Thersites [Ther-síte-eez]. Only member of the rank-and-file to play a part in the *Iliad*, slapped down by Odysseus.

Tydeus [Tied-yoos]. Father of Diomedes, the hero of an earlier siege of Thebes.

TROJANS AND ALLIES OF *TROY*

The Trojan Royal Family (see 20.215–40)

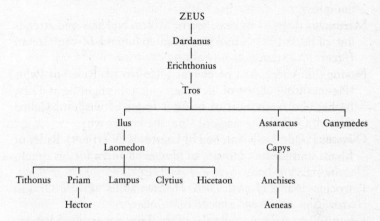

Aeneas [Inn-ée-us]. Son of the goddess *APHRODITE* and mortal *Anchises* [Ank-éye-sees]. Second-in-command to *Hector*. The hero of Virgil's *Aeneid*, a Roman epic (19 BC) about *Aeneas* leaving *Ilium* after it was sacked by Greeks and founding the Roman race in Italy.

Andromache [And-ró-mack-ee]. Daughter of *Eëtion*, the ruler of *Thebe* [Thée-bee]. Wife of *Hector* and mother of *Astyanax*.

Antenor [Ant-ée-nor]. A *Trojan* leader who advised his countrymen to give up Helen.

Astyanax [Ast-éye-an-ax]. Son of *Hector* and *Andromache*.

Briseis [Briss-áy-iss]. Daughter of *Briseus* from *Lyrnessus*. When Achilles sacked the town, he took *Briseis* captive. Agamemnon subsequently took her from him to compensate himself for the loss of *Chryseis*.

Cassandra [Cass-ánd-ra]. Daughter of *Priam* and *Hecabe*. After the sack of *Ilium*, Agamemnon took her home with him, and she was murdered by his wife Clytaemnestra. She was a prophetess who, because she rejected the advances of *APOLLO*, was doomed always to tell the truth and never to be believed.

Chryseis [Cry-sáy-iss]. Daughter of *Chryses* [Crý-seez], the priest of *APOLLO* at *Chryse* [Crý-see] in *Troy*. She was captured at *Thebe* by Achilles and allotted to Agamemnon, who was forced by *APOLLO*'s plague to give her back to her father.

Deiphobus [Day-íff-obb-us]. Son of *Priam* and *Hecabe*. A *Trojan* leader. ATHENE likens herself to him when she deceives *Hector* into standing and fighting against Achilles.

Dolon [Dóll-on]. Son of *Eumedes*. A wealthy young *Trojan* who was very fond of horses.

Eëtion [Ee-étt-ee-on]. Father of *Andromache*, killed (as his sons were) by Achilles.

Glaucus [Gl-ór-kus]. Son of *Hippolochus*. A *Trojan* ally from *Lycia*, second-in-command to his cousin *Sarpedon*.

Hecabe [Héck-a-bee]. Wife of *Priam*, to whom she bore many sons, including *Hector, Paris, Helenus* and *Deiphobus*.

Hector. Son of *Priam* and *Hecabe*. Married to *Andromache* (with a son *Astyanax*); leader of the *Trojan* and allied armies, and *Troy*'s greatest fighter. Scathing of his elder brother *Paris*.

Helenus [Héll-enn-us]. Son of *Priam* and *Hecabe*. Like his sister *Cassandra*, he was gifted with second sight.

Idaeus [Eye-dáy-us]. Chief herald to *Priam*.

Ilus [Éye-lus]. Grandfather of *Priam*. Ilium is the 'city of *Ilus*'.

Laomedon [Lay-ómm-edd-on]. Treacherous early ruler of *Troy* renowned for not keeping to agreements, for example to give Heracles his famous horses for rescuing his daughter from a sea-monster, or to pay POSEIDON for building the walls round *Ilium*.

Pandarus [Pánd-ar-us]. Son of *Lycaon*. An ally of *Troy* from *Lycia*. Expert, but treacherous, archer.

Paris. Son of *Priam* and *Hecabe*. Apparently junior to his brother *Hector* (but see under *Hector*). Homer refers throughout to his abduction of Helen as the cause of the war but makes only one passing reference to the famous judgement by *Paris* of the three goddesses, *APHRODITE*, HERA and ATHENE, when he was serving as a shepherd on *Mount Ida* [Éye-da].

Polydamas [Poll-ídd-a-mus]. Son of *Panthous*. One of the ablest of the *Trojan* leaders. He is a cautious, clear-headed strategist whom Homer uses as a warning figure for *Hector*.

Priam [Pr-éye-am]. Son of *Laomedon*, and descendant of *Dardanus* son of ZEUS (hence 'Dardanian'). Aged ruler of Troy.

Sarpedon [Sar-pée-don]. Son of ZEUS and leader of the *Trojan* allies from *Lycia*.

GODS

APHRODITE [Aff-rod-éye-tee]. Daughter of ZEUS; mother of *Aeneas*; lover of the War-god *ARES*; a goddess primarily associated with sexual impulses. Since *Paris* selected her as the loveliest of the three goddesses, she fights on the *Trojan* side. Called 'Cyprian' because of her famous cult-centre on Cyprus.

APOLLO [A-póll-oh]. Son of ZEUS and *LETO*, also called *Phoebus*. God of prophecy, sickness and health, and stringed instruments (hence of the lyre and the bow). The sudden deaths of men (not by violence) are attributed to his arrows. He fights on the *Trojan* side.

ARES [Aír-eez]. Son of ZEUS and HERA; the god of war, called 'most hateful' of the gods by ZEUS. He fights on the *Trojan* side, and in the battle of the gods is ignominiously disposed of by ATHENE.

ARTEMIS [Árt-emm-iss]. Daughter of ZEUS and *LETO*, and sister of *APOLLO*; the goddess of hunting and wild animals. She used her arrows to administer a peaceful death for women. On the *Trojan* side.

ATHENE [Ath-ée-nee]. Daughter of ZEUS, also called PALLAS ('Lady'?, 'Mistress'?, 'Youthful'?) ATHENE. Goddess of war, wisdom and the arts and crafts. Strongly pro-Greek because of her defeat in the judgement of *Paris*; works together with HERA against the *Trojans*. 'Grey-eyed' could mean 'owl-eyed', the owl being her special bird. 'Triton-born' may possibly mean that, after ZEUS gave birth to

ATHENE from his head, she was then brought up by the River Triton in Greece. 'Atrytone' [A-trý-tonn-ee] remains unexplained.

CRONUS [Crónn-us]. Husband of RHEA [Rée-ah] and father of ZEUS, POSEIDON, HADES and HERA. He was deposed from power by ZEUS, who defeated him in battle and hurled him, with his TITAN supporters, deep underground. He came to power by slicing off his father URANUS' genitals with a sickle (hence ZEUS is 'son of sickle-wielding Cronus').

DELUSION (in Greek *atê* [art-air]). Daughter of ZEUS. She is the personification of blind folly – the impulse to do something irrational and stupid, with disastrous consequences. See 'Personification' in Appendix 1.

EILEITHYIA [Ay-lay-thwée-ya]. Daughter of HERA. Goddess of labour in childbirth.

FURY/FURIES. Gods of the underworld who preserve the natural order of things, guard oaths and punish unnatural acts (including disrespect for parents).

HADES [Háy-deez]. Son of CRONUS and RHEA. God of the dead, who received the underworld as his portion when he and his brothers ZEUS and POSEIDON divided the world between them. Associated with horses.

HEBE [Hée-bee]. Daughter of ZEUS and HERA. Cup-bearer and handmaiden of the gods.

HEPHAESTUS [Heff-éye-stus]. Son of ZEUS and HERA. Master craftsman and architect of Olympus. Pro-Greek. In Homer he was born a cripple and thrown out of Olympus by ZEUS for trying to rescue his mother HERA when ZEUS tied her up.

HERA [Héar-ah]. Daughter of CRONUS and RHEA, sister and wife of ZEUS. Strongly pro-Greek, always plotting with ATHENE against ZEUS and occasionally being punished by him (see under 'Heracles'). Goddess of marriage and motherhood. 'White-armed' perhaps because a fair skin was valued; 'ox-eyed' perhaps because she was associated with the cow in prehistoric ritual.

HERMES [Hér-meez]. Son of ZEUS and Maia. The ambassador of the gods, though in the *Iliad* IRIS is used more often than HERMES as go-between. Called 'guide', as he guided the dead down to HADES; called 'slayer of Argus', a many-eyed monster sent by HERA to watch over Io, a young woman ZEUS loved. ZEUS ordered HERMES to get rid of it.

IRIS (= 'rainbow'). Messenger of the gods.

LETO [Lée-toe]. Mother of *APOLLO* and *ARTEMIS* by ZEUS.

MUSE. Goddess of memory, who helps the poet sing about events from long ago.

OCEAN. The ancient god whose great river, Greeks believed, circled the world.

POSEIDON [Poss-áy-don]. Son of CRONUS and RHEA, and a younger brother of ZEUS. He received the sea as his domain when the three brothers, ZEUS, POSEIDON and HADES divided the world by lot between them. God of elemental forces, for example earthquakes. Pro-Greek because he built the walls of *Ilium* for the treacherous *Trojan* ruler *Laomedon*, but received no 'pay' for his work.

STRIFE (in Greek, *eris*). Sister of *ARES* the War-god – another personification. It was she who threw the golden apple marked 'to the most beautiful' among the gods (see p. xiii).

THETIS [Thétt-iss]. Daughter of the Old Man of the Sea (Nereus). A Sea-nymph who was married to a mortal, Peleus, father of her only child, Achilles. Always at her son's side when he needs help.

TITANS [Tíe-tuns]. Powerful gods who supported CRONUS in his fight against his son ZEUS. They were thrust deep underground when ZEUS defeated them.

XANTHUS [Xán-thus]. God of the *Trojan* River *XANTHUS*, called '*Scamander*' by mortals; also the name of a river in *Lycia*.

ZEUS [Z-yoos]. Son of CRONUS and RHEA. Sky and Weather-god (hence 'lord of the lightning-flash', 'cloud-gatherer', 'far-thunderer' and so on). Strongest of all the gods and therefore the supreme Olympian deity, the 'Father'. He agrees to support Achilles in his feud with Agamemnon and shows some sympathy for the *Trojans*, in particular *Hector* and *Priam*.

Further Reading

THE *ILIAD*

D. L. Cairns (ed.), *Oxford Readings in Homer's 'Iliad'* (Oxford: Oxford University Press, 2001).

M. W. Edwards, *Homer: Poet of the 'Iliad'* (Baltimore: Johns Hopkins University Press, 1987).

S. L. Schein, *The Mortal Hero: An Introduction to Homer's 'Iliad'* (Berkeley: University of California Press, 1984).

S. Shankman (ed.), *The 'Iliad' of Homer*, transl. Alexander Pope (Harmondsworth: Penguin, 1996), complete with Pope's wonderful 'Observations' and 'Poetical Index'.

O. P. Taplin, *Homeric Soundings: The Shaping of the 'Iliad'* (Oxford: Clarendon Press, 1992).

HOMER

H. W. Clarke, *Homer's Readers: A Historical Introduction to the 'Iliad' and 'Odyssey'* (Newark: Associated University Presses, 1981).

J. Griffin, *Homer on Life and Death* (Oxford: Clarendon Press, 1980).

J. B. Hainsworth, *The Idea of Epic* (Berkeley: University of California Press, 1991).

J. Latacz, *Homer: His Art and his World* (Ann Arbor: University of Michigan Press, 1996).

E. V. Rieu, revised by D. C. H. Rieu, *Homer: The Odyssey* (Harmondsworth: Penguin, 1991; new edition 2003).

COMMENTARIES

On the Greek
G. S. Kirk (General Editor), *The Iliad: A Commentary* (6 vols.,
  Cambridge: Cambridge University Press, 1985–93).
W. Leaf, *The Iliad* (2 vols., London: Macmillan, 1886).
M. M. Willcock, *The 'Iliad' of Homer* (2 vols., London: Mac-
  millan, 1978–84).

In translation
Peter Jones, *Homer's 'Iliad': A Commentary on Three Transla-
  tions* (London: Duckworth, 2003). The translations in ques-
  tion are this one; Martin Hammond, *Homer: The Iliad*
  (Harmondsworth: Penguin, 1987); and Richard Lattimore,
  The Iliad of Homer (Chicago: University of Chicago Press,
  1951).
N. Postlethwaite, *The 'Iliad' of Homer: A Commentary* (Exeter:
  Exeter University Press, 2000).
M. M. Willcock, *A Companion to the 'Iliad'* (Chicago: Univer-
  sity of Chicago Press, 1976).

LEARNING ANCIENT GREEK

Peter Jones, *Learn Ancient Greek* (London: Duckworth, 1998),
  a simple introduction, based on a series in the *Daily
  Telegraph*.

CLASSICS TODAY

There are two associations for members of the general public
who live in the UK: *Friends of Classics*. This is for adults with
a love of the ancient world, however creaky their knowledge of
it. It organizes seminars, social events and outings, and produces
a biennial colour magazine (ed. Peter Jones). Write to Jeannie
Cohen, 51 Achilles Road, London NW6 1DZ

The Classical Association. The CA organizes lectures at local universities, school reading competitions and an AGM, and publishes regular newsletters. Write to The CA, Institute of Classical Studies, Senate House, Malet Street, London WC1E 7HU.

For details of classical summer schools for students and adults in ancient Greek, Latin, and Greek and Roman history and culture, write to: The Joint Association of Classical Teachers, Institute of Classical Studies, Senate House, Malet Street, London WC1E 7HU.

1. A reconstruction of Homer's imagined battlefields, as viewed from a point above Imbros, looking south

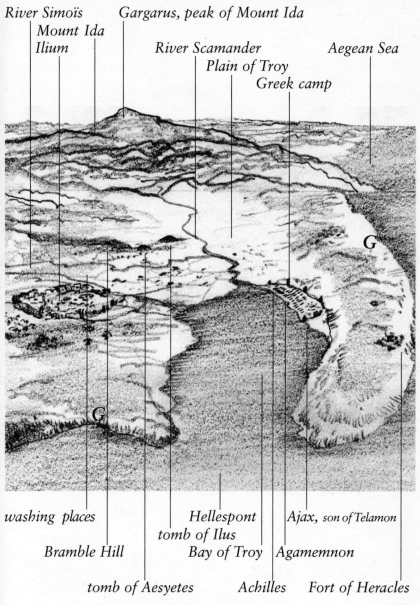

River Simoïs

Mount Ida

Ilium

Gargarus, peak of Mount Ida

River Scamander

Plain of Troy

Greek camp

Aegean Sea

washing places

Bramble Hill

tomb of Aesyetes

Hellespont
tomb of Ilus

Bay of Troy

Achilles

Ajax, son of Telamon

Agamemnon

Fort of Heracles

G=possible alternative sites for Greek camp

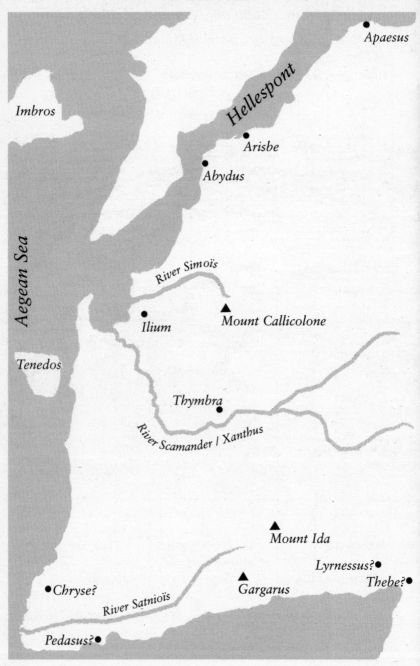

2. The Troad

Apaesus

Hellespont

Imbros

Arisbe

Abydus

River Simoïs

Aegean Sea

Ilium ▲ Mount Callicolone

Tenedos

Thymbra

River Scamander / Xanthus

▲ Mount Ida

Lyrnessus?●

●Chryse? ▲ Gargarus ●Thebe?

River Satnioïs

Pedasus?●

3. Trojan places and contingents

Trojans and allies in italics, contingents in capitals.
For Paeonians see map 5.

CICONES

THRACIANS

River Sangarius

PHRYGIANS

Samothrace
ZELEIA
MYSIANS
PERCOTE•
ADRESTEIA
DARDANIANS
River Aesepus

PAPHLAGONIANS →
Imbros
HALIZONES →
Ilium• TROJANS

▲ Mount Ida *(central peak Gargarus)*
Lemnos *Tenedos*

LARISA

MAEONIANS

Lesbos
River Hyllus
Lake Gygaea
River Hermus

I o n i a
▲ Mount Sipylus
▲ Mount Tmolus
River Cayster

CARIANS

River Xanthus

LYCIANS

COS

SYME

RHODES

4. Homeric Greece

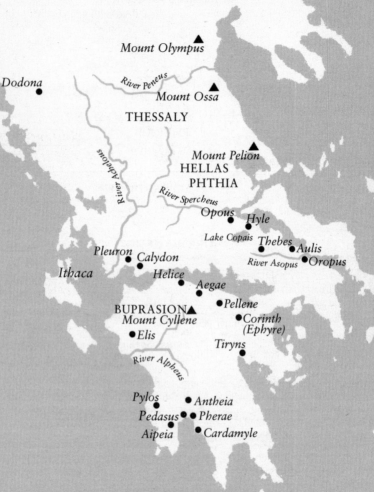

5. Greek contingents at Troy
For Cos, Syme and Rhodes see map 3.

PAEONIANS

PHILOCTETES?

CYPHUS?
TRICCE   ARGISSA

ORMENION?

PHERAE
PHYLACE

MAGNETES

MYRMIDONS

LOCRIS

EUBOEA
(Abantes)

ORCHOMENUS

AETOLIA
DULICHIUM   PHOCIS

BOEOTIA
ATHENS

CEPHALLENIA

ARCADIA

ELIS   MYCENAE

SALAMIS

ARGOS

PYLOS
LACEDAEMON

CRETE

Preliminaries

CONVENTIONS

1. On my use of 'Greeks', please see Notes on this Revision, 5.
2. In the summaries to each book and the marginal notes, and all other sections, Greek names and places are printed in roman type (e.g. Achilles, Argos), Trojan names and places are in italics (e.g. *Hector, Ilium*). Since Troy had many allies (cf. 2.804, 4.437), '*Trojan*' covers everyone on the Trojan side, wherever they come from. The names of gods are printed in capitals (ZEUS), pro-Trojan gods in italic capitals (*APOLLO*).
3. There are many ways of representing Greek names in English. Rieu used the traditional Anglicized forms, though he opted to follow Homer when he had a choice of ending a name with -*e* or -*a* (thus ATHENE, not ATHENA). I have followed his practice throughout, though I have changed ZEUS' wife from HERE to HERA to avoid confusion, and have converted the Greek hero Aias (an exact transliteration of the Greek name) back to his Anglicized name Ajax, which Rieu avoided because in his time that was the name universally associated with a popular brand of kitchen cleaner.

Other translations and books often prefer to use forms that more nearly represent ancient Greek, for example not 'Achilles' but 'Akhilleus' or 'Achilleus'. On the whole issue, see my *An Intelligent Person's Guide to Classics* (London: Duckworth, 2000), pp. 138–9.

A NOTE ON HOMER'S STYLE

Homer constantly gives characters and objects little descriptions. People are always being called for example 'godlike', 'lord', 'lord of men', and so on. More specifically, Achilles is 'swift-footed', ZEUS is a god 'who drives the storm-cloud', *APOLLO* is the 'Archer-god' or 'lord of the silver bow' and HERA 'white-armed'. Ships are 'hollow' or 'swift' (even when beached, like a parked 'fast car'), *Ilium* a town 'with fine walls', and so on.

'Son of' is especially popular, since fathers are important figures in Homer's world. So ZEUS is 'son of Cronus', Achilles 'son of Peleus', Agamemnon and Menelaus 'son(s) of Atreus'. Humans can even be credited with a divine father or mother, a high compliment. 'Olympian-born' means (literally) 'born of a god' and 'Olympian-bred' means 'brought up by a god' (see 'Some general epithets' in Appendix 1).

As well as these small repeated descriptions, whole sentences, sometimes whole speeches or scenes, are verbally repeated. Speeches nearly always end 'So X spoke' or 'With these words'. These repetitions are intentional. They are all part of Homer's way of composing and are there to be enjoyed (see Introduction, p. xxviii, for the technical explanation).

For 'supplication' or 'entreaty', common throughout the *Iliad*, see the Index.

The Iliad

I

PLAGUE AND WRATH

The Greek army is led by Agamemnon (son of Atreus). It is besieging *Ilium*, a town in the region of *Troy* whose ruler is *Priam*; it is the tenth year of the war (2.134).

To satisfy their desire for booty, the Greeks carry out raids on local towns. Human captives are especially prized. They are kept as slaves or sold for ransom. After one such raid, the young girl *Chryseis* is selected as an appropriate prize for Agamemnon. But *Chryseis* is the daughter of *Chryses*, a local priest of *APOLLO* ...

1–7: The poet announces his theme and asks the goddess (the Muse, goddess of memory) to 'sing', through him, the destructive anger of the greatest Greek fighter Achilles (son of Peleus).

8–52: [1st day] *Chryses* offers a ransom for his daughter, which Agamemnon brutally rejects. *APOLLO* sends a plague on the Greeks.

[Nine-day plague]

53–120: [10th day] Achilles calls an assembly, at which Agamemnon agrees to return *Chryseis*, but demands immediate compensation.

121–307: Achilles and Agamemnon quarrel over compensation. The insulted Achilles threatens to walk out. The goddess ATHENE prevents Achilles killing Agamemnon and promises him massive rewards for the insult. When the much respected Nestor fails to reconcile the two, Achilles stalks out of the fighting, taking his companion Patroclus and their troops (the Myrmidons) with him.

308–48: The mission to return *Chryseis* sets off, and Agamemnon's heralds seize Achilles' girl *Briseis*.

348–430: Achilles appeals for help to his divine mother THETIS.

430–92: *Chryseis* is handed over, and the plague ends [11th day].

[Eleven-day absence of the gods, beginning from the 9th day, 1.424.]

493–530: [21st day] THETIS supplicates a reluctant ZEUS and persuades him to make the Greeks start losing. That will force them to take Achilles back – with due compensation and the return of *Briseis*.

531–611: ZEUS quarrels with his wife HERA, who supports the Greeks. HEPHAESTUS restores the peace, and the gods turn to feasting and song. Night falls.

Anger – sing, goddess, the anger of Achilles son of Peleus, that accursed anger, which brought the Greeks endless sufferings and sent the mighty souls of many warriors to Hades, leaving their bodies as carrion for the dogs and a feast for the birds; and Zeus' purpose was fulfilled. It all began when Agamemnon lord of men and godlike Achilles quarrelled and parted.

Which of the gods was it that made them quarrel? It was Apollo, son of Zeus and Leto, who started the feud because he was furious with Agamemnon for not respecting his priest Chryses.
10 So Apollo inflicted a deadly plague on Agamemnon's army and destroyed his men.

Chryses had come to the Greeks' swift ships to recover his captured daughter. He brought with him an immense ransom and carried the emblems of the Archer-god Apollo on a golden staff in his hands. He spoke in supplication to the whole Greek army and most of all its two commanders, Agamemnon and Menelaus, the sons of Atreus:

'Sons of Atreus and you other Greek men-at-arms; you hope to sack Priam's town and get home in safety. May the gods that live on Olympus grant your wish. Now respect the Archer-god
20 Apollo son of Zeus, accept this ransom and release my beloved daughter.'

Then all the other Greeks shouted in agreement. They wanted to see the priest respected and the splendid ransom taken. But this was not at all to Agamemnon's liking. He cruelly and bluntly dismissed the priest:

'Old man, don't let me catch you loitering by the hollow ships today or coming back again in the future, or you may find the god's staff and emblems a very poor defence. That girl I will not release. She will grow old in Argos, in my household, a long way from her country, working at the loom, sharing my bed. Now get out and don't provoke me, if you want to save your skin.' 30

So he spoke, and the old man was afraid and did as he was told. He went off without a word along the shore of the sounding sea. But when he had gone some distance, the old man poured out prayers to lord Apollo, son of lovely-haired Leto:

'Hear me, Apollo, lord of the silver bow, protector of Chryse and holy Cilla, and mighty ruler over Tenedos! Plague-god, if ever I built a temple that pleased you, if ever I burnt you offerings 40 of the fat thighs of bulls or goats, grant me this wish. Make the Greeks pay with your arrows for my tears.'

So he spoke in prayer, and Phoebus Apollo heard him and came down in fury from the heights of Olympus, his bow and covered quiver on his back. With every movement of the furious god, the arrows rattled on his shoulders, and his descent was like nightfall. He settled down some way from the ships

[Day 1]
APOLLO avenges *Chryses*: the plague

and shot an arrow, with a terrifying twang from his silver bow. He attacked the mules first and the swift dogs; then he aimed 50 his sharp arrows at the men, and struck again and again. Day and night, packed funeral pyres burned.

For nine days the god's arrows rained down on the camp. On the tenth, Achilles had the men summoned to assembly, an idea the goddess white-armed Hera gave him in her concern for the Greeks whose destruction she was witnessing. When everyone had arrived and the gathering was complete, swift-footed Achilles rose and spoke to them:

'Agamemnon son of Atreus, what with the ravages of the fighting and the plague, any of us that are not dead by then will soon, I think, have to sail for home. Come, let us consult 60 some prophet or priest or some interpreter of dreams (dreams, as you know, are sent by Zeus) and find out from him why Phoebus Apollo is so angry with us. He may be offended at

some broken vow or failure in our rites. If so, he may be willing
to accept an offering of unblemished sheep and goats and save
us from the plague.'

With these words Achilles sat down, and Calchas
son of Thestor rose to his feet. As a prophet, Calchas
had no rival in the camp. Past, present and future
held no secrets from him; and it was his second sight
– a gift he owed to Apollo – that had guided the
70 Greek ships to Ilium. He had their interests at heart as he rose
and addressed them:

'Achilles dear to Zeus, you have instructed me to account for
the anger of lord Apollo the Archer-god; and I will do so. But
listen to me first and swear an oath to use all your eloquence
and strength to look after me and protect me. I ask this of you,
being well aware that I am about to infuriate a man whose
authority is great among us and whose word is law to all the
80 Greeks. An ordinary mortal is no match for anyone in authority
he angers. Even if his superior swallows his anger for the
moment, he will still nurse his grievance till the day when he
can settle the account. Consider, then, whether you can guaran-
tee my safety.'

Swift-footed Achilles replied and said:

'Put your mind at rest and tell us everything you have learnt
from the god. For by Apollo son of Zeus, the very god to whom
you pray, Calchas, when you reveal your prophecies – I swear
that as long as I am alive and look on the earth, not one of all
the Greeks here by the hollow ships will raise a fist against you,
90 not even if the man you mean is Agamemnon, who now claims
to be far the best of all.'

Then the matchless prophet took heart and said:

'Apollo has found no fault with any broken vows or failures
in our rites. Agamemnon insulted his priest, did not free his
daughter and refused the ransom – that is why Apollo made us
suffer and will continue to do so. He will not release us from
this loathsome plague till we give the dark-eyed girl back to
her father, without recompense or ransom, and send a sacred
100 offering to the priest's town of Chryse. Appease him like that,
and we might persuade him to relent.'

[Day 10] The
assembly:
Calchas'
revelation

With these words Calchas sat down, and the warrior son of
Atreus, wide-ruling Agamemnon, leapt up, enraged. His heart
seethed with fury, and his eyes were like flames of fire. With a
menacing look he spoke first to Calchas:

'Prophet of evil, never yet have you said a word to my advan-
tage. It's always trouble you revel in predicting. Not once have
you delivered a positive prophecy – not once! And now you
hold forth as the army's prophet, telling the Greeks that the
Archer-god Apollo is persecuting them because I refused the   110
splendid ransom for the girl Chryseis. And why? Because I
wanted to have her at home myself. Indeed, I like her better than
my wife Clytaemnestra. Chryseis is quite as beautiful and no
less clever or skilful with her hands.

'Still, I am willing to give her up, if that appears the better
course. I want my army alive and well, not dead or dying. But
give me another prize at once or I will be the only one of us
without one. That cannot be right. You can all see for yourselves   120
that the prize I was given is on its way elsewhere.'

Swift-footed godlike Achilles replied:

'Most glorious Agamemnon, unequalled in your   The argument
greed, where will the great-hearted Greeks find you   over prizes
a fresh prize? I have yet to hear of any store of common prop-
erty we have laid by. The plunder we took from captured
towns has been distributed. It cannot be right to ask the men
to reassemble that. No: give the girl back now, as the god de-
mands, and we will compensate you three, four times over,
if Zeus ever allows us to sack this Trojan town with its fine
walls.'

Lord Agamemnon replied and said: 130

'You are a great warrior, godlike Achilles, but don't imagine
you can trick me into that. I am not going to be outmanoeuvred
or persuaded by you. "Give up the girl", you say, in order to
keep your own prize safe. Do you expect me to sit tamely by,
while I am robbed? No: if the army is prepared to give me a
fresh prize, they must choose one to my taste to make up for my
loss. If not, I shall come and help myself to your prize, or Ajax's,
or maybe I shall walk off with Odysseus'. And what an angry
man I shall leave behind me!

140   'However, we can deal with all that later. For the moment, let us run a black ship down into the bright sea, carefully select her crew, load the animals for sacrifice and put the girl herself, fair-cheeked Chryseis, on board. And let some adviser be in charge, Ajax, Idomeneus, godlike Odysseus, or you yourself, Achilles, most impetuous of all Greeks, to offer the sacrifice and win us back Apollo's favour.'

Swift-footed Achilles gave him a black look and replied:

150   'You shameless, self-centred . . . ! How can you expect any of the men to comply with you willingly when you send them on a raid or into battle? It was no quarrel with Trojan warriors that brought *me* here to fight. They have never done *me* any harm. They have never lifted oxen or horses of mine, nor ravaged my crops back home in fertile Phthia, nurse of warriors. The roaring seas and many a dark range of mountains lie between us.

Achilles threatens to return home

'We joined your expedition, you shameless swine, to please you, to get satisfaction from the Trojans for Menelaus and

160   yourself, dog-face – a fact you utterly ignore. And now comes this threat from you, of all people, to rob me of my prize, in person, my hard-earned prize which was a tribute from the army. It's not as though I am ever given a prize equal to yours when the Greeks sack some prosperous Trojan town. The heat and burden of the fighting fall on me, but when it comes to dealing out the spoils, it is you that takes the lion's share, leaving me to return to my ships, exhausted from battle, with some pathetic portion to call my own.

'So, I shall now go back home to Phthia. That is the best thing

170   I can do – to sail home with my beaked ships. I can see no point in staying here to be insulted, while I pile up wealth and luxuries for you.'

Agamemnon lord of men replied:

'Run for it, then, by all means, if that's the way you feel. I am not going down on bended knees to entreat you to stay here on my account. There are others with me who will treat me with respect, and Zeus wise in counsel is first among them. Of all the Olympian-bred lords here, you are the most hateful to me. Rivalry, war,

Agamemnon dismisses Achilles

fighting – these are the breath of life to you. If you *are* a great
warrior, it is because the god made you so. Go home now with
your ships and your men-at-arms and rule your Myrmidons.   180
I have no interest in you whatsoever. Your resentment leaves
me cold.

'But here is a threat: in the same way as Phoebus Apollo is
robbing me of Chryseis, whom I propose to send off in my
ship with my crew, I will come in person to your hut and
take away fair-cheeked Briseis, your prize, Achilles, to let you
know how far I am your superior and to teach others to
shrink from claiming parity with me and playing the equal to
my face.'

So he spoke, and his words infuriated Achilles. In his manly
chest, his heart was torn whether to draw the sharp sword from   190
his side, thrust his way through the crowd and disembowel
Agamemnon, or control himself and check his angry impulse.
These thoughts were racing through his mind, and he was just
drawing his great sword from his sheath when Athene came
down from the skies. The goddess white-armed Hera had sent
her because she felt equally close to both men and was concerned
for them.

Athene stood behind Achilles and seized him by his auburn
hair. No one but Achilles was aware of her; the rest saw nothing.
Achilles was amazed. He swung round, recognized Pallas Athene   200
at once – so wonderful was the light from her eyes – and spoke
winged words:

'Why have you come here this time, daughter of
Zeus who drives the storm-cloud? Is it to witness
Agamemnon's humiliating affront? I tell you bluntly
and, believe me, I mean it: he stands to pay for this
insolence with his life.'

ATHENE
prevents
Achilles killing
Agamemnon

The goddess grey-eyed Athene replied:

'I came from the skies to cool your fury, if you will listen to
me. The goddess white-armed Hera sent me because she feels
equally close to both of you and is concerned for you. Come   210
now, give up this quarrel and take your hand from your sword.
Insult him with words instead and tell him what you mean to
do. I tell you bluntly and I *do* mean it: the day shall come when

splendid gifts three times as valuable as what you have now lost
will be laid at your feet because of that humiliating affront.
Hold your hand, then, and do as we tell you.'

Swift-footed Achilles replied and said:

'Goddess, a man must respect what you and Hera say, how-
ever angry he may be. Better for him if he does. The gods listen
to the man who goes along with them.'

220   He spoke, placed his heavy hand on the silver hilt, drove the
long sword back into its scabbard and complied with Athene,
who then set out for Olympus and the palace of Zeus who drives
the storm-cloud, where she rejoined the other gods.

Not that Achilles curbed his anger. He rounded bitterly on
Agamemnon and said:

'You drunkard, you, with your eyes of a dog and heart of a
doe! You never have the courage to arm yourself and go into
battle with the men, let alone join the pick of the Greeks in an
ambush – you'd sooner die. It suits you better to remain in
230   camp, walking off with the prizes of anyone who contradicts
you – a leader who grows fat on his own people! But then, you
rule over nobodies: otherwise, son of Atreus, this outrage would
prove your last.

'But I tell you bluntly, and I am going to take a solemn oath
on this staff in my hands. Once cut from its stem in the hills, it
can never put out leaves or twigs again. The bronze axe stripped
it of its bark and foliage: it will sprout no more. The men who
in the name of Zeus safeguard our traditions now hold it when
they give judgement. By this I solemnly swear that the day is
240   coming when the Greeks one and all will miss Achilles badly,
and you in your despair will be powerless to help them as they
fall in their multitudes to man-slaying Hector. Then you will
tear your heart out in remorse for giving no respect to the best
of the Greeks.'

So spoke the son of Peleus, flung down the staff with its golden
studs and resumed his seat, leaving Agamemnon thundering at
him from the other side. But Nestor now leapt up, eloquent
Nestor, the clear-voiced orator from Pylos whose speech flowed
sweeter than honey off his tongue. He had already seen two
250   generations of men born, grow up and die in sacred Pylos, and

now he ruled the third. He had their interests at heart as he rose
and addressed them:

'What can I say? This is indeed enough to make
Greece weep! How happy Priam and his sons would
be, how all the Trojans would rejoice, if they could
hear you at each other's throats, you, the two best
Greeks when it comes to giving advice and fighting!

Nestor's
reconcili-
ation fails

'Now listen to me. You are both my juniors. What's more, I   260
have mixed in the past with even better men than you and never
failed to carry conviction with them, the finest men I have ever
seen or shall see, men like Peirithous and Dryas shepherd of the
people, Caeneus, Exadius, godlike Polyphemus and Aegeus' son
Theseus, a man like the gods. These Lapiths were the strongest
men that earth has bred, the strongest men who pitted them-
selves against the strongest enemies – the mountain-dwelling
Centaurs, whom they violently destroyed. These were the men
I left my home in Pylos to join. I travelled far to meet them –   270
they invited me, personally – and I fought my own campaign.
Not a soul on earth today could live with those men in battle –
and they listened to what I said and followed my advice. You
two do the same. It's for your own good to go along with what
I tell you.

'You, Agamemnon, though you have the authority, do not
rob him of his girl. The Greek army gave her to him first. Let
him keep his prize. And you, Achilles, give up your desire to
cross swords with your leader. Through the authority he derives
from Zeus, a leader who holds the sceptre of power has more
claim to our respect than anyone else. Even if you, with a
goddess for mother, are the better fighter, yet Agamemnon is   280
your superior since he rules more people. Agamemnon, cool
your fury; I, Nestor, entreat you to put aside your anger against
Achilles who is a mighty tower of strength for every Greek in
the hell of battle.'

Lord Agamemnon replied and said:

'Venerable sir, all that is very true. But this man here wants
no superiors: he wants to dominate everyone, to lord it over
everyone and to give us each our orders, though I know one
person who is not going to stand for that. What if the everlasting   290

gods did make a spearman of him? Does that entitle him to hurl
insults – ?'

Abruptly, godlike Achilles replied:

'A pathetic little nonentity I shall be called, for sure, if I give
in to you at every point, no matter what you say. Issue your
commands to the rest. Don't tell me what to do. I have done
with taking your orders. And I'll tell you something else, and
you bear it in mind. I am not going to fight you, or anyone else,
with my bare hands for this girl's sake. You Greeks gave her to
me, and now you take her back. But there's much else by my
swift black ship that is mine, and you will take none of that
against my will. Come on, just try, so that everyone here can see
what happens. Your black blood will soon be flowing down my
spear.'

The war of words was over. The two stood up and dismissed
the assembly by the Greek ships. Achilles, with Menoetius' son
Patroclus and his Myrmidon troops, made off to his hut and
ships; while Agamemnon launched a swift ship into the water,
chose twenty rowers, loaded the offering of cattle for sacrifice
to the god and seated fair-cheeked Chryseis on board. Quick-
thinking Odysseus went as their leader and, when everyone
was aboard, they set off along the highways of the sea.

Meanwhile Agamemnon ordered the army to purify itself by
bathing. When they had done this and thrown the dirty water
into the waves, they offered perfect sacrifices of bulls and goats
to Apollo on the shore of the murmuring sea. The smell of
sacrifice, mixed with the curling smoke, went up into the sky.

While the army was engaged on these duties in the camp,
Agamemnon did not forget his quarrel with Achilles and the
threat he had made at the assembly. He spoke to Talthybius and
Eurybates, his heralds and busy attendants:

'Go to Achilles' hut, take fair-cheeked Briseis by
the hand and bring her here. If he refuses to let her
go, I shall come in force to fetch her myself, which
will be all the worse for him.'

So he spoke, and bluntly dismissed them. The two made their
unwilling way along the shore of the murmuring sea till they
reached the Myrmidons' huts and ships, where they found

300

310

320

Agamemnon
has *Briseis*
fetched

Achilles himself sitting by his own black ship. It gave him no 330
pleasure to see them. They came to a halt, too terrified and
embarrassed before their lord to address him or ask anything.
But he realized what was going on and spoke out:

'Heralds, ambassadors of Zeus and men, welcome. Come in.
My quarrel is not with you but with Agamemnon, who sent you
here to fetch the girl Briseis. Come, Olympian-born Patroclus,
bring the girl out and hand her over to these men. I shall count
on them to be my witnesses before the blessed gods, before men
and before the obstinate Agamemnon as well, if the Greeks ever 340
need me again to save them from some terrible disaster. That
man is raving mad, incapable of understanding the past or the
future, let alone how the army is going to survive when it's
fighting for its life by the ships.'

So he spoke, and Patroclus did as his dear companion had
told him, brought out fair-cheeked Briseis from their hut and
gave her up to the two men, who made their way back along
the line of the ships: the girl went unwillingly with them.

Withdrawing from his men, Achilles broke into tears. He sat
down by himself on the shore of the grey sea and looked out 350
across the boundless ocean. Then, stretching out his arms, he
poured out prayers to his mother:

'Mother, since you, a goddess, bore me to live the
briefest of lives, surely high-thundering Olympian
Zeus owes me some measure of respect. But he pays
me none – not even a little. Look how wide-ruling
Agamemnon son of Atreus has dishonoured me. He
took my prize, made off with her in person and now he has her
for himself.'

Achilles
appeals to
his mother
THETIS

So he spoke in tears, and his lady mother heard him where
she sat in the depths of the sea with her old father. She rose
swiftly from the grey water like a mist, came and sat by her 360
weeping son, stroked him with her hand and said:

'My child, why these tears? Why this sorrow? Tell me, don't
keep it to yourself. We must share it.'

Swift-footed Achilles sighed heavily and said:

'You know and, since you know, why should I tell you the
whole story? We went to Thebe, Eëtion's sacred town, sacked

it and brought back all the plunder. The sons of the Greeks
shared it out among themselves in the proper way and chose
370 fair-cheeked Chryseis for Agamemnon. Then Chryses, priest of
the Archer-god Apollo, came to the ships of the bronze-
armoured Greeks to recover his captured daughter. He brought
with him an immense ransom and carried the emblems of the
Archer-god Apollo on a golden staff in his hands. He spoke in
supplication to the whole Greek army, and most of all its two
commanders, Agamemnon and Menelaus, the sons of Atreus.
Then all the other Greeks shouted in agreement. They wanted
to see the priest respected and the splendid ransom taken. But
this was not at all to Agamemnon's liking. He cruelly and bluntly
dismissed the priest.

380   'So, the old man went back in anger; but Apollo listened to
his prayers – the priest was very dear to him – and launched his
deadly arrows at the Greek army. The men fell thick and fast,
since the god's arrows rained down on every part of the broad
Greek camp. At last a prophet who understood the god's will
explained the matter to us. I was the first to rise and advise them
to appease the god. This made Agamemnon furious. He leapt
to his feet and threatened me. And now he has carried out his
390 threats. The dark-eyed Greeks are taking Chryseis to Chryse in
a swift ship with offerings for the god, while Agamemnon's
heralds have just gone from my hut with the girl Briseis, whom
the army gave to me.

THETIS
asked to
intervene
with ZEUS

'So now, if you have any power, protect your son.
Go to Olympus and, if anything you have ever said
or done has warmed the heart of Zeus, remind him
of it as you supplicate him. For instance, in my
father's house I often heard you proudly telling us
how you alone among the gods once saved Zeus who darkens
the clouds from a terrible disaster when some of the other
400 Olympians – Hera, Poseidon and Pallas Athene – had plotted
to throw him in chains. You, goddess, went and had him
released. You immediately summoned to high Olympus that
monster with a hundred arms – the gods call him Briareus, but
mankind Aegaeon – a giant more powerful even than his father.
He took up his position beside Zeus son of Cronus, exulting in

his glory, and the blessed gods slunk off in terror, leaving Zeus free.

'Sit by him now, take him by the knees and remind him of that. Persuade him, if you can, to help the Trojans and to fling the Greeks back on their ships, pen them hard against the sea and massacre them. That would teach them the true measure of their leader. Make wide-ruling Agamemnon son of Atreus realize the delusion he is under in giving no respect to the best of all the Greeks.'

Thetis replied in tears:

'My son, my son! Cursed in my child-bearing, was it for this I nursed you? If only you could have been left to pass your days without tears or trouble beside the ships, since destiny has given you so short a life, no time at all. As it is, you are not only doomed to an early death but also to a most miserable life. It was indeed to an evil destiny that I brought you into the world.

'Nevertheless, I will go to snow-capped Olympus to tell all this myself to Zeus who delights in thunder, and I will see whether I can move him. Meanwhile, stay by your swift ships, keep up your anger against the Greeks and take no part in the fighting. Yesterday, I must tell you, Zeus left for Ocean to join the matchless Ethiopians at a feast, and all the gods went with him. But in twelve days' time he will be back on Olympus, and then I shall go to his bronze-floored palace where I will fall on my knees at his feet. I am convinced he will do what I ask.'

With these words she departed and left Achilles there, anger mounting in his heart at the treatment of his well-girdled woman Briseis, whom they had taken from him against his will.

Meanwhile Odysseus and his crew reached Chryse with the sacred offerings. When they had brought their ship into the waters of the deep-bayed port, they gathered up the sails and stowed them in the black ship's hold, quickly slackened the forestays, dropped the mast into its crutch, rowed the ship into her moorings, threw out anchor-stones from the prow into the sea, tied up the stern hawsers on land and disembarked on to the beach.

410

420

430

[Day 11]
Chryseis is
returned to
her father

The cattle for the Archer-god Apollo were landed, and Chryseis
440   stepped ashore from the seafaring vessel. Quick-thinking
Odysseus then led the girl to the altar, gave her back into her
father's arms and said:

'Chryses, Agamemnon lord of men has ordered me to bring
you your daughter and to make a sacred offering of oxen to
Apollo on the Greeks' behalf, in the hope of pacifying the god
who has been inflicting sorrow and mourning on our men.'

With these words he handed the girl over into the arms of her
father, who joyfully welcomed his beloved child.

The sacred offering of oxen to do honour to the god was
quickly set in place round the well-built altar. The men rinsed
450   their hands and took up the sacrificial grains. Then Chryses
lifted up his hands and prayed aloud:

'Hear me, Apollo, lord of the silver bow, protector of Chryse
and holy Cilla, mighty ruler over Tenedos! You heard me
when I prayed to you before; you showed your respect for
me and struck a great blow at the Greek army. Now grant
me a second wish and lift the loathsome plague from the
Greeks.'

So he spoke in prayer, and Phoebus Apollo heard him. When
they had made their prayers and thrown the grain over the
victims, they first drew back the animals' heads, slit their throats
460   and skinned them. Then, for the god's portion, they cut out the
thigh bones, wrapped them in folds of fat and laid raw meat
from the rest of the animal above them. These pieces the old
priest burnt on wooden spits while he poured libations of red
wine over them and the young men gathered round him with
five-pronged forks in their hands. When the god's portion had
been consumed by fire, they ate the offal and then carved the
rest of the victims into small pieces, pierced them with skewers,
roasted them carefully and drew them all off.

When their work was done and the meal prepared, they
feasted, and no one went without a fair share. Their hunger and
470   thirst satisfied, the young men filled the mixing-bowls to the
brim with wine and went round the whole company, pouring
some into each cup for a libation to the god. And for the rest of
the day the young Greek warriors sang and danced to appease

the god with a beautiful hymn celebrating the Archer Apollo, to
which he listened with delight.

When the sun set and darkness fell, they lay down to sleep by
the hawsers of their ship. But when early-born, rosy-fingered
Dawn appeared, they set sail for the broad Greek camp, taking
advantage of a favourable breeze the Archer-god had sent them.
They put up their mast and spread the white sail. The wind filled   480
its belly, and a dark wave hissed loudly round her keel as the
vessel gathered way and sped through the swell, forging ahead
on her course. So they returned to the broad Greek camp, where
they dragged the black ship high up on the sandy shore and kept
it upright with wooden props. That done, they dispersed to their
several huts and ships.

But Olympian-born son of Peleus swift-footed Achilles was
sitting by his ships, nursing his anger. He had not only kept   490
away from the fighting but had attended no meetings of the
assembly where men win glory. He stayed where he was, eating
his heart out and longing for the sound and fury of battle.

Eleven days went by, and at dawn on the twelfth the everlast-
ing gods returned in full strength to Olympus, with Zeus at their
head. Thetis, remembering her son's instructions, emerged in
the morning from the waves of the sea, rose into the broad sky
and reached Olympus. She found far-thundering Zeus sitting
away from the rest of the gods on the highest of Olympus' many
peaks. She sank down in front of him, put her left arm round   500
his knees, took his chin in her right hand and in supplication
spoke to lord Zeus son of Cronus:

'Father Zeus, if ever I have served you well among
the gods by word or deed, grant me this wish: give   [Day 21]
honour to my son. He is already singled out for an   THETIS
early death, and now Agamemnon lord of men has   supplicates
dishonoured him. He took his prize, removed her in   ZEUS
person and now he has her for himself. But you at least do him
honour, Olympian Zeus wise in counsel, and let the Trojans
have the upper hand till the Greeks pay back my son and increase   510
the honour in which he is held.'

So she spoke, and Zeus who marshals the clouds made no
reply. He sat in silence for a long time, with Thetis clinging to

his knees as she had done throughout. Then she asked once more:

'Promise me faithfully and bow your head in agreement, or else, since you have nothing to fear by doing so, refuse; then I shall know for sure that no other god is less respected than I am.'

Much perturbed, Zeus who marshals the clouds replied:

'This is going to mean trouble! You will make me fall foul of my wife Hera when she heaps me with abuse for this, as she
520 will. Even as things are, she slanders me constantly before the other gods and accuses me of helping the Trojans in this war.

'However, leave me now, or Hera may notice us; and I will see the matter through. But first, to reassure you, I will bow my head in agreement – and the immortals recognize no surer guarantee from me than that. When I seal a promise with a nod, there can be no failure to fulfil it, no going back, no deception.'

The son of Cronus spoke and nodded his sable brows. The
530 divine locks rolled forward from the lord god's immortal head, and great Olympus shook.

ZEUS nods
to THETIS;
HERA's rage
The agreement was made, and the two now parted. Thetis plunged down from glittering Olympus into the salt-sea depths, while Zeus departed for his own palace. There the whole company of gods rose from their seats in their Father's presence. There was no one that dared to keep his seat as he approached; they all stood up as he came in.

So Zeus sat down on his throne; and Hera had seen, and knew that he and silver-footed Thetis, daughter of the Old Man of the Sea, had hatched a plot between them. At once she spoke to Zeus with cutting words:

540 'Which god has been hatching plots with you this time, you arch-deceiver? How like you it is to wait till my back is turned and then cook up some secret schemes, on your own. You have never been willing to confide in me.'

The Father of men and gods replied to her:

'Hera, don't expect to learn all my decisions. You would find the knowledge hard to bear, although you are my wife. What it is right for you to hear, no man or god shall know before you.

But when I choose to take a step without referring to the gods,
don't cross-examine me about it.'   550

Ox-eyed lady Hera replied:

'Dread son of Cronus, what are you suggesting now? Surely
it was never my way to pester you with questions; you are at
liberty to make whatever decisions you like. But now I have a
terrible fear you have been talked round by silver-footed Thetis,
daughter of the Old Man of the Sea. She sat with you this
morning and took you by the knees. This makes me suppose
you have given your word to her to honour Achilles and let the
Greeks be slaughtered in their multitudes by their ships.'

Zeus who marshals the clouds replied and said: 560

'Remarkable! You can never stop "supposing". I can keep no
secrets from you. But there is nothing you can *do* – except to
turn me even more against you, which will be all the worse for
yourself. If things are as you say, you may take it that my will
is being done. Sit there in silence and obey me, or all the gods
on Olympus will be of no help in keeping me off when I lay my
unconquerable hands on you.'

So he spoke, and ox-eyed lady Hera was afraid and,
restraining her feelings, sat down in silence. The Sky-gods in   570
Zeus' palace were filled with consternation, till at last the great
craftsman Hephaestus, who sided with his mother white-armed
Hera, began to address them:

'This is going to mean trouble, and we are not
going to put up with it, with you two squabbling over
mere mortals and setting the gods at loggerheads. It
will be impossible to enjoy a good feast with so much
trouble in the air. I do advise my mother, who knows

HEPH-
AESTUS
restores the
peace

well enough what is best, to make her peace with my dear Father
Zeus, or she may draw another rebuke from him and the feast
be entirely spoilt. If he wanted to, the Olympian lord of the   580
lightning flash, our superior by far, could blast us all from our
seats. No, Mother, deal with him tactfully, and the Olympian
will be gracious to us again.'

So he spoke, hurried forward with a two-handled cup, put it
in his mother's hands and said:

'Mother, be patient and swallow your resentment, or, much

as I love you, I may see you thrashed here in front of me. A
distressing sight for me, but I will be unable to do anything to
590 help you. The Olympian is a hard god to resist. Why, once
before, when I was trying to save you, he seized me by the foot
and hurled me from the threshold of Olympus. I flew all day
and, as the sun sank, I fell, all the life knocked out of me, on
Lemnos, where I was picked up and looked after by the Sintians.'

So he spoke, and the goddess white-armed Hera smiled and
took the cup from her son, still smiling. Then Hephaestus went
on to serve the rest in turn, beginning from the left, with sweet
nectar which he drew from the mixing bowl; and a fit of helpless
600 laughter seized the blessed gods as they watched him bustling
up and down the hall.

So the feast went on, all day till sundown. No one went short
of the pleasures of food or music: Apollo played his magnificent
lyre and the Muses sang, voice answering glorious voice. But
when the bright lamp of the sun had set, they all went home to
bed in the separate houses that the famous lame god Hephaestus
with his supreme skill had built for them. Olympian Zeus, lord
610 of the lightning flash, retired to the bed where he usually rested
when sweet sleep overcame him. There he went up and slept,
with Hera of the golden throne beside him.

2

A DREAM, A TESTING
AND THE CATALOGUE
OF SHIPS

1–207: [Night of 21st day] ZEUS sends a dream that makes Agamemnon think the Greeks are about to win. [22nd day: first day of combat] When Agamemnon tests the morale of the men, they charge for the ships to return home. ATHENE alerts Odysseus, who restrains the senior men and hits out at the ranks.

207–393: The assembly reconvenes and a common soldier Thersites abuses Agamemnon. Odysseus thrashes Thersites, to applause. Odysseus and Nestor give morale-boosting speeches. The Greeks prepare for battle.

394–483: The army feeds, Agamemnon offers a sacrifice and a prayer. Nestor suggests the troops now assemble. The troops are marshalled with ATHENE's help.

484–779: The catalogue of Greek ships.

780–815: The goddess IRIS alerts the *Trojans* and their leader *Hector* to the Greek threat.

816–77: The catalogue of *Trojan* contingents.

The other gods and all the fighting men slept through the night, but there was no such soothing sleep for Zeus. He was wondering how to honour Achilles and have the Greeks slaughtered in multitudes by their ships. He decided that the best way would be to send Agamemnon son of Atreus a destructive dream. So he spoke to one with winged words:

'Off you go, destructive dream, to the Greek ships. Go to Agamemnon in his hut and repeat to him exactly what I say. Tell him to prepare his long-haired Greeks for battle at once. His chance of capturing the Trojans' town with its broad streets has come; the immortals that live on Olympus are no longer divided on that issue. Hera's entreaties have brought us all round, and the Trojans' fate is sealed.'

So he spoke, and the dream heard his instructions and left. It was soon at the Greek ships, where it sought out Agamemnon and found him lying fast asleep in his hut. Assuming the appearance of Nestor, son of Neleus, Agamemnon's most valued adviser, it stood over his head and said:

'You sleep, son of the wise horse-tamer Atreus. It is not right for one in authority who has an army in his charge, a man with much on his mind, to sleep all night. Listen to me now and understand that I come from Zeus who, far off as he is, is much concerned on your behalf and pities you. He tells you to prepare your long-haired Greeks for battle at once. Your chance of capturing the Trojans' town with its broad streets has come; the immortals that live on Olympus are no longer divided on that issue. Hera's entreaties have brought them all round, and the Trojans' fate is sealed by Zeus. Remember what I have said and do not forget it, when you emerge from sweet sleep.'

With these words the dream went off, leaving Agamemnon with a false picture of the future in his mind. He imagined he would capture Priam's town that very day, the fool. He little knew what Zeus intended, nor all the sufferings and sorrows he had in store for both sides in the heat of battle.

When he woke from his sleep, the divine voice was all about him. He sat up, got to his feet and put on a fine, soft, new-made tunic and over that a great cloak. He bound a fine pair of sandals on his gleaming feet, slung a silver-riveted sword round his shoulders, picked up his ancestral, indestructible sceptre and with this in his hand walked down to the ships of the bronze-armoured Greeks.

When the goddess Dawn reached high Olympus, announcing the new day to Zeus and the other gods, Agamemnon ordered his clear-voiced heralds to summon the long-haired Greeks to assembly. The heralds cried their summons, and the warriors quickly gathered.

But first Agamemnon arranged a council of his senior advisers beside the ship of Nestor, lord of Pylos, and when he had called them together, he outlined his carefully considered plan:

'Friends, I was visited in my sleep by a dream from the gods which came to me through the immortal night, and in its appearance, size and physique, it looked very similar to godlike Nestor. It stood above my head and instructed me as follows: "You sleep, son of the wise horse-tamer Atreus. It is not right 60 for one in authority who has an army in his charge, a man with much on his mind, to sleep all night. Listen to me now and understand that I come from Zeus who, far off as he is, is much concerned on your behalf and pities you. He tells you to prepare your long-haired Greeks for battle at once. Your chance of capturing the Trojans' town with its broad streets has come; the immortals that live on Olympus are no longer divided on that issue. Hera's entreaties have brought them all round, and the Trojans' fate is sealed by Zeus. Remember what I have said." 70 With that it flew away, and I woke up.

'To work, then: we must get the troops under arms. But first, as is my right, I am going to test them by a speech in which I shall tell them to take to their many-benched ships and sail for home. You must dissuade them from all sides.'

With these words Agamemnon sat down, and Nestor, who was lord of sandy Pylos, got up. He had their interests at heart as he rose and addressed them:

'Friends, rulers and leaders of the Greeks, if any other Greek 80 had told us of a dream like this, we should have thought it false and distanced ourselves from it. But as it is, the man who claims to be best of the Greeks saw it. To work, then: we must get the troops under arms.'

With these words he moved off, signalling the end of the meeting. The other sceptred lords stood up after Nestor and followed the example of this shepherd of the people, and the army hurried forward as troops of swarming bees do, streaming out in relays from a hollow rock. The bees fly in clusters towards the spring flowers and settle in swarms, some here, some there. 90 So the many troops of men marched in squads from their ships and huts in front of the wide sea-shore to the assembly. Rumour, the messenger of Zeus, spread through them like fire, speeding their steps.

And now the assembly became the scene of turmoil. As they sat down, the ground groaned beneath their weight, and above the pandemonium the shouting of nine heralds could be heard, calling them to come to order, stop the din and pay attention to their Olympian-bred leaders. When after some difficulty the troops were brought to order in their seats and had settled down and stopped their chatter, Lord Agamemnon rose holding his sceptre, which Hephaestus himself had made. Hephaestus gave it to lord Zeus son of Cronus, and Zeus to Hermes, the guide and slayer of Argus. Lord Hermes presented it to Pelops the great charioteer, and Pelops passed it on to Atreus, shepherd of the people. When Atreus died, he left it to Thyestes rich in flocks; and he in turn left it to Agamemnon to carry, to be a token of his lordship over many islands and all Argos. Leaning on this sceptre, he spoke to the Greeks:

'Friends, Greek warriors, servants of the War-god Ares, Zeus son of Cronus has seriously deluded me, a crushing blow. That perverse god once solemnly assured me that we would sack Ilium with its fine walls and return home; but now his advice turns out to be an evil deception, and he is telling me to return home to Argos in disgrace, with half my army lost. It appears that this is what almighty Zeus, who has brought down the high towers of many a town and will destroy others yet, has decided, such is his absolute power.

Agamemnon tests the troops, who run

'But what a scandal, what a tale for our descendants' ears, that such a large and excellent force as ours should be engaged so ineffectually, with no final end in sight, in an unsuccessful struggle with a weaker enemy. If we and the Trojans swore a solemn truce and each side held a count, the enemy reckoning only native Trojans and we Greeks numbering off in tens, with the idea that each of our groups should have a Trojan to pour out its wine – many a group would go without a wine-steward. Such I believe to be the odds we enjoy against the Trojans in the town itself.

'But they have numerous spear-wielding allies from many

towns, who thwart me at every turn and defeat all my efforts to sack prosperous Ilium. Nine of great Zeus' years have now passed. The timbers of our ships have rotted, and their rigging has perished. Our wives and little children sit at home and wait for us. Meanwhile the task we set ourselves when we came here remains undone. So I suggest we all do what I now propose – board ship and home to the land of our fathers! The Trojans' 140 town with its broad streets will never fall to us.'

So he spoke, and his words went straight to the heart of every man in that crowd, except those who had attended the advisory council, and the whole assembly was swayed like the great rollers of the Icarian sea when they are swollen by a south-easter rushing down from Father Zeus' clouds. As the west wind rushes tumultuously down to sway a deep harvest of corn, and the ears of the crop bend under it, so the whole assembly was swayed. They charged, shouting, for the ships. 150 The dust they kicked up with their feet hung high overhead. They shouted to each other to get hold of the ships and drag them down into the bright sea. They began clearing out the ships' runways. They even started shifting the props from under the hulls and, in their desire to be off, made a din that reached the sky.

Then the Greeks would have returned home in defiance of destiny, if Hera had not spoken her mind to Athene:

'Athene Atrytone, daughter of Zeus who drives the storm-cloud, this is a disaster! The Greeks will run away and sail home over the broad back of the sea to the land of their fathers and leave Helen here for Priam and the Trojans to boast about 160 – Helen, for whom so many of her countrymen have died on Trojan soil, far from their own fatherland. But go down among these bronze-armoured Greeks at once and use your eloquence to stop them. Deal with them man by man. Don't let them drag the curved ships down into the sea.'

So she spoke, and the goddess grey-eyed Athene complied. She came swooping down from the heights of Olympus and, soon reaching the Greek's swift ships, found Odysseus, equal in invention to Zeus, rooted to the spot. He had not even touched his good

ATHENE gets Odysseus to stop the rout

170 black ship: he was in complete despair. Grey-eyed Athene went
up to him and said:

'Olympian-born son of Laertes, resourceful Odysseus, are
you all going to run off like this, falling aboard your many-
benched ships to get home to the land of your fathers, and
leaving Helen here for Priam and the Trojans to boast about –
Helen, for whom so many of her countrymen have died on
Trojan soil, far from their own fatherland? Don't stay here any
180 longer, but go down among the Greek army. Use your eloquence
to stop them. Deal with them man by man. Don't let them drag
the curved ships down into the sea.'

So she spoke, and he recognized the voice of the goddess and
set out at a run, throwing off his cloak to be picked up by
Eurybates, his Ithacan attendant. He went straight to Agamem-
non, borrowed from him his indestructible ancestral sceptre
and with this in his hand went down among the ships of the
bronze-armoured Greeks. When he came upon a lord and a man
of rank, he would stand beside him and persuade him gently to
stop:

190 'You there, it is not right to threaten you: you are no coward.
But go back to your seat yourself and make your men do the
same. You do not really know what Agamemnon has in mind.
This is only an experiment with the men. He will soon take it
out on them. Did we not all hear what he said at the council?
He will be angry with the troops and may well punish them for
this. Olympian-bred rulers have their pride, upheld in authority
and championed as they are by Zeus wise in counsel.'

When he saw any ordinary warrior shouting his companions
on, he struck him with the sceptre and yelled orders at him:

200 'You there, get back to your seat and wait for orders from
your superiors! Coward and weakling, you count for nothing
in battle or council. We cannot all be leaders here; and mob rule
is a bad thing. Let there be one commander only, one ruler, who
is given the sceptre of power and the right to rule by Zeus, son
of sickle-wielding Cronus.'

So Odysseus acted, asserting his authority over the army; and
now they all flocked back to the assembly from their ships and
huts with a noise like the waves of the sounding sea which

thunder along the length of a beach when the deep lifts up its   210
voice.

They all sat down and were brought to order in
their places, but for one man who refused to hold his   Thersites
tongue. This was Thersites, who loved the sound of   abuses
his own voice and had a large store of insulting   Agamemnon
language at his disposal. He used this gratuitously and offen-
sively to needle his masters whenever he thought it would raise
a laugh among the troops. He was the ugliest man that had
come to Ilium. He was bandy-legged and limped. His hunched
shoulders almost met across his chest; and his head rose to a
point where a few short hairs sprouted. Nobody loathed the   220
man more than Achilles and Odysseus, since he was always
abusing them, but now it was against godlike Agamemnon that
he aimed a shrill torrent of insults. The Greeks felt nothing but
anger and resentment at him. Shouting at the top of his voice he
directed an abusive lecture at Agamemnon:

'Son of Atreus, what are you blaming us for now? What more
do you want? Your huts are full of bronze, and since we Greeks
always give you first choice when we plunder a town, you have
the pick of any number of women too. Maybe you are short of
gold, a ransom which some horse-taming Trojan will come   230
along with from the town to free a son of his who has been tied
up and brought in by myself or another of the men? Or a new
girl for you to sleep with and keep all to yourself, though it is
not right for you as our leader to create trouble for the army
like this.

'As for you, my feeble friends, disgraces that you are – Greek
women, I cannot call you men! – let's sail for home anyway and
leave this man here in Troy to brood over his prizes all by
himself. He'll soon find out how much he depends on us. Why,
only a little while ago he dishonoured Achilles, a far better man
than he is. He took his prize, removed her in person and now   240
has her for himself. But Achilles hasn't lost his temper. He is
relaxed about it. Otherwise, Agamemnon, that outrage would
have been your last.'

So spoke Thersites, abusing Agamemnon shepherd of the
people. But godlike Odysseus was quickly at his side and,

looking blackly at him, attacked him and taught him a
sharp lesson:

Odysseus
silences
Thersites   'Thersites, what a brilliant speaker you are – of
pure drivel. Hold your tongue and stop arguing with
your leaders. No one else does. In my view, you are
the worst of all the Greeks that followed the sons of
250 Atreus to Ilium. So you had better stop criticizing and hurling
insults at them with an eye to getting home. Nobody here knows
exactly how this business will end. We may return in triumph;
we may not. But all you do is sit there and insult Agamemnon
son of Atreus, shepherd of the people, for the generosity the
Greek warriors show him. Your speech was one long sneer.

'But I tell you bluntly and I mean it. If I catch you once again
acting as mindlessly as this, let my head be parted from my
260 shoulders and Telemachus be called no son of mine, if I don't
get my hands on you, strip you of your clothes – the cloak and
tunic that cover your genitals – thrash you, throw you out of
the assembly under an ignominious hail of blows and send you
blubbering back to the ships.'

So he spoke, and struck him on the back and shoulders with
the sceptre. Thersites cowered and burst into tears. A bloody
bruise raised by the gold-studded sceptre swelled up on the
man's back. He sat down, terrified and in pain, looked helplessly
270 around and brushed away a tear. The others, disgruntled though
they were, had a good laugh at him. They looked at each other
and said as one man:

'Well done! There's many a fine thing to Odysseus' credit,
what with his brilliant ideas and leadership in battle. But shut-
ting up that ranting windbag in assembly is by far the best thing
he has done for us. I don't think the great Thersites will be in a
hurry to come here again and sling abuse and insults at our
leaders.'

So the gathering spoke. And now Odysseus, sacker of towns,
rose to speak with the sceptre in his hand. Grey-eyed Athene,
280 disguising herself as a herald, stood beside him and called the
assembly to order, so that Greeks at the back as well as the front
could hear his speech and consider his advice. Odysseus had
their interests at heart as he rose and addressed them:

'Lord Agamemnon, it seems the Greeks are deter-
mined to turn you into an object of contempt before
all mankind and to break the promise they made you
on the voyage here from horse-grazing Greece, that
you would never sail home till you had sacked Ilium
with its fine walls. The way they whimper to each other about   290
getting back, they might be little children or widowed wives!
Not that I deny that our efforts here are enough to send any
man away frustrated. A sailor on board his ship will start to get
restless when winter gales and rising seas have cooped him up
in harbour and kept him from his wife for even a month; but
we have hung on here for nine long years. Small blame, then, if
the troops are getting restless by the ships.

'Yet it would be humiliating, after staying here for so long, to
return home empty-handed! Be patient, my friends. Hold out a
little longer, till we find out whether our priest Calchas proph-   300
esies the truth or not. We all know what I mean: in fact you all
saw the thing for yourselves – those whom the demons of death
have not since come to carry away.

'It seems like only yesterday. The Greek ships were gathering
at Aulis, ready to bring trouble to Priam and the Trojans. We
were making perfect sacrifices to the gods on their holy altars
round a spring under a fine plane-tree at the foot of which the
sparkling water was gushing out, when a great sign appeared.
A snake with blood-red markings on its back, an intimidating
creature which Olympian Zeus himself had released into the
light of day, darted out from below an altar and made straight   310
for the tree. There was a brood of young sparrows on the highest
branch, helpless little things nestling under the leaves – eight
birds in all, or nine, counting the mother of the hatch. All of
them, cheeping piteously and with their mother fluttering round
and wailing for her dear children, were eaten by the snake. It
got the mother too: it coiled itself up to strike and seized her by
the wing as she flew past shrieking. But when it had devoured
them all, mother and young, the god who had caused it to
appear, Zeus son of sickle-wielding Cronus, transformed it and
turned it into a stone.

'We stood there transfixed by what had happened. But once   320

*Odysseus re-
minds troops
of Calchas'
prophecy*

this awe-inspiring prodigy had intruded on our sacrifice, Calchas interpreted the omen then and there: "Why are you silent, you long-haired Greeks? It was for us that Zeus wise in counsel staged this prophetic scene. It was late in coming and will be late in fulfilment; but its glorious memory will not die. There were eight young sparrows, making nine with their mother, and all of these, mother and hatch, were devoured by the snake. Nine, then, is the number of years we shall have to fight over Ilium, and in the tenth its broad streets will be ours."

330   'That is what Calchas prophesied, and all he said is coming true. So, you Greek men-at-arms, you must all stand your ground till we capture Priam's great town.'

So he spoke, and the Greeks thundered out loud to show how well they had liked this speech from godlike Odysseus. Their intimidating roar echoed round the ships. Then Nestor the Gerenian charioteer addressed them too:

Nestor encourages Agamemnon

'Well! You might be little children with no interest in war at all, to judge by all this talk. What will become of our agreements 340 and oaths? We may as well throw on to the fire all our plans and strategies, all our pledges sealed in wine, our right hands in which we place such trust. Words are the only weapons we are using now and, given how long we have been here, *they* will get us nowhere.

'Agamemnon, be true as always to your firm resolve and lead the Greeks into the thick of the action. If there are one or two traitors among us, scheming to sail for home before they find out whether Zeus was telling us the truth, let them rot – they 350 will not succeed. For I am convinced that Zeus the almighty son of Cronus nodded his approval of us on the day we got aboard our swift ships to bring death and destruction to the Trojans. There was a flash of lightning on our right, a sign that all would be well. Let there be no scramble to get home, then, till every man of you has slept with a Trojan wife and taken revenge for all the sweat and tears Helen has caused you. But if anyone does have a violent urge to be off, he has only to touch his well-benched black ship and, as far as everyone else is concerned, he will be ensuring his own death and destiny.

'Now, my lord, think things over carefully and take advice 360 from another. Here is my own: it is not to be put aside lightly. Sort your men out, Agamemnon, into their tribes and clans, so that clan helps clan and the tribes support each other. If you do this and the Greeks comply, you will find out who are the cowards and who the brave among your commanders and troops. For each man will be fighting at his brother's side, and you will soon find out whether it is the gods' will that stands between you and the sack of Ilium, or the cowardice of your warriors and their incompetence in battle.'

Lord Agamemnon replied and said:

'One more debate where you, venerable sir, have carried all 370 before you! Father Zeus, Athene and Apollo, give me ten such advisers as Nestor, and the town of lord Priam would soon be captured, sacked and turned over to Greek hands! But Zeus who drives the storm-cloud, the son of Cronus, *will* torment me. He entangles me in pointless bickering and rows. Look at the way Achilles and I quarrelled and exchanged insults over a girl, though it was I who lost my temper first. If ever he and I can see eye to eye once more, there will be no stay of execution for the Trojans, not for 380 a moment.

Agamemnon regrets his quarrel

'Now let us eat and prepare ourselves for battle. Sharpen your spears, adjust your shields, see that your horses are fed, check your chariots and be ready to battle it out grimly all day. There will be no respite, not for a moment, till night comes and separates the forces. The strap of a man's shield will be soaked with the sweat from his chest; his hand will weary on his spear; his horses pulling at his polished chariot will be covered in 390 lather. And as for anyone I see who prefers to loiter by the beaked ships far from battle, nothing can save him: he is for the dogs and birds.'

So he spoke, and the Greeks thundered out loud, like a wave against the rocky promontory of a high headland when the south wind descends and whips up the seas. The waves raised by winds from all quarters never leave it in peace from any direction.

    They rose from the assembly at once and dispersed among the ships, where they lit fires in their huts and fed. Each man, as he sacrificed to one of the immortal gods, prayed that he might come through the grind

400 of battle with his life. Agamemnon lord of men himself sacrificed a fatted five-year-old ox to Zeus almighty son of Cronus and invited the senior advisers of the Greeks to attend – Nestor first of all, then lord Idomeneus; the two Ajaxes; Diomedes son of Tydeus; and for a sixth, Odysseus, equal in invention to Zeus. Menelaus, master of the battle-cry, came without needing an invitation, since he knew very well how heavy his brother Aga-

410 memnon's burden was. Standing round the ox they took up the sacrificial grains. Lord Agamemnon addressed them and prayed:

'Zeus, greatest and most glorious, god of the black cloud, dwelling in the skies! Grant that the sun may not set and darkness fall before I bring Priam's smoke-blackened palace crashing down, send his gates up in flames and rip the tunic on Hector's chest. And at his side let many of his friends fall and bite the dust.'

420 So he spoke, but Zeus did not grant his prayer. He accepted the offering but in return doubled his load of misery.

When they had made their prayers and thrown the grain over the victim, they first drew back the animal's head and slit its throat and skinned it. Then for the god's portion they cut out the thigh bones, wrapped them in folds of fat and laid raw meat from the rest of the animal above them. These pieces they burnt on spits stripped of leaves, then pierced the entrails and held them over the flames. When the god's portion had been consumed by fire, they ate the offal and then carved the rest of the victim into small pieces, pierced them with skewers, roasted them carefully and drew them all off.

430 When their work was done and the meal prepared, they feasted and no one went without a fair share. Their hunger and thirst satisfied, Nestor the Gerenian charioteer began and spoke his mind to them:

'Most glorious son of Atreus, Agamemnon lord of men, let

us not prolong this meeting any more nor put off the work that the god has set our hands to. Come, let the heralds of the bronze-armoured Greeks gather the troops from the ships for battle. Then we could go round the whole Greek army together and soon unleash the dogs of war.' 440

So he spoke, and Agamemnon lord of men complied. He gave immediate orders to his clear-voiced heralds to call the long-haired Greeks to battle stations. They cried their summons and the men quickly gathered. The Olympian-bred lords under Agamemnon bustled about marshalling the troops, and with them went grey-eyed Athene.

She was holding her splendid cloak, the unfading, everlasting aegis from which a hundred golden tassels flutter, all beautifully woven, each worth a hundred head of cattle. Darting about 450 with this she raced through the ranks, urging the men forward and filling the heart of every Greek with the courage to do battle and fight the enemy relentlessly. At once the prospect of battle became sweeter to them than returning in their hollow ships to the land of their fathers.

As destructive fire ravages a great forest on the mountain heights and the glint of the flames is seen from far away, so, as they fell in, the dazzling glitter of their magnificent bronze armour flashed through the air to the skies.

The Greek
army gathers

Like the many flocks of birds – geese, cranes or long-necked 460 swans – that gather in the Asian meadow by the streams of Cayster and wheel around here and there, revelling in their flight, and with a great racket spread out over the ground, and the meadow is filled with sound, so the many groups poured from their ships and their huts on to the plain of the River Scamander; and the earth beneath resounded intimidatingly to the tramp of marching men and horses' hooves, as they took their positions in the flowery meadow of Scamander, countless, as many as the leaves and flowers in their season.

Like the many groups of busy flies that swarm around the 470 sheepfold in spring, when the milk splashes the pails, so many long-haired Greeks were drawn up on the plain against the Trojans, determined to smash through them.

Like goatherds who easily sort out their wandering flocks of goats when they have become mixed up at pasture, so the commanders deployed men here and there to advance to battle; and in among them moved lord Agamemnon, with head and eyes like those of Zeus who delights in thunder,
480 with a waist like the War-god's and a chest like Poseidon's. Like a bull that stands out clearly from all the cattle in a herd, conspicuous among the assembled cows, so Zeus made Agamemnon look that day, conspicuous among the crowd and eclipsing all other warriors.

The catalogue of Greek ships

Tell me now, you Muses that live on Olympus, since you are goddesses, are present everywhere and know everything, while we men have only hearsay to go on and know nothing – tell me who were the leaders and commanders of the Greeks? As for the rank and file, I could not name or even count them, not if I had ten tongues and ten
490 mouths, a voice that could never tire and a heart of bronze – unless you, Muses of Olympus, daughters of Zeus who drives the storm-cloud, remind me how many came to Ilium. So I shall list the captains and their ships from first to last.

Boeotia

The contingent from Boeotia was commanded by Peneleos, Leitus, Arcesilaus, Prothoenor and Clonius. The towns the Boeotians came from were Hyrie and stony Aulis, Schoenus and Scolus; Eteonus with its many ridges; Thespeia and Graea and spacious Mycalessus; Harma,
500 Eilesion and Erythrae; Eleon, Hyle and Peteon; Ocalea and the stronghold of Medeon; Copae, Eutresis and Thisbe rich in doves; Coronea and grassy Haliartus; Plataea, Glisas and the stronghold of Lower Thebes; sacred Onchestus, Poseidon's lovely grove; Arne with its many vines; and Mideia, holy Nisa and remote Anthedon. This contingent under their com-
510 manders came in fifty ships with a hundred and twenty young Boeotians in each.

Orchomenus

The contingent from Orchomenus, men from Aspledon and Minyan Orchomenus, was commanded by Ascalaphus and Ialmenus. These two were sons of Ares. Astyoche, a modest young girl, had conceived them in the palace of her father Actor son of Azeus; she had gone upstairs with the mighty War-god and slept with him in secret. They had come in thirty hollow ships.

The contingent from Phocis was commanded by Schedius and Epistrophus, sons of the great-hearted Iphitus son of Naubolus. The towns they came from were Cyparissus and rocky Pytho; holy Crisa, Daulis and Panopeus; around Anemoreia and Hyampolis and the bright River Cephisus; and Lilaea, where the Cephisus rises. This contingent came under their commanders in forty black ships. Their leaders marshalled the Phocian ranks and set them in their battle stations next to the Boeotians on the left.

Phocis

520

The contingent from Locris was led by swift-footed Ajax son of Oïleus, the lesser Ajax – not such a man as Ajax son of Telamon, indeed inferior by far. He was short and wore linen body-protection; but no Greek was his equal in spearmanship. The towns his following had come from were Cynus, Opous and Calliarus; Bessa, Scarphe and lovely Augeiae; Tarphe and Thronion and around the streams of the River Boagrius. This contingent came under Ajax's command in forty black ships manned by the Locrians who live across the straits from holy Euboea.

Locris

530

The contingent from Euboea consisted of the Abantes, breathing courage. The towns these men came from were Chalcis, Eretria and Histiaea with its many vines; Cerinthus by the sea and the high fortress of Dius; and Carystus and Styra. These were all captained by Elephenor, ally of the War-god, son of Chalcodon and leader of the great-hearted Abantes. His followers were quick on their feet; they wore their hair long at the back, fighters hoping to lunge with their ash spears and rip through the armour on their enemies' chests. This contingent came under Elephenor's command in forty black ships.

Euboea

540

The next contingent came from the stronghold of Athens, the community of great-hearted Erechtheus. Erechtheus was a child of the fruitful Earth who was brought up by Athene daughter of Zeus. She had established him at Athens in her own rich temple where Athenian youths offer him bulls and rams ever year. This contingent was commanded by

Athens

550

Menestheus son of Peteos. He had no rival on earth in the art of handling infantry and chariots. Nestor was the only competition, and he was an older man. The Athenians came under Menestheus' command in fifty black ships.

Salamis

The contingent from Salamis was led by Ajax son of Telamon in twelve ships. He beached them where the Athenian force was stationed.

Argos

The contingent from Argos contained men from the towns of Argos and well-walled Tiryns; from
560 Hermione and Asine with their deep gulfs; from Troezen, Eionae and vine-clad Epidaurus; and from Aegina and Mases. They were commanded by Diomedes, master of the battle-cry, and Sthenelus, son of far-famed Capaneus. Euryalus, a godlike man, son of lord Mecisteus son of Talaus, had come as third in command. But Diomedes, master of the battle-cry, was in charge of the whole force. This contingent came under their commanders in eighty black ships.

Mycenae

The contingent from Mycenae contained men from the stronghold of Mycenae, from wealthy
570 Corinth and well-built Cleonae; from Orneiae and lovely Araethyrea; from Sicyon, where Adrestus reigned in early years; from Hyperesie and lofty Gonoessa, Pellene and around Aegion; and from the whole length of the coast and the broad lands of Helice. Lord Agamemnon son of Atreus commanded these men in their hundred ships. His following was by far the finest and most numerous. He armed himself in gleaming bronze, exultant,
580 and stood out among all the other warriors because he was the best man, commanding by far the largest force.

Lacedaemon

The contingent from hollow Lacedaemon contained men from that lovely land with its many ravines; and men from Pharis, Sparta and Messe rich in doves; from Bryseiae and lovely Augeiae; from Amyclae and the seaside town of Helos; and from Oetylus and Laas. Menelaus, master of the battle-cry, brother of Agamemnon, commanded their sixty ships. They had a station separate from the Mycenaean contingent. Menelaus strode among them, confident in his readiness for action and urging them to battle. Nobody was more

eager than he to take revenge for all the sweat and tears Helen 590
had caused them.

The contingent from Pylos came from there and *Pylos*
from lovely Arene; from Thryon, where the River
Alpheus is forded; from handsome Aepy; from Cyparisseis,
Amphigeneia, Pteleus and Helos; and from Dorion, where the
Muses met Thamyris the Thracian poet and ended his career
while he was on his way from Oechalia and the home of Oechal-
ian Eurytus. He had boasted that he would win a singing compe-
tition even if the Muses themselves, daughters of Zeus who
drives the storm-cloud, were to take part. This angered them.
They paralysed him, robbed him of the divine gift of song 600
and made him forget his lyre. Nestor the Gerenian charioteer
commanded these men. They had come in ninety hollow ships.

The contingent from Arcadia came from the lands *Arcadia*
where Mount Cyllene lifts its peak and Aepytus was
buried, where men are trained in hand-to-hand fighting. The
towns they came from were Pheneus, Orchomenus rich in sheep,
Rhype and Stratie and windy Enispe; Tegea and lovely Manti-
nea, Stymphelus and Parrhasie. Lord Agapenor son of Ancaeus
commanded their sixty ships. Many Arcadians, expert fighters, 610
boarded each ship. Agamemnon lord of men had himself given
Agapenor the well-benched ships in which to cross the wine-
dark sea, as the Arcadians knew nothing of seafaring.

The contingent from Elis came from Buprasion *Elis*
and as much of the bright land of Elis as lies between
Hermine, furthest Myrsinus, the Olenian Rock and Alesion.
They had four commanders, each with ten swift ships filled
with these troops from Elis. Amphimachus son of Cteatus and 620
Thalpius son of Eurytus, grandsons of Actor, commanded two
squadrons; mighty Diores, son of Amarynceus, the third; and
godlike Polyxeinus, the son of lord Agasthenes, Augeas' son,
the fourth.

The contingent from Dulichium came from there *Dulichium*
and the sacred Echinean Islands across the sea from
Elis. Meges, equal of Ares and son of Phyleus, commanded
them. Phyleus was a charioteer dear to Zeus who had quarrelled

630   with his father and migrated to Dulichium. This contingent
      came under Meges' command in forty black ships.

                        The contingent from proud Cephallenia was led by
      Cephallenia
                        Odysseus. It contained men from Ithaca and Neritos
      with its quivering leaves, from Crocyleia and rugged Aegilips;
      from forested Zacynthus and Samos and the mainland opposite
      the islands. Odysseus, equal in wisdom to Zeus, commanded
      these men. This contingent came under his command in twelve
      ships with crimson-painted bows.

                        The contingent from Aetolia was led by Thoas,
      Aetolia
                        Andraemon's son. It contained men from Pleuron
640   and Olenus, Pylene, Chalcis by the sea and rocky Calydon.
      Thoas led them because the sons of great-hearted Oeneus
      were dead; so was Oeneus himself; and so was auburn-
      haired Meleager, on whom lordship over all the Aetolians
      had devolved. This contingent came under Thoas' command in
      forty black ships.

                        The contingent from Crete was led by the great
      Crete
                        spearman Idomeneus. It contained men from
      Cnossus, from well-walled Gortyn, from Lyctus, Miletus, chalky
      Lycastus, Phaestus and Rhytion, welcoming towns all of them,
650   and other troops that had their homes in Crete with its hundred
      towns. The great spearman Idomeneus and Meriones, equal of
      the murderous War-god Ares, led these troops. This contingent
      came under their two leaders' command in eighty black ships.

                        The contingent from proud Rhodes was brought
      Rhodes
                        by Tlepolemus, the tall and handsome son of Her-
      acles, in nine ships. The Rhodians occupy three separate parts
      of the island, Lindus, Ialysus and chalky Cameirus. The famous
      spearman Tlepolemus who led these forces was son of mighty
      Heracles by Astyocheia. Heracles carried her off from Ephyre
660   and the River Selleïs after sacking many of their chieftains'
      strongholds. Tlepolemus, when he had grown to manhood in
      the palace at Tiryns, killed his own father's uncle, Licymnius,
      ally of the War-god, who was an old man by then. Tlepolemus
      immediately built some ships, gathered a large following and fled
      overseas, menaced as he was by the other sons and grandsons of
      mighty Heracles. Thus, as a fugitive and after many hardships,

he reached Rhodes. His people settled in three districts according to their tribes and enjoyed the favour of Zeus son of Cronus, lord of gods and men, who showered untold wealth on them.   670

The contingent from Syme was brought by Nireus in three trim ships. Nireus was son of Aglaia and lord Charopus, the handsomest Greek that came to Ilium with the exception of matchless Achilles. But he was a weakling and his following was small.

Syme

The contingent from Cos, city of Eurypylus, contained men from that island and Nisyrus, Crapathus and Casus and the Calydnian Isles. It was led by Pheidippus and Antiphus, the two sons of lord Thessalus son of Heracles. This   680 contingent came in thirty hollow ships.

Cos

The Myrmidon contingent contained men that lived in Pelasgian Argos, from Alus and Alope, from Trachis, Phthia and Hellas land of lovely women. They were called Myrmidons, Hellenes and Achaeans. Achilles led their fifty ships. But at this time they had forgotten the sound and fury of war, since there was no one to marshal them in battle-order; for swift-footed godlike Achilles was lying by his ships, furious over fair-cheeked Briseis, the girl he had won from   690 Lyrnessus by the sweat of his brow when he sacked Lyrnessus itself and stormed the walls of Thebe and brought down the spear-men Mynes and Epistrophus, the sons of lord Euenus, Selepus' son. He lay there pining for this girl. But he was soon to arise.

Myrmidons

The contingent from Phylace contained men from there and from flowery Pyrasus, Demeter's sanctuary; from Iton mother of sheep, Antron by the sea and Pteleus deep in grass. Warlike Protesilaus led them while he lived, but by now the black earth had received him. So his wife was left in   700 Phylace, her cheeks lacerated and his house half-built. He had been the first of the Greeks to leap ashore, but a Trojan killed him as he did so. However, his followers were not left without a chief, though they did miss their leader. Podarces, ally of the War-god and son of Phylacus' son Iphiclus, lord of many sheep, commanded them. Podarces was a brother of the great-hearted Protesilaus, a younger brother, the warlike Protesilaus being both the older and the better man. So their troops did not

Phylace

710 lack a leader, though they missed excellent Protesilaus. This
contingent came under his command in forty black ships.

Pherae   The contingent from Pherae contained men who
came from there by the Boebeian Lake and from
Boebe, Glaphyrae and well-built Iolcus. Admetus' son Eumelus
led them in their eleven ships. Queenly Alcestis, Pelias' most
beautiful daughter, had borne him to Admetus.

Philoctetes'   Philoctetes the great archer brought a contingent
men   in seven ships, men from Methone, Thaumacie, Meli-
boea and rugged Olizon. Each was manned by fifty
720 oarsmen trained to fight with the bow. But Philoctetes lay in
agony on the lovely isle of Lemnos where the Greek army had
left him, suffering from the poisonous bite of a malignant water
snake. So he lay there pining, but the Greeks by their ships were
soon to think once more of lord Philoctetes. However, his
followers were not left without a chief, though they did miss
their leader. Medon, the bastard son of Oïleus, whom Rhene
bore to Oïleus sacker of towns, commanded them.

Tricce   The contingent from Tricce, from Ithome with
its terraced hills and from Oechalia, the city of
730 Oechalian Eurytus, was led by two sons of Asclepius, the admir-
able healers Podaleirius and Machaon. This contingent came in
thirty hollow ships.

Ormenion   The contingent from Ormenion and the spring
of Hypereia, from Asterion and the white towers of
Titanus, was led by Eurypylus, Euaemon's splendid son. This
contingent came under his command in forty black ships.

Argissa   The contingent from Argissa and from Gyrtone,
Orthe, Helone and the white town of Oloosson
740 was led by resolute Polypoetes with Leonteus, both Lapiths.
Polypoetes was son of Peirithous, son of immortal Zeus. Famous
Hippodameia had conceived him for Peirithous on the day when
Peirithous took his revenge on the Centaurs, shaggy people of
the wilds, expelled them from Mount Pelion and drove them
into the hands of the Aethices. Polypoetes was not alone but
shared his command with Leonteus, ally of the War-god and
son of proud Coronus son of Caeneus. This contingent came
under their leaders' command in forty black ships.

From Cyphus, Gouneus brought a contingent in twenty-two ships, consisting of Enienes and resolute Peraebians who built their homes round wintry Dodona and tilled the fields by the delectable Titaressus; this river pours its lovely stream into the Peneus, yet does not mingle with the silver eddies of Peneus but floats along on top of them like olive-oil, being a part of the waters of Styx, the river of the dread oath.

Cyphus

750

The Magnetes came in a contingent led by Prothous son of Tenthredon. The Magnetes lived by the Peneus and by Mount Pelion of the trembling leaves. These were the men that swift Prothous led. This contingent came under his command in forty black ships.

The Magnetes

These then were the leaders and commanders of the Greeks. Now you tell me, Muse, of all the men and horses that crossed with Agamemnon and Menelaus, which were by far the best?

760

Best Greek men and horses, except Achilles

Of the horses, the best by far were the mares of Admetus which his son Eumelus drove. Swift as birds, they were alike in coat and age and of exactly equal height. These mares had been reared in Peraea by Apollo lord of the silver bow to strike panic in the ranks.

Of the men, Ajax son of Telamon was by far the best but only while Achilles was in a rage since he, matchless son of Peleus, was the finest man of all and drove the finest horses. But he was lying now by his seafaring beaked ships, nursing his implacable anger against Agamemnon son of Atreus, shepherd of the people. Meanwhile on the beach his men amused themselves with archery and throwing discuses and spears; the horses stood idle, each by its own chariot, munching clover and parsley from the marsh; their masters' chariots lay covered up inside their huts; and the men themselves, who missed their war-loving chief, strolled aimlessly about the camp and did no fighting.

770

The Greeks advanced as if fire was grazing over the whole land. Earth groaned beneath them, as it does when Zeus who delights in thunder is angry and lashes the ground above the giant Typhoeus in the Arimean mountains, where people say Typhoeus sleeps. So the earth groaned loudly under the feet of marching men as they advanced at speed across the plain.

780

IRIS warns
the *Trojans*

The messenger goddess swift Iris, quick as the wind, was sent to the Trojans by Zeus who drives the storm-cloud with the bad news. They had all 790 gathered, young and old alike, in assembly at Priam's gates. Swift-footed Iris came up to them and spoke in a voice like that of Priam's son Polites, who because of his speed was posted as lookout for the Trojans on top of old Aesyetes' tomb, waiting for an attack from the Greek ships. Swift-footed Iris spoke with his voice:

'Venerable sir, you are still as fond of interminable talk as you were in peace-time. But inescapable war is upon us. Indeed, I have taken part in many battles, but I have never seen so great 800 and formidable a force. They are advancing over the plain to fight at the town, like the leaves of the forest or the sands of the sea. Hector, I urge you above all to do as I say. In his great town, Priam has many allies. But these scattered foreigners all speak different languages. Let their own commanders in each case issue orders to them, draw up their people and lead them out to battle.'

So she spoke, and Hector did not fail to recognize the words of a goddess and immediately dismissed the assembly. They rushed to arms. The gates were all thrown open and the whole 810 army charged out, foot-soldiers and charioteers. The noise they made was tremendous.

Outside the town and some way off in the plain, there is a high mound with open ground on every side, which men call Bramble Hill, but the immortals call the tomb of dancing Myrine. It was here that the Trojans and their allies were marshalled for battle.

The catalogue
of *Trojan*
troops

Priam's son, great Hector of the flashing helmet, was in charge of the Trojans. With him marched by far the finest and most numerous force, keen spearmen all of them.

The Dardanians were led by Anchises' admirable son Aeneas, 820 whom celestial Aphrodite conceived for Anchises, goddess sleeping with mortal, on the slopes of Mount Ida. Aeneas was not in sole command, but was supported by Antenor's two sons,

Archelochus and Acamas, both experienced in every kind of fighting.

The men that lived in Zeleia, under the lowest spurs of Mount Ida and drank the dark water of Aesepus – a prosperous Trojan clan – were led by the famous son of Lycaon, Pandarus, whose bow was a gift from Apollo himself.

The men from Adresteia and the land of Apaesus, from Pityeia and the steep slopes of Tereia, were led by Adrestus and 830 Amphius in his linen body-protection, the two sons of Merops of Percote, who was the ablest prophet of his day and had forbidden his sons to go off to the killing fields. But they would not listen to him: the demons of death led them on.

The men who lived in Percote, Practius and in Sestus, in Abydus and holy Arisbe, were commanded by Asius son of Hyrtacus, leader of men, whom his big and glossy horses had brought from Arisbe beside the River Selleïs.

Hippothous was in command of the tribes of Pelasgian 840 spearmen who lived in fertile Larisa. Hippothous was joined in command by Pylaeus, ally of the War-god: they were the two sons of Pelasgian Lethus, son of Teutamus.

Acamas and the warrior Peiros led the Thracians whose lands are bounded by the swift-flowing Hellespont.

Euphemus, son of Olympian-bred Troezenus son of Ceas, led the warlike Cicones.

Pyraechmes commanded the Paeonians with their curving bows. They had come from far, from Amydon and the banks of the broad River Axius – the Axius, whose waters are the most 850 beautiful that flow over the earth.

Manly Pylaemenes led the Paphlagonians from the lands of the Eneti, from which wild mules come. The Eneti lived in Cytorus, round Sesamon, in impressive homesteads by the River Parthenius, in Cromna, Aegialus and lofty Erythini.

Odius and Epistrophus led the Halizones from distant Alybe, the native home of silver.

Chromis and Ennomus were in command of the Mysians. Ennomus was an augur. But all his bird-lore did not save him from the black hand of death. He fell a victim to swift-footed 860

Achilles in the river-bed when he was making havoc of the Trojans and their allies.

Phorcys and godlike Ascanius led the Phrygians, eager for battle, from remote Ascania.

The Maeonians were led by Mesthles and Antiphus, the sons of Talaemenes, whose mother was the Gygaean Lake. These two led the Maeonians whose native land is under Tmolus.

Nastes led the Carians, who do not speak Greek. They lived in Miletus, thickly wooded Mount Phthires, the streams of Maeander and Mycale with its steep peak. These were the men whom Amphimachus and Nastes brought – Nastes and Amphimachus, the splendid sons of Nomion. Amphimachus went into battle decked in gold like a girl, the fool. Not that it saved him from an ugly end. He fell to swift-footed Achilles, there in the river-bed; and warlike Achilles made off with the gold.

Sarpedon and matchless Glaucus led the Lycians, from distant Lycia and the eddying River Xanthus.

3

A DUEL AND A TROJAN
VIEW OF THE GREEKS

When everyone had been drawn up, each contingent under its leader, the Trojans advanced with shrieks and cries like cranes which, screaming from the skies, fly from the onset of winter and its unnatural downpours. Shrieking, they make for the rivers of Ocean to bring death and destruction to the Pygmies, launching their wicked assault from the air. But the Greeks moved forward in silence, breathing courage, filled with determination to stand by one another.

As the south wind wraps a mist around the mountain-tops – bad news for the shepherd but better than night for a thief, and a man can see no farther than he can throw a stone – so dense a cloud of dust arose from their marching feet as they advanced at speed across the plain.

When the armies had come within range of each other,

godlike Paris stepped out from the Trojan ranks. He was decked
out with a leopard's skin on his back and a curved bow and
a sword. Brandishing two bronze-headed spears, he chal-
20 lenged all the best of the Greeks to meet him face-to-face in
mortal combat.

Paris re-
treats from
Menelaus

When warlike Menelaus saw Paris striding
towards him in front of the enemy ranks, he was as
delighted as a lion that comes across a great carcass
and finds it is an antlered stag or wild goat; he is
starving and greedily devours it in spite of all the efforts of
the quick dogs and strong young hunters to drive him off. So
delighted was Menelaus, when his eyes fell on godlike Paris, for
he thought his chance had come of paying back the man who
had wronged him. Fully armed, he immediately leapt from his
chariot to the ground.

30   When godlike Paris saw Menelaus emerging through the front
ranks, his heart failed him completely and he retreated into his
own contingent of warriors to avoid death. Like a man who
catches sight of a snake in a wooded ravine and sharply recoils,
knees trembling, and retreats, pale-faced, so godlike Paris dis-
appeared back into the mass of proud Trojans, terrified of
Menelaus son of Atreus.

Hector saw him and attacked him sharply:

'Paris, you parody, with your wonderful looks, you sex-
40 crazed seducer, you should never have been born, or married.
How I wish that were the case! Far better that than to be
the disgrace you are now, trusted by nobody. How the long-
haired Greeks must cackle when they see us make a cham-
pion of a man because of his good looks, not his strength of
purpose or courage.

Hector abuses
Paris: duel
with *Menelaus*
proposed

'Can you be the same man who picked a crew,
crossed the waves in your seafaring ships, mixed with
foreigners and carried off a beautiful woman from a
distant land, and from a warrior family too, Helen,
50 to be a scourge to your father, to the town and to
the whole people, to cause our enemies to rejoice and you to
hang your head in shame? And won't you now stand up to
warlike Menelaus? Then you would soon find out the kind of

man he is whose luscious wife you stole. Your lyre would not help you at all, nor Aphrodite's gifts, your lovely locks and pretty face, when you mixed with the dust. But the Trojans are too soft. Otherwise you would have been stoned to death long ago for the trouble you have caused.'

Godlike Paris replied:

'Hector, your taunts are justified, nothing more than I deserve. Your heart is tireless, like an axe in the hands of a carpenter, hewing through the wood. The carpenter's skill shapes a ship's timbers, but the axe gives him the strength he needs. So with you – your strength of purpose remains indomitable. But don't hold against me the irresistible gifts I have from golden Aphrodite. The glorious gifts which the gods themselves choose to lavish on a man are not to be despised; no man ever acquires them by his own efforts.

'But now, if you want me to do battle and fight, make the rest of the Trojans and all the Greeks sit down and let me and warlike Menelaus meet in the middle to fight it out over Helen and all the property I brought back with her. The one who wins and proves himself the better man can take all the property and the woman home, while you others can then swear solemn oaths of friendship with the enemy and remain in fertile Troy, while the Greeks return to horse-grazing Thessaly and Achaea with its lovely women.'

So he spoke, and Hector was delighted at his proposal. He stepped out into no-man's-land and, grasping his spear by the middle, pushed the Trojan ranks back. They all sat down; but the long-haired Greeks began to shoot at him, making Hector the target for their arrows and stones. Then Agamemnon lord of men gave a great shout:

'Greeks, enough! Men, stop shooting! Hector of the flashing helmet looks as if he has something to say.'

So he spoke, and the troops abandoned their attack and immediately fell silent. Hector then spoke to both sides:

'Trojans and Greek men-at-arms, hear from me what Paris, who began this trouble between us, now proposes. He suggests the rest of the Trojans and all the Greeks ground their arms while he and warlike Menelaus meet in the middle and fight it out over Helen and all the property Paris brought back with her. The one who wins and proves himself the better man can take all the property and the woman home, while we others can then swear solemn oaths of friendship.'

So he spoke and was received in complete silence by them all. Then Menelaus, master of the battle-cry, spoke to them:

'Listen now to me too. I am the chief sufferer here, but I intend the Greeks and Trojans to part in peace this day, having had quite enough to endure as a result of this dispute between me and Paris – who began it all. May the man who is marked out by death and destiny meet his end, and then the rest of you will soon be reconciled.

Menelaus welcomes the duel

'You Trojans bring two sheep, a white ram and a black ewe, for the Earth and the Sun; and we will bring another ram for Zeus. And let mighty Priam be fetched so that he can take the oath himself, since he has arrogant and unscrupulous sons and we do not want to see an oath in the name of Zeus wrecked by treachery. Young men are never dependable, but when an old man takes a hand in such affairs, he considers the future as well as the past, and the result is the best for both parties.'

So he spoke, and the Greeks and Trojans were delighted at the prospect of a reprieve from the painful business of fighting. They drew up their chariots in ranks, got down and removed their equipment, which they laid on the ground at close intervals; there was little open space left around. Hector dispatched two heralds at full speed to the town to fetch the sheep and summon Priam; lord Agamemnon sent Talthybius off to the hollow ships and told him to bring back a lamb. Talthybius complied with godlike Agamemnon.

Meanwhile Iris the messenger-goddess brought the news to white-armed Helen, disguising herself as Helen's sister-in-law, Laodice, the most beautiful of Priam's daughters, who was married to lord Helicaon, Antenor's son. She found Helen in the hall at work on a great web of purple cloth for folding double, into which she was weaving some of the many trials that the Trojans and Greeks had suffered for her sake at the hands of the War-god Ares. Swift-footed Iris went up to her and said:

'My dear sister, come and see how strangely the Trojan and 130 Greek warriors are behaving. A little while ago they were making war with all its tears against each other in the plain and looked as thought they meant to fight to the death. But now the battle is off and they are sitting there in silence, leaning on their shields, with their long spears stuck in the ground beside them, while Paris and warlike Menelaus are to fight a duel with their great spears – over you. The winner is to claim you as his wife.'

IRIS summons Helen

With these words the goddess filled Helen's heart with sweet longing for her former husband, her parents and the town she 140 had left. She immediately covered her head in a veil of white linen and, with the soft tears running down her cheeks, set out from her room, not alone, but attended by two waiting-women, Aethre daughter of Pittheus and ox-eyed Clymene. In a little while they reached the Scaean gate.

At this gate, Priam was sitting in conference with the elders of the town Panthous and Thymoetes, Lampus and Clytius, Hicetaon, servant of the War-god Ares, and Ucalegon and Antenor, both sensible men. Old age had brought their fight- 150 ing days to an end but they were excellent speakers, these Trojan elders, sitting there on the tower like cicadas perched on a tree in the woods trilling lightly away. When they saw Helen coming to the tower, they whispered winged words to each other:

'No one could blame the Trojans and Greek men-at-arms for suffering so long for such a woman's sake. She is fearfully like the immortal goddesses. All the same, and lovely as she is, let her sail home and not stay 160 here, a scourge to us and our children after us.'

Trojan elders admire Helen

So they spoke, and Priam called out to Helen:

'Dear child, come here and sit in front of me, so that you can see your former husband and your relatives and friends. I don't hold you responsible for any of this, but the gods. It is they who brought on me this war against the Greeks, with all its tears.

'And now you can tell me the name of that awe-
Priam invites
inspiring man over there, that fine, tall Greek. There
Helen to
are certainly others who are taller but I have never
identify Greeks
set eyes on a man so handsome and imposing. He
170 looks every inch a leader.'

Helen, goddess among women, replied:

'I respect and admire you, my dear father-in-law. I wish I had
chosen to die in misery before I came here with your son,
deserting my bridal bed, my relatives, my darling daughter and
the dear friends with whom I had grown up. But things did not
fall out like that, and so I spend my life in tears.

'Now I will tell what you wished to know. The
Agamemnon
man you pointed out is Agamemnon, son of Atreus,
180 a good ruler and a mighty spearman too. He was my brother-in-
law once, slut that I am – unless all that was a dream.'

So she spoke, and the old man gazed at Agamemnon in
admiration and said:

'Happy son of Atreus, child of fortune, blessed by the gods –
how many thousands of Greeks serve under you! I went to
Phrygia once, land of vines, and there I saw numerous Phrygians
with their galloping horses, and the armies of Otreus and god-
like Mygdon all encamped by the banks of the River Sangarius.
I was their ally and took my place among them that time the
Amazons, women who were a match for men, came up to the
190 attack. But even they were not as numerous as these dark-eyed
Greeks.'

The old man noticed Odysseus next and asked:

'Tell me now, dear child, who that man is. He is shorter than
Agamemnon but broader in the shoulders and chest. He has left
his armour lying on the bountiful earth, and there he goes, like
the leader of a flock, inspecting the ranks. He reminds me of a
fleecy ram moving among a great flock of white sheep.'

Then Helen, child of Zeus, replied:

200 'That is quick-thinking Odysseus, son of Laertes. He was
brought up on Ithaca, a rugged island, and is master
Odysseus and
of all kinds of manoeuvres and strategies.'
Menelaus
Then sensible Antenor spoke in reply:

'Madam, you are quite right. I know, because godlike

Odysseus once came here on a mission on your behalf with warlike Menelaus, and I was their host. I entertained them in my own palace and got to know not only what they looked like but how intelligently they thought. In assembly with the Trojans, 210 when all were standing, Menelaus with his broad shoulders was the taller, but Odysseus was the more imposing of the two when they were both seated.

'When their turn came to express their views in public, Menelaus spoke fluently, not at great length but very clearly, being a man of few words who kept to the point, though he was the younger of the two. By contrast, whenever quick-thinking Odysseus sprang up to speak, he stood there and looked up from under eyes firmly fixed on the ground; he did not swing the speaker's staff either backwards or forwards but held it stiffly, as though he had never handled one before. You would have taken him for some surly or simply stupid 220 fellow. But when he liberated that great voice from his chest and poured out words like the snows of winter, there was no man alive who could compete with him. When we looked at him then, we were no longer surprised at the thought of his appearance.'

Ajax was the third man Priam noticed and asked:

'Who is that other fine, tall Greek, head and shoulders above the rest?'

Helen of the long robes, goddess among women, replied:

'That is awe-inspiring Ajax, a tower of strength to the Greeks. And there next to him is Idomeneus, standing among 230 the Cretans like a god, with his Cretan captains gathered round him. Warlike Menelaus often used to entertain him in our house when he paid us a visit from Crete.

'Now I have picked out all the dark-eyed Greeks I can recognize and name, except two commanders I cannot find – horse-taming Castor and the great boxer Pollux, my brothers, borne by the same mother as myself. Either they did not join the army from lovely Lacedaemon, or 240 they did arrive in their seafaring ships but are unwilling to take part in the fighting on account of the disgrace attached to my name and the many insults they might hear.'

Ajax and
Idomeneus

So she spoke, but the life-giving earth already held them fast over there in Lacedaemon, in the dear land of their fathers.

Heralds, meanwhile, were bringing through the town the oath-offerings for the gods, two sheep and a goatskin full of gladdening wine, the fruit of the soil. The herald Idaeus, who carried a gleaming mixing-bowl and golden cups, came up to Priam and roused him to action:

250 'Up, son of Laomedon. The commanders of the Trojans and Greek forces are calling for you to come down to the plain and swear a solemn oath. Paris and warlike Menelaus are going to fight it out with their spears for the woman. The winner will take the woman, property and all. We others can then swear oaths of friendship with the enemy and remain in fertile Troy, while the Greeks return to horse-grazing Thessaly and Achaea with its lovely women.'

Sacrifice

So he spoke, and the old man shuddered; but he told his men to yoke the horses to his chariot, and 260 they promptly complied. Priam mounted and held the horses steady on the reins, Antenor got into the superb chariot beside him and they drove their fast horses through the Scaean gate towards the plain.

When they reached the assembled armies, they stepped down from the chariot on to the bountiful earth and walked to a spot between the Greeks and Trojans. Agamemnon lord of men and quick-thinking Odysseus rose at once; and noble heralds herded together the oath-offerings for the gods, mixed wine in the 270 bowl and poured some water on their leaders' hands. Then Agamemnon drew the knife that he always carried beside the great scabbard of his sword and cut some wool from the lambs' heads. The wool was distributed among the Trojan and Greek leaders by the heralds. Agamemnon then raised his hands and prayed aloud:

Oaths

'Father Zeus, you that rule from Mount Ida, greatest and most glorious; and you the Sun who see and hear everything; you Rivers and you Earth; and you Powers of the world below that make the dead pay if they have sworn a 280 false oath – I call on you to witness our solemn oaths and see they are kept.

'If Paris kills Menelaus, he is to keep Helen and all her property, and we shall sail away in our seafaring ships. But if auburn-haired Menelaus kills Paris, the Trojans must surrender Helen and all her property and make the Greeks compensation on a scale that future generations shall remember. And if, in the event of Paris' death, Priam and his sons refuse to meet this demand, I shall stay here and fight for satisfaction until the war   290 is finished.'

He spoke, slit the lambs' throats with the relentless bronze and dropped them gasping on the ground, where life ebbed from them: the knife had removed their spirit. Then they drew wine from the mixing-bowl into cups and, as they poured it on the ground, they prayed to the immortal gods. Greeks and Trojans said as one man:

'Zeus, greatest and most glorious, and you other immortal gods! May the brains of whichever party breaks this treaty be   300 poured out on the ground as that wine is poured, and not only theirs but their children's too; and other men possess their wives.'

So they spoke, but Zeus son of Cronus did not yet grant their prayers. Now Priam son of Dardanus addressed them:

'Hear me, Trojans and Greek men-at-arms. I am now going back to windswept Ilium, since I cannot bear to look on while my own dear son fights warlike Menelaus. Zeus and the other immortal gods must know already which of the two is going to his doom.'

Godlike Priam spoke, put the lambs into the chariot, mounted   310 himself and held the horses steady on the reins; Antenor got into the superb chariot beside him and the two drove off on their way back to Ilium.

Hector son of Priam and godlike Odysseus proceeded to measure out the ground and then to place lots in a bronze helmet and shake them to see which of the two should throw his bronze spear first. The *Priam* leaves, lots are drawn; the duel watching armies prayed with their hands raised to the gods. Greeks and Trojans said as one man:

'Father Zeus, you that rule from Mount Ida, greatest and   320 most glorious! Let the man who brought these troubles on both peoples die and go down to the house of Hades; and let firm oaths of friendship be made.'

So they spoke, and now great Hector of the flashing helmet shook the helmet, averting his eyes. Paris' lot immediately leapt out. The troops then sat down in rows, each man by his high-stepping horses where his ornate armour lay.

330   Then godlike Paris, husband of lovely-haired Helen, put on his magnificent armour. First he placed fine leg-guards on his shins, fitted with silver ankle-clips. Then he put on body-armour. It belonged to his brother Lycaon and fitted him too. Over his shoulder he slung a bronze silver-riveted sword, then a great heavy shield. On his mighty head he placed a well-made helmet with a horsehair crest, the plume nodding frighteningly from the top. Then he took up a powerful spear that fitted his grip.

340   Warlike Menelaus also armed in the same way; and when both had got themselves ready, each behind his front line, they strode out between the two forces, looking daggers. The Trojans and Greeks watched spellbound. The two men took up their positions not far from each other within the measured piece of ground and brandished their weapons in mutual fury.

First Paris hurled his long-shadowed spear, and it hit Menelaus' round shield. But it did not break through and the tip was bent back by the stout shield. Then Menelaus attacked with his
350   spear, with a prayer to Father Zeus:

'Grant me revenge, Lord Zeus, on godlike Paris, the man who wronged me in the beginning. Use my hand to bring him down so that our children's children will still shudder at the thought of wronging a host who has offered them friendship.'

He spoke, balanced his long-shadowed spear and hurled it. It hit Paris' round shield. The heavy weapon pierced the glittering shield, forced its way through the ornate body-armour and
360   ripped right on through the side of Paris' tunic. But Paris had swerved and so avoided dark death. Menelaus then drew his silver-riveted sword, swung it back and brought it down full on the ridge of his enemy's helmet. But the sword shattered on the helmet and fell in pieces from his hands. Menelaus gave a groan and looked up to the broad sky:

'Father Zeus, there is no god more spiteful than you. I thought

I had paid Paris back for his wickedness, and now my sword breaks in my hands when I have already thrown my spear for nothing and never touched the man!'

He spoke and, hurling himself at Paris, seized him by the horsehair crest and, turning him round, began to drag him back   370 into the Greek lines. Paris was choked by the pressure on his tender throat of the embroidered helmet-strap which he had tied tightly under his chin; and Menelaus would have hauled him off and won unutterable glory, but for the quickness of Aphrodite daughter of Zeus, who saw what was happening and broke the strap made of leather from a slaugh-   *APHRODITE* tered ox. So the helmet came away empty in Mene-   rescues *Paris*; laus' clenched fist. The warrior swung it round and   takes him to tossed it into the Greek lines, where it was picked up   Helen by his loyal troops, and launched himself at Paris again in the hope of killing him with his bronze spear. But   380 Aphrodite hid Paris in a dense mist and whisked him away – an easy feat for an immortal – and put him down in his own perfumed, fragrant bedroom. Then she went herself to summon Helen.

Aphrodite found Helen on the high tower, surrounded by Trojan women. The goddess put out her hand, tugged at her sweet-smelling robe and spoke to her in the disguise of an old woman she was very fond of, a wool-worker who used to comb the wool for Helen when she lived in Lacedaemon. Mimicking this woman, celestial Aphrodite spoke to her:

'Come here! Paris wants you to go home to him. There he is   390 in his bedroom, on the inlaid bed, dazzling in looks and dress. You would never believe he had just come in from a duel. You would think he was going to a dance or had just stepped off the floor and sat down to rest.'

So she spoke, and her words went straight to Helen's heart. But when she noticed the superb neck, desirable breasts and sparkling eyes of the goddess, she was shocked and spoke to her:

'Mysterious goddess, why are you trying to lead me on like this? You are plotting, I suppose, to carry me off to some still   400 more distant town, in Phrygia or lovely Maeonia, to gratify some other favourite of yours who may be living in those parts. Or is it that Menelaus has beaten Paris and wants to take me back home, me, his loathsome wife – so now you have come here to try to lure me back to Paris?

'No, go and sit with him yourself. Forget you are a goddess. Never set foot on Olympus again but go and agonize over Paris, go and pamper him, and one day he may make you his wife – or his concubine. I refuse to go and share that man's bed again – it would be quite wrong. There is not a woman in Troy who would not blame me if I did. I have enough trouble to put up with already.'

Enraged, celestial Aphrodite spoke to her:

APHRODITE orders Helen to make love to Paris

'Obstinate wretch! Don't get the wrong side of me, or I may desert you in my anger and detest you as vehemently as I have loved you up till now, and provoke Greeks and Trojans alike to such hatred of you that you would come to a dreadful end.'

So she spoke, and Helen, child of Zeus, was terrified. She wrapped herself up in her shining white robe and went off in silence. Not one of the Trojan women saw her go: she had a protecting divinity to guide her.

When they reached Paris' superb house, the waiting-women in attendance at once turned to their tasks while Helen, goddess among women, went to her lofty bedroom. There the goddess herself, laughter-loving Aphrodite, picked up a chair, carried it across the room and put it down for her in front of Paris. Helen, daughter of Zeus who drives the storm-cloud, sat down on it but refused to look her husband in the face and attacked him:

'So you are back from the battlefield – and I was hoping you had fallen there to the mighty warrior who was once my husband! You used to boast you were a better man than warlike Menelaus – a finer spearman, stronger in the arm. Go and challenge him to fight again, then! But if you take my advice, you will think twice before you offer single combat to auburn-haired Menelaus – or you may end by falling to his spear.'

Paris replied and said:

'My dear, don't say such hurtful things about me and my courage. Menelaus has just beaten me, with Athene's help. But

I too have gods to help me and next time I shall win. Come, let   440
us go to bed together and enjoy the pleasures of love. Never has
such desire overwhelmed me, not even in the beginning when I
carried you off from lovely Lacedaemon in my seafaring ships
and spent the night making love to you on the isle of Cranae –
never till now have I felt such desire for you, or has such sweet
longing overwhelmed me.'

He spoke, and made a move towards their elaborate bed,
leading her to it. His wife followed him, and there the two lay
down together.

Meanwhile Menelaus was prowling through the ranks like a
wild beast, trying to find godlike Paris. But not a man among   450
the Trojans and their famous allies could point him out to
warlike Menelaus. Not that, if anyone had seen him, they would
have hidden him out of friendship. They loathed him, all of
them, like black death. Then Agamemnon lord of men spoke to
them:

'Trojans, Greeks and allies, listen to me. Menelaus has clearly
won. Now give up Helen from Argos and all her property
and make compensation on a scale that future generations will   460
remember.'

So spoke the son of Atreus, and the Greeks all applauded.

4

THE OATH IS BROKEN AND BATTLE JOINED

The fighting starts in this book (see p. xxxiv). When battle is joined, the warrior advances to battle in a two-horse chariot driven by his charioteer. He fights from his chariot, or dismounts to fight on the ground with the chariot in close attendance. He fights mainly with the spear, either 'hitting' with a throw from long range, or 'stabbing' from short range.

Two types of battle are distinguished: the standing fight, when both sides advance and retreat, and the 'panic' or 'rout', when one side turns tail and runs for it. Homer carefully indicates what stage the battle is at; for example, when one side is on the retreat, they die from wounds in the back. The general mass of warriors fighting on foot receives only occasional background mention. Battle encounters are dramatic and highly charged moments. They attract a large number of similes, which seem to cluster at such points (see p. xxxvii).

1–72: ZEUS wonders whether HERA and ATHENE would agree to making peace between the Greeks and *Trojans*. The goddesses, who hate the *Trojans*, refuse, and ATHENE descends to restart the fighting.

73–219: ATHENE persuades the *Trojan* archer *Pandarus* to shoot Menelaus. ATHENE herself takes care to deflect the shot, so that it only grazes him.

220–421: Agamemnon surveys his troops, praising Idomeneus, Ajax, Teucer and Nestor, but rebuking Menestheus, Odysseus and Diomedes.

422–544: Battle is joined. *APOLLO* and ATHENE urge on the two sides.

The gods, meanwhile, had sat down in assembly with Zeus on Olympus' golden floor. Lady Hebe served them with nectar, and they drank each other's health from cups of gold as they looked out over the Trojans' town.

Zeus son of Cronus now tried to irritate Hera by needling her, though he did not really mean what he said:

'Two of the goddesses are on Menelaus' side – Hera from Argos and Athene from Alalcomenae. But they are happy just to sit up here and watch; whereas laughter-loving Aphrodite is 10 always at Paris' side, shielding him from death. Only a moment ago she whisked him off when he thought his end had come. Nevertheless, victory has certainly gone to warlike Menelaus, and we should now consider what to do next. Are we to stir up evil war again, with all the sound and fury of battle, or shall we make peace between the two sides? Subject to your approval, this would mean that lord Priam's town would survive, and Menelaus take Helen back . . .'

ZEUS proposes *Ilium*'s survival; HERA disagrees

So he spoke, and Athene and Hera muttered darkly to each 20 other. They were sitting close together, plotting trouble for the Trojans. Athene held her tongue and said nothing, but glared at Father Zeus, seething with indignation. Hera, however, could not contain her rage and spoke out:

'Dread son of Cronus, what are you suggesting now? How can you think of making all my efforts count for nothing, the pains I took, the sweat that poured from me as I toiled round in my chariot and gathered the army to make trouble for Priam and his sons? Do what you like, then: but not all the rest of us gods will approve.'

Angrily, Zeus who marshals the clouds replied: 30

'You are impossible! What injury can Priam and his sons have done you, to account for the vehemence of your desire to sack the well-built town of Ilium? You would satisfy your rage only if you stormed through the gates and long walls and ate up Priam, his children and the rest of the Trojans raw. Act as you see fit. I don't wish this difference of ours to develop into a serious breach.

'But I will tell you something else, and you bear it in mind.

40 When it is *my* turn to desire the sack of a town and I choose one
where favourites of yours are living, make no attempt to curb
my anger, but let me have my way, since I have given in to
you this time of my own accord, though much against my
inclination. For of all the towns that mortal men live in under
the sun and starry sky, I prized sacred Ilium closest to my heart,
with Priam and the people of Priam of the good ash spear. My
altar never lacked its share of generous offerings, libations of
wine and the fat from burnt sacrifice, the honour that gods have
been granted as our right.'

50   Ox-eyed lady Hera replied:
'The three towns *I* love best are Argos, Sparta and Mycenae
with its broad streets. Sack those, whenever they incur your
hatred. I shall not make a stand on their behalf nor begrudge
them to you. But even if I do object and refuse to permit their
destruction, I shall achieve nothing – you are far too strong for
me. And yet my efforts must not count for nothing, because I
too am divine, and our parentage is one. Further, among all the
60 daughters of sickle-wielding Cronus I take precedence in two
respects – because I am the eldest by birth, and also because I
am your acknowledged wife and you are lord of all the gods.

'However, let us yield to one another in these matters, I to
you and you to me. The rest of the immortal gods will then
follow our example. Now immediately instruct Athene to visit
the Trojan and Greek battle lines, and try to arrange for the
Trojans to be the first to break the oaths made with the proud
Greeks.'

So she spoke, and the Father of men and gods complied. At
once he spoke to Athene with winged words:
70   'Off with you immediately to the Trojan and Greek battle
front, and try to arrange for the Trojans to be the first to break
the oaths made with the proud Greeks.'

With these words he encouraged Athene, who had already set
her heart on action. She came swooping down from the heights
of Olympus like a meteor that Zeus, son of sickle-wielding
Cronus, discharges as a warning to sailors or to some great army
on the land: blazing, it shoots out a mass of sparks. That was
how Pallas Athene looked as she sped to earth and leapt in

among the troops. The horse-taming Trojans and Greek men-at-arms were awe-struck at the sight. They looked at each other and said as one man: 80

'This means dreadful war and all the sound and fury of battle are on us again, or Zeus, controller of war on earth, is to make peace between us.'

So Greeks and Trojans talked. Meanwhile Athene disguised herself as a man and slipped into the Trojan ranks in the likeness of Laodocus, a mighty spearman. She was trying to find godlike Pandarus and she found him, the handsome and mighty son of Lycaon, standing there beside the powerful 90 shield-bearing force that had come under his command from the River Aesepus. She went up to him and spoke winged words:

'Pandarus, shrewd son of Lycaon, you should do what I say. If you could bring yourself to shoot a flying arrow at Menelaus, you would cover yourself in glory and put every Trojan in your debt, lord Paris most of all. He would be the first to come forward with splendid gifts, if he saw Menelaus warlike son of Atreus brought down by a shot from you and laid out on the sad funeral pyre. Come, shoot at illustrious Menelaus and promise the 100 renowned Lycian-born Archer-god Apollo an impressive offering of first-born lambs when you get back home to sacred Zeleia.'

ATHENE
tells *Pandarus*
to shoot at
Menelaus

So spoke Athene, and she persuaded the fool. Then and there he unsheathed his polished bow. It was made from the horns of a full-grown wild goat that he himself had shot in the chest. He had been lying in wait for the animal and hit it as it emerged from its rocky hiding place; there it fell, on its back. The horns on its head, measuring over a metre across, had been prepared by 110 a craftsman in horn who fitted them into the wooden bow-stave, made it all smooth and put a golden hook for the bowstring at the end.

Pandarus then placed the bow firmly against the ground, bent and strung it, while his brave troops surrounded him with their shields to protect him from attack by the warlike Greeks before he could get a shot at Menelaus. Then he took off the

lid of his quiver and picked out a feathered arrow, as yet unused,
black pain concealed within it. He quickly fitted the sharp
arrow to the string and promised the renowned Lycian-born
120 Archer-god Apollo an impressive offering of first-born lambs
when he got back home to sacred Zeleia. He notched the
arrow into the ox-gut string, gripped it by the end and drew
it back, till the string was touching his chest and the arrow's
iron tip lay alongside the bow. When he had bent the great
bow into a circle, it gave a crisp twang, the string sang out,
and the sharp arrow leapt into the air, eager to wing its way
into the enemy ranks.

ATHENE   But the blessed immortal gods did not forget you,
            Menelaus, and first of these was the war-leader
protects   Athene, daughter of Zeus, who took her stand in
Menelaus   front of you and warded off the piercing missile,
130 turning it away just so much from your flesh, like a mother
brushing a fly away from her gently sleeping child. With her
own hand she guided it instead to where the golden buckles of
the belt fixed together and the body-armour overlapped. So the
sharp arrow struck the fastened belt. It punched through this
ornate belt and drove on through both the richly worked body-
armour and through the kilt that Menelaus wore as a last line
of defence against flying weapons. This did more than all the
rest to save him, though the arrow did penetrate that too. In the
140 end the arrow just grazed his mortal flesh, and at once the dark
blood came flowing from the wound.

As a woman from Caria or Maeonia stains ivory with purple
dye to make a cheek-piece for a horse; it is put in store, and
every charioteer prays to see it on a horse of his; but it is in store
to delight a ruler, as an adornment for his horse and badge
of honour for his charioteer – so, Menelaus, blood stained
your handsome thighs and shins and ran down to your fine
ankles.

Agamemnon lord of men shuddered when he saw the dark
150 blood streaming from the wound. Warlike Menelaus himself
shuddered too, though when he saw that the arrow-head and
its bindings had not sunk in, he recovered his composure. But

lord Agamemnon gave a deep groan, as did his men, took Menelaus by the hand and said:

'My dear brother, it was your death, then, that I swore to when I took the oath and sent you out alone to fight for us against the Trojans, who have shot you now and trampled on the sacred oaths. But oaths sealed by our right hands and solemnized with libations of wine and the blood of lambs cannot have been sealed in vain. Olympian Zeus may postpone the penalty, but he exacts it, in full, in the end, and oath-breakers pay a heavy price – they pay with their own lives and their wives' and children's too. But deep in my heart I know well the day is coming when sacred Ilium will be destroyed, together with the people of Priam and Priam himself of the good ash spear. Zeus son of Cronus, from his high throne in Olympus where he lives, will himself shake out the dark aegis of destruction over all of them in his anger at this perjury of theirs. All this will happen without fail.

Agamemnon laments Menelaus' wound

'Yet if you die, Menelaus, if your life has really run its destined course, how bitterly I shall lament you. And what a storm of criticism I would face on my return to dusty Argos! For the Greeks will at once be set on getting home. We should be forced to abandon Helen here for Priam and his men to boast over, while the earth would rot your bones as you lay here in Troy, the site of your failed mission. Some arrogant Trojan will jump up and down on the tomb of illustrious Menelaus and say "May every quarrel picked by Agamemnon end like this – a failed expedition, retreat in empty ships and brave Menelaus left behind!" That is how they will talk – and I shall pray for the broad earth to swallow me.'

Auburn-haired Menelaus comforted him and spoke:

'Put your mind at rest and don't alarm the men. The sharp arrow did not reach a vital spot. Before it got so far, it was stopped by my metal belt, the body-armour underneath and the kilt which bronze-smiths made for me.'

Lord Agamemnon replied and said:

'If only you are right, dear Menelaus! But a healer will treat the wound and apply herbs to relieve the pain.'

He spoke and addressed Talthybius the godlike herald:

Machaon is
called to heal
Menelaus

'Talthybius, fetch Machaon here as quickly as possible, son of the matchless healer Asclepius, to see Menelaus. Some Trojan or Lycian archer who knows his business well has hit him with an arrow: glory for him, grief for us.'

So he spoke, and the herald heard, complied and made his
200 way through the ranks of bronze-armoured Greeks, searching for the warrior Machaon. He found him standing with his men, the powerful shield-bearing force that had come under his command from Tricce where the horses graze. He went up to him and spoke winged words:

'Quick, Machaon, son of Asclepius, lord Agamemnon has sent for you to see Menelaus. Some Trojan or Lycian archer who knows his business well has hit him with an arrow: glory for him, grief for us.'

So he spoke, and his words went straight to Machaon's heart. He set off through the ranks of the great Greek army. When
210 they reached the spot where Menelaus lay wounded, with all the commanders gathered round him in a circle, Machaon took his place in the middle and at once extracted the arrow from the close-fitting belt, though the pointed barbs broke as the head was pulled out. Then he undid the metal belt, the body-armour underneath and the kilt which bronze-smiths had made. When he found the place where the sharp arrow had pierced the flesh, he sucked out the blood and skilfully applied soothing herbs from the supply with which the sympathetic centaur Cheiron had once equipped his father Asclepius.

220 While they were attending to Menelaus, master of the battle-cry, the ranks of shield-bearing Trojans advanced to the attack. The Greeks once more put on their armour, their will to fight renewed.

Agamemnon
surveys the
troops

Then you would not see godlike Agamemnon dozing or hiding or unwilling to fight, but eager for the battle where men win glory. He decided not to use his horses and bronze-inlaid chariot. So the pair were led aside by his attendant Eurymedon, son of Ptolemy, snorting

as they went. But Agamemnon was careful to instruct the man
to keep them close at hand, in case he grew weary at any point   230
while he worked his way as commander round the great army.
Then he set out on foot to make his tour of inspection of the
troops.

When he came upon any of his Greeks with their swift horses
who were up and doing, he stopped and encouraged them:

'Greeks, never relax that fighting spirit of yours! Perjurers
will get no help from Father Zeus. The men who first broke the
oaths are going to have their own smooth flesh devoured by
vultures, while we will carry off their dear wives and little
children on board our ships, when we have sacked their citadel!'

On the other hand, if he found any shrinking from the ugly   240
business of war, he turned on them sharply and angrily:

'Greeks, you despicable loud-mouths, have you no shame?
Why do you stand there, bewildered, like fawns that dash across
the plain and exhaust themselves and stop, because they have
no more will to resist? That's what you look like, standing there,
bewildered, instead of fighting. Or are you waiting for the
Trojans to threaten our well-built ships drawn up on the grey
sea-shore in the hope that Zeus will lay a protecting hand over
you?'

So he made his commander's tour of inspection of the troops.   250
In his tour of the throng of men, he came upon the Cretans, the
troops that armed for battle under warlike Idomeneus. In the
forefront was Idomeneus himself, brave as a boar; while Mer-
iones urged on the troops at the rear. Agamemnon lord of men
was delighted when he saw them and at once spoke warmly to
Idomeneus:

'Idomeneus, of all my Greeks with their swift
horses, there is not one I honour more than you, on   Idomeneus
the battlefield, on other missions and at feasts for senior advisers
when the Greek leaders mix themselves sparkling wine. When   260
the rest of the long-haired Greeks have drunk up their portion,
your cup stands full, like mine, to drink from as you wish. Off,
then, into battle and be the man you have always said you were!'

Idomeneus commander of the Cretans said in reply:

'Son of Atreus, you can rely on my loyal support and the

solemn assurance I gave you when this business began. Inspire
the rest of the long-haired Greeks, so that we can join battle at
270 once, now that the Trojans have broken their oaths. As for
them, they can look forward to nothing but death and disaster,
since they first broke the oaths.'

Ajax and
Teucer

So he spoke, and Agamemnon passed on, well
pleased. In his tour of the throng of men, he came
upon the two brothers, Ajax and Teucer. The pair
were putting on their helmets and had a cloud of infantrymen at
their back. As a goatherd in his lookout sees a cloud approaching
across the sea, driven by a roaring west wind; the goatherd is
some way off but, black as pitch, the cloud advances at him
across the sea bringing a great whirlwind in its wake, and he
280 shudders when he sees it and drives his flocks into a cave –
such were the close-packed ranks of Olympian-bred young men
under the two brothers, dark, bristling with shields and spears
as they moved off into battle. Lord Agamemnon was delighted
to see them and spoke winged words:

'Ajax and Teucer, leaders of the bronze-armoured Greeks, I
have no orders – encouraging you would be quite out of place!
Your very leadership inspires your men to fight their best. Father
Zeus, Athene and Apollo, if only everyone had your attitude!
290 The town of lord Priam would soon be captured, sacked and
turned over to Greek hands.'

Nestor

With these words Agamemnon left them and
moved on to the others. There he came across Nestor
the clear-voiced speaker from Pylos, whom he found preparing
his men to fight and marshalling them under their leaders,
great Pelagon, Alastor and Chromius, lord Haemon and Bias
shepherd of the people. Nestor stationed his charioteers with
their horses and chariots in the front and at the back his many
brave foot-soldiers, to serve as rearguard. He placed his inferior
300 troops in the middle so that even the unwilling would be forced
to fight. He told his charioteers, whom he was instructing first,
to keep control of their horses and not get entangled in the
mêlée:

'Don't think bravery and skill entitle a charioteer to charge
forward and fight the Trojans on his own. And don't let anyone

drop behind and weaken the whole force. When a man in his own chariot comes within reach of the enemy, he should try a spear-thrust. That is the best tactic. This is the discipline and courage that enabled our forefathers to storm towns and fortifications.'

So old Nestor used the experience he had gained in battles long ago to inspire his troops. Lord Agamemnon was delighted to see him and spoke winged words:

'Venerable sir, how happy I could be if your spirit were matched by the vigour of your limbs, and your strength was unimpaired! But age, which no one can escape, lies heavy upon you. If only you could pass it on to someone else and rejoin the ranks of youth!'

Then Nestor the Gerenian charioteer replied to him:

'Son of Atreus, I too could wish most heartily to be the man I was when I killed godlike Ereuthalion. But the gods do not grant us all their favours at one time. I was a young man then; now age presses hard upon me. Yet for all that I shall still be with my charioteers and in command. Their tactics and orders come from me – that's the privilege of age – even if the spear is left to younger men than myself, who can rely on their muscle.'

So he spoke, and Agamemnon moved on, well pleased. Next he found Peteos' son the horse-driver Menestheus. This man and his Athenian troops, champions of the battle-cry, were standing idle; and nearby was quick-thinking Odysseus with his Cephallenian troops, a substantial force, standing idle too. The call to battle had not yet reached their ears, since the Trojan and Greek troops had only just begun to move into action. So they stood there and waited for some other Greek contingent to advance against the Trojans and signal the start of the fighting. When he noticed this, Agamemnon lord of men attacked them and spoke winged words:

'You, Menestheus, son of a noble father, and you, Odysseus, master of sharp practice, always looking out for number one, why are you hanging back like this and leaving others to advance? You ought to be taking your place in the front line, ready to bear the heat of battle. You two are the first to get an invitation from me when we lay on a feast for

310

320

330

Odysseus

340

the senior advisers. On such occasions you're quite happy to take your fill of roast meat and sweet wine for as long as you want. But now you seem happy to stand by and watch while ten contingents of Greeks fall on the enemy with their spears before you make a move.'

Quick-thinking Odysseus gave him a black look and replied:

350 'Son of Atreus, why do you say such a thing? How can you maintain that, when we Greeks unleash the dogs of war against the horse-taming Trojans, we shirk the fighting? You'll have your wish, if that's what is troubling you, and see the father of Telemachus at grips with the front ranks of these horse-taming Trojans. As for you, you're all hot air.'

When lord Agamemnon realized that Odysseus was angry, he smiled and answered with an apology:

'Olympian-born son of Laertes, resourceful Odysseus, I am not really attacking you and I have no more orders to give. I

360 know in your heart of hearts you are well disposed to me. In fact, we see eye to eye. On, then; I'll make up for it later if I have said anything offensive. May the gods scatter it to the winds.'

With these words Agamemnon left them and moved on to the others. He found Tydeus' son great-heated Diomedes stationary there among the horses and finely built chariots. Sthenelus son of Capaneus stood close at hand. Seeing him, Agamemnon lord of men attacked him and spoke winged words:

370 'Diomedes son of that dauntless charioteer Tydeus, what can I say? Why are you hanging back like this, just eyeing the lines of battle? It was not your father Tydeus' habit to hang back but to come to grips with the enemy way out in front of his men. That is what people say who saw the man at work. They say he

Diomedes (contrasted with Tydeus) was the best of them all. I myself never met or saw him, though he did come to Mycenae once, not to fight but on a personal mission with godlike Polyneices in search of reinforcements. It was the time they were attacking the sacred walls of Thebes to drive out

380 Eteocles. They entreated our people to provide adequate support, and our people were sympathetic and promised all they asked for.

'But Zeus made us change our minds with some unfavourable

omens. So Tydeus and his men left Mycenae. When they had
gone some way along the road and reached the meadows and
reedy banks of the River Asopus near Thebes, the Greeks sent
Tydeus with a message into the town. He entered and found a
large group of Thebans, the people of Cadmus, feasting in the
palace of their leader, mighty Eteocles. But even as a visitor,
alone among a crowd of Thebans, Tydeus showed no fear. He
challenged them to athletic contests and won easily in every
case, since he had Athene to help him.   390

'This infuriated the horse-racing Thebans and, when Tydeus
left, they gathered and laid an ambush in his path, fifty men
with two leaders, Maeon, a man like the gods, and resolute
Polyphontes. But Tydeus dealt with them and brought them to
a nasty end. He killed the whole party except the one he sent
back to Thebes (acknowledging signs from the gods, he let
Maeon go).

'That was Tydeus from Aetolia. You are his son. But you do
not fight as he did, though you may be better when it comes to   400
talking.'

So he spoke, and mighty Diomedes made no reply. He duti-
fully accepted the rebuke from the leader he respected. But
Sthenelus son of illustrious Capaneus replied:

'Son of Atreus, you know the facts: don't lie about
them. I say we are far better men than our fathers.   Diomedes
We *did* succeed in capturing seven-gated Thebes.   silences
With a weaker force, we stormed more powerful   Sthenelus
defences than they ever faced, because we trusted in Zeus'
help and the signs that the gods sent us; but our fathers were
destroyed through their own recklessness. So don't talk to me   410
about our fathers in the same breath as us.'

Mighty Diomedes gave Sthenelus a black look and said:

'Be quiet, man, and listen to me. I am not going to quarrel
with Agamemnon shepherd of the people for encouraging the
Greeks to fight. It is he who will get the credit if the Greeks beat
the Trojans and capture sacred Ilium; but at the same time, if
the Greeks are defeated, he will also get the grief. Come: time
for the two of us to call up that fighting spirit of ours!'

He spoke and, fully armed, leapt from his chariot to the

420   ground. As he charged into action, the bronze rang terrifyingly
       on his chest. The bravest heart might well have quailed.

       As the waves of the ocean under a westerly gale race one after
       the other on to a booming beach; far out at sea the white
       horses rise, then break and crash thunderously on the shore and,
       arching up, climb headlands and send the salt spray flying – so,
       one after the other, the Greek contingents moved relentlessly
       into battle. Each leader was issuing orders to his own command,
430   but the men advanced in silence. You would not think so large
       an army was on the march or had a voice, so silent were they,
       in fear of their commanders. Their ornate armour glittered as
       they advanced, rank on rank.

       As for the Trojans, like sheep that stand in their thousands
       in a rich man's yard, yielding their white milk and bleating
       incessantly because they hear their lambs, so a hubbub went up
       through the great army. Their speech and dialects were all
       different, as they spoke a mixture of languages – the troops
       hailed from many parts.

       The War-god Ares spurred on the Trojan forces, and grey-
440   eyed Athene the Greeks. Terror and Panic accompanied her,
       and so did implacably determined Strife, the sister and ally of
       man-slaying Ares. Small at first, she soars upward and, though
       her feet are still on the ground, reaches high Olympus with her
       head. Now she too swept in among the Trojans and Greeks,
       filling them with hatred of one another and ensuring the death-
       cries of more and more men.

Battle is joined   The armies advanced and met in a single space
                       with a clash of shields, spears and bronze-armoured
       warriors. The bossed shields collided and a great roar went up
450   – the screams of the dying, the jeers of the victors – and the earth
       ran with blood. As two mountain rivers in winter, fed by their
       great springs higher up, meet in full spate in some deep ravine,
       while far off in the mountains a shepherd hears the thunder, such
       were the yelling and turmoil as the two armies came to grips.

Antilochus kills   Antilochus was the first to kill his man, brave
     Echepolus   Echepolus, who was fighting in full armour in
                       the Trojan front ranks. Antilochus hit him on the
460   ridge of his plumed helmet. The bronze spear hit

Echepolus' forehead and pierced right through the bone. Darkness engulfed his eyes and he crashed, like a tower, in the thick of the action.

As he fell, lord Elephenor, leader of the great-hearted Abantes, seized him by the feet and tried to drag him quickly out of range, eager to strip him of his armour. But the attempt was short-lived, since Agenor saw him dragging the body away. With his bronze spear he stabbed Elephenor in the side which his shield had left exposed as he bent over. Agenor brought him down, life left him, and a grim struggle between Trojans and Greeks developed over him. They leapt at each other like wolves, and man grappled with man.

Agenor kills Elephenor

470

Then Ajax son of Telamon hit Anthemion's son Simoïsius, an unmarried young man at the prime of his youth. His mother bore him by the banks of the River Simoïs when she was returning from Mount Ida where her father and mother had taken her to see to their sheep. So they called him Simoïsius. His life was too short to repay his parents for their loving care, for it ended when he met the spear of great-hearted Ajax. As the young man advanced among the front ranks, Ajax hit him in the chest by the right nipple. The bronze spear went clean through his shoulder, and he crashed to the ground in the dust like a poplar which grows in the hollow of a great water-meadow, its trunk trimmed and the branches sprouting out at the top. A chariot-maker cuts it down with his gleaming axe to make the wheel-rims for a beautiful chariot; but he leaves it now to lie and season on the bank. So Ajax slaughtered Anthemion's son Simoïsius.

Ajax kills *Simoïsius*

480

Now Priam's son brightly armoured Antiphus threw a sharp spear at Ajax through the crowd. Antiphus missed his man but hit Leucus, one of Odysseus' brave comrades, in the groin as he was dragging Simoïsius away. The body fell from Leucus' hands, and he himself came crashing down on top of it.

490

Odysseus was infuriated when he saw Leucus killed. His bronze armour glittering, he advanced through the front ranks up to the enemy lines, where he took his stand and, looking carefully round, threw his gleaming spear. The Trojans leapt back when

Antiphus kills Leucus; Odysseus kills *Democoön*

they saw it coming. But Odysseus' spear did not leave his hand
for nothing. It hit Democoön, a bastard son of Priam, who had
500 joined Priam from the town of Abydus. He was standing by his
horses when Odysseus, infuriated by his companion's death, hit
him with his spear on the temple, and the bronze tip passed
right through and came out the other side. Darkness engulfed
Democoön's eyes; he thudded to the ground, and his armour
clattered about him.

At this glorious Hector and the Trojan front ranks fell back,
while the Greeks gave a great shout, dragged in the bodies and
pushed forward. This filled Apollo, who was watching from
Pergamus – Ilium's highest point – with indignation, and he
shouted to the Trojans:

APOLLO   'On with you, horse-taming Trojans! Never give
rallies the   Greeks best in your will to fight! They are not made of
Trojans   stone or iron. Their flesh can't keep out penetrating
                  spears when they are hit. And what's more, Achilles,
510 son of lovely-haired Thetis, is not fighting, but nursing his
heart-tearing anger by the ships.'

So the awe-inspiring god spoke from the citadel, while the
Greeks were encouraged by Athene, Triton-born, most glorious
daughter of Zeus, who went through the ranks herself spurring
on any Greek she saw holding back.

Peiros kills   Now destiny shackled Diores. He was hit by a
Diores; Thoas   jagged stone on the right leg near the ankle. The man
kills Peiros   who threw it was the Thracian leader Peiros who
                  came from Aenus. The shameless rock completely
520 shattered the two tendons and the bones; and Diores fell back-
wards in the dust, stretching his hands out to his friends and
gasping for life. But Peiros, the man who had hit him, ran up
and stabbed him by the navel with his spear. All his innards
gushed out on to the ground, and darkness engulfed his eyes.

As Peiros sprang away, however, Thoas from Aetolia hit him
in the chest with his spear, below the nipple, and the bronze
530 point sank into his lung. Thoas then came up to him, pulled the
heavy spear from Peiros' chest and, drawing his sharp sword,
struck him full in the belly. He took Peiros' life but he did not
get his armour. For Peiros' men, the Thracians with their hair

in top-knots, surrounded him. They held their long spears steady in their hands and forced Thoas, great, powerful and noble though he was, to retreat. Shaken, he withdrew.

So these two, Peiros and Diores, lay stretched in the dust at each other's side, one of them leader of the Thracians, the other of the bronze-armoured Eleans. And many others lay dead around them.

Indeed, this was no idle skirmish. Anyone arriving fresh in the middle of this battle uninjured by throw or thrust of a sharp spear – he would have needed Athene to shield him from the hail of missiles and lead him by the hand – would have soon found that out. Trojans and Greeks that day lay there in their multitudes, stretched out alongside each other, face down in the dust.

540

5
DIOMEDES' HEROICS

Pallas Athene now inspired Diomedes son of Tydeus with determination and bravery, so that he might eclipse all the Greeks and win heroic glory. She made his shield and helmet glow with a steady blaze, like Sirius the autumn star which rises from its bath in Ocean to shine brightest of all. Such was the fire she made blaze from his head and shoulders as she thrust him into the very heart of the battle where the fighting was at its most confused.

There was a Trojan called Dares, rich and handsome, who
was a priest of Hephaestus. He had two sons Phegeus and
Idaeus, both experienced in every kind of fighting. These two
detached themselves from the rest and launched themselves
against Diomedes in their chariot, while he went to
meet them on foot. When they had come within
range of each other, Phegeus was the first to hurl his
long-shadowed spear. But the spear-point passed over Diom-
edes' left shoulder and did not hit him. Then Diomedes son of
Tydeus replied with his bronze spear. It did not leave his hand
for nothing.

Diomedes kills Phegeus

It hit Phegeus in the middle of the chest and knocked him
out of the superb chariot, which Idaeus then also deserted by
leaping out of it, not daring to stand over his brother's body.
And black destiny would have got him too, if Heph-
aestus had not come to the rescue and wrapped him
in night, saving him so that his aged priest Dares,
their father, might not be utterly broken by grief.
Great-hearted Diomedes drove the men's horses off and told his
followers to take them back to the hollow ships.

HEPH-AESTUS rescues Idaeus

When the great-hearted Trojans saw that one of
Dares' sons had fled for his life and the other been
killed beside the chariot, panic threatened. Then
grey-eyed Athene took the wild War-god Ares by the
hand and said:

ATHENE leads ARES out of battle

'Ares, murderous Ares, butcher of men and sacker of towns,
is it not time for us to let the Trojans and Greeks fight it out and
leave it to Father Zeus to decide who will win the glory? Let us
two leave the field of battle before we make him angry.'

So she spoke, led wild Ares out of the fight and made him sit
down on the high bank of the River Scamander.

As a result, the Greeks pushed back the Trojans and
each of their leaders killed his man. First Agamemnon
lord of men hurled great Odius, leader of the Hali-
zones, out of his chariot. Odius was the first to turn, and
Agamemnon stabbed him with his spear in the middle of the
back between his shoulders and drove it on through his chest.
He thudded to the ground, and his armour clattered about him.

Greeks kill six Trojans

Next Idomeneus killed Phaestus, who had come from fertile Tarne in Maeonia. Just as Phaestus was getting into his chariot the great spearman Idomeneus pierced his right shoulder with his long spear. Phaestus crashed out of the chariot and hateful darkness engulfed him. Idomeneus' followers then stripped his body.

Then Menelaus son of Atreus caught the brilliant hunter
50 Scamandrius with his sharp spear. Scamandrius was a great man for the chase, who had been taught by the goddess Artemis herself how to bring down any kind of wild game that lives in the mountain forests. But Artemis who delights in arrows was of no help to him now, nor were the long shots that had won him fame. As Scamandrius fled before him, the great spearman Menelaus son of Atreus stabbed him with his spear in the middle of the back between his shoulders and drove it on through his chest. He crashed down on his face, and his armour clattered about him.

Next, Meriones killed Phereclus son of Tecton, Harmon's
60 son, who could turn his hand to the most intricate kind of work. Pallas Athene had no greater favourite. It was he who had built for Paris those balanced ships that had started all the trouble and proved such a curse to the whole Trojan people – and eventually to himself, since he knew nothing of the oracles of the gods. Meriones pursued him and, when he caught him, hit him in the right buttock. The spear-head passed clean through to the bladder under the pubic bone. He dropped to his knees with a scream, and death enveloped him.

70 Then Meges killed Pedaeus, an illegitimate son of Antenor's whom bright Theano, Antenor's wife, had conscientiously brought up like a child of her own to please her husband. The great spearman Meges caught this man up and hit him with his sharp spear on the nape of the head. The point came through between his teeth and cut out the root of his tongue. He collapsed in the dust and bit the cold bronze with his teeth.

Meanwhile Eurypylus killed godlike Hypsenor, who served as priest to the River-god Scamander and was honoured like
80 a god by the people. As Hypsenor fled before him, glorious Eurypylus closed in at full tilt and slashed at his shoulder with

his sword. His great arm was shorn off and fell bleeding to the ground. Inexorable destiny and purple death closed his eyes.

So they fought it out in the heat of battle. As for Diomedes himself, you could not have told to which army, Trojan or Greek, he belonged. He stormed across the plain like a winter torrent in spate, bursting dykes as it races along; when the skies open, neither close-packed embankments nor walls built to   90
protect fertile gardens can contain its sudden onslaught, and far and wide it flattens the good work of industrious farmers – so the dense ranks of the Trojans were thrown into confusion by Diomedes, unable for all their numbers to withstand him.

But when Pandarus, Lycaon's splendid son, saw Diomedes storming across the plain and driving the ranks in confusion ahead of him, he lost no time but bent his curved bow, took aim and hit him, as he raced *Pandarus wounds Diomedes*
ahead, in the right shoulder on a plate of his armour. Piercing the plate, the bitter arrow went right on through, and his body-   100
armour was spattered with blood. Pandarus gave a great shout:

'Great-hearted Trojans, forward and at them, charioteers! The best man they've got is hit, and after a shot like that I don't think he'll last much longer, if it really was lord Apollo son of Zeus who sped me on my way here when I left Lycia.'

So he spoke, boasting. But the flying arrow did not bring Diomedes down. He fell back, came to a halt by his horses and chariot and spoke to his charioteer, Capaneus' son Sthenelus:

'Quick, Sthenelus old friend, get down from the chariot and   110
draw this wretched arrow from my shoulder.'

So he spoke, and Sthenelus leapt from his chariot to the ground, came over to him and pulled the arrow right through the shoulder and out the other side. The blood came gushing out through his strongly woven tunic, and Diomedes, master of the battle-cry, prayed to Athene:

'Listen to me, daughter of Zeus who drives the storm-cloud, Atrytone. If ever in the past you wished me and my father Tydeus well and stood by us in the heat of battle, be kind to me again, Athene. Let me kill Pandarus. Bring me within range of the man who shot me before I saw him. And now he's boasting about it and saying I won't see the light of day much longer.'   120

ATHENE
helps Diomedes
to recognize
gods
So he spoke in prayer, and Pallas Athene heard him and removed the heaviness from his legs and arms. She went up to him and spoke winged words: 'Now, Diomedes, you can fight the Trojans in full confidence! I have filled your heart with the fearless determination of your father Tydeus, the shield-bearing charioteer. Also, I have swept the mist from your eyes and made you able to distinguish gods from men. Now, in case a god comes here to try you out, do not fight with any of them – with one exception only. If Aphrodite daughter of Zeus comes into battle, stab her with your sharp spear.'

With these words grey-eyed Athene left, and Diomedes went and engaged once more with the front ranks. Even without Athene, he had been determined to fall on the enemy again, and now he possessed three times the determination, like a lion which a shepherd in charge of the fleecy sheep on an outlying farm has wounded as it leaps over the fence but failed to kill. He only rouses the lion to greater fury; but now he cannot keep it off, so it gets in among the folds, and the abandoned sheep run in panic. They are left piled up in heaps against each other, and the lion, as determined as ever, jumps the high wall and escapes – with such determination did mighty Diomedes charge the Trojans.

Diomedes kills
eight *Trojans*
He killed Astynous and Hypeiron shepherd of the people. He hit the one above the nipple with his bronze spear and struck the other with his great sword on the collar bone by the shoulder, severing the shoulder from neck and back.

He left them lying there and went after Abas and Polyidus, sons of Eurydamas, an old man who interpreted dreams. But the old man interpreted no dreams for these two when they set out for Troy, and Diomedes killed them both.

Then he went after Xanthus and Thoön, sons of Phaenops, both late-born. Phaenops was old now and ailing and had no other son to whom he could leave his wealth. Diomedes killed them both, depriving them of their precious lives and leaving their father only tears and a broken heart. He never welcomed them home alive from the war. Relatives divided up the estate.

Diomedes' next victims were two sons of Dardanian Priam, Echemmon and Chromius, who were riding in the same chariot. As a lion pounces on cattle grazing peacefully at pasture and breaks the neck of an ox or heifer, so Diomedes gave them no option but brutally forced them out of their chariot, stripped them of their armour and gave their horses to his men to drive to the ships.

Aeneas, seeing what havoc Diomedes was making of the Trojan lines, set out through the battle and hail of missiles in search of godlike Pandarus. When he found Lycaon's handsome mighty son, he went up to him and said:

Aeneas urges
Pandarus to
shoot
Diomedes

'Pandarus, what's happened to your bow, your winged arrows, your reputation as an archer? You are supposed to be the best archer Lycia can boast, better than any we have in Troy. So lift your hands in prayer to Zeus and let fly at that man over there. I don't know who he is, but he's having it all his own way, and has done us a great deal of harm already and brought many of our best men down – unless it's an angry god, resentful at some shortcoming in our rites. If it is, his anger is taking a heavy toll.'

Pandarus, splendid son of Lycaon, replied:

'Aeneas, adviser to the bronze-armoured Trojans, if you ask me, that man is Diomedes, to the life. I recognize him by his shield and plumed helmet. I know his horses too when I see them. On the other hand, it may be a god: I don't know for sure. But if it *is* the man I take him for, warlike Diomedes, I can see the hand of the gods in this frenzied attack. Some god must surely be standing by him, wrapped in a mist, to have made my flying arrow swerve when it was dead on course. Because I *have* shot at him already – and I hit him in the right shoulder, clean through the plate of armour. I certainly thought that would see him off to Hades. Yet somehow I failed to kill him. So perhaps it *is* some resentful god, after all.

'And here am I, without a chariot or horses to carry me. In my father Lycaon's palace, let me tell you, I have eleven splendid chariots fresh from the joiner's, brand new. They are still under their protective cloths, and a couple of horses stand by each one, munching white barley and rye. There in the palace before I left for Troy, my old father, the spearman Lycaon, told me time and again that I should lead men into the thick of the action from a horse-drawn chariot. But I would not listen to him – better for me if I had. I wanted to spare my horses, who had always had plenty to eat, in case fodder ran short in a town under siege.

'So I left and came to Ilium on foot, relying on my archery. Not, as it turns out, that archery was going to do me any good. I have already shot two of their best men, Diomedes and Menelaus, and in each case I scored a hit and drew blood – no doubt about it. But I only roused them to greater efforts. No, destiny was not looking kindly on me when I took my curved bow from its peg that day I set out with my contingent for lovely Ilium to serve godlike Hector. But if ever I get home again and set eyes on the land of my fathers, my wife and my great house with its high roof, I'll be ready to let anyone cut my head off then and there, if I don't smash this bow with my own hands and throw it on the blazing fire. It's surplus baggage.'

Aeneas leader of the Trojans spoke in reply:

'No more speeches like that, *please*. Things are not going to change till you and I confront him in full armour from a chariot and find out what he's made of. Come, get into this chariot and you will see what horses bred by my ancestor Tros are like, and how quickly they can cover the ground in pursuit or retreat. They'll get us safely back to Ilium, if Zeus gives Diomedes son of Tydeus the glory. Come on, take the whip and reins, and when the time comes I'll dismount and do the fighting. Or you take on the man, while I look after the horses.'

Aeneas invites Pandarus into his chariot

The splendid son of Lycaon replied:

'Aeneas, take the reins yourself and drive your own horses. They'll pull the curved chariot better with their usual charioteer behind them, if we have to run away from Diomedes. They might take fright and not respond, if they missed your voice, and refuse to take us from the battle. Then great-hearted Diomedes would close in, finish us off and drive away our horses. So handle the chariot and horses yourself and, when the man charges, I will take him on with my spear.'

With these words they mounted the ornate chariot and, filled 240 with determination, directed their swift horses at Diomedes. Splendid Sthenelus, son of Capaneus, saw them coming and promptly spoke to Diomedes with winged words:

'Diomedes son of Tydeus, my pride and joy, here come two mighty men determined to fight you – a formidably powerful pair. One is the expert bowman, Pandarus, who can boast he is Lycaon's son. The other is Aeneas, who can name matchless Anchises as his father and Aphrodite as his mother. Quick, let's retreat in the chariot. No more storming about on foot in the 250 front line like this, or you may lose your life.'

Mighty Diomedes gave him a black look and replied:

'Don't talk to me of flight. I do not think you will persuade me. It's not in my nature to evade a fight or run away and hide. My desire to win is as strong as ever. No chariot for me, either; I will go to meet them as I am. Pallas Athene does not allow me to run in terror. As for those two, their swift horses will not save *both* of them from us and get them home, even if one of them escapes.

Diomedes plans to capture Aeneas' horses

'And I will tell you something else, and you bear it in mind. If all-wise Athene lets me win and kill them both, leave our own 260 horses here – you can tie the reins to the rail – and concentrate on the horses of Aeneas. Seize *them* and drive them away from the Trojans towards our lines. I tell you, they are bred from the same stock as those that far-thundering Zeus gave Tros in compensation after he had stolen his son Ganymede; and *they* were the best horses in the world. They were passed down to Laomedon, and Anchises lord of men stole the breed by putting mares to them without Laomedon's knowledge. Six foals 270 resulted. Anchises kept four for himself and reared them in his own stables, but gave the last two, masters of the rout, to his son Aeneas for use in battle. If we could capture them, we'd win heroic glory.'

As they were discussing this, their opponents came up, urging on their swift horses. Splendid Pandarus was first to speak:

'Bold and brilliant Diomedes, son of noble Tydeus, evidently my flying missile, my bitter arrow, didn't bring you down. Well, I shall try with a spear this time and see what that will do.'

280   He spoke, balanced his long-shadowed spear and hurled it. It hit Diomedes' shield. The bronze point pierced it and reached Diomedes' body-armour. Pandarus gave a great shout over him:

Diomedes kills
Pandarus

'A hit – clean through the flank! I don't think you'll last much longer now! What a triumph you've given me!'

Unperturbed, mighty Diomedes said:

'Missed! You never touched me. But I reckon, before you two have done, one or the other is going to fall and glut the War-god Ares, that shield-bearing warrior, with his blood.'

290   With these words he threw. His spear, guided by Athene, came down on top of Pandarus' nose by the eye and passed between his white teeth. His tongue was cut off at the root by the relentless bronze, and the point came out under his chin. He crashed out of the chariot. His bright, glittering armour clattered about him, and his swift horses shied away. Life and spirit left him there.

Aeneas now leapt down from his chariot with his shield and long spear, fearing the Greeks might try to rob him of the body.
300   He stood over it like a lion in the pride of its power, covering the body with his spear and round shield, determined to kill all comers, shouting his intimidating war-cry.

Diomedes picked up a rock, a tremendous feat. Not even two men today could manage it, but Diomedes tossed it about quite easily on his own. With this he hit Aeneas on the hip where the thigh turns in the hip-joint – the cup-bone, as they call it. He crushed the cup-bone and broke both sinews too, and the skin was ripped away by the jagged boulder. The warrior sank to his knees and supported himself with one great hand on the ground;
310   but the world went black as night.

APHRODITE
rescues Aeneas

Then Aeneas lord of men would have perished there and then, but for the quickness of his mother divine Aphrodite who had conceived Aeneas for Anchises when he was herding cattle. Seeing what had happened, she threw her white arms round her dear son and drew

a fold of her shimmering robe in front of him, to protect him
from flying weapons and any fatal spear in the chest from the
Greeks with their swift horses.

While Aphrodite was rescuing her son from the battle,
Sthenelus, not forgetting the instructions he had received from   320
Diomedes, tied his horses' reins to the chariot-rail, left them
there some way from the mayhem and went for Aeneas' pair
with their lovely manes.

Seizing these, he drove them out of the Trojan
into the Greek lines, where he handed them over to   Diomedes wounds
Deipylus, a close friend whom he liked more than   *APHRODITE*
any man of his own age and with whom he saw eye to eye. After
telling Deipylus to drive the pair back to the hollow ships,
Sthenelus mounted his own chariot, grasped the glittering reins
and immediately drove his powerful horses keenly off in search
of Diomedes.

Diomedes, meanwhile, had gone himself in hot pursuit of   330
Aphrodite with his relentless spear, knowing what a timid god-
dess she was, not one of those that play a dominating part in
the battles of mankind, such as Athene or Enyo, sacker of towns.
After a long chase through the crowd he caught up with her and
leapt to the attack. He made a lunge at her with his sharp spear
and stabbed her soft hand at the base of the palm. The point,
slicing through the imperishable robe which the Graces had
made for her, pierced her flesh where the palm joins the wrist.
Out came the goddess' immortal blood, the ichor that runs in   340
the veins of the blessed gods, who eat no bread and drink
no sparkling wine and so are bloodless and called immortals.
Aphrodite gave a piercing scream and dropped her son, but
Phoebus Apollo took him in his arms and wrapped him in a
dark-blue cloud to protect him from any fatal spear in the chest
from the Greeks with their swift horses. Diomedes, master of
the battle-cry, gave a great shout over her:

'Aphrodite daughter of Zeus, be off from the battlefield and
its slaughter! Isn't it enough for you to seduce the feeble wits of
women? If you persist in interfering in battle, I think you will   350
be taught to tremble at the very mention of it, wherever you
hear it.'

So he spoke, and Aphrodite withdrew, bewildered and in considerable discomfort. Her lovely skin was darkening with blood and she was hurting from the pain, but Iris, quick as the wind, took charge of her and led her out of the tumult. To the left of the battlefield Aphrodite found the wild War-god Ares, seated on the ground, with his spear and horses resting on a bank of cloud. Sinking to her knees, she entreated her brother for the loan of his horses with the golden headpieces:

360   'See me safe, dear brother. Let me have your horses to get me back to Olympus where the immortals have their home. I'm in agony. I've been stabbed by a mortal, Diomedes, who is in a mood now to fight with Father Zeus himself.'

APHRODITE retreats to Olympus   So she spoke, and Ares gave her the horses with the golden headpieces. Aphrodite mounted the chariot in some distress but Iris got in beside her, took the reins in her hands and lashed the horses with the whip to get them moving. The willing pair flew off; and before long they reached steep Olympus where the gods have their home. There swift Iris, quick as the wind, brought the horses to a halt, unyoked them from the chariot and threw

370   ambrosial fodder down beside them, while celestial Aphrodite went to her mother Dione and sank down at her knees. Dione took her daughter in her arms, stroked her with her hand and spoke to her:

'My darling child, which of the Sky-gods has foolishly treated you like this, as if you had done something wicked in public?'

Laughter-loving Aphrodite replied:

'The son of Tydeus, dauntless Diomedes, stabbed me because I was rescuing my own beloved son Aeneas from the battle – the son who means more to me than anyone! This war is no longer

380   a struggle between Trojans and Greeks: the Greeks are fighting now against the gods as well.'

Dione, celestial goddess, replied:

DIONE on the gods' suffering   'Endure, my child, and put up with it, despite your distress. Many of us that live here on Olympus have suffered at the hands of men in our attempts to inflict serious injury on one another.

'Ares, for one, had to suffer when Otus and mighty Ephialtes, children of Aloeus, threw him in chains. He spent thirteen months trussed up in a bronze jar. And that would have been the end of the insatiable War-god Ares, if beautiful Eriboea his stepmother had not told Hermes what they had done. Ares' strength was already failing him when, despite the formidable shackles that held him, Hermes spirited him away.   390

'Hera suffered too when Heracles mighty son of Amphitryon hit her in the right breast with a three-barbed arrow – she was in absolute agony.

'And dread Hades had to suffer, like the rest, when that same Heracles, son of Zeus who drives the storm-cloud, shot him with a flying arrow at Hell's gate among the dead and hurt him very badly. Sick at heart and in excruciating pain, Hades found his way to high Olympus and Zeus' palace. The arrow had   400
driven into his shoulder muscles and was giving him considerable distress. However, Paeëon the healer spread pain-killing herbs on the wound and healed him; for, after all, he was immortal. But what a self-willed monster that Heracles was! He cared so little what wickedness he set his hand to that he harassed the very gods who live on Olympus with his bow!

'As for your trouble, it was grey-eyed Athene who told the man to chase you. What a fool Diomedes is! He has no idea how short life is for the man who fights the immortals. For him, there is no homecoming from war and its horrors, no little children gathering at his knee to call him "father". So let   410
Diomedes, mighty man though he is, take care that no god more formidable than you comes out to fight him, or one day his wife noble Aegialea, wise daughter of Adrestus, will awaken the household she loves from sleep, bewailing the loss of her young husband, the best of the Greeks, horse-taming Diomedes.'

She spoke, and wiped the ichor from Aphrodite's wrist with her hands. The wound healed and the severe pain was relieved.

Athene and Hera had missed nothing of this and turned mockingly to Zeus. The goddess grey-eyed Athene began and   420
spoke her mind:

'Father Zeus, will you be offended by what I say?

The gods tease
APHRODITE

Aphrodite must have been at work again, luring Greek women into the arms of the Trojans whom she loves so vehemently. One of these lovely-robed Greek women was evidently wearing a gold brooch, and Aphrodite scratched her dainty hand on it as she patted her and egged her on.'

So she spoke, and the Father of men and gods smiled, called golden Aphrodite and said:

'Warfare, my child, is not for you. You take charge of the
430 marriage-bed and its passions. Leave fleet-footed Ares and Athene to look after military matters.'

As they discussed this with one another, Diomedes, master of the battle-cry, flung himself once more at Aeneas. He knew that Apollo himself had taken him under his protection, but he had no respect even for that great god and persisted in his efforts to kill Aeneas and strip him of his impressive armour. Three times he flung himself at Aeneas, determined to kill him, and three times Apollo knocked his glittering shield aside. But when like something superhuman he charged for the fourth time, the Archer-god Apollo gave a terrible cry:

440 'Think, Diomedes, and give way! Don't aspire to be our equal! Immortal gods and men that walk on the ground are not the same breed.'

APOLLO
warns
Diomedes

So he spoke, and Diomedes fell back just a little to avoid the wrath of the Archer-god; and Apollo removed Aeneas from the battlefield to the holy citadel of Pergamus in Ilium where his temple stood. There, in the great inner shrine, Leto and Artemis who delights in arrows not only healed him but made him more splendid than ever.

Meanwhile Apollo, lord of the silver bow, created a phantom
450 which looked exactly like Aeneas, armour and all. Round this phantom, Trojans and Greeks hacked at each other from behind the oxhide shields, great and small, that protected their chests. Then Phoebus Apollo spoke to wild Ares:

'Ares, murderous Ares, butcher of men and sacker of towns, won't you take a hand and drive this man Diomedes out of the fighting? He's in a mood to fight Father Zeus himself. He began by closing with Aphrodite and stabbing her in the wrist and then he flung himself, like something superhuman, at me.'

With these words Apollo withdrew and sat down on the 460 heights of Pergamus in the town, while Ares the destroyer disguised himself as Acamas, the swift leader of the Thracians, and slipped in among the Trojans to rally them. He began by giving instructions to the Olympian-bred sons of Priam:

'Sons of Olympian-bred lord Priam, how much longer are you going to let your men be slaughtered by the Greeks? Till they are storming the town gates? Aeneas son of great-hearted Anchises lies low – a warrior we honour in the same breath as godlike Hector. Come on now, and rescue our brave comrade from the mayhem.'

ARES urges on the *Trojans*

With these words he put fresh heart and courage into every 470 man. Then Sarpedon rebuked godlike Hector.

'Hector, where is the spirit you used to show? You talked of holding the town without troops or allies, single-handed but for your brothers and brothers-in-law. But I look around and can't see a single one. They are cowering like dogs before a lion, while we do the fighting, though we came in only as your allies.

Sarpedon abuses *Hector*; *Aeneas* returns

'Take me. It was a long, long journey *I* made to reinforce you. It is a far cry from Lycia and the eddying River Xanthus, where I left my dear wife, baby son and great possessions too, which 480 every poor man would love to get his hands on. Nevertheless, I make my Lycians fight and am myself as determined as ever to meet my man in battle, even though I own nothing here the Greeks could loot or carry off.

'Meanwhile you just stand there, and don't even tell your men to make a stand or fight in defence of their women! Take care, or you'll be caught like fish in a net and fall easy prey to your enemies, who will be sacking your prosperous town any day now. You can plead with the leaders of your allies, but your priority day and night should be to make a deter- 490 mined stand yourself and give no one any grounds for harsh criticism.'

So spoke Sarpedon, and Hector was stung by his rebuke. Fully armed, he immediately leapt from his chariot to the ground and, brandishing a pair of sharp spears, went everywhere among his men, urging them to fight and rousing their spirit for grim battle. As a result the Trojans turned and faced the Greeks, but the Greeks held their ground in massed formation and did not retreat. As the wind carries the chaff across the sacred threshing-floor when men are winnowing and, as the winds rise, the golden-haired goddess Demeter separates the grain from the chaff, and the heaps of chaff gradually whiten – so the Greeks were whitened from above by the dust which the horses' hooves kicked up through the ranks into the bronze sky as their chariot-eers wheeled them round to rejoin them again; and the enemy were engaged full on at close quarters.

But now the wild War-god Ares, ranging everywhere, threw a veil of darkness over the battle to help the Trojans. He was carrying out the orders he had from Phoebus Apollo of the golden sword. Phoebus had told him to put fresh heart into the Trojans when he saw Pallas Athene, who was on the Greeks' side, withdraw. Moreover, Apollo himself made Aeneas leave the rich shrine where he had taken sanctuary and filled this shepherd of the people with new determination. So Aeneas took his place once more among his troops, who were delighted to find him still alive and see him come back sound of limb and fired with determination. Not that they had time to ask him any questions: there was far too much fighting to do, stirred up by Apollo, lord of the silver bow, man-slaying Ares, and implacably determined Strife.

The Greeks on their side were spurred on to fight by the two Ajaxes, Odysseus and Diomedes. They needed little encouragement. No onslaught of the Trojan made them run for cover, however hard it was pressed home. They stood their ground like the motionless clouds with which Zeus caps the mountain peaks in calm weather, when sleep overcomes the powerful north wind and the other boisterous breezes that, with their shrill blasts, send the shadowy clouds scudding – so the Greeks held firm against the Trojans and refused to panic. Agamemnon went through their ranks, issuing orders:

'Fellow warriors, be men. Keep your courage up and in the
heat of the battle fear nothing but dishonour in each other's   530
eyes. When warriors fear disgrace, more are saved than killed.
There's no honour or salvation to be found in flight.'

He spoke, made a swift throw with his spear
and hit a leading fighter and companion of great-   Agamemnon
hearted Aeneas, Deicoön son of Pergasus. Since he   kills *Deicoön*
was always quick to fight among the front ranks, Trojans
honoured him like one of lord Priam's sons. Lord Agamem-
non hit him on the shield. It failed to protect him. The bronze
spear pierced it and drove on through the belt into his ab-
domen. He thudded to the ground, and his armour clattered   540
about him.

Aeneas replied by killing two of the best of the Greeks, Cre-
thon and Orsilochus whose father Diocles lived in well-built
Pherae. Diocles was a man of substance, tracing his descent
from the god of the river Alpheus which flows at large through
the region of Pylos. The River-god first bore Ortilochus, who
ruled over many. He was father of great-hearted Diocles who in
turn had these twin sons Crethon and Orsilochus, both experi-
enced in every kind of fighting. When they were of age, they   550
embarked with the Greeks in their black ships for Troy to win
compensation for Agamemnon and Menelaus. But there
the adventure ended – in their death. As a pair of lions are
brought up by their mother in deep forest thickets on moun-
tain heights, and prey on cattle and fat sheep, and plunder
farmers' yards till they themselves fall victims to men with
bronze weapons – so these two were killed by Aeneas and fell,   560
like tall pines.

Their death filled warlike Menelaus with pity. His
bronze armour glittering, he advanced through the   Menelaus and
front ranks brandishing his spear. Ares spurred   Antilochus drive
him on, intending him to be killed by Aeneas. But   off *Aeneas*
Antilochus, son of great-hearted Nestor, saw what Menelaus
was doing and followed him through the front lines, fearing
some disaster might overtake this shepherd of the people and
bring all their efforts to nothing. Menelaus and Aeneas, both

determined to fight it out, were already aiming their sharp spears
570 at one another as Antilochus came up to Menelaus and took his
place beside him; and when Aeneas saw the two men making
this united stand, he did not hold his ground, agile fighter though
he was. So Menelaus and Antilochus dragged the bodies of
Crethon and Orsilochus back into the Greek lines, and after
handing over the luckless pair to their men, went back and
fought in the front ranks once more.

Pylaemenes   Then they killed Pylaemenes, Ares' equal, com-
and Mydon   mander of the great-hearted shield-bearing Paphla-
killed   gonians. He was standing stock still when the great
                     spearman Menelaus stabbed him with his spear on
580 the collar bone. Meanwhile Antilochus hit his attendant and
charioteer Mydon, who was wheeling his horses round. Anti-
lochus hit him full on the elbow with a rock, and the reins, white
with their ivory decoration, dropped from his hands and fell in
the dust. Antilochus leapt in and drove his sword into the man's
temple. With a gasp, he fell headlong from the well-made chariot
up to his head and shoulders in the dust. For a while he stuck
there, since it happened to be deep at that point. Then his horses
kicked him down and laid him flat on the ground. With a lash
of the whip Antilochus drove the horses back into the Greek
army.

590 Across the ranks Hector had observed these two and now
made towards them, shouting. He was supported by a powerful
following of Trojans who were led on by the War-god Ares
Hector rallies   and the goddess Enyo. Enyo brought Confusion with
the Trojans   her, the shameless destroyer, while Ares brandished
                   in his hand an awe-inspiring spear and strode, now
in front of Hector, now behind him.

When Diomedes, master of the battle-cry, saw them, he was
shaken. Like a traveller crossing a great plain who halts help-
lessly beside a fast-flowing river rushing towards the sea, takes
one look at the seething foam and turns back in his tracks, so
600 Diomedes drew back and said to his troops:

'Men, no wonder we've been impressed by godlike Hector's
bravery and ability as a fighter: he always has one of the gods
with him to save his skin. Ares is with him now, disguised as a

man. Retreat then, but facing the enemy. We must not offer
battle to the gods.'

So he spoke, and the Trojans were on them and Hector killed
two men, Menesthes and Anchialus, neither lacking the will to
fight, who were riding in one chariot.

Their death filled great Ajax son of Telamon with pity. Taking   610
his stand close by them, he let fly with a glittering spear and hit
Amphius, a rich man, who lived in Paesus and owned many
cornfields. But destiny had brought him to Troy to serve as an
ally of Priam and his sons. Ajax son of Telamon hit him on the
belt. The long-shadowed spear stuck in his abdomen,
and he thudded to the ground. But when glorious   *Ajax kills*
Ajax ran up to strip him of his armour, the Trojans   *Amphius*
met him with a volley of glittering spears, many of which he
took on the shield. Nevertheless, he planted his foot on the body   620
and dragged his bronze spear out. But he could not remove the
man's own fine armour from his back – the spears were too
much for him. Moreover, he was afraid of being surrounded
and overpowered by the proud Trojans, who faced him in
formidable numbers with their spears at the ready. So they
forced him, great, powerful and noble though he was, to retreat.
Shaken, he withdrew.

So they battled it out in the thick of the action.
Inexorable destiny then thrust Tlepolemus, the fine,   *Sarpedon*
tall son of Heracles, into conflict with godlike Sarpe-   *is wounded*
don. When these two had come within range of each other, one   630
a son, the other a grandson of Zeus who marshals the clouds,
Tlepolemus was the first to speak:

'Sarpedon, adviser to the Lycians, what made you come here,
just to skulk and hide? You don't know what a battle is. They
are liars when they call you a son of Zeus who drives the
storm-cloud: you are nothing like the sons he used to have. How
different, by all accounts, from mighty Heracles, my all-daring,
lion-hearted father, who once came here to get Laomedon's   640
mares and, with only six ships and a pretty small force of men,
sacked Ilium and widowed its streets. You have all the heart of
a coward, and your troops are on their last legs. You may be a
strong fighter yourself but I don't think your journey here from

Lycia will help the Trojans much. No, you're going to fall to me and pass through the gates of Hades!'

Sarpedon, leader of the Lycians, spoke in reply:

'Tlepolemus, Heracles did indeed sack sacred Ilium but only because of the stupidity of one man, noble Laomedon, who
650 repaid his services with insults and refused to let him have the mares he had come so far to get. As for you, I tell you dark death and destruction await you at my hands: conquered by my spear, you will surrender the glory to me and your life to the god Hades, famed for his horses.'

So spoke Sarpedon, and the other raised his ash spear. The great weapons leapt from their hands at one and the same time. Sarpedon hit Tlepolemus in the middle of the neck. The painful spear passed right through, and black night came down and
660 engulfed his eyes. At the same moment Tlepolemus' spear hit Sarpedon in the left thigh. The point pressed eagerly on and grazed the bone; but, for the moment, his father Zeus saved him from death.

Godlike Sarpedon was carried from the fight by his men. The great spear dragged along and weighed him down: in their haste, no one had noticed it or thought of pulling it out of his thigh so that he could use his legs. They had enough to do just to see him safe.

On the other side, the Greek men-at-arms carried off Tlepo-
670 lemus. Godlike enduring Odysseus noticed and was furious. The thoughts raced through his mind whether to start in pursuit of Sarpedon son of loud-thundering Zeus or do further execution on the Lycians. But destiny did not intend the mighty son of Zeus to fall to Odysseus' bronze spear, and so Athene turned his fury on the Lycian ranks. Then and there he killed Coeranus, Alastor and Chromius, Alcander and Halius, Noemon and Prytanis. Indeed, Odysseus would
680 have gone on to kill even more of the Lycians, but for the sharp eye of great Hector of the flashing helmet. His bronze armour glittering, he advanced through the front ranks, striking terror into the Greeks. Sarpedon son of Zeus was delighted he had come and appealed to him:

'Hector son of Priam, rescue me and don't leave me lying here

Odysseus kills seven Lycians

at the mercy of the Greeks. Then may I die in your town. It is clear I wasn't meant to return home to the land of my fathers after all and bring happiness to my dear wife and little son.'

So he spoke, but Hector of the flashing helmet made no reply and raced past him. He made it his first priority to thrust the 690 Greeks back and kill as many of them as he could. But godlike Sarpedon was removed by his men and laid under a lovely oak-tree, sacred to Zeus who drives the storm-cloud. There his close companion, mighty Pelagon, ex- *Sarpedon* tracted the ash spear from his thigh. A mist descended *is rescued* over Sarpedon's eyes and he fainted. But presently he came to. The north wind played about him and, drained though he was, revived him.

But the Greeks, faced by the War-god Ares and Hector in his bronze armour, did not run in panic to their black ships nor 700 counter-attack, but fell back steadily as they became aware of Ares' presence on the Trojan side. And who were the first and last of them to fall there to Hector son of Priam and to bronze-armed Ares? Godlike Teuthras was the first; then Orestes tamer of horses; Trechus, an Aetolian spearman; Oenomaus; Oenops' son Helenus; and Oresbius with *Hector* and his glittering belt, who lived in Hyle on the shores of *ARES* kill six Lake Copais where he looked after his rich estate, *Greeks* with other Boeotians for neighbours in the fertile countryside. 710

When the goddess white-armed Hera saw the Greeks being slaughtered in the heat of the battle, she immediately spoke to Athene with winged words:

'Child of Zeus who drives the storm-cloud, Atrytone, this is disastrous. If we let deadly Ares run wild like this, what of the promise we made to Menelaus when we told him he would sack Ilium with its fine walls before he returned home? Come: time for the two of us to summon up that fighting spirit of ours!'

So she spoke, and the goddess grey-eyed Athene complied. Hera, ancient goddess, daughter of great Cronus, went off to 720 get ready her horses with their golden headbands. The goddess Hebe quickly fixed the chariot's two *HERA* and bronze wheels, each with eight spokes, on the ends *ATHENE* help of the iron axle. The inner rims of these wheels are *the Greeks*

made of imperishable gold, while bronze tyres are fitted to the outside – wonderful to see – and the hubs that rotate on each axle are made of silver. The bodywork was constructed of plaited gold and silver straps, with a double railing round it. A
730 silver shaft ran out from the front. To the end of this shaft Hebe tied the beautiful golden yoke and attached the fine gold straps. Eager for the sound and fury of battle, Hera led her swift horses under the yoke.

On her father's threshold Athene, daughter of Zeus who drives the storm-cloud, took off the soft embroidered robe she had made and worked with her own hands, replaced it with a tunic and over that put on the armour of Zeus who marshals the clouds, in preparation for war's work with all its tears. Then she threw round her shoulders the terrifying fringed aegis. It
740 was encircled with Fear, Strife, Force, chilling Pursuit and the Gorgon's head, a ghastly monster, the awe-inspiring, potent emblem of Zeus. On her head she put her double-ridged golden helmet with its four plates, adorned with fighting men of a hundred towns. Then she stepped into the fiery chariot and took up the long, thick, heavy spear with which she breaks the ranks of warriors when she, the almighty Father's child, is roused to anger.

Hera immediately leaned forward to whip on her horses, and of their own accord the gates of Olympus thundered open for them. These are kept by the Seasons, the wardens of the broad
750 sky and Olympus, whose task it is to roll the gates of heavy cloud away from the entrance or roll them back. Through these gates the goddesses directed their horses, spurring them on with the whip.

They found Zeus sitting apart from the other gods on the highest of Olympus' many peaks. The goddess white-armed Hera brought her pair to a halt and questioned high Zeus son of Cronus:

ATHENE to attack ARES   'Father Zeus, aren't you angry at Ares' savagery and the sight of all these fine Greek warriors he has slaughtered without rhyme or reason? I cannot bear
760 to watch. But your Cyprian daughter Aphrodite and Apollo lord of the silver bow are sitting back and enjoying every

minute of it, unleashing this madman who knows neither right nor wrong. Father Zeus, will you be angry with me if I give him a severe beating and chase him from the battle-field?'

Zeus who marshals the clouds replied and said:

'Not at all. Get to work, and set the war-leader Athene on him. She's well used to teaching Ares a few painful and humiliating lessons.'

So he spoke, and the goddess white-armed Hera complied. She lashed the horses with the whip, and the willing pair flew off between the earth and starry sky. These proud, snorting horses of the gods cover in one stride the distance a man can see 770 when he looks out from a watchtower over the wine-dark sea into the hazy beyond. But when they reached Troy and the place where the two flowing Rivers Simoïs and Scamander meet, there the goddess white-armed Hera stopped her horses and released them from the yoke. She hid them in a mist, and Simoïs made ambrosia spring up for them to eat. Then the two goddesses set out on foot, strutting like pigeons, eager to bring help to the Greek army.

They made for the part of the battlefield where the best of 780 the Greeks had rallied in numbers round great horse-taming Diomedes and were standing at bay like flesh-eating lions or wild boars who are not easily worn down. There the goddess white-armed Hera stopped and shouted, imitating the brazen voice of great-hearted Stentor, who could shout like fifty:

'Shame on you, Greeks! Contemptible creatures, admired only for your looks! In the days when godlike Achilles came out and fought, the Trojans never showed themselves in front of the Dardanian gate: they were too afraid of his massive spear. 790 But now the Trojans are fighting far from their town and by your very ships!'

With these words she put fresh heart and courage into every man. Meanwhile the goddess grey-eyed Athene made straight for Diomedes son of Tydeus. She found him with his chariot and horses, airing the wound that Pandarus had given him with his arrow. Under the broad shoulder-strap of his round shield the sweat was irritating it. Troubled by this and with his arm

aching, he had lifted up the strap and was wiping the dark blood
away. The goddess laid her hand on his horses' yoke and said:

800   'Tydeus had a son, but how unlike himself! Tydeus was
            a little man, but what a fighter! He even fought when
ATHENE
            I had forbidden him to do anything like dashing off
 abuses
            into battle, the time he was sent alone to Thebes on
Diomedes
            a mission to a crowd of Thebans. I told him to
(5.99, 131)
            enjoy his feast quietly in the palace. So, like the
tremendous-hearted man he always was, he went and challenged
the young Thebans to athletic contests and won all the events
easily – he had me to help him! And here am I now. I stand
810 beside you; I shield you from harm; and I tell you to fight the
Trojans with my blessing – and you are either exhausted by
your efforts and unable to stir a limb, or paralysed with fear.
You are no son of Tydeus or grandson of warlike Oeneus.'

    Mighty Diomedes replied to her and said:

    'I know who you are, goddess, daughter of Zeus who drives
the storm-cloud, and I will speak to you openly, hiding nothing.
I'm not paralysed with fear or indecision. All I am doing is to
keep in mind the instructions you yourself gave me. You told
820 me not to fight against the blessed gods except for Aphrodite
daughter of Zeus. If *she* came into the fight, you said I could
stab her with my bronze spear. But it's Ares who is carrying all
before him. When I saw that, I fell back and told the rest of the
Greeks to rally round me.'

    The goddess grey-eyed Athene replied:

    'Diomedes son of Tydeus, my pride and joy, don't be afraid
of Ares or any other god. You have me to help you! Quick now
830 – drive your horses straight at him. Let him have it at short range.
Don't be intimidated by wild Ares, that mad, double-dealing
delinquent. Earlier on he gave Hera and myself his word to fight
against the Trojans and help the Greeks – and now he has
forgotten all he said and is fighting on the Trojan side.'

    With these words she reached out and dragged Diomedes'
charioteer Sthenelus out of the back of the chariot. He quickly
leapt down, and the eager goddess took his place in the chariot
beside godlike Diomedes. The oak axle groaned aloud at the
weight it had to carry, a formidable goddess and a mighty

warrior. Pallas Athene seized the reins and whip and drove   840
the horses straight off in the direction of Ares. At that mo-
ment he was removing the armour from awe-inspiring Peri-
phas, the best man in the Aetolian force. Spattered with blood
he was busy stripping his victim. To conceal her approach
from this imperious deity, Athene put a cap of invisibility on
her head.

Directly the butcher Ares saw godlike Diomedes,
he left awe-inspiring Periphas to lie where he had   *ARES*
killed him and made straight for horse-taming Diom-   *wounded*
edes. When the two had come within range of each other, Ares   850
lunged at Diomedes with his bronze spear over the yoke and
reins of Diomedes' chariot, determined to kill him. But the
goddess grey-eyed Athene, catching the shaft in her hand, thrust
it up above the chariot where it hit thin air. Diomedes, master
of the battle-cry, then attacked him with his bronze spear and
Pallas Athene drove it home into the lower part of Ares' belly
where he wore a protective kilt round his middle. There Diom-
edes stabbed him, tearing through his fair flesh. Diomedes
immediately drew out his spear, and bronze-clad Ares let out a   860
yell as loud as the war-cry of nine or ten thousand men clashing
on the field of battle. Terror gripped the Greeks and Trojans,
such was the scream from the insatiable War-god.

Bronze-clad Ares rose in a cloud into the broad skies, looking
to Diomedes like the column of black air that issues from the
clouds when a tornado springs up in the boiling heat. He rapidly
reached the gods' home on steep Olympus and sat down by
Zeus, feeling very sorry for himself. He showed Zeus the im-   870
mortal blood pouring from his wound and mournfully spoke
winged words:

'Father Zeus, aren't you angry at the sight of this
savagery? We gods have to put up with the most   *ZEUS heals*
frightful indignities from each other whenever we do   *ARES*
mankind a favour – and it's all your fault. We are all at logger-
heads with you because of that brainless daughter of yours,
damned Athene, who creates chaos wherever she can. The rest
of us gods on Olympus bow to your will and are subject to you.
But when it comes to *her*, you don't say or do a thing to check

880 her: you let her have her head, because she is the child you bore yourself, a killer for a daughter.

'Now she has encouraged insolent Diomedes to run wild among the immortal gods. He began by charging Aphrodite and stabbing her in the wrist; and then he flung himself like something superhuman at *me*. I am quick enough on my feet to have escaped. Otherwise, I would have had a long and painful time there among the grisly piles of dead on the battlefield, or come away crippled for life by his blows.'

Zeus who marshals the clouds gave Ares a black look and replied:

'You shifty hypocrite, don't come whining to me. I hate you
890 more than any other god on Olympus. Rivalry, war, fighting – these are the breath of life to you. Your mother Hera too has the same headstrong and ungovernable temper. I have always found it hard to control her by word of mouth alone. I suspect it was she that started this business and got you into trouble.

'However, I don't intend to let you suffer any longer, since you are my own flesh and blood and your mother is my wife. But if any other god had fathered such a killer, you would long ago have found yourself in a deeper hole than those Titans I buried when I came to power.'

So he spoke and told Paeëon to heal him. Paeëon spread
900 soothing herbs on the wound and healed it – Ares was not made of mortal stuff. As fig-juice busily thickens milk, which is liquid but quickly curdles as it is stirred, so rapidly did Paeëon heal wild Ares. Hebe bathed him and gave him lovely clothing to put on; and he sat down by Zeus son of Cronus, exulting in his glory.

Meanwhile the two goddesses, Hera from Argos and Athene from Alalcomenae, came back to the palace of great Zeus. They had checked the butcher Ares in his murderous assault.

6

HECTOR AND
ANDROMACHE

1–72: The Greeks enjoy some success. Agamemnon and Nestor urge
the Greeks to show no mercy.

73–118: The prophet *Helenus* advises *Aeneas* and *Hector* to rally the
Trojans and then orders *Hector* to tell the women of *Troy* to make
an offering to ATHENE to try to stop Diomedes' rampage.

119–236: *Glaucus* and Diomedes meet in battle (story of *Bellerophon*).

237–368: *Hector* arrives in *Ilium* and meets his mother *Hecabe*. The
offering to ATHENE is made (in vain) and *Hector* converses with
Paris and Helen.

369–495: *Hector* converses with his wife *Andromache* who has their
baby *Astyanax* with her.

495–529: *Hector* and *Andromache* part, as if for the last time, and
Hector and *Paris* meet up and return to battle.

So the Trojans and Greeks were left to carry on the grim struggle
without divine interference, and the battle kept swaying this
way and that across the plain as volleys of bronze-headed spears
were exchanged, midway between the River Simoïs and the
streams of Scamander.

Ajax son of Telamon, a tower of strength to the
Greeks, was the first to break the Trojan line and
give his friends the scent of victory, when he hit
the best fighter that the Thracians had, the tall and
splendid Acamas. Ajax hit him on the ridge of his plumed
helmet. The bronze spear hit him on the forehead and pierced
right through the bone, and darkness engulfed his eyes.

Next, Diomedes, master of the battle-cry, killed Axylus, who

*Greeks kill
fourteen
Trojans*

10

came from well-built Arisbe. He was a man of substance, with a wide circle of friends: he lived in a house by the road-side and entertained everyone. But none of these friends came forward now to tackle the enemy for him and save him from an ugly end. Diomedes killed the pair of them, him and his attendant Calesius who was serving as his charioteer, and they both sank to the world below.

20   Euryalus killed Dresus and Opheltius and then raced after Aesepus and Pedasus, whom the Water-nymph Abarbarea had borne to matchless Bucolion. Bucolion was a son of proud Laomedon (the first child Laomedon had, born in secret). Bucolion was shepherding his flocks when he met the Nymph and made love to her. She conceived and bore him twin boys. But Euryalus ended their resistance, laid low their bright young limbs and stripped the armour from their shoulders.

30   Resolute Polypoetes slaughtered Astyalus; Odysseus killed Pidytes of Percote with his bronze spear, as did Teucer the godlike Aretaon. Antilochus son of Nestor killed Ablerus with his glittering spear, and Agamemnon lord of men slew Elatus, who lived by the banks of sweet-flowing Satnioïs in steep Pedasus. The warrior Leitus killed Phylacus in mid-flight, and Eurypylus dispatched Melanthius.

      Menelaus ordered to kill Adrestus   Meanwhile Menelaus, master of the battle-cry, had captured Adrestus alive. This man's pair of horses, bolting across the plain, had become entangled in a tamarisk bush, snapped off the shaft
40   where it was fixed to the curved body of the chariot and galloped off on their own towards the town, where the rest had stampeded off in panic. Adrestus himself was thrown out of the chariot beside the wheel, flat on his face in the dust; and he soon had Menelaus son of Atreus standing over him with a long-shadowed spear in his hand. Adrestus threw his arms round Menelaus' knees and supplicated him:

'Son of Atreus, take me alive and you will get a ransom that will be well worth it. My father is rich and has plenty of treasure in his house, bronze and gold and wrought iron. He would offer
50   you an immense ransom, if he heard I had been taken back to the Greek ships alive.'

So he spoke, and Menelaus was inclined to agree. And indeed he was just about to tell his attendant to take him back to the fast Greek ships, when Agamemnon came running up, shouting disapprovingly at him:

'Menelaus, my soft-hearted brother, why are you so concerned for these men? Did the Trojans treat you as handsomely when they stayed in your palace? No: we are not going to leave a single one of them alive, down to the babies in their mothers' wombs – not even they must live. The whole people must be wiped out of existence, with none to shed a tear for them, leaving no trace.' 60

With this sound advice Agamemnon made Menelaus change his mind. He pushed the warrior Adrestus away from him with his hand, and lord Agamemnon stabbed him in the flank. The man fell on his back, and Agamemnon put his foot on his chest and drew out the ash spear.

Nestor then called out to the Greeks in a loud voice:

'Friends, Greek warriors, servants of the War-god Ares! No looting now! No lingering behind to get back to the ships with the biggest share! Let us kill Trojans. Afterwards, at your leisure, you can strip the dead on the battlefield.' 70

With these words he put fresh heart and courage into every man; and it looked as though the Trojans, weakened and demoralized, would be driven back into Ilium by the war-loving Greeks. But at this point, Priam's son Helenus, the best prophet in Troy, went up to Aeneas and Hector and said:

'Aeneas and Hector, more than all the other Trojans and Lycians together you two bear the brunt of the fighting because, whatever the enterprise, you have never failed us in the council-chamber *Hector to sacrifice to ATHENE* or on the battlefield. Now make a stand here. Visit every part 80 of the battlefield yourselves and regroup the troops in front of the gates before they run for it, fall into their women's arms and make the enemy happy men. When you two have rallied all our forces, we'll stand our ground and fight the Greeks here, exhausted though we are – we have no choice in the matter.

'Meanwhile, Hector, go into the town and speak to our

mother. Tell her to collect the older women at the temple of grey-eyed Athene on the town heights and unlock the doors of 90 the holy shrine. Let her choose a robe from her palace, the loveliest and biggest she can find in the house and the one most precious to her, and lay it on the knees of lovely-haired Athene. And let her promise to sacrifice in her shrine a dozen year-old heifers that have never worked, if only she will have pity on the town and on the Trojans' wives and little children and keep that savage spearman and master of the rout, Diomedes, clear of sacred Ilium. He, in my opinion, is now our most powerful Greek adversary. We were never so terrified even of Achilles, 100 leader of men, and said to be a goddess' son. But Diomedes here is quite uncontrollable and not a man can hold him.'

So he spoke, and Hector complied. Fully armed, he immediately leapt from his chariot to the ground and, brandishing a pair of sharp spears, went everywhere among his men, urging them to fight and rousing their spirit for grim battle. As a result the Trojans turned and faced the Greeks, who now gave ground and killed no more of the enemy. Indeed, the Trojans rallied so effectively that the Greeks thought some god must have come 110 down from the starry sky to help them. Hector then called out to the Trojans in a loud voice:

'Proud Trojans and famous allies, be men, my comrades, and call up that fighting spirit of yours, while I go into Ilium to tell our elders and our wives to pray to the gods and promise them a sacrifice.'

With these words Hector of the flashing helmet went off towards the town. As he walked, the dark leather rim of the bossed shield slung over his shoulder tapped him above and below, on the ankles and on the back of the neck.

Glaucus son of Hippolochus and Diomedes son of Tydeus 120 now approached one another in the space between the two armies, determined to do battle. When they had come within range of each other, Diomedes, master of the battle-cry, spoke first:

Glaucus and
Diomedes meet

'What mortal man are you, sir? I have not seen you in battle where men win glory – till now. Yet in facing the long-shadowed spear in my hand you have shown far greater courage than any of your comrades. Pity those fathers whose sons face me in my fury!

'But if you are one of the immortals descended from Olympus, I am not the man to fight against the gods of the skies. Why, not even powerful Lycurgus, Dryas' son, survived his quarrel with the gods of the skies for very long. This murderous Lycurgus chased the nurses of the wild god Dionysus down from the holy hills of Nysa, and they all scattered the god's emblems to the ground as he struck them with his ox-goad. Dionysus fled and found sanctuary under the salt sea waves where the Sea-nymph Thetis took him to her bosom, terrified and shaking violently from Lycurgus' threats. But the immortals who live at ease resented what Lycurgus had done – and Zeus struck him blind. He did not live long after that, since all the immortals hated him. So I will not be fighting against the blessed gods.

'But if you are one of us mortals who eat the fruit of the earth, come on, and the sooner your fate will be sealed.'

Glaucus, glorious son of Hippolochus, spoke:

'Great-hearted Diomedes, why ask after my family? The family of man is like the leaves of the trees. The wind scatters them on the ground, but the trees burst into bud and grow fresh leaves when the spring comes round. So with the family of man: one generation grows, the other fades. But if you really wish to learn about my family, I will tell you. Most people know my story already.

'There is a town called Ephyre in a corner of Argos where the horses graze. Here lived a man called Sisyphus, a man as crafty as they come. Aeolus was his father's name. Sisyphus had a son called Glaucus; and Glaucus in his turn was father of matchless Bellerophon.

Story of Bellerophon

'The gods endowed Bellerophon with fine looks and every desirable manly virtue. But Zeus made him subject to Proetus from Argos, who was far more powerful; and Proetus, who had trouble in mind for Bellerophon, expelled him from the town. The reason was that Proetus' wife godlike Anteia was mad for him to make secret love to her. But prudent Bellerophon was a man of sound principles and refused. So Anteia went to lord Proetus with a lying tale and said: "Proetus, Bellerophon wanted to seduce me, but I refused. Kill him, or may you die your-self."

'So she spoke, and Proetus was enraged at what he heard. He stopped short of putting Bellerophon to death – he did not think it right to do so – but instead sent him off to Lycia carrying a fatal message, a folded tablet on which he had written signs
170 with a deadly meaning. Proetus told Bellerophon to hand this tablet to his father-in-law, the ruler of Lycia, thus ensuring Bellerophon's death.

'The journey was smoothly overseen by the gods and, when Bellerophon reached Lycia and the flowing River Xanthus, he was welcomed as an honoured guest by the ruler of those broad lands. His host entertained him for nine days and slaughtered an ox every day. But when rosy-fingered Dawn rose for the tenth day, he questioned Bellerophon, asked to see what message he had brought from Proetus and was given the tablet with the fatal instructions that Proetus had sent.

'The Lycian ruler's first step was to order Bellerophon to kill
180 the raging Chimaera, a creature born of the gods, not men. She had a lion's head, a serpent's tail and the body of a goat; and her breath came out in terrible blasts of burning flame. But Bellerophon let himself be guided by the gods and succeeded in killing her. His second mission was to fight the illustrious Solymi – Bellerophon spoke of that as the most terrific battle he had ever fought against men. And by way of a third task, he killed the Amazons, women who were a match for men.

'But the ruler of Lycia thought of something different and set a clever trap to catch him on his return from this adventure. He picked out the best men in all Lycia and stationed them in
190 ambush. Not one of them came home – matchless Bellerophon killed them all. In the end, he realized Bellerophon was a true son of the gods. So he kept him in Lycia and gave him his daughter's hand and half his kingdom, while the Lycians also sectioned off a piece of their best land with rich vineyards and cornfields for him to cultivate.

'Bellerophon's wife bore him three children – Isander, Hippo-lochus and Laodameia, who slept with Zeus wise in counsel and became the mother of the godlike warrior Sarpedon. But the

time came when Bellerophon incurred the enmity of all the gods   200
and wandered off in solitude across the Aleian Plain, eating his
heart out and avoiding all contact with men. Ares, the insatiable
War-god, killed his son Isander in battle with the illustrious
Solymi, and Artemis, whose chariot has golden reins, killed
Laodameia in anger.

'That left Hippolochus – and they say I am his son. He sent
me to Troy and often used to tell me always to be the best and
excel all others and never disgrace our forefathers who were
by far the best men in Ephyre and Lycia.   210

'That, then, is my family; that is the blood I claim as mine.'

So he spoke, and Glaucus' tale delighted Diomedes, master
of the battle-cry. He stuck his spear into the bountiful earth and
warmly addressed this shepherd of the people:

'Surely your family and mine are linked by old-
established ties. Godlike Oeneus my grandfather   *Glaucus* and
once entertained matchless Bellerophon in his palace   Diomedes
and kept him there for twenty days, after which they   exchange
gave each other the usual splendid gifts that host and   armour
guest exchange. Oeneus gave Bellerophon a belt bright with
purple, and Bellerophon gave Oeneus a gold two-handled cup   220
which I left behind at home when I set out here for Troy. (As
for my father Tydeus, however, I don't remember him, as I was
only a baby when he joined the Greek expedition that was
destroyed at Thebes.) So now you will have a good friend in me
in the heart of Argos, and I shall have you in Lycia if ever I visit
that country.

'So let us avoid each other's spears even in the tumult of
battle, since there are plenty of other Trojans and their famous
allies for me to kill, if the god provides them and I have the
speed to catch them, and plenty of Greeks for you to slaughter,
if you can. And let us exchange our armour so that everyone   230
will know our grandfathers' friendship has made friends of us.'

With these words they leapt from their chariots, took each
other by the hand and gave their word of honour. But Zeus
robbed Glaucus of his wits since he exchanged his golden
armour for Diomedes' bronze, a hundred oxen's worth for the
value of nine.

Meanwhile Hector had reached the oak-tree at the Scaean gate and was at once besieged by Trojan wives and daughters running up to ask about their sons and brothers, their husbands 240 and their friends. He told them all in turn to pray to the gods. Grief was in store for many.

Then he made his way to Priam's magnificent palace. It was fronted with rows of polished columns, and in the main building behind there were fifty apartments of polished stone adjoining each other, where Priam's sons slept with their wives. His daughters had separate quarters, on the other side of the courtyard, where twelve adjoining bedrooms had been built for them, of polished stone and well roofed in. Here Priam's sons-in-law 250 slept with their honoured wives.

Hector meets Hecabe

Hector was met at the palace by his gentle, generous mother Hecabe who was coming in with Laodice, the most beautiful of her daughters. Putting her hand in his she said:

'Hector! Why have you left the brave conflict to come here, my child? It is true, then, that those hateful Greeks are getting the better of us in the fighting round the town; and your spirit moved you to return here and lift your hands in prayer to Zeus on the town's heights. But wait a moment while I fetch you some sweet wine, so that you can first make a libation to Father 260 Zeus and the other immortals and then, if you like, refresh yourself with a drink as well. Wine is a great comfort to a weary man, and you must be exhausted after fighting so hard for your loved ones.'

Great Hector of the flashing helmet replied:

'My lady mother, don't bring me any delicious wine or you will deprive me of my strength and leave me unfit to fight. And I shrink from offering Zeus sparkling wine with unwashed hands. A man cannot pray to Zeus, who darkens the clouds, when he is bespattered with blood and filth.

270   'No, it is you who must pray. Collect the older women and go with offerings to the temple of the war-leader Athene. Choose a robe, the loveliest and biggest you can find in the house and the one most precious to you, and lay it on the knees of lovely-haired Athene. Promise to sacrifice in her shrine a dozen

year-old heifers that have never worked, if only she will have
pity on the town and on the Trojans' wives and little children
and keep that savage spearman and mighty master of the rout,
Diomedes, clear of sacred Ilium.

'Go, then, to the war-leader Athene's shrine, while I go after   280
Paris and order him out, though I doubt he is willing to listen
to me. Indeed, I wish the earth would open and swallow him
up. What a scourge Olympian Zeus raised him to be for the
Trojans, great-hearted Priam and his sons! If I could see him on
his way down to Hades' halls, I would say my troubles were
over.'

So he spoke, and Hector's mother went into the palace and
gave instructions to her waiting-women. While these were going
round the town to collect the older women, she went down to
the scented storeroom where she kept her embroidered robes.
These were the work of Sidonian women whom godlike Paris   290
himself had brought across the sea from Sidon, on the same
journey he escorted highborn Helen back to Ilium. Hecabe
picked out the longest and most richly decorated of these as a
gift for Athene. It had lain underneath all the rest and glittered
like a star. With this she set out, and a number of the older
women hurried along at her side.

When they reached the temple of Athene on the
town heights, the doors were opened for them by   *Trojan*
fair-cheeked Theano, daughter of Cisses and wife of   offering to
horse-taming Antenor, who had been made priestess   ATHENE
of Athene by the Trojans. With a loud cry in which everyone   300
joined, the women lifted their hands to Athene, while fair-
cheeked Theano took the robe, laid it on Athene's knees and
prayed to the daughter of great Zeus:

'Lady Athene, protectress of cities, celestial goddess, break
Diomedes' spear. Bring him crashing headlong down in front of
the Scaean gate. And we will sacrifice here and now in your
shrine a dozen year-old heifers that have never worked, if only
you will have pity on the town and on the Trojans' wives and   310
little children.'

So Theano prayed, but for answer Pallas Athene shook her
head.

So the women prayed to the daughter of great Zeus, and
Hector made his way to the fine house where Paris lived. Paris
had built it himself using the best workmen to be found in
the fertile land of Troy. They built it for him complete with
sleeping-quarters, hall and court-yard, close to the houses of
Priam and Hector on the town heights. There Hector dear to
Zeus stepped inside. He was carrying a spear five metres long.
320 The bronze point glittered in front of him, and a gold ring
clamped the socket tight to the shaft.

Hector meets
Paris (3.380 ff.)

He found Paris in his bedroom, seeing to his
superb armour, his shield and body-armour, and
examining his curved bow, while Helen sat beside
him with her waiting-women and supervised their excellent
work. Seeing Paris, Hector attacked him sharply:

'What do you think you are doing? It doesn't do you much
credit to sit and sulk by yourself like this, while our men are
falling in action round the town and its steep walls. It's your
fault this town flares with the sound and fury of battle, and you
330 would be the first to quarrel with anyone else you found shirking
the horrors of war. Back into action with you now, before the
town goes up in flames!'

Godlike Paris replied:

'Hector, your taunts are justified, nothing more than what I
deserve. But let me say something, and you listen and pay
attention too. I am not sulking. I have no grudge against the
Trojans, but came and sat down in my room to wallow in my
grief. However, my wife has just been gently urging me to re-
turn to the front. And I think she is right – victory switches
340 from one man to another. So give me a moment while I arm for
battle, or else go on ahead and I will follow. I can soon catch
you up.'

So he spoke, but Hector of the flashing helmet made no reply.
Helen now warmly addressed Hector:

'My brother-in-law, what a cold, evil-minded slut I am! How
I wish that, on the very day when my mother bore me, the
storm-fiend had swept me off into the mountains or into the
waves of the sounding sea, to be overwhelmed before all this
could happen. And next to that, since the gods have ordained

things to this evil end, I wish I had found a better husband, one   350
with some feelings for the anger and contempt that his fellow
men had for him. But as it is, this husband of mine hasn't a
brain in his head and never will; though one day he will pay for
it, if I am not mistaken.

'But come in now, my dear brother-in-law, and sit down on
this chair. No one in Troy bears a greater burden of responsi-
bility for the fighting than you – and all because of me, slut
that I am, and Paris' blind folly. Zeus surely has an evil end in
store for us, intending us to figure in the songs of people yet
unborn.'

Great Hector of the flashing helmet replied:

'Helen, you are very kind, but don't ask me to sit down. You   360
will not persuade me. I am already anxious to return and help
the Trojans who miss me badly when I am gone. What you can
do is to hurry this fellow up. And he had better get a move on
himself. Then he could catch me up before I leave the town,
since I intend to look into my own house to see my house-slaves
and my dear wife and little boy. I can't tell whether I shall ever
come back to them again, or the gods have destined me to fall
to the Greeks this very day.'

With these words Hector of the flashing helmet took his leave
and soon reached his own welcoming house. But he did not find   370
his white-armed wife Andromache at home. She had gone up to
a tower on the wall with her child and well-robed waiting-
woman and was standing there crying her heart out. Failing to
find his matchless wife in the house, Hector went to the threshold
and said to the serving-women:

'Women, tell me what's happened. Where has white-armed
Andromache gone to from the house? Is she visiting one of my
sisters or my brothers' well-robed wives? Or has she gone to
Athene's shrine where the rest of the Trojan woman with their   380
lovely hair are interceding with that august goddess?'

A busy serving-woman replied:

'Hector, since you order me to tell the truth, she is not visiting
your sisters or your brothers' well-robed wives and she has not
gone to Athene's shrine with the rest of the women to pray to
that august goddess. She has gone to the great tower of Ilium.

She had heard that our men were being ground down, and the Greeks were well on top. So she rushed out like a woman possessed and must have arrived at the walls. The nurse followed her with the baby in her arms.'

390   So spoke the serving-woman, and Hector raced out of the house and retraced his steps down the well-built streets. He had crossed the great town and reached the Scaean gate – his route out on to the plain – when Andromache herself, who married him with a rich dowry, came running up to meet him. Andromache was the daughter of great-hearted Eëtion, the Cilician ruler who lived below the woods of Mount Placus in Thebe-under-Placus. It was his daughter that the warrior Hector had married.

Hector meets Andromache

Andromache came to meet him, and her waiting-woman
400   carried the little boy in her arms, their baby son and Hector's darling, lovely as a star, whom Hector called Scamandrius, but everyone else Astyanax, 'Town-lord', because his father was the one defence of Ilium.

Hector looked at his son and smiled, but said nothing. Andromache, bursting into tears, went up to him, put her hand in his and said:

'Hector, you are possessed! This determination of yours will be the death of you. You have no pity on your little boy or your luckless wife, who will soon be your widow, when the Greeks
410   kill you in a massed attack. And when I lose you, I might as well be dead. There will be no comfort left when you have met your end – nothing but grief.

'And I have no father or lady mother either. My father Eëtion fell to godlike Achilles when he sacked our welcoming town, Cilician Thebe with its high gates. But though Achilles killed Eëtion, he did not think it right to strip the body. He cremated him in his ornate arms and built a grave-mound above him;
420   and the mountain Nymphs, daughters of Zeus who drives the storm-cloud, planted elms around it.

'I had seven brothers too at home. In one day, all of them went down into Hades. Godlike swift-footed Achilles killed them all while they were looking after their shambling cattle and white sheep. As for my mother, who ruled in Thebe under

the woods of Mount Placus, Achilles brought her here with the
rest of his spoils, but freed her for an immense ransom, and later
she died peacefully in her father's house at the hands of Artemis
who delights in arrows.

'So Hector, you are father and mother and brother to me, as   430
well as my strong husband. Have pity on me now. Stay here on
the tower and don't make your boy an orphan and your wife a
widow. Rally the Trojans by the fig-tree there, where the wall is
easiest to scale and the town most open to attack. Three times
already, their best men led by the two Ajaxes, celebrated Ido-
meneus, Agamemnon, Menelaus and brave Diomedes have
assaulted that point and tried to break through. Someone who
knows the oracles must have told them about it or else they
have their own reasons for attacking there.'

Great Hector of the flashing helmet replied: 440

'Andromache, I too have all this constantly on my mind. But
if I hid myself like a coward and slunk from the fighting, I
would feel nothing but shame before the Trojans and the Trojan
women in their trailing gowns. My heart would not be in it
either, since I have trained myself always to be a good warrior,
to take my place in the front line and try to win glory for my
father and myself.

'But deep in my heart I know well the day is coming when
sacred Ilium will be destroyed, together with the people of Priam
and Priam himself of the good ash spear. Yet what distresses   450
me is not only the thought of what the Trojans will suffer, or
Hecabe herself, or lord Priam, or my brothers who, for all their
numbers and bravery, will be brought down in the dust at enemy
hands, but much more the thought of you, when you are dragged
off in tears by some bronze-armoured Greek, your freedom
gone.

'I see you there in Greece, labouring away for some other
woman at the loom or carrying water from some foreign
spring, Messeis or Hypereia, much against your will, unable
to do anything about it. "There goes the wife of Hector" they   460
will say when they see your tears. "He was the greatest of the
horse-taming Trojans who fought it out round Ilium." That is
what they will say, and you will feel fresh grief at the loss of

the one man who might have kept you free. But may the earth be piled high over my dead body before I hear your cries as they drag you off.'

Hector's child

With these words glorious Hector reached out for his boy. But the child shrank back with a cry to the bosom of his girdled nurse, alarmed by his father's appearance, 470 terrified by his bronze helmet with its horsehair plume that he saw nodding frighteningly from the top. His father and lady mother burst out laughing. Glorious Hector quickly took his helmet off and put it, all shining, on the ground. Then he kissed his dear son, dandled him in his arms and prayed to Zeus and the other gods:

'Zeus and you other gods, grant that this boy of mine becomes, like me, pre-eminent among the Trojans; as strong and brave as I; a mighty ruler of Ilium. May people say, when 480 he comes back from battle, "Here is a man much better than his father." Let him bring home the bloodstained armour of the enemy he has killed and delight his mother's heart.'

With these words Hector handed the boy into the arms of his wife, who took him to her fragrant bosom, laughing through her tears. When her husband saw this, pity overcame him. He stroked her with his hand and said:

'Dear heart, I beg you, don't distress yourself too much. No one is going to send me down to Hades before my time, though death itself, I think, is something no man, coward or hero, can 490 escape, once he has come into this world. You go home now and attend to your work, the loom and the spindle, and tell the waiting-women to get on with theirs. War is men's business; and this war will be the business of every man in Ilium, myself above all.'

With these words glorious Hector picked up his helmet with its horsehair plume. His wife set out for home, weeping profusely and with many a backward look. She soon reached the welcoming palace of man-slaying Hector, found many of her waiting-women inside and stirred them all to lamentation. They 500 mourned for Hector in his own house, though he was still alive, thinking he would never survive the fury of the Greeks' assault and come home from the battle.

Paris too had not lingered in his high house. *Hector* and
Directly he had put on his impressive ornate armour, *Paris* return to
he hurried out through the town, making the most battle
of his speed. As a stabled horse breaks his halter at
the manger where he feeds and, hooves thudding, gallops off
across the fields to his usual bathing-place in the sweet-flowing
river, exultant; he tosses his head; his mane streams in the wind
along his shoulders; he knows how beautiful he is, and his feet 510
carry him skimming over the ground to the horses' haunts and
pastures – so Paris, Priam's son, resplendent as the shining sun
in his armour, came down from the citadel of Pergamus in Ilium,
laughing as he ran.

He soon caught up with his brother godlike Hector, just as
he was leaving the spot where he had been exchanging intimacies
with his wife. Godlike Paris spoke first:

'My dear brother, have I been too leisurely and kept you
waiting when you wanted to be off, and not come at the time
you told me to?'

Hector of the flashing helmet replied and said: 520

'What a strange man you are. No reasonable man could make
light of your performance in battle: you have plenty of courage.
But you are too ready to give up and refuse to fight. And it
distresses me to hear such shameful things said about you by
the Trojans, who are suffering so much on your account.

'But let's be off. Later we will make up for anything we may
have said, if Zeus ever lets us drive the Greeks from our soil and
celebrate our freedom with drink-offerings in the palace to the
everlasting Olympian gods.'

7

AJAX FIGHTS HECTOR

With these words glorious Hector rushed out through the gate with his brother Paris, both eager to do battle and fight. As a god answers exhausted sailors' prayers and sends them a breeze when their limbs are weak from the effort of driving their polished pine oars through the sea, so the two of them re-appeared like an answer to the Trojans' prayers.

Trojans kill Greeks

Then Paris killed Menesthius, who lived at Arne and was the son of lord Areithous the Maceman and ox-eyed lady Phylomedusa. Hector with his sharp spear stabbed Eioneus in the neck under the bronze rim of his helmet and brought him down. Meanwhile the Lycian leader

10

Glaucus, throwing a spear across the lines of battle, struck
Iphinous on the shoulder just as he was leaping up behind his
fast mares. He fell from his chariot to the ground and crumpled
up.

When the goddess grey-eyed Athene saw Greeks being slaugh-
tered in the heat of battle, she came swooping down from the
heights of Olympus to sacred Ilium. But Apollo, who desired a   20
Trojan victory, saw her from the citadel Pergamus in Ilium and
started out to intercept her. The two met by the oak-tree and
lord Apollo son of Zeus spoke first:

'Daughter of great Zeus, why have you so eagerly   ATHENE and
come down from Olympus? With what high purpose   APOLLO plan
in mind? Since the destruction of the Trojans does   Hector's duel
not move you at all, do you want to switch victory
to the Greeks? But if you care to listen to me, I have a better
plan. Let us end the fighting and the bloodshed for the moment.   30
They can fight again another day, and go on till they reach their
goal in Ilium, since you goddesses have set your hearts on razing
this town to the ground.'

The goddess grey-eyed Athene replied:

'So be it, Archer-god. That is what I too had in mind when I
came from Olympus to visit the battlefield. But how do you
propose to stop the men from fighting?'

Lord Apollo son of Zeus replied:

'We could rouse the fighting spirit in horse-taming Hector and
make him challenge one of the Greeks to take him on face-to-face   40
in mortal combat. The Greeks would be put on the spot and
would send out someone to fight a duel with godlike Hector.'

So he spoke, and the goddess grey-eyed Athene complied.
Priam's son Helenus was able to divine what these gods had
agreed and went straight up to his brother Hector and addressed
him:

'Hector son of Priam, equal in wisdom to Zeus, you should
allow yourself to be guided by your brother. Make the Trojans
and Greeks sit down and then challenge the best of the Greeks   50
to take you on face-to-face in mortal combat. Your time has not
yet come to die and meet your destiny. I have this from the
immortal gods themselves.'

So he spoke, and Hector was delighted at what he heard. He
stepped out into no-man's-land and, grasping his spear by the
middle, pushed the Trojan ranks back. They all sat down, and
Agamemnon made the Greeks do the same. Athene and Apollo
lord of the silver bow also sat down, in the form of vultures, on
60 a tall oak sacred to Zeus who drives the storm-cloud. They
enjoyed the sight of all these warriors sitting there, rank upon
rank, rippling with shields, helmets and spears. Like ripples
spreading over the sea when the west wind first springs up, and
the surface darkens under it, so the ranks of Greeks and Trojans
sat down on the plain.

Hector addressed the two armies:

Hector issues   'Trojans and Greek men-at-arms, hear a proposal
the challenge   I am moved to make. High-throned Zeus has not
(22.256)   brought our oaths to fulfilment. It's clear he has
                   trouble in store for both sides till the day when you
70 bring down the Trojans' city with its fine towers, or succumb to
us yourselves beside your seafaring ships.

'Now you have in your army the finest men in all Greece. Let
the man who is willing to take me on step forward, in front of
everyone, as your champion against godlike Hector. And here
are the conditions I lay down, with Zeus for witness. If your
man kills me with his long-pointed spear, he can strip me of my
arms and take them back to your hollow ships; but he must let
80 them bring my body home, so that the Trojans and their wives
can cremate it in the proper manner. If I kill your man and
Apollo gives me the glory, I shall strip off his armour and bring
it to sacred Ilium, where I shall hang it in Apollo's shrine; but I
shall send his body back to your well-benched ships, so the
long-haired Greeks can bury him properly and build a grave-
mound over him by the broad Hellespont. Then one day some
future traveller, sailing by in his many-oared ship across the
wine-dark sea, will say: "This is the monument of some great
90 warrior of an earlier day who was killed in action by glorious
Hector." That is what he will say, and my fame will never
die.'

So he spoke and was received in complete silence by them all.
They were ashamed to refuse his challenge, but afraid to accept

it. Eventually Menelaus rose to his feet and, saddened at heart, reproached them bitterly:

'What does this mean, you big mouths, you women? I cannot call you men. Not a single Greek willing to meet Hector? This is the last straw, our final humiliation. Very well then, sit there and rot, the whole lot of you, gutless no-hopers to a man. I will arm and fight him myself. The gods above will decide who wins.'

With these words he put on his splendid armour. And that, Menelaus, would have been the end of you, since Hector was by far the better man, if the Greek leaders had not leapt up and held you back, and if the son of Atreus himself, wide-ruling Agamemnon, had not seized you by the right hand and spoken:

'You are mad, Olympian-bred Menelaus. There is no call for such foolishness. Withdraw, however distressing it may be for you. Don't fight a better man just to make a contest of it. Others quail before Hector. Even Achilles feared to meet him in battle where men win glory, and Achilles is a far better man than you. So go back now and sit down among your men, and the Greeks will find someone else to fight for them against this man. Hector may be fearless and never able to get enough fighting, but I still think even he will be glad to rest his weary limbs, if he escapes with his life from the heat of this deadly encounter.'

With this sound advice Agamemnon changed his brother's mind, and he was persuaded to step down; and joyfully his attendants took the armour from his shoulders. Then Nestor rose to his feet and addressed the Greeks:

'This is a disgrace, enough to make Greece weep! How Peleus the old horseman would grieve, Peleus, that brave adviser and orator of the Myrmidons, who took such delight, when I stayed with him once, in finding out from me the parentage and pedigree of every Greek. If it came to his ears that those same men were now all cowering before Hector, he would lift up his hands to the gods and beg them to let his spirit leave his body and descend to Hades' halls.

'Ah, Father Zeus, Athene and Apollo, if only I could be as young as I was when the men of Pylos gathered to fight the spearmen from Arcadia at the

Menelaus's challenge stopped

Nestor's story of Ereuthalion

swift River Celadon, below the walls of Pheia, by the streams of
Iardanus! We were challenged by their best man, Ereuthalion.
He was like a god and carried on his shoulders the armour of
lord Areithous – the great Areithous who was surnamed the
Maceman by his compatriots and their girdled wives, because
140 he never fought with a bow or spear but used an iron mace
to smash his way through the enemy ranks. Lycurgus killed
Areithous, not by superior strength, but by cunning. He caught
him in a narrow pass where his iron mace could not save him.
Before the Maceman could bring it into play, Lycurgus pierced
him through the middle with his spear and brought him crashing
to the ground on his back. Then he stripped Areithous of the
armour bronze-clad Ares had given him, and afterwards wore
it himself when he went into battle. Later, when Lycurgus had
grown old in his palace, he let his attendant Ereuthalion wear
150 it; and so it came about that Ereuthalion challenged our cham-
pions in Areithous' armour.

'And no one dared take up the challenge; they were all
throughly terrified. But I was bold enough to take him on, and
rash enough – but then I was the youngest of them all. So I
fought him, and Athene gave me the glory. He was the tallest
and strongest man I have ever killed. He lay there, a giant of a
man, sprawling this way and that.

'Ah, if only I were still as young, and with all my powers
intact! Then Hector of the flashing helmet would soon have his
fight. As it is, I see before me the best men in all Greece – and
160 not one that has the will to stand up to Hector!'

So the old man reproached them, and nine men in all then
sprang up. Agamemnon lord of men was the first to rise. He was
followed by mighty Diomedes son of Tydeus; and these by the
two Ajaxes, clothed in martial valour; and these, again, by
Idomeneus and Idomeneus' attendant Meriones, equal of the
murderous War-god Ares; and these by Eurypylus, Euaemon's
noble son. Thoas son of Andraemon got up too, and so did
godlike Odysseus. When all these had volunteered to fight
170 godlike Hector, Nestor the Gerenian charioteer addressed
them:

'Draw lots to decide who is to be chosen. The Ajax wins
lottery to fight
Hector winner will not only benefit the Greeks but also reap a rich reward himself, if he escapes with his life from the heat of this deadly encounter.'

So he spoke, and each of them marked his own lot and put it into the helmet of Agamemnon son of Atreus, while the troops raised their hands to the gods and prayed. They looked up to the broad skies and said as one man:

'Father Zeus, let it be Ajax or Diomedes or Agamemnon   180
himself, lord of golden Mycenae.'

So they spoke, and Nestor the Gerenian charioteer shook the helmet and out leapt the lot they had hoped for – that of Ajax. A herald carried it round the circle from left to right, showing it to each of the Greek leaders, and each in turn disowned it when he failed to recognize his mark. At last, as he took the lot round the group, he came to the man who had marked it and put it in the helmet, glorious Ajax himself. Ajax reached out. The herald came up and put the lot in his hand. Ajax recognized his mark and was thrilled. He threw it on the ground at his feet   190
and said:

'Friends! The lot is mine! And I am delighted, because I think I shall defeat godlike Hector. But, while I am arming for the fight, pray to lord Zeus son of Cronus, and pray in silence, so that the Trojans cannot overhear you. Or pray out loud! We are afraid of nobody whatever. No one is going to have his way with me and make me run, either by brute force or because I lack the skill: after all, I should be surprised to find I was born and bred a complete novice on Salamis.'

So he spoke, and they then prayed to lord Zeus son of Cronus.   200
They looked up to the broad skies and said as one man:

'Father Zeus, you that rule from Mount Ida, greatest and most glorious! Answer Ajax's prayer and grant him a brilliant victory. But if you hold Hector dear too and wish him well, let neither man be beaten and the fight be drawn.'

So they spoke, and Ajax armed himself in his dazzling bronze. When all his armour was on, he set out like awe-inspiring Ares, god of war, going to join battle among men brought together to

210 fight by Zeus, their hearts set on soul-destroying combat. So awe-inspiring Ajax, a tower of strength for the Greeks, rose and went into battle, smiling a grim smile, taking great strides as he went, brandishing his long-shadowed spear. The Greeks, when they saw him, were overjoyed, but there was not a Trojan whose knees did not tremble. Even Hector's heart beat faster. But it was too late now for him to turn tail and slink back among his men, since it was his will to fight that had made him throw down the challenge.

And now Ajax drew near, carrying a shield like a tower,
220 made of bronze and seven layers of oxhide. Tychius the master leather-worker, who lived at Hyle, had made this glittering shield for him with the hides of seven well-fattened bulls, which he overlaid with an eighth layer of bronze. Holding this shield in front of him, Ajax son of Telamon went right up to Hector and defied him:

The duel 'Hector, you're now going to discover, in single combat, what sort of champions the Greeks have at their disposal, even when they can't count on Achilles, lion-hearted breaker of men. At the moment he is lying by his
230 seafaring beaked ships, nursing his implacable anger against Agamemnon son of Atreus, shepherd of the people. But for all that, we have men who can stand up to you, and plenty of them. So take the first throw and start the duel.'

Great Hector of the flashing helmet said:

'Olympian-born Ajax, son of Telamon, leader of men, don't try to scare me like a feeble child or a woman who knows nothing about warfare. I know all about fighting and killing. I know how to handle my toughened oxhide shield and swing it to right or left – the real skill of work with a shield. I know how
240 to charge in among the confusion of the chariots; and in a standing fight I know all the steps of the War-god's deadly dance. But enough: seeing the man you are, I have no desire to steal a shot at you when you aren't looking, but to throw openly, if I can hit you.'

He spoke, balanced his long-shadowed spear and hurled it. It struck the formidable, sevenfold shield of Ajax on its metal sheath, the eighth and outermost layer. The untiring bronze tore through six layers, but was held up by the seventh hide. Then Olympian-born Ajax in turn hurled his long-shadowed spear. It hit Hector's round shield. The heavy weapon pierced the glittering shield, forced its way through the ornate body-armour and ripped right on through the side of Hector's tunic. But Hector had swerved and so avoided dark death.

And now the pair, when each had pulled the long spear out of his shield, fell on each other like flesh-eating lions, or wild boars whose strength is not to be despised. Hector thrust at the centre of Ajax's shield with his spear, but it did not break through and the tip was bent back. Then Ajax leapt in and stabbed at Hector's shield. The spear passed clean through and stopped Hector in his tracks: it grazed his neck and the dark blood spurted out.

Yet even so Hector of the flashing helmet did not give up the fight. He drew back and with his great hand picked up a large and jagged piece of black rock that was lying on the ground, hurled it at Ajax's formidable sevenfold shield and struck it in the middle on the boss, making the bronze ring out. But Ajax then picked up an even bigger rock, which he swung and hurled at Hector, putting his full weight into it. This millstone of a boulder crumpled his shield and swept him off his feet. There Hector lay, jammed in the shield, stretched on his back. But Apollo quickly had him up on his feet again.

And now they would have closed and hacked at one another with their swords, if heralds, ambassadors of Zeus and men, had not intervened, Talthybius on the Greek side and Idaeus on the Trojan, both sensible men. They raised their sceptres between the combatants, and Idaeus, a herald rich in wisdom, spoke his mind:

'Dear sons, give up now and break off the fight. Cloud-gatherer Zeus holds you both dear, and you are both fine spearmen – we all of us know that. Also, it is nearly dark. It is sensible to take that into account.'

Ajax son of Telamon replied and said:

'Idaeus, tell Hector to call it off. It was his will to fight that made him throw down the challenge to all our best men. Let him make the first move. I will do as he does.'

The duel ends; gifts exchanged

Great Hector of the flashing helmet said:

290 'Ajax, the god has given you size, strength and ability, and you are the best spearman on your side. Let us bring today's duel to an end. We can fight some other time, till the powers above decide between us, and one of us wins. Also, it is nearly dark. It is sensible to take that into account.

'Then you will bring joy to the Greeks back at the ships, your friends and relatives above all; while I too shall get a warm welcome in lord Priam's town from the Trojans and the Trojan ladies in their trailing gowns, who will enter the sacred assembly to offer up prayers in my name. But first let us both exchange 300 prestigious gifts, so that Trojans and Greeks alike can say: "These two fought each other in soul-destroying combat, but were reconciled and parted friends."'

With these words he gave Ajax his silver-riveted sword, which he handed over with its scabbard and sword-belt; and at the same time Ajax gave Hector his brilliant purple belt.

So the two parted. Ajax went back into the Greek lines, while Hector rejoined the Trojan forces. His men were delighted to see him return to them safe and sound from the fury of Ajax's 310 invincible assault. They escorted him back to the town, hardly able to believe he was alive. Meanwhile, on the other side, the Greek men at arms conducted Ajax, elated by his victory, to godlike Agamemnon.

When they reached his huts, Agamemnon lord of men offered a five-year-old bull on their behalf to almighty Zeus son of Cronus. They skinned and prepared it by cutting up the carcass. They deftly carved it into small pieces, pierced these with skewers, roasted them carefully and drew them all off. When their 320 work was done and the meal prepared, they feasted, and no one went without a fair share, though the warrior son of Atreus, wide-ruling Agamemnon, honoured Ajax with the whole length of the back.

Their hunger and thirst satisfied, a proposal was put to them by the old man Nestor, whose wisdom had often proved itself in the past. He had their interests at heart as he rose and addressed them:

'Agamemnon and you other Greek chieftains, the Greek army has suffered heavy losses. The cruel War-god has darkened the banks of Scamander with the blood of our dead, whose souls have gone down to Hades.

Nestor's defensive wall

330

'So at dawn you should announce a truce. Then let us all get to work together, bring the dead in here with oxen and mules and burn them not far from the ships, so that each of us can take the bones back home to their children when we return to the land of our fathers. Let us then make them one communal grave-mound over the pyre on the plain.

'Then we should immediately construct high-towered walls against it to protect the ships and ourselves, with well-fitted gates that leave room for chariots to drive through. And a little way outside the wall, we should dig a deep ditch parallel with the walls all round the camp to keep out enemy chariots and infantry, in case the proud Trojans start putting the pressure on us some day.'

340

So he spoke, and they all approved.

Meanwhile, at the doors of Priam's palace on the town heights of Ilium, the Trojans held a frightened and confused assembly. Sensible Antenor spoke first:

'Trojans, Dardanians and allies, hear a proposal which I feel compelled to make. Enough is enough: let us give Helen back to Agamemnon and Menelaus, along with all the property that came with her. By fighting on as we are doing, we have cheated on the oaths. No good that I can see will ever come of that, unless we act as I suggest.'

350

So Antenor spoke and sat down. Godlike Paris, husband of lovely-haired Helen, stood up and in reply spoke winged words:

Paris rejects return of Helen

'Antenor, that was an unusually ill-disposed speech of yours. You know you could have thought of something better. But if you really do mean what you say, then the gods themselves must have scrambled your brains.

360

'I shall now tell you horse-taming Trojans my views and declare outright that I will not give up my wife. On the other hand, I am willing to return all the goods I brought home with me from Greece and to add something of my own.'

So Paris spoke and sat down. Dardanian Priam, wise as the gods, stood up, and he had their interests at heart as he rose and addressed them:

'Trojans, Dardanians and allies, listen to what I feel compelled
370 to say. For the moment, take your supper in the town as usual. Remember to mount guard and keep alert, every man of you. At dawn let Idaeus go to the hollow ships and convey to Agamemnon and Menelaus the offer we have heard from Paris, who started the quarrel. And Idaeus can make a further sensible suggestion: he can ask the Greeks whether they are willing to refrain from hostilities till we have burnt our dead. We can fight some other time, till the powers above decide between us and one of us wins.'

380 So he spoke, and the Trojans heard and agreed. They took their supper at their posts, and at dawn Idaeus went to the hollow ships where he found the Greeks, attendants of Ares, in conference by the stern of Agamemnon's ship. The herald stood among them and spoke out clearly:

[Day 23]   'Agamemnon and you other leaders of Greeks,
Greeks refuse   Priam and the other noble Trojans have instructed
peace-terms   me to deliver an offer from the man who started our
                  quarrel, Paris, if it meets with your approval. All the property Paris brought away with him to Troy in his hollow
390 ships – and would to God he had perished first – he is willing to return, with additions of his own. But he says he will not give up glorious Menelaus' wife, though I can assure you the Trojans have urged him to do so. Furthermore, they instructed me to ask whether you are willing to refrain from hostilities while we burn the dead. We can fight some other time, till the powers above decide between us and one of us wins.'

So he spoke and was received in complete silence by them all. Eventually Diomedes, master of the battle-cry, spoke up:

400 'At this stage let no one accept Paris' offer of possessions or Helen either. Any fool can see the Trojans' doom is sealed.'

The Greeks to a man roared their approval, delighted at

the words of horse-taming Diomedes. Lord Agamemnon then
addressed Idaeus:

'Idaeus, you have heard for yourself the Greek view. That is
their answer and I am pleased to agree. The cremation of the
bodies is another matter. To that I raise no objection. When
men are dead and gone, one cannot grudge their bodies swift   410
propitiation by fire. A truce, then; and let loud-thundering Zeus,
husband of Hera, witness it.'

With these words he sealed the oath by lifting up his sceptre
to all the gods. Idaeus then withdrew and made his way back
once again to sacred Ilium, where the Trojans and Dardanians
had gathered and were all seated in assembly, awaiting the
herald's return. When Idaeus reached them, he stood in the
middle and reported his news.

Then they prepared themselves at once for their double task,
some to bring in the dead and others to fetch wood; while on
the other side, parties of Greeks from their well-benched ships
hurried off on the same duties.   420

The sun, climbing into the sky from the deep and   The dead
peaceful Stream of Ocean, was already lighting up   cremated
the fields with his first beams when the Trojan and
Greek parties met. Even so, they found it difficult to recognize
the individual dead bodies until they had washed away the
congealed blood with water. Then, as they lifted them on to the
waggons, the hot tears flowed. As for the Trojans, great Priam
had forbidden his men to cry aloud. So with heavy hearts they
piled up their dead on the pyre in silence and, when they had
cremated them, returned to sacred Ilium. So too, on their side,   430
the Greek men-at-arms with heavy hearts piled up their dead on
the pyre and, when they had cremated them, returned to their
hollow ships.

Before dawn on the next day, when the night had   [Day 24] The
a hint of daylight, a working-party of Greek troops   Greek wall
gathered by the pyre. Over the pyre they made one   built
communal grave-mound in the plain, and con-
structed high-towered walls against it to protect the ships and
themselves, with well-fitted gates which left room for chariots
to drive through. And a little way outside the wall, they dug a   440

long ditch parallel with the walls, deep and broad, and planted a row of stakes along it.

So the long-haired Greeks worked away. But the gods seated with Zeus, lord of the lightning flash, were watching the great work of the bronze-armoured Greeks in some amazement. Poseidon the earthshaker began and spoke his mind:

POSEIDON complains (12.1–35)

'Father Zeus, is there no mortal left in the whole wide world who will inform us gods of his plans? Can't you see that the Greeks have thrown a wall round their ships and dug a ditch along it, without 450 offering impressive sacrifices to the gods? Its fame will spread as far as the dawn extends, and the wall that I and Phoebus Apollo built with such labour for the warrior Laomedon will be forgotten.'

Angrily, Zeus who marshals the clouds replied:

'Powerful earthshaker, what are you talking about? Leave it to other gods less determined and tenacious than yourself to be alarmed at this development; and rest assured it is your fame that will spread as far as the dawn extends. Besides, you can go 460 to work once the Greeks have sailed back to the land of their fathers – break down the wall, scatter the fragments in the sea, cover the long beach once more with sand and so obliterate this great wall.'

While the gods were talking together in this way, the sun set and the Greeks finished their task. They slaughtered some oxen in their huts and took their supper.

Greek supply ships come in

A number of ships had put in from Lemnos with cargoes of wine. They came from Euneus, the son Hypsipyle had borne to Jason shepherd of the people, 470 and he had included a thousand measures of sweet wine as a special gift for Agamemnon and Menelaus. The long-haired Greeks now supplied themselves with wine from these ships, some in exchange for bronze, some for gleaming iron, others for hides or live cattle, others again for war-captives. It was a sumptuous meal they prepared. All night long the Greeks feasted themselves, while in the town the Trojans and their allies did the same.

But all night long Zeus wise in counsel, brewing evil for them

in his heart, kept thundering ominously. They turned pale
with fear and poured wine on the ground from their cups. Not   480
a man dared to drink before he had made a libation to the
almighty son of Cronus. Then they lay down and took the gift
of sleep.

8

HECTOR TRIUMPHANT

As saffron-robed Dawn spread over the world, Zeus who delights in thunder called the gods to an assembly on the highest of Olympus' many peaks. He opened it himself, and everyone paid close attention:

[Day 25, second combat day]

ZEUS' warning

'Listen to me, all you gods and goddesses, so that I can tell you what I feel compelled to say. I am determined to bring this business to a speedy close, and with that end in view I give you my ruling, which no god or goddess must attempt to defy – you must accept it, every one of you.

'If I find any god taking independent action and going to help   10
the Trojans or Greeks, he shall be thrashed and indecently
packed off back to Olympus. Or I will seize him and hurl him
into the gloom of Tartarus, far, far away, where the deepest of
all chasms yawns below the world, where the Iron Gates are,
and the Bronze Threshold, as far below Hades as the earth is
under the skies. That will teach you how far I am the most
powerful of all the immortals.

'Come on, you gods, try me, if you like, and find out for
yourselves. Tie a golden rope to Olympus and take the other   20
end of it, all of you, gods and goddesses together. Try as hard
as you like, you will never drag Zeus the high counsellor down
from the skies to the ground. But if I cared to pull in earnest
from my end, I could haul the lot of you up here, and the earth
and sea as well. Then I would make the rope fast to a spur of
Olympus and leave everything to dangle in mid-air. That is how
much stronger I am than gods and men.'

So he spoke and was received in complete silence by them
all. The bluntness of his words had taken them completely by
surprise. Eventually the goddess grey-eyed Athene spoke: 30

'Father of ours, son of Cronus, lord supreme, we all know
well enough you are invincible. But we are sorry for the Greek
spearmen, who will be left to their wretched fate – destruction.
However, we will refrain from fighting, as you command, and
shall concentrate instead on offering helpful advice to the
Greeks, so that they will not all come to grief because of your
anger.'

Zeus who marshals the clouds smiled and said:

'Have no fear, Triton-born Athene, dear child. I was not in
earnest and do not mean to be unkind to you.'   40

With these words Zeus harnessed to his chariot his two swift
horses with their hooves of bronze and flowing manes of gold.
He dressed himself in gold, picked up his splendid golden whip,
mounted his chariot and lashed the horses with the whip to get
them moving. The willing pair flew off midway between the
earth and starry sky and brought him to Gargarus, a peak of
Mount Ida of the many springs, the mother of wild beasts,
where he has a precinct and smoking altar. There the Father of

50 men and gods pulled up his horses, freed them from the yoke
and wrapped them in a dense mist. Then he sat down on the
heights, exulting in his glory and looking out over the Trojans'
town and Greek ships.

Meanwhile the long-haired Greeks snatched a meal in their
huts and then armed; while on the other side, in the town, the
Trojans also prepared themselves for battle. There were fewer
of them, yet they were still determined to confront the enemy
face-to-face, driven as they were by the need to fight for their
wives and children. The gates were all thrown open, and with a
great din their whole army, foot-soldiers and charioteers,
60 poured out. The armies advanced and met in a single space
with a great clash of shields, spears and bronze-armoured
warriors. The bossed shields collided and a great roar went
up – the screams of the dying, the jeers of the victors – and the
earth ran with blood.

The Greeks
retreat
Right through the morning, while the blessed light
of day grew stronger, volley and counter-volley
found their mark and men kept falling. But when the
sun was high in the sky, the Father held out his golden scales,
70 and putting death that lays men low in either pan, on one side for
the horse-taming Trojans, on the other for the bronze-armoured
Greeks, raised the balance by the middle of the beam. The beam
came down on the Greeks' side, spelling doom for them. Their
destiny settled on the bountiful earth, while that of the Trojans
went soaring up to the broad sky. Zeus thundered out from
Mount Ida and launched a flash of vivid lightning at the Greek
troops, who were confounded by it. Terror drained the colour
from every man.

Then, neither Idomeneus nor Agamemnon could bring
themselves to hold their ground. Nor could the two Ajaxes,
80 attendants of Ares. Gerenian Nestor, guardian of the Greeks,
was the only one to delay, not because he wanted to but because
his third horse, the trace-horse, was in trouble. Godlike Paris,
husband of lovely-haired Helen, had hit it with an arrow on the
top of the crown where the mane starts to grow on a horse's
head, a deadly spot. In its agony it reared up, since the point

sank into its brain; and writhing round with the arrow in it, the trace-horse threw the other horses into confusion.

Nestor rushed in with his sword and was slashing at this horse's reins when Hector's horses came galloping up through the mayhem, with their daring charioteer, Hector himself, behind them. The old man would then and there have lost his life but for the quick eye of Diomedes, master of the battle-cry, who saw the danger and shouted loudly to Odysseus for help:

Diomedes saves Nestor (5.323)

90

'Olympian-born son of Laertes, resourceful Odysseus, where are you off to, melting like a coward into the crowd, your shield slung behind you? If you don't watch out, someone'll hit you in the midriff with a spear as you run for it. But stop and help me keep this brute off old Nestor.'

So he spoke, but all-daring, godlike Odysseus did not hear him properly and sped by on his way to the Greeks' hollow ships. Now on his own, Diomedes none the less engaged with the front ranks, made a stand in front of Nestor's chariot and spoke winged words:

100

'Venerable sir, these young warriors are proving too much for you. You're exhausted, with all those years to carry too. That attendant of yours is useless and your horses too slow. Come, get into this chariot and you'll see what horses bred by Tros are like and how quickly they can cover the ground in pursuit or retreat. I took them from Aeneas only the other day, these masters of the rout. Let our attendants take charge of your horses, while you and I drive this pair at the Trojans. Hector will soon know if I too have in my hand a spear raging for blood.'

110

So he spoke, and Nestor the Gerenian charioteer complied. So their two powerful attendants, Sthenelus and genial Eurymedon, took charge of Nestor's mares while Nestor and Diomedes both mounted Diomedes' chariot. Nestor took up the gleaming reins and started the horses with the whip. They were soon within range of Hector, and Diomedes let fly at him as he came charging up. He missed, but instead got Hector's attendant and charioteer

Diomedes kills Eniopeus

120   Eniopeus. He hit him by the nipple on his chest, with the horses'
reins in his hands. He crashed out of the chariot and his horses
shied. Life and spirit left him there.

His charioteer's death wrung Hector's heart but, sorry as he
was for his comrade-in-arms, he left him lying there and went
off in search of another daring charioteer. His fast horses were
not long without a driver. He soon found daring Archeptolemus,
made him get up behind the speedy pair and handed him
the reins.

130   Irreparable disaster threatened the Trojans now
and they would have been driven into Ilium like
ZEUS'   lambs into a pen, if the Father of men and gods
thunderbolt   had not been alert and acted quickly. With a terrific
warns Nestor   thunderclap, he launched a dazzling bolt of lightning
and guided it to earth in front of Diomedes' horses. There was
a dreadful flash of burning sulphur. The horses shied and backed
up under the chariot. The gleaming reins dropped from Nestor's
hands and, terrified, he said to Diomedes:

'Diomedes, quick, turn the horses round and get out of here.
140   Don't you see you can expect no help from Zeus? He is giving
Hector all the glory – for today. Another day our turn will come,
if he wishes it. However mighty a man may be, he will never
deflect the will of Zeus, who is far more powerful.'

Diomedes, master of the battle-cry, replied:

'All that, venerable sir, is very true. But it really hurts me to
think of Hector standing up and saying to the Trojans: "Dio-
medes ran away from me and didn't stop till he reached the
150   ships." That is how he'll boast, and when he does, may the wide
earth swallow me up!'

Nestor the Gerenian charioteer replied:

'Son of mighty Tydeus, what are you saying! Hector can call
you a coward and weakling to his heart's content, but he won't
convince the Trojans and Dardanians, nor those proud shield-
bearing Trojans' wives whose strong husbands you've hurled in
the dust.'

                           With these words he wheeled the horses round and
Hector mocks   drove them back in flight across the mayhem. Hector
Diomedes   and the Trojans followed them with a tremendous

roar and a hail of deadly missiles. Then great Hector of the   160
glittering helmet raised a shout of triumph over Diomedes:

'Diomedes, the Greek charioteers used to honour you with
pride of place, the choicest meat and never empty cups. Now
they will despise you. I can see you always were a woman. Off
with you, cry-baby! You won't find me standing aside while you
climb our walls or carry off our women in your ships! I'll see
you off to Hades first!'

So he spoke, and Diomedes' heart was torn whether to turn
his horses and take Hector head on. Three times he considered
the possibility, and three times Zeus wise in counsel thundered   170
from Mount Ida as a sign to the Trojans that the battle was
turning their way. Hector then called out to the Trojans in a
loud voice:

'Trojans, Lycians and you Dardanians that like your fight-
ing hand to hand, be men, my comrades, and call up that
fighting spirit of yours! I'm convinced Zeus is in earnest
about granting me victory and a great triumph, and disaster for
the Greeks – fools that they are, to have gone and made those
flimsy, futile walls, which will not resist my onslaught for a
moment.

'As for the ditch they have dug, our horses will jump that
with ease. And once I get among the hollow ships, remember   180
the battle-cry – "Fire!" I'll send their ships up in flames, the
Greeks will panic in the smoke and I'll slaughter them then and
there by their vessels.'

With these words Hector called to his horses and spoke to
them:

'Now you two repay me for the attentions lavished on you
by Andromache, daughter of great-hearted Eëtion, who always
put honey-sweet wheat in front of you first and mixed wine
with it for you to drink at your leisure, before she ever served   190
me, her strong husband. After them, now, at the gallop, and
let us capture Nestor's shield, whose fame reaches the skies –
solid gold, they say, handgrips and all – and then tear from
Diomedes' shoulders the inlaid body-armour Hephaestus made
for him. If we could get our hands on those two pieces, I'd
expect the Greeks to take to their swift ships this very night.'

So he spoke, boasting, and the lady Hera was furious. Shaking
her throne and making high Olympus tremble, she addressed
200 the great god Poseidon:

POSEIDON
refuses help to
Greeks
'What's going on, powerful earthshaker? Even you
cannot find any pity in your heart for the slaughtered
Greeks! Yet at Helice and Aegae they bring you many
pleasing offerings. Once you wished them victory.
Now, if we who are on the Greek side made up our minds to
keep far-thundering Zeus from interfering and to drive back the
Trojans, he *would* feel sorry for himself, sitting all alone there
on Mount Ida.'

Greatly disturbed, the lord of the earthquake replied:

'What are you suggesting now, Hera? These are wild words
210 indeed. I certainly have no wish to join the others in a fight
against Zeus, who is so much stronger than all of us!'

While they were talking together in this way, the whole area
away from the ships, between the ditch and the wall, was filled
with chariots and shield-bearing men penned in by Hector,
equal of the swift War-god Ares, now that Zeus had granted
him the glory. Indeed, he would have had the ships in flames, if
the lady Hera had not put it into Agamemnon's head to take
action and rally the Greeks before it was too late.

220
He raced along past the huts and ships, clutching
a large purple cloak in his fist, and took his stand on

HERA spurs
Agamemnon
to action
the bulging black hull of Odysseus' ship. This stood
in the centre of the line, so that a shout would carry
to either end, to the huts of Ajax son of Telamon or
those of Achilles. Both these two had had confidence enough in
their own bravery and strength to draw up their ships on the
extreme flanks. From this point, Agamemnon sent his voice
ringing out to the whole Greek army:

'Shame on you, Greeks! Contemptible creatures, admired
only for your looks! What's become of those proud claims that
230 we were the finest force on earth? What of the idle boasts you
made that time in Lemnos, when you were gorging your-
selves on beef and drinking from bowls brimful of wine? You
said that in a fight you could each stand up to a hundred, no,
two hundred, Trojans! But today the whole crowd of us is no

match for Hector alone; and he, before long, will have the ships going up in flames.

'Father Zeus, have you ever deluded any mighty leader like this before and robbed him of all his glory? Yet I can say that on my unhappy journey here in my ship I never overlooked a single one of your fine altars. On every one of them I burnt the   240 fat and thighs of bullocks in my eagerness to sack the Trojans' city with its fine walls. Then, Zeus, grant me this prayer at least. Allow us to escape with our lives, if nothing else, and don't let the Trojans overwhelm us like this!'

So Agamemnon spoke, and the Father was moved by his tears. With a nod of his head he signalled that his army would be saved, not destroyed, and at the same time released an eagle – most effective of prophetic birds – with a fawn in its talons, the offspring of some swift doe. The eagle dropped this fawn by the superb altar of Zeus where the Greeks used to sacrifice to Zeus   250 god of omens; and when they realized that the bird came from Zeus, they fell on the Trojans once more, their will to fight renewed.

Then not one of the many Greek charioteers could claim he had raced Diomedes to the ditch and driven out before him to engage the enemy. He was easily the first to kill a helmeted Trojan, Agelaus, who had swung his horses round in flight. As he turned, Diomedes stabbed him with his spear in the middle of the back between his shoulders and drove it on through his chest. He crashed   260 from his chariot and his armour clattered about him.

The Greeks rally; Teucer's success

Diomedes was followed by Agamemnon and Menelaus; these by the two Ajaxes, clothed in martial valour; and these, again, by Idomeneus and his attendant Meriones, equal of the murderous War-god Ares, and by Eurypylus. The ninth to come, drawing his curved bow, was Teucer and he took up his position behind the shield of Ajax son of Telamon. Ajax would move his shield slightly aside; Teucer would then peer about for a target in the crowd and shoot. Then, as the man he hit dropped   270 dead, Teucer, like a child running for shelter to its mother, took cover once again with Ajax who hid him behind his glittering shield.

Who was the first of the Trojans to fall to matchless Teucer? Orsilochus; then Ormenus and Ophelestes, Daetor and Chromius and godlike Lycophontes; and Amopaon, Polyaemon's son, and Melanippus. All these in swift succession he brought down to the bountiful earth. Agamemnon lord of men was delighted when he saw the havoc Teucer was causing with
280 his mighty bow among the Trojan ranks. He went up to him and spoke his mind:

'Teucer, dear friend, son of Telamon, leader of men, carry on like this and you will save the Greeks and bring glory to your father Telamon, who took you under his roof and reared you even though you were an illegitimate son. Repay him now with glory, far away as he is. I tell you truly and I mean it: if Zeus who drives the storm-cloud and Athene ever let me sack the well-built town of Ilium, I will hand you the first prize of honour
290 after my own, a tripod, or a pair of horses with their chariot, or a woman to share your bed.'

Matchless Teucer replied and said:

'Most glorious Agamemnon, why flog a willing horse? I'm doing all I can, without stopping. From the moment we pushed them back towards Ilium, I have been watching for chances to kill the enemy. I have shot eight long-pointed arrows, and each has found its mark in the flesh of some brave young warrior. But here's a mad dog I cannot hit.'

300   He spoke and launched another arrow at Hector,
            longing to bring him down. He missed, but the arrow
Teucer misses   landed in the chest of one of Priam's strong sons,
Hector; kills   handsome Gorgythion, whose mother, lovely Casti-
two Trojans   aneira with a figure like a goddess, had come from
Aesyme to be married to Priam. As a poppy's head tilts to one side, weighed down in the garden by its seed and the showers of spring, so Gorgythion's head, weighed down by his helmet, dropped to one side.

Once more, longing to bring him down, Teucer launched an
310 arrow at Hector. He missed this time too, since Apollo turned the arrow aside, but he did hit Archeptolemus, Hector's daring charioteer, by the nipple on his chest, as he was charging into

battle. He crashed from his chariot and his swift horses shied. Life and spirit left him there.

His charioteer's death wrung Hector's heart but, sorry as he was for his comrade-in-arms, he left him there and called on his brother Cebriones, who happened to be near, to take the horses' reins. Cebriones heard him and complied. Hector himself leapt 320 to the ground from his shining chariot with a terrible shout, picked up a lump of rock and made straight for Teucer, whom he had determined to kill.

Teucer took a sharp arrow from his quiver and notched it to the string. As he drew the string back, *Hector* Hector's jagged stone hit him on the shoulder, a vulner- *smashes* able spot where the collar bone connects the neck and *Teucer's bow* shoulders. The bowstring snapped; his fingers and wrist went numb; he sank to his knees; and the bow dropped from his hand. But Ajax did not disregard his brother's fall. Running 330 up, he stood over Teucer and covered him with his shield. Then two of their loyal comrades, Mecisteus and godlike Alastor, lifted him up on their shoulders and carried him off, groaning heavily, to the hollow ships.

Olympian Zeus now put fresh heart into the Trojans, and they drove the Greeks right back to their deep ditch. Hector, elated and irresistible, led from the front. As a hound in full cry after a lion or a wild boar snaps at its flank and hindquarters 340 and follows every twist and turn, so Hector pursued the Greeks, killing the hindmost all the time as they ran before him. They turned in panic and ran through the line of the stakes and across the ditch, suffering heavy losses at the hands of the Trojans, and did not stop till they reached the ships. There they halted, calling to one another for help; and every man lifted up his hands and poured out prayers to all the gods. But there was Hector, turning his lovely-maned horses this way and that, glaring at them with the eyes of Gorgo or the murderous War-god.

Seeing them, the goddess white-armed Hera felt pity and 350 spoke to Athene with winged words:

'This is disastrous, daughter of Zeus who drives the storm-cloud. Can't we intervene, even at the last minute, to prevent the Greeks being killed? They are going to be left to their wretched fate – destruction – mown down by this one man's onslaught. See what Hector has done to them already! And now there is no stopping him in his mad assault.'

The goddess grey-eyed Athene replied:

'Nothing would please me more than to see his mad assault cut short and him drop dead at Greek hands on his native soil.

360 But my father's in a mad and evil mood himself, obstinate old wretch that he is, always blocking my plans. He never remembers how often I went to help his son Heracles when the tasks Eurystheus set him became too much for him. Heracles had only to whimper to the skies and Zeus would send me speeding down to get him out of trouble. I wish my prophetic heart had warned me of all this when Eurystheus sent Heracles down to the house of Hades, warden of the gates, to bring the hound of hell back up from the depths of Erebus: then I would have made sure he never re-crossed the torrents of the River Styx.

HERA and ATHENE help the Greeks

370 'But now Zeus loathes me and is letting Thetis have her way, because she kissed his knees, took his chin in her hand and begged him to bring honour to Achilles sacker of towns. Yet the day will come when he will call me his grey-eyed darling once more. In the meantime, however, you get our horses ready, while I go into the palace of Zeus who drives the storm-cloud and arm for war. I want to see whether this son of Priam, Hector of the flashing helmet, will be pleased when we two appear in the lines of battle; or whether it is now the turn of the Trojans to fall dead by the Greek ships and glut the dogs and the birds
380 of prey with their fat and flesh.'

So she spoke, white-armed Hera complied and this august goddess, daughter of great Cronus, went off to get ready her horses with their golden headbands. On her father's threshold, Athene, daughter of Zeus who drives the storm-cloud, took off the soft embroidered robe she had made and worked with her own hands, replaced it with a tunic and over that put on the armour of Zeus, who marshals the clouds, in preparation for war's work with all its tears. Then she stepped into the fiery

chariot and took up the long, thick, heavy spear with which she   390
breaks the ranks of warriors when she, the almighty Father's
child, is roused to anger. Hera immediately leaned forward to
whip on her horses, and of their own accord the gates of
Olympus thundered open for them. These are kept by the
Seasons, the wardens of the broad sky and of Olympus, whose
task it is to roll the gates of heavy cloud away from the entrance
or roll them back. Through these gates, the goddesses directed
their horses spurred on by the whip.

When Father Zeus saw them from Mount Ida, he was enraged
and at once told Iris of the golden wings to convey a message to
them:

'Off with you, swift-footed Iris! Make them turn back. Don't
let them meet me face to face. It would not be a good idea for   400
them to fight *me*. But I say bluntly and I mean it: I will ham-
string the swift horses they are driving, hurl them
both from their chariot and smash it to pieces. Ten   IRIS warns
rolling years will not be enough to heal them of the   HERA and
wounds my thunderbolt will inflict. That will teach   ATHENE
my grey-eyed daughter what it means to fight against her father.
As for Hera, I am not so much hurt and angered by *her*. Defying
me comes naturally to her.'

So he spoke, and Iris, quick as the wind, sped off on her
mission. From the peaks of Mount Ida she arrived on high   410
Olympus. On its rugged heights she met the two goddesses at
the outer gates, stopped them and delivered Zeus' orders:

'Where are you hurrying off to? What's the purpose of this
mad adventure? The son of Cronus forbids you to assist the
Greeks. Hear what he threatens – and he will keep his word.
He will hamstring the horses you are driving, hurl you both
from your chariot and smash it to pieces. Ten rolling years
will not be enough to heal you of the wounds his thunder-
bolt will inflict. That will teach you, his grey-eyed daughter,   420
what it means to fight against your father. As for Hera, he is not
so much hurt and angered by *her*. Defying him comes naturally
to her. But you have gone too far, you barefaced bitch, if you
really dare to brandish that awe-inspiring spear of yours at
Zeus.'

With these words swift-footed Iris took her leave. Then Hera spoke to Athene:

'Oh dear, daughter of Zeus who drives the storm-cloud, I've changed my mind. We two will not go to war with Zeus on man's behalf. Let chance settle who is to live or die. Zeus must decide in his own mind between the Trojans and Greeks, as is only right.'

With these words she turned their chariot back. The Seasons unyoked their lovely-maned horses, tethered them at their ambrosial mangers and tilted the chariot against the white-plastered courtyard walls. The two goddesses then rejoined the other gods and sat down on golden chairs, thoroughly disgruntled.

ZEUS reasserts his authority

Meanwhile Father Zeus left Mount Ida, drove his chariot and horses at speed to Olympus and arrived at the seat of the gods. The famous earthshaker Poseidon unyoked his horses, put his chariot on its stand and covered it with a cloth. Far-thundering Zeus himself sat down on his golden throne, and great Olympus shook beneath his feet.

Athene and Hera, sitting alone by themselves apart from Zeus, said nothing to him and asked no questions. But he realized what was going on and said:

'Athene and Hera, why so disgruntled? You cannot, surely, be worn out by the battle where men win glory in which you killed so many of those Trojans you hate so intensely. Now, all the gods in Olympus could never turn *me* from my path, such is my determination and invincible might. But you two were trembling in every shining limb before you ever saw the battle-field and battle's grim horrors. I tell you bluntly, and I would have seen to it: you would not have returned home in your own chariot to Olympus where the gods live, because my thunderbolt would have wrecked it.'

So he spoke, and Athene and Hera muttered darkly to each other. They were sitting close together, plotting trouble for the Trojans. Athene held her tongue and said nothing, but glared at Father Zeus, seething with indignation. But Hera could not contain her rage and spoke out:

'Dread son of Cronus, what are you suggesting now? We all

know well enough you are invincible. But we are sorry for the Greek spearmen, who will be left to their wretched fate – destruction. However, we will refrain from fighting, as you command, and shall concentrate instead on offering helpful advice to the Greeks, so that they will not all come to grief because of your anger.'

Zeus who marshals the clouds replied and said:

'At dawn tomorrow, if you are interested, ox-eyed lady Hera,   470
you will witness Zeus behaving even more mightily, destroying much of the Greek army. For I tell you, imperious Hector will give his enemies no rest till swift-footed   ZEUS fore-
Achilles rises up again beside the ships on the day   tells Patroclus'
when the Greeks, in desperate straits, are fighting   death (16.855)
at the very sterns of their vessels over the body of the dead Patroclus.

'That is divinely decreed. As for yourself, your fury leaves me unmoved. For all I care, you can go off to the lowest limits of land and sea and join my old Titan enemies Iapetus and Cronus, sitting there sunk in the depths of Tartarus, cut off from the   480
pleasures of the beams of Hyperion the sun and of the breezes. Get even that far in your wanderings, and your resentment will still leave me unmoved. No one is more of a bitch than you.'

So he spoke, and white-armed Hera made no reply. Now the bright lamp of the sun dropped into Ocean, drawing black night in its train across the fruitful earth. The Trojans had not wished the day to end, but for the Greeks the welcome dark night came like an answer to their prayers.

Glorious Hector withdrew the Trojans from the Greek ships and summoned a meeting beside the swirling river, in an open   490
space where the ground was clear of bodies; and they got down from their chariots to hear what Hector dear to Zeus had to say. He was carrying a spear five metres long; the bronze point glittered in front of him, and a gold ring clamped the socket tight to the shaft. Leaning on this spear, he addressed his troops:

'Trojans, Dardanians and allies, listen to me. I had
hoped to destroy the ships and all the Greeks with   Hector's
them before going home to windswept Ilium. But   hopes
night intervened. It was that, more than anything, that has saved   500

the Greeks and their ships by the sea-shore. But now, we can only do as night dictates and prepare to eat. Unyoke and feed your lovely-maned horses. Then quickly go and fetch cattle and fat sheep from the town and supply yourselves with delicious wine and bread from your houses.

'Then collect quantities of wood. We must have plenty of fires burning all night long till dawn and light up the whole sky. We don't want the long-haired Greeks launching out over the broad back of the sea and making a dash for home in spite of the darkness. We certainly mustn't leave them to embark at their leisure. Let's give each of them something to think about at home – an arrow or a sharp spear in the back as they jump on board – to teach them, and others like them, to think twice before bringing war with all its tears on the horse-taming Trojans.

'In Ilium itself, our heralds must call out boys and grey-haired old men to camp out all round the town on the walls that the gods built us, while our womenfolk keep a big fire burning in every home. In addition, regular guards must be mounted so that no enemy raiding-party can steal into the town while the troops are away. Those, great-hearted Trojans, are my orders; let them be carried out.

'So much, then, for the needs of the moment. As for tomorrow, I say this to you. I pray in good hope to Zeus and all the other gods that I shall be able to drive away these doomed dogs whom the demons of death brought here in their black ships. During the night, we must keep guard on our position. But at the first light of dawn, we will arm and unleash the dogs of war by their hollow ships. Then I shall see whether mighty Diomedes son of Tydeus can drive me back from the ships to Ilium's walls, or whether I shall bring him down with my spear and carry off his bloodstained arms. He will learn in the morning whether he has it in him to stand up to my spear. More likely, as tomorrow's sun goes up, he will lie there in the front line, run through, with many of his contingent dead around him. If only I could be as certain of immortality and eternal youth and being honoured as Athene or Apollo are honoured, as I am certain this day will prove disastrous to the Greeks!'

So Hector spoke, and the Trojans shouted approval. They

freed their sweating horses from the yokes and tethered them with straps, each man by his own chariot. They went quickly and fetched cattle and fat sheep from the town, supplied them- selves with delicious wine and bread from their houses and collected quantities of wood. Soon the breeze was taking the smell of sacrifice up to the skies.   550

So all night long, buoyed up with hopes, they sat along the lines of battle, and many fires burned. As the stars in the sky stand out in all their splendour round the bright moon, when the upper air is still; when every lookout place, headland and mountain ravine stands out, and infinite upper air floods down from the skies; when every star is visible, and the shepherd rejoices in his heart – so many were the fires, lit by the Trojans, that could be seen in   560 front of Ilium between the streams of Scamander and the Greek ships. There were a thousand fires burning on the plain, and round each one sat fifty men in the light of its blaze, while horses stood beside their chariots, munching white barley and rye, and awaiting Dawn on her golden throne.

The *Trojans* camp out on the plain

9

THE EMBASSY TO
ACHILLES

1–181: [Evening and night before 26th day] Agamemnon is desperate,
and Nestor proposes that an apology be made to Achilles. Agamem-
non sketches the compensation he will offer. An embassy consisting
of Phoenix, Odysseus and Ajax is sent.

182–429: Achilles welcomes and feeds the embassy, and Odysseus
makes the offer, adding an appeal to Achilles' sense of pity. Achilles
rejects it outright, saying he will return home next day.

430–622: Phoenix tries to persuade Achilles, remembering how he
came to Achilles' home and raised him. He appeals to him in the
name of the gods of supplication (LITAE), and tells the story of
Meleager who also rejected gifts. Achilles says he will think again
about returning home.

622–55: Ajax appeals to Achilles in the name of friendship. Achilles
says he will consider returning to battle if the *Trojans* threaten his
ships.

656–713: The embassy returns, and Odysseus reports its failure. Dio-
medes says it was always going to be a waste of time, and they must
just fight on.

While the Trojans kept their watch, the Greek army was
haunted by panic and chilling thoughts of flight. All their leaders
were overwhelmed with inconsolable grief at their losses. As the
north and west winds suddenly descend from Thrace to whip
up the teeming sea; white horses cap the darkening rollers, and
seaweed piles up all along the beach – so Greek morale was
shattered.

Agamemnon, wandering about in complete despair, told his 10
clear-voiced heralds to summon every man by name
to an assembly, but not to call out loud and alert   *[Evening, day 25]*
the Trojans. He himself played a leading part in this   Greek assembly;
task. The men sat down to the assembly in some   Diomedes' rebuke
desperation. Agamemnon rose, weeping tears like a   (4.370)
dark spring trickling black streaks of water down a steep rock-
face. Sighing heavily, he addressed the Greeks:

'Friends, rulers and leaders of the Greeks, Zeus son of Cronus
has seriously deluded me, a crushing blow. That perverse god
once solemnly assured me that we would sack Ilium with its fine 20
walls and return home; but now his advice turns out to be an
evil deception, and he is telling me to return home to Argos in
disgrace, with half my army lost. It appears that this is what
almighty Zeus, who has brought down the high towers of many
a town and will destroy others yet, has decided, such is his
absolute power. So I suggest we all do what I now propose –
board ship and home to the land of our fathers! The Trojans'
town with its broad streets will never fall to us.'

So he spoke and was received in complete silence by them all.
For a long time everyone sat there, speechless and dejected. 30
Eventually Diomedes, master of the battle-cry, spoke out:

'Agamemnon son of Atreus, I will begin by taking issue with
you over your stupid proposal – here in open assembly, com-
mander, as is normal practice – and you must not be offended.

'You took it on yourself the other day to call my courage in
question in front of the troops. You said I was a weakling and
a coward. Well, every Greek, young and old, knows how far
that is the case. Then again, Zeus, son of sickle-wielding Cronus,
has granted you some things, but not others. He gave you the
sceptre of power and the honour it brings with it, but he did not
give you courage – and courage is the secret of authority. You
amaze me – do you really believe the Greeks are the cowards 40
and weaklings you say they are? If you, for one, have set your
heart on getting away, then go. The way is clear, and all your
ships are drawn up by the sea, the whole great fleet of them that
brought you from Mycenae. But the rest of the long-haired

Greeks are going to stay till we conquer Troy. Or let them scramble back home in their ships as well. We two, I and my charioteer Sthenelus, will fight on till we reach our goal in Ilium. We are here because the god wants us to be.'

50   So he spoke, and all the Greeks shouted their approval, delighted at the words of horse-taming Diomedes. Now the charioteer Nestor rose to speak:

Nestor proposes a special council

'Diomedes, you are a formidable warrior in a fight, and in debate you have no rival of your age; no one here will object to your speech or contradict a word of it. But it was beside the point. You certainly talked sensibly to the Greek leaders in terms appropriate to your age, but you are a young man – there's no denying it – and in fact you could be my 60 youngest son. But I am much older than you are, and it is now time for me to speak out and take the whole situation into consideration. And no one will look down on what I have to say, not even lord Agamemnon; for that man is indeed an outlaw from clan, law and home who is in love with the bitter taste of internal discord.

'For the moment, we must take the night into account and eat. Sentries must be posted at intervals along the ditch outside the wall. That is a duty I leave to the younger men. After that, Agamemnon, since you rank the highest here, you must take the 70 initiative. Invite your senior advisers to a feast. It is the right way to proceed and can do you no harm. Day by day Greek ships bring wine to you over the broad seas from Thrace. Your huts are full of it; and as ruler over many people, it is for you to offer hospitality. When you have gathered us all together, you must listen to the man who gives you the best advice. We Greeks certainly all need the best and most reliable we can get, with all those Trojan camp-fires so close to our ships. Who finds *them* a pleasant sight? This one night will sink or save the whole expedition.'

So he spoke, and they heard and agreed. Armed sentries 80 went out at the double under the command of Nestor's son Thrasymedes shepherd of the people; Ascalaphus and Ialmenus, children of the War-god; Meriones, Aphareus, and Deipyrus; and godlike Lycomedes, Creon's son. There were seven captains of the guard, and a hundred young men marched behind each, armed with long spears. They took their posts midway between the ditch and the wall, where each contingent lit a fire and laid out food.

Meanwhile Agamemnon led the whole party of senior advisers to his huts and had a heartening meal served up. They helped themselves to the good things spread before them and, when their hunger and thirst were satisfied, the old man Nestor, whose wisdom had won the day before, expounded his plan. He had their interests at heart as he rose and addressed them:

'Most glorious Agamemnon son of Atreus, lord of men, with you my speech begins and it will end with you. You are ruler over many people, for whose guidance Zeus granted you the sceptre and the authority to take decisions. So you, above all, must both give and listen to advice and carry out the suggestions that others may feel bound to put forward in the common interest. You will get the credit, whatever the proposal.

Nestor recommends conciliating Achilles (1.275)

'Now I will tell you how things seem to me – because no one will come up with a better analysis than mine. I formed it at the time and have not altered it, since the moment, Olympian-born Agamemnon, you infuriated Achilles by going to take the young girl Briseis from his hut. We were all against it; and I for one did my best to dissuade you. But your arrogant temper got the better of you, and you dishonoured a man of the highest distinction, whom the gods themselves respected, by taking and keeping his prize. Even at this late hour, then, we should consider how to talk him round and appease him with soothing gifts and winning words.'

Agamemnon lord of men replied:

'Venerable sir, your account of my blind folly is the truth. Deluded I was – I for one cannot deny it. The man Zeus takes to his heart and honours – as he now does that man to the point of crushing the Greeks – is worth a whole army. But since I gave in to a lamentable impulse and committed this act of blind folly, I am willing to make amends and give him limitless compensation.

'Before you all, I list the prestigious gifts I have in
mind: seven tripods untarnished by the flames; ten
talents of gold; twenty cauldrons of gleaming copper;
and twelve powerful racehorses whose speed has made winners
of them. Why, with nothing more than the prizes they have
won for me, a man would not be badly off or short of precious
gold.

Agamem-
non's gifts

130   'I will give him seven women skilled in arts and crafts, women
of exceptional beauty that I chose out of the spoils when he
captured thriving Lesbos. I will give him these and, with them,
the woman I took from him, the daughter of Briseus. Moreover,
I shall give him my solemn oath that I have never been in her
bed and slept with her, as men and women do. All these gifts
shall be put in his hands at once.

'Later, if the gods permit us to sack Priam's great town, let
him come in with us when we are sharing out the spoils, load
his ship with gold and bronze to his heart's content, and pick
140   out twenty Trojan women for himself, the loveliest he can find
after Greek Helen.

'And if in due course we get back to Argos, the most fertile of
all lands, he can become my son-in-law, and I will honour him
as I do Orestes, my beloved son, who is being brought up there
in the lap of luxury. I have three daughters in my strong palace,
Chrysothemis, Laodice and Iphianassa. Of these he shall choose
for his own whichever he likes best and take her back to Peleus'
house, without the usual bride-gifts. Indeed, I will give *him*
gifts, generous ones, more than anyone has ever given with his
daughter.

'Not only that, but I will give him seven prosperous towns:
150   Cardamyle, Enope and grassy Hire; holy Pherae and Antheia
with its deep meadows; beautiful Aepeia and Pedasus rich in
vines. They are all near the sea, in the farthest part of sandy
Pylos. Their people are rich in flocks and cattle. They will
honour him with their gifts as though he were a god and, being
under his authority, give him rich dues.

'All this I will do for him the moment he abandons his anger.
Let him surrender. We all know it is because Hades is so implac-
able and unyielding that he is more hated by mortals than any

other god. Yes, let him submit to me, since I rank higher than   160
he does and am older as well.'

Nestor the Gerenian charioteer replied:

'Most glorious Agamemnon son of Atreus, lord of men,
nobody could say your offer to lord Achilles was not generous.
Very well then, we must now send an urgent deputation to
Achilles' hut. I will nominate the men myself, and they must not
refuse the duty. First of all Phoenix, dear to the gods, must lead
the way, then great Ajax and godlike Odysseus. Of the heralds,
Odius and Eurybates are the men to go with them. Now fetch   170
water for our hands and call for silence, so that we can pray to
Zeus son of Cronus and ask him to have pity on us.'

So he spoke, and everything he said met with their
approval. Heralds at once poured water over their   *The embassy*
hands, and the young men filled the mixing-bowls to   *to Achilles*
the brim with wine and went round the whole company, pouring
some into each cup for a libation to the god. When they had
poured their libations and drunk as much as they wished, the
envoys set out from Agamemnon's hut. Glancing from one man   180
to another, but with an especial eye for Odysseus, Nestor gave
them full instructions to do their utmost to win over matchless
Achilles.

They walked together along the shore of the sounding sea
with many a prayer to the earthshaker Poseidon who encircles
the world that it might be easy to win over Achilles' proud heart.
When they came to the Myrmidons' huts and ships, they found
him entertaining himself on a tuneful lyre, a beautifully ornate
instrument with a silver crossbar which he had taken from
the spoils when he destroyed Eëtion's town. With this he was
entertaining himself, singing of the famous deeds of heroes. He
was alone but for Patroclus, who was sitting opposite him in   190
silence, waiting for him to stop singing.

The envoys drew near, godlike Odysseus leading, and halted
in front of him. Achilles was amazed, sprang to his feet still
holding his lyre and came forward from the chair where he
had been sitting. Patroclus too got up when he saw the men.
Extending his hand, swift-footed Achilles said:

'Welcome – to my dear friends! Something urgent must have

brought you here, you who are dearest of all the Greeks to me, however angry I am with them.'

200 With these words godlike Achilles led them into his hut and seated them on chairs with purple coverings. Then he turned quickly to Patroclus, who was standing nearby, and said:

'Bring out a bigger bowl, Patroclus, mix less water with the wine and give every man a cup. Here are my dearest friends under my own roof.'

So he spoke, and Patroclus did as his companion asked. He put down a hefty chopping-block in the firelight, and laid on it the backs of a sheep and a plump goat and the lower back of a great hog, rich in fat. Automedon held these for him while
210 Achilles jointed them and then carved up the joints and spitted the slices. Meanwhile, Patroclus stoked up the fire. When it had burnt down and the flames had died away, he spread out the embers and laid the spits above them, resting them on the supports, after he had sprinkled the meat with salt. When he had roasted it and heaped it up on platters, Patroclus fetched some bread and set it out on the table in handsome baskets; and Achilles divided the meat into portions. This done, Achilles took a chair by the wall opposite godlike Odysseus and told his
220 companion Patroclus to sacrifice to the gods. Patroclus threw the ritual pieces on the fire, and they all helped themselves to the good things spread before them. Their hunger and thirst satisfied, Ajax nodded to Phoenix. But godlike Odysseus caught the signal and, having filled his cup with wine, drank to Achilles:

Odysseus makes the offer
'Your health, Achilles! With all these appetizing dishes set before us we are certainly not short of our share of feasts, either in Agamemnon's hut or here again in yours.

'But at the moment the pleasures of the table are far from our thoughts. We are staring disaster in the face, Olympian-bred Achilles, and the prospect appals us. Unless *you* put on a show
230 of force, it is in the balance whether our ships will be saved or destroyed.

'The proud Trojans and their famous allies have taken up positions right next to the ships and our defensive wall. Their camp is bright with fires. They are convinced there is now nothing left to stop them from falling on the vessels. Zeus son of Cronus showers them with favourable omens, his lightning flashing on the right.

'And Hector is running wild, elated and irresistible. He puts complete trust in Zeus and respects neither man nor god in the mad-dog frenzy that possesses him. His one prayer is for the goddess Dawn to break at once, when he is promising to hack the peaks from the sterns of our ships as trophies, see the ships devoured by fire, smoke us out and slaughter us by the hulls. My big fear is the gods will let him carry out his threats – that it may be our destiny to perish here in Troy, far from Greece where the horses graze.

'Up with you then, if even at this late hour you want to rescue the exhausted troops from the Trojans' fury. You for one will regret it later when disaster has finally struck, since there will be no way of finding a remedy. Give some thought, before that stage is reached, to saving the Greeks from catastrophe.

'My old friend, when your father Peleus sent you from Phthia to join Agamemnon, he gave you this advice: "My son, Athene and Hera, if that is their will, are going to give you the strength. What *you* must do is keep a firm grip on that proud spirit of yours. Fellow feeling is better. Avoid destructive quarrels, and Greeks young and old will look up to you all the more."

'That was the old man's advice – which you have forgotten. But late as it is, yield, now. Give up this heart-rending anger. Agamemnon is ready to make you ample compensation the moment you relent. If you will listen, I will enumerate the gifts he promised in his hut:

'Seven tripods untarnished by the flames; ten talents of gold; twenty cauldrons of gleaming copper; and twelve powerful racehorses whose speed has made winners of them. With nothing more than the prizes they have won, a man would not be badly off or short of precious gold.

'He will give you seven women skilled in arts and crafts, women of exceptional beauty that he chose out of the spoils when you captured thriving Lesbos. He will give you these and, with them, the woman he took from you, the daughter of Briseus. Moreover, he will give you a solemn oath that he has never been in her bed and slept with her, my lord, as men and women do. All these gifts shall be put in your hands at once.

280 'Later, if the gods permit us to sack Priam's great town, you can go in with them when they are sharing out the spoils, load your ship with gold and bronze to your heart's content and pick out twenty Trojan women for yourself, the loveliest you can find after Greek Helen.

'And if in due course we get back to Argos, the most fertile of all lands, you can become his son-in-law, and he will honour you as he does Orestes, his beloved son, who is being brought up there in the lap of luxury. He has three daughters in his strong palace, Chrysothemis, Laodice and Iphianassa. Of these you can choose for your own whichever you like best and take her back to Peleus' house, without the usual bride-gifts. Indeed, 290 he will give *you* gifts, generous ones, more than anyone has ever given with his daughter.

'Not only that, but he will give you seven prosperous towns: Cardamyle, Enope and grassy Hire; holy Pherae and Antheia with its deep meadows; beautiful Aepeia and Pedasus rich in vines. They are all near the sea, in the farthest part of sandy Pylos. Their people are rich in flocks and cattle. They will honour you with their gifts as though you were a god and, being under your authority, give you rich dues.

'All this he will do for you, the moment you abandon your 300 anger. But if your loathing of Agamemnon, gifts and all, outweighs every other consideration, at least take pity on the Greeks in their camp. They are ready to drop and will honour you like a god. Indeed, you would cover yourself with glory in their eyes, since now you could even kill Hector himself. He reckons he has no equal among all the Greeks whom the ships brought here and he may even come within range of you, in the grip of his destructive madness.'

Swift-footed Achilles replied and said:

'Olympian-born son of Laertes, resourceful Odysseus, I had 310 better tell you point-blank how I feel and what I am going to do, because I don't want relays of you coming here, sitting down and whining and whimpering on at me. I loathe like

Hades' gates the man who thinks one thing and says
another. So now I will tell you how I see matters.

Achilles rejects
the offer
(1.213)

'I don't think Agamemnon son of Atreus or the
rest of the Greeks will win me over, since all along
men have been given no reward for battling relentlessly with the
enemy day in, day out.

'The man who stays put gets the same share as the man who
fights his best. Cowards and brave men are given equal respect.
The same death awaits the man who does much, and the man   320
who does nothing.

'All I have suffered by constantly risking my life in battle has
left me no better off than anyone else. As a bird brings every
morsel she finds to her unfledged chicks, however hard it goes
with *her*, so I have spent many a sleepless night and fought
through many a bloody day, battling with men for the sake of
women.

'Look: I have captured twelve towns by sea and eleven by
land across fertile Troy. From each of them I won a magnificent   330
haul of treasure, the whole of which I brought back every time
and gave to Agamemnon. To the son of Atreus! Who had stayed
put, by the ships. And I'd hand it all over, and he'd take it and
dole it out in little bits here and there, and keep the lion's share
for himself. Our leading men still have the prizes he gave them,
safe and sound in their possession. I am the only one he has
robbed, the *only* one. And he has taken the wife I love, too.
Well, he can have her – to his heart's content.

'Why do the Greeks have to fight the Trojans? Well, why did
the son of Atreus raise an army and bring it here? Was it not for
lovely-haired Helen? So are they the only men on earth who   340
love their wives, these sons of Atreus? No, every decent, right-
minded man loves and cherishes his own woman, as I loved that
girl with all my heart, even though she was a war-captive. But
now he has snatched my prize from my arms and cheated me,
don't let him try his tricks on me again. I know him too well.
He won't win me over.

'No, Odysseus, he'd better work out with you and the rest of
the leadership how to save the ships from going up in flames.
After all, he has already done *miracles* without me. Look, he's

350 built a wall and dug a ditch along it, a fine broad ditch, complete
with stakes! But even so he cannot keep mighty, man-slaying
Hector out. Why, in the days when I took the field with the
Greeks, nothing would have induced Hector to start a fight any
distance at all from the town walls. He'd come no farther than
the Scaean gate and the oak-tree – though once he *did* wait for
me there on my own and only just escaped with his life.

'But as it is, I now have no desire to fight godlike Hector. So
tomorrow I am going to sacrifice to Zeus and all the other gods,
then load and launch my ships. First thing in the morning, if
360 you want to and are interested, you will see my ships crossing
the teeming Hellespont and my men straining at the oar. And in
three days, given a good crossing by Poseidon, I will be home in
fertile Phthia. I have great wealth there which I left behind when,
to my cost, I came here; and now I will enrich it further by what
I bring back – the gold, the red copper, the well-girdled women
and the grey iron that fell to me as my ordinary share of booty,
for what it is worth. But *the* prize he gave me, he humiliatingly
withdrew – that's what lord Agamemnon did to me, that son of
Atreus.

'Tell him all I say and tell him in public. Then the rest of the
370 army can make their feelings clear when he tries to cheat any
other Greek. He is utterly shameless, but still the dog cannot
even bring himself to look me in the eye. He'll get no advice or
action from me. He has cheated me and played me false. He
won't take me in again. Once is enough. He can go to hell in his
own good time. Zeus wise in counsel has removed his brains.

'I hate his gifts and value *him* at one splinter. Not if he gave
380 me ten or twenty times as much as he possesses or could raise
elsewhere, or all the revenues of Orchomenus or Thebes –
Egyptian Thebes where the houses are stuffed with treasure,
and through every one of a hundred gates two hundred warriors
ride out with their chariots and horses – not if he gave me
gifts numerous as grains of sand or specks of dust, would
Agamemnon ever win me over, until he has paid back the whole
heart-rending insult.

'I'm marrying no daughter of Agamemnon son of Atreus. She
390 could be as lovely as golden Aphrodite and as skilful as grey-eyed

Athene. I would still not marry her. He can choose some other Greek for her, someone on his own exalted plane, more elevated than me. If the gods allow me to get safely home, my father Peleus will, I am sure, find me a wife. Up and down Hellas and Phthia there are plenty of Greek girls, daughters of nobles who protect their towns. I have only to choose the one I want and make her my own. There were often times at home when my heart's one desire was to make some well-matched girl my lawful wife and enjoy the fortune my old father Peleus had made.   400

'For nothing, as I now see it, equals the value of life – not the wealth they say prosperous Ilium possessed in earlier days, when there was peace, before the coming of the Greeks, nor all the treasure piled up behind the stone threshold of Phoebus Apollo in rocky Delphi. Cattle and fat sheep can be lifted. Tripods and chestnut horses can be procured. But you cannot lift or procure a man's life, when once the breath has left his lips.

'My divine mother, silver-footed Thetis, says that destiny has   410
left two courses open to me on my journey to the grave. If I stay here and fight it out round Ilium, there is no home-coming for me, but there will be eternal glory instead. If I go back to the land of my fathers, my heroic glory will be forfeit, but my life will be long and I shall be spared an early death.

'And another thing: I would encourage all the rest of you to sail for home too. You are never going to reach your goal in the steep streets of Ilium. Far-thundering Zeus has stretched   420
out a protecting hand over that town, and its people have taken heart.

'So leave me now and report my message to the Greek leaders, freely, as is the privilege of advisers. Then they can think up some better way of saving the ships and all their troops beside them, since this plan, which they thought up as a result of my implacable anger, will not work. But Phoenix can stay here and spend the night with us. Then he can embark for home with me in the morning, if he wants to. There will be no compulsion.'

So he spoke, and was received in complete silence by them   430
all. The bluntness of his words had taken them completely by surprise. Eventually the old charioteer Phoenix spoke up, bursting into tears, so afraid was he for the Greek ships:

'Glorious Achilles, if you really are thinking of
sailing home and are so obsessed by your anger that
you refuse to save the ships from going up in flames,
what is to become of me without you, dear child? How could I
possibly stay here, alone? Your father Peleus made me your
guardian when he sent you off from Phthia to join Agamemnon.
440 You were a mere boy then with no experience of war, that great
leveller, or of debate where men make their mark. It was to
teach you all these things, to make a speaker of you and a man
of action, that he sent me with you. But I could not bring
myself to be separated from you, dear child, not even if the god
promised to strip off my years and turn me into the fine young
man I was when I first left Hellas with its lovely women.

'I ran away because of a quarrel with my father, Amyntor.
His anger with me was down to a lovely-haired woman he
450 intended to bring home. He was passionate about her, which
was humiliating for his wife, my mother. So my mother entreated
me to sleep with the woman first, and thus make her dislike the
old man. I consented and did so. My father guessed at once and
with solemn curses called on the hateful Furies to make me
childless, so he would never have to lift a son of mine on to his
lap; and over time the gods, Zeus of the underworld and august
Persephone, fulfilled his curses.

'I then planned to put my father to the sword. But one of the
460 gods restrained me. He made me think of public opinion and of
the reproaches I would incur, and how the Greeks must not
know me as a father-killer. After that, I could not bring myself
to remain any longer in my angry father's house. Naturally,
my kinsmen and cousins were all for keeping me there at
home and gathered round in entreaty, pleading hard with me.
Many fat sheep and shambling cattle with crooked horns
were slaughtered; many a fine fat hog was spitted over the
flames for singeing; and many a jar of the old man's wine was
drunk.

470   'For nine nights they camped beside me, taking it in turns to
go on guard, and keeping two fires burning, one under the
colonnade of the walled yard, and the other in the forecourt
outside the door of my sleeping-quarters. But on the tenth dark

night I broke open the close-fitting doors of my bedroom and escaped. I easily cleared the courtyard wall, and not one of the men or waiting-women on guard saw me. Then I fled far across spacious Hellas and came as a suppliant to fertile Phthia, mother of flocks, and your father lord Peleus. He welcomed me warmly 480 and loved me as a father loves his son, an only, cherished son, heir to a great estate. He made me a rich man and gave me a populous district to rule, and I settled down on the borders of Phthia as lord of the Dolopes.

'Since then, godlike Achilles, all my loving devotion has gone into making you the great man you are. You would refuse to go out to a feast or touch your food at home unless I was there; I always had to take you on my knees and feed you, cutting up your meat for you and holding the wine to your lips. You would 490 often soak the front of my tunic, dribbling wine all down it – just like a baby! Yes, I went through a great deal for you and worked myself to the bone, aware that the gods were not going to send me a son of my own. So I tried to make *you* my son, godlike Achilles, so that you would save me some day from a miserable end.

'Master your tremendous pride, Achilles. You have no need to be so stubborn. Even the gods themselves, for all their greater majesty, honour and power, are capable of being swayed. When someone has gone too far and done wrong, they supplicate gods with sacrifice and soft prayers, libations and 500 burnt-offerings, to turn them from their anger.

'There are goddesses of supplication, Litae, daugh- The LITAE ters of almighty Zeus. These Litae are wrinkled crea- tures, limping, eyes askance, who make it their business to pursue Delusion. But Delusion is strong and sure-footed, because she is quick enough to leave them all behind. Roaming the world, Delusion brings mankind to grief. But the Litae come after and put the trouble right. The man who respects these daughters of Zeus when they approach him is greatly blessed by them, and they listen to his prayers. But when a man hardens 510 his heart and rebuffs them, they go and supplicate Zeus, asking that Delusion accompany the man so that he comes to grief and pays the price.

'This applies to you, Achilles. You must give the daughters of
Zeus that same respect that bends even great men to yield. If
Agamemnon had not made you a generous offer with the
promise of more to come, but had persisted in his vindictiveness,
I would not be asking you to cast your anger to the winds and
help the Greeks now, however great their need. But as it is, he
is not only offering you a great deal now but guaranteeing much
520   more, as well as choosing the most distinguished men from the
whole army to come and supplicate you, men who are your own
dearest friends among the Greeks. Don't scorn their message or
their mission here – though up till now, no one could have
blamed you in the slightest for your anger.

'We all know famous stories of the past when great heroes
behaved like this and worked themselves up into a fury of rage,
yet proved amenable to gifts and yielded to persuasion. I can
remember a case myself from long ago. It's nothing new, but
we're all friends here. I'll tell you the story.

530   'The Curetes were fighting the warlike Aetolians at the town
of Calydon, and losses were heavy on both sides. The Aetolians
were defending their lovely town of Calydon, and
the Curetes doing all they could to sack it. The
trouble had been started by the goddess of the golden
throne Artemis. She had taken offence when lord Oeneus of
Calydon had failed to make her any harvest-offering on the
sacred hill in his estate. All the other gods enjoyed rich sacrifices;
it was only this daughter of great Zeus to whom he offered
nothing. Perhaps he forgot her, perhaps he did not intend to do
it – in either case, it was a seriously deluded act.

'In her rage, Artemis who delights in arrows launched at him
540   a foaming wild boar with flashing tusks, which settled down to
do much damage, ravaging Oeneus' orchards. It strewed the
ground with the tall trees it brought tumbling down, rooting
them up, fruit and all. But at last Oeneus' son Meleager killed
it. He had to raise huntsmen and hounds from many towns to
do this, since the beast was far too powerful to be dealt with by
just a few – even so, it still laid many of them on the sad funeral
pyre. But then Artemis started the hue and cry of battle over the
destination of the carcass: she set the Curetes and Aetolians at

The story of
Meleager

each other's throats over who should be awarded the prize of the beast's head and shaggy hide.

'In the war that ensued, as long as Meleager was in the 550 battlefield, things went badly for the Curetes who were unable to hold their ground outside Calydon's walls, for all their numbers. But many a sensible man at times finds his heart swelling with rage, and this is what happened to Meleager now. He got into a fury with his mother Althaea, withdrew from the fighting and stayed at home with his wife, lovely Cleopatra.

'(Cleopatra's mother was slim-ankled Marpessa, and her father was Idas, in his time the strongest man on earth. Phoebus Apollo once snatched Marpessa away, and Idas took on Apollo with his bow to defend his wife's honour. When she had been 560 seized by the Archer-god Apollo, Marpessa mourned as a king-fisher does its mate; and that is why, later, Marpessa and Idas had given Cleopatra the nickname Alcyone, kingfisher, because of her mother.)

'Anyway, Meleager took to his bed with Cleopatra and nursed his heart-rending anger. This anger had been caused by his mother Althaea's curses. Meleager had quarrelled with Althaea's brother, his uncle, over who should get the prize from the boar-hunt and killed him. So his mother in her grief had begged the gods to kill her son Meleager, falling on her knees, 570 deluging her lap with tears and beating the bountiful earth with her fists as she called on Hades and august Persephone. And the Fury that walks in the dark heard her from Hell, and his heart was implacable.

'So before long there arose the noise and commotion of the Curetes at the town gates, battering at the walls. And now the Aetolian elders supplicated Meleager to come out and fight. They sent him a deputation of the leading priests and promised him a great gift. They told him he could choose an estate of fifty acres for his own use, half vineland and half open ploughland, 580 to be carved out of the richest part of the lovely Calydonian plain. Again and again the old charioteer Oeneus prayed to Meleager. He stood on the threshold of his lofty bedroom and shook the solid wooden doors, imploring his son. Again and again his sisters and his lady mother supplicated him too, though

this only made him more obstinate. Again and again his com-
rades-in-arms tried, the dearest and most cherished friends he
had. Even so they could not win him over.

'But then the Curetes began scaling the walls and setting fire
to the great town, and the missiles started hailing down on
590 the bedroom itself. At that point, Meleager's well-girdled wife
Cleopatra supplicated him in tears. She pictured all the miseries
people suffer when their town is captured: they kill the men, fire
levels the town, the enemy carry off the children and low-girdled
women. Her recital of these disasters touched his heart, and he
came out and put on his gleaming armour. In this way, by
yielding to his personal feelings, he saved the Aetolians from
disaster. But the only result was that his friends gave him none
of the many splendid gifts they had earlier offered. He saved
them, but got nothing by it.

600 'Don't, I beg you, think as he did; don't, dear friend, let some
god make you follow his example. When the ships are already
on fire, it will be all the more difficult to save them. No; come
while gifts are still to be had, and the Greeks will treat you like
a god. If you plunge into the killing fields with no such gifts,
you will not be so respected, even though you turn defeat into
victory.'

Swift-footed Achilles replied to him and said:

'Olympian-bred Phoenix, my dear old friend; I
Achilles' reply
to Phoenix have no need of the Greeks' honour. I believe I am
honoured because Zeus decrees it so, and this will
610 keep me by my beaked ships as long as breath remains in my
body and strength in my limbs.

'And I tell you something else, and you bear it in mind. Don't
undermine my resolution with a display of weeping and wailing
designed to curry favour with Agamemnon. You must not side
with him, or I, who side with you, may come to hate you. Injure
the man who injures me – that's your duty, if you're with me;
and if you are, then come back and rule my dominions equally
with me, share all my privileges.

'These men will report back to the Greeks. Meanwhile,
you stay here yourself – there is a soft bed for you to sleep

on – and at daybreak we will decide whether to go home or not.'

He spoke, and quietly signalled to Patroclus with a move- 620
ment of his eyebrows to make up the bed for Phoenix, so
that the others might think of getting on their way as soon
as possible. Ajax, godlike son of Telamon, now spoke his
mind:

'Olympian-born son of Laertes, resourceful Odys-
seus, let's go. It seems to me our mission is doomed   Ajax's speech
to failure, this time at any rate. Bad as the news is, we must
report it at once to the Greeks, who are no doubt sitting up
waiting for us. Achilles has hardened his once noble heart and
become quite unreasonable – no thought for the affection of us, 630
his comrades, who held him in the highest regard in the whole
camp. And so obstinate! After all, even in cases of murder a
man accepts a blood-price for the death of a brother or a son.
And the killer does not even have to leave his country, if he
compensates the next of kin, since that compensation holds the
family's anger and injured feelings in check.

'But you, Achilles – the gods have worked you up into this
implacable fury over a girl, one, single girl. And here we are,
offering you seven of the very best and a great deal more besides.
Be gracious. Respect your obligations as our host. We are under 640
your roof, representing the whole Greek army, and we wish for
nothing better than to remain your closest and dearest friends
among all the Greeks.'

Swift-footed Achilles replied to him and said:

'Olympian-born Ajax, son of Telamon, leader of
men, I agree with pretty much everything you seem   Achilles' reply
to be saying. But my heart swells with anger when   to Ajax
I think of what happened and the disgraceful way in which
Agamemnon treated me in public, like some refugee who
counted for nothing.

'Go now and make my decision public. I shall not contemplate 650
bloodshed and warfare again until Hector reaches the huts
and ships of my Myrmidons, killing Greeks as he comes, and
destroys the ships by fire. However keen to attack he may be,

Hector will, I think, be halted when he reaches *my* huts and black ship.'

So he spoke, and each of them took up a two-handled cup, offered a libation and made their way back along the line of ships, with Odysseus at their head.

Patroclus told his men and the waiting-women to make up a
660 comfortable bed for Phoenix as soon as possible. When the women made up the bed as he had ordered with fleeces, a rug and a fine linen sheet, the old man lay down and waited for the coming of divine Dawn. Achilles himself slept in a corner of his well-built hut with a woman he had brought from Lesbos, fair-cheeked Diomede. Patroclus slept in the corner opposite. He too had a companion, fair-girdled Iphis, whom godlike Achilles had given him after capturing steep Scyros, Enyeus' town.

The envoys reached Agamemnon's huts and were no sooner
670 inside than the Greek lords leapt to their feet, drank to them in welcome from every side with golden cups and bombarded them with questions. Agamemnon lord of men was the first to speak:

'Tell me, celebrated Odysseus, great glory of the Greeks – will he save the ships from being burnt or does he refuse? Is that proud spirit of his still in the grip of his anger?'

All-daring godlike Odysseus replied:

Odysseus on
failed embassy
'Most glorious Agamemnon son of Atreus, lord of men, the man has no intention of extinguishing his rage. In fact he is angrier than ever. He rejects you
680 and your gifts. He says you can find out for yourself among the Greeks how to save the ships and men. Meanwhile he threatens to drag his own ships down to the sea at dawn. And he said he advised all the rest of us to sail for home as well: "You are never going to reach your goal in the steep streets of Ilium. Far-thundering Zeus has stretched out a protecting hand over that town, and its people have taken heart." Those were his words.

'Of my fellow envoys, Ajax and the two heralds, both sensible
690 men, are here to bear me out. But the old man Phoenix is sleeping there. Achilles pressed him to stay so that he could embark with

him for home in the morning if he wished to, though he said there would be no compulsion.'

So he spoke and was received in complete silence by them all. The bluntness of his words had taken them completely by surprise. For a long time they sat there, speechless and dejected. Eventually Diomedes, master of the battle-cry, spoke out:

'Most glorious Agamemnon son of Atreus, lord of men, you should never have supplicated matchless Achilles and made him such a lavish offer. He is an arrogant man at the best of times, and now you have merely reinforced that arrogance. Well, we'll   700
leave it to him whether he sails or stays. He'll fight again when his heart tells him to, and the god moves him.

'So I suggest we all do what I now propose. For the moment, go to bed – you have satisfied yourselves with the food and wine that a man needs to keep up his strength and courage. When lovely, rosy-fingered Dawn appears, you, Agamemnon, must deploy your infantry and chariots in front of the ships; you must inspire them; and you must fight in the front line yourself.'

So he spoke, and the leaders all shouted their approval,   710
delighted at the words of horse-taming Diomedes. They made their libations and retired to their several huts, where they lay down and took the gift of sleep.

DIOMEDES AND ODYSSEUS: THE NIGHT ATTACK

1–193: Agamemnon and Menelaus cannot sleep for worry about the Greek situation, so they call a council and check on the sentries.

194–298: At the council Nestor suggests a night spying mission on the *Trojan* camp. Diomedes and Odysseus volunteer.

299–468: *Hector* invites a *Trojan* to spy on the Greek camp: *Dolon* volunteers and sets off. Odysseus and Diomedes catch *Dolon*, milk him for information and kill him.

469–579: Odysseus and Diomedes slaughter the sleeping *Thracians* and their leader *Rhesus*, take his famous horses and return in triumph.

All the Greek leaders spent the rest of the night by the ships, wrapped in the soft arms of sleep. But Agamemnon son of Atreus, shepherd of the people, had too much on his mind for easeful rest.

As Zeus, husband of lovely-haired Hera, flashes lightning to herald a hailstorm, deluge or blizzard and mantle the fields with snow, or to open the gaping jaws of bitter war, so Agamemnon
10 uttered groan after groan from the depths of his being, and his heart trembled with fear. When he glanced out across the Trojan plain, he was amazed by the innumerable Trojan fires burning in front of Ilium, the music of their various reed-pipes and the voices of their troops. And when he looked at the Greek ships and his own army, he tore the hair from his head by the roots, appealing to Zeus in Olympus, and groaned loud in his great heart.

In the end he could think of nothing better than to go straight to Nestor son of Neleus in the hope that together they might hit on some unbeatable plan for saving the expedition from disaster. 20 So he got up, put on his tunic, bound a pair of fine sandals on his gleaming feet, threw over his shoulders the glossy pelt of a great tawny lion, which came down to his ankles, and picked up his spear.

Sleep did not come easily to Menelaus either. He too was obsessed by anxiety for the Greeks, who for his sake had come to Troy across a great expanse of water to start this audacious campaign. He threw a spotted leopard's skin round his broad shoulders, took up his bronze 30 helmet and put it on, picked up his spear in his great hand and set out to rouse his brother, lord of all the Greeks and honoured like a god by his people. He found him by the stern of his ship, slinging his fine armour on his shoulders. Agamemnon was delighted to see him; but Menelaus, master of the battle-cry, was the first to speak:

Menelaus' anxiety

'My dear brother, why are you arming like this? Are you sending a man out to spy on the Trojans? I am much afraid you won't find anyone willing to accept that duty. It would take a brave heart indeed to venture out alone through the immortal 40 night and spy on the enemy camp.'

Lord Agamemnon replied and said:

'Olympian-bred Menelaus, you and I need a plan, and a clever one, to protect and secure the Greeks and our ships, now that Zeus has turned against us. It's clear that Hector's offerings mean more to him than ours. That a single man – and no son of 50 the gods either – should do the damage in the course of a day that Hector has done to our army is something quite outside my experience. But the fact remains that he has struck us blows which we will feel to our cost for many a long day to come.

'But set off now past the ships and fetch Ajax and Idomeneus, while I go to godlike Nestor and tell him to get up. I want him to visit the guard-posts, which are so important, and keep the sentries on their toes. They will pay more attention to him than to anyone, since his own son and Idomeneus' attendant Meriones are in command. We put them in special charge.'

Menelaus, master of the battle-cry, replied: 60

'Very well, but what instructions do you have for me? Am I to stay with Ajax and Idomeneus and wait for you to join us? Or run back to you when I've given them their orders?'

Agamemnon lord of men replied:

'Stay with them, or you and I may miss each other among all the paths that cross the camp. And speak up to the men wherever you go. Tell them to remain on the alert, and mention their lineage and father's name. Compliment them all 70 and don't stand on ceremony. We too must do our part: Zeus seems to have decreed serious hardship for us at the moment of our birth.'

Nestor awakened

With these careful words of instruction Agamemnon dismissed his brother, and himself went in search of Nestor shepherd of the people. He found him lying on a soft bed beside his hut and black ship. At his side lay his ornate arms, a shield, two spears, and a shining helmet; also the glittering belt the old man put on when he armed himself to lead his men into the killing fields: for whatever the danger, he made 80 no concessions to wretched old age. Nestor, raising himself on his elbow and lifting his head, called out and challenged Agamemnon:

'Who goes there, wandering about the camp alone, close to the ships, at dead of night, when everyone else is asleep? Are you looking for a stray mule or one of your friends? Speak up, but stay where you are till you answer. What's your business here?'

Agamemnon lord of men replied:

'Nestor son of Neleus, great glory of the Greeks, you will recognize Agamemnon son of Atreus, the man Zeus has singled 90 out for unending trouble as long as breath remains in my body and strength in my limbs. I'm wandering about because I am much too worried about the war and our plight to enjoy a moment's sleep. I am so afraid for my people that my self-control has deserted me. I'm beside myself. My heart is leaping out of my chest, and my knees trembling.

'But you aren't sleeping any better than I am. If you want something to do, come with me and visit the sentries, to make sure they haven't fallen asleep from exhaustion and lack of rest,

forgetting all about their duties. The enemy are camped very 100
close, and we know nothing of their plans. They might even be
up for a night attack.'

Nestor the Gerenian charioteer replied:

'Most glorious Agamemnon lord of men, Zeus wise in counsel
is not going to let Hector realize all the high hopes he is presently
entertaining. On the contrary, I reckon Hector will have even
more to worry about than ever, if Achilles has a change of heart
and abandons his present unrelenting rage. Of course I will go
with you.

'But let us wake some of the others in their turn – Diomedes
the great spearman, Odysseus, swift-footed Ajax son of Oïleus 110
and strong Meges. Someone should also go and call up the other
two, godlike Ajax son of Telamon and lord Idomeneus, whose
ships are at the end of the line and some way off.

'But what's up with Menelaus? I like and respect him, but I
do feel critical of him, and won't hide my feelings, even if it
makes you angry. He should not be asleep at a time like this,
leaving all the work to you. He ought to have been up and doing
among all our leading men, entreating them to lend a hand. The
situation is desperate.'

Agamemnon lord of men said:

'Venerable sir, there are times when I would indeed be glad 120
to see you taking him to task. He is often inclined to do nothing
and let things slide, not through laziness or stupidity, but
because he looks to me to take the lead. Tonight, however, he
got up well before me and came to see me. I have already sent
him out to call up the two men you mentioned. So let's be going.
We shall find them with the sentries outside the gates, where I
told them to meet.'

Nestor the Gerenian charioteer replied:

'In that case, no one will have a word to say against him or
fail to pay attention when he takes command and urges them 130
on.'

With these words he got into his tunic and bound a pair of
fine sandals on his gleaming feet. Next he put on a purple cloak
and fastened it with a brooch – it was a long double-folding
cloak with a thick nap on the wool. Finally he picked up a strong

spear with a sharp point of bronze, and set out on his way past the ships of the bronze-armoured Greeks.

The first man that Nestor the Gerenian charioteer woke up was Odysseus, equal in invention to Zeus. He gave him a call 140 and, as soon as he heard it, Odysseus came out of his hut and questioned his visitors:

Other Greeks roused

'Why are you wandering about on your own through the men's huts and the ships at this time of night? What brings you here? It must be something serious.'

Nestor the Gerenian charioteer replied:

'Olympian-born son of Laertes, resourceful Odysseus, don't be annoyed with us. The Greeks are indeed in serious trouble. But come along with us, and let's wake up some of the others we ought to consult before deciding whether to leave or fight on.'

So he spoke, and quick-thinking Odysseus went into his hut, slung his ornate shield on his back and followed them. They 150 went next to Diomedes son of Tydeus and found him lying there, some way outside his hut, with his armour. His men were sleeping round him with their shields for pillows. The spiked butt-ends of their spears were stuck in the ground, and the bronze points flashed in the distance like lightning from Father Zeus. The warrior was asleep, with the hide of a farmyard ox underneath him and a glossy rug drawn under his head. Nestor the Gerenian charioteer went up to him, gave him a kick, woke him up and said jokingly:

'Wake up, son of Tydeus! Why are you sleeping in luxury all 160 night long? Has it escaped your notice that the Trojans are camped out near our ships on the high ground just above us, and virtually nothing separates us?'

So he spoke, and Diomedes, who had woken and leapt up at great speed, spoke winged words:

'You're a tough one, my old fellow. Always on the go. Haven't we got any younger men to do the rounds and wake up all the leaders? You're quite impossible, old man.'

Nestor the Gerenian charioteer said:

170   'My friend, all that is very true. I have my handsome sons and

plenty of troops to do the rounds and call people up. But we are in a critical position, on a razor's edge – an unpleasant death for every Greek, or else deliverance. However, if you are feeling sorry for me – and you *are* the younger man – go yourself and wake up Meges and swift-footed Ajax son of Oïleus.'

So he spoke, and Diomedes threw round his shoulders the glossy skin of a great lion, which reached to his feet, picked up his spear and went on his way. When he roused the two men from their huts, he brought them along with him.

The party then visited the guards at their posts, but failed to catch any of their leaders asleep. They were all sitting there with their weapons, on the alert. As dogs keep uneasy watch over their flocks in a farmyard, having heard some savage animal coming down from the mountains into a wood and the hue and cry of men and hounds behind it, and all thoughts of sleep are banished, so sweet sleep was banished from the eyes of the sentries as they kept watch throughout that unfriendly night. All their attention was turned towards the plain to catch the first sign of any Trojan movement.

Old Nestor was delighted to see them like this, encouraged them and spoke winged words:

'That's the way, lads. Carry on. Let no one take a nap, or we'll give the enemy something to cheer about.'

With these words he crossed the ditch, followed by the Greek leaders who had been summoned to the council. Meriones and Nestor's noble son Thrasymedes came with them too, having been invited to assist at the conference. Leaving the ditch behind them, they sat down in an open place where the ground was clear of bodies. It was the very spot where imperious Hector had turned back from slaughtering the Greeks when night descended on the battlefield. Seated there, they started to exchange ideas. Nestor the Gerenian charioteer began and spoke his mind:

'My friends, couldn't someone with enough daring and confidence pay these arrogant Trojans a visit, on the chance of cutting off a straggler from the enemy? He might even overhear some talk about their intentions, and so find out whether they mean to stay in their

Nestor proposes a night sortie (8.491)

210 advanced position by our ships or retreat back into town, after inflicting this defeat on the Greeks. If he discovered that and returned in one piece, his fame would spread world-wide. He'll be splendidly rewarded too. Every ship's commander will give him a black ewe with its suckling lamb, a reward second to none, and he will be invited to all their dinners and ceremonial feasts.'

So he spoke and was received in complete silence by them all. Then Diomedes, master of the battle-cry, addressed them:

220 'Nestor, this adventure appeals to me. The Trojan camp isn't far off either. I'll visit it. But if someone else came with me, I'd feel more comfortable and also more inclined to take a risk. When men work in pairs, one sees advantages the other would miss, while a man on his own may see the possibilities, but lack the necessary imagination and intelligence.'

So Diomedes spoke, and many volunteered to go with him. Both the Ajaxes, attendants of Ares, wished to go. So did Meriones; and Nestor's son Thrasymedes was eager. The famous
230 spearman Menelaus also volunteered; and daring Odysseus also wanted to steal in among the Trojan troops – adventure was always dear to him. Agamemnon lord of men now addressed them:

'Diomedes son of Tydeus, my pride and joy, pick the companion you want, the very best of the volunteers. There are plenty of them. Don't let undue deference make you leave the better man and take the worse out of respect for his birth, not even if he is of higher rank.'

240 So he spoke, in terror for his brother auburn-haired Menelaus. Diomedes, master of the battle-cry, then addressed them:

Diomedes and Odysseus volunteer

'If you really are instructing me to choose my companion myself, how could I overlook godlike Odysseus, who puts a willing heart and soul into everything he does, and Pallas Athene loves him too? With this man beside me, we could go through blazing fire and still get back. His intelligence is without equal.'

All-daring godlike Odysseus said:

'Diomedes, don't sing my praises – or faults. You are talking
250 to men who know all this already. Let's be off. The night is well

advanced – it's nearly dawn. The stars are past their zenith, and a good two-thirds of the night is gone, leaving us the third watch only.'

With these words they slung on their formidable gear. The Resolute Thrasymedes gave Diomedes a two-edged sword, as he had left his own behind beside his ship, together with a shield. On his head he put an oxhide helmet without cheek-plates or crest, of the sort called 'skull-cap', which young men wear to protect their heads.

Meriones gave Odysseus a bow, a quiver and a sword, and put a cleverly made leather helmet on his head. On the inside there was a strong lining of interwoven straps, onto which a felt cap had been sewn in. The outside was cleverly adorned all round with rows of white tusks from a shiny-toothed boar, the tusks running in alternate directions in each row. This helmet originally came from Eleon where Autolycus stole it from Amyntor by breaking into his well-protected house. Autolycus gave it to Amphidamas of Cythera to take to Scandaea; and Amphidamas gave it to Molus in return for hospitality. Molus, in his turn, gave it to his son Meriones to wear, and now it was Odysseus' head that it served to protect.

Armed in this formidable manner the pair set out, leaving all the chieftains there. Pallas Athene sent them a lucky omen, a heron close to their path on the right. The night was too dark for them to see the bird, but they heard it squawk and Odysseus, pleased by the omen, offered a prayer to Athene:

They arm and pray to ATHENE

'Hear me, daughter of Zeus who drives the storm-cloud, you that stand by me in all my adventures and never forget me when I go into action. Tonight, Athene, show me your special favour, and grant that we come back to the ships with some great deed to our credit, which will give the Trojans something to think about.'

Diomedes, master of the battle-cry, followed him with a prayer of his own:

'Daughter of Zeus, Atrytone, hear me also. Be with me as you were with my godlike father, Tydeus, when he went into Thebes as ambassador for the Greeks, leaving their army on the banks

of the Asopus. He went there with an offer of peace for the
Thebans; but on his way back he performed heroics, seeing off
290 their ambush in which you helped him, celestial goddess, with
your keen support. Stand willingly by me now and watch over
me, and in return you shall have from me a year-old heifer,
broad in the brow, which has never worked or been led under
the yoke. She will be sacrificed to you with gold leaf round her
horns.'

So they prayed; and Pallas Athene heard them. When their
prayers to the daughter of great Zeus were finished, they set out
through the black night like a pair of lions, picking their way
through the slaughter, the bodies, the armour and the black
blood.

300 Hector did not allow the proud Trojans much time to sleep
either. He called together all the leading men, their
Dolon vol-
unteers for
rulers and leaders and, when he had gathered them
round him, put a carefully considered plan to them:
Hector's night
raid
'Will anyone take on and see through this job I
have in mind? There will be a rich reward, which I
can guarantee. I will give the best chariot and pair of thorough-
breds in the Greek camp to the man who dares – it will mean
glory for him – to approach their ships and find out whether
310 they are guarded as usual or whether, as a result of their defeat
at our hands, they are already discussing the possibility of flight,
and are so utterly exhausted that they are not troubling to keep
watch during the night.'

So he spoke and was received in complete silence by them all.
But among the Trojans present was the son of the sacred herald
Eumedes, Dolon, a rich man with plenty of gold and bronze.
His appearance was certainly unattractive, but he was fast on
his feet; and in a family of six he was the only son. This man
then spoke his mind to Hector and the Trojans:

'Hector, the adventure appeals to me. I volunteer to ap-
320 proach the Greek ships and find out the situation. But first, will
you hold up this staff and swear to give me the horses and
bronze-inlaid chariot that matchless Achilles drives? I shan't be
useless as a spy, or fall below your expectations. I mean to go ·
right through the camp till I come to Agamemnon's ship, where

I assume their leaders will be discussing whether to retreat or fight on.'

So he spoke, and Hector took the staff in his hands and gave Dolon his oath:

'Let Zeus himself, loud-thundering husband of Hera, hear me swear that no other Trojan shall ride behind those horses, and   330
you will pride yourself on them for the rest of your days.'

So he spoke, swore an oath that was not to be fulfilled, and sent him on his way. Dolon at once slung his curved bow on his shoulders, threw the pelt of a grey wolf over it, put a weasel-skin cap on his head and, picking up a sharp spear, set out from the camp in the direction of the ships. Not that he was destined to come back from them with news for Hector. However, once he had put behind him the crowds of horses and men in the camp, he sped keenly on his way.

Olympian-born Odysseus saw him coming towards them and   340
said to Diomedes:

'Here comes a man from the enemy camp, Dio-   *Dolon* caught
medes, maybe to spy on our ships, or strip some of   and questioned
the bodies – I can't say which. Let's wait for him to
get past us a little. Then we leap out and grab him. If he's too fast for us, menace him with your spear and force him all the time towards our ships and away from his camp, so that he can't slip back into Ilium.'

With these words they turned off and lay down among the dead beside the path. Dolon in complete ignorance passed by   350
them at a run. When he was as far ahead as the width of a day's ploughing by mules (and they are better than oxen at dragging a jointed plough through the deep soil), the two men gave chase. Dolon stopped when he heard the footsteps behind him, imagining they were friends coming from the Trojans to turn him back because Hector had changed his orders. But when they were less than a spear's throw away, he saw they were the enemy and sprinted off in flight.

They were after him in a flash. As a couple of experienced,   360
sharp-toothed hunting dogs relentlessly pursue a fawn or hare flying before them through wooded country and screaming as it goes, so Diomedes and Odysseus sacker of cities relentlessly

chased down their man, heading him off from his own side. In fact, escaping as he was towards the Greek ships, Dolon was just about to run into the sentries when Athene gave Diomedes an extra turn of speed so that no Greek could boast he had hit Dolon before Diomedes could get him. Threatening him with his spear, mighty Diomedes spoke:

370 'Stop, or you get it with my spear; and then I don't think you'll have long to live.'

He spoke and threw, but deliberately missed the man. The head of the polished spear passed over his right shoulder and stuck in the ground. Dolon came to a halt, terrified, stuttering, his teeth chattering, white with fear. His two pursuers came panting up and pinned him by the arms. He burst into tears and said:

'Take me alive, and I will pay my own ransom. I have bronze
380 and gold and wrought iron at home. My father would offer you an immense ransom from it if he heard I had been taken back to the Greek ships alive.'

Quick-thinking Odysseus replied and said:

'Pull yourself together, man, and don't worry about dying. Now answer my questions and tell me exactly. Where are you off to, leaving your camp like this and coming to our ships, alone, at the dead of the night, when everyone else is asleep? Was it to strip some of the dead? Or did Hector send you, to spy around our ships? Or was it your own initiative?'

390 Trembling, Dolon replied:

'I was a fool – Hector deluded me, against my better judge-ment, by promising me the horses and bronze-inlaid chariot of noble Achilles. He wanted me to make my way through the dark into enemy territory and find out whether the ships were guarded as usual, or whether, as a result of your defeat at our hands, the Greeks were already discussing the possibility of flight and were so utterly exhausted that they weren't troubling to keep watch through the night.'

400 Quick-thinking Odysseus smiled and replied:

'So you were after the big prize, were you, the horses of warlike Achilles! But they are hard to master and difficult to drive, at any rate for a mere man, or anyone but Achilles, whose mother is a goddess. Now answer my questions and tell me exactly. Where did you leave Hector, shepherd of the people, when you came here just now? Where is his equipment lying? Where are his horses? How are the Trojans' sentries disposed, and where are the rest of them sleeping? And what are they planning to do next? Do they mean to stay in their advanced position by our ships, or retreat back into the town after inflicting this defeat on the Greeks?' 410

Dolon son of Eumedes replied:

'I'll answer all your questions exactly. First, Hector is conferring with his advisers by the grave-mound of the divine Ilus, away from all the noise. As for your question about the sentries, sir, no special guard was mounted to watch the camp or keep a lookout. The Trojans have their watch-fires, and the men detailed for duty stay awake and encourage each other to keep alert. Our various allies are asleep. They leave it to us to keep watch: *their* women and children aren't lying close at hand.' 420

Quick-thinking Odysseus replied and said:

'How do you mean? Are your allies sleeping in the same parts of the camp as the horse-taming Trojans, or somewhere else? Be precise: I want to know.'

Dolon son of Eumedes replied:

'I'll answer all your questions exactly. The Carians and the Paeonians with their crooked bows are over by the sea, with the Leleges, the Caucones and the godlike Pelasgi. The Lycians, the lordly Mysians, the Phrygians who fight on horseback and the Maeonian charioteers were assigned ground in the direction of Thymbra. *Dolon's disclosure and death* 430

'But why ask for all these details? If your idea is to infiltrate the Trojan camp, there are the Thracians over there: they have just arrived and are way off at the very end of the line. Rhesus their lord is with them. That man has the loveliest and biggest horses I have ever seen. They are whiter than snow and run like the wind. His chariot is beautifully finished with gold and silver, and he has brought some awe-inspiring pieces of golden armour with him too, a fantastic sight. Men really shouldn't wear such things; they are fit only for the immortal gods. 440

'But now take me to your ships, or tie me up tight and leave me here. You can then can go and check whether I've told you the truth or not.'

Mighty Diomedes gave him a black look and replied:

'Dolon, you have given us excellent news, but don't imagine you're going to get away, now that you have fallen into our
450 hands. If we ransom you now or let you go, you will return to the Greek ships some other time, either to spy or meet us in open fight. But if I take you and kill you, you will never be a nuisance to the Greeks again.'

He spoke, and Dolon, raising his great hand, was just about to touch his captor's chin in supplication when Diomedes slashed at him with his sword and caught him full on the neck. He cut through both sinews, and Dolon's head met the dust while he was still speaking. They took the weasel-skin cap from his head and stripped him of his wolf's pelt, his curved bow and
460 long spear. Then godlike Odysseus held up the trophies in his hand for Athene, goddess of spoils, to see, and spoke in prayer to her:

'Let these gladden your heart, goddess, since we shall again call on you for help before any other immortal in Olympus. Help us now in our raid on the sleeping Thracians and their horses.'

So he spoke, raised the bundle clear of his head and placed it high up in a tamarisk bush. Then he gathered a handful of reeds and fresh tamarisk twigs to mark the spot clearly, so that they should not miss it when they came back through the darkness of the night.

The two now went ahead, threading their way through the
470 armour and black blood, and before long reached the Thracian contingent. The men were asleep, tired out by their exertions, and their fine equipment was neatly piled in three rows on the ground beside them. A pair of horses stood by each man. Rhesus slept in the centre, with his swift horses beside him tied by the reins to the end of the chariot-rail. Odysseus saw him first and pointed him out to Diomedes:

'That's our man, Diomedes, and there are the horses men-tioned by Dolon, the man we killed. Now put that tremendous
480 strength of yours about. No time to stand about fiddling with

your weapons. Quick! Get the horses clear! Or you kill the men, and I'll see to the horses.'

So Odysseus spoke, and grey-eyed Athene breathed strength into Diomedes, who laid about him with his sword, this way and that. Hideous groans rose from the dying men, and the earth ran red with blood. Like a lion that has found some untended sheep or goats and leaps on them with murder in its heart, so Diomedes son of Tydeus dealt with the Thracians.

Rhesus' horses stolen

He slaughtered twelve of them and, as he came to each and put him to the sword, quick-thinking Odysseus seized the body by the foot from behind and dragged it out. His purpose was to leave the way clear for the lovely-maned horses, who were unaccustomed to their new masters and might be frightened if they trod on a body. Then Diomedes came upon lord Rhesus, the thirteenth victim he robbed of his sweet life, breath gasping out of him. An evil dream had come to stand over him that night – Diomedes son of Tydeus, through the planning of Athene.

490

Meanwhile all-daring Odysseus unfastened the horses from the chariot, tied them together with straps and galloped them out of the crowded space with a lash of his bow, since it had not occurred to him to pick up the shining whip that had lain in the ornate chariot. Directly he was clear, he gave a whistle, to let godlike Diomedes know.

500

But Diomedes was in no hurry, wondering what was the most daring thing he could do next – get hold of the chariot where the ornamented armour lay and drag it out by the shaft? Hoist it up and carry it off? Kill more Thracians? These thoughts were racing through his mind when Athene came up to him and said:

'Son of great-hearted Tydeus, think about getting home to the hollow ships, or you may reach them in full flight. Some other god might wake the Trojans.'

510

So she spoke, and Diomedes, recognizing the voice of the goddess, mounted at once. Odysseus struck the horses with his bow, and off they flew to the Greek ships.

None of this had escaped the watchful eye of Apollo lord of the silver bow. When he saw how Athene was dancing attendance on Diomedes, he was enraged with her and descended on

the great Trojan army, where he roused one of the Thracian advisers, Hippocoön, a brave kinsman of Rhesus. Hippocoön
520 leapt up from sleep and, when he saw the empty places where the horses had been standing and men gasping out their lives in hideous carnage, he shrieked and called on his dear companion by name. Utter chaos ensued as shouting Trojans came running to gaze, appalled, on the terrible things the two men had done before escaping back to the hollow ships.

Diomedes and Odysseus return triumphant
When Odysseus and Diomedes reached the spot where they had killed Hector's spy, Odysseus dear to Zeus pulled up their swift horses, and Diomedes jumped down and handed up the bloodstained arms to him. Then he mounted again and lashed the horses
530 with the whip. The willing pair flew off towards the hollow ships, eager to reach their journey's end.

Nestor was the first to hear hoof-beats and said:

'My friends, rulers and leaders of the Greeks, can I be mistaken, or am I right? I must speak up – the sound of racing horses came to my ears. If only Odysseus and mighty Diomedes were to be driving some fine horses at speed here from the Trojan camp! But I am terribly afraid the Trojans are on the warpath, and our two best men are in trouble.'

540 The last words were hardly out of his mouth when the two arrived. They jumped down to the ground, and were welcomed by their friends with much shaking of hands and many exclamations of delight. Nestor the Gerenian charioteer was first to question them:

'Tell me, celebrated Odysseus, great glory of the Greeks, how did you get hold of these horses? By infiltrating the Trojan camp, or did some god meet you on the way and make you a present of them? They shine like the rays of the sun. I am always meeting the Trojans in battle – in fact I can claim that I never stay behind by the ships, old as I am for a fighting man – but I have never
550 seen or imagined horses like these. I think you met a god, and he gave them to you. Zeus who marshals the clouds is very fond of you both, and so is his daughter, grey-eyed Athene.'

Quick-thinking Odysseus replied and said:

'Nestor son of Neleus, great glory of the Greeks, the gods

have greater powers than men and, if one of them wished to make us a present, he could easily produce an even finer pair. But to answer your question, venerable sir, these horses have only just arrived, and they are Thracian. Brave Diomedes killed their master and the twelve best men in the contingent beside   560
him. The thirteenth man (beside Rhesus) was the spy we caught near the ships, sent to reconnoitre our camp by Hector and the rest of the noble Trojans.'

With these words he drove the horses across the ditch, laughing, and the other Greeks followed him, exultant. When they reached Diomedes' well-built hut, they tied the pair up with leather straps at the mangers where Diomedes' own swift horses stood munching their honey-sweet barley. Odysseus put Dolon's bloodstained equipment in the stern of his ship, until they could   570
prepare their sacrifice to Athene.

Then they waded into the sea to wash the sweat from their shins, neck and thighs. When the waves had removed the sweat from their bodies and they felt refreshed, they went and bathed themselves in polished baths. Then, after washing and covering themselves liberally with olive-oil, they sat down to eat, and from a full mixing-bowl drew off sweet wine and poured libations to Athene.

11

ACHILLES TAKES
NOTICE

1–83: [26th day: third day of combat] Agamemnon arms for battle. All the gods except STRIFE stay away, while ZEUS watches from Olympus.

84–180: Agamemnon enjoys success, and the *Trojans* retreat.

181–283: ZEUS descends to *Mount Ida* and tells *Hector* to re-join the battle when Agamemnon is wounded. This happens, and Agamemnon leaves the field.

284–342: *Hector* enters the battle successfully, but Odysseus and Diomedes fight back.

343–400: Diomedes stuns *Hector*, who retreats and recovers. But *Paris* shoots Diomedes in the foot. Diomedes leaves the field.

401–97: Odysseus, now stranded, fights back, but is wounded. Ajax and Menelaus rescue him. Ajax storms forward.

497–598: *Paris* wounds the Greek doctor Machaon; Nestor takes him back to the ships. Ajax slowly retreats before *Hector* and is helped by Eurypylus, but *Paris* shoots Eurypylus in the thigh. The Greek defence rallies.

599–803: Achilles sees Nestor conveying Machaon from the field and sends Patroclus to find out what is going on. Nestor tells Patroclus a long story about his (Nestor's) youthful exploits – a revenge raid against the Eleans, defeat of the Elean counter-attack and Menoetius' advice to Patroclus. Nestor urges Patroclus to get permission to return to the fighting himself, in Achilles' armour.

804–48: Patroclus helps the wounded Eurypylus.

When Dawn had risen from the bed where she sleeps with noble Tithonus to bring daylight to the immortals and to men, Zeus sent down cruel Strife to the Greek ships with the emblem of battle in her hands. She took her stand on the bulging black hull of Odysseus' ship. This stood in the centre of the line, so that a shout would carry to either end, to the huts of Ajax son of Telamon or those of Achilles. Both these had had confidence enough in their own bravery and strength to draw up their ships on the extreme flanks. Standing there the goddess uttered her great and terrible war-cry, filling the heart of every Greek with mighty courage to do battle and fight the enemy relentlessly. At once the prospect of battle became sweeter to them than returning in their hollow ships to the land of their fathers.

Agamemnon shouted orders to his troops to prepare for battle and himself put on his gleaming bronze armour. First he placed fine leg-guards on his shins, fitted with silver ankle-clips. Then he put on body-armour that Cinyras had once presented to him as a gift of friendship. News had reached Cinyras in Cyprus of the great Greek expedition that was about to sail for Troy, and he had sent this body-armour to gratify its leader. It was made of strips, ten of dark-blue inlay, twelve of gold, and twenty of tin. On either side three dark-blue snakes rose up towards the opening for the neck, looking like the rainbow that Zeus fixes on a cloud as a portent to mankind below.

[Day 26, third combat day]

Agamemnon arms

Next Agamemnon slung his sword over his shoulder. Gold rivets glittered on the hilt but the sheath was of silver, with gold rings for attaching to its shoulder-strap. Then he took up his lively, man-covering shield, a superbly decorated piece, with its ten concentric rings of bronze and twenty white studs of tin circling a dark inlaid boss in the middle. A horrible Gorgon's head with fearsome eyes was set like a wreath round the centre and, on either side of that, Panic and Rout were depicted. It was fitted with a silver-decorated shoulder-strap, round which a writhing snake of blue inlay twisted, in different directions, the three heads that grew from its single neck.

On his head Agamemnon placed a helmet with metal plates on either side, four ridges and horsehair crest: the plume nodded frighteningly from the top. Finally he picked up a pair of strong, sharp bronze-headed spears. Beams from the bronze armour he

wore flashed into the distant sky, and Athene and Hera thun-
dered in answer, glorifying Agamemnon lord of golden
Mycenae.

The warriors each left their chariots in their drivers' charge
with instructions to draw them up in proper order on the outer
side of the ditch, while they themselves hurried forward across
50   the ditch in their full equipment. The tumult of battle filled the
air that early morning. They formed their line along the ditch
some time before their drivers, though these were only a little
way behind them. But Zeus son of Cronus fanned dire confusion
among them and from the upper air released showers of blood,
since he intended to send many mighty souls to Hades.

On their side too the Trojans lined up on the high ground of
the plain, round great Hector, matchless Polydamas, Aeneas,
whom the Trojan people honoured like a god, and Antenor's
60   three sons, Polybus, godlike Agenor and young Acamas looking
like the immortals. Hector was in the front ranks carrying his
circular shield. Like a menacing star that at one moment can be
seen shining out from behind the clouds, and the next moment
sinks behind them into shadow, so Hector was seen, now in the
front ranks, now in the rear, spurring them on. His bronze
armour flashed like the lightning that comes from Father Zeus
who drives the storm-cloud.

And now, like reapers who, starting from opposite
sides of a rich man's field, drive swathes through his
wheat or barley, and the handfuls of cut ears keep
on falling, so the Trojans and Greeks leapt at each
70   other and started the killing. Neither side contemplated fatal
flight. The confrontation brought them head to head, and they
charged in like wolves.

Strife who deals in sorrow rejoiced when she saw them. She
was the only one of the gods to witness this action. The rest
were not on the battlefield but sitting at home uninvolved, each
in his lovely house built on the folds of Olympus. They were all
at loggerheads with Zeus who darkens the clouds, because he
80   wished to give the Trojans the glory. But Father Zeus cared
nothing for the gods. He had slipped away from them and sat
down on his own a long way off, exulting in his glory, and

Battle joined;
the gods stay
clear (8.10)

looking down on the Trojan town and the Greek ships, on the
flashing bronze, the killers and the killed.

Right through the morning, while the blessed light of day
grew stronger, volley and counter-volley found their mark and
men kept falling. But about the time that a woodman prepares
a mid-morning meal in a mountain dell and, his arms weary
from felling the tall trees, feels he has done enough and yields
to the thought of delicious food, at that time the Greeks, calling   90
to their companions across the ranks, summoned up their cour-
age and broke the enemy lines.

Agamemnon was first to charge in and killed the
Trojan Bienor, shepherd of the people, and after him   Agamemnon
his comrade and charioteer Oïleus. Oïleus had leapt   kills six
down from his chariot to oppose him. But as he   Trojans
moved in to the attack, Agamemnon stabbed him in the forehead
with his sharp spear. The heavy bronze helmet failed to stop the
spear, and it pierced both the metal and the bone and spattered
all the inside of the helmet with his brains. So he ended Oïleus'
assault.

Agamemnon, after stripping off their tunics, left the dead men
there, chests gleaming, and went on to kill Isus and Antiphus,   100
two sons of Priam, one a bastard and the other legitimate, both
in the one chariot. The bastard Isus was driving it; excellent
Antiphus was beside him. This pair had been caught before by
Achilles as they shepherded their flocks on the spurs of Ida. He
had tied them up with willow-shoots, but afterwards accepted
ransom and released them. And now they met wide-ruling
Agamemnon. He hit Isus with his spear above the nipple on his
chest; he struck Antiphus beside the ear with his sword and
hurled him out of the chariot. Then with all speed he stripped   110
the splendid armour from the pair, recognizing them as he
did so: he had seen them before by his own swift ships when
swift-footed Achilles had brought them in from Mount Ida.

As a lion easily crunches up the little fawns of a speedy doe,
breaking into her lair and seizing them in his powerful jaws and
robbing them of their tender life; even if the doe is close at hand,
she cannot help them: she is terrified herself and off she flies,
crashing through the forest undergrowth and sweating in her

120 haste to save herself from the powerful beast's attack – so the
Trojans could not save these two from destruction, but were
themselves in flight from the Greeks.

Agamemnon next attacked Peisander and resolute Hippo-
lochus, sons of warlike Antimachus. He, hoping for splendid
bribes of gold from Paris, had dissuaded the Trojans from
returning Helen to Menelaus. But now it was his two sons that
were captured by lord Agamemnon. They were in one chariot
and were trying to control their swift horses. But the horses
were in confusion, since the gleaming reins had slipped from the
130 charioteers' hands. Agamemnon sprang at them like a lion, and
without even dismounting they appealed to him:

'Son of Atreus, take us alive and you will get a ransom that
will be well worth it. Antimachus our father is rich. He has
plenty of treasure in his house, bronze and gold and wrought
iron. He would offer you an immense ransom if he heard we
had been taken back to the Greek ships alive.'

So, tearfully, they addressed Agamemnon with pitiful words.
But there was no pity in the voice that answered them:

'If you two are sons of warlike Antimachus, he is the man
who once argued in the Trojan assembly that Menelaus, who
140 had come there on an embassy with godlike Odysseus, should
be killed on the spot and not allowed to return to Greece. You
shall now pay for your father's disgraceful insult.'

He spoke and hitting Peisander in the chest with his spear
knocked him out of the chariot and pushed him to the ground,
flat on his back. Hippolochus leapt down from the chariot, but
Agamemnon killed him on the ground. He slashed off his arms
and head with his sword and sent the trunk rolling like a log
through the crowd.

Agamemnon now left the two there and charged in where the
fighting was at its most confused, backed by the rest of the
150 Greek men-at-arms. Foot-soldiers and charioteers forced their
opposite numbers to run and slaughtered them with their spears,
while from the ground the dust rose, kicked up by the horses'
thundering hooves. And all the while lord Agamemnon, shout-
ing to the Greeks, followed up and killed.

As a raging fire attacks a thickly wooded forest; a billowing wind blows the flames back and forth, and uprooted bushes fall headlong before the fire's onslaught – so the routed Trojans were mown down by Agamemnon's onslaught. Many a pair of horses tossed their heads and rattled their empty chariots down the lines of battle, missing their charioteers who lay sprawled on the ground, far more enticing to the vultures than to their wives.

Zeus kept Hector away from the flying missiles, the dust, the slaughter, the blood and the mayhem, and Agamemnon continued his chase, calling out loud to the Greeks. The Trojans swept back over the middle of the plain, past the grave-mound made in olden days for Ilus son of Dardanus and past the wild fig-tree, making for the town. Yelling, Agamemnon stayed hot in pursuit, spattering his invincible hands with gore.

Trojans routed; IRIS rallies Hector

But when the Trojans reached the Scaean gate and the oak-tree, they came to a halt and waited there for the others. These were still flying in panic over the open plain, like cattle when a lion stampedes a herd at dusk, and sudden death comes to a solitary heifer: it seizes her, breaks her neck with its powerful jaws and then devours her blood and entrails – so lord Agamemnon pursued them, always killing the hindmost, and they fled in panic. Many a charioteer was toppled out of his chariot by him, face-first or on his back, such was his raging onslaught with the spear.

He had almost reached the town and its steep walls, when the Father of men and gods descended from the skies to take up position on the heights of Mount Ida with its many springs. He had a thunderbolt in his hands and sent off golden-winged Iris with a message:

'Off with you, swift Iris, and give Hector this message from me. As long as he sees Agamemnon, shepherd of the people, storming along the front line and mowing down the Trojan ranks, let him give ground, but tell his men to continue battling it out in the thick of the action with the enemy. But directly Agamemnon is hit by a spear or arrow and takes to his chariot, then I will give Hector strength to kill until he reaches the well-benched ships, the sun sets and blessed darkness intervenes.'

So he spoke, and swift Iris, quick as the wind, complied. She
sped down from the peaks of Mount Ida to sacred Ilium. There
she found godlike Hector, son of wise Priam, standing in his
finely built chariot with its horses. Swift-footed Iris went up to
him and said:

200   'Hector son of Priam, equal in wisdom to Zeus, Father Zeus
has sent me down to deliver his word to you. As long as you see
Agamemnon, shepherd of the people, storming along the front
line and mowing down the Trojan ranks, give ground but tell
your men to continue battling it out in the thick of the action
with the enemy. But directly Agamemnon is hit by a spear or
arrow and takes to his chariot, then he will give you strength to
kill until you reach the well-benched ships, the sun sets and
blessed darkness intervenes.'

210   With these words swift-footed Iris withdrew. Fully armed,
Hector immediately leapt from his chariot to the ground and,
brandishing a pair of sharp spears, went everywhere among his
men, urging them to fight and rousing their spirit for grim battle.
As a result the Trojans turned and faced the Greeks, but the
Greeks on their side reinforced their ranks. Thus the battle was
set, the two armies faced each other, and Agamemnon, eager to
lead the fighting from the front, was the first to leap on the enemy.

     Tell me now, you Muses that have your home on Olympus,
220 who was the first of the Trojans or their famous allies to face
Agamemnon?

           Agamem-   It was Iphidamas son of Trojan Antenor, tall and
           non kills   handsome, who had been brought up in the fertile
           Iphidamas   country of Thrace, mother of sheep. His grandfather
                            Cisses, father of his mother fair-cheeked Theano,
had raised him from infancy in his own palace and, when
Iphidamas reached the stage of youthful ambition, had done his
best to keep him at home by offering him his daughter's hand.
But Iphidamas had no sooner married her than he left the bridal
chamber in pursuit of glory against the Greeks. He sailed with
twelve beaked ships, left them in harbour at Percote and himself
230 reached Ilium on foot. This was the man who now confronted
Agamemnon son of Atreus.

     When they had come within range of each other, Agamemnon

missed with his spear, and it flew wide. Iphidamas stabbed Agamemnon on the belt under his body-armour and threw the whole weight of his body into it, keeping a firm grip on the spear. But he failed to pierce the glittering belt: when his spear-point met the silver, it bent like a bit of lead. Wide-ruling Agamemnon got his hand on the shaft and, pulling it towards him with the fury of a lion, dragged it out of the man's grasp. Then with his sword he hit him on the neck and brought him down.   240

So there Iphidamas fell, to sleep the unbreakable sleep – a pitiable end, helping his fellow Trojans, far from his wife, the new bride from whom he had had no joy, though he had given so much for her. He had already handed over a hundred head of cattle and promised a thousand more sheep and goats from his countless flocks. And now Agamemnon son of Atreus stripped his body and went off with his splendid armour into the Greek ranks.

When admirable Coön, Antenor's eldest son, realized what had happened, grief for his fallen brother blinded him, and 250 he came up side-on, unnoticed by godlike Agamem- non, and struck him below the elbow in the middle of the forearm. The glittering spear-point went right on through. Agamemnon lord of men convulsed; but, far from giving up the fight and withdrawing, he charged at Coön, bran- dishing his weathered spear. Coön had got hold of Iphidamas' foot and was hurriedly dragging his brother into the crowd, calling on all the best men to help. As he did so, Agamemnon stabbed him with his bronze spear under his bossed shield and 260 brought him down. Then he went up to him and cut his head off over the body of Iphidamas. So at the hands of lord Agamemnon these sons of Antenor fulfilled their destiny and went down to the house of Hades.

Agamemnon is wounded

As long as the warm blood was still welling up from his injury, Agamemnon continued to harry the enemy ranks with spear, sword and boulders. But when the blood stopped flowing and the wound began to dry, he felt stabbing pains. As sharp pangs seize a woman in child- birth, the bitter pangs that are sent by the Eileithyiae, goddesses 270

Agamemnon retreats

of labour, who are daughters of Hera and dispense its bitter pains – such were the stabbing pains Agamemnon felt. He leapt into his chariot, told his charioteer to drive to the hollow ships and, in considerable distress, sent his voice ringing out to the whole Greek army:

'Friends, rulers and leaders of the Greeks, keep the furious battle away from our seafaring ships, since Zeus wise in counsel has not allowed me to fight the Trojans all day long.'

280   So he spoke, and his charioteer whipped his lovely-maned horses towards the hollow ships. The willing pair flew off, and their chests were flecked with foam, their bellies grey with dust, as they carried off their wounded lord far from the battlefield.

When Hector saw Agamemnon withdraw, he called out to the Trojans and Lycians in a loud voice:

'Trojans, Lycians and you Dardanians that like your fighting hand to hand, be men, my comrades, and call up that fighting spirit of yours! Their best man is gone and Zeus son of Cronus has given me a great victory. Drive your horses straight at these

290   mighty Greeks and win a greater victory yet!'

With these words he put fresh heart and courage into every man. As a hunter sets his white-fanged hounds on a savage wild boar or a lion, so Hector son of Priam, equal of the murderous War-god Ares, set the proud Trojans on the Greeks. Fearlessly, he took his own place in the forefront and flung himself into the battle like a squall that sweeps down from the mountains and lashes the blue waters of the sea.

300   And who were the first and last that fell to Hector son of Priam, now that Zeus gave him the victory? Asaeus

Hector kills   first, and Autonous and Opites; Dolops son of Cly-
nine Greeks   tius, Opheltius and Agelaus; Aesymnus, Orus and resolute Hipponous. These were the first Greek leaders he killed. Then he fell on the ranks, as a storm-force north-west wind batters and scatters the clouds blown up by a clear southwesterly: the great rollers start their forward march, and the foam flies high on the roaring blast of the swirling wind – so the enemy fell in multitudes before the onslaught of Hector.

310   Irreparable disaster now threatened the Greeks who in their

flight would soon have reached the ships and fallen there, had not Odysseus called out to Diomedes son of Tydeus:

'Son of Tydeus, what's the matter with us? Where's that fighting spirit of ours gone? Here, my old friend, make a stand with me. We will never live it down if Hector of the flashing helmet captures the ships.'

Mighty Diomedes replied to him and said:

'Of course I'll stand with you and take what comes. But it won't help us for very long. Zeus who marshals the clouds has decided he'd rather see the Trojans win than us.'

He spoke, flung his spear at Thymbraeus, hit him on the left 320 nipple and knocked him out of his chariot, while Odysseus dealt with Molion his godlike attendant. Leaving these two where they fell – and for them there was no more fighting – the pair dashed into the crowd and ran riot, as a couple of wild boars turn fearlessly and charge the hounds that are chasing them. So they rounded on the Trojans and destroyed them, giving the Greeks a welcome pause for breath in their flight from godlike Hector.

Diomedes and Odysseus kill seven Trojans

A chariot and two leaders of the people then fell to them. They were the two sons of Merops of Percote, the ablest prophet of his day. He had forbidden his sons to go off to the killing 330 fields, but these two, led on by the demons of death, had not listened to him. And now the great spearman Diomedes took their life and stripped them of their glorious arms, while Odysseus killed and stripped Hippodamus and Hypeirochus.

Then Zeus, looking down from Mount Ida, intensified the battle on both sides, and for a time the slaughter became mutual. Diomedes stabbed Agastrophus the warrior son of Paeëon on the hip-joint with his spear. This man had been unable to escape, as his chariot was nowhere near: utterly deluded, Agastrophus 340 had left his charioteer holding the horses some way off, while he had charged into the front line on foot. This cost him his life.

But Hector, looking sharply across the ranks, launched himself at Diomedes and Odysseus with a great shout, which brought the Trojan ranks after him. When Diomedes, master of the battle-cry, saw him, he was shaken. He turned at once to Odysseus, who was close at hand, and said:

'Trouble's looming. Here comes imperious Hector. Come on, let's make a stand and drive him off.'

350   He spoke, balanced his long-shadowed spear and hurled it. He had aimed at Hector's head and did not miss, striking him on the crest of the helmet. But the bronze spear rebounded from the bronze and never reached his fine flesh: it was stopped by the triple layers of the vizored helmet which Phoebus Apollo had given him.

Diomedes drives off Hector

Hector promptly retreated without looking back and disappeared into the crowd. Sinking to his knees, he supported himself with one great hand on the ground, and then the world went black as night. Meanwhile Diomedes was following up his spear-throw across the front lines to the spot where it had fallen.
360   So Hector had time to come to, leap once more into his chariot and drive off into the crowd. He had escaped dark death. But mighty Diomedes, rushing up with his spear, said:

'You dog, once more you've saved your skin – but only just. Phoebus Apollo took care of you again: you must pray to him as the spears thud around you. But we shall meet once more and then I'll finish you off, if I too can find some god somewhere to help me. For the moment I'll attack anyone else I can find.'

He spoke and proceeded to strip his earlier victim Agastrophus.

370   Now Paris, husband of lovely-haired Helen, aimed his bow at Diomedes shepherd of the people, leaning for cover against the column on the grave-mound which men had made for an earlier Trojan leader, Ilus son of Dardanus. As Diomedes was engaged in removing the ornate body-armour from mighty Agastrophus' chest, the shield from his shoulder and his heavy helmet from his head, Paris drew the bow and shot. The arrow did not leave his hand for nothing. Hitting Diomedes on the flat of his right foot, it went right through and stuck in the earth. Paris, with a happy laugh, leapt out from his cover and spoke in triumph over Diomedes:

Paris wounds Diomedes

380   'Got you! I didn't shoot for nothing. I only wish I'd hit you in the belly and killed you. Then the Trojans, who tremble at you like bleating goats at a lion, would have had some respite from their trouble.'

Unperturbed, mighty Diomedes answered him:

'Typical archer – loud mouth, all hairstyle and bedroom eyes! If you faced me man to man with real weapons, you would find your bow and arrows a poor defence. As it is, you're boasting about scratching my foot. I might as well have been hit by a woman or naughty little boy, for all I care. A shot from a cowardly nonentity never hurt anyone. But *my* weapons show their edge rather differently. One touch from them and a man is dead. His wife lacerates her cheeks and his children have no father. The earth turns red with his blood, and there he rots, with more vultures than girls clustering round him.'   390

So he spoke, and the great spearman Odysseus came up and covered him. Diomedes sat down under his protection and drew the sharp arrow from his foot. Pain stabbed through him, and in considerable distress he got into his chariot and told his charioteer to drive back to the hollow ships.   *Diomedes retreats*   400

Left to himself without a single Greek to support him, since they were all in flight, the great spearman Odysseus was perturbed and reflected on the situation:

'Damn. What am I to do now? It would be pure cowardice to run for it, frightened by the odds against me; but even more unpleasant to be trapped alone, now that Zeus has put all the rest of the Greeks to flight. But why talk to myself like this? I know cowards run from the battlefield; but the brave warrior must stand unflinching, to kill or be killed.'   410

While these thoughts raced through Odysseus' mind, shield-bearing Trojan ranks bore down and surrounded him. They brought themselves nothing but trouble. As strong young huntsmen and their hounds harry a wild boar which emerges from the depths of its lair, sharpening up its white tusks in its crooked jaws; they rush at it from every side; there is a noise of gnashing teeth; but formidable as the boar is, they hold their ground against it – so the encircling Trojans harried Odysseus dear to Zeus.   *Odysseus kills five Trojans*

First Odysseus leapt at matchless Deïopites with his sharp spear and stabbed down on his shoulder from above. Next he killed Thoön and Ennomus. Chersidamas then jumped down   420

from his chariot but Odysseus stabbed him with his spear in the
crutch under his bossed shield. He fell in the dust and clutched
at the earth. Leaving them where they fell, Odysseus with his
spear stabbed Charops, son of Hippasus. He was a brother of
wealthy Socus, a godlike mortal who, advancing to defend him,
took his stand in front of Odysseus and said:

430   'Celebrated Odysseus, with your relish for con-tricks and
combat, today you will either triumph over both sons of Hip-
pasus and boast about the splendid pair you have killed and
stripped, or be brought down by my spear and die yourself.'

               With these words he stabbed at Odysseus' round

Socus wounds
and is killed
by Odysseus shield. The heavy weapon pierced the glittering
shield, forced its way through the ornate body-
armour and ripped the flesh clean off Odysseus' side,
though Pallas Athene did not allow it to penetrate his innards.

440 Odysseus knew it had not touched a vital spot, drew back and
said to Socus:

   'Miserable wretch, your doom is sealed. You have stopped
me fighting the Trojans, but I tell you dark death and destruction
await you this day: conquered by my spear, you will surrender
the glory to me and your life to the god Hades, famed for his
horses.'

   He spoke, and Socus turned and started to run. As he turned,
Odysseus stabbed him with his spear in the middle of the back
between his shoulders and drove it through his chest. He
thudded to the ground, and godlike Odysseus triumphed over
him:

450   'Ah, Socus, son of Hippasus the brave charioteer! So death
after all was too quick for you, and you did not escape. *Your*
eyes, poor wretch, will not be closed in death by your father
and your lady mother, but the carrion birds will gather round
you with their flapping wings and tear your body to pieces. But
when *I* die, I shall have funeral honours from the god-
like Greeks.'

               With these words he pulled Socus' heavy spear out

Menelaus calls
for help of his own wound and bossed shield. Blood gushed
up as the point came out, and Odysseus was in serious

460 distress. When the Trojans saw the blood, they called to each

other across the ranks and attacked him in a body. Odysseus gave ground, shouting to his friends for help. He called three times at the top of his voice, and warlike Menelaus, hearing his cries, turned quickly to Ajax, who happened to be near, and said:

'Olympian-born Ajax son of Telamon, leader of men, I can hear great Odysseus crying out. It sounds as though the Trojans have cut him off in the thick of the action and overpowered him. You and I had better charge in to the rescue. I am afraid it   470
will be all up with him if we leave him stranded like that, great warrior though he is. What a loss to the Greeks that would be!'

With these words he led the way, and godlike Ajax went with him.

They soon found Odysseus, Trojans crowding round him like tawny jackals in the mountains round an antlered stag wounded by an arrow from a huntsman's bow; it has the speed to leave the man behind, as long as the blood flows warm and its legs carry it; but when the arrow has sapped its strength, the flesh-eating jackals devour it in the shadowy woods of the mountains;   480
a god then brings a predatory lion on the scene; the jackals scatter: it is the lion's turn to feed – just so, many brave Trojans crowded round warlike, quick-thinking Odysseus who, by lunging out with his spear, managed to keep death at bay.

But now Ajax with his towerlike shield came up and covered him. The Trojans scattered in all directions, and warlike Menelaus took Odysseus by the arm and led him through the crowd while an attendant brought up Menelaus' chariot.

Ajax then flung himself on the Trojans and killed Doryclus,   490
a bastard son of Priam's; next he stabbed Pandocus and Lysander and Pyrasus and Pylartes. As a river in spate, swollen by the winter rains, rushes down from *Ajax kills five* the mountains to the plain, sweeping up dead oaks *Trojans* and pines and carrying piles of driftwood to the sea – so glorious Ajax stormed across the plain and fell on the enemy, destroying horse and man.

Hector knew nothing of all this. He was engaged on the far left by the banks of River Scamander, where the slaughter was   500
heaviest and the tumult of battle filled the air round great Nestor

and warlike Idomeneus. Hector was in the thick of it here, creating havoc with chariot and spear and mowing down the Greek youth.

Paris hits
Machaon;
Nestor rescues
him

Yet even so the godlike Greeks would not have given ground to him, if Paris, husband of lovely-haired Helen, had not halted Machaon, shepherd of the people and the best warrior there, by hitting him with a three-barbed arrow in the right shoulder. The Greeks, breathing courage, were terrified he might be captured
510 as the battle swayed, and Idomeneus at once spoke to godlike Nestor:

'Quick, Nestor son of Neleus, great glory of the Greeks, into your chariot, pick up Machaon and drive with all speed to the ships. A healer like him, who can cut out arrows and apply soothing herbs, is worth a thousand others.'

So he spoke, and Nestor the Gerenian charioteer complied. He mounted his chariot and Machaon, son of Asclepius the matchless healer, got in beside him. Nestor lashed the horses
520 with the whip, and the willing pair flew off towards the hollow ships, eager to reach their journey's end.

Cebriones, Hector's charioteer, saw that the Trojans elsewhere had been put to flight and spoke his mind to Hector:

'Hector, here are we, engaged with the Greeks on the very fringe of the battle while the rest of the Trojans are running off in chaos, chariots and all. Ajax son of Telamon is sweeping them before him: I recognize him easily – he has that broad shield on his shoulders. Let's drive over there and join in where the charioteers and infantry are launching their strongest
530 assault, where men are killing each other and the tumult of battle fills the air.'

With these words Cebriones whipped his lovely-maned horses with his whistling lash. Hearing the stroke, they swept the chariot off at a gallop towards the Trojans and Greeks, trampling dead men and shields alike. The whole axle of the chariot and the rails that ran round it were sprayed with the blood thrown up by the horses' hooves and the wheel-rims. Hector was eager to get in among the throng of fighting men, to charge and break through. But though his arrival brought terrible

confusion to the Greeks, and he did not shrink from using his
spear, he avoided battle with Ajax son of Telamon, and made   540
his presence felt among the rest of the enemy with spear and
sword and boulder.

Father Zeus on his high throne then made Ajax
retreat. He lost his nerve and came to a halt. Then,   *Ajax slowly*
looking anxiously about him, he swung his sevenfold   *withdraws*
shield across his back, turned in retreat and step by step gave
ground, like a wild beast, with many a backward look. As dogs
and farm hands drive a tawny lion from a cattle-yard: they have   550
stayed awake all night to protect the choicest of their cattle from
its jaws but, hungry for meat, the lion keeps on charging; but it
does no good by it; showers of spears and blazing torches hurled
at it by strong hands scare it off for all its appetite, and at
dawn it slinks off, disappointed – so, equally disappointed, Ajax
retreated from the Trojans, much against his will and acutely
conscious of the danger to the Greek ships.

As a stubborn donkey passing a cornfield defies the boys in
charge of him – though stick after stick has often been broken
round his ribs – and goes in and helps himself to the rich standing   560
crop: the children continue to beat him, but their efforts are
feeble, and they just about manage to drive him out, but not
before he has eaten all he wants – so the proud Trojans and their
famous allies dogged the steps of great Ajax son of Telamon,
stabbing at the centre of his shield with their spears. At times
Ajax would call up that fighting spirit of his, wheel and hold the
ranks of the horse-taming Trojans at bay; and then once more
he would turn and resume his retreat. In this way he managed
to fend off the whole force that was threatening the ships,
standing and laying about him halfway between the Trojans   570
and Greeks. Many spears launched from strong arms were
halted in their forward flight by his great shield, while many
others fell short before they could enjoy white flesh and stuck
in the earth, thirsting to take their fill.

When splendid Eurypylus noticed Ajax labouring
under this hail of missiles, he ran up to support   *Eurypylus kills*
him, let fly his glittering spear and struck Apisaon,   *Apisaon;*
shepherd of the people, in the liver under the midriff, *Paris' reply*

580 bringing him down at once. Then, charging up, he began to take
the armour from his shoulders. But as Eurypylus stripped his
man, godlike Paris saw him, quickly bent his bow at him and
hit him with an arrow in the right thigh. The shaft broke off in
his thigh and slowed him down, but he retreated into his own
contingent of warriors to avoid death. He then sent his voice
ringing out to the whole Greek army:

'My friends, rulers and leaders of the Greeks, turn, make a
stand and save Ajax from destruction. He's under a hail of
590 missiles, and I cannot see how he can disengage himself. Rally
round great Ajax son of Telamon!'

So spoke the wounded Eurypylus, and they closed and
rallied round Ajax, crouching behind sloped shields, with
their spears up at the ready. Ajax came to meet them and,
when he reached his own contingent, turned about and stood
his ground.

               So they fought on like blazing fire. Meanwhile the
Achilles mares of Neleus' breed, sweating as they ran, were
dispatches carrying Nestor from the battlefield and with him
Patroclus Machaon shepherd of the people. Swift-footed god-
600 like Achilles, who had been watching the uphill work of battle
and the Greeks' unhappy retreat from the stern of his wide-
bellied ship, saw him and took note. He called at once to his
companion Patroclus, shouting for him from the ship. Hearing
the call in his hut, Patroclus equal of Ares came out; and that
was the beginning of his end. The strong son of Menoetius spoke
first:

'Why did you call, Achilles? What do you want me for?'

Swift-footed Achilles replied and said:

'Godlike son of Menoetius, my pride and joy, now I think the
610 Greeks will be gathering at my knees in supplication! They
are in desperate straits. But go now, Patroclus, and ask Nestor
who is the wounded man he is taking from the battlefield. Seen
from behind, he looks exactly like Machaon son of Asclepius,
but the horses raced past in such a hurry that I could not see his
face.'

So he spoke, and Patroclus complied with his companion and
set off at a run along the Greeks' huts and their ships.

When Nestor and Machaon reached Nestor's hut, they
stepped down from the chariot to the bountiful earth while   620
Eurymedon, the old man's attendant, unyoked the
horses. The men then stood in the breeze by the   Nestor and
sea-shore to dry the sweat from their tunics, and   Machaon
after that went inside and took a seat. Lovely-haired reach safety
Hecamede prepared them a drink. Nestor had won her when
Achilles sacked Tenedos; she was the daughter of great-hearted
Arsinous, and the Greeks had picked her out for Nestor because
he was their wisest adviser.

First she pushed up a handsome polished table with blue
inlaid feet. On this she placed a bronze dish with an onion as   630
seasoning for the drink, some yellow honey and barley bread;
and beside these a magnificent cup adorned with gold rivets,
which the old man had brought from home. It had four handles,
and on top of each, facing one another, two gold doves were
dipping in their beaks. There were two supports underneath.
Anyone else would have found it difficult to shift the cup from
the table when it was full, but Nestor, old as he was, could lift
it with ease. This woman like the goddesses poured Pramnian
wine into the cup, grated into it some goat's milk cheese with a   640
bronze grater, sprinkled white barley on top and, when she had
finished, told them to drink.

They had quenched their parching thirst and were
agreeably engaged in conversation, when Patroclus   Patroclus
suddenly appeared in the doorway, a mortal like a   reaches
god. The old man saw him, got up from his polished   Nestor's hut
chair, took him by the hand, brought him in and told him to sit
down. But Patroclus from the other side refused and explained:

'No time for sitting down, my venerable lord; you will not
persuade me. That man who sent me to find out the wounded
man you just brought in – he commands respect. He is easy to   650
annoy. But, as I can see for myself that it is Machaon, shepherd
of the people, I will go back at once and report to Achilles. You
know well enough, Olympian-bred sir, what a difficult man he
is, quite capable of finding fault without reason.'

Nestor the Gerenian charioteer replied:

'Why is Achilles so concerned about a few Greek casualties,

when he knows nothing about the disaster affecting the whole
army? Our very best men are lying by the ships, hit by missiles
660 or stabbed. Mighty Diomedes has been hit; Odysseus the great
spearman has been stabbed; so has Agamemnon; Eurypylus has
had an arrow in his thigh; and here is another I have just brought
from the battlefield, hit by an arrow. Yet Achilles, great warrior
that he is, feels no concern or pity for the Greeks. Is he waiting
till, in spite of all we can do, our ships go up in flames beside
the sea and we in turn are destroyed? Certainly *my* strength is
not what it was or my limbs as supple.

670   'Ah, if only I were still as young and with all my powers
                    intact, as I was when we and the Eleans came to
Nestor recalls   blows over some cattle-raids, and I killed strong
routing the   Itymoneus who lived in Elis. I was raiding his herds
Eleans
                    by way of reprisal for what their ruler Augeas lord
of the Eleans had done to us, and while Itymoneus was defending
them I hit him with a spear and killed him, and his rustic
followers scattered in panic. We drove off a vast quantity of
booty from the plain – fifty herds of cattle, and as many flocks
680 of sheep, droves of pigs and scattered herds of goats, as well as
a hundred and fifty chestnut horses, all of them mares and many
with foals beside them. In the night we drove them in to my
father Neleus' town of Pylos, and Neleus was delighted that so
much had fallen to me in my first military encounter.

       'At dawn our town-criers summoned everyone who had debts
owed to them by Eleans to attend. Our leading men in Pylos
held a meeting and divided up the spoils: many of our people
were owed compensation by the Eleans. Indeed, we in Pylos
were seriously weakened at that time – the few of us that were
690 left. The reason was that, in previous years, mighty Heracles
had come and done his worst to us, and all our best men had
been killed. I alone had survived out of the twelve sons that
matchless Neleus had had – all the rest had perished. As a result
the arrogant Elean warriors had been in the habit of humiliating
us, and done us great wrong with their plundering.

       'But after my raid, the old lord Neleus had now got a herd of
cattle and a great flock of sheep out of our spoils: he chose three
hundred for himself, together with their shepherds. The point

was that the Eleans owed him a good deal of compensation. This was because Neleus had sent a four-horse chariot to Elis to run in their games and compete for a tripod. But their ruler 700 Augeas had kept them and sent back their charioteer deprived of his horses and with an insulting message. Neleus had resented the wording of this as much as Augeas' actions. So now he helped himself liberally to the booty, leaving the remainder to the people to divide in such a way that no one should go short of their proper share.

'So we were dealing with this business in Pylos and sacrificing to the gods at various points in the town. But on the third day, the whole of Elis, chariots and foot-soldiers, bore down on us at great speed, and with them marched the two Moliones who 710 were still lads at the time with no experience of war. There is an outlying stronghold called Thryoessa perched on a steep hill overlooking the River Alpheus on the borders of sandy Pylos. Their aim was to destroy this place; so they laid siege to it and overran the surrounding plain. But in the night Athene came speeding down from Olympus and warned us to arm for battle. She did not find us unwilling; in fact the whole force she raised in Pylos was spoiling for a fight. But Neleus did not wish me to arm. He felt I knew too little about serious fighting and hid my horses from me. All the same, Athene so arranged the battle 720 that, even though I went on foot, I outshone even our own charioteers.

'There is a river called Minyeius which falls into the sea near Arene. Here our charioteers halted till bright dawn, while the foot-soldiers came streaming up. From that point a rapid march under arms brought us by noon to the sacred River Alpheus. There we made fine boundary sacrifices to almighty Zeus and also offered a bull to the River-god, a bull to Poseidon and an unworked heifer to grey-eyed Athene. We ate the sacrificial meal 730 in our several contingents and settled down for the night on the banks of the stream, every man fully armed.

'The confident Eleans meanwhile were besieging the citadel of Thryoessa, determined on its downfall; but they witnessed a tremendous feat of arms instead. No sooner had the sun shown his face above the horizon than we gave battle, with a prayer to

Zeus and Athene; and when the two armies engaged, the first
man fell to me and I took over his horses.

'He was a spearman called Mulius, a son-in-law of Augeas,
740   married to his eldest daughter auburn-haired Agamede, who
knew every magic herb that grows in the wide world. As he
came at me, I struck him with my bronze-headed spear and he
crashed in the dust. I leapt into his chariot and took my place in
the front rank. The confident Eleans broke and ran in all direc-
tions when they saw their chariot-leader, their best fighter,
brought to earth. But I was after them like a black storm. I
captured fifty chariots, and the two occupants of each were all
brought down by my spear and bit the dust. In fact I would have
750   killed the twin Moliones too, had not their father, Poseidon the
wide-ruling earthshaker, hidden them in a thick mist and rescued
them from the battlefield.

'Yes, Zeus gave us Pylians a great victory there. We chased
them across open country, killing the men and gathering up
their splendid armour, till our chariots were rolling through the
corn lands of Buprasion and we reached the Olenian Rock and
the place called Alesion Hill. At that point Athene turned our
forces back, and there I killed and left my last man. Our chariot-
760   eers withdrew from Buprasion and drove back to Pylos, all of
them giving glory to Zeus among the gods and to Nestor among
men.

'That was me, in my day – long ago as it all was. By compari-
son, Achilles is the only one who is going to get any advantage
from *his* brilliance in battle – though he will shed many a
remorseful tear when it is too late and the army is destroyed.

Patroclus'   'My dear friend, your father Menoetius gave you
father's advice   instructions that day he sent you from Phthia to join
                  Agamemnon. I and godlike Odysseus were in the
house and we heard everything he told you. We had come to
Phthia and the welcoming palace of Achilles' father Peleus to
770   recruit troops from the bountiful land of Achaea. There we
found the warrior Menoetius and yourself and Achilles with
you. Peleus the old charioteer was burning the fat thighs of an
ox in his stable-yard in honour of Zeus who delights in thunder.
He had a golden cup in his hand and was pouring a libation of

sparkling wine as the sacrifice was burning, while you two were
preparing the meat.

'At that moment, Odysseus and I appeared at the gate.
Achilles was amazed and sprang to his feet, took us by the
hand, brought us in, told us to sit down and set beside us the
food that hospitality requires. When we had satisfied our hunger   780
and thirst, I began to speak, urging you and Achilles to join us.
You were more than willing, and your fathers both started
giving you advice. While the old man Peleus exhorted his son
Achilles always to be the best and excel all others, Menoetius
was giving you his own advice: "My son, Achilles is of nobler
birth than you and he is also by far the stronger man. But you
are older than he is. It is for you to give him sound advice, make
suggestions and give him a lead which he will follow to his own
advantage."

'Those were your old father's instructions – which you have   790
forgotten. But even so you could still speak to warlike Achilles
to see if he will do what you say. Who knows? With some divine
help, your suggestions might stir him to change his
mind. A friend's advice is often the most effective.   Nestor
But if he is privately deterred by some prophecy,   suggests
some word from Zeus that his lady mother has told   Patroclus'
him, let him at least allow *you* to take the field with   return (16.40)
the Myrmidon contingent at your back, if perhaps you might
bring salvation to the Greeks. Let him give you his own fine
armour to fight in, so that the Trojans take you for him and
break off the battle. That would give our weary troops some   800
breathing space – there is little enough respite in war. The
Trojans have fought to the point of exhaustion, and you, being
fresh, might well drive them back to the town from our ships
and huts.'

So he spoke, and his words went straight to Patroclus' heart.
He set off at a run past the line of ships to rejoin Achilles. As he
ran past the ships of godlike Odysseus – the place where they
held their assemblies, conducted public business and had put up
their altars to the gods – Eurypylus met him, limping back from
the battle with the wound from an arrow in his thigh. Sweat   810
was pouring from his head and shoulders and dark blood gushed

from his painful wound, though his mind was not affected. Strong Patroclus was moved to compassion at the sight and mournfully spoke winged words:

'Wretched rulers and leaders of the Greeks, so now it seems you were destined to glut the swift dogs of Troy with your white flesh, far from your dear ones and the land of your fathers. But
820 tell me, Eurypylus, is there any hope of holding awe-inspiring Hector in check, or will the Greeks fall to his spear and be destroyed today?'

The wounded Eurypylus replied:

Patroclus tends Eurypylus' wound
'Olympian-born Patroclus, there will be no salvation for the Greeks now; they will fall by their own black ships. All our former champions are lying there already, hit by Trojan missiles or stabbed, and all the time the enemy grows stronger. But at least you can take *me* and see me safe to my black ship, then cut the arrow out from
830 my thigh, wash off the blood with warm water and spread soothing herbs on the wound, the excellent ones you learnt about from Achilles who was taught by Cheiron, most honest of Centaurs. As for our healers Podaleirius and Machaon, I think one of them is lying wounded in camp in need of a good healer himself, while the other is still in the field resisting the Trojans' frenzied attack.'

The strong son of Menoetius replied:

'How can we have got into this situation? What are we to do, Eurypylus? I am on my way with a message for warlike Achilles
840 from Gerenian Nestor, guardian of the Greeks. But I'm not going to abandon you in your distress.'

He spoke, put his arm round his waist and supported this shepherd of the people back to his hut. When Eurypylus' attendant saw him, he spread some hides on the floor, and there Patroclus laid him down, cut the sharp point of the arrow out of his thigh with his knife and washed away the dark blood from the wound with warm water. Then he crushed the root of a bitter herb with his hands and applied it. It was a pain-killer, which promptly did its work. The wound began to dry, and the blood stopped flowing.

12

HECTOR STORMS
THE WALL

While brave Patroclus was attending to the wounded Eurypylus in his hut, general fighting broke out between the Greeks and Trojans. It did not look as though the Greeks' ditch and the wide wall behind it could hold out much longer.

When the Greeks had built this wall with the ditch alongside to protect their ships, they had failed to make impressive offerings to the gods and so to ensure a safe haven for them and the vast spoils they had taken. The wall was built without the goodwill of the immortal gods, and it did not last for long. While Hector was alive, Achilles angry and lord Priam's town 10 unsacked, the great Greek wall survived. But later, when all the best of the Trojans were dead and many of the Greeks too (though some survived); when Priam's town had been sacked in the tenth year of the siege and the Greek expedition had sailed for home; then Poseidon and Apollo decided to destroy the wall by unleashing upon it the force of all the rivers that run down from the range of Mount Ida to the sea.

20   The names of the rivers were Rhesus, Heptaporus, Caresus, Rhodius, Granicus, Aesepus, divine Scamander and Simoïs, on whose banks many a shield and helmet and many a warrior of that half-divine generation had fallen in the dust. When that day came, Phoebus Apollo brought all these rivers together at one mouth and for nine days he flung their waters at the wall, while Zeus rained without ceasing to submerge it the quicker. Trident in hand, Poseidon the earthshaker himself directed the torrent, washed out to sea all the wooden and stone foundations that 30 the Greeks had laid with such labour and levelled the shore of the fast-flowing Hellespont. When the wall had been destroyed, he covered the wide beach once more with sand and turned the rivers back into the channels down which their lovely streams had run before.

The wall's eventual destruction (7.459)

All this remained to be done by Poseidon and Apollo in the future. At the moment, however, the wall stood solid, and the hue and cry of battle flared up round it, the woodwork of its towers reverberating to the enemy's missiles. The Greeks, cowed by Zeus' scourge, were penned in and trapped beside their ships 40 by their fear of Hector, the mighty master of the rout, who was fighting in the front ranks like a hurricane.

As a wild boar or lion twists this way and that among the hounds and huntsmen to defy them in its strength: the men close their ranks, confront it like a wall and pelt it with showers of spears; but there is no fear or thought of flight in the boar's dauntless heart – its very courage kills it; time and again it turns and tries some new point in the ranks; and wherever it charges, the ranks give way – so Hector went up and down among his 50 men, urging the charioteers to cross the ditch. But not even his own swift horses would cross for him. They were frightened by its width and halted at the brink, neighing shrilly: it was certainly not easy to leap over or cross in any way. Both banks were

overhanging along its entire length, and on top there was a row
of pointed stakes, close-set and strong, which the Greek troops
had planted there to keep out their enemies. So no horses pulling
a chariot could easily break through to the other side.

The foot-soldiers, however, were keen to attempt the crossing,
and Polydamas went up to daring Hector and said: 60

'Hector and you other Trojan and allied com-
manders, it would be unwise to drive our chariots   *Polydamas* sug-
over the ditch. It's almost impossible to cross: there   gests attacking
are the sharp stakes along the edge, and close behind   wall on foot
comes the Greek wall, leaving the charioteers no room to dis-
mount and fight – and so narrow a strip that I am certain there
would be casualties. If high-thundering Zeus is really on our
side, has evil in mind for the Greeks and means to wipe them
out, there is nothing I want more than to see them being   70
destroyed here and now, far from Greece, with no trace left. But
if they regroup and launch a counter-attack from the ships, and
we get entangled in the ditch, I don't think a single man would
escape to bring the news to Ilium. So I suggest we all do what I
now propose. Let our attendants hold our horses at the ditch
while we, on foot and fully armed, follow Hector in massed
formation. The Greeks won't stand up to us, if their doom really
is sealed.'

So spoke Polydamas, and his timely advice seemed excellent   80
to Hector. Fully armed, he immediately leapt from his chariot to
the ground, and all the other Trojans abandoned their formation
and did the same when they saw Hector dismount. They all left
their chariots in their drivers' charge, with orders to hold their
horses in good order there at the ditch. Then, dividing up, they
organized themselves into groups and lined up behind their own
leaders in five contingents.

Of these, the best and biggest was the one com-
manded by Hector and matchless Polydamas. None   The *Trojan*
showed greater enthusiasm to breach the wall and   battle order
fight by the hollow ships. Cebriones, Hector's charioteer –   90
Hector had replaced him in his chariot with an inferior fighter
– was third in command. The second contingent was led by
Paris, Alcathous and Agenor; and the third by two of Priam's

sons, Helenus and godlike Deiphobus, with, as third in com-
mand, the warrior Asius whose huge, sleek horses had brought
him from Arisbe and the River Selleïs. Aeneas, handsome son
of Anchises, led the fourth contingent supported by two sons of
100 Antenor, Archelochus and Acamas, men experienced in every
kind of fighting. Fifth, Sarpedon commanded the renowned
allies, and had appointed under him Glaucus and warlike
Asteropaeus, whom he considered beyond question the best
men among the allies next to himself, he being the finest warrior
of them all. They drew up in close formation, oxhide shields
touching, and resolutely advanced on the Greeks, in the confi-
dence that nothing could stop them now from falling on the
enemy ships.

Of the Trojans and their famous allies, all except Asius son
of Hyrtacus adopted the tactics suggested by admirable Poly-
110 damas. But Asius, commander of men, refused to abandon
his chariot and charioteer and decided instead to advance
on the ships, chariot and all. He was a fool. He was not des-
tined to evade the evil demons of death and to drive back his
chariot and pair in triumph from the ships to windswept
Ilium. Before that, in the spear of noble Idomeneus, a hateful
fate engulfed him.

Lapiths repel
Asius   Asius drove at the left flank of the ships where the
                                  Greeks had a crossing that they used when returning
                                  from the plain. Here Asius drove his chariot and
120 horses over and, coming to the gateway, found the doors had
not been closed nor the long bar slid in place. The defenders
were holding them open to give stragglers escaping from the
battlefield a chance to reach the ships. So Asius in his chariot
made straight for the gate and his contingent followed, yelling
shrilly. They thought the Greeks could not stop them now but
would be slaughtered beside their ships.

The fools. At the gate they met two champions, proud sons
of the warlike Lapith race. One was mighty Polypoetes son of
130 Peirithous, and the other was Leonteus, equal of the murderous
War-god Ares. This pair had planted themselves in front of the
high gate, like lofty mountain oaks that resist the wind and rain
for ever, supported by their long and sturdy roots. So the two,

relying on the strength of their arms, awaited the onslaught of great Asius and did not retreat. The Trojans, massing themselves around lord Asius, Adamas his son, Iamenus, Orestes, Thoön 140 and Oenomaus, held up their leather shields and with a mighty shout made straight for the wall.

For a while, the two Lapiths had been encouraging the Greek men-at-arms inside the ramparts to defend their ships from that point. But when they saw the Trojans storming the wall and the Greeks yelling and panicking, they charged right out and fought in front of the gate, like a pair of wild boars in the mountains, facing a noisy mob of men and dogs: they charge with glancing blows, crushing and rooting up the undergrowth around them, noisily clashing their teeth, till at last they are hit by someone's 150 spear and killed – so the shining bronze on the chests of the Lapiths clashed as it met the enemy's blows. They put up a mighty defence, trusting in their own strength and in the men on the wall above, who were flinging stones down from the well-built ramparts in defence of their lives, their camp and seafaring ships. Rocks came pelting to the ground like snow flakes in a fierce blizzard which sends the dark clouds scudding and thickly blankets the bountiful earth. So the rocks flew from the hands of Greek and Trojan alike. Helmets and bossed shields 160 rang out harshly as the great boulders hit them.

Then Asius groaned, slapped his thighs and in exasperation spoke out:

'So, Father Zeus, you are an absolute born liar. I never thought those Greek warriors could withstand our determination and invincible tenacity. But they're like supple-waisted wasps or bees that build their home by a rocky path and won't be driven from the hive, but stay and defend their children against the huntsmen 170 – in just the same way those two Greeks want to kill or be killed before they give way from the gate.'

So he spoke, but his words had no effect on Zeus, who had made up his mind to let Hector have the glory. Meanwhile other Trojan contingents had carried the fighting to other gates. But it would be difficult for me to tell the whole story, as if I had the abilities of a god. All along the stone wall fierce fires broke out, and the hard-pressed Greeks were compelled to fight for their

180   very ships. All the gods who had taken their side were in the
depths of despair.

But here it was the two Lapiths who now went on
the offensive. Peirithous' son Polypoetes threw his
spear and hit Damasus on his bronze-sided helmet.
The helmet failed to repel it, and the point smashed
right through the bone, spattering all the inside of the helmet
with his brains. So he ended Damasus' assault. Next, he killed
Pylon and Ormenus.

The Lapiths
kill eight
Trojans

Meanwhile Leonteus ally of the War-god flung his spear at
190   Hippomachus and caught him on the belt. Then he drew his
sharp sword from its sheath and dashed into the throng, where
he closed in on Antiphates and struck him. Antiphates was
hurled to the ground flat on his back. Then in swift succession
Leonteus brought Menon, Iamenus and Orestes to the bountiful
earth.

While the Lapiths were stripping the shining armour from
these men, the young Trojan warriors under Polydamas and
Hector, who formed the best and biggest of the contingents and
had shown the greatest eagerness to breach the wall and set the
ships on fire, were still standing along the ditch, hesitating to
200   advance. The reason was that, just as they were going to cross,
a bird of omen had suddenly appeared to them, an eagle flying
high across the front of the army from right to left, with a
blood-red snake in its talons. This ominous creature was alive
and still struggling: it had not let up on its will to fight. Twisting
back on itself, it bit its captor on the breast beside the neck. At
this the eagle, in agony, released its hold, let the snake drop to
the ground among the troops and with a loud cry sailed away
down the wind.

The Trojans were appalled when they saw the snake lying
there writhing about in their midst, a sign from Zeus who drives
210   the storm-cloud. Polydamas went straight up to daring Hector
and said:

'Hector, as a rule you object when I offer sound advice at our
assemblies. It is, of course, *entirely* unfitting for your humble
servant to disagree with you either in the council-chamber or
on the battlefield; he must only exalt your authority. But once

again I am now going to speak my mind and say what I think best.

'We ought not to advance and fight the enemy around his ships. I know exactly what will happen, if that bird of omen does not lie. Just as we were going to move forward, an eagle flew high across the front of the army from right to left with a blood-red snake in its talons. The snake was alive, and the bird 220 dropped it before its reached its nest – it failed to get it home and give it to its young. In the same way, even if by a great effort we succeed in breaking down the Greek gate and wall and the enemy give way, we will not be able to make an orderly withdrawal from the ships over the same ground. We will have to leave many Trojans behind, and the Greeks, fighting in defence of their ships, will slaughter them. That is how a prophet who really understood such omens and had the army's confidence would interpret this sign.'

Hector of the flashing helmet gave him a black look and said: 230

'Polydamas, that was an unusually ill-disposed speech of yours. You know you could have thought of something better. But if you really do mean what you say, then the gods themselves must have scrambled your brains. Loud-thundering Zeus himself made and confirmed to me certain promises. These you tell me to forget; *Hector* rejects interpretation of omen and instead you would have me base my actions on long-winged birds, who do not interest me at all. In fact I don't care whether they fly to the right towards the morning sun or to the left into the western gloom. Let's pin our faith in the will of great Zeus, 240 who governs all mankind and the gods as well.

'Fight for your country – that is the best and only omen. But why should *you* fear war and its ravages? Even if the rest of us are slaughtered wholesale by the Greek ships, you need have no fear for your own safety – you aren't the man to stand and fight it out. That said, if you personally shrink from the fighting or dissuade any of the others from battle, you will lose your life – 250 and it will be my spear that ends it.'

With these words Hector led off, and his men came after him with a mighty roar. From the mountains of Ida Zeus who delights in thunder unleashed a hurricane that raised the dust and blew it straight at the ships, bewildering the Greeks and glorifying Hector and the Trojans.

Trusting in this sign of divine favour and their own strength, they now made determined efforts to breach the great Greek wall, tearing away the parapets, pulling down the battlements
260 and levering up the projecting buttresses that the Greeks had sunk into the ground outside to support the wall. By undermining these they hoped to bring down the wall itself. But the Greeks would not give way. They closed up gaps in the battlements with their oxhide shields and from there pelted the enemy as they came up beneath the wall.

The Ajaxes hearten Greek defenders
The two Ajaxes ranged everywhere along the walls, issuing orders and putting fresh heart into their men. Some they encouraged but others, who had abandoned all resistance, they harshly rebuked:

'Friends, it takes all sorts to make an army – the good, the
270 bad and the indifferent – and today there is work for every man of you. But you know this well enough yourselves. You have your leaders' orders: no one must turn back to the ships. Forward instead, straight at the enemy, urging each other on and trusting that Olympian Zeus, lord of the lightning-flash, will let us counter this attack and chase the enemy back to their town.'

So the two Ajaxes, cheering the troops on, inspired the Greeks for battle.

As snowflakes fall thick and fast on a winter day when Zeus
280 wise in counsel starts the snow falling and shows his missiles to men: he puts the winds to sleep, and it snows without ceasing till he has covered the high mountain tops and the bold headlands of the coast and the clover meadows and the farmers' fields; till even the shores and inlets of the grey sea are under snow, and the waves cannot resist it as they come rolling in; everything is blanketed by the blizzard sent by Zeus – so the stones flew thick and fast in both directions as the Greeks pelted the Trojans and the Trojans the Greeks. The whole length of the wall thundered to volleys of rocks.

290 But even then glorious Hector and his Trojans would not have broken down the gate in the wall and the long bar, if Zeus wise in counsel had not launched his son Sarpedon against the

Greeks, like a lion falling on cattle. Sarpedon held his fine round
shield in front of him – made of beaten bronze, hammered out
by the smith and backed with hide after hide, stitched together
with gold wire running right round it. With this in front of him
and brandishing two spears, Sarpedon set out like a mountain
lion who has long been in need of meat; impelled by his proud   300
heart, he even assaults a strongly protected farmstead to make
an attempt on the sheep; even if he finds herdsmen on the spot
guarding the sheep with a ring of dogs and spears, he has no
mind to be chased away without making an attempt on the
fold, and either leaps in and seizes a sheep, or is himself struck
down in the front ranks by a spear from a quick hand – so
godlike Sarpedon's courage impelled him to assault the wall and
break through the battlements. At once he addressed Glaucus,
Hippolochus' son:

'Glaucus, why are we most of all singled out for honour at   310
home in Lycia, with pride of place, the choicest meat and never
empty cups? Why do they all look up to us as gods?
And why do we cultivate a great estate on the banks   *Sarpedon*
of the River Xanthus, with lovely orchards and splen-   *on heroism*
did fields of wheat? All this now obliges us to take our places in
the front ranks of the Lycians and fling ourselves into the flames
of battle. Only then will our Lycian men-at-arms say of us:
"Well! These are no dishonourable lords of Lycia that rule over
us and eat fat sheep and drink the best sweet wine: they are   320
indomitable and fight in the forefront of the Lycians."

'My friend, if, after living through this war, we could be sure
of becoming ageless and immortal, I should not fight in the front
line nor send you out into the battle where men win glory. But
the world is not like that. A thousand demons of death hover
over us, and nobody can escape or avoid them. So in we go,
whether we yield the victory to some other man, or he to us.'

So he spoke, and Glaucus did not turn back or disagree, and
the two went forward at the head of a great Lycian force.   330

When he saw them coming, Menestheus shud-   *Sarpedon*
dered: it was against his sector of the Greek ramparts   *and Glaucus*
that the menace was directed. Looking along the wall   *attack the wall*
for some commander who could save his contingent

from disaster, he saw the two Ajaxes, those gluttons for battle, standing quite near, along with Teucer who had just come from his hut. But it was impossible to make himself heard by shouting. The noise was tremendous and the very sky was assaulted by the din as shields, crested helmets and gates were struck again
340 and again (the gates had all been closed by now and the Trojans were crowding round trying to break them down and force their way in). At once Menestheus sent the herald Thoötes with a message to Ajax son of Telamon:

'Quick, godlike Thoötes, run and call Ajax, or rather both Ajaxes. That would be best of all. Death is staring us in the face here. The Lycian leaders have thrown in an overwhelming force and so far they've proved powerful opposition in the heat of battle. But if our men have a battle on their hands over there too, let's at least have brave Ajax son of Telamon, and tell him
350 to bring Teucer the expert bowman with him.'

So he spoke, and the herald heard, complied and set off at a run along the Greek wall. When he reached the two Ajaxes, he went up and spoke to them at once:

The two Ajaxes defend

'You Ajaxes, leaders of the bronze-armoured Greeks, Menestheus tells you to come over, if only for a little while, and lend him a hand in his difficulties, preferably both of you. That would be best of all. Death is staring us in the face there. The Lycian leaders have thrown in
360 an overwhelming force and so far they've proved powerful opposition in the heat of the battle. But if you have a battle on your hands over here too, at least let brave Ajax son of Telamon come, and bring Teucer the expert bowman with him.'

So he spoke, and great Ajax son of Telamon complied. He then spoke to Ajax son of Oïleus with winged words:

'Ajax, you and powerful Lycomedes stay here and tell the Greeks to keep the enemy engaged, while I go and deal with the situation over there. I'll soon be back when I have shored up their defence.'

370 With these words Ajax son of Telamon set off and his half-brother Teucer went with him, with Pandion carrying Teucer's curved bow. They went along behind the wall and so reached the sector commanded by great-hearted Menestheus, where the

pressure was intense. Here the mighty Lycian rulers and leaders were climbing the battlements like a dark hurricane. They hurled themselves at the enemy, and the tumult of battle rose.

Ajax son of Telamon was the first to kill his man, a comrade of Sarpedon's, great-hearted Epicles. He hit him with a jagged 380 lump of rock that he picked up inside the wall from on top of a heap beside a battlement. Even the strongest young man of our generation would have found it difficult to lift with both hands, but Ajax heaved it above his head and flung it, crushing the helmet with its four plates and smashing the man's skull to pieces. Epicles dropped like a diver from the high tower and the spirit left his bones.

Epicles and *Alcmaon killed; Glaucus wounded*

Meanwhile Teucer hit powerful Glaucus son of Hippolochus with an arrow as he charged at the high wall. Teucer saw his arm exposed and hit it, ending Glaucus' interest in the fight. Glaucus at once jumped unobtrusively down from the wall, so 390 that the Greeks might not see he was wounded and gloat over him.

Sarpedon was horrified when he realized that Glaucus was gone. But it did not diminish his own will to fight. He stabbed at Alcmaon with his spear, hit him and dragged the weapon out. The man came with it, falling headlong from the wall, and his ornate bronze armour clattered about him.

Then Sarpedon got his mighty hands on the battlement. He gave a pull, and a whole length of the breastwork came away, exposing the top of the wall. He had made a breach for the hordes.

The Ajaxes hold off Sarpedon

Ajax and Teucer now took him on together. Teucer hit him 400 with an arrow on the gleaming shoulder-strap that ran across his chest and supported his man-covering shield. And though Zeus saved Sarpedon from destruction, not wishing that his son should meet his doom by the sterns of the ships, Ajax charged in and stabbed at his shield. The weapon failed to penetrate, but it stopped Sarpedon in his tracks, and he withdrew a little from the battlements. Even so he did not retreat completely. He was still filled with hopes of glory and, wheeling round, he shouted to his godlike Lycians:

'Lycians, where is that old fighting spirit of yours? Strong as
410 I am, I can hardly breach the wall on my own and open up our
way to the ships. Rally round! The more the better!'

So he spoke, and the Lycians, fearing their leader's dis-
approval, attacked in greater numbers than ever around their
leader. But the Greeks on their side reinforced the contingents
behind the wall, and the struggle that ensued was desperate for
both sides. The mighty Lycians could not break down the Greek
wall and open up a way to the ships, nor were the Greek
spearmen able to force back the Lycians once they had gained a
420 foothold by the wall.

As two men quarrel over the boundary-markers in a common
field, each with measuring-sticks in their hands, fighting for
their fair share in a narrow strip of ground: that was the distance
they were kept apart by the battlements. Over the battlements,
Trojans and Greeks hacked at each from behind their oxhide
shields, great and small, that protected their chests. Many a
warrior's flesh felt the stab of the sharp bronze spear when they
swung round and bared their backs, or when they were pierced
430 through the shield itself. All along, the towers and battlements
were drenched with blood from both sides, Trojan and Greek.

And yet the Trojans were unable to set their enemies on the
run. The Greeks held on, like a careful wool-worker who holds
up her scales to balance the wool against the weights and check
the accuracy of the meagre pittance she is earning for her chil-
dren. The struggle was as tight and even as that, till the moment
when Zeus gave the upper hand to Hector son of Priam, who
was the first to leap inside the Greek wall. Hector sent his voice
ringing out to the whole Trojan army:

440 'On with you, horse-taming Trojans! Smash the Greek wall
and fire the ships!'

So he spoke, and there was no Trojan ear that did not catch
his stirring call. Massing together, they charged at the wall and
began to scale the parapet with sharp spears in their hands. But
Hector seized and brought along a rock that was lying in front
of the gate. Broad at the base and coming to a point, it would
have taxed the strength of the two best men in any town of the
present generation to lever it up from the ground on to a waggon.

But Hector handled it effortlessly on his own. Zeus, son of   450
sickle-wielding Cronus, had made it light for him.

As a shepherd easily picks up a ram's fleece in one
hand, carries it off and scarcely feels the weight, so   *Hector* smashes
Hector lifted up the rock and brought it towards the   Greek gate
planking that made up the high, strong, well-fitted double gates,
which were held on the inside by two beams sliding in from
either gate-post, locked by a single bolt. Hector went right up
to them and bracing himself, legs well apart for maximum
power, hurled the rock, hit the doors full in the middle and
smashed it out of its pivots on either side. The force of the throw
propelled the rock through, and there was a great roar from the   460
gate as the planks were smashed to splinters by the impact of
the stone and the bars gave way.

In leapt glorious Hector, face dark as nightfall. He held two
spears in his hands and the bronze of his body-armour gleamed
with a baleful light. None but a god could have met and held
him as he sprang through that gate. And now, with fire flashing
from his eyes, he wheeled round to the crowd behind him and
called on the Trojans to cross the wall. His men responded to
his summons. Some swarmed over the wall; others poured in
through the gate itself. The panic-stricken Greeks fled back to   470
their hollow ships, and all hell broke loose.

13
THE BATTLE AT
THE SHIPS

1–9: ZEUS, confident that no god will interfere in the battle, looks elsewhere (cf. 8.10).

10–205: POSEIDON takes advantage. He fills the two Ajaxes with renewed vigour and rallies the rest of the Greeks. Ajax drives off *Hector*.

206–539: POSEIDON encourages Idomeneus to take the lead. Idomeneus meets Meriones: they exchange views on the meaning of bravery and make for the battle. Idomeneus enjoys success, and *Deiphobus* fights back.

540–672: General fighting ensues.

673–837: *Hector* finds many *Trojans* dead or wounded but leads the *Trojans* back to the attack. Ajax taunts *Hector* who, despite an omen, replies in kind. The *Trojans* charge, and general fighting breaks out.

When Zeus had brought Hector and the Trojans up to the Greek ships, he left both sides there to endure the unending struggle and tears and turned his shining eyes away into the distance, where he concentrated his gaze on the lands of the horse-breeding Thracians, the Mysians who fight hand to hand, the lordly Hippemolgi who drink mares' milk and the Abii, the most civilized of men on earth. Not another glance of his bright eyes did he give to Troy. He did not expect that any of the immortals would come down to help either the Trojans or the Greeks.

10   None of this had escaped the watchful eye of the earthshaker lord Poseidon. He too had sat down high on the topmost peak of wooded Samothrace and was watching the battle spellbound.

From here the whole of Mount Ida, as well as Priam's town and the ships of the Greeks, could be seen. Sitting there after he had risen from the sea, he pitied the Greeks in their hour of defeat and was enraged with Zeus.

POSEIDON helps the Greeks

So now he strode at speed down the rocky slope. The high hills and forests shook under the immortal feet of the descending god. He took three strides and with the fourth reached Aegae, 20 his goal, where his impressive palace built of gleaming gold stands under the depths of the waters, and will stand for ever. There he harnessed to his chariot his two swift horses with their hooves of bronze and flowing manes of gold. He dressed himself in gold, picked up his splendid golden whip, mounted his chariot and drove out across the waves. The dolphins did not fail to recognize their master. On every side, they emerged from their caves and gambolled at his coming. The sea made way for him in its delight, the chariot flew along and the bronze axle 30 remained dry below as his bounding horses carried him towards the Greek ships.

Midway between Tenedos and rugged Imbros there is a large cavern down in the deep sea. Here Poseidon the earthshaker unyoked and left his horses. He put ambrosial fodder down beside them and tied their legs with golden hobbles which they could neither break nor shake off, to make sure they stayed there till their master's return. Then he made his way to the Greek camp.

Here, like a high wind or a conflagration, the massed Trojans 40 were sweeping on with implacable determination in the wake of Hector son of Priam, shouting and yelling as one. They were now hopeful of capturing the ships and killing all the best of the Greeks beside them. But at this moment Poseidon, the earth-shaker who encircles the world, emerged from the depths of the sea to put fresh heart into the Greeks. Borrowing the form and tireless voice of Calchas, he first addressed the two Ajaxes, both already intent on combat:

'Ajaxes, you two can save the Greek army, if you fight with your old courage and entertain no cowardly thoughts of panic. The Trojans have climbed the great wall in force, but for all 50

POSEIDON
inspires the
Ajaxes

their invincible tenacity, I have no fears for the rest of the front where the bronze-armoured Greeks will hold them all in check. It is here I dread disaster, where that rabid dog Hector, who boasts that his father was almighty Zeus, is leading their advance like a raging fire. If some god could only make you see that this is the place for you two to stand fast and rally the rest, you could still drive him off from your ships, for all his fury and the encouragement he gets from Olympian Zeus himself.'

The earthshaker who encircles the world spoke and, touching
60 them with his staff, filled them both with resolution and energy and banished the heaviness from their legs and arms. Then, like a swift hawk, which leaves its position high up on a rocky precipice, poises, and swoops to chase some other bird across the plain, Poseidon the earthshaker disappeared from their sight. Of the two Ajaxes, it was swift Ajax, Oïleus' son, who first knew him for a god. He immediately spoke to Ajax son of Telamon:

'Ajax, it was one of the gods that live on Olympus who urged us just now to fight by the ships. He took the prophet's form
70 but he was not Calchas, our prophet. His heels and the backs of his knees as he left us were proof enough for me – it's not hard to recognize a god. Not only that, but I feel a change in my heart. I'm much more eager to do battle and fight. My feet and hands are itching to be at them.'

Ajax son of Telamon replied to him and said:

'I feel the same: my mighty hands are itching on my spear; my spirit is roused; my feet are eager to be off. Single-handed, I'd
80 be happy to meet Hector son of Priam in all his implacable determination.'

While the two Ajaxes were talking together in this way, savouring the will to fight which the god had put into their hearts, Poseidon was stirring up the Greeks behind the lines, who were trying to recover their spirits beside their swift ships. They were not only weakened physically by complete exhaustion but also demoralized at the sight of the Trojans who had swarmed across the great wall in such numbers. When they looked at them, their eyes filled with tears and they saw no hope of salvation.

But now, with the ease of a god, the earthshaker went in   90
among the ranks and urged them on. Teucer was the first he
visited and roused, with Leitus, the warrior Peneleos, Thoas,
Deipyrus and finally Meriones and Antilochus, champions of
the battle-cry. He urged them on and spoke winged words:

'Greeks, shame on you, young warriors! You are
the very men on whose bravery I had relied to save   POSEIDON
our ships. If *you* give up because the fight is so   rallies other
desperate, the day for our conquest by the Trojans   troops
has indeed arrived. Well, well, what an astonishing sight, a   100
fearful thing I never dreamt of seeing – the Trojans at our very
ships! In the old days, they were like the cowardly does that trot
through the woods in their weak and aimless way, food for
jackals, panthers and wolves, with no will to fight in them.
That's how the Trojans used to behave, taking care never for a
moment to stand up to any determined assault from us.

'But now they have left their town far behind them and are
fighting by the hollow ships, all through the incompetence of
our leader and the slackness of the troops, who are so disgusted
with their leader that they would rather die beside their fast   110
ships than defend them. Yet even if the whole blame does
rest with Agamemnon son of Atreus for insulting swift-footed
Achilles, we have no excuse whatever for giving up the struggle.

'But brave men can recover: let's be quick to put things right.
For instance, it is not a pretty sight to see you, who are numbered
among the best men in the army, slackening that fighting spirit
of yours like this. I could forgive some feeble wretch for giving
up the struggle. But you are different, and with you I quarrel
heartily. You weaklings, this slackness of yours will make a bad   120
situation far worse. Think, each of you, of the shame of your
conduct and how outraged others will be at it in a crisis like this
when Hector, master of the battle-cry, has broken down the
gate and the long bar and is fighting by the very ships!'

With these stirring words Poseidon who encircles the world
rallied the Greeks. Strong ranks formed up under the two
Ajaxes, such as would have made the War-god himself or Athene
who drives on armies think twice. There stood the very pick of
their best men awaiting godlike Hector and the Trojans, an

130 impenetrable hedge of spears and sloping shields, shield to shield, helmet to helmet, man to man. So close were the ranks that, when they moved their heads, their crested helmets with their shining plates touched and the spears overlapped as they brandished them in their sturdy hands. Their minds were fixed on facing the enemy and they were eager for the clash.

The Trojans advanced in a mass and Hector led them, sweeping forward like a boulder bounding down a rocky slope, when a river swollen by winter rain dislodges it over the edge of a plateau and washes away the little stones which hold the 140 misbegotten thing. Leaping high in the air, it hurtles down through echoing woods and then runs on unchecked till it reaches level ground, where it stops rolling, much against its will – so Hector threatened for a while to reach the sea with ease through the Greek camp and ships, killing as he went.

Hector is halted

But when he ran into that solid block of men, he stopped short, hard against them; and the Greeks facing him lunged at him with their swords and curved spears and forced him to retreat. Shaken, Hector withdrew, but sent his voice ringing out to the whole Trojan army:

150 'Stand by me, Trojans, Lycians, and you Dardanians that like your fighting hand to hand! The Greeks will not hold me up for long, packed together though they are like stones in a wall. They will give before my spear, if it is true I was brought here by the best of all gods, Hera's loud-thundering husband!'

With these words he put fresh heart and courage into every man, and his brother Deiphobus fearlessly strode out among them, holding his rounded shield in front of him as he stepped carefully forward, advancing under its cover.

160 Meriones let fly at him with a glittering spear. And he did not miss his man: he hit his rounded oxhide shield. But the long shaft, far from passing through, broke off at the socket – Deiphobus had held the leather shield at arm's length, being afraid of a spear from warlike Meriones. Meriones now retreated into his own contingent of warriors. He was enraged both at the loss of his broken spear and at missing a kill, and he went off at once to the Greek camp and ships to fetch the long spear that he had left in his hut.

Meriones breaks his spear

But the rest fought on and the tumult of battle filled the air. Teucer son of Telamon was the first to kill his man, the spearman 170 Imbrius, son of the horse-owner Mentor. He had lived at Pedaeum before the Greek expedition came and was married to Medesicaste, an illegitimate daughter of Priam's. But when the Greeks arrived in their rolling ships, Imbrius returned to Ilium, distinguished himself among the Trojans and lived with Priam who treated him like one of his own children. Teucer stabbed this man below the ear with his long spear, which he then pulled out. Imbrius fell like an ash-tree that has stood as a landmark on a high hill-top, until 180 it is cut down by an axe and brings its delicate foliage to the ground. So Imbrius fell, and his ornate bronze equipment rang about him.

Teucer kills Imbrius

Teucer ran up, eager to get his armour off, and as he did so, Hector let fly at him with his glittering spear. But Teucer was on the lookout and managed by a hair's breadth to avoid the weapon, which struck Amphimachus' chest as he rushed into the fray. He thudded to the ground, and his armour clattered about him.

Hector kills Amphimachus

As Hector dashed in to tear the close-fitting helmet from great-hearted Amphimachus' temples, Ajax aimed at him with 190 his glittering spear. But no part of his body was exposed; he was completely protected by his intimidating bronze armour, and all Ajax hit was the boss of his shield. Yet the force of the blow was so great that Hector had to give ground and leave the two dead men to be recovered by the Greeks. Amphimachus was conveyed into their lines by Stichius and Menestheus, the Athenian leaders, while Ajax and Teucer, fired up with that fighting spirit of theirs, seized Imbrius' body.

Like a couple of lions which have snatched a goat away from under the noses of the goatherd's sharp-toothed dogs and lift it clear of the ground as they carry it off in their jaws 200 over the dense bushes, so the helmeted Ajax and Teucer held Imbrius aloft and stripped him of his armour. And in his fury at Amphimachus' death, Ajax cut Imbrius' head from his soft neck and with a swing sent it whirling like a ball through the crowd to drop in the dust at Hector's feet.

When Poseidon saw his grandson Amphimachus killed in the heat of the battle, he was bitterly angry and went along by the Greeks' huts and ships to stir them up and make trouble for the Trojans. He met
²¹⁰ Idomeneus the famous spearman. Idomeneus had been with a member of his own contingent who had just come out of the fight with a spear-wound in the back of his knee. This man had been carried in by his comrades, and Idomeneus, after instructing the healers, was going to his own hut, with every intention of returning to the fight, when the lord earthshaker accosted him. Poseidon imitated the voice of Thoas, Andrae-mon's son, who ruled the Aetolians in Pleuron and mountainous Calydon and was honoured like a god by the people:

'Idomeneus, adviser of the Cretans, what has become of all
²²⁰ the threats that the Greeks used to make against the Trojans?'

Idomeneus the Cretan leader replied:

'Thoas, as far as I can see no individuals are to blame. We all know how to fight. Nobody is paralysed with fear or has run away from this horrible battle in panic. This is how almighty Zeus must want it to be – the Greeks destroyed here, far from Greece, with no trace left. But you, Thoas, never waver in battle and are good at inspiring others when you see them giving up.
²³⁰ So don't slacken now. Give every man their orders.'

Poseidon the earthshaker replied:

'Idomeneus, may the man who does not fight his best today never come home from Troy but stay here to delight the dogs! Come, take your arms and follow me. We must get on with this business together, if the pair of us are going to be of any use. Even the poorest fighters turn into brave men when they stand side by side; and you and I know how to take on the very best.'

With these words the god went back again into the turmoil,
²⁴⁰ and Idomeneus made his way to his well-built hut, put on his splendid armour, seized a couple of spears and came out looking like the lightning that Zeus takes in his hand and discharges from glittering Olympus to flash into the distant sky as a sign for mankind. That was how the bronze gleamed on Idomeneus' chest as he ran.

He had hardly left his hut when he was met by Meriones his

brave attendant, who had come to fetch a bronze spear. Powerful Idomeneus said:

'Dearest comrade-in-arms, son of my brother Molus, swift-footed Meriones, why have you left the battlefield to come here? 250 Are you hit and in pain from a weapon? Or have you come with some message for me? I have no desire to sit in my hut myself, but am eager for the fight.'

Sensible Meriones replied:

'Idomeneus, adviser of the bronze-armoured Cretans, I've come for a spear, hoping to find one left in your hut. I broke the one I had when I hit the shield of proud Deiphobus.'

Idomeneus the Cretan leader replied:

'If it's a spear you want, you will find one, or twenty, leaning 260 against the white-plastered wall by the entrance to my hut. They are Trojan spears: I take them from the men I kill. I don't believe in fighting the enemy at a distance. Hence my collection of spears and bossed shields, helmets and glittering body-armour.'

Bravery discussed

Sensible Meriones replied:

'I too have plenty of Trojan weapons in my hut and my black ship, but not where I can pick them up at once. And I don't consider my courage has deserted me either. Whenever battle is 270 joined where men win glory, I take my place in the front line. You are the last of the bronze-armoured Greeks I should have expected to be blind to my ability – you've seen it for yourself.'

Idomeneus the Cretan leader replied:

'No need for you to dwell on that. I know how brave you are and how you would prove it if we were all being gathered by the ships for an ambush. There's nothing like an ambush for bringing a man's worth to light and picking out the wretches from the brave. The wretch changes colour all the time, peering about him this way and that; he can't sit still for nervousness, 280 but fidgets about, shifting from one foot to the other; his heart thumps in his chest as he conjures up death's demons and his teeth chatter. But the brave man never changes colour at all and is not unduly afraid from the moment he settles down in ambush with the rest; all he prays for is to come to grips with the enemy as soon as possible.

'At such a time no one would find fault with your determination and tenacity. If you were hit in action by an arrow or spear, it would not be behind, on your neck or back, that it
290 would fall; it would seek out your chest or belly as you rushed forward into the intimacy of battle in the front line.

'But we mustn't stay here and chatter like little boys, or people may become resentful. Go into my hut and get yourself a spear.'

So he spoke, and Meriones equal of swift Ares snatched up a bronze spear from inside the hut and went after Idomeneus, fully intent on battle. The two were like murderous Ares and
300 his son, fierce and indomitable Rout, before whom the most resolute warrior turns tail, setting out for the wars: they march from Thrace to join the Ephyri or the great-hearted Phlegyans, to bring victory to one side and turn a deaf ear to the prayers of the other – so Meriones and Idomeneus, leaders of men, set out for the battle, bronze armour glittering.

Meriones spoke his mind first:

'Idomeneus son of Deucalion, at what point do you want to enter the fight? On our right, in the centre, or on the left? It's
310 there, I imagine, the Greek defence is most likely to break down.'

Idomeneus the Cretan leader replied:

'There are others to look after the ships in the centre. The two Ajaxes are there, and so is Teucer, the best archer we have and a good man too in a standing fight. Hector is fired up for battle, but they'll give him his fill of fighting, however formidable he is. Indeed, for all his desire to fight, he won't find it easy to overcome their determination and invincible tenacity, as he must before he sets the swift ships on fire – unless Zeus himself
320 helps and hurls a flaming brand among them. Great Ajax son of Telamon will never yield to any mortal man who eats the bread of mother earth and can be cut by bronze or brought down by a great boulder. Ajax would not give way even to Achilles breaker of the battle-line – or at any rate not in a standing fight, though neither he nor anyone else can run like Achilles. So let's make for the left here; and we'll soon find out whether we are going to yield victory to some other man, or he to us.'

So he spoke, and Meriones led off in the direction indicated by Idomeneus and they reached the front.

When the Trojans saw Idomeneus come up like a fire in his courage and his attendant with him, both in their ornate arms, they called to each other across the ranks to attack him in a body, and mass battle was engaged by the sterns of the ships. As, on a day when the dust lies thick on the roadways, currents of air driven by howling winds raise a great, confused dust-cloud, so the front lines massed, and in the chaos every man longed to kill his opponent with his sharp bronze spear. The battlefield of death bristled with the long flesh-cutting spears they wielded, and the eye was dazzled by the glint of bronze from the shimmering helmets, newly polished body-armour and gleaming shields as the two armies came together. None but the most stony-hearted man would have enjoyed the sight and not recoiled.

POSEIDON vs. ZEUS

So the mighty sons of Cronus, Poseidon and Zeus, took different sides and brought terrible sufferings on the warriors. Zeus had in mind a victory for the Trojans and Hector, with a view to honouring swift-footed Achilles. But he did not mean the Greek army to be utterly destroyed in front of Ilium: he was honouring Thetis and her strong-willed son. Poseidon, on the other hand, had emerged stealthily from the grey sea to join the Greeks and inspire them. It distressed him to see them being beaten by the Trojans and he was furious with Zeus. Yet the two gods' descent and parentage were the same, though Zeus was the older and the wiser. For this reason Poseidon was careful not to help the Greeks openly. He took the form of a man and in that disguise kept moving about the army, urging the troops on.

So the gods pulled alternately on the rope of this violent and evenly balanced battle, to make it taut over the two sides. The rope was indestructible and no one could break it; but it broke many men.

Idomeneus, though he was no longer a young man, flung himself into the fight with a shout to his troops. He struck panic into the Trojans by killing Othryoneus, an ally who had joined them from

Idomeneus kills Othryoneus and Asius

330

340

350

360

Cabesus. Drawn by news of the war, this man was a newcomer
to Troy who had asked Priam for the hand of Cassandra, the
most beautiful of his daughters. Instead of giving him gifts for
his bride, he had promised to do great things and drive the
Greeks from his shores, whether they liked it or not. Old Priam,
accepting the offer, had promised him his daughter's hand; and
it was on this understanding that Othryoneus took part in the
fighting.

370 But now Idomeneus let fly at him with a glittering spear and
caught him as he swaggered about. The bronze body-armour he
was wearing did not serve him well: the spear struck him in the
middle of his belly, and he thudded to the ground. Idomeneus
triumphed over him and said:

'Othryoneus, I congratulate you on your betrothal to
Priam's daughter – subject, of course, to your part of the con-
tract being duly fulfilled. We too could do business with you on
the same lines. We will send over to Greece for the loveliest of
Agamemnon's daughters and make her your bride, if you will
380 help us sack the prosperous citadel of Ilium. Step this way with
me to our seafaring ships, where we can come to terms about
your marriage. You will find our price for brides is not exor-
bitant.'

With these words the warrior Idomeneus took him by the
foot and began to drag him away through the thick of the action.
But now Asius came to the rescue. He was on foot in front of
his chariot, which the charioteer kept so close to him that the
horses were breathing down his neck. Asius did his best to kill
Idomeneus. But Idomeneus was too quick for him. He stabbed
him with his spear in the throat under the chin and drove the
point right through. Asius crashed down as an oak crashes down
390 or a poplar or a towering pine, which woodsmen cut down in
the mountains with their newly sharpened axes to make timbers
for a ship. So Asius lay stretched in front of his chariot and
horses, gurgling and clutching at the bloody dust.

His charioteer, losing such wits as he possessed,
had not even the presence of mind to turn his horses
round and slip out of his enemies' hands. Resolute
Antilochus pinned him with a spear through his

*Antilochus
kills Asius'
charioteer*

middle. Again, the bronze body-armour he was wearing did not serve him well: the spear struck him in the middle of his belly. With a gasp he fell headlong from the well-built chariot and Antilochus, son of great-hearted Nestor, drove his horses out of the Trojan into the Greek lines.

Deiphobus, distressed at Asius' death, came up close to Idomeneus and let fly with a glittering spear. *Deiphobus hits Hypsenor* But Idomeneus was on the lookout and avoided the bronze spear by sheltering behind the rounded shield he always carried. It was built of concentric rings of oxhide and of glittering bronze and was fitted with a couple of cross-struts. He crouched under cover of this, and the bronze spear flew over him, drawing a hollow note from the shield as it grazed its edge. But the spear had not flown from Deiphobus' strong arm for nothing. It struck Hypsenor son of Hippasus, shepherd of the people, in the liver under the midriff, bringing him down at once. Deiphobus boasted of his triumph over him in a loud voice:

'So Asius does not lie unavenged! Even on his way to the mighty gate-keeper Hades, I feel he will travel with a light heart now I've given him an escort.'

So he spoke, and his boasting stung the Greeks. It went straight to the heart of warlike Antilochus in particular who, for all his sorrow, did not forget his comrade but ran to stand over him and cover him with his shield. Then two of their trusty men, Mecisteus and worthy Alastor, lifted him from the ground and carried him off to the hollow ships, groaning heavily.

But Idomeneus was still brimming with energy. His one desire was to bring black night down on a Trojan's eyes or to thud to the ground himself in saving the Greeks from destruction. His next victim was the warrior Alcathous, son of Aesyetes and son-in-law of Anchises, whose eldest daughter, Hippodameia, was his wife. Her father and lady mother at home adored her; indeed, there was no other woman of her age with such beauty, skill and intelligence. So the best man in broad Troy had married her – the man Poseidon now killed at Idomeneus' hands. Poseidon put Alcathous in a trance and so shackled his limbs that he

could neither retreat nor leap aside, but was standing there, motionless, like a gravestone or tall, leafy tree when the warrior Idomeneus stabbed him with his spear full in the chest and
440   smashed through his bronze armour.

Idomeneus kills Alcathous and taunts Deiphobus

Up to this moment it had saved him from death, but now it rang out drily as the spear cut through. Alcathous thudded to the ground. The spear was fixed in his heart and its dying palpitations shook the spear to the very butt till at last the imperious War-god Ares stilled its force. Idomeneus boasted of his triumph over him in a loud voice:

'Deiphobus, do we reckon my three victims are a fair exchange for the one you were boasting about so much? Come on, you *lucky* fellow, tackle me yourself and learn the quality of one of
450   Zeus' offspring who is visiting your land. It was Zeus who established our line. He first fathered Minos, lord of Crete; matchless Deucalion was Minos' son; and I am Deucalion's lord over many people in broad Crete; and now my ships have brought me here to bring trouble on you and your father and everyone in Troy.'

So he spoke, and Deiphobus' heart was torn whether to retreat and call on one of his great-hearted compatriots for support, or to see what he could do alone. Deciding that he had better look for help, he went after Aeneas and found him standing idle
460   behind the lines: Aeneas always bore godlike Priam a grudge because Priam gave him such little respect, though he was as good a man as any. Deiphobus went up to him and spoke winged words:

'Aeneas, adviser of the Trojans, you're badly needed for the rescue of Alcathous, your brother-in-law. If you care for your family at all, come and help me save your sister's husband, who lived in your house and looked after you as a child. The great spearman Idomeneus has just killed him.'

So he spoke, and his words went straight to the heart of
470   Aeneas, who went after Idomeneus, fully intent on battle. But

Aeneas advances against Idomeneus

Idomeneus was not to be scared off like a little boy. He waited for him like some mountain boar, confident in his strength, who faces a crowd of huntsmen advancing on him in a lonely spot: his back bristles, his eyes flame like fire and he sharpens his tusks, eager to take on men and dogs – so the great spearman Idomeneus awaited the onslaught of Aeneas and gave no ground at all. But he did call for support, looking especially to Ascalaphus, Aphareus and Deipyrus as well as Meriones and Antilochus, champions of the battle-cry. Calling on them, he spoke winged   480 words:

'Here, friends, help! I'm alone and in fear of an attack from swift-footed Aeneas, who is making for me now. He is a mighty killer in a fight; and he has the great advantage of youth. If our ages were matched as our courage is now, there would soon be a triumph for Aeneas or myself.'

So Idomeneus spoke, and, united in their resolution, his companions all closed in and rallied round him, crouching behind sloped shields. But Aeneas, on his side, also called upon his friends, looking for help to Deiphobus, Paris and godlike   490 Agenor, his fellow leaders in the Trojan army. The troops backed him too, like sheep following the leader of the flock from the pasture to drink at a stream, delighting the shepherd. So Aeneas was pleased to see the body of men behind him.

They now fought at close quarters over Alcathous' body with their long spears, and the bronze armour rang intimidatingly on their chests as they aimed at each other across the ranks. But there were two warriors, Aeneas and Idomeneus,   500 equals of Ares, who surpassed all the rest in their desire to slice into each other's flesh with their cruel spears.

Aeneas threw at Idomeneus first. But Idomeneus was on the lookout and avoided his bronze spear, which flew by and hit the ground, quivering: it had *Oenomaus* and Ascalaphus killed leapt from his strong hand for nothing. Then Idomeneus threw. He hit Oenomaus full in the belly, smashing a plate in his armour, and his bowels gushed through. Oenomaus fell in the dust, clutching at the ground. Idomeneus dragged his long-shadowed spear out of the body but, overwhelmed as he was by missiles, was unable to strip the man's fine arms and armour   510 from his shoulders. He was no longer quick enough to dash in and recover his own throw or avoid someone else's; and being too slow on his feet to save his life by running, he fought where he stood and so kept death at bay.

Now as he moved slowly off, Deiphobus, who continued to bear a grudge against him for his taunts, hurled his glittering spear at him. For the second time he missed Idomeneus; but the spear hit Ascalaphus, a son of Ares. The heavy weapon went 520 right through his shoulder, and he fell in the dust and clutched at the ground. But it was only later that his imperious father, deep-voiced Ares, heard that his son had fallen in the thick of the action. At the moment he was sitting high up on Olympus under the golden clouds, where he was detained by the plan of Zeus together with the rest of the immortal gods for whom the war was also out of bounds.

It was now over Ascalaphus that they fought each other at close quarters. Deiphobus had just torn the glittering helmet from his head when Meriones, equal of swift Ares, leapt in and struck his arm near the shoulder with a spear. The helmet with its heavy vizor dropped 530 from his hand and fell to the ground with a clang; and like a vulture Meriones swooped in again, withdrew the weighty spear from his arm and then retreated into his own contingent of warriors. Polites, Deiphobus' brother, putting his arm round his waist, supported him out of the battle and brought him to his swift horses, who were waiting for him behind the fighting with their charioteer and his decorated chariot. They carried him off to the town, groaning heavily and racked with pain, blood pouring from the fresh wound in his arm.

Meriones
wounds
Deiphobus

540   But the rest fought on, and the tumult of battle filled the air. Aeneas now charged in and with his sharp spear stabbed Aphareus, who was facing him, in the throat. The man's head jerked backwards; he crumpled up under his shield and helmet, and heart-crushing death engulfed him. Meanwhile, Antilochus, seizing a moment when Thoön's back was turned, leapt in and stabbed him. He sheared off the whole vein that runs up the back to the neck. Thoön dropped backwards in the dust, stretching his hands out 550 to his comrades-in-arms. Antilochus fell on him and began to strip him of his armour, but kept a sharp look-out, for the

Death of
Aphareus and
Thoön

Trojans started coming up on every side. They stabbed at his broad and glittering shield, but they could not so much as scratch the smooth skin of Antilochus' neck with their cruel spears. For this son of Nestor's was protected by Poseidon the earthshaker, even under a hail of spears as fierce as this. Unable to shake off his enemies, Antilochus wheeled round to face them, now on this side, now on that. His spear was never still for a moment but shook as he brandished it, threatening to throw it at a distant opponent or lunge at close range.

Antilochus was just preparing to throw into the crowd when Adamas son of Asius, who had watched for the chance, leapt in and stabbed at the centre of his shield with his sharp spear. Sable-haired Poseidon denied it Antilochus' life and blunted its force, with the result that half of it stuck in the shield like a charred stake, while the other half fell to the ground. Adamas retreated into his own contingent of warriors to avoid death. 560

But Meriones followed him as he withdrew and hit him with his spear between the navel and genitals, where death in battle comes most painfully to wretched mortals. There the spear went home, and Adamas, collapsing, writhed round it, as a wild mountain bull twists about when herdsmen have caught and roped it and bring it in against its will. So the stricken fighter writhed, but not for long – only till the warrior Meriones came up and pulled the spear out of his flesh. Then darkness engulfed his eyes.

Adamas and Deipyrus killed 570

Helenus then closed with Deipyrus and struck him on the temple with his big Thracian sword, slicing through his helmet-strap. The dislodged helmet fell to the ground and was picked up by a Greek as it rolled among the fighters' feet. Black night came down and engulfed Deipyrus' eyes. 580

Menelaus, master of the battle-cry, was distressed when he saw this and made for the warrior lord Helenus with a menacing shout, brandishing a sharp spear. Helenus drew his bow, and the two were ready to let fly at the same moment, one with a sharp spear, the other with an arrow from the string. Helenus struck Menelaus' chest with his arrow on a plate of his body-armour, but it ricocheted

Helenus is wounded by Menelaus

off. As black beans or chickpeas on a broad threshing-floor leap
590 from the flat shovel with the whistling wind and the winnower's
force behind them, so the painful arrow ricocheted off Mene-
laus' body-armour and flew away into the distance. But Mene-
laus, master of the battle-cry, struck Helenus on the hand in
which he was holding his polished bow, and the bronze spear
went clean through his hand into the bow. Helenus retreated
into his own contingent of warriors to avoid death, with his
hand hanging down at his side and dragging the ash spear along.
The spear was withdrawn from his wound by great-hearted
600 Agenor, who bound up the hand with a sling made of twisted
wool which his attendant was able to give him.

Menelaus kills   Peisander now made straight for illustrious Mene-
Peisander and   laus. It was an evil destiny that led him on this path,
abuses the   with death at the end of it, death, Menelaus, in the
Trojans   heat of battle with you. When the two men had come
                    within range of each other, Menelaus missed – his
spear swerved wide. Peisander stabbed the shield of illustrious
Menelaus, but was unable to drive the spear through. The broad
shield held it up, and the spear snapped at the socket. Peisander
was delighted at the hit, scenting victory. But now Menelaus
610 drew his silver-riveted sword and charged him. Peisander from
under his shield brought out a fine bronze axe with a long,
smooth haft of olive-wood. They met; and Peisander hit the
ridge of Menelaus' helmet on the top, just below the horsehair
plume. But Menelaus caught Peisander, as he charged at him,
on the forehead above the base of the nose. The bones cracked
and his eyes, all bloody, dropped in the dust at his feet. He
doubled up and fell. Menelaus put his foot on his chest, stripped
off his armour and spoke in triumph:

620   'That's how you'll be retreating from the Greek ships, you
insolent Trojans, always spoiling for a fight! Not that you are
amateurs in other forms of abusive and shameful behaviour.
Look at how you abused me, you dirty dogs, when you broke
the laws of hospitality and defied the wrath of loud-thundering
Zeus, protector of guests, who is going to bring Ilium tumbling
down before long. You stole my wife and sailed away with her
and much of my wealth for no reason at all, since you had been

hospitably treated in her palace. And now you won't be satisfied till you have sent our seafaring ships up in flames and slaughtered us. You're spoiling for a fight, but one day you'll be stopped. 630

'Ah, Father Zeus, they say you are wiser than any man or god – and all this is your doing! You are so indulgent towards these Trojan bullies, who have a passion for evil and an insatiable desire for the din of battle, that great leveller. People tire of everything, even of sleep and love-making, of sweet music and the elegant dance. Everyone would far rather satisfy themselves with these things than war, but the Trojans are gluttons for it.'

With these words matchless Menelaus stripped the blood-stained armour from the body and gave it to his men. Then he went and engaged once more with the front ranks. 640

No sooner was he there than he was attacked by Harpalion, son of lord Pylaemenes, who had come with his father to the Trojan War, never to return to his own country again. Closing with Menelaus, Harpalion thrust at the centre of his shield with a spear; but being unable to drive the spear through, he retreated into his own contingent of warriors to avoid death, keeping a lookout on every side for any missile that might come his way. As he withdrew, Meriones shot him with a bronze-headed arrow and hit him in the right buttock. The arrow went clean through his bladder and came out under the pubic bone. Harpalion collapsed at once, gasped out his life in the arms of his friends and lay stretched out on the ground like a dead worm, while the dark blood poured out of him and soaked the earth. Gathering round him, the great-hearted Paphlagonians lifted him into a chariot and with heavy hearts drove him to sacred Ilium. His weeping father went with them. There was no compensation for his son's death. 650

Meriones kills Harpalion

But the slaughter of Harpalion roused Paris to anger, since this Paphlagonian had been his guest, and he shot an arrow in fury for his friend. There was a Greek called Euchenor, son of the prophet Polyidus, a man of substance and good birth who lived in Corinth. When he 660

Paris kills Euchenor

embarked for Troy, he knew well enough the grim fate that awaited him, since his old father, good Polyidus, had often told him he must either die in his bed of a painful disease or sail with the Greeks and be killed at Troy. So he went, avoiding the heavy forfeit the Greeks would have demanded for not serving, and
670 saving himself from hateful illness and the pain he did not wish to bear. Paris now hit him with his arrow under the jaw and ear. Life left his limbs at once, and hateful darkness engulfed him.

So they fought on like blazing fire. But Hector dear to Zeus, who had not been kept informed, had no idea that on the left of the ships his troops were being slaughtered by the Greeks. Indeed, the Greeks came close to winning, so effectively did Poseidon, the earthshaker who encircles the world, inspire them, besides putting his own efforts into their defence. So Hector was still on the attack in that part of the front where he had first
680 broken the shield-bearing Greek ranks and stormed the gate and wall, and where the ships of Ajax son of Oïleus and Protesilaus were drawn up on the shore of the grey sea. There the protecting wall had been lower than elsewhere, and the Greek infantry and chariots were putting up the fiercest defence.

Greek gate
defended
against *Hector*

The troops at this point, the Boeotians, the Ionians with their long tunics, the Locrians, Phthians and splendid Eleans, had the utmost difficulty in holding off godlike Hector's attack on the ships and were quite unable to thrust him back: he came at them like fire.
690 Picked men from Athens were fighting here, led by Menestheus, supported by Pheides, Stichius and brave Bias; while the Eleans were commanded by Meges, Amphion and Dracius; and the Phthians by Medon and resolute Podarces. One of these, Medon, was a bastard son of godlike Oïleus and so a brother of Ajax. But he had been exiled for homicide and lived in Phylace, having killed a kinsman of his step-mother Eriopis, the wife of Oïleus. Podarces, the other, was a son of Iphiclus the son of Phylacus. These two in their full armour were fighting to defend
700 the ships in front of the Phthians and side by side with the Boeotians.

Ajax swift son of Oïleus was never separated even for a

moment from Ajax son of Telamon. As a pair of dark-faced oxen strain at the jointed plough in fallow ground, each as hard as the other; with the sweat pouring out at the base of their horns and separated only by their polished yoke, they press on down the furrow till they reach the turning point at the end of the field – so these stood alongside each other, cheek by jowl. The son of Telamon was backed by a fine, strong body of men who relieved him of his shield when he was overcome by the heat and fatigue; but the great-hearted son of Oïleus was not accompanied by his Locrian troops, who had no stomach for the standing fight since they did not possess appropriate arms – bronze helmets with crests, rounded shields and ash spears. They relied on bows and slings of well-twisted wool. It was with these weapons that they had followed their leader to Ilium and after their arrival used them extensively to break through the Trojan ranks. So now, while the troops in their ornate armour engaged the Trojans and bronze-clad Hector in the front line, the Locrians kept shooting at them from well out of sight in the rear. The Trojans, thrown into confusion by the arrows, began to lose their will to fight.

Then they would have made a miserable retreat back from the Greek ships and huts towards windswept Ilium, had not Polydamas gone up to daring Hector and said:

'Hector, you are an obstinate man when it comes to taking good advice. Just because the god gave you uncommon fighting ability, you like to think you know better than anyone else about tactics too. But you cannot possibly take responsibility for everything. The god gives men differing gifts. One man can fight, another dance, another sing poetry to the lyre; and yet another is endowed by far-thundering Zeus with a good brain, to the advantage of many of his friends. It saves them from disaster time and again, as *he* knows even better than they do.

Polydamas tells Hector to regroup

'However, I will tell you what I think best. The fighting has blazed up all round you in a ring. Our great-hearted men certainly stormed the wall, but having done so some are now standing idle under arms, while others are scattered among the Greek ships and fighting against odds. So withdraw and call in

710

720

730

740

all your best men. We could then consult and settle the whole question whether to fall on their ships, if the god wishes to give us a decisive victory, or failing that to withdraw from them intact. I, for one, am afraid the Greeks are going to pay us back for what we did to them yesterday. They have got a man biding his time beside their ships who is insatiable for battle; and I can't believe he will keep out of the fighting altogether.'

So spoke Polydamas, and his timely advice seemed excellent
750 to Hector. He replied and spoke winged words:

'Polydamas, stay here and keep all the best men round you, while I go and deal with the situation over there. I shall soon be back when I've given them my orders.'

He spoke and sped away, looking like a snow-capped peak, and as he passed swiftly through the Trojan ranks and those of their allies, he shouted to his men. They all ran up when they heard Hector's voice and massed themselves round Panthous' son, amiable Polydamas. But Hector went up and down the
760 front line looking to see if he could find Deiphobus, strong lord Helenus, Adamas son of Asius or Asius himself, son of Hyrtacus. He found not one of them alive or uninjured. Two had fallen to the Greeks and lay dead by the sterns of the ships, while the others were back within the town wall, wounded at long or short range. But he did find one man quickly enough, on the left flank of the battlefield with all its tears, and that was godlike Paris, husband of lovely-haired Helen. Paris was encouraging his men and urging them into battle. Hector went up to him and insulted him:

'Paris, you parody, with your wonderful looks, you sex-
770 crazed seducer, where, I ask you, are Deiphobus and strong lord Helenus, Adamas son of Asius, and Asius son of Hyrtacus? And where, please, is Othryoneus? This is indeed the end of steep Ilium, from top to bottom. There is nothing for you now but death.'

Godlike Paris replied:

Paris tells Hector of Trojan losses

'Hector, you're blaming an innocent man in your rage. If I have ever shrunk from fighting, my mother still did not bear an utter coward; and from the moment you told your men to attack by the ships,

we've held our ground here and kept the Greeks engaged relent-
lessly. The friends you ask about are killed, except Deiphobus   780
and strong lord Helenus who have withdrawn. Each was
wounded by a long spear in the arm, but Zeus saved their lives.

'Lead us now wherever you wish. We'll follow you with a
will and, I think, with no lack of courage either, so far as we are
able. What a man cannot do, however committed, is fight
beyond his ability.'

With these words the warrior Paris pacified his brother, and
they went off together into the sound and fury of battle, which
was raging now round Cebriones and matchless Polydamas,   790
Phalces, Orthaeus, godlike Polyphetes, Palmys, and Ascanius
and Morys, who had arrived as replacements from fertile
Ascania on the morning of the previous day, and now Zeus
inspired them to fight.

The Trojans came on like an angry squall that
swoops down from Zeus' thunder-laden sky: it   Ajax and
throws the ocean into indescribable turmoil, where   *Hector*
innumerable waves of the sounding sea hiss and arch exchange
their foaming backs in a never-ending procession –   threats
so the Trojans came on behind their leaders, rank after rank,   800
glittering with bronze, and with Hector, equal of the mur-
derous War-god Ares, at their head. In front of him he held his
rounded shield with its close layers of hide and covering of
beaten bronze, and his gleaming helmet nodded on his temples.
Hector sprang forward and probed the enemy line at various
points in the hope that it would break before him as he charged
under the cover of his shield. But he did not shake the Greeks'
resolution. Ajax first challenged him, striding confidently
forward:

'*Brilliant* Hector, do come closer. Why are you trying to   810
terrify the Greeks like this? We do know something about war;
it is just that we have been under Zeus' evil whip. I suppose you
imagine you're going to destroy our ships. But we too have
hands ready to fight for them and likely to capture your fine
town and sack it, long before you get our ships. As for you, I
say the time is drawing near when you will take to your heels
and pray to Father Zeus and the other gods to make your

820   lovely-maned horses faster than falcons as they carry you back
      home to Ilium in clouds of dust.'

         As he spoke a bird flew by on the right, a high-soaring eagle.
      The Greek troops were heartened by the omen and shouted for
      joy. But glorious Hector replied:

         'Ajax, you've got it wrong, you great oaf. What are you
      talking about? If only I could be as certain of spending my days
      as the son of Zeus who drives the storm-cloud, with the lady
      Hera as my mother, and be honoured as Athene and Apollo are
      honoured, as I am of this day proving disastrous to the Greeks,
      all of them. You'll die with the rest of them, if you dare to stand
830   up to my long spear which is going to feast on your lily-white
      skin. Yes, you'll fall by your own ships, and your flesh and fat
      shall glut the Trojan dogs and birds of prey.'

         With these words Hector led off, and his men came after him
      with a mighty roar, while the whole force behind them took up
      the cry. The Greeks answered with their own war-cry and,
      summoning up their courage, awaited the onslaught of the
      Trojans' best. The clamour from the two armies reached the
      upper air and the very eye of Olympus.

14

ZEUS
OUTMANOEUVRED

1–152: Nestor finds Odysseus, Diomedes and Agamemnon all wounded. Odysseus attacks Agamemnon for cowardice. POSEI-DON heartens Agamemnon with a speech.

153–360: HERA decides to send ZEUS to sleep by making love to him. She decks herself out, gets *APHRODITE*'s love charm and persuades SLEEP to join her. HERA and ZEUS make love and ZEUS falls asleep. SLEEP tells POSEIDON he can carry on helping the Greeks.

361–439: POSEIDON rallies the Greeks, and Ajax takes *Hector* out of the fighting with a rock.

440–522: A series of killings ensues. The *Trojans* are routed and run.

The din was so great that it reached the ears of Nestor who was drinking in his hut, and he spoke to Machaon with winged words:

'Godlike Machaon, we must consider what to do. The cries of our brave young men are growing louder by the ships. You sit here for the time being and drink your sparkling wine, till Hecamede has heated some water and washed the congealed blood from your wound. I'll find some place where I can see what is going on.'

With these words Nestor picked up a well-made shield of gleaming bronze that was lying in his hut and belonged to his son horse-taming Thrasymedes, who was using his father's. He took a strong spear too with a sharp bronze point and had no sooner stepped outside his hut than he saw a shocking sight –

the Greeks in full rout with the proud Trojans close on their
heels. The Greek wall had fallen.

As the great open sea heaves under a soundless swell; it
vaguely senses the onset of a whistling gale, but the waves cannot
begin their march this way or that till the wind sets in decisively
20 from one quarter or the other – so the old man faltered between
two courses, unable to make up his mind whether to join the
Greeks with their swift horses in the fight or to seek out Agam-
emnon shepherd of the people. In the end he decided the best
thing was to go to Agamemnon. Meanwhile, the fighting and
slaughter continued, and the hard bronze rang out on men's
bodies as it met the thrust of sword or curved spear.

On his way, Nestor fell in with the leaders who
had been wounded, Diomedes, Odysseus and Agam-
emnon. They were coming up from their ships which
were stationed on the shore of the grey sea a long
30 way from the present fighting. The reason was that the first ships
to arrive had been hauled up well inland on the plain, and it
was by their sterns that the wall had been built. For the beach
itself, wide as it was, had proved unable to hold all the ships,
and the Greeks, cramped for room, had drawn them up in rows
covering the whole seaboard of the long bay from headland to
headland. So, in order to get a view of the battle, the leaders
were making their way inland together, propping themselves up
on their spears, deeply depressed. When they met the old man
40 Nestor, their hearts sank further. Lord Agamemnon spoke to
him and said:

'Nestor son of Neleus, great glory of the Greeks, why have
you turned your back on the killing fields and come down here?
I am afraid imperious Hector is going to carry out the threat he
made in the speech to his men – that he would never fall back
from the ships to Ilium till he had sent them up in flames and
slaughtered us as well. That was the promise he made them, and
now everything he said is coming true. Hell! The whole army
50 must be as furious with me as Achilles is, if they refuse to make
a stand by the sterns of the ships.'

Nestor the Gerenian charioteer replied:

'Some such disaster is certainly upon us, and high-thundering

Greek despair
(11.252, 377,
437)

Zeus himself could not avert it. We thought the wall was an impregnable defence for the ships and ourselves. That has now fallen, and our men are faced with a long and desperate fight beside the swift ships. Look as hard as you will, you cannot tell whether the Greeks are being chased and harried from the front or the rear, so confused is the slaughter – and the din reaches the skies. We should now consider what to do next – if thinking can do any good. But I don't advise we go into battle ourselves. No wounded man can fight.'

Agamemnon lord of men replied:

'Nestor, since the fighting has reached the sterns of ships, and neither the strong wall nor the ditch that cost the Greeks so much effort has been of any use, though they looked on them as an impregnable defence for the ships and ourselves, then this, I suppose, is how almighty Zeus must want it to be – the Greeks destroyed here, far from Greece, with no trace left. I felt this when he was helping the Greeks with all his heart and I realize it now, when he is exalting the Trojans to the level of the blessed gods and has reduced us to impotence.

'So I suggest we all do what I now propose. Let's drag down the ships that were drawn up next to the sea, launch them on the bright water and moor them well out, till night allows us to drag down all the rest – unless the Trojans go on fighting even then. There is nothing to be ashamed of in running from disaster, even by night. It's better to save one's skin by running than to be caught.'

Quick-thinking Odysseus gave him a black look and said:

'Agamemnon, why do you say such a thing? Damn you, you should have taken charge of some tin-pot army instead of leading people like ourselves, obliged by Zeus to see wars through to their bitter end from cradle to grave till one by one we drop. So this is how you propose to bid farewell to the Trojans' city with its broad streets, for which we have suffered so much! Hold your tongue, or the men may get wind of this idea of yours which nobody with any sense would ever put into words – least of all a man in authority with a huge army like yours to command.

'I think you've lost your mind to expect us, in the middle of a

60

70

80

Odysseus: do not abandon war

90

pitched battle, to drag our ships into the sea and to give the Trojans, who are masters enough of the situation already, everything they've ever prayed for. They will wipe out the whole expedition. The Greeks will never keep a steady front while their ships are being dragged down into the sea. They will do nothing but look over their shoulders and lose all their will to fight. That will be the fatal effect of your tactics, commander.'

Agamemnon lord of men replied:

'A harsh rebuke, Odysseus! But I admit you're right. Very well, then, I will not instruct the men to drag the ships into the sea against their inclination. But now one of *you* must come forward with a sounder scheme than mine. Seniority does not matter. I shall be pleased to hear him.'

Diomedes, master of the battle-cry, spoke out:

'The man we need is close at hand. We shall not have far to seek, if you are willing to admit it and not resent the fact that I am the youngest man among you. After all, I too can boast of a noble father and family.

'My father was Tydeus, whose bones lie buried under a grave-mound in Thebes. And he was descended from Portheus, who had three matchless sons, living in Pleuron and steep Calydon – Agrius, Melas and lastly Oeneus the charioteer, my father's father, who was the bravest of them all. Oeneus did not move from his old home, but Zeus and the other gods must have planned a different life for my father Tydeus, who left for Argos, where he married one of Adrestus' daughters and settled in luxury with a house, some good cornland, many private orchards and plenty of livestock. And there was no Greek to compare with him in spearmanship.

'But you must have heard all this and know whether it is true. So you cannot take exception to any proposal I put forward (if it is a good one) on the grounds of a humble, cowardly background. What I now suggest is that we visit the battlefield – indeed we must, wounded though we are. When we are there, let us ourselves refrain from fighting and keep out of range of their missiles, or one of us may be wounded again. But what we *can* do is to press others into the fight, those, I mean, who, though

Diomedes suggests visiting the troops

previously loyal, have distanced themselves and kept out of it.'

So he spoke, and they heard and agreed. Agamemnon lord of men led off, and they all set out.

None of this had escaped the watchful eye of the famous earthshaker Poseidon. Disguising himself as an old man, he went after them and, taking hold of Agamemnon's right hand, spoke winged words:

'Agamemnon, no doubt Achilles is rejoicing in his black heart 140 as he sees the Greeks put to flight and slaughtered, fool that he is, without a grain of sense. Well, let him go to hell: god blind him. As for you, my lord, the blessed gods are not yet completely ill-disposed towards you. On the contrary, the day is still coming when the Trojan captains and commanders will fill the wide plain with dust and you, with your own eyes, will see them fleeing to their town from your ships and huts.'

POSEIDON
heartens
Agamemnon

With these words Poseidon sped off across the plain with a great shout, as loud as the war-cry of nine or ten thousand warriors joined in battle. Such was the cry that came from the 150 throat of the lord earthshaker and filled the heart of every Greek with mighty courage to do battle and fight the enemy relentlessly.

Now Hera of the golden throne, looking out from where she stood on the summit of Olympus, was quick to observe how Poseidon, her brother and brother-in-law, was bustling about on the field of battle, and she rejoiced. But she also saw Zeus sitting on the highest peak of Mount Ida of the many springs, and the sight filled her with disgust.

So ox-eyed lady Hera began to wonder how she could hood- 160 wink Zeus who drives the storm-cloud; and she decided the best way to do it was this. She would deck herself out to her best advantage and visit him on Mount Ida. If, as well might be, he succumbed to her beauty and desired to make love to her, she would flood his eyes and sharp mind with soothing, forgetful sleep.

HERA
plans to seduce
ZEUS (8.10)

Accordingly she made her way to her bedroom that had been built for her by her own son Hephaestus who, when he had hung the heavy doors on their posts, fitted them with a secret

lock which no other god could open. Hera went in and closed the polished doors behind her. She began by removing every
170 stain from her desirable body with ambrosia and then lavishly anointing herself with the ambrosial oil with which her dress was scented; this only had to flutter in the bronze-floored palace of Zeus for its scent to spread through earth and sky alike. With this she smoothed her lovely skin and hair, then combed her hair and with her own hands plaited her shining locks and let them fall in their divine beauty from her immortal head. Next she put on an ambrosial robe that Athene had woven smooth, then finished and richly embroidered. She fastened it across her
180 breast with golden clasps and, at her waist, tied a girdle from which a hundred tassels hung. In the pierced lobes of her ears she fixed two shining earrings, each a thing of brilliant grace with its cluster of three drops. Then the celestial goddess covered her hair with a beautiful new head-dress which was as bright as the sun; and last of all, she bound a fine pair of sandals under her shimmering feet.

When she had decked herself out to look her best, she left her bedroom, beckoned Aphrodite away from the other gods and spoke her mind:
190 'I wonder, dear child, whether you will do me a favour, or refuse because you are annoyed with me for helping the Greeks, while you are on the Trojans' side.'

Aphrodite daughter of Zeus replied:

'Hera, august goddess, daughter of great Cronus, tell me what is in your mind and I shall gladly do what you ask of me, if I can and if the task is not impossible.'

The lady Hera deceptively replied:

'Give me Love and Desire, the powers by which you yourself
200 subdue gods and men alike. You see, I am going to the ends of the fruitful earth to visit Ocean, forefather of the gods, and mother Tethys, who treated me kindly and brought me up in their own home after taking me from my mother Rhea, when far-thundering Zeus made my father Cronus a prisoner under the earth and the murmuring sea. I am going to see them and bring their interminable quarrels to an end. They have not been sleeping

APHRODITE gives HERA her magic charm

together for a long time now, as a result of an angry row. If by
talking the matter over I could win them round and bring them
together again in bed, I should win their affection and esteem   210
for ever.'

Laughter-loving Aphrodite said:

'To refuse a request from you, that sleep in the arms of Zeus
the supreme, would be both wrong and impossible.'

She spoke and undid from her breast the charm decorated
with ornaments in which all her magic resides, Sexual Pleasure
and Desire and Intimacies and Sweet Persuasion, that turn even
wise men into fools. She placed this in Hera's hands and said:

'There, take this charm with its ornaments and keep it in your
bosom. All my magic resides in this, and I have no doubt that   220
you will come back from your mission successful.'

So she spoke, and ox-eyed lady Hera smiled and, as she tucked
the charm into her bosom, she smiled again.

Aphrodite daughter of Zeus went home, and Hera sped down
from the summit of Olympus. First she dropped to the Pierian
range and to lovely Emathia; then passed swiftly over the snowy
mountains of the horse-breeding Thracians, the very highest
peaks, but never setting foot on the ground. From Athos she
travelled over the foaming sea and so came to Lemnos, town of   230
lord Thoas, where she found the god of Sleep, brother of Death.
Putting her hand in his she said:

'Sleep, lord of all gods and all mankind, if ever you
listened to me in the past, do what I ask of you now   HERA
and I shall be grateful to you for ever. Seal the bright   persuades
eyes of Zeus for me in sleep, directly I have lain in   SLEEP to help
love with him, and in return I will give you a beautiful chair,
imperishable, golden, which the lame god Hephaestus, my own
son, will make and finish for you, with a footstool underneath   240
it, on which you could rest your gleaming feet as you dine.'

Sweet Sleep replied and said:

'Hera, august queen, daughter of mighty Cronus, I should
think it a small matter to put any of the other eternal gods to
sleep, even Ocean Stream himself, forefather of all. But I dare
not go near Zeus son of Cronus or send him to sleep, unless he
asks me to do so himself.

'I have learnt my lesson from the task you once set me before,
250   when Heracles, that arrogant son of Zeus, set sail from Ilium
after sacking the Trojans' town, and you made up your mind
to make trouble for him. I gently lulled Zeus who drives the
storm-cloud to sleep, while you raised a terrible tempest at sea
and carried Heracles off to the prosperous island of Cos, far
from all his friends. Zeus was enraged when he awoke. He
hurled the gods about in his palace and looked for me every-
where as the chief culprit. I would have been thrown from
Olympus into the sea and never heard of again, if Night, who
overpowers gods and men alike, had not rescued me. I found
260   sanctuary with her, and Zeus, for all his fury, had to stop and
think twice before doing something that swift Night would
not like. And now you come to me once more with another
impossible request!'

Ox-eyed lady Hera said:

'Sleep, why are you so worried about this? Can you really
think that far-thundering Zeus will exert himself in defence of
the Trojans as he did when it was the abduction of his very own
son, Heracles, that had enraged him? Come, do as I wish and I
will give you one of the younger Graces in marriage. She shall
be called your wife.'

270   So she spoke, and Sleep was delighted and replied:

'Very well, swear to me now by the inviolable waters of Styx,
grasping the bountiful Earth with one hand and the shimmering
Sea with the other, so that all the gods who are below with
Cronus may be our witnesses; and promise you will give me
one of the younger Graces, Pasitheë, whom I have desired all
my life.'

So he spoke, and the goddess white-armed Hera agreed and
gave him her oath in the way he had prescribed, naming all the
gods under Tartarus, who are called Titans. When she had
280   sworn and completed the oath, the two wrapped themselves in
mist and set out, leaving the towns of Lemnos and Imbros
behind them and travelling fast. They reached Mount Ida of the
many springs, the mother of wild beasts, by way of a promontory
at its foot, Lecton, where they first left the sea and passed over
the dry land, causing the treetops to sway beneath their feet. But

now, to avoid the eye of Zeus, Sleep came to a halt and climbed up into a tall pine-tree, the tallest on Ida, which reached through the mist up into the clear air above. There he perched, hidden by the branches, in the form of a songbird of the mountains   290
which is called bronze-throat by the gods and eagle-owl by men.

Meanwhile Hera rapidly drew near to Gargarus, the highest peak of lofty Ida. Zeus who marshals the clouds saw her, and at the first look desire overwhelmed his heart, as in the days when they had first made love and gone to bed together without their parents' knowledge. He went up to her and said:

'Hera, what business brings you here from Olympus? And why no horses and chariot to drive in?'

The lady Hera deceptively replied: 300

'Oh, I am going to the ends of the fruitful earth to visit Ocean, forefather of the gods, and mother Tethys, who treated me kindly and brought me up in their own home. I am going to see them and bring their interminable quarrels to an end. They have not been sleeping together for a long time now, as a result of an angry row. As for my horses . . . oh, they are waiting at the foot of Ida, ready to carry me back over the water and the solid land. But at the moment I have come here from Olympus to see *you*. I was worried you might become angry with me   310
afterwards, if I paid a visit to the deep Stream of Ocean without letting you know.'

Zeus who marshals the clouds replied and said:

'Hera, that's a journey you can postpone. Come, let us to bed and the delights of love. Never has such desire, for goddess or mortal, flooded and over-whelmed my heart; no, not when I loved Ixion's wife who bore Peirithous, wise as the gods; or Danaë of the slim ankles, daughter of Acrisius, who gave birth to Perseus, the greatest   320
hero of his time; or the far-famed daughter of Phoenix, who bore me Minos and godlike Rhadamanthus; or Semele, or Alcmene in Thebes, whose son was lion-hearted Heracles, while Semele bore Dionysus, mankind's delight; or lady Demeter with her lovely hair, or incomparable Leto; or you yourself – never have I felt such desire for you, or has such sweet longing overwhelmed me.'

HERA seduces ZEUS

The lady Hera replied deceptively:

330 'Dread son of Cronus, what *are* you suggesting now! Suppose
we do as you wish and make love on the heights of Ida, everyone
will see everything. What will happen if one of the eternal gods
saw us sleeping together and ran off to tell the rest? I certainly
wouldn't relish the idea of rising straight from such a bed and
going back to your palace. Think of the scandal! No, if it really
is your pleasure to do this, you have a bedroom that your own
son Hephaestus built for you, and the doors he made for it are
340 solid. Let us go and lie down there, since bed takes your fancy.'

Zeus who marshals the clouds replied and said:

'Hera, don't be afraid any god or man will see us. I'll hide
you in a golden cloud. Even the sun, whose rays provide him
with the keenest sight in all the world, will not be able to see
through it.'

The son of Cronus spoke and took his wife in his arms; and
the divine earth sent up spring flowers beneath them, dewy
clover and crocuses and a soft and crowded bed of hyacinths,
350 to lift them off the ground. In this they lay, covered by a beautiful
golden cloud, from which a rain of glistening dewdrops fell.

While the Father lay peacefully on top of Mount Gargarus,
with his arms round his wife, conquered by sleep and love, sweet
Sleep flew off to the Greek ships to tell the earthshaker who
encircles the world the news. He went up to him and spoke
winged words:

'Poseidon, help the Greeks now with all your heart and give
them the upper hand, if only for a short time, while Zeus still
360 slumbers. I sent him into a deep and gentle sleep after Hera had
tricked him into making love to her.'

POSEIDON
rallies the
Greeks

With these words Sleep went off among the famous
nations of mankind, leaving Poseidon more enthusi-
astic than ever in his championship of the Greeks.
With a great leap forward into the front ranks, he
issued his orders:

'Greeks, are we going once more to leave the victory to Hector
son of Priam, to let him destroy the ships and win the glory? He
says he will and boasts about it – but only because Achilles sits
in a fury by his hollow ships. Yet Achilles will not be missed so

very much, if the rest of us can only rouse ourselves to stand by one another.

'So I suggest we all do what I now propose. Let's equip 370 ourselves with the best and biggest shields in the camp, put dazzling helmets on our heads and go into the fight with the longest spears we can lay our hands on. I myself will take command and I don't think Hector son of Priam will stand up to us long, for all his determination. Let every warrior who has proved his worth in battle, but carries a small shield, hand it over to a weaker man, and equip himself with a larger shield.'

So he spoke, and they heard and agreed. Wounded as they were, the leaders themselves, Diomedes, Odysseus and Aga- 380 memnon, prepared their men for the struggle, visiting the ranks and interchanging their arms, so that the best warriors were now the best equipped, giving their inferior weapons to inferior troops. When all had put on their gleaming bronze, they set out with the earthshaker Poseidon at their head, carrying his long and fearful sword in his great hand. The sword is like a lightning flash. No one may engage with Poseidon in battle, and men shrink from him in terror.

On the other side glorious Hector brought the Trojans into battle order. And now the most appalling fight of all was staged by sable-haired Poseidon and glorious Hector, one battling for 390 the Greeks, the other for the Trojans. As the two sides met with a deafening clamour, the sea surged up to the Greeks' huts and their ships. But neither the thunder of breakers on the beach, driven in from the deep by a stinging northerly gale; nor the roar of flames when fire attacks the forest in a mountain ravine; nor the call of the wind in the high foliage of the oaks when it rises to a scream in its wrath, is so loud as the terrible war-cry 400 that the Trojans and Greeks raised as they fell upon each other.

Glorious Hector first hurled a spear at Ajax as he turned directly towards him. He did not miss, but *Ajax stuns* hit Ajax where the two shoulder-straps, one for his *Hector* shield and one for his silver-riveted sword, met across his chest, and they saved his tender flesh. Hector was frustrated that the swift spear had left his hand to no purpose and retreated into his own contingent of warriors to avoid death. As he withdrew,

410 great Ajax son of Telamon picked up one of the many boulders
that had been used to support the ships and had rolled among
the feet of the combatants, and with this hit Hector on the chest
just below the neck over the rim of his shield, making him spin
like a top and stagger about in all directions. As an oak is
uprooted by a lightning-stroke from Father Zeus: it gives off a
terrifying reek of sulphur, unnerving all who happen to be near
– the violence of great Zeus' bolt is a frightening thing – so
Hector in all his might was brought down in the dust. His
second spear fell from his hand; he crumpled up under his shield
420 and helmet, and the ornamented bronze armour clattered
about him.

The Greek men-at-arms rushed towards him with triumphant
cries, hoping to drag him off, and rained spears on him. But no
one had a chance to stab or hit this shepherd of the people. He
was surrounded too quickly by the best Trojans, Polydamas,
Aeneas and godlike Agenor, Sarpedon lord of the Lycians and
matchless Glaucus. And of the rest there was no one that neg-
lected his leader. They all held their rounded shields in front of
him. Then, putting their arms underneath him, his comrades
lifted him up and carried him out of the fighting to his swift
430 horses, who were waiting for him behind the fighting with their
charioteer and his decorated chariot. They carried him off to
the town, groaning heavily.

But when they reached the ford of the sweetly flowing river,
eddying Scamander whose father is immortal Zeus, Hector's
men lifted him from the chariot, laid him on the ground and
poured water over him. Hector recovered and opened his eyes.
He got to his knees and coughed up dark blood. Then he sank
back once more on the ground, and the world went black as
night before his eyes. He had not yet recovered from the blow.

440   When the Greeks saw Hector withdraw, they fell on the
            Trojans more keenly, their will to fight renewed. First
Satnius, Pro-   swift Ajax son of Oïleus charged with his sharp-
thoenor and   pointed spear and stabbed Satnius, whom a flawless
Archelochus   Nymph had borne to his father, Enops, when he was
killed   tending his herds on the banks of the River Satnioïs.
The famous spearman Ajax leapt in and stabbed him in the side.

Satnius fell on his back, and the Greeks and Trojans locked in
a fierce tussle around him. The famous spearman Polydamas
son of Panthous, coming to the rescue, hit Prothoenor on the   450
right shoulder. The heavy spear held its course through his
shoulder, and he fell in the dust and clawed the earth. Polydamas
boasted of his triumph over him in a loud voice:

'That was another spear from the strong arm of Panthous'
proud son that did not fly to no purpose, but found its home in
a Greek's flesh! He can use it as a staff as he goes down to
Hades' halls.'

So he spoke, and his boasting stung the Greeks. It went
straight to the heart of Ajax, warlike son of Telamon, in particu-
lar, who had been nearest the spot where Prothoenor fell. He   460
quickly threw his glittering spear at the retreating Polydamas.
Polydamas himself avoided certain death by leaping to one side.
It was Antenor's son, Archelochus, who received the spear. The
gods meant him to die, and it hit him where the head meets the
neck on the topmost segment of the spine. It severed both
tendons and, as he fell, his forehead, mouth and nose hit the
ground well before his legs and knees. Ajax shouted back at
matchless Polydamas:

'Think it over, Polydamas, and tell me frankly – doesn't this   470
man's death make up for Prothoenor's? To judge by his looks,
he was certainly no coward or low-born – more like a brother
or son of horse-taming Antenor. The family likeness is striking.'

Ajax spoke, knowing well enough whom he had
killed, and Trojan hearts sank. But Acamas stood   *Promachus*
protectively over Archelochus, who was his brother,   *and Ilioneus*
and when a Boeotian called Promachus tried to drag   *killed*
off the body by the feet, he stabbed him with his spear. Acamas
boasted of his triumph over him in a loud voice:

'You Greeks, loud-mouths, so free with your threats –
trouble and misery are not reserved for us alone. We've had our   480
losses: yours are coming. Look at your man Promachus, put to
sleep by my spear in prompt repayment for my brother's death.
That's what a man prays for – a relative to survive him and
avenge his fall.'

So he spoke, and his boasting stung the Greeks. It went

straight to the heart of Peneleos in particular. He made for
Acamas, but Acamas did not stand up to his attack and it
490 was Ilioneus who fell to lord Peneleos. He was son of the
sheep-owner Phorbas, a favourite in Troy of the god Hermes
who had made him a rich man. But Ilioneus' mother had given
Phorbas no other child, and now Peneleos struck him under the
eyebrow in the socket of the eye. The spear dislodged his eyeball,
pierced the eye-socket and came out at the back of his head. He
sank back, stretching out both his hands. But Peneleos, drawing
his sharp sword, hit him full on the neck and brought head and
helmet tumbling down to the ground. The heavy spear was still
stuck in the eye as Peneleos raised it aloft, like a poppy-head,
500 for the Trojans to see, and spoke in triumph:

'Trojans, do me a favour and instruct Ilioneus' father and
mother to start lamenting him at home. After all, the wife of
Promachus, son of Alegenor, will never have the happiness of
seeing *her* husband return when we Greeks sail from Troy.'

So he spoke, and the knees of all the Trojans trembled, and
each man peered around to find some escape from sudden death.
Tell me now, you Muses that have your homes on
Olympus, who was the first Greek to take a blood-
stained set of armour from the enemy, now that the
510 famous earthshaker Poseidon had swayed the battle in their
favour? It was Ajax son of Telamon who began by stabbing
Hyrtius, leader of the lionhearted Mysians. Next Antilochus
killed Phalces and Mermerus; Meriones slew Morys and Hippo-
tion; and Teucer slew Prothoon and Periphetes. Then Menelaus
stabbed Hyperenor shepherd of the people in the side. Tearing
its way through, the bronze spear let out his innards; his life
hurried out through the gaping wound, and darkness engulfed
520 his eyes. But it was to Ajax, swift son of Oïleus, that the greatest
number fell: for when Zeus started a panic, there was nobody
like Ajax for chasing the routed enemy on foot.

*Greeks slaugh-
ter Trojans*

THE GREEKS AT BAY

1–261: The *Trojans* retreat in panic from the Greek camp. ZEUS wakes up, furious, and turns on HERA, who claims innocence. ZEUS foretells the deaths of Patroclus and *Hector*, calls off POSEIDON (who reluctantly obeys) and orders *APOLLO* to revive *Hector* and restore the *Trojans'* victorious assault.

262–389: *Hector* returns invigorated to battle. The Greeks panic and run. *APOLLO* kicks down the Greek defences, and the *Trojans* swarm round the ships.

390–405: Patroclus, hearing the noise, leaves the wounded Eurypylus and returns to Achilles.

405–564: *Hector* and Ajax rally their own sides: general fighting.

565–746: ZEUS spurs on *Hector*, and the Greeks retreat further back among their ships. Ajax defends the ships with a huge pike, but slowly has to yield.

The fleeing Trojans re-crossed the stakes and ditch, many falling at the hands of the Greeks, and did not stop till they reached their chariots. As they paused there, panic-stricken and pale with terror, Zeus, who was still lying on the heights of Mount Ida beside Hera of the golden throne, awoke and leaping to his feet took in the situation – the Trojans thrown back and the Greeks in hot pursuit; lord Poseidon helping in the chase; and Hector lying on the ground with his comrades sitting round him.

Hector was breathing in some discomfort and coughing up 10 blood. He was still dazed, since the man who had hit him was by no means the feeblest in the Greek ranks. The Father of men and gods was filled with pity at the sight of him. He gave Hera a terrifying black look and spoke his mind:

ZEUS accuses
HERA of
deception

'Hera, you are incorrigible. It is through *your* treacherous tricks that godlike Hector has been stopped from the fighting and the Trojans routed. I have half a mind to give you a good thrashing and let you be the first to enjoy the consequences of your wretched antics again. Have you forgotten the time when I strung you up with a couple of anvils hanging from your feet and your hands
20   lashed together with a golden chain you could not break? There you dangled, up in the air and in among the clouds; and the gods on high Olympus, though they stood around you in despair, found it impossible to set you free. I seized anyone I caught in the attempt; I hurled him from my threshold and, when he reached the ground, the breath was knocked right out of him.

'But even that did not relieve the heartache I felt for godlike Heracles when you, after persuading the gales to help you in your evil schemes, had sent him scudding over the murmuring sea before a northerly gale. You swept him off in the end to the prosperous island of Cos. But I rescued him from Cos and
30   brought him back to Thessaly where the horses graze, after all he'd been through.

'I am reminding you of this to put a stop to your deceptions and to teach you how little good has come of that love-making of yours, which you tricked me into when you came here from Olympus.'

So he spoke, and ox-eyed lady Hera shuddered and spoke winged words:

'Now let my witnesses be Earth, and the broad skies above, and the falling waters of Styx – the greatest and most solemn oath the blessed gods can take – and your sacred head, and our
40   own bridal couch, by which I would never dare to perjure myself: it is not my fault that Poseidon the earthshaker is doing Hector and the Trojans harm and helping the Greeks. I can only suppose he was sorry for the Greeks when he saw them hard-pressed beside the ships and felt it necessary to take action.

Indeed, I would be quite ready to advise him to go wherever you told him to, Zeus who darkens the clouds.'

So she spoke, and the Father of men and gods smiled and, replying, spoke winged words:

'Ox-eyed lady Hera, if from now on I could count on you to support me in the council of the gods, Poseidon would soon come round and see eye to eye with you and me, however much he might be otherwise inclined. However, if you have told me the full, exact truth, go back now to the gods and order Iris and Apollo the renowned Archer-god to come here. I want Iris to visit the bronze-armoured Greeks and tell lord Poseidon to stop fighting and go home; and Phoebus Apollo to bring Hector back into the battle after breathing new energy into him and making him forget the pain that is causing him such distress.

ZEUS foretells Achilles' return (15.596)

'Phoebus must then sow panic among the Greeks and make them run for it. They will fall back as far as the many-benched ships of Achilles son of Peleus, who will send his companion Patroclus into the fight. Patroclus, after killing a number of his brave enemies, including my own son godlike Sarpedon, will fall to the spear of glorious Hector in front of Ilium; and godlike Achilles, infuriated at Patroclus' death, will kill Hector himself. From that moment on, I will arrange a steady Greek counter-attack from the ships till the day when the Greeks capture steep Ilium, helped by Athene's advice.

'But in the meantime I remain hostile to the Greeks and will not permit any other of the immortals to come down to their assistance until the wishes of Achilles are fulfilled, in accordance with the promise I gave him (and confirmed with a nod of my head) that day when the goddess Thetis put her arms round my knees and supplicated me to give honour to her son Achilles, sacker of cities.'

So he spoke, and the goddess white-armed Hera complied and set out from Mount Ida for high Olympus. Like the speed of thought of a man who has travelled widely and in his sharp mind thinks 'I wish I were there, or there', and instantly brings it all to mind, so quickly the eager lady Hera flew.

On reaching the peak of Olympus, she presented herself to

the immortal gods who were assembled in the palace of Zeus.
When they saw her, they all leapt to their feet and drank her
health. Ignoring the rest, Hera accepted a cup from fair-cheeked
Themis, who was the first to come running up to her and speak
to her with winged words:

90   'Hera, what brings you here? You look flustered. You must
be beating a hasty retreat from your husband, the son of
Cronus!'

The goddess white-armed Hera replied:

'Divine Themis, no questions about that. You know yourself
how arrogant and uncompromising he can be. But if you will
give a lead by beginning the gods' feast in the palace, you
and the rest shall hear all about the wicked schemes Zeus is
contemplating. And in case anyone is sitting happily down to
feast, I can assure them that the news will not please everybody,
man or god.'

100   With these words the lady Hera took her seat, and up and
down the hall of Zeus the gods were filled with conster-
nation, for though there was laughter on Hera's lips, there was
no warmth in her forehead or dark brows. Angrily she addressed
the company:

                'What fools we have been! What idiots, to quarrel
HERA warns   with Zeus! Yet here we are, still determined to have
of ZEUS' will   a go at stopping him, if not by talking, then by force.
And all the while he simply sits there, by himself, showing not
the slightest interest. He could not care less about us. He knows
that, for sheer brute force, he is without question first among
the gods. As a result, you all have to take whatever troubles he
may send you lying down! For example, if I am not mistaken, a

110 calamity has already overtaken Ares. A son and favourite of his,
Ascalaphus, has fallen in action. Imperious Ares does claim to
be his father, does he not?'

So she spoke, and Ares slapped his sturdy thighs with the flat
of his hands and in anguish said:

'Gods who live on Olympus, don't get angry with me now if
I go down to the Greek ships and avenge the slaughter of my
son, even if it is my destiny to be struck down by Zeus' thunder-
bolt and join the bodies in the blood and dust.'

So he spoke and called to his sons Panic and Rout to yoke his horses, while he himself put on his glittering armour.   120

And now another quarrel, even greater and more disastrous than the last, would have broken out between Zeus and the immortals, if Athene in her terror for the whole divine community had not leapt

ATHENE prevents *ARES*' revenge (13.519)

from her chair and dashed out after Ares through the porch. She snatched the helmet from his head, the shield from his shoulders and put away the bronze spear she took from his sturdy hand. She then gave the wild War-god a piece of her mind:

'You maniac! You idiot! You're done for. You clearly don't have ears to hear with. Reason, restraint – all gone. Did you not   130
hear what we were told by Hera, who has come straight from Olympian Zeus? Or do you really wish to get a thrashing for yourself and to be chased back to Olympus with your tail between your legs, while the rest of us reap the whirlwind you've sown? I tell you, Zeus will leave those proud Trojans and Greeks without a moment's thought, come straight here to Olympus and cause absolute mayhem, seizing each of us in turn, innocent and guilty alike. Take my advice, then, and forget your anger for your son. Many a finer and stronger man than he has been killed before now and will be killed in the future. It would be   140
very difficult to protect the family and children of every man on earth.'

With these words Athene led the wild War-god back to his chair. Hera then called Apollo and Iris, who is messenger of the immortal gods, out of the palace and spoke winged words:

'Zeus requires you two to go with all speed to Mount Ida. When you have reached the palace and appeared before him, you will carry out whatever orders he gives you.'

With these words the lady Hera went back in again and sat down on her throne, and the pair flew off at speed. When they   150
reached Mount Ida of the many springs, mother of sheep, they found far-thundering son of Cronus sitting on the summit of Gargarus, enveloped in a perfumed mist. They came and stood before Zeus who marshals the clouds. He had no fault to find

with them, since they had carried out his wife's instructions promptly. He first spoke to Iris with winged words:

'Off with you, swift Iris. Inform lord Poseidon of everything
160 I say and tell him no lies. Instruct him to stop fighting, retire
from the battlefield and either rejoin the company of
the gods or withdraw into his own bright sea. If he
chooses to ignore my explicit commands, let him
think carefully about it and consider whether, power-
ful though he is, he would be able to resist an attack
from me, who is by far the stronger god and his senior by birth.
Not that he hesitates on that account to behave as my equal,
even though the other gods all live in terror of me.'

POSEIDON
told not to
help the
Greeks

So he spoke, and swift Iris, quick as the wind, complied and
170 set out from Mount Ida for sacred Ilium. Like snow or chilling
hail that falls from the clouds at the onset of a bitter north wind,
so quickly the eager Iris flew. She went straight up to the famous
earthshaker and said:

'Sable-haired god, you who encircle the world, I have come
here with a message from Zeus who drives the storm-cloud. He
orders you to stop fighting, retire from the battlefield and either
rejoin the company of the gods or withdraw into your own
bright sea. If you choose to ignore his explicit commands, he
180 threatens to come here and take you on in person. He instructs
you not to engage in combat with him, since he is by far the
stronger god and your senior by birth. Not that you hesitate on
that account to behave as his equal, even though the other gods
all live in terror of him.'

Indignant, the famous earthshaker replied:

'This is outrageous! Zeus may be powerful but it is sheer
arrogance for him to talk of forcing me, his equal in prestige, to
bend my will to his. There are three of us brothers, all sons of
Cronus and Rhea: Zeus, myself and Hades, the lord of the dead.
Each of us was given his own domain when the world was
190 divided into three parts. We cast lots, and I received the grey sea
as my inalienable realm, Hades drew the darkness below and
Zeus was allotted the broad sky in the upper air among the
clouds. But the earth was left common to all of us, and high
Olympus too.

'So I am not going to live at Zeus' beck and call. Powerful though he is, let him stay quietly in his own third of the world. And don't let him try to scare me with threats of violence, as if I were some out-and-out coward. He'd do better to issue his nasty threats to his own sons and daughters. He is their Father, and they are duty bound to listen when he orders them about.'

Swift Iris, quick as the wind, replied: 200

'Sable-haired god, you who encircle the world, do you really wish me to convey this blunt and uncompromising reply back to Zeus? Won't you change your mind a little? It is the mark of a noble mind to be swayed. And you know how the avenging Furies always support elder brothers.'

POSEIDON reluctantly agrees to desist

Poseidon the earthshaker said:

'Goddess Iris, all that is very true. It is noble, too, for a messenger to show such tact. But it really hurts to be insulted   210 and bullied by a god with whom destiny has decreed that I should share the world on equal terms. However, I will give in now, though not without resentment. But I will tell you something else, and this is a serious word of warning. If Zeus, against my wishes and those of the war-leader Athene, Hera, Hermes and lord Hephaestus, spares high Ilium and will not have it sacked, giving the Greeks a resounding victory, let him know there will be an irreparable breach between the two of us.'

With these words the earthshaker left the Greek army and withdrew into the sea. The Greek warriors missed him badly.

Then Zeus who marshals the clouds addressed Apollo: 220

'Go now, dear Phoebus, to bronze-armoured Hector. The earthshaker who encircles the world has by now retired into the bright sea to avoid the full weight of my anger. Indeed, if we had come to blows, everyone would have heard of it, even the gods who

APOLLO told to restore Hector (14.412)

live with Cronus in the world below. But it was a far better thing for both of us that, resentful though he was, he should have yielded to me without taking me on – otherwise there would certainly have been much sweat before matters could have been settled.

'Now take my fringed aegis in your hands, give it a fierce

230 shake and strike panic into the Greek warriors. And make glorious Hector your special concern, Archer-god. Fill him with tremendous energy until such time as the Greeks reach their ships and the Hellespont in panic. At that point, I myself will decide what must be said and done to give them a breathing-space from battle.'

So he spoke, and Apollo turned no deaf ear to his father's words but swooped down from the mountains of Ida with the speed of a dove-destroying hawk, which is the fastest thing on wings. Godlike Hector, son of wise Priam, was no longer 240 prostrate when he found him, but sitting up. He had just regained consciousness and could recognize the friends about him, having ceased to pant and sweat from the moment when Zeus who drives the storm-cloud had willed his recovery. The Archer-god Apollo came up to him and said:

'Hector son of Priam, why are you sitting here away from your troops and in such a sad state? Have you been hurt?'

In a feeble voice Hector of the flashing helmet replied:

'What god are you, my lord, and why do you come to me for news? Don't you know that, as I was killing Greeks by the outer line of ships, Ajax, master of the battle-cry, hit me on the chest 250 with a lump of rock and knocked all the fight out of me? Indeed, I thought I was going to breathe my last today and descend among the dead in Hades' halls.'

Lord Apollo the Archer-god replied:

'Take heart! Trust the ally that Zeus son of Cronus sends you from Mount Ida to take his place beside you and protect you – myself, Phoebus Apollo of the golden sword, who in days gone by have saved not only you but your lofty citadel as well. Up, now! Command your many charioteers to drive at the gallop 260 right up to the hollow ships, and I will go ahead of them, making a way over the ditch for the horses and putting the Greek warriors to flight.'

With these words he breathed tremendous energy into this shepherd of the people. As a stabled horse breaks his halter at the manger where he feeds and, hooves thudding, gallops off across the fields to his usual bathing-place in the sweet-flowing river, exultant; he tosses his head; his mane streams in the wind along his shoulders; he knows how beautiful he is, and his feet carry him skimming over the ground to the horses' haunts and pastures – so Hector lightly and easily now sprinted off when   270 he heard the god speak, urging on his charioteers.

The Greeks were like rustics with a pack of hounds chasing an antlered stag or wild goat. It takes refuge in some well-shaded wood or steep rocky outcrop: it was not, after all, destined to be caught by them. Then suddenly a bearded lion, roused by their cries, appears in their path and, for all their determination, sends them running – so the Greeks had been advancing steadily in mass formation, stabbing with their swords and curved spears. But when they saw Hector once more marshalling his men, they were filled with consternation, and their hearts sank.   280

Thoas, Andraemon's son, then addressed the Greeks. He was by far the finest of the Aetolians, skilled with the spear and a good man in a standing fight. Moreover, there were few Greeks who could get the better of him in the assembly when they competed to give the best advice. He had their interests at heart as he rose and addressed them:

'Well, well, what a miracle – Hector risen from the dead! Just when we were all thinking that Ajax son of Telamon had finished him off, some god has taken him in hand and brought   290 him back to life, as though he hadn't killed enough of us already. And there is more of that to come. Hector would not be back in the front line threatening us like this, if loud-thundering Zeus had not put him there.

Thoas prepares the Greeks to face Hector

'So I suggest we all do what I now propose. Let the main body retreat to the ships, while we that claim to be the best men in the army make a stand, with our spears up at the ready, in the hope of holding Hector's first attack. For all his determination, I have an idea he'll think twice about engaging with such a Greek force.'

So he spoke, and they heard and agreed. They gathered in   300 their best men to form a closed battle-line against Hector and his Trojans, under the leadership of Ajax, lord Idomeneus, Teucer, Meriones and Meges. Behind them, the main force retreated to the Greek ships.

APOLLO
routs the
Greeks

The Trojans advanced in a mass and Hector led them, striding confidently forward. In front of him, with a mist round his shoulders, went Phoebus Apollo, holding the lively aegis, grimly resplendent
310 with its fringe, the very aegis that the bronzesmith Hephaestus had given to Zeus to strike panic into men. With this in his hand, Apollo led the Trojan army.

But the Greeks awaited them in mass formation. A deafening roar went up from either side, and arrows leapt from the string. Many spears launched from strong arms landed in young warriors' bodies, while many others fell short before they could enjoy white flesh and stuck in the earth, thirsting to take their fill.

As long as Phoebus Apollo kept the aegis steady in his hands, volley and counter-volley found their mark and men kept falling.
320 But the moment came when, looking the Greeks full in the face, he shook the aegis at them and gave a great shout. Then their hearts were bewildered, and all the fight went out of them. As two wild animals stampede a herd of cows or some great flock of sheep in the depths of the dark night, emerging all of a sudden when the herdsman is not there, so the demoralized Greeks were routed. It was Apollo himself who had unleashed panic among them and gave the Hector and his Trojans the glory.

Trojans kill
eight Greeks

Having broken the Greek ranks, the Trojans began to pick off the Greeks one by one. Hector killed Arcesilaus and Stichius, one a leader of the bronze-
330 armoured Boeotians and the other a loyal follower of great-hearted Menestheus. Meanwhile Aeneas slew Medon and Iasus. Medon was an illegitimate son of godlike Oïleus and so a brother of Ajax; but he lived in Phylace a long way from the land of his fathers, because he had killed a kinsman of his step-mother Eriopis, Oïleus' wife. Iasus was one of the Athenian leaders and his father was Sphelus. Polydamas killed Mecisteus; Polites
340 killed Echion in the front line; and godlike Agenor slew Clonius. Deiochus, as he joined the other front ranks in their flight, was hit from behind at the base of the shoulder by Paris, whose bronze spear passed clean through him.

While the victors were stripping the dead men of their arms, the Greeks, dashing in panic this way and that and entangled in their own ditch and palisade, were forced to take refuge behind the wall. Seeing this, Hector called out to the Trojans in a loud voice:

'On to the Greek ships! Forget about seizing the bloodstained armour! Any straggler I see, anyone who does not follow me there, I'll put to death on the spot. What's more, he'll get no   350
funeral from his relatives and womenfolk. The dogs will tear his body in front of Ilium.'

With these words, and swinging his arm right back, he whipped on his horses and sent a great cry across the Trojan ranks. His charioteers to a man gave an answering shout and with a mighty roar drove on their horses and chariots.

In front of them Phoebus Apollo easily kicked in the banks of the deep ditch and piled them into the middle, making a broad and ample causeway, wide as the distance a man throws a spear when he is testing his strength. Here they poured across rank after rank, led by Apollo, holding up his precious aegis. Then,   360
with equal ease, the god knocked down the Greek wall, as a boy at the seaside knocks down a sandcastle: he builds it to amuse himself, as children do, and then with his hands and feet wrecks the whole thing for fun – so you, Apollo, wrecked the Greeks' arduous efforts and sowed panic among them.

APOLLO kicks down the Greek defences

The Greeks did not stop till they reached the ships. There they halted, calling to one another for help, and every man lifted up his hands and poured out prayers to all the gods, none more fervently than Gerenian Nestor, guardian of the Greeks, who   370
stretched out his arms to the starry sky:

'Father Zeus, if ever any of us back in Greece with its rich cornfields burnt you the fat thigh of an ox or sheep as he prayed for a safe return, and you promised it to him with a nod of your head, remember that moment now, Olympian; save us from this day of death; and don't let the Trojans overwhelm the Greeks so completely.'

So he spoke in prayer, and Zeus wise in counsel thundered loud when he heard the prayer of the ancient son of Neleus.

But when the Trojans heard the thunderclap of Zeus who

380 drives the storm-cloud, they fell on the Greeks more fiercely than ever, their will to fight renewed. As a great roller on the high seas tumbles over the sides of a ship when a storm whips up the waves and drives them on, so with a roar the Trojans swept across the wall, lashing their horses on. In a moment they were fighting hand to hand by the ships, the Trojans from their chariots with their curved spears, and the Greeks from high up on the black sterns where they had climbed, with the great pikes – built up in sections and tipped with bronze – which they kept on board for fights at sea.

390   Now Patroclus, so long as the Greeks and Trojans were fighting for control of the wall and were some way from the ships, sat with amiable Eurypylus in his hut and, while entertaining him with his talk, applied herbs to his ugly wound to soothe away the pain. But when he saw the Trojans swarming across the wall and heard the Greeks yelling and panicking, he gave a groan, slapped his thighs with the flat of his hands and said in his distress:

Patroclus leaves
Eurypylus
(11.843)

'Eurypylus, I can't stay here with you any longer, however 400 much you need me. It's critical out there. Your attendant must look after you while I hurry back to Achilles and do my best to make him fight. Who knows? With some divine help, my suggestions might stir him to change his mind. A friend's advice is often the most effective.'

Even as he spoke, his feet were on the move.

Meanwhile the Greeks resolutely resisted the oncoming Trojans but, though they outnumbered them, were unable to drive them back from the ships. Nor, for their part, were the Trojans able to break the Greek lines and get through to their ships and 410 camp. As a string stretched along a ship's timber enables a skilful carpenter who has mastered his trade under the guidance of Athene to draw a straight line, so battle was pulled tight, neither front line yielding an inch.

Ajax vs. Hector;
Caletor killed

While parties of his men attacked at other ships, Hector made straight for illustrious Ajax and the two of them fought it out over the one vessel. Hector could not drive Ajax off it and set it on fire, and Ajax was equally unable to repel Hector once the god had brought him

to the spot. Then glorious Ajax hit Caletor in the chest with a   420
spear as he was carrying fire to the ship. Caletor thudded to the
ground, and the brand dropped from his grip. Hector, seeing
his cousin fall in the dust in front of the black ship, called out
to the Trojans and Lycians in a loud voice:

'Trojans, Lycians and you Dardanians that like your fighting
hand to hand, don't yield an inch in this narrow space we are
in! Caletor's been killed in action round the ships! Rescue him,
or the Greeks will have his armour off him!'

With these words he flung a glittering spear at Ajax, but   430
missing him, he struck Lycophron from Cythera, Ajax's atten-
dant, who had come to live with him after killing a
man in sacred Cythera. Lycophron was standing by   Lycophron
Ajax when Hector's sharp bronze spear struck him   and *Cleitus*
on the head above the ear. He tumbled backwards   killed
from the ship's stern to the ground and crumpled up in the dust.
Ajax shuddered and called to his brother:

'Dear Teucer, we've lost our faithful friend Lycophron, who
came from Cythera to live with us; and we thought as much of
him as we did of our own parents. Great-hearted Hector has   440
just killed him. Where are your deadly arrows and the bow you
had from Phoebus Apollo?'

So he spoke, and Teucer understood him and, running to his
side with his curved bow and full quiver, began at once to direct
his arrows at the Trojans. The first man he hit was Cleitus, an
attendant to noble Polydamas. Teucer hit him with the reins in
his hands. He was in trouble with his horses, having driven them
into the thick of the foot-soldiers where the fighting was at its
most confused, with the idea of doing Hector and the Trojans a
good turn. He met disaster at once from which no one could   450
save him, though they would have wanted to. The fatal arrow
struck him in the back of the neck and brought him crashing
down from his chariot. His horses shied and ran away, with the
empty chariot rattling off behind them, till lord Polydamas, who
had been the first to notice what had happened, intercepted
them. He handed them over to Astynous and urgently told the
man to watch his movements and keep the horses close at hand.
Then he went and engaged once more with the front ranks.

Teucer aimed his next arrow at bronze-armoured Hector. He
460 would have put an end to the battle by the Greek ships had
he struck and killed Hector in the hour of his glory. But Zeus,
who is too wary to be caught, was looking after Hector and
had kept an eye on Teucer. He robbed him of his triumph by
snapping the twisted string of his trusty bow as he was taking
aim at his man. The bronze-weighted arrow swerved off-course
and the bow fell from his hand. Teucer shivered and said to
his brother Ajax:

'Damn! Some evil power is thwarting everything
Teucer aban-   we try in battle today! It has knocked the bow out of
dons his   my hand and broken the fresh string I bound on this
broken bow   morning to take the strain of my leaping arrows.'
470 Great Ajax son of Telamon replied:
'Well, old friend, abandon your bow and all those arrows,
now that some god with a grudge against the Greeks has made
them of no use. Pick up a spear instead, sling a shield over your
shoulder and so meet the enemy – and give a lead to the rest of
our men. Let's call up our will to fight and, even if the Trojans
defeat us, make them pay heavily for our ships.'

So he spoke, and Teucer laid his bow down in his hut and
480 slung a shield of fourfold leather on his shoulder. On his mighty
head he placed a well-made helmet with a horsehair crest, the
plume nodding frighteningly from the top. Then he took up a
powerful spear tipped with sharp bronze and, setting out at a
run, was soon at Ajax's side.

When Hector saw Teucer's weapons were out of commission,
he called out to the Trojans and Lycians in a loud voice:

'Trojans, Lycians, and you Dardanians that like
Hector and   your fighting hand to hand, be men, my comrades,
Ajax rally   and call up that fighting spirit of yours here by the
their sides   hollow ships! I saw with my own eyes how one of
their best men was stopped by Zeus from shooting any more.
490 There is no mistaking help from Zeus. He makes it plain, both
to the side for whom he is planning victory and to those he is
weakening and refusing to help. See how he is weakening Greek
resistance and supporting us! Mass together, then, and attack
the ships. If anyone is hit or stabbed and meets his fated end,

so be it. He will have fallen for his country, and that's no dishonourable death. He will leave his wife and children safe for the future and his house and land secure, once these Greeks have sailed back to the land of their fathers.'

So Hector spoke and put fresh heart and courage into every man. Ajax on his side immediately called out to his followers: 500

'Shame on you, Greeks! Today we have no choice but to perish here or save the ships and live. Or do you think you'll all get home on foot if Hector of the flashing helmet takes the ships? He is desperate to set them on fire – can't you hear him driving his whole army on? And believe me, he's not inviting them to a dance but to fight. Our only hope, our only strategy, is to face them in battle, hand to hand, and man to man. Whether we live 510 or die, it's better to settle the matter once and for all than let a weaker enemy squeeze the life out of us in the heat of the battle by the ships.'

So Ajax spoke and put fresh heart and courage into every man. Now Hector killed Schedius, a Phocian chieftain; Ajax killed noble Laodamas, an infantry commander; and Polydamas slew Otus from Cyllene, *Otus and Croesmus killed* a leader of the great-hearted Eleans and a friend of Meges. Meges, when he saw this, leapt at Polydamas, but Polydamas 520 avoided his attack by recoiling – Apollo was not going to let him fall in the front line – and Meges missed.

Meges then stabbed Croesmus full in the chest with his spear. Croesmus thudded to the ground, and Meges began to strip the armour from his shoulders. But as he did so, he was assaulted by Dolops who was an expert with the spear. This man was a son of Lampus – the best son he had and a practised fighter – and grandson of Laomedon. Attacking at close range, Dolops pierced the centre of Meges' shield with his spear. But Meges was well served by the stout body-armour he was wearing, with 530 its metal plates. His father Phyleus had brought this armour from Ephyre and the River Selleïs, where his host, Euphetes lord of men, had made him a gift of it to wear when he went to war and protect him from his enemies. Now it also saved his son from destruction.

Meges stabbed with his sharp-pointed spear at the plumed

crown of Dolops' bronze helmet and sheared the horsehair crest
clean off the top. The whole ornament, resplendent in its fresh
purple dye, fell in the dust. But Dolops did not despair

Dolops killed   of winning; he stood his ground and fought on. What
540 he did not notice was that warlike Menelaus, spear in hand, had
come to Meges' help and crept up on his flank. Menelaus hit
him in the shoulder from behind, and the eager spear-point
forced its way through and came out at his chest. Dolops fell
headlong, and Menelaus and Meges rushed in to strip the bronze
armour from his shoulders.

Hector called on all his relatives to rally and singled out
mighty Melanippus for rebuke. This man, before the invasion,
had lived at Percote where he grazed his shambling cattle. But
when the Greeks arrived in their rolling ships, he returned to
550 Ilium, distinguished himself among the Trojans and lived with
Priam who treated him like one of his own children. Hector
shouted angrily at him:

Hector and   'Melanippus, are we to take things lying down like
Ajax rally men this? Is it nothing to you that they have killed your
cousin Dolops? Or don't you see them helping them-
selves to his armour? Come with me now. We can't grapple at
long range with these Greeks any longer – either we destroy them
or they destroy lofty Ilium from top to bottom and slaughter all
our people.'

With these words Hector led the way, and godlike Melanippus
went with him.

560 Meanwhile great Ajax son of Telamon was stirring up the
Greeks:

'Fellow warriors, be men, think of your reputations, and in
the heat of battle fear nothing but dishonour in each other's
eyes! When warriors fear disgrace, then more are saved than
killed. There is no honour or safety to be found in flight.'

So he spoke, and though they scarcely needed this encourage-
ment to defend themselves, the Greeks took his words to heart
and ringed their ships with a fence of bronze. But Zeus still
urged the Trojans to attack.

Menelaus, master of the battle-cry, then spurred on Anti-
lochus:

'We have nobody younger than you, Antilochus, and no one quicker on his feet or bolder in a fight. Why not race out and see if you can bring a Trojan down?' 570

With these words Menelaus withdrew but he had inspired Antilochus. He leapt out from the front line and, looking carefully round, let fly with his glittering spear. The Trojans leapt back when they saw it coming. But his spear did not leave his hand for nothing. He caught proud Melanippus beside the nipple on his chest as he was advancing into battle. Melanippus thudded to the ground, and night enveloped his eyes. Antilochus pounced on him like a hound leaping on a stricken fawn that a huntsman has killed 580 and brought down with a lucky shot as it started from its lair. So, Melanippus, did resolute Antilochus leap at you to strip you of your arms.

Antilochus kills Melanippus

But godlike Hector, who had seen what he had done, came running up through the mêlée to confront him; and Antilochus, brisk fighter though he was, did not await his arrival. He ran for it like a wild beast that has done wrong in killing a dog or herdsman and takes to its heels before a crowd is put together to chase it. So Nestor's son Antilochus fled, pursued by deafening cries and a hail of deadly missiles from the Trojans and 590 Hector. But he turned and stood his ground when he reached his own contingent.

The Trojans now stormed the ships like flesh-eating lions, fulfilling the orders of Zeus who filled them with tremendous energy and bewildered the spirits of the Greeks by denying them all success and encouraging their enemies. He was planning to give Hector the glory, so that he could hurl unquenchable fire on the beaked ships and satisfy all the unreasonable demands of Thetis: Zeus wise in counsel was waiting to see the blaze of a ship on fire. 600 From that moment, he intended the Trojans to be thrust back from the ships and the Greeks to be victorious. All this was in his mind as he spurred on Hector son of Priam to attack the hollow ships.

ZEUS spurs Hector on (15.58)

Not that Hector lacked determination. He raged like Ares the spear-wielding War-god, or like destructive fire in the thickets

of a deep forest in the mountains. There was foam on his mouth;
his eyes flashed under lowering brows; and his helmet swayed
610 menacingly on his temples as he fought. Zeus himself was
Hector's ally in the sky, selecting him alone from that great
crowd of men for honour and glory, since he had but a short
time to live. Pallas Athene was already speeding on the day
when he should fall to Achilles, mighty son of Peleus.

Hector's aim was to break the enemy line and, wherever he
saw the greatest numbers and best-armed men, he put it to the
test. But he failed to break through, for all the ferocity of his
assault. Packed as tight as the stones in a wall, the Greeks held
620 firm like a great sheer cliff that faces the grey sea and resists the
onslaught of the howling winds and vast waves roaring on at it;
so resolutely did the Greeks stand up to the Trojans and never
turn to flight.

At last, his fiery armour blazing all round him, Hector burst
into their midst. He fell on them as a great tossing wave, whipped
up by the winds and the clouds, breaks against a ship; she is
completely hidden by the spray; the terrifying blast of the wind
howls in her sail; and the crew, shocked and panicking, are
saved from destruction by a hair's breadth – so Greek morale
was utterly shattered.

630 Hector fell on them like a murderous lion coming across
Hector kills cattle grazing in numbers in the pastures of some
Periphetes great water-meadow; the herdsman is inexperienced
in fighting off the beast from the carcass of an animal,
so he keeps level with the front or rear of the herd and leaves
the lion to strike at the centre and devour his kill, while the rest
of the herd scatters in panic – so the whole Greek force was
miraculously put to flight by Hector and Father Zeus. Hector
killed just one Greek.

His victim was a Mycenean, Periphetes son of Copreus.
Copreus had been the messenger of lord Eurystheus, employed
640 to deliver Eurystheus' instructions to mighty Heracles about his
labours. But this worthless father had produced a far better son
in all respects: Periphetes was a fast runner, a good warrior and
one of the most intelligent men in Mycenae. He now handed
Hector yet greater glory. He had just turned to run when he

tripped against the rim of his shield which he carried to keep
missiles off and which came down to his feet. Thus entangled,
he fell backwards and, as he hit the ground, his helmet clanged
balefully round his temples, at once attracting Hector's notice.
He ran up to him and drove a spear into his chest, killing him   650
in the very presence of his dear companions, who could do
nothing to help their comrade, for all their distress at his death,
since godlike Hector had terrified them all.

Very soon the Greeks were in among their ships and protected
by the sterns of those that had been drawn up first. But the
Trojans poured in too, and the Greeks were forced to fall back
from the first line to their adjoining huts. There they re-grouped
and came to a halt, not scattering all over the camp, but kept
together by a sense of shame and fear and the constant encour-
agement they shouted to each other. In particular Gerenian
Nestor, guardian of the Greeks, appealed in supplication to each   660
and every man in his parents' name:

'Be men, my friends, and think of your reputation among
others! Each of you remember your children too and your
wives, your property and your parents, whether they are alive
or dead. For the sake of your absent dear ones, I beg you – stand
firm! Don't turn and run!'

So Nestor spoke and put fresh heart and courage into every
man; and Athene cleared away from their eyes the strange mist
that had befogged them. There was daylight now on both sides,
over the ships and the field of battle, that great leveller. Hector,   670
master of the battle-cry, and his men were now visible to all the
Greeks, both those who were standing unengaged in the rear as
well as those fighting beside the swift ships.

Great-hearted Ajax was not pleased by the idea of
joining the Greeks who had stood back from the   Ajax desper-
fighting. Instead, he kept moving up and down the   ately defends
raised half-decks of the ships with great strides,   the ships
swinging in his hands a huge pike ten metres long, made of
sections pegged together and designed for sea-battles. As an
expert trainer harnesses together four horses and gallops them   680
in from the plain to a big town down a busy road: many men
and women look on in admiration as he keeps jumping from

one mount to another, without slipping, as they race along – so Ajax, taking enormous strides, kept moving from one ship's deck to another, and his voice reached the sky as he exhorted the Greeks with tremendous shouts to defend their ships and huts.

Hector was equally unwilling to linger among the crowd of
690 his Trojan men-at-arms. As a tawny eagle swoops on a flock of birds – geese, cranes or long-necked swans – that are feeding by a river, so Hector dashed to the front and made straight for a blue-prowed ship. Zeus with his great hand urged him on from behind and spurred his men to follow.

So once again an intense struggle broke out around the ships. You would think they had gone fresh and unwearied into the fight, so eagerly did they come to grips. But this was the attitude
700 of the combatants: the Greeks felt they were in for disaster and would be destroyed, but every Trojan there was filled with the hope of burning the ships and killing the Greek warriors. Such were their expectations as they closed in conflict.

Hector at last got his hands on the stern of a ship. It was the speedy seafaring vessel that had brought Protesilaus to Troy, thought it never carried him home again to the land of his fathers. Round this ship the Greeks and Trojans hacked away at each other hand to hand. It was not a matter now of keeping their distance and weathering volleys of arrows or spears on
710 either side, but, united in resolution, they stood man to man and fought it out with sharp axes and hatchets, long swords and curved spears. Many a fine black-hilted sword fell to the ground from warriors' hands, and many another was cut from their shoulders as they fought. The earth ran black with blood.

Hector, once he had laid hold of the ship, never let go but kept his hands on the stern-post and shouted to the Trojans:

Hector calls for fire

'Bring fire! Mass and charge! This is the day, worth all the rest, when Zeus allows us to destroy their ships! They came here against the will of the gods
720 and started all our troubles. But that was through the cowardice of our elders. When I wished to carry the fighting up to the ships, they stopped me and held back my troops. But as surely

as far-thundering Zeus blinded us then, he is backing us today and sweeping us on!'

So he spoke, and they fell on the Greeks with even greater ferocity. Ajax himself, overwhelmed by missiles, could no longer hold his position but, in fear of death, gave way a little and retreated from the ship's afterdeck towards the two-metre cross-bench amidships. There he stood on the alert and, when any 730 Trojan came up with a blazing torch, he fended them off from the ships with his pike. And all the time, in that terrifying voice of his, he was calling to the Greeks:

'Friends, Greek warriors, attendants of Ares, be men, my comrades, and call up that fighting spirit of yours! Do you imagine we have allies in the rear or a better wall to keep off disaster? There is no walled town nearby with reinforcements to save the day. We are in a plain controlled by Trojan men-at-arms; the sea is at our backs; and the land of our fathers is a 740 long way off. So our only salvation is to fight! There's no tenderness in war!'

He spoke and kept thrusting furiously with his sharp pike. Whenever a Trojan came near the hollow ships with a burning brand (in the hope of gratifying Hector who was urging them on) Ajax was ready and hit him with the enormous weapon. He stabbed twelve men like that, hand to hand in front of the ships.

16

THE DEATH OF
PATROCLUS

While this battle was raging round the well-benched ship, Patroclus came up to Achilles shepherd of the people, weeping hot tears like a dark spring trickling black streaks of water down a steep rock-face. Swift-footed godlike Achilles felt pity when he saw him and spoke to him with winged words:

'Patroclus, why are you in tears, like a little girl running along beside her mother and begging to be carried, tugging at her skirt to make her stop, although she is in a hurry, and looking tearfully up at her till at last she picks her up? That, Patroclus, is how you look, with the soft tears rolling down your cheeks. Have you something to tell our Myrmidon troops, or myself? Some news from our home in Phthia that has reached you

10

privately? They say your father Menoetius is still alive, and my
father Peleus certainly is, with his Myrmidons around him. If
either of them were dead, we should indeed have cause for grief.
Or perhaps you are weeping for the Greeks, who are being
slaughtered by the hollow ships because of their stupidity? Tell
me, don't keep it to yourself. We must share it.'

Sighing heavily, charioteer Patroclus, you replied: 20

'Achilles son of Peleus, by far the greatest of the
Greeks, don't be angry at what I say. It's the Greeks   Patroclus
– they are in terrible distress. All our best men are   criticizes
lying by their ships, hit or stabbed. Mighty Diomedes   Achilles
son of Tydeus has been hit; the great spearman Odys-   (15.399)
seus has been stabbed; so has Agamemnon; and Eurypylus has
had an arrow in his thigh. Healers are attending them with all
the remedies at their command to try to heal their wounds.

'But you, Achilles, you are impossible. God preserve me from   30
the bitterness you harbour! You and your disastrous great-
ness – what will future generations have to thank *you* for, if
you do nothing to prevent the Greeks' humiliating destruction?
You are quite pitiless. Peleus was not your father, or Thetis
your mother. No, the grey sea and the sheer cliffs produced
you and your unfeeling heart. But if you are privately de-
terred by some prophecy, some word from Zeus that your lady
mother has told you, at least allow *me* to take the field with the
Myrmidon contingent at my back, if perhaps I might bring
salvation to the Greeks. Give me your own armour to fight in,   40
so that the Trojans take me for you and break off the battle.
That would give our weary troops some breathing space – there
is little enough respite in war. The Trojans have fought to the
point of exhaustion, and I, being fresh, might well drive them
back to the town from our ships and huts.'

So Patroclus spoke in supplication, the great fool. In doing
so, he was simply invoking his own destiny and a dreadful death.
Greatly disturbed, swift-footed Achilles replied:

'Olympian-born Patroclus, what are you talking about? There
is no prophecy I know of that I should be paying attention to,   50
and my lady mother has passed on to me no word from Zeus.
But it really hurts me when a man who is my equal wants to rob

me and take away the prize I won, just because he has more
power. After all I have been through in this war, that really
hurts me. The army gave me that girl as my prize; I had sacked
a walled town; I had won her with my own spear. And now lord
Agamemnon son of Atreus snatched her from my arms as if I
were some refugee who counted for nothing.

60   'But that's over and done with: let it go. I was wrong in
supposing a man could nurse his anger for ever, though I had
intended to do so till the tumult and the fighting reached my
own ships. Arm yourself, then, in my famous battle gear and
lead my warlike Myrmidons into battle, now that a dark cloud
of Trojans is indeed swirling threateningly round our ships, and
the Greeks are clinging on to a narrow strip of ground with the
beach at their back. The whole town has turned out against us,
its courage restored.

70   'No wonder, when they cannot see the helmet on *my* head
glinting in their faces. They would soon take to their heels and
fill the gullies with their dead, if lord Agamemnon had kindly
feelings towards me. As it is, the Greeks are having to defend
the very camp itself. Diomedes' spear is no longer raging in his
hands to save the Greeks from destruction; and I have not
even heard loathsome Agamemnon barking out his orders. It is
man-slaying Hector's shouts that ring in my ears, as he hounds
on his Trojans. Their cries fill the whole plain: they are trouncing
the Greeks.

80   'Nevertheless, Patroclus, you must save the ships. Attack with
             all your force before the Trojans send them up in
    Patroclus   flames and cut us off from home. But listen while I
  allowed back
     to fight   tell you exactly how I want things to be: I want you
             to win *me* great honour and glory in the eyes of all
the Greeks, so that they give my lovely woman back to me and
provide splendid gifts as well. So return to me directly you have
driven the Trojans from the ships. Even if loud-thundering
Zeus offers you the chance of winning glory for yourself, don't
entertain any dreams of fighting on without me against these
90   war-loving Trojans. You will diminish my honour.
    'So don't lead the Myrmidons on to Ilium in the flush of

victory, killing Trojans as you go, or one of the eternal gods from Olympus may cross your path. The Archer-god Apollo loves these Trojans dearly. But turn back when you have lit the way to victory at the ships and leave the rest to do the fighting on the plain. Ah, Father Zeus, Athene and Apollo, if only no Trojan could get away alive, not one, and no Greek either, and we two could survive the massacre to tear off Troy's holy diadem of towers single-handed!' 100

While Achilles and Patroclus were talking together in this way, the moment came when Ajax could no longer hold his position. He was conquered by the will of Zeus and over-whelmed with spears from the hands of the proud Trojans. His shining helmet, its stout plates struck again and again on both sides, rang terrifyingly about his temples. His left shoulder ached from the prolonged effort of swinging his shield, though even so the volleys of enemy spears were unable to knock it aside. He was panting hard and the sweat streamed from all his limbs. He 110 had no time to catch his breath. Everywhere, disaster piled on disaster.

Tell me now, you Muses that live on Olympus, how the Greek ships were first set on fire! Hector went right up to Ajax, struck Ajax's ash pike with *Hector* fires the ships his great sword below the socket of the point and sheared the head clean off. Ajax continued wielding the now headless pike as before, the head finally hitting the ground with a clang a long way below him. Deep in his great heart Ajax realized with a shudder that the gods were taking a hand in the affair and that 120 high-thundering Zeus, intent on a Trojan victory, was thwarting all his battle plans. So he fell back out of range; the Trojans threw blazing brands into the swift ship; and in a moment she was wrapped in inextinguishable flames.

So the fire swirled round her stern. But Achilles slapped his thighs and said to Patroclus:

'Up, Olympian-born Patroclus, charioteer! I can see a blaze of fire roaring up by the ships. They mustn't capture them and cut off our retreat! Quick, get your armour on while I assemble the men.'

130   So he spoke, and Patroclus armed himself in the gleaming
           bronze. First he placed fine leg-guards on his shins,
Patroclus arms;   fitted with silver ankle-clips. Then he put on Achilles'
the Myrmidons   body-armour, glittering and starry. Over his shoul-
muster   der he slung his bronze, silver-riveted sword, then his
great, heavy shield. On his mighty head he placed his well-made
helmet with a horsehair crest, the plume nodding frighteningly
from the top. Then he took up two powerful spears that fitted
140 his grip. The only weapon of matchless Achilles he did not take
was Achilles' long, thick, heavy spear. No Greek could wield
this but Achilles, who alone knew how to handle it. It was made
from an ash-tree on the top of Mount Pelion and had been a
gift from Cheiron to Achilles' father Peleus, to bring death to
warriors.

        Patroclus ordered Automedon to yoke the horses at once. He
thought more highly of Automedon than of anyone except
Achilles breaker of the battle-line, having found that in action
he could be completely relied on to keep within calling distance.
So Automedon yoked up for him divine Xanthus and Balius,
150 who could race with the winds. Podarge, the storm-filly, had
foaled these for their sire the Western Gale when she was grazing
in the meadows beside Ocean Stream. Automedon then put in
as a trace-horse the thoroughbred Pedasus, whom Achilles
had brought away with him when he captured Eëtion's town.
Pedasus was only a mortal horse but he could keep up with the
immortal pair.

        Achilles went the rounds of his huts and got all his Myrmidons
under arms. They were like flesh-eating wolves, hearts filled
with boundless courage, who have brought down a great
antlered stag in the mountains and tear at it, and their jowls
160 run red with blood; then they go off in a pack to lap the black
water from the surface of a dark spring with their slender
tongues, belching out the gore; their hearts are fearless, and
their bellies growl – so the captains and commanders of the
Myrmidons surged forward to fall in under the command of
Patroclus, Achilles' brave attendant. And there stood warlike
Achilles himself, encouraging the charioteers and the shield-
bearing infantry.

Each of the fifty swift ships that Achilles had brought to Troy had a crew of fifty men at the oars. He had appointed five 170 commanders whom he trusted to lead them, but he was the most powerful and in overall command. Menesthius of the flashing body-armour had led the first line of ships. He was son of the divine River Spercheus and beautiful Polydora was his mother, a daughter of Peleus. He was thus the child of a woman bedded by a god, the tireless stream Spercheus. But in name he was the son of Borus, because Borus son of Perieres had openly married his mother, giving a handsome dowry.

Warlike Eudorus had commanded the second line. He was the illegitimate son of Polymele daughter of Phylas, a beautiful 180 dancer. The great god Hermes slayer of Argus had fallen for her when he saw her dancing in a chorus for Artemis of the golden distaff, goddess of the hunt. Gracious Hermes took her straight up to her bedroom unobserved, slept with her and made her the mother of this splendid child, Eudorus the great runner and fighter. When the baby had been brought into the light by Eileithyia, the goddess of labour, and saw the rays of the sun, a powerful chieftain, Echecles son of Actor, married the mother after giving an untold bride-price and took her 190 home with him. So Eudorus' old grandfather Phylas devotedly raised and looked after the baby, surrounding him with love as if he were his own son. Warlike Peisander had commanded the third line. Of all the Myrmidons he was the best spearman after Patroclus. The old charioteer Phoenix had led the fourth and noble Alcimedon the fifth.

When Achilles had drawn them all up, men with their commanders in their proper ranks, he addressed them bluntly:

'Myrmidons, let none of you forget what you have been 200 threatening to do to the Trojans here by the ships while I indulged my anger. There is not one of you who did not abuse me: "Obstinate son of Peleus, your mother suckled you with bile, not milk; you brute, holding your men back by the ships against their will. Let's take to our seafaring vessels and sail home again, since you are in the grip of such pernicious rage." That's what you said about me when you all got together. Well now, a bit of real work has come your way, the sort of fight you have been longing for. So, brave hearts, let the Trojans have it!'

210   So he spoke and put fresh heart and courage into every man, and the ranks closed when they heard their lord. As a mason fits together blocks of stone when he builds the wall of a high house to make sure of keeping out the wind, so tightly packed were their helmets and their bossed shields. They stood so close together, shield to shield, helmet to helmet, man to man, that when they moved their heads, the glittering peaks of their plumed helmets met. And in front of them all Patroclus and Automedon stood ready for battle, two men united in their

220   resolution to fight in the forefront of the Myrmidons.

But Achilles went off to his hut, where he lifted the lid of a beautiful inlaid chest which his mother silver-footed Thetis had packed with tunics, wind-proof cloaks and thick rugs, and put on board ship for him to take on his journey. In this he kept a lovely cup, from which he alone drank the sparkling wine and which he himself used for libations to no other god but Father Zeus. He took it from the chest and, after purifying it

230   with sulphur, rinsed it in a lovely stream of water, washed his hands and drew off some sparkling wine. Then, standing in the middle of the forecourt, he prayed and, looking up into the sky, poured out the wine. Zeus who delights in thunder did not fail to notice him:

Prayers for
Patroclus'
return

'Lord Zeus, god of Dodona, god of the Pelasgi, you that live far away and rule over wintry Dodona, surrounded by your interpreters the Helloi, who leave their feet unwashed and sleep on the ground; you listened when I prayed to you before and you honoured me by striking a mighty blow at the Greek army. Now grant me

240   another wish. I myself am going to stay here by the ships, but I am sending my comrade with many of my Myrmidons into battle. Grant him victory, far-thundering Zeus, and fill his heart with daring, so that Hector finds out whether my attendant knows how to fight on his own or whether his hands rage invincibly only when *I* throw myself into the grind of battle. And directly he has driven the tumult and the fighting back from the ships, let him come back to me here at my own ships safe and sound with all my armour and close-fighting companions.'

So Achilles spoke in prayer, and Zeus wise in counsel heard him. One half the Father granted, but not the other. The Father 250 agreed that Patroclus should drive the tumult and the fighting back from the ships, but not that he should come back safely from battle. When Achilles had made his libation and prayer to Father Zeus, he went back into his hut and put the cup away in the chest. Then he came out and stood in front of his hut. He still wished to witness the dreadful clash between Trojans and Greeks.

Meanwhile the armed contingents under great-hearted Patroclus advanced and fearlessly attacked the Trojans. They came swarming on like roadside wasps that boys always like to 260 tease, stirring them up in their nest by the road, the young fools: they turn them into a public menace, and if a traveller comes by and unintentionally disturbs them, these brave hearts fly out one and all and protect their little ones – with their courage and spirit the Myrmidons swarmed out in a mass from the ships, and the tumult of battle filled the air. Patroclus then called out to his troops in a loud voice:

'Myrmidons, companions of Achilles, be men, my comrades, 270 call up that fighting spirit of yours and win glory for the son of Peleus, the best man in the Greek camp, with the best warriors under him. Make wide-ruling Agamemnon son of Atreus realize the delusion he is under in giving no respect to the best of all the Greeks.'

So Patroclus spoke and put fresh heart and courage into every man. They fell on the Trojans in a mass and their intimidating roar echoed round the ships.

When the Trojans saw strong Patroclus and his attendant Automedon beside him in all the brilliance of their bronze armour, panic threatened and the ranks began to waver, since 280 they thought swift-footed Achilles must have abandoned his anger and reconciled himself with Agamemnon. Every man looked anxiously around to find some escape from sudden death.

Patroclus was the first to throw a glittering spear. He hurled it straight into the mass of men where the fighting was at its most confused round the stern of

Patroclus kills Pyraechmes

Protesilaus' ship and struck Pyraechmes, who had brought his
Paeonians in their plumed helmets from Amydon and the broad-
flowing River Axius. He hit him in the right shoulder. With a
290   groan Pyraechmes fell on his back in the dust, and his Paeonian
troops ran for it. By killing their leader and finest fighter,
Patroclus had sown panic among them all. Patroclus, having
swept them from the ships, extinguished the fire that was blazing
there, leaving the vessel half-burnt. Meanwhile the Trojans
fell back with a tremendous din. The Greeks poured forward
between the ships, and all hell broke loose.

Like lightning-gatherer Zeus shifting a dense cloud from the
high summit of a great mountain, when every look-out place
300   and headland and mountain ravine stands out, and infinite
upper air floods down from the skies – so the Greeks saved their
ships from going up in flames and for a while could breathe
more freely, but they had not done with the fighting. The Trojans
had been forced back from the black ships, but not as yet in
headlong rout. They still confronted them.

Greeks kill   Having broken the Trojan ranks, the Greeks
nine *Trojans*   started picking off their men one by one. Brave
                       Patroclus was first to throw his sharp spear at
Areilycus and hit him in the thigh just as he had turned. The
310   bronze point drove through and broke the bone; the man fell
headlong to the ground. Meanwhile warlike Menelaus struck
Thoas in his chest, which he had left exposed above his shield,
and brought him down. Amphiclus charged at Meges, but Meges
kept his eye on him and got in first with a spear-thrust on the
top of the leg where a man's muscle is very thick. The spear-point
tore through the tendons, and darkness enveloped Amphiclus'
eyes.

Then one of Nestor's sons Antilochus stabbed Atymnius with
his sharp spear and drove the bronze head through his side.
Atymnius crashed down in front of him. But Maris, infuriated
320   by his brother's death, charged at Antilochus, spear in hand,
and planted himself in front of the body. However, before he
could do any damage, another son of Nestor, godlike Thrasy-
medes, made a swift lunge at his shoulder and did not miss. The
point of his spear, striking the base of the arm, tore it away from

the muscles and completely dislocated the arm-bone. Maris thudded to the ground, and darkness enveloped his eyes. Thus these two men were killed by two brothers and went down to the underworld. Brave spearmen of Sarpedon's contingent, they were the sons of Amisodarus who had reared the Chimaera, the raging monster that brought so many men to grief.

Ajax son of Oïleus dashed into the mêlée where Cleobulus   330 had tripped up and took him alive. But he killed him soon enough with a blow to the neck from his hilted sword, warming the whole blade with blood. Inexorable destiny and purple death closed his eyes. Next, Peneleos and Lycon charged at each other. Each had made a bad throw with his spear and missed the other. So now they ran at one another with their swords. Lycon struck the cone of the other's plumed helmet and his sword broke off at the hilt. But Peneleos slashed Lycon in the neck behind the ear and his sword-blade sliced right through. Nothing held but   340 a piece of skin, and from that Lycon's head dangled down as he sank to the ground.

Meriones, too fast for Acamas, caught him up and stabbed him in the right shoulder as he was about to mount his chariot. Acamas crashed out of the chariot and a mist descended on his eyes. Meanwhile, Idomeneus struck Erymas on the mouth with his relentless bronze. The metal point of the spear penetrated under his brain and smashed the white jaw-bones. His teeth were knocked out; both his eyes filled with blood; and gasping for breath, he blew blood through his mouth and nostrils. Death's black cloud enveloped him.   350

So each of these Greek chieftains killed his man. Just as predatory wolves harry lambs or kids and snatch them away from their mothers when they have become separated on the mountains through the shepherd's carelessness, and the wolves seize their chance to pick off the timid creatures – so the Greeks harried the Trojans. The Trojans could think only of tumultuous retreat, and all the fight went out of them.

It was now the one desire of great Ajax son of Telamon to hit bronze-clad Hector with his spear. But Hector was no in-experienced fighter. He protected his broad shoulders with his   360 bull's hide shield, and his ear was alert to the whistle of arrows

and thud of spears. He was well aware that the enemy's
reinforcements had won them the day, but even so he held his
position and tried to save his loyal men.

Hector and   As Zeus unleashes a tempest after clear weather,
the Trojans   driving storm-clouds into the skies from Olympus, so
turn to run   the Trojans started yelling and panicking, and they
                fled across the Greeks' defensive ditch in no semblance
of order. Hector's speedy horses carried him off, arms and all,
and he left to their fate the men who had become unintentionally
370 ensnared by the ditch. For many a pair of swift war-horses
snapped off their shafts at the yoke as they tried to climb the
ditch, leaving their master's chariot behind.

Patroclus chased them with slaughter in his heart, urging on
the Greeks relentlessly, while yelling, panicking Trojans, now
separated from each other, filled every track. Swirls of dust went
rolling up to the clouds as their strong horses made at full speed
for the town, leaving the Greek ships and their huts behind
them. Wherever Patroclus saw the greatest numbers of chariots
in wild retreat, there he followed up, yelling threats. Men
tumbled headlong from their chariots beneath his axles, and
380 their chariots flipped over. But Patroclus' immortal swift horses,
the splendid gift given by the gods to Achilles' father Peleus,
pressed on without a check and cleared the ditch at a single
bound. It was Hector he was after, Hector he yearned to kill.
But Hector's swift horses carried him to safety.

As in autumn the whole countryside grows dark and heavy
with rain under a stormy sky when Zeus sends torrential
downpours; he is angry, and rages at men who deliver crooked
rulings in public assembly and drive justice out, regardless of
390 the eye of the gods. All the streams run in spate, torrents scar
the terraced hillsides, and rivers rush headlong down from the
mountains with a great roar into the turbid sea, washing away
the fields – such was the din that went up from the Trojan
chariots as they fled.

Patroclus kills   Patroclus had by now cut off the nearest Trojan
                contingents and was herding them back towards the
twelve Trojans   ships. He defeated all their efforts to get back to
Ilium and there, between the ships, the river and the high wall,

he kept charging in and killing men, exacting the penalty for so
many Greek dead. First he threw his shining spear at Pronous
and hit him on the chest which he had left exposed above his   400
shield: this brought him down, and he thudded to the ground.
Next he attacked Thestor, who was sitting hunched up in his
polished chariot. This man had lost his senses, and the reins had
slipped from his hands. Patroclus came up beside him and
stabbed him on the right side of the jaw, driving the spear
between his teeth. Then, using the spear as a lever, he hoisted
him over the chariot-rail, as a fisherman sitting on a jutting rock
pulls a lively fish out of the sea with his line and shining hook.
So with his bright spear Patroclus hauled his gaping catch out
of the chariot and dropped him on his face to die where he fell.   410
Next, as Erylaus rushed at him, he hit him with a rock full on
the head. Inside the heavy helmet the man's skull was split in
two; he fell face downward on the ground, and heart-crushing
death engulfed him. Then Patroclus dealt with Erymas, Ampho-
terus and Epaltes; Tlepolemus, Echius and Pyris; Ipheus,
Euippus and Polymelus, bringing them down in swift succession
to the bountiful earth.

When Sarpedon saw how his beltless Lycians were falling   420
to Patroclus son of Menoetius, he turned on his godlike
warriors:

'Shame on you, Lycians! Where are you off to? Come on,
now! I'm going to take on that man over there. I intend to find
out who it is that's carrying all before him and has done the
Trojans so much harm already, bringing down so many of our
best men.'

He spoke and, fully armed, leapt from his chariot to the
ground, and on the other side Patroclus, when he saw him, did
the same. As two vultures with their crooked claws and curved
beaks fight on a rocky height and scream as they fight, so the
two men, uttering defiant cries, made for each other.   430

Zeus, son of sickle-wielding Cronus, saw what was
happening and took pity on them. Then he spoke to
Hera, his sister and wife:

ZEUS weeps
for his son *Sar-
pedon* (5.662)

'This is an unhappy business! My son Sarpedon,
dearest of men, is destined to be killed by Patroclus son of

Menoetius. I wonder now – I am in two minds. Shall I snatch him up and set him down alive on Lycia's rich soil, far from the war with all its tears? Or shall I now let him fall at Patroclus' hands?'

Ox-eyed lady Hera replied:

440 'Dread son of Cronus, what are you suggesting now? Are you proposing to reprieve from the pains of death a mortal man whose destiny has long been settled? Do what you like, then; but not all the rest of us gods will approve.

'But I will tell you something else, and you bear it in mind. If you send Sarpedon home alive, consider whether some other god might not want to do the same for a son of his in the heat of battle. Many of those fighting it out round Troy are the sons of gods who would resent your action bitterly. If Sarpedon is

450 dear to you and your heart grieves for him, let him fall in the thick of the action against Patroclus and, when the breath of life has left him, send Death and sweet Sleep to take him up and bring him to the broad realm of Lycia, where his relatives and retainers will give him burial with a grave-mound and monument, the honour that is due to the dead.'

So she spoke, and the Father of men and gods complied. But he did send down a shower of bloody raindrops to the earth in

460 tribute to his dear son whom Patroclus was about to kill in fertile Troy, far from the land of his fathers.

When the two had come within range of each other, Patroclus threw. He hit famous Thrasydemus, lord Sarpedon's fine attendant, in the lower belly and brought him down. Sarpedon, throwing second with his shining spear, missed Patroclus but struck his horse Pedasus on the right shoulder. The horse keeled over, gasping for breath, fell whinnying in the dust, and its life

470 departed. The other two horses sprang apart; the yoke creaked under the strain; and their reins became entangled, since their trace-horse lay in the dust. But the great spearman Automedon soon found the remedy. He drew the long sword from his sturdy thigh, jumped down and deftly cut the trace-horse clear. The pair straightened themselves up and were pulled in by the reins, and the two men resumed their soul-destroying duel.

Sarpedon then missed with a glittering spear; the point passed harmlessly over Patroclus' left shoulder and failed to make its mark. But Patroclus threw his spear, and the weapon did not 480 leave his hand for nothing. It struck Sarpedon where the lungs enclosed his dense heart, and he crashed down as an oak crashes down or a poplar or a towering pine which woodsmen cut down in the mountains

Sarpedon calls on *Glaucus* and dies

with their newly sharpened axes to make timbers for a ship. So Sarpedon lay stretched in front of his chariot and horses, gurgling and clutching at the bloodstained dust. As a lion gets in among a herd and kills a proud tawny bull among the shambling cows, and the bull, dying under the lion's jaws, bellows – so Sarpedon, leader of the shield-bearing Lycians, struggled 490 defiantly to speak as he yielded up his life to Patroclus, and called on his dear companion:

'Glaucus, old friend, champion among men, now's the time to show your bravery and ability as a fighter. Now make deadly war your one desire, if you have it in you. Run to our Lycian leaders everywhere and urge them on to rally round Sarpedon. Then fight over me with your own spear. Every day of your life you will bear the blame and disgrace if you let the Greeks strip me of my arms, here where I fell beside their ships. Hold firm, 500 then, with all your strength and throw every man we have into the fight.'

As Sarpedon spoke, the end that is death enveloped his eyes and cut short his breath. Patroclus put his foot on his chest and withdrew the spear from his flesh. The innards came with it: he had drawn out the spear-point and the man's life together. Close by, the Myrmidons held on to Sarpedon's snorting horses, who were ready to bolt now they had left their masters' chariot.

Glaucus was distraught when he heard Sarpedon's call. His inability to help him wrung his heart; and he gripped his dam- 510 aged arm with his good hand, hurting as he was from the arrow-wound that Teucer, defending his companions, had given him when he charged at the high Greek wall. Then he prayed to the Archer-god Apollo:

Glaucus healed
(12.389); *Hector*
rallies (12.397)
'Listen to me, lord, you who are somewhere in
the rich land of Lycia or in Troy; wherever you are,
you can hear a man in distress, as I am now. I've
received this cruel wound. The pain driving through
my arm is excruciating; the blood refuses to dry up; my shoul-
520 der's paralysed; I can't hold my spear steady or go out and fight
the enemy. And now our best man has been killed, Sarpedon
son of Zeus. But Zeus will not lift a finger, even for his own son.
But you, lord Apollo, heal this cruel wound, soothe away the
pain and give me strength to call on the Lycians and urge them
into battle, while I fight over the body of the dead man myself.'

So he spoke in prayer, and Phoebus Apollo heard him and at
once relieved the pain, dried up the dark blood from the ugly
wound and filled him with fresh energy. Glaucus realized what
had happened and rejoiced that the great god had responded so
530 quickly to his prayer. He went at once to all the Lycian leaders
everywhere and urged them to rally round Sarpedon. Then he
went striding off to find some Trojans also, Polydamas and
godlike Agenor, Aeneas and bronze-armoured Hector. He went
up to them and spoke winged words:

'Hector, you have completely forgotten your allies, who are
giving their lives for you far from their dear ones and the land
540 of their fathers. You show no eagerness to help them. Sarpedon,
leader of the shield-bearing Lycian, lies dead. He was the upright
and strong defender of the Lycian realm, and now the bronze-
clad War-god Ares has cut him down under Patroclus' spear.
Make a stand by him, my friends. Think of the shame of it, if
the Myrmidons, angry for the many Greeks who fell to our
spears beside their swift ships, should take Sarpedon's arms and
desecrate his body.'

So he spoke, and the Trojans could not contain their
overwhelming, inconsolable grief, since Sarpedon, though a
550 foreigner, had been a mainstay of their town and the finest
warrior among the many he had brought with him. Eager to
avenge him, they made straight for the Greeks with Hector in
the forefront, infuriated by Sarpedon's death.

Meanwhile manly Patroclus spurred on the Greeks. First he
spoke to the Ajaxes, both already intent on combat:

'You two Ajaxes, now make it your mission to fight off the enemy like the men you have always been, or even better. Sarpedon lies dead. He was the first man to storm the Greek wall. Let's see if we can capture and mangle his body, strip the armour from his back and at the same time slaughter some of the friends who will protect him.' 560

So he spoke, and they were already spoiling for the fight. And now, when the two forces, Trojans and Lycians on the one side, Greeks and Myrmidons on the other, had strengthened their ranks, they joined battle over the fallen Sarpedon with terrifying cries. The armour on men's bodies rang aloud, and Zeus eclipsed the field of battle in dreadful night to make the struggle over his dear son all the more murderous.

At first the Trojans were able to repel the dark-eyed Greeks, who lost one of the best men in the Myrmidon force, godlike Epeigeus. He had at one time been ruler of prosperous Budeion but, having killed a brave relative, he took sanctuary with Peleus and his wife silver-footed Thetis, who sent him to Ilium land of horses in the company of Achilles, breaker of men, to fight the Trojans. Epeigeus had just laid his hands on Sarpedon's body when glorious Hector hurled a rock which struck him on the head. Inside the heavy helmet his skull was split in two; he fell face down across the body, and heart-crushing death engulfed him. 580 570

Epeigeus and *Sthenelaus* killed

Patroclus, distressed at his comrade's loss, raced through the front line like a swift falcon when it scatters the jackdaws and the starlings. That was how you, charioteer Patroclus, flew at the Lycians and Trojans, in fury at the death of your friend. Patroclus threw a boulder at the neck of Sthenelaus and smashed the tendons. The Trojan front line and glorious Hector himself fell back before his onslaught. As far as a man throws a long, light spear when he is doing his best in the games or in battle against an enemy thirsting for his blood, so far did the Trojans withdraw and the Greeks press forward. 590

Glaucus, leader of the shield-bearing Lycians, was the first to halt. He turned and killed great-hearted Bathycles, who lived in Hellas and stood out as one of the most prosperous of the Myrmidons. Bathycles

Bathycles and *Laogonus* killed

was about to catch him up when Glaucus suddenly turned on his pursuer and stabbed him with his spear in the middle of the chest. He thudded to the ground. The loss of this brave man 600 was a heavy blow to the Greeks; but the Trojans were delighted and massed in numbers round Glaucus.

The Greeks, however, had lost none of their fight and still bore energetically down on the enemy. It was now the turn of Meriones to kill a Trojan man-at-arms, daring Laogonus who was priest of Idaean Zeus and was honoured by the people like a god. Meriones struck him under the jaw and ear. Life swiftly left his limbs, and hateful darkness engulfed him.

Aeneas then hurled a spear at Meriones, hoping to catch him 610 as he strode forward under cover of his shield. But Meriones was on the look-out and avoided the bronze spear. He ducked under it, and the long shaft stuck in the ground behind him, its butt-end quivering till the imperious War-god Ares took away its force. Aeneas was enraged and said:

'Meriones, you may be a fine dancer, but my spear would have stopped you for good and all, if only I'd hit you.'

The famous spearman Meriones said:

620 'Aeneas, powerful though you are, it would be difficult for you to extinguish the fire of everyone you met in action. You are made of mortal stuff like the rest of us, and if I caught you in the belly with a sharp spear, you would, for all your strength and confidence, immediately yield the glory to me and your life to the god Hades, famed for his horses.'

Aeneas and Meriones exchange taunts

So he spoke, and Patroclus, brave son of Menoetius, reproved him:

'Meriones, you're too fine a warrior to spend your time making speeches. Believe me, old friend, the Trojans are not going to be pushed back from Sarpedon's body by a few insults; 630 the earth will cover many a man first. Battles are won by deeds; the council-chamber is the place for words. This is no time to talk, but to fight.'

With these words he led the way and godlike Meriones went with him. Like the crashing that rises from woodcutters at work in a mountain glade, and the noise is heard a long way off, so

from the broad earth there rose the thud of bronze, leather and
well-made shields as men stabbed at each other with swords
and curved spears. Even the sharpest eye would never have
recognized godlike Sarpedon, enveloped as he was from head to   640
foot in weapons, blood and dust. Men swarmed round his
body as flies in a sheepfold buzz round the brimming pails in
spring-time when the vessels overflow with milk.

So they swarmed round the body and, as they did so, Zeus
never shifted his shining eyes from the thick of battle but kept
them always fixed on the men, thinking to himself about the
killing of Patroclus. He was in two minds whether to let him
fall to glorious Hector's spear in the thick of the action over
godlike Sarpedon and let Hector strip the armour from his   650
shoulders, or whether to allow Patroclus to bring still more of
his enemies to grief. In the end Zeus decided the best thing was
for Patroclus, Achilles' fine attendant, to drive the Trojans and
bronze-armoured Hector back towards the town, taking many
lives.

So Zeus made a coward of Hector. He leapt into
his chariot and wheeled it round for flight, shouting
to the other Trojans to take to their heels – he knew
Zeus had tipped the sacred scales against him. At
that, not even the mighty Lycians stood their ground; they
fled one and all. They had seen their own lord hit in the heart   660
and lying where the dead were heaped. For in the fierce conflict
Zeus had staged, many a man had been killed over Sarpedon's
body.

ZEUS turns Hector to flight

So the Greeks stripped the gleaming bronze armour from
Sarpedon's shoulders. Brave Patroclus son of Menoetius handed
it to his men and told them to take it to the hollow ships. Then
Zeus who marshals the clouds addressed Apollo:

'Quick, dear Phoebus, go and take Sarpedon out
of range and, when you have wiped the dark blood
off, carry him to some distant spot and wash him in
running water, anoint him with ambrosia and wrap
him in an immortal robe. Then send him to be borne away by   670
Sleep and his twin-brother Death, those swift attendants, who
will quickly set him down in broad Lycia's fertile realm where

APOLLO to save Sarpedon's body

his relatives and retainers will give him burial with a grave-mound and monument – the honour that is due to the dead.'

So he spoke, and Apollo did not turn a deaf ear, but descended from the mountains of Ida into the mayhem of the fight. At once he took godlike Sarpedon out of range and, carrying him to some distant spot, washed him in running water, anointed him with ambrosia and wrapped him in an immortal robe. Then he sent him to be borne away by Sleep and his twin-brother Death, those swift attendants, who quickly set him down in broad Lycia's fertile realm.

Patroclus, with a shout to his charioteer Automedon, went in pursuit of the Trojans and Lycians. He was completely deluded, the blind fool. Had he kept to his orders from Achilles, he would have saved himself from the evil destiny which is dark death. But the will of Zeus always prevails over men. Zeus can easily make a brave man run away and lose a battle, but at another time that very same god will urge him on to fight. Now he put heart into Patroclus.

Who was the first man, who the last, to fall to you, Patroclus, as the gods summoned you to your death? Adrestus first, and Autonous and Echeclus; Perimus, Epistor and Melanippus; and then Elasus and Mulius and Pylartes. All these Patroclus killed, though the rest of them had had the sense to run. He was raging so unstoppably with his spear that the Trojans' city with its high gates would now have fallen to the Greeks under Patroclus if Phoebus Apollo had not taken his stand on the well-built tower with death in mind for Patroclus and salvation for the Trojans. Three times Patroclus scaled an angle of the high wall and three times Apollo hurled him off, thrusting back his glittering shield with his immortal hands. But when he came on like something superhuman for the fourth time, the god gave a terrible shout and spoke winged words:

APOLLO warns Patroclus

'Back, Olympian-born Patroclus! The town of the proud Trojans is not destined to be captured by your spear nor even by Achilles, who is a far better man than you.'

So he spoke, and Patroclus retreated a good way back to avoid the wrath of the Archer-god Apollo.

Hector had pulled up his horses at the Scaean gate. There he debated whether to drive into the mêlée once more and fight, or to order all his men to withdraw into the town. He was still in two minds when Phoebus Apollo appeared beside him, resembling vigorous and powerful Asius, horse-taming Hector's uncle (Asius was a brother of Hecabe and a son of Dymas who lived in Phrygia on the banks of the River Sangarius). In this disguise Apollo son of Zeus said: 720

'Hector, why have you stopped fighting and neglected your duty? I wish I were as much your better as you are mine! Then you would soon regret your withdrawal from battle. Off with you now and set your powerful horses at Patroclus. You could catch him yet, and Apollo grant you the victory.'

With these words the god went back into the battling crowd, and glorious Hector told warlike Cebriones to lash his horses into the fight. Apollo, merging with the throng, created terrible mayhem among the Greeks and gave the upper hand to Hector and the   730 Trojans. But Hector ignored the rest of the Greeks and, killing none of them, drove his powerful horses straight at Patroclus. Patroclus on his side leapt from his chariot to the ground with his spear in his left hand.

Hector launched at Patroclus

With the other he picked up a jagged, sparkling stone – his hand just covered it – and, refusing to retreat before Hector, threw it with all his force. He did not throw in vain: the sharp stone caught Hector's charioteer Cebriones, famous Priam's illegitimate son, on the forehead, with the horses' reins still in his hands. It shattered both his   740 eyebrows, crushing the bone; and his eyes fell out and rolled in the dust at his feet. He fell back out of the well-built chariot like a diver, and life left his bones. Mocking him, charioteer Patroclus, you said:

Patroclus kills Cebriones

'Well, well! How light on his toes, judging by that acrobatic somersault! Now, if the delightful dive he has taken from the chariot on to the plain is anything to go by, he'd satisfy the hunger of lots of people by doing the same at sea. Even in the roughest weather he could leap off a boat and grope about for molluscs. I never knew the Trojans had such acrobats!'   750

With these words he advanced to claim the body of the
warrior Cebriones, springing like a lion that has been wounded
in the chest while assaulting the folds, and his courage is the
death of him. With such determination, Patroclus, did you hurl
yourself at Cebriones.

Hector on the other side leapt from his chariot to the ground,
and the two fought for Cebriones like a pair of lions on the
mountain heights, each as hungry and fearless as the other,
disputing the dead body of a stag. So, with the body of Cebriones
760 between them, these two champions of the battle-cry, Patroclus
and glorious Hector, longed to hack into each other's flesh with
their cruel spears. Hector got hold of Cebriones' head and never
once let go; Patroclus, at his end, clung to a foot; and the rest of
the Trojans and Greeks joined in the fierce confrontation.

Like the east and south winds tussling with one another in a
mountain glen, setting the dense wood heaving, beech and ash
and smooth-barked cornel: their long boughs lash each other
770 with a terrifying sound, and the branches snap noisily – so the
Trojans and Greeks leapt at one another and destroyed. There
was no thought of fatal flight on either side. The ground where
Cebriones fell was peppered with sharp spears and feathered
arrows that had leapt from the bowstring; huge rocks struck
shields and sent staggering those that fought about him. And
there great Cebriones lay, in a swirl of dust, great even in his
fall, his charioteering days forgotten.

While the sun was high in the sky, volley and counter-volley
found their mark and men kept falling. But when the sun began
to drop – towards the time when the ploughman unyokes his ox
780 – the Greeks got the upper hand in defiance of destiny. They
dragged the warrior Cebriones out from among the weapons
and the yelling Trojans, and stripped the armour from his back.

APOLLO But Patroclus, with murder in his heart, leapt on
assaults the enemy. Three times he charged with an intim-
Patroclus idating yell, like impetuous Ares, and three times he
killed nine men. But when he leapt in like something
superhuman for the fourth time, then, Patroclus, the end was in
sight. In the heat of the battle, Phoebus encountered you,
Phoebus most terrible.

Patroclus had not seen him coming through the mayhem; the god had wrapped himself in a thick mist for this meet- 790 ing. He stood behind Patroclus now and, striking his back and broad shoulders with the flat of his hand, he made Patroclus' eyes spin and knocked the helmet off his head. With its heavy vizor it rolled clattering away under the horses' hooves, and its plume was defiled with blood and dust. It had not been allowed to defile that crested helmet in the dust before, when it pro- tected the head and handsome face of godlike Achilles. But now Zeus granted it to Hector to wear, since he was very close to 800 death. The long-shadowed spear, huge, thick and heavy with its head of bronze, was shattered in Patroclus' hands. The fringed shield with its strap fell from his shoulder to the ground; and lord Apollo son of Zeus undid the body-armour on his chest.

A fatal blindness overtook Patroclus. His shining limbs were paralysed; and as he stood there in a daze, a Dardanian called Euphorbus, son of Panthous, came up behind him at close range, threw a sharp spear and hit him in the middle of the back between the shoulders. This Euphorbus was the best spearman, runner and horseman of his years and in this very battle (the first he had fought as a charioteer learning the art of war) he had already brought twenty men from their chariots to the 810 ground. He was the first, then, to let fly at you, charioteer Patroclus. But he did not kill you. After pulling out the ash spear from his flesh, he ran back and mingled with the crowd. He did not stay to fight Patroclus, defenceless though he was.

And now, overcome by the god's blow and Euphorbus' spear, Patroclus began to retreat into his own contingent of warriors to avoid death. When Hector saw great-hearted Patroclus wounded and in retreat, he made his way towards him through 820 the ranks and, coming up, stabbed him with his spear in the lower belly, driving the bronze clean through. Patroclus thudded to the ground, throwing the whole Greek army into conster- nation. As a lion's will to fight overpowers an indomitable wild boar when the fearless pair battle it out in the mountains over a little stream; both wish to drink there, but the lion's strength prevails and his panting enemy is overcome – so, after killing

many men himself, Menoetius' strong son fell to a close-range
thrust from Hector, who now spoke to him in triumph with
winged words:

830   'Patroclus, you probably thought you'd sack our town,
make Trojan women slaves and ship them off to the
land of your fathers. You innocent! In their defence,
Hector's swift horses were racing into battle – I,
Hector, finest spearman of the war-loving Trojans,
who stand between them and the day of slavery. As for you,
vultures are going to eat you on this very spot. Miserable wretch!
Even great Achilles did not save you. I can imagine all the
instructions he gave you on your way out, while he stayed
behind: "Charioteer Patroclus, don't come back to the hollow
840   ships till you have ripped through the tunic on man-slaying
Hector's chest and soaked it with his blood." That, I imagine,
is what he must have said; and like an idiot you took him at his
word.'

Patroclus' death (15.65, 8.476)

    Fading fast you replied, charioteer Patroclus:

    'Hector, boast loud and long while you can. Zeus and Apollo
handed you that victory. *They* conquered me. It was an easy
task: they took the armour from my back. If twenty men like
you had confronted me, they would all have fallen to my
spear. No: it was deadly destiny and Leto's son Apollo that
850   did for me. Then came a man, Euphorbus; you are the third
of them all to kill me. But I will tell you something else, and
you bear it in mind. You too, I swear it, have not long to live.
Already you stand in the shadow of death and inexorable des-
tiny, slaughtered at the hands of Achilles, the matchless son of
Peleus.'

    As he spoke, the end that is death enveloped him. Life left his
limbs and took wing for the house of Hades, bewailing its lot
and the youth and the manhood it had left behind. But glorious
Hector spoke to him again, though he was gone:

    'Patroclus, why prophesy an early end for me? Who knows –
860   Achilles, son of lovely-haired Thetis, may still get there first,
dispatched with a blow from my spear.'

    With these words Hector put his foot on Patroclus to with-
draw his bronze spear from the wound, and trod the body off it

to lie face upwards on the ground. Then without a pause he
went after Automedon, Achilles' godlike attendant, with his
spear. He was eager to hit him. But Automedon was carried out
of harm's way by his speedy immortal horses, the splendid gift
that Peleus had received from the gods.

THE STRUGGLE OVER
PATROCLUS

Warlike Menelaus son of Atreus did not fail to notice that Patroclus had been overcome in battle by the Trojans. He advanced through the front ranks, bronze armour glittering, and stood over Patroclus' body as a mother-cow stands protectively over the first calf she has brought into the world. So auburn-haired Menelaus stood over Patroclus and guarded the body with his spear and round shield, determined to kill anyone who advanced against him.

But Panthous' son, Euphorbus of the ash spear, had not lost
10 interest in the body of matchless Patroclus. Coming close up to it, he said to Menelaus: 'Olympian-born Menelaus son of Atreus, leader of men, get back; leave the dead man and don't

touch his bloodstained armour. I was the first of the Trojans and their famous allies to hit Patroclus with a spear in the heat of battle. So allow me to win heroic glory in Trojan eyes, or I will hit you and take your precious life.'

Furious, auburn-haired Menelaus said:

'Father Zeus, it is no good thing to boast so arrogantly. The courage of the panther, the lion and the murderous wild boar, the most high-spirited and defiant beast of all, is, it seems, nothing to compare with the pride of these sons of Panthous with their famous ash spears! Yet your brother, mighty Hyperenor, did not long survive to enjoy the delights of youth when he insulted and stood up to me in battle. He said I was the most contemptible of the Greek men-at-arms. But I seem to remember that it was not on his own feet that he went home to delight his loving wife and cherished parents. And I'll cut *you* down to size as I did him, if you take me on. Get back now, join the rabble, and don't stand up to me, or you will come to grief. Only a fool is wise after the event.'

Menelaus taunts and kills Euphorbus

So he spoke but did not persuade him. Euphorbus replied and said:

'This very day, Olympian-born Menelaus, you are going to pay the price for my brother, whom you killed and boast about, and whose wife you left a widow in her new bridal chamber. You caused his parents untold tears and misery; yet I could still wipe away the tears of that unhappy pair if I brought back your head and armour and put them in the hands of Panthous and his wife godlike Phrontis. But our business will not long remain unsettled or uncontested – victory or defeat!'

With these words he stabbed Menelaus' round shield. But the spear did not break through and the tip was bent back by the stout shield. Then Menelaus son of Atreus attacked with his spear and a prayer to Father Zeus. As Euphorbus drew back, Menelaus stabbed him in the base of the throat and threw the whole weight of his body into it, keeping a firm grip on the spear. The point went clean through his soft neck. He thudded to the ground, and his armour clattered about him. His hair, lovely as the Graces', and the curls he used to bind with gold

and silver spirals were all drenched with blood. Like the shoot
of an olive-tree that a gardener nurtures in a place of its own,
where there is enough water for it to drink and grow fine and
healthy; the breezes of all the winds shake it, and it bursts into
white blossom, but suddenly there is a great gust of wind which
uproots it from its trench and lays it flat on the ground – such
was Panthous' son, Euphorbus of the ash spear, when Menelaus
60 killed him and stripped him of his armour.

Disguised
APOLLO
stirs *Hector*

As a mountain lion which has confidence in its
own strength pounces on the finest heifer in a grazing
herd; it seizes her, breaks her neck with its power-
ful jaws and then, tearing at her, devours her blood
and entrails; all round it the dogs and herdsmen create a ter-
rific din, but keep their distance; they have no desire to close
in, and are green with fear of it – so not a single Trojan had the
70 daring to come near illustrious Menelaus. Then Menelaus
would have found it easy to take Euphorbus' splendid armour
if Phoebus Apollo had not grudged him it and sent Hector equal
of Ares to attack him. Apollo went to Hector in the disguise of
a man called Mentes, a leader of the Cicones, and spoke winged
words:

'Hector, at the moment you are running around in pursuit of
the unattainable – the horses of warlike Achilles, which are hard
to master and difficult to drive, at any rate for a mere man, or
anyone but Achilles, whose mother is a goddess. Meanwhile
80 warlike Menelaus is standing over Patroclus' body and has killed
the best man in Troy: Euphorbus, son of Panthous, will never
fight again.'

With these words the god went back into the heart of the
battle, and Hector's heart was wrung with grief. But presently
he peered across the ranks and saw the pair of them, Menelaus
removing the impressive arms and Euphorbus lying on the
ground, the blood pouring from the stab-wound. Yelling shrilly,
Hector advanced through the front ranks, his bronze armour
glittering, looking like the inextinguishable flames in the furnace
of the blacksmith god Hephaestus. Menelaus did not fail to
90 recognize his war-cry. Disturbed he reflected on the situation:

'What shall I do? If I abandon these fine arms and the body

of Patroclus, who fell here fighting to avenge wrongs done to me, any Greek who sees me will rightly be angry. But if, to save face, I fight with Hector and the Trojans single-handed, I am likely to be cut off and surrounded, since Hector of the flashing helmet is bringing all his Trojans with him.

'But why talk to myself like this? When a man decides, without the good will of the gods, to fight another who enjoys their favour, he has disaster coming to him. Surely then, no Greek is   100
going to be angry to see me giving way to Hector, who is fighting with the gods on his side. If only I knew where Ajax, master of the battle-cry, was, the pair of us could call up our old will to fight, even with the god against us, and go to see if we could save the body for Achilles son of Peleus. That would make the best of a bad situation.'

While these thoughts raced through his mind, the Trojan ranks bore down on him with Hector at their head. Abandoning Patroclus' body, Menelaus turned and retreated, but with many a backward look, like a bearded lion being chased from the fold with spears and shouts by the shepherds and their dogs; he feels   110
the chill of fear in his brave heart and much against his will abandons the farmyard – so Menelaus withdrew from Patroclus' body. But he turned and stood his ground when he reached his own contingent, looking everywhere for great Ajax son of Telamon. He saw him presently, out on the left flank, exhorting and urging on his men to fight, since Phoebus Apollo had filled them with an unnatural panic. Menelaus ran up to him at once and said:

'Ajax, over here, old friend! Patroclus is dead. Hurry! We   120
might at least save the body for Achilles. It's been stripped – Hector of the flashing helmet has taken his armour.'

So he spoke, and his words went straight to warlike   *Hector* takes
Ajax's heart. He and auburn-haired Menelaus set off   Patroclus'
through the front lines.   armour

Hector was beginning to haul away the body. He had removed Patroclus' famous armour and now he wanted to behead him with his sharp sword, drag off the trunk and give it to the dogs of Troy. But when Ajax came up with his towerlike shield, Hector retreated into his own contingent and leapt on to his   130 chariot. He gave the beautiful armour to some Trojans to take back to Ilium, where it would make his reputation. Meanwhile Ajax covered Patroclus with his broad shield and stood at bay like a lioness over its cubs: leading them through the forest, it is confronted by huntsmen; breathing defiance, it knits its eyebrows together in a frown that covers its eyes – so Ajax planted himself by Patroclus. Warlike Menelaus son of Atreus took his stand back to back with him, anguish growing in his heart.

140   Glaucus son of Hippolochus, leader of the Lycian forces, looked blackly at Hector and reproached him sharply:

Glaucus rounds on Hector   'Hector, with your wonderful looks, you're useless in battle. Your heroic reputation hides a coward after all. Ask yourself how you are going to save the town and its people with nobody to help you but the native Trojans; since none of the Lycians will be going out to fight against the Greeks for Ilium. All along, they have been given no reward for battling relentlessly with the enemy day in, day out. What hopes has a lesser man of being rescued by you in a tight

150   corner when you have callously left Sarpedon, your guest and comrade-in-arms, like carrion in Greek hands? You and your people owed much to him while he was alive; yet you cannot bring yourself to save him from the dogs.

'So now, if I have any influence with the Lycians, we go home. And that will mean the end for Troy. Why, if the Trojans had any real courage, the fearless spirit that enters into men who are fighting their enemies tooth and nail in defence of their country, we should soon drag Patroclus into Ilium. And if that

160   man's dead body could be brought out of the battle and into Priam's great town, the Greeks would at once return Sarpedon's beautiful armour, and we could bring Sarpedon's body back into Ilium. Such is the man to whom Patroclus was attendant, the best warrior in the Greek camp, with the best men at close combat under his command.

'But you could not bring yourself, with the enemy war-cry ringing in your ears, to face great-hearted Ajax, to look him in the eye and fight it out with him – because he is the better man.'

Looking blackly at him Hector of the flashing helmet replied:

170   'Glaucus, what's made a man like you talk so insolently? I

cannot believe it. I always took you for the wisest man in the whole of fertile Lycia. As it is, you have destroyed my faith in your judgement by talking like this and suggesting I dared not stand up to awe-inspiring Ajax. Believe me, fighting and the noise of chariots do not frighten me. But the will of Zeus who drives the storm-cloud always prevails. He can easily make a brave man run away and lose a battle, but at another time that very same god will urge him on to fight.

'But come here, my friend, and stand by my side, and see what I can do; see whether you are right and I shall prove a coward all day long, or whether I can stop some of these Greeks, determined as they are, from fighting any longer over Patroclus' body.' 180

With these words he called out to the Trojans in a loud voice:

'Trojans, Lycians and you Dardanians that like your fighting hand to hand, be men, my comrades, and call up that fighting spirit of yours! I am going to put on the armour of matchless Achilles, the fine armour I took from mighty Patroclus when I killed him.'

With these words Hector of the flashing helmet left the battle-field and ran after his men who were carrying the famous armour of Achilles son of Peleus to the town. He soon caught them up, since they had not gone far and he ran fast. 190 Then he changed his equipment, standing far from the battlefield with all its tears, telling his war-loving Trojans to take his own arms to sacred Ilium and putting on the imperishable armour of Achilles which the Sky-gods had given to his father Peleus. Peleus, when he grew old, had passed it on to his son. But the son did not grow old in his father's armour.

ZEUS pities *Hector* in Achilles' armour

When from afar Zeus who marshals the clouds saw Hector equipping himself in the arms of godlike Achilles, he shook his head and said to himself: 200

'Unhappy man! Little knowing how close you are to death, you are putting on the imperishable armour of a mighty man of war, before whom all others tremble. And it was you that killed his comrade, brave and gentle Patroclus, and improperly stripped the armour from his head and shoulders. Well, for the moment at any rate I grant you supremacy. But you must pay for it. There will be no homecoming for you from battle, and your wife Andromache will never take the famous armour of Achilles from your hands.'

The son of Cronus spoke and nodded his sable brows in confirmation.

210   The armour fitted Hector's body well, the savage spirit of the terrible War-god now entered him and power and fresh vigour filled his limbs. Uttering his piercing war-cry, he went in search of his renowned allies and presented himself before all of them, resplendent in the armour of great-hearted Achilles. To rouse their spirits he went up and spoke to each of them in turn: to Mesthles and Glaucus; to Medon and Thersilochus; to Asteropaeus, Deisenor and Hippothous; to Phorcys and Chromis and Ennomus the prophet. Urging them on, he spoke winged words:

220   'Hear me, you countless tribes of allies that live round about. I neither sought nor needed mere numbers when I summoned each of you here from your own towns. What I wanted was men who would be fully committed to fighting the war-loving Greeks in defence of the women and little children of Troy. That is why I impoverish my own people by demanding they supply you with gifts and provisions and so keep your courage high.

Hector and Menelaus rouse their men

    'Turn, then, and straight at the enemy, every one of you, to live or die! That is the intimacy of battle. To the man who forces 230 Ajax back and brings Patroclus, dead though he is, into the Trojan lines, I will give half the spoils, keeping the other half myself, so that he will share the glory equally with me.'

So he spoke, and they lifted their spears and charged at the Greeks with full force, filled with high hopes of retrieving the body from Ajax son of Telamon. The innocents – Ajax was going to take many a life over Patroclus' body. Then Ajax spoke to Menelaus, master of the battle-cry:

    'My old friend, Olympian-born Menelaus, I'm beginning to think we'll never get safely back from this fight. I am not only 240 very afraid Patroclus' body will soon be glutting the Trojan dogs and birds, but also of the perilous situation we'll be facing, with a cloud of war called Hector swirling up on all sides. Death is staring us in the face. Quick! Call the Greek chieftains! Somebody might hear.'

So he spoke, and Menelaus, master of the battle-cry, complied and sent his voice ringing out to the whole Greek army:

'Friends, rulers and leaders of the Greeks! All you who drink your wine at the public cost by the side of Agamemnon and   250
Menelaus; who share in the command and derive your honour and glory from Zeus; it is impossible for me to pick out every commander – the battle's flaring up everywhere. Here, every one of you, without being named! Think of the disgrace, that the dogs of Ilium should have Patroclus to toy with!'

So he spoke, and swift Ajax son of Oïleus heard every word of this and was the first to come running up to Menelaus through the mayhem. He was followed by Idomeneus and Idomeneus' attendant Meriones, equal of the murderous War-god Ares. As for the rest that came behind to reinforce the   260
Greek line, where is the man who could remember all their names?

The Trojans advanced in a mass, and Hector led them. As a great wave roars against the current flowing out of the mouth of a sky-fed river, and the sea-shore's headlands on either side boom thunderously as the sea washes back – with such a roar did the Trojans advance. But united in their resolution, the Greeks faced them, making a fence of their bronze shields round Patroclus. Moreover Zeus son of Cronus spread a thick mist about their gleaming helmets. He had no quarrel with Patroclus   270
while he was alive and serving as Achilles' attendant, and loathed the thought of his becoming carrion for the enemy dogs of Troy. So now he roused Patroclus' comrades-in-arms to fight in his defence.

At first the Trojans flung back the dark-eyed Greeks, who abandoned the body and gave ground before them. Even so, the proud Trojans did not succeed in killing any of them with their spears, for all their efforts. But the Trojans did start dragging off the body. The Greeks, however, were not going to be separated from it for long. They were soon rallied by Ajax, who, next to matchless Achilles, was the best-looking and best fighter of   280 all the Greeks. He charged through the front line, fierce as a wild boar in the mountains who easily scatters the hounds and lively young huntsmen as it turns at bay in the glades. So glorious Ajax charged and easily scattered the ranks of Trojans, who had gathered round Patroclus and made up their minds that *they* were going to win the glory and drag his body into the city.

290   Hippothous, glorious son of Pelasgian Lethus, had tied his sword-belt round the tendons of Patroclus' ankle and was hauling him by the foot through the thick of the action. He hoped to do Hector and the Trojans a favour. But he did himself a bad one, since he soon ran into trouble from which no one, however willing, could save him. Ajax rushed up to him through the crowd and from close range struck him through his bronze-cheeked helmet. The plumed helmet, hit by the great spear and mighty hand behind it, was split apart by the spear-point, and the man's blood and brains came gushing out along the spear-socket. Hippothous collapsed. He let the foot of great-hearted Patroclus drop from

*Hippothous,
Schedius,
Phorcys killed*

300   his hand to the ground and fell there next to it, face forward on the body. He was a long way from fertile Larisa and could never repay his parents for their care; his life had been too short when Ajax's spear cut him off.

Now Hector hurled a glittering spear at Ajax. But Ajax was on the lookout and just avoided the bronze spear, which hit a man called Schedius, best of the Phocians, who ruled over many and whose home was in the impressive town of Panopeus. Hector struck him under the middle of the collar bone. The

310   bronze spear-point went right through and emerged below his shoulder. He thudded to the ground, and his armour clattered about him.

In his turn, Ajax stabbed warlike Phorcys full in the belly as he stood over Hippothous and smashed a plate of his body-armour. The spear-point let out his innards and, falling in the dust, he clutched at the ground. The Trojan front and glorious Hector himself fell back, while the Greeks with a triumphant cry dragged away the bodies of Phorcys and Hippothous and removed the armour from their shoulders.

Weakened and demoralized, the Trojans would have been

driven back into Ilium by the war-loving Greeks, who would   320
thus, by their sheer brute force, have won a victory in defiance
of the will of Zeus, if Apollo had not roused Aeneas. The god
took the form of a herald, Periphas, who was kindly disposed
to Aeneas, having grown old as a herald in the service of Aeneas'
old father Anchises. In this disguise, Apollo son of Zeus spoke
to him:

'Aeneas, if the gods were indeed against you, how
could you hope to save lofty Ilium? I have known   *APOLLO*
men who saved their country, even though their own   rallies *Aeneas*
people were inferior, by relying on their own brute force, their
bravery and their numbers. But Zeus is on our side! He wants   330
us to beat the Greeks. And yet you are scared out of your senses
and refuse to fight.'

So he spoke, and Aeneas looked him in the face and knew
him for the Archer-god Apollo. He gave Hector a great shout:

'Hector and all you Trojan and allied commanders, it's a
shameful thing to let the war-loving Greeks drive us, weak-
ened and demoralized, back into Ilium! Besides, one of the
gods came up to me just now and told me that Zeus the high
counsellor is still our ally in this war. So let's make straight at 340
the Greeks and make sure they don't find it too easy to take the
dead Patroclus back to their ships.'

So Aeneas spoke and leapt forward to make a
stand well in front of the foremost fighters. As a   Leiocritus and
result the Trojans turned about and faced the Greeks.   *Apisaon* killed
Then Aeneas stabbed Leiocritus. This man was a brave follower
of Lycomedes, and his death filled war-loving Lycomedes with
pity. He ran up, stood beside him and let fly with his glittering
spear which hit Apisaon, shepherd of the people, in the liver
under the midriff, bringing him down at once. Apisaon was one
of those that had come from fertile Paeonia. In fact, he was their 350
best warrior next to Asteropaeus.

His death filled warlike Asteropaeus with pity, and he now
charged with a will at the Greeks himself. But it was too late to
accomplish any good. They had surrounded Patroclus with
a fence of shields and levelled spears. Awe-inspiring Ajax in
particular was going round issuing strict orders to them all: no

one was to back off from the body, and no one to break away
and fight out in front. They were all to stick close to Patroclus
and fight hand to hand.

360   Such were awe-inspiring Ajax's orders, and the earth was
soaked with crimson blood, and men fell in heaps, the Trojans
and their proud allies mingling their corpses with the Greek
dead. For the Greeks did not fight a bloodless battle either. And
yet they lost far fewer men: all the time they remembered to
protect each other from death inn the mayhem.

> Battle in the mist

So they fought on like fire, and you would not
have thought the sun and moon were still func-
tioning, since a mist had spread over that part of the
battlefield where the pick of the men were disputing the body
370 of Patroclus. Elsewhere, however, the Trojans and the Greek
men-at-arms were battling without that problem under a clear
sky. There was brilliant sunshine everywhere and not a cloud in
sight above the plain or on the hills. The fighting was desultory;
they kept their distance and avoided trouble from each other's
spears. It was only in the centre that the best of the Greeks were
suffering badly from the mist and the battle in which they were
being ground down by the brutal spears. Two men, illustrious
Thrasymedes and Antilochus, had not yet heard that matchless
380 Patroclus had been killed. They thought he was still alive and
fighting Trojans in the front line of battle. They were fighting
some way away, looking out for casualties and signs of panic in
their own contingent, as Nestor had told them to do when he
urged them from the black ships into battle.

But the great, grim struggle continued unabated all day long.
All the while knees, shins, feet, hands and eyes streamed with
the sweat of the exertions of those who were battling it out over
390 the brave attendant of swift-footed Achilles. As a man gives his
people a great bull's hide soaked in fat for stretching; they take
the hide, stand round in a ring and stretch it, and the moisture
soon comes out while the fat sinks in and, with many hands
tugging at it, it is stretched tight in every part – so both sides
tugged the body to and fro between them in that restricted
space. Each party had high hopes, the Trojans of dragging
Patroclus into Ilium and the Greeks of bringing him back to the

hollow ships. They ground savagely away at each other over the body; not even Ares who drives on armies, or Athene at her angriest, would have been displeased by the sight. Such was the agonizing struggle Zeus extended that day over man and horse   400
alike in the battle for Patroclus.

Godlike Achilles had as yet no inkling of Patroclus' death. They were fighting a long way from the swift ships under the walls of Ilium, and it never entered his head that Patroclus had been killed. He thought of him as pressing on to the very gates of the town, but then returning safe and sound. He certainly never expected him to sack the town without him – or with him, either. He had often been told this was not to be by his own mother, who used to give him private information about almighty Zeus' plans. Not that she   410
told him now of the disaster that had occurred, the death of his dearest companion.

Achilles' ignorance

Over the dead man, meanwhile, the others with their pointed spears were locked in an unending struggle and killing one another. The bronze-armoured Greeks said to a man:

'Comrades, there is no honour in falling back to our hollow ships. If we let the horse-taming Trojans drag this body into their town and win the glory, the best thing to happen would be for the black earth to swallow us here where we stand!'

And on their side, the great-hearted Trojans said: 420

'Comrades, even if all of us are destined to be killed beside this body, no one must retreat.'

So they spoke and gave each other fresh heart. So the fight continued, and an iron din rose up through the murmuring air and struck the bronze sky.

Far from the conflict, the horses of Achilles had been weeping ever since they learnt that their chario-teer had been brought down in the dust by man-slaying Hector. Automedon, Diores' strong son, did all he could with them: he tried lashing them with his whistling   430
whip; he tried coaxing them; he tried threats. But the pair refused either to go back to the ships and the broad Hellespont, or into battle with the Greeks. Firm as a gravestone planted on the

ZEUS pities Patroclus' horses

barrow of a dead man or woman, they stood motionless in front of their beautiful chariot, their heads bowed to the earth. Hot tears ran from their eyes to the ground as they mourned for their lost charioteer, and their luxuriant manes, falling to the
440   ground from the collar on both sides of the yoke, were soiled in the dust.

Zeus son of Cronus took pity on the pair when he saw their grief. He shook his head and said to himself:

'Poor beasts! Why did we give you, who are ageless and immortal, to lord Peleus, who is doomed to die? Did we mean you to share the sorrows of unhappy men? For of all creatures that breathe and creep about on the earth, there is none so miserable as man. But Hector shall not drive you and your
450   ornate chariot. That I will not have. Is it not enough that he has the armour and exults as he does?

'No, I will fill your legs with energy and your hearts with courage, so that you can at least save Automedon and bring him back from the battle to the hollow ships. For I still intend to give the glory to the Trojans, to go on killing Greeks till they reach the well-benched ships, the sun sets and blessed darkness intervenes.'

With these words Zeus breathed energy into the horses. They shook the dust from their manes and galloped off with their fast chariot to join the Trojans and Greeks. Behind them, Automedon took on the fighter's role, though he grieved bitterly for his companion, and charged into battle with his chariot like
460   a vulture after geese. His horses' speed made it easy for him to avoid becoming entangled in the mêlée of Trojans, and as easy to dash into it and pursue an enemy through the crowd.

But he could not kill the men he chased. Alone as
Alcimedon   he was in the speeding chariot, he found it impossible
rejoins the   to control his swift horses and at the same time bring
fight   his spear into play. At last, however, his companion
Alcimedon saw him. He came up behind the chariot and said to Automedon:

'Automedon, what god has robbed you of your intelligence
470   and put this pointless idea in your head? Look at the way you're taking on the front-line Trojans single-handed, when your

companion has been killed and Hector himself is swaggering about in the armour of Achilles.'

Automedon son of Diores said:

'Alcimedon, was there anyone like you for mastering and controlling the strength of these immortal horses – except Patroclus, wise as the gods, while he lived? But now death and destiny have claimed him. So take the whip and shining reins yourself, while I get down and fight.'   480

So Automedon spoke and dismounted, while Alcimedon leapt into the fast war-chariot and quickly seized the whip and reins. Glorious Hector saw them and said to Aeneas, who happened to be near:

'Aeneas, adviser of the bronze-armoured Trojans, I see the horses of swift-footed Achilles coming into battle with an in-competent pair of charioteers. I think we could capture them, if, that is, you'd care to help me. Those two would never stand   490 and fight if you and I attacked them.'

So he spoke, and Aeneas strong son of Anchises complied; so the two men went forward, protecting their shoulders with their shields of dried and toughened oxhide on to which much bronze had been hammered. Chromis and godlike Aretus both went with them and they had great hopes of killing the men and driving off their high-necked horses. The innocents: they were not about to disengage from Automedon without bloodshed.

Meanwhile Automedon prayed to Father Zeus and was filled with power and fresh vigour. At once he spoke to Alcimedon   500 his trusted friend:

'Alcimedon, keep near me with the horses; let me feel their breath on my back. If Hector isn't killed in the front line himself, I don't think there'll be any holding him in his determination till he has killed both of us, jumped up behind Achilles' beautiful horses and put the Greek ranks to flight.'

Automedon
calls for help

With these words he called to the Ajaxes and Menelaus:

'You two Ajaxes, commanders of the Greeks, and you, Mene-laus, entrust your best men to stand over the body there and   510 hold the enemy off, while you come to help us keep death at bay. We're still alive here in the battle with all its tears, but Hector and Aeneas, best of the Trojans, are bearing down on us at speed. But since everything that happens is in the lap of the gods, I'll try a throw myself and leave the rest to Zeus.'

Automedon kills *Aretus*

He spoke, balanced his long-shadowed spear and hurled it. It hit Aretus' round shield. This failed to stop it, and the spear pierced it and drove on through

520 his belt into his abdomen. As a strong man with a sharp axe strikes a farmyard ox behind the horns and then cuts its throat, and the ox springs forward and then collapses, so Aretus sprang forward and then fell on his back. The sharp spear quivered in his guts and drew the life from him. Hector then threw a glittering spear at Automedon. But he was on the lookout and avoided the bronze weapon. He ducked under it, and the long shaft stuck in the ground behind him, its butt-end quivering till the imperious War-god Ares took away its force.

530 And now they would have been at one another's throats with their swords, if the two Ajaxes, who had come up through the press in answer to their comrade's call, had not caused their determined opponents to disengage. Frightened of such a pair, Hector, Aeneas and godlike Chromius drew back, leaving the stricken Aretus to lie where he fell. Automedon equal of swift Ares stripped him of his arms and spoke in triumph over him:

'That consoles me somewhat for Patroclus' death, though he was a better man than the one I've killed.'

540 With these words he lifted the bloodstained armour into his chariot and mounted it himself, his feet and hands covered in blood like a lion that has eaten a bull.

Once more, conflict with all its tears and pain raged fiercely around Patroclus, since Athene brought it on. She came down from Olympus to give a lead to the Greeks on the instructions of far-thundering Zeus, who had changed his mind. Like a shimmering rainbow that Zeus stretches across the skies to warn mankind of war, or the coming of a chilly storm that

550 stops work in the fields and discomforts the flocks – so Athene, wrapping herself in a shimmering mist, plunged in among the Greek troops and stirred up one and all. First she urged on

mighty Menelaus, who happened to be nearest. Borrowing the shape and tireless voice of Phoenix, she said:

'It's you, Menelaus, who will hang your head in shame at the reproach, if the swift dogs are allowed to maul the loyal friend of noble Achilles under the walls of Ilium. Hold firm, then, with all your strength and throw every man we have into the fight.'

ATHENE inspires Menelaus

Menelaus, master of the battle-cry, replied:

560

'Phoenix, my venerable lord and ancient friend, I only wish Athene would give me strength and keep the missiles off. Then I should gladly make a stand and fight for Patroclus, whose death has struck me a cruel blow. But Hector has the terrifying energy of fire. He's on an unstoppable rampage with his spear. Zeus is handing him the glory.'

So he spoke, and grey-eyed Athene was delighted that Menelaus had prayed to her before all other gods. She strengthened his shoulders and knees and implanted in his chest the daring of 570 a fly which is so fond of human blood that it returns to its attack however often a man brushes it away. With such daring did the goddess fill his heart, and he took his stand beside Patroclus' body and threw his glittering spear.

There was a Trojan called Podes. He was a man of wealth and breeding, and Hector held him dearer than any other Trojan, since they were the best of companions at feasts. This man was struck on the belt by auburn-haired Menelaus' spear as he started to run away. The spear went right through him; he thudded to the ground, and Menelaus son of Atreus dragged 580 Patroclus' body away from the Trojans and gave it to his men.

But now Apollo stood by Hector and urged him on. The god went up to him disguised as Phaenops, who came from Abydus and was Hector's favourite among his foreign guests. In this disguise the Archer-god Apollo said:

'Hector, what Greek will ever fear you again if you let yourself be scared by Menelaus, who has been a soft touch so far? But now he has come and lifted out the dead man on his own and killed your loyal friend Podes, a brave man in the front line.' 590

So he spoke, and a black cloud of grief descended on Hector. He advanced through the front ranks, bronze armour glittering.

And at this moment Zeus, who had hidden Mount Ida under clouds, discharged a lightning flash with a great clap of thunder and, taking up his gleaming fringed aegis, shook it out, gave victory to the Trojans and filled the Greeks with panic.

Peneleos from Boeotia was the first of them to turn and run. He had been steadily facing the enemy when a spear from
600 Polydamas, who had come up and thrown from short range,

Peneleos and Leitus wounded

hit him on the top of the shoulder. It was a glancing blow but the spear-point grazed the bone. Then Hector at close quarters stabbed Leitus in the wrist and ended his interest in the fight. Leitus, knowing he could no longer expect to handle a spear and take on the enemy, gave one look round and fled.

As Hector went in pursuit of Leitus, Idomeneus son of Deucalion threw at Hector and hit his body-armour by the nipple on his chest. But the long spear broke at the socket, and the Trojans gave a yell. Hector retaliated with a spear at Idomeneus, who by now had mounted a chariot. He just missed him but hit
610 Coeranus, who had come to the war from well-built Lyctus in Crete as attendant and charioteer of Meriones. Coeranus had galloped to the rescue of Idomeneus, who had set out from the ships that day on foot and would otherwise have pre-

Coeranus killed

sented the enemy with a great triumph. So Coeranus was the salvation of Idomeneus and preserved his life; but he lost his own to man-slaying Hector, whose spear and its socket, hitting him under the jaw and ear, knocked all his teeth out and cut his tongue in half. Coeranus crashed
620 out of the chariot, dropping the reins on the ground. Meriones stooped down, picked them up from the ground with his own hands and said to Idomeneus:

'Now whip the horses on till you reach the ships. You don't need me to tell you we have lost the day.'

So he spoke, and Idomeneus lashed the lovely-maned horses back to the hollow ships. He was a frightened man.

Menelaus and great-hearted Ajax were also well aware that Zeus was working to give the Trojans victory. Great Ajax son of Telamon began and spoke his mind:
630 'This is hopeless! Any fool can see Father Zeus himself is

helping the Trojans. Every spear they throw hits its mark. Whether an incompetent or expert throws it, Zeus sees it to its target, while all ours fall ineffectually to the ground like this.

'Well, we shall have to come up with an effective tactic of our own for bringing the body away and pleasing our comrades behind by getting safely back to them. They must be watching us in some anxiety and wondering whether anything can stop man-slaying Hector in his determined onslaught from swooping down on our black ships. If only one of our men could run   640 with a message to Achilles – I don't believe he has even heard the dreadful news of his dear companion's death. But I can't see the man for the task: men and horses are all lost in this mist. Father Zeus, get us out of it and give us a clear sky, so that at least we can see what we're doing. As long as we are in the light, kill us too, since that is what you want.'

So he spoke, and the Father, moved by this tearful outburst, quickly cleared away the darkness and dispersed the mist. The   650 sun burst through, bringing the whole battlefield into view. Then Ajax said to Menelaus, master of the battle-cry:

Antilochus to inform Achilles

'Now look around you, Olympian-born Menelaus, and see whether you can spot great-hearted Nestor's son, Antilochus. If he's still alive, tell him to run quickly to warlike Achilles with the news that his dearest companion is dead.'

So he spoke, and Menelaus, master of the battle-cry, complied. He set off like a lion that retreats from a farmyard when it is tired of pitting itself against the dogs and men: they have stayed awake all night to protect the choicest of their cattle from his jaws but, hungry for meat, the lion keeps on charging. But   660 it does no good by it. Showers of spears and blazing torches hurled at it by strong hands scare it off for all its appetite, and at dawn it slinks off disappointed – so Menelaus, master of the battle-cry, retired from the body of Patroclus. He did not wish to go at all since he was much afraid that the Greeks, as the result of dire panic, might make the enemy a gift of it. He gave Meriones and the two Ajaxes full orders:

'You two Ajaxes, leaders of the Greeks, and you, Meriones,

670   now's the time to remember poor, gentle Patroclus. To every
one of us he was the soul of kindness while he lived. Now death
and destiny have claimed him.'

With these words auburn-haired Menelaus went off, peering
all round him like an eagle, which is said to have the sharpest
sight of any bird in the sky: however high in the air, it still spots
the swift hare crouching under a leafy bush and swoops down,
seizes it and takes its life – so, Olympian-born Menelaus, did
680   your brilliant eyes range everywhere among your many men, to
see whether Nestor's son Antilochus was still alive. Menelaus
quickly spotted his man on the far left of the battle, encouraging
his troops and driving them on to fight. Auburn-haired Mene-
laus went up to him and said:

'Olympian-born Antilochus, come here and let me tell you
the dreadful news. How I wish it had never happened! You must
have seen for yourself that the god has already brought disaster
to the Greeks and victory to the Trojans. But now the best of all
690   the Greeks is dead – Patroclus. It is an enormous loss for us.
Now run to the ships at once, let Achilles know and tell him to
come to the rescue immediately and bring the body safely back
to his ship. It has been stripped. Hector of the flashing helmet
has his armour.'

So he spoke, and Antilochus was horrified at what he heard.
For a while he was unable to speak; his eyes filled with
tears; the words stuck in his throat. But he did not ignore Mene-
laus' orders and set off at a run after handing his armour to
his admirable attendant Laodocus, who was manoeuvring his
700   horses up and down beside him. He ran, weeping, from the
battlefield to tell Achilles the bad news.

Nor did you, Olympian-born Menelaus, wish to stay and
help the weary Pylian troops whom Antilochus had left,
though they missed their leader badly. Instead, Menelaus put
godlike Thrasymedes in command and himself returned to stand
over Patroclus. He ran up to the two Ajaxes and immediately
said:

'I've sent our man to the ships with the message for Achilles.
710   But I dare not hope Achilles will come at once, however angry
he may be with Hector – he can't fight the Trojans without his

armour. We'll have to come up with an effective tactic of our own for bringing back the body and saving our own lives from these yelling Trojans.'

Great Ajax son of Telamon replied:

'You're quite right, noble Menelaus. You and Meriones get your shoulders under the body, lift it up and get it out of the fighting as fast as you can, while the pair of us stay and keep Hector and the Trojans engaged. We Ajaxes share the same 720 name and spirit. This is not the first time we've fought in a tight corner side by side.'

So he spoke, and with a tremendous effort the two men hoisted Patroclus up off the ground. The pursuing Trojans gave a shout when they saw the Greeks carrying off the body and charged like hounds that launch themselves at a wounded boar in front of the young huntsmen: for a while the hounds race after him, determined to tear him to pieces, but when the boar, relying on its strength, turns on them, they recoil and bolt in all directions – so for a 730 time the Trojans followed up in a mass, stabbing with their swords and curved spears. But when the two Ajaxes turned and made a stand against them, their colour changed and none of them had the courage to charge in and fight over the body.

So, full of determination, Menelaus and Meriones carried Patroclus' body from the battlefield and brought it to the hollow ships. The battle extended round them as uncontrollable as a fire that suddenly blazes up and sweeps through a town, and the houses are consumed in a mighty conflagration and a powerful wind roars on the flames – so the incessant din from 740 fighting men and chariots followed after them as they went. As mules put all their energy into dragging a log or some huge ship's timber down from the mountains by a rocky track, wearing themselves out with their exertions, heaving and sweating, so, full of determination, they carried off the body.

Behind them, the two Ajaxes held back the enemy, as a wooded ridge that lies in a continuous line across the countryside holds back the floods and withstands the destructive torrents of mighty rivers, diverting them all over the plain and 750 thrusting them back, and the rivers do not break through even

Greeks retreat with Patroclus' body

when they pour down in spate – so all the time the two Ajaxes fended off the Trojans who attacked the rear. But the Trojans and two men in particular, Aeneas son of Anchises and glorious Hector, kept after them. As a flock of starlings or jackdaws takes wing, screaming in confusion, when they see a falcon after them, spelling death to their nestlings, so the Greek warriors, confused and yelling, fled before Aeneas and Hector and lost the will to fight. Many a fine weapon fell at and around the ditch as the Greeks ran for it. But there was no let-up in the conflict.

18

ACHILLES' DECISION

1–147: Antilochus brings news of Patroclus' death. Achilles collapses in grief, and his mother THETIS, hearing his cries, arrives with her Sea-nymphs to lament. Achilles says he will have his revenge by killing *Hector* and ignores THETIS' warning that his death will follow soon after *Hector*'s.

148–242: Achilles makes an appearance on the battlefield and with ATHENE's help routs the *Trojans* with a shout. Patroclus' body is brought back to the Greek camp [night before 27th day].

243–314: Terrified by Achilles' return, the *Trojans* hold an assembly. *Polydamas* recommends withdrawal to *Ilium*; *Hector*, wrongly convinced ZEUS is on his side, rejects this advice and wins *Trojan* approval to continue the attack next morning.

314–68: Achilles laments Patroclus, foreseeing his own death but anticipating revenge on *Hector*. The body is washed, anointed and clothed, and lamentation continues throughout the night. HERA gloats to ZEUS over her success in bringing Achilles back into the fighting.

369–467: THETIS arrives at HEPHAESTUS' home and asks for armour.

468–617: HEPHAESTUS returns to his forge to make armour for Achilles. The shield is described in detail.

So they fought on like blazing fire. Meanwhile Antilochus, swift-footed messenger, came to Achilles with his news and found him in front of his beaked ships. Achilles harboured a premonition of what had already happened and, disturbed, was reflecting on the situation:

'What's going on? Why are the long-haired Greeks stam-
peding wildly for their ships across the plain? I pray the gods
have not brought about the grief and suffering my mother once
10   predicted for me. She told me that, while I was still alive, the
best of the Myrmidons would fall to the Trojans and leave the
light of day. And now I am sure Menoetius' brave son Patroclus
is dead. The hothead! I ordered him to come back here when
he'd saved the ships from the flames and not fight it out with
Hector.'

While these thoughts raced through his mind, noble Anti-
lochus, Nestor's son, halted before him, hot tears pouring down
his cheeks, and gave him the agonizing news:

'What can I say, son of warlike Peleus? You are about to hear
20   dreadful news. If only it weren't true. Patroclus lies dead. They
are fighting over his body. It's been stripped. Hector of the
flashing helmet has your armour.'

Achilles collapses at the news

So he spoke, and a black cloud of grief engulfed
Achilles. He picked up the sooty dust in both his
hands and poured it over his head. He begrimed his
handsome features with it, and black ashes settled
on his sweet-smelling tunic. Great Achilles lay spread out in the
dust, a giant of a man, clawing at his hair with his hands and
mangling it. The female slaves he and Patroclus had captured
30   shrieked aloud and in their grief ran out of doors to surround
warlike Achilles. They beat their breasts with their hands and
sank to the ground. On the other side Antilochus, shedding tears
of misery, gripped Achilles' hands. Achilles was sobbing out his
noble heart, and Antilochus was afraid he might take a knife
and cut his throat.

Achilles let out an intimidating cry, and his lady mother heard
him where she sat in the depths of the sea beside her ancient
father. Then she herself took up the cry of grief, and there
gathered round her every goddess, every Nereid that was in the
deep salt sea. Glauce was there and Thaleia and Cymodoce;
40   Nesaea, Speio, Thoe and ox-eyed Halie; Cymothoe, Actaee and
Limnoreia; Melite, Iaera, Amphithoe and Agaue; Doto, Proto
too, Pherusa and Dynamene; Dexamene, Amphinome and
Callianeira; Doris and Panope and famous, far-sung Galatea;

Nemertes and Apseudes and Callianassa; Clymene came too,
with Ianeira, Ianassa, Maera, Oreithuia, lovely-haired Ama-
theia, and other Nereids of the salt-sea depths. The silvery cave   50
was full of Nymphs. With one accord they beat their breasts,
and Thetis led them in their lamentations:

'Listen to me, my sister Nereids, and know the   THETIS brings
sorrows of my heart. How wretched I am, unhappy   her Nereids to
mother of the best of men! I brought into the world   mourn
a matchless son, a mighty man, greatest of warriors.
I nursed him as one tends a little plant in a garden bed and he
shot up like a sapling. I sent him to Ilium in his ships to fight
against the Trojans; and never again now shall I welcome him   60
home to Peleus' house. And yet he has to suffer, every day he
lives and sees the sun; and I can do no good by going to his side.
But I *will* go, none the less, to see my dear child and hear what
anguish has come to him in his absence from the fighting.'

With these words she left the cave. The rest went with her,
weeping, and on either side of them the surging sea fell back.
When they reached fertile Troy, they came up one by one on to
the beach where the Myrmidon ships had been drawn up on the
shore round swift Achilles. His lady mother went up to him as   70
he lay groaning there and with a piercing cry took her son's
head in her hands and lamenting spoke winged words:

'My child, why these tears? Why this sorrow? Tell me, don't
keep it to yourself. What you prayed for when you lifted up
your hands to Zeus has been fulfilled by him: the Greeks have
been penned in at the ships because of your absence and suffered
the ugly consequences.'

Swift-footed Achilles sighed heavily and said:

'Mother, the Olympian has indeed done what I asked. But
what satisfaction can I get from that, now that my dearest   80
companion is dead, Patroclus, who was more to me than any
other of my men, whom I loved as much as my own life? I have
destroyed Patroclus. And Hector who killed him has stripped
him of my armour, my awe-inspiring, wonderful, magnificent
armour that the gods gave as a splendid gift to Peleus on the
day they brought you to the bed of a mortal man in marriage.
How I wish you had stayed there with the deathless salt-sea

Nymphs, and Peleus had taken home a mortal wife! But as it
is, you became my mother; and now, to multiply *your* sor-
rows too, you are going to lose your son and never welcome
him home again. For I have no wish to live and linger in the
world of men, unless, before all else, Hector is hit by my spear
and dies, paying the price for slaughtering Patroclus son of
Menoetius.'

Thetis said in tears:

'If that is so, my child, you do not have long to live; you are
doomed to die immediately after Hector –'

Deeply disturbed, swift-footed Achilles replied:

'Then let me die immediately, since I let my com-
panion be killed when I could have saved him. He
has fallen, far from the land of his fathers, needing
my help to defend him from death. But now, since I shall never
see the land of my fathers again, since I have proved no defence
for Patroclus or for all my many other comrades whom godlike
Hector killed, but have sat here by my ships, an idle burden on
the earth, a man who fights like no other in all the Greek army,
though others are better in debate ... ah, how I wish rivalry
could be banished from the world of gods and men, and with it
anger, which makes the wisest man flare up and spreads much
sweeter than dripping honey through his whole being, like
smoke – anger such as lord Agamemnon has now provoked
in me!

'But however much it still rankles, it is now over and done
with: let it go. We must master our pride. We have no choice.
So now I will go and seek out Hector, the destroyer of that dear
life. As for my death, when Zeus and the other immortal gods
appoint it, I will welcome it. Even mighty Heracles could not
escape his doom, dear as he was to lord Zeus son of Cronus,
but was laid low by destiny and Hera's bitter anger. So I too
shall lie low in death, if the same destiny awaits me.

'But now, may I win heroic glory! I will make these Trojan
women and full-girdled daughters of Dardanus wipe the tears
from their tender cheeks with both their hands as they raise
the funeral dirge, to teach them that I have been away from

*Achilles
accepts death*

battle too long. And you, Mother, as you love me, don't keep
me from battle. You will never persuade me now.'

The goddess silver-footed Thetis replied:

'Indeed, my child, it would be no bad thing for you to save
your exhausted comrades from the death that stares them in the
face. But your fine, sparkling bronze armour is in Trojan hands.   130
Hector of the flashing helmet is swaggering about in
it himself – not, I think, that he will glory in it long,   THETIS
for he is very near death. So don't throw yourself   promises fresh
into the grind of battle till you see me here again. I   armour
shall come back at sunrise tomorrow with a fine set of armour
from lord Hephaestus.'

With these words she turned away from her son and spoke to
her sister Nereids:

'Plunge now into the broad bosom of the deep and make your   140
way to the Old Man of the Sea and our father's house. Tell
him everything. I myself am going to high Olympus to ask the
famous blacksmith Hephaestus whether he would like to give
my son an impressive set of shining armour.'

So she spoke, and the Nymphs now disappeared from view
into the waves of the sea, and the goddess silver-footed Thetis
set out for Olympus to fetch an impressive set of armour for her
dear son.

While she was on her way to Olympus, the Greek
men-at-arms, escaping with cries of terror from man-   *Hector* almost
slaying Hector, streamed back to the ships and the   takes Patroclus'
Hellespont. It was almost more than they could do   body
to drag the body of Achilles' attendant Patroclus out of range   150
of the missiles. The Trojan infantry and chariots and Hector,
like fire in his courage, caught up with it again. Three times
glorious Hector, coming up behind and shouting for his men's
support, seized it by the feet and tried to drag it back; three
times the two Ajaxes, clothed in martial valour, flung him back
from the body.

But Hector's resolution was unshaken. When he was not
hurling himself into the mêlée, he stood his ground, shouting   160
his great battle-cry, and he never once fell back. As shepherds

in the fields are unable to chase a famished tawny lion off its
kill, so the bronze-armoured Ajaxes could not chase Priam's
son Hector away from the body. In fact Hector would have
hauled it away and won unutterable glory, if swift Iris, quick as
the wind, had not come running down from Olympus to tell
Achilles to prepare for battle. Hera sent her without telling Zeus
and the other gods. Coming up to Achilles she spoke winged
words:

170   'Up, son of Peleus, most impetuous of men – rise and defend
Patroclus! They're fighting tooth and nail for him, and men are
killing men beside the ships, the Greeks in their efforts to
protect his body, the Trojans in the hope of haul-
ing it away to windswept Ilium. Glorious Hector
above all is determined to drag off Patroclus. He
wants to cut his head from his soft neck and stick it on the
palisade. So get up! Stop lying there! You should feel ashamed
that Patroclus might become the plaything of the dogs of Ilium.

180 It's you who'll be disgraced if he goes mutilated to the dead
below.'

IRIS rouses
Achilles

Swift-footed godlike Achilles replied:
'Divine Iris, which of the gods sent you to me with this
message?'
Swift Iris, quick as the wind, replied:
'It was Hera, honourable wife of Zeus, that sent me. The son
of Cronus who sits on high was not told, nor was any other of
the gods that live on snowy Olympus.'
Swift-footed Achilles replied and said:
'But how can I go into action? They've got my armour, and
my own mother has forbidden me to prepare for battle till I

190 see her back here. She promised to bring me fine arms from
Hephaestus. I don't know of anyone else whose armour I could
wear, except maybe the shield of Ajax son of Telamon. But he,
I expect, will be in his place in the front line, causing havoc with
his spear for the dead Patroclus.'
Swift Iris, quick as the wind, replied:
'We gods are well aware your famous armour has been taken.
But go to the ditch anyway, as you are, and show yourself to
the Trojans. They may be unnerved by you and break off the

battle. That would give your weary troops some breathing space   200
– there is little enough respite in war.'

With these words swift-footed Iris took her leave, and Achilles dear to Zeus rose up. Athene threw her fringed aegis round his mighty shoulders and the celestial goddess also crowned him with a golden cloud around his head, and from it a blaze of light shone out. Just as smoke goes up to the skies from a town on some far-away beleaguered island which enemy troops are besieging: all day long the men fight a desperate battle from their town walls, but   210 at sunset beacon-fires blaze up one after the other, and the light shoots up into the sky for neighbours to see and come to the rescue in their ships – so the gleam from Achilles' head reached the skies.

[Night 26]
Patroclus' body
is rescued

He went beyond the wall and took his stand by the ditch; but, remembering his mother's careful instructions, did not join the Greeks in battle. There he stood and gave a shout, while in the distance Pallas Athene raised the war-cry too. This threw the Trojans into unutterable chaos. Like the piercing sound that rings out from a trumpet when a town is surrounded by murder-   220 ous enemies, such was Achilles' piercing cry. The Trojans heard his bronze voice, and panic threatened. Even the lovely-maned horses sensed death in the air and began to pull their chariots round. Their charioteers were dumbfounded as they saw the inexhaustible fire, fed by the goddess grey-eyed Athene, blaze fearfully from the head of great-hearted Achilles son of Peleus. Three times godlike Achilles sent his voice ringing out over the ditch, three times the Trojans and their famous allies were thrown into chaos. Twelve of their best men perished then and   230 there, entangled among their own chariots and spears.

Meanwhile, with thankful hearts the Greeks pulled Patroc-lus out of range. They laid him on a bier and his dear com-panions gathered round him, weeping. Swift-footed Achilles accompanied them, and the hot tears poured down his cheeks when he saw his faithful companion lying on the bier pierced by the sharp bronze spear. He had sent him into battle with his chariot and horses, never to welcome him home on his return.

240   Ox-eyed lady Hera now told the tireless sun to return, unwill-
ingly, into the Stream of Ocean. The sun set, and the godlike
Greeks enjoyed a respite from the fierce struggle and war, the
great leveller.

The Trojans on their side withdrew from the heat of battle,
unyoked the swift horses from their chariots and, before think-
ing of food, gathered together to assess the situation. Nobody
dared sit down, and they held the meeting on their feet, since all
of them had been appalled by Achilles' reappearance after his
long absence from war and its agonies. The discussion was
250   begun by wise Polydamas, the only man among them who
looked into the future as into the past. He was a comrade of
Hector's – they were born on the same night – but he was the
champion in debate, Hector in battle. He had their interests at
heart as he rose and addressed them:

'Consider both sides of the question very carefully,
Polydamas
my friends. It is my opinion that, at this distance from
advises retreat
the walls, we ought to withdraw into the town now
(8.553)
and not wait for daylight here in the open by the
ships. So long as Achilles was at loggerheads with lord Agamem-
non, the Greeks were easier to deal with, and I too enjoyed the
260   night we spent beside the ships and the hopes we entertained of
capturing their rolling ships. But now I am terrified of swift-
footed Achilles. He is a proud man. He will never be content to
stay in the plain, where we and the Greeks meet each other on
equal terms, but will make our very town and womenfolk his
target.

'Believe me, we must now retreat to Ilium. Otherwise, I know
what will happen. For the moment, the blessed night has checked
Achilles. But if tomorrow he charges out in full armour and
catches us here, well, you won't find him hard to recognize. The
270   man who gets away from him and reaches sacred Ilium will
thank his stars. It's Trojan flesh the dogs and vultures will be
feasting on.

'I pray my words are not an omen! But if, despite your
misgivings, you follow my advice, we will keep our army
together in the market-place tonight, while the town will be
safely protected by its walls, high gateways and great wooden

doors fitted to them, firmly closed. At daybreak, fully armed, we will take our position along the battlements; and if Achilles wants to leave the ships and take us on round the walls, so much the worse for him. When he has exhausted his high-necked horses trotting them up and down below the walls, he will have   280 to drive them back to the ships again. However great his anger, it will not allow him to force his way inside. He will never sack the town. The swift dogs will have him first.'

Hector of the flashing helmet gave him a black look and said:

'Polydamas, the man who tells us to retreat and shut ourselves up in the town no longer talks my language. Aren't you sick of being cooped up inside those walls? There was a time when the wealth of Priam's town, its gold and bronze, was the talk of all the world. But that has passed. Our houses have been emptied   290 of their treasure; most of it has been bartered away to Phrygia and lovely Maeonia, since great Zeus came to hate us. Now, at the very moment when the son of sickle-wielding Cronus has allowed me to win glory by the ships and drive the Greeks back against the sea, don't put such notions in the people's heads, you ignorant fool. Not that a single Trojan will follow your lead anyway. I'll see to that.

Hector disagrees; prepares to fight

'So I suggest we all do what I now propose. Let the whole army eat in its several contingents, not forgetting to mount guard and the need for every man to keep alert. As for any   300 Trojan who is over-anxious about his possessions, he should collect them and give them to the people to grow fat on – better for the people to enjoy them than the Greeks! At daybreak, fully armed, we will unleash the dogs of war by their hollow ships. If godlike Achilles really has returned to battle by the ships, so much the worse for him, if that's what he wants. I'm not going to shirk a fight and run away from him. I shall meet him face to face and we shall see who wins the victory. The War-god has no favourites and kills the would-be killer.'

So Hector addressed them, and the Trojans shouted their   310 approval, the fools. Pallas Athene had destroyed their judgement. Polydamas, whose strategy was sound, received no

support at all, but they applauded Hector and his bad advice.
And now the whole army settled down to eat.

All night long the Greeks lamented and mourned for
Patroclus. Achilles son of Peleus was their leader in the loud
dirge. He laid his man-slaying hands on his companion's chest
and groaned again and again, like a bearded lion when a hunts-
320 man has stolen its cubs from a thicket: it comes back too late,
grieves for its loss and follows the man's trail through glade after
glade, hoping to track him down, and bitter anger overwhelms
it – so, groaning heavily, Achilles spoke to his Myrmidons:

'What a fool I was! They were idle words I let fall
that day when I was reassuring Patroclus' warrior
father Menoetius in Peleus' palace. I said I would
bring back his famous son to him at Opous after the
sack of Ilium, laden with his share of plunder. But
Zeus makes havoc of the schemes of men; and now both of us
are destined to redden with our blood one patch of earth here
330 in the land of Troy. I shall never be welcomed again on my
return home by Peleus the old charioteer and my mother Thetis,
but the earth I stand on will cover me.

*Achilles
laments over
Patroclus'
body*

'So then, Patroclus, since I too am going below, but after you,
I shall not hold your funeral till I have brought back here the
armour and the head of Hector, who slaughtered you in your
greatness. And at your pyre I am going to cut the throats of a
dozen splendid sons of Troy, to vent my anger at your death.

'Till then, you shall lie as you are by my beaked ships,
340 lamented and mourned for day and night by the Trojan women
and full-girdled daughters of Dardanus whom we worked hard
to capture, with our own hands and our long spears, when we
sacked the fertile towns of men.'

With these words godlike Achilles told his companions to
stand a great three-legged cauldron over the fire and wash the
congealed blood from Patroclus' body as soon as possible. They
set a large cauldron over the glowing fire, filled it with water
and brought wood for kindling underneath it. The flames began
to lick the belly of the cauldron, and the water grew warm.
When it came to the boil in the gleaming bronze, they washed
350 the body, anointed it with olive oil and filled the wounds with

an ointment nine years old. Then they laid it on a bier and covered it from head to foot with a fine linen cloth, over which they spread a white cloak. And for the rest of the night the Myrmidons gathered round swift-footed Achilles to lament and mourn for Patroclus.

Zeus spoke to his wife and sister Hera:

'So you have had your way once more, ox-eyed lady Hera, and roused swift-footed Achilles. Anyone might think the long-haired Greeks were children of your own.'

HERA
rejoices at
success (4.34)

Ox-eyed lady Hera replied:

360

'Dread son of Cronus, what are you suggesting now? Surely even a human, a mere mortal not equipped with such wisdom as ours, is likely to get what he wants on someone else's behalf. How then could I, who claim to be the greatest of goddesses both by right of birth and also because I am your acknowledged wife and you are lord of all the gods – how could I in my rage at the Trojans possibly refrain from making trouble for them?'

While they were talking together in this way, silver-footed Thetis made her way to the starry palace of Hephaestus, which the little club-foot god had built, with his own hands, of imperishable bronze; it shone out among the houses of the gods. She found Hephaestus hard at work and sweating as he bustled about at the bellows in his forge. He was making a set of twenty tripods to stand round the walls of his well-built hall. He had fitted golden wheels to all their feet so that they could run off to a meeting of the gods and return home again, all self-propelled – an amazing sight. They were not quite finished: he still had to put on the ornamental handles and was fitting these and forging the rivets.

THETIS
visits HEPH-
AESTUS

370

Hephaestus was engaged on this task, which called for all his skill, when the goddess silver-footed Thetis arrived. Charis, the famous lame god's wife, beautiful in her shimmering head-dress, came out of the house and saw her. Putting her hand in Thetis', she said:

380

'Long-robed Thetis, what brings you to our house? You are an honoured and welcome guest, though previously you have not been in the habit of visiting us. But come with me indoors and let me offer you hospitality.'

With these words the celestial goddess led her in and seated
390 her on a beautiful, decorated silver chair with a footstool underneath. Then she called to Hephaestus the famous blacksmith and said:

'Hephaestus! Come here! Thetis wants to ask a favour of you.'

The famous lame god replied:

'Thetis here? The very goddess whom I revere and honour for saving me in my hour of distress when my mother, the bitch, wanted to get rid of me because I was a cripple and threw me out of the skies into the sea! How I would have suffered then, if the sea-goddesses, Thetis and Eurynome daughter of Ocean with its circling stream, hadn't taken me to their hearts. I stayed
400 nine years with them making metal jewellery – brooches, earrings, rosettes and necklaces – there in their vaulted cave, lapped by the never-ending Stream of Ocean seething with foam. No one on earth or in Olympus knew the secret but Eurynome and Thetis who had rescued me. And here is Thetis in our house, lovely-haired Thetis! I must certainly repay her for saving me. Entertain her hospitably, till I have put away my bellows and all my tools.'

410 Hephaestus spoke and raised his monstrous, panting bulk
from the anvil. He limped, but he was nimble enough
. HEPH-   on his stunted legs. He turned the bellows away from
AESTUS   the fire, collected all the tools he used and put them
leaves his   in a silver chest. Then he sponged both sides of his
forge   face, his hands, his solid neck and hairy chest, put
on his tunic, picked up a thick staff and came limping from the forge.

Waiting-women hurried along to help their master. They were made of gold, but looked like real girls and could not only speak
420 and use their limbs but were also endowed with intelligence and had learned their skills from the immortal gods. While they scurried round to support their lord, Hephaestus moved unsteadily to where Thetis was seated, himself sat down on a polished chair and putting his hand in hers said:

'Long-robed Thetis, what brings you to our house? You are an honoured and a welcome guest, though previously you have not been in the habit of visiting us. Tell me what is in your mind, and I shall gladly do what you ask of me, if I can and if the task is not impossible.'

Bursting into tears, Thetis replied:

'Hephaestus, of all the goddesses on Olympus, is there a single one who has had such anguish and misery to endure as I have, beyond all others, at the hands of Zeus? I, to begin with, was the Sea-nymph whom he picked out from all the rest to force into marrying a human, Peleus son of Aeacus; and much against my will I had to endure the bed of a mortal, who lies at home now, crushed by miserable old age. But Zeus had more to follow. He gave me a son to bear and bring up, greatest of warriors. I nursed him as one tends a little plant in a garden bed and he shot up like a sapling. I sent him to Ilium in his ships to fight against the Trojans; and never again now shall I welcome him home to Peleus' house. And yet he has to suffer, every day he lives and sees the sun; and I can do no good by going to his side.

'Now lord Agamemnon has taken from his arms the girl the Greek army gave him as a prize. He has been eating his heart out in grief at her absence. In consequence the Trojans have been able to pin the Greeks back among their ships, from which they will not let them move. Greek ambassadors were sent to supplicate Achilles and listed many prestigious gifts. But he refused them: he was not going to save them from disaster himself. However, he lent his armour to Patroclus and sent him out into battle with a strong force behind him. They fought all day by the Scaean gate and would have sacked Ilium that very day, if Apollo had not given Hector the glory by killing brave Patroclus in the front line, after he had made havoc of the Trojan ranks.

'So I have come to throw myself at your knees and ask you to give my son, who is so soon to die, a shield and helmet, a pair of fine leg-guards for his shins fitted with ankle-clasps, and body-armour. His former set of armour was lost when his loyal companion was overwhelmed

Achilles' new armour

430

440

450

460

by the Trojans; and Achilles is lying on the ground, pouring his heart out over him.'

The famous lame god replied:

'Take heart. Don't worry about any of this. I only wish it were as easy for me to save him from the pains of death when dread destiny confronts him, as to provide him with a magnificent set of armour, which will be the wonder of everyone who sees it.'

With these words Hephaestus left her there and went back to his forge, where he turned the bellows on the fire and told them 470 to get to work. The bellows – there were twenty of them – blew through the nozzles and gave healthy blasts from different directions, fast or slow to suit the needs of the busy blacksmith, depending on the stage the work had reached. He then placed in the crucibles over the fire imperishable bronze and some tin and precious gold and silver. Then he put a great anvil on its stand and gripped a powerful hammer in one hand and a pair of tongs in the other.

He began by making a large and heavy shield,
The shield: which he decorated all over and round which he
constellations   placed a bright triple rim of gleaming metal and fitted
480 with a silver shoulder-strap. The shield consisted of five layers, and he made all sorts of decorations for it, executed with consummate skill.

He made earth, sky and sea, the tireless sun, the full moon and all the constellations with which the skies are crowned, the Pleiades, the Hyades, great Orion and the Bear, also called the waggon. This is the only constellation never to bathe in Ocean Stream, but always wheels round in the same place and looks across at Orion the Hunter with a wary eye.

490 Next he made two beautiful towns full of people. In one of them weddings and feasts were in progress. They
Marriage   were bringing the brides through the streets from their homes, accompanied by blazing torches, and the wedding-hymn could be heard loud and clear. Young men danced, whirling round to the sound of pipes and lyres, and women stood by the doors of their houses to admire the sight.

But the men had gathered in the meeting-place, where a

dispute had arisen between two men who were in
conflict about the compensation for a man who had   Court case
been killed. One side claimed the right to solve the problem by
meeting the demand, and was showing the people the full extent   500
of his offer; but the other refused all compensation. Both parties
insisted that the issue should be settled by an expert; and both
sides were cheered by their supporters in the crowd, whom the
heralds were attempting to control. The expert elders sat on
smooth stone seats in a sacred circle; they received in their hands
the speaker's staff from the clear-voiced heralds; and the two
sides rushed over to them as they each gave judgment in turn.
Two talents of gold – one from each side – were displayed in
the centre: they were the fee for the elder who delivered the
soundest judgment.

The other town was under siege from two armies, which were
shown in their glittering armour. The besiegers were unable to   510
agree whether to sack the place outright, or to take half the
goods that the lovely town contained in return for surrender.
But the townspeople had not yet given up: they were secretly
preparing an ambush. Leaving the walls defended
by their wives and little children, together with the   Siege and
older men, they advanced under the leadership of   ambush
Ares and Pallas Athene. These were gold, wore golden clothes
and looked as big and beautiful in their armour as gods should,
standing out above their troops who were on a smaller scale.
When the townsmen had found a likely place for an ambush in   520
a river-bed where all the cattle came to drink, they sat down
there in their shining bronze armour and posted two scouts in
the distance to watch for the arrival of the sheep and cattle with
their crooked horns belonging to the besieging army. These
soon appeared in the charge of two herdsmen, who were playing
on their pipes and suspected no trap.

The men who had laid the ambush saw them, charged out
and promptly rounded up the herds of oxen and the fine flocks
of white sheep, killing the shepherds. But when the besiegers,   530
who were sitting in debate, heard the commotion raised by this
attack on their herds, they immediately mounted the chariots
behind their high-stepping horses and made for the scene of

action, which they quickly reached. A pitched battle ensued
on the banks of the river, and volleys of bronze spears were
exchanged. Strife and Panic were co-operating, and there was
the dreadful Demon of Death, laying her hands on a freshly
wounded man who was still alive and on another not yet
wounded, and dragging a body by its foot through the crowd.
The cloak on her shoulders was red with human blood; and the
540   warriors met and fought and dragged away each other's dead,
just as real warriors do.

Next he placed on it a large field of soft, rich fallow,
Ploughing   ploughed three times. A number of ploughmen were
driving their teams of oxen across it, up and down. When they
reached the ridge at the end of the field and had to turn, a man
would come up and hand them a cup of delicious wine. Then
they turned back down the furrows, keen to reach the other end
through the deep fallow soil. The field, though it was made of
gold, grew black behind them, as a field does when it is being
ploughed. It was a miraculous piece of work.

550   He also placed on it a lord's estate where hired reapers were
at work with sharp sickles in their hands. Handfuls
Reaping   of corn were falling to the ground one after the other
along the lines cut by the reapers, while others were being tied
up with bindings by the sheaf-binders following behind. There
were three sheaf-binders at work, and boys were at hand,
promptly picking up the sheaves and carrying them off in their
arms to be stored. And there among them was the lord himself,
staff in hand, standing quietly by the point the reapers had
reached, delighted. Under an oak-tree some way from the reap-
ing, his attendants were preparing a feast. They were busy with
a great ox they had slaughtered, and the women were sprinkling
560   the meat with handfuls of white barley for the labourers' supper.

Next he placed on it a vineyard laden with grapes.
Grape harvest   It was beautiful and made of gold, but the bunches
of grapes were black, and the supporting poles showed up
throughout in silver. All round it, Hephaestus ran a ditch of
blue inlay and, outside that, a fence of tin. There was a single
pathway by which the pickers approached the vineyard to gather
the vintage; and young girls and light-hearted boys were carrying

off the delicious fruit in baskets. In the middle of them a boy
was playing delightfully on a tuneful lyre and singing the song   570
of Linus, quite beautifully, in a high voice. They all kept time
with him and followed, singing and shouting, with dancing feet.

He created a herd of straight-horned cattle,   Cattle-herding
making the animals of gold and tin. They were moo-
ing as they hurried from the byre to feed where the rushes
swayed beside a murmuring stream. Four golden herdsmen
marched with the cattle, and there were nine swift dogs accom-
panying them. But at the head of the herd a pair of fearsome
lions had seized a bellowing bull that roared aloud as it was   580
being dragged off. The young men and dogs were running up to
the rescue. But the lions had torn open the great bull's hide and
were lapping up its dark blood and entrails. It was in vain that
the shepherds were setting their swift dogs on them and urging
them forward: when it came to sinking their teeth into the lions,
the dogs were having none of it. They stood there at close range,
barking, but were careful to avoid them.

The famous lame god created a big grazing ground
for white-fleeced sheep, in a beautiful valley, with   Sheep-flocks
farm buildings, pens and well-roofed huts.

Next the famous lame god cleverly depicted a dancing-floor,   590
like the one Daedalus designed in the spacious town
of Cnossus for lovely-haired Ariadne. Youths and   Dancing
marriageable maidens were dancing there holding each other
by the wrists, the girls in fine linen shawls, the men in closely
woven tunics showing a faint gleam of oil, the girls with lovely
garlands on their heads, the men with daggers of gold hanging
from their silver belts. Here they circled lightly round on accom-   600
plished feet, like the wheel which fits neatly in a potter's hands
when he sits down and tests it to see if it will spin; and here they
ran in lines to meet each other. A large crowd stood round
enjoying the delightful dance. A godlike singer of tales sang with
them to the lyre, while a couple of solo dancers led off and spun
round among the people.

Then, round the very rim of the superbly con-
structed shield, he placed the mighty Stream of   Ocean
Ocean.

610   When he had finished the great, heavy shield, he made
Achilles' body-armour brighter than blazing fire. Then he made
a massive helmet to fit on his temples. It was beautifully decor-
ated, and he put a gold crest on top. He also made him leg-guards
of soft tin for his shins.

    When the famous lame god had finished every piece, he gath-
ered them up and laid them before Achilles' mother. She took
the glittering armour from Hephaestus in her arms and swooped
down like a falcon from snow-clad Olympus.

19

THE FEUD ENDS

1–144: [27th day: fourth day of combat] THETIS delivers Achilles' new armour. Achilles summons an assembly, expresses his regret for the past, his willingness to renounce his anger and his desire to return to battle. Agamemnon blames DELUSION for his actions, describes how even ZEUS was deluded by HERA and agrees to hand over the compensation.

145–237: Achilles wants to return to battle at once, but Odysseus says the men must be fed.

238–356: Agamemnon's gifts are fetched. *Briseis* laments for Patroclus. At ZEUS' suggestion, ATHENE secretly feeds Achilles with ambrosia and nectar.

357–424: The Greeks come out for battle – bronze armour flashes, the earth resounds – and Achilles arms himself, taking his father's spear. The horse Xanthus prophesies Achilles' death.

As saffron-robed Dawn rose from the river of Ocean to bring daylight to the immortals and to men, Thetis reached the Greek ships with the god's gifts in her hands. She found her son Achilles prostrate, with his arms round Patroclus. He was weeping bitterly and many of his men stood round him lamenting. The celestial goddess went up to them and, putting her hand in her son's, said:

'My child, the man who lies here was struck down by the will of the gods. For all your grief, let him be now and take this impressive armour I have brought you from Hephaestus. It is utterly magnificent. No mortal has ever worn anything like it.'

With these words the goddess laid the intricately worked armour before Achilles. It rang out loud, and all the Myrmidons shook with fear. They could not endure to look at it and backed away. But the more Achilles looked, the deeper his anger against Hector grew, and from beneath their lids his eyes shone fearfully like flames. He picked up the god's splendid gifts and handled them with delight. When he had taken in all their intricate work, he spoke to his mother with winged words:

[Day 27, fourth combat day]
THETIS protects Patroclus

'Mother, this armour of the god's – this is indeed the workmanship we might expect from the immortals. No human could have made it. So now I will arm for battle. But I am terribly afraid that in the meantime flies will defile the body of brave Patroclus by settling on the open wounds and breeding worms in them. Life has gone out of him, and all his flesh may rot.'

The goddess silver-footed Thetis replied:

'My child, have no worries about any of this. I shall arrange to keep off those pests, the flies that devour the bodies of men killed in battle. Patroclus could lie here for a whole year, and still his flesh would be preserved – indeed, it might be better than now. But go and summon the Greek warriors to assembly, renounce your anger against Agamemnon shepherd of the people, and then immediately arm for battle and clothe yourself in valour.'

With these words she breathed supreme confidence into her son; and, to save Patroclus from decay, she treated his body with ambrosia and red nectar which she dripped through his nostrils.

Meanwhile godlike Achilles went along the beach shouting at the top of his voice to call out the Greek warriors. As a result, even the men who usually stayed with the ships (the helmsmen in charge of the steering-oars and the on-board stewards who dealt out provisions) came to the assembly, now that Achilles had reappeared after his long absence from war and its agonies. The two attendants of Ares, resolute Diomedes and godlike Odysseus, came limping in, still troubled by their wounds and

Wounded leaders' assembly (11.251, 373, 434)

leaning on their spears. They came and sat down in the front of   50
the assembly, and last of all came Agamemnon lord of men. He
too was suffering, from the wound that Coön son of Antenor
had given him with his bronze-headed spear in the thick of the
action.

When all the Greeks were gathered together, swift-footed
Achilles stood up and spoke to them:

'Agamemnon son of Atreus, has it proved a good thing, either
for you or me, to keep up this soul-destroying rivalry about a
girl, which has brought us such anguish? I only wish Artemis
had killed her with an arrow on board ship, that day I won her   60
when I sacked Lyrnessus. Fewer Greeks would then have bitten
the dust of the broad earth, slaughtered by the enemy, while I
sat apart in my implacable fury. It was only Hector and the
Trojans who profited by our quarrel. The Greeks, I think, will
have cause to remember it for many a long day. But however
much it still rankles, it is now over and done with: let it go. We
must master our pride. We have no choice.

'So I now renounce my anger. There is no need for me to
nurse it any longer. But come, summon the long-haired Greeks   70
to battle immediately, so that, if the Trojans insist on camping
out by our ships, I can pit myself against them once
more. I reckon that any Trojan who dodges my spear   Achilles
and comes out of this battle alive will be only too   renounces his
glad to rest his weary limbs.'   anger (9.646,
                                                                              1.488)
So he spoke, and the Greek men-at-arms shouted
for joy when they heard the great-hearted son of Peleus dis-
claim his anger. Agamemnon lord of men then addressed
them from his seat, rather than rising and speaking from the
centre:

'Friends, Greek warriors, attendants of Ares, when a man
stands to speak, as Achilles has just done, it is only courteous to
give him a hearing and not interrupt, which even the experienced   80
orator finds hard to cope with. How can anyone talk or hear,
when everyone is making an uproar to drown out the shrillest
speaker? Now, I am going to clarify my position to Achilles in
particular, but all the rest of you pay attention and take in what
I say.

'The Greeks have often insulted me, making the
very point with which the last speech began. But I
was not to blame. It was Zeus and Destiny and
the Fury that walks in darkness that blinded my
judgement that day at the assembly when I took Achilles' prize
90 for myself. What could I do? At such moments a god takes
complete command – Delusion, eldest daughter of Zeus who
blinds us all, damn her. She never touches the ground with those
soft feet of hers but flits over men's heads, corrupting them and
shackling one man after another.

'Why, even Zeus was blinded by her once, and they say he
is the best of all men and gods. Hera and her feminine wiles
tricked him on the day when Alcmene was going to give birth
to mighty Heracles in Thebes with its crown of battlements.
100 Zeus boasted to all the gods: "Listen to me, all you gods and
goddesses, so that I can tell you what I feel compelled to say.
This day Eileithyia, goddess of labour, will bring into the light
a baby, born of a family with my blood in their veins, who will
have dominion over all his neighbours."

'The lady Hera set a trap for Zeus and said: "That's a lie – as
time will show, a prophecy that you will not fulfil. Come now,
Olympian, swear me a solemn oath that the child delivered by
110 the woman between her feet this day, who comes of a family
with your blood in its veins, shall indeed have dominion over
all his neighbours." So she spoke, and Zeus saw no trickery in
this and swore a great oath. In so doing, he was completely
deluded.

'Hera swooped down from the summit of Olympus and hur-
ried to Argos in Achaea, where, as she knew, the noble wife of
Sthenelus son of Perseus also had a baby on its way, but was
only seven months gone. Hera brought this child into the light
of day prematurely and postponed Alcmene's delivery by
restraining the goddesses of childbirth. Then she went to Zeus
120 and personally gave him the news: "Father Zeus, lord of the
vivid lightning, just to let you know a noble child *has* been born
today, who is to have dominion over the Greeks. They have
called him Eurystheus, and his father is Sthenelus, son of Perseus

ZEUS and
Delusion
(2.377, 9.119)

– of *your* family. So it is no disgrace for him to have dominion over the Greeks."

'So she spoke, and it was a bitter blow to Zeus and stung him very badly. In his rage, he seized Delusion by her glossy hair and, swearing a mighty oath that this goddess who blinds everyone should never set foot in Olympus and the starry sky again, he whirled her round his head and hurled her down from the starry   130 skies. Delusion quickly found herself in the world of men. But Zeus could not think of her without a groan when he saw Heracles, his own beloved son, labouring away at the humiliating tasks set him by Eurystheus.

'It was the same with me. When great Hector of the flashing helmet was once more slaughtering Greeks at the sterns of the ships, I could not forget Delusion who blinded me that day. But since I *was* blinded and Zeus robbed me of my wits, I am willing to make amends and grant immense compensation. So prepare yourself for battle and give a lead to the rest of the army. As   140 for the gifts, I am ready to produce all that godlike Odysseus promised when he went to you yesterday in your hut. Or if you like, restrain your desire for battle for a while, and my attendants will fetch your gifts from my ship, so that you will be able to see I am giving you the very best.'

Swift-footed Achilles replied and said:

'Most glorious son of Atreus, Agamemnon lord of men, it is up to you if you want to produce the gifts, as would be right, or keep them. But now, let us call up our old will to fight – immediately. There is serious work to be done. We ought not to stay here chatting away and wasting time. As each of you sees Achilles in the front line once again   150 destroying Trojan ranks with his bronze spear, so let him keep that image in his mind as he fights the enemy.'

Achilles wants to fight now

Quick-thinking Odysseus replied and said:

'You are a great warrior, godlike Achilles, but you must not order the men to march against Ilium and take on the enemy without having eaten something first. The battle will not soon be over, once the two forces are engaged and the god has breathed his fire into them.

Odysseus says the men need food

160 Tell the men rather to take some food and wine by the ships –
their courage and stamina depend on it. It's impossible for a
man to stand up to the enemy all day long till sunset without
food. His heart may be set on fighting, but exhaustion takes him
unawares, hunger and thirst set in and his legs give way under
him. But when a man has had his fill of wine and food before
170 an all-day battle, his spirit is up and his strength doesn't flag till
the fight is broken off.

'So, dismiss the troops and tell them to prepare a meal. As
for the gifts, let lord Agamemnon bring them into the middle
of the assembly so that everyone can see them for themselves,
and you can be satisfied. Further, let him stand up before the
whole army and swear on oath that he has never been in the
girl's bed and slept with her. In return, Achilles, you must show
a gracious and forgiving spirit. Then let Agamemnon make it
180 up to you with a rich feast in his hut, so that you will not feel
you have been sold short. Agamemnon, you will be more ready
in the future to give others their due. It is no disgrace for a ruler
to make up in full for trouble he has begun.'

Agamemnon lord of men said:

'Odysseus son of Laertes, I am delighted to have heard your
views. Nothing was missing: you dealt properly with every
point. I am not only ready but anxious to take the oath you
suggest and I will not swear falsely in the sight of the god. But
meanwhile let Achilles wait here, though he is eager for action,
190 and all the rest of you remain in your places too, till the gifts are
brought from my hut and we can make a pact on oath. You
yourself, Odysseus, are the man I entrust with this task. Pick
out some young men, the best you can find in the whole force,
go to my ship and fetch all the gifts we promised Achilles
yesterday, and bring the women too. And let Talthybius get a
boar ready for me at once to sacrifice to Zeus and the Sun in the
presence of this whole great army.'

Swift-footed Achilles replied and said:

200 'Most glorious son of Atreus, Agamemnon lord of men, you
ought to be taking these steps at some other time, when there is
a lull in the fighting and my blood is not up, as it is now. But

our men who fell to Hector when Zeus gave him the glory are still lying mangled out on the plain – and you and Odysseus are urging us to eat! I would make the men fight now, fasting and hungry, and then prepare a huge meal for them at sunset after we have avenged the insult done to us. Till that's done, no food or drink will pass my lips, with my companion lying dead in my hut, pierced by the sharp bronze spear, his feet lying towards the door and his comrades weeping round him. None of your proposals interests me – only slaughter and bloodshed and the groans of the dying.'

Achilles to fight; gifts brought

Quick-thinking Odysseus replied and said:

'Achilles, son of Peleus, greatest of the Greeks, you are a stronger man than I and not a little better with the spear, but in view of my greater age and experience, my judgement is much sounder than yours. That being so, prepare yourself for what I am about to say.

'Men have soon had enough of pitched battle: their weapons may scatter heaps of dead over the ground like straw, but after Zeus, controller of war on earth, has tipped the scales to decide who wins, the resulting reward for their risk is small. You wish the troops to express their grief at a man's death by fasting. That is impossible. Day after day, one after the other, men fall in their hundreds – would we ever find rest from struggle and suffering? No: we must steel our hearts, bury our dead and let one day's tears suffice.

'All those who have survived the carnage must now turn their thoughts to food and drink, so that we can carry on the struggle without let-up to the bitter end with our bronze armour – *that* never tires – on our backs. So let none of you hold back and wait for any second call to action. This *is* the summons. There will be trouble for anyone left behind at the ships. The whole army must advance together and unleash the dogs of war against those horse-taming Trojans.'

He spoke and chose to help him illustrious Nestor's sons, with Meges, Thoas, Meriones, Lycomedes and Melanippus, and they set out for Agamemnon's hut. Once there, no sooner said than done: they fetched out from his quarters the seven tripods he had promised Achilles, the twenty cauldrons of gleaming copper and the twelve horses; and immediately after, the seven women skilled in arts and crafts, fair-cheeked Briseis making the eighth. Then Odysseus who had weighed out ten talents of gold, led the way back, followed by the other young Greeks carrying the gifts.

250   They laid them down in the middle of the assembly, and Agamemnon rose to his feet. Beside him stood Talthybius, whose voice was like a god's, holding a boar in his arms. Agamemnon drew out the knife that hung by the great scabbard of his sword and made the first offering by cutting a little hair from the boar's head and lifting up his hands in prayer to Zeus, while the Greeks all sat quietly in their own places in the proper way, listening to their leader. He looked up into the broad skies and prayed:

260   'I call on Zeus, highest and best of the gods, and then on the Earth and Sun and the Furies who punish men for perjury in the world below, to be my witnesses that I never laid hands on the girl Briseis to bring her to my bed, or for any other purpose. She stayed in my hut unmolested. If a word of this is false, may the gods inflict on me all the sufferings that they impose on those who take their names in vain.'

Agamemnon and Achilles renounce the quarrel

He spoke and cut the boar's throat with the relentless bronze. Talthybius took the carcass and with a swing flung it out over the broad expanse of the grey sea for the fish to eat. Then Achilles rose to address the war-loving Greeks:

270   'Father Zeus, what tremendous delusions you inflict on men! Agamemnon would never have provoked me to such lasting bitterness nor stubbornly taken the girl against my will, if Zeus had not wanted a Greek massacre. But go now, take your meal, and then to battle!'

So he spoke, and quickly dismissed the assembly. They scattered to their several ships, and the Myrmidons took charge of the gifts and carried them off to godlike Achilles' ship 280 where they placed them in his hut and sat the women down. The horses were driven in among his own herd by his noble attendants.

But when Briseis, who looked like golden Aphro-
dite, saw Patroclus lying there, mangled by the sharp
bronze spear, she gave a piercing scream, threw her-
self on his body and tore with her hands at her
breast and tender neck and fair cheeks. Lovely as the
goddesses, she spoke in tears:

Briseis (1.346)
and Achilles
mourn
Patroclus

'Oh, Patroclus, my heart's delight! Oh, my misery! I left you
in this hut alive when I went away; and now I have come back,
commander of men, to find you dead. Such is my life, an endless   290
chain of disaster. I saw the husband to whom my father and my
lady mother gave me mangled in front of his town by the cruel
spear; and I saw my three brothers, my dear brothers, borne by
the same mother as myself, all meet their doom. But you, when
swift-footed Achilles killed my husband and sacked lord Mynes'
town, you would not even let me weep; you said you would
make me Achilles' lawful wife and take me in your ships to
your home in Phthia and give me a wedding-feast among the
Myrmidons. You were always so gentle with me. So in death I   300
mourn you inconsolably.'

So she spoke in tears, and the other women took up the cry,
each one recalling through Patroclus her own misfortunes. As
for Achilles, the Greek chieftains gathered round and entreated
him to take food. But he refused with a groan:

'If you have any regard for my wishes, I entreat you, don't
ask me to satisfy my thirst and hunger now. My grief is too
dreadful. I intend to hold out, at all costs, till sunset.'

With these words he dismissed the rest, but Agamemnon
and Menelaus stayed, and so did godlike Odysseus, Nestor,   310
Idomeneus and Phoenix the old charioteer. They tried to
comfort him in his anguish. But his heart would find no com-
fort till he hurled himself into the jaws of bloody battle.
Memories came crowding round, and with many a sigh he said:

'How often you yourself, my most unhappy and beloved
companion, have set a delicious meal before me in this hut, with
speed and skill, when the Greeks were set to bring war with all
its tears on the horse-taming Trojans. As it is, you lie mangled
here, and my heart rejects all thought of food. Not that I lack   320
it. I lack you.

'I could have suffered no crueller blow than this, not even the news of my father Peleus' death, who is no doubt shedding soft tears in Phthia at this moment for me, the dear son he has lost – while I am fighting Trojans in a foreign land for wretched Helen's sake; nor even if they told me my own son godlike Neoptolemus was dead, who is growing up in Scyros, if he is still alive anywhere. And yet I liked to think that I alone would perish here in Troy, far from Thessaly where the horses
330 graze, and that you, Patroclus, would get home to Phthia and be able to fetch my son from Scyros in a fast black ship and show him everything, my possessions and slaves and great high-roofed palace. Now surely Peleus, if he is not dead and gone by now, is only half-alive, crushed by the burden of old age and in daily expectation of the dreadful news that I myself am dead.'

So Achilles spoke in tears, and the leaders took up the cry, each of them remembering what he had left at home.

340   Zeus son of Cronus took pity on them when he saw their grief and immediately spoke to Athene with winged words:

ATHENE   'My child, you have deserted your favourite. Is
feeds Achilles   there then no longer any room in your heart for
              Achilles, who is sitting there in front of his high-beaked ships mourning for his dear companion and fasting, refusing to touch a thing, while all the rest have gone to eat? Go and distil some nectar and lovely ambrosia into his chest to save him from starvation.'

With these words he spurred on Athene, who had already set her heart on action. She swooped down from the skies through
350 the upper air like a shrieking, long-winged sea-bird. While the Greeks were arming themselves throughout the camp, she distilled nectar and lovely ambrosia into Achilles' chest to preserve him from the pangs of hunger. This done, she made her way back to her almighty Father's palace, as the troops poured out from among the swift ships. Like cold snowflakes teeming thickly down from the sky before the onset of a clear-born
360 northerly gale, so thickly did the shining helmets, bossed shields, plated armour and ash spears emerge from the ships. Brightness lit up the sky, the whole earth round about laughed at the glitter

of bronze, and the land resounded to the thunder of marching feet.

In the middle of all this, godlike Achilles armed for battle. He ground his teeth, his eyes blazed like flames of fire and unendurable grief consumed him *Achilles arms for battle* as he put on the divine gifts that Hephaestus had made for him, raging against the Trojans. First he placed fine leg-guards on his shins, fitted with silver ankle-clips. Then he put on his body-armour and slung his bronze, silver-riveted sword over his shoulder. Then he took up the great, heavy shield, whose brightness flashed into the distance like the moon's. Like the gleam that sailors catch at sea from a fire burning on a lonely upland farm, when the winds drive them unwillingly from home over the teeming seas, such was the gleam that went up into the sky from Achilles' ornamented shield. Next he picked up his massive helmet and placed it on his head. It sparkled like a star, and above it danced the golden plumes that Hephaestus had lavished on the crest. Godlike Achilles tried himself in the armour to see if it fitted and allowed his splendid limbs free movement. It was like a pair of wings to this shepherd of the people and lifted him up. Finally he took his father's spear from its case, long, thick and heavy. No Greek could wield this but Achilles, who alone knew how to handle it. It was made from an ash-tree on the top of Mount Pelion and had been a gift from Cheiron to Achilles' father, Peleus, to bring death to warriors.

Meanwhile Automedon and Alcimedon were busy seeing to the yoking of the horses. They fitted the yoke-straps round their chests, put the bits in their mouths and drew the reins back into the chariot. Then Automedon picked up a shining whip that fitted his grip and leapt in behind the pair. Achilles, armed for battle, followed him in, resplendent in his armour like the shining sun, and called to his father's horses in a terrible voice:

'Xanthus and Balius, Podarge's legendary foals, try this time to think more carefully about bringing your charioteer back to his friends alive when the fighting is done, instead of leaving him dead on the battlefield as you left Patroclus.'

From under the yoke flashing-footed Xanthus replied. He had lowered his head so his mane came tumbling down from the yoke-pad and swept the ground. The goddess white-armed Hera had endowed him with human speech:

Achilles' horse
predicts his death

'Indeed, imperious Achilles, we will once more bring you safely home today. But the day of your death is drawing near; and it is not we who will be the cause of it, but a great god and inexorable destiny. Nor was it by our laziness or lack of speed that the Trojans were enabled to strip the armour from Patroclus' shoulders. It was the best of gods, Apollo son of lovely-haired Leto, who killed him in the front line and let Hector have the glory. We could run with the speed of the west wind – and they say nothing is faster – but you are still destined to fall in battle at the hands of a god and of a man.'

As he spoke, the Furies struck him dumb. Angrily swift-footed Achilles replied:

420   'Xanthus, why prophesy my death? There is no need. I know well enough I am destined to perish here, far from my dear father and mother. But I am still not going to stop till I have given the Trojans their fill of battle.'

He spoke, raised the battle-cry among the leaders and drove his powerful horses forward.

ACHILLES ON
THE RAMPAGE

So beside the beaked ships the Greeks armed for battle led by
you, son of Peleus, always spoiling for a fight, and on the other
side the Trojans too lined up on the high ground of the plain.
At the same time, from the summit of rugged Olympus Zeus
ordered Themis to call the gods to assembly, and she went the
rounds and summoned them to his palace. Apart from Ocean,
not a single River stayed away, nor did any of the Nymphs that
haunt delightful woods, the sources of streams and the grassy
water-meadows. They all came to the cloud-gatherer's house   10
and sat down in the polished colonnade that Hephaestus with
his supreme skill had made for Father Zeus.

When they had all gathered in the palace, earthshaker Posei-
don (who had not ignored the goddess' call but came up out of
the sea to join them and sat down in their midst) inquired what
purpose Zeus had in mind:

'Lord of the vivid lightning, why have you ordered the gods to assemble? Are you concerned for the Trojans and Greeks? Battle between the two of them is very close to flaring up.'

Zeus who marshals the clouds replied and said:

20   'Earthshaker, you know what is in my mind and why I have summoned this gathering. Yes, they do concern me, dying as they are. Nevertheless I am going to stay here seated in some glen on Olympus from which I can enjoy the divine spectacle – since I now give the rest of you my permission to join the Trojans and Greeks and give your help to either side, as the inclination takes you. My reason is that, if Achilles fights the Trojans without intervention from you, the Trojans will not stand up to him for a moment. Even before this, they would take one look at him and run; but now he has been embittered by the loss of his
30 companion, I am afraid he will cheat destiny and storm the walls of Ilium.'

Gods allowed to support their favourites (8.10)

So spoke the son of Cronus and provoked unstoppable conflict. The immortals at once set out for the scene of action in two hostile groups. Hera and Pallas Athene made their way to the Greek ships. So did Poseidon who encircles the world and Hermes the runner, incomparably astute. Hephaestus accompanied them, exulting in his strength, for though he limped, his stunted legs were nimble enough. To the Trojan side went Ares of the flashing helmet, flowing-haired Apollo, Artemis who
40 delights in arrows, Leto, River Scamander and laughter-loving Aphrodite.

Up to the moment when the gods became involved, the Greeks carried all before them. Achilles had reappeared after his long absence from war and its agonies, and the limbs of all the Trojans shook in terror at the sight of swift-footed son of Peleus, resplendent in his arms, equal of the murderous War-god Ares. But when the Olympians joined the ranks of men, Strife who drives on armies rose in all her strength. While Athene raised her war-cry, standing now by the ditch beyond the Greek wall,
50 and now sending her voice down the thundering shore, she was answered on the other side by Ares, who resembled a black squall and screamed his orders to the Trojans, at one moment

from the heights of the citadel, and at the next from the banks
of River Simoïs, as he ran along the slopes of Callicolone.

So the blessed gods, encouraging the two forces,
threw them at each other's throats and at the same
time opened up the bitter rivalry in their own ranks.
Up on high the Father of men and gods thundered
ominously, and down below Poseidon caused the boundless
earth and lofty mountain-tops to shake. The foothills and peaks
of Mount Ida of the many springs were shaken; Ilium and the   60
Greek ships trembled; and in the underworld Hades, lord of the
dead, took fright and leapt with a cry from his throne. He was
afraid earthshaker Poseidon might split open the ground above
his head and expose to mortal and immortal eyes the horrible
decaying chambers that fill the gods themselves with loathing.

*Hades almost
splits open
with the noise*

Such was the cosmic crash of gods joining in conflict. Poseidon
was faced by Phoebus Apollo with his winged arrows, and the
goddess grey-eyed Athene by Ares; Hera was confronted by
Apollo's sister, Artemis of the golden distaff who delights in   70
arrows; Leto by the strong runner Hermes, and Hephaestus by
the mighty eddying River, who is called Xanthus by the gods
and Scamander by mankind. So they went to war, god against
god. As for Achilles, he wished for nothing better than to
meet Hector son of Priam in the turmoil: he wanted Ares the
shield-bearing warrior to gorge himself on his blood. But
Apollo who drives on armies immediately intervened to fill   80
Aeneas with determination and send him to confront Achilles
son of Peleus. Disguising himself and imitating the voice of
Lycaon, one of Priam's sons, Apollo son of Zeus said:

'Aeneas, adviser of the Trojans, what has be-
come of all your threats? Did you not tell the Trojan
leaders over the wine-cups that you would face
Achilles son of Peleus man to man?'

*APOLLO
launches
Aeneas at
Achilles*

Aeneas replied and said:

'Lycaon, why do you order me to pit myself against the proud
son of Peleus? I have no stomach for it, since this will not be the
first time I have been confronted by him. Once before, he turned   90
me to flight with his spear under Mount Ida, when he raided
our cattle and sacked Lyrnessus and Pedasus, where the Leleges

live. On that occasion I was saved by Zeus who gave me the determination and speed of foot, or I should have fallen to Achilles and Athene. She had gone ahead of him to protect him and told him to slaughter the Leleges and Trojans with his spear.

'So it is impossible for any mortal to fight Achilles. He always has a god with him to keep death at bay. Quite apart from that, his spear has a way of flying straight and true and never stopping till it lands in human flesh. However, if a god decides to keep things equal between us, Achilles will not have an easy victory, even though he does like to think he is made of bronze.'

Lord Apollo son of Zeus said:

'Warrior, come, invoke the deathless gods yourself! They say you are the son of Aphrodite daughter of Zeus, while Achilles is born of a lesser god. Aphrodite is a daughter of Zeus, but Thetis has only the Old Man of the Sea for her father. Straight at him, then, with the hard bronze! And don't let his threats and insults put you off.'

With these words Apollo breathed tremendous energy into this shepherd of the people, who advanced through the front ranks, his bronze armour glittering. But the goddess white-armed Hera was not taken unawares and, when she saw Aeneas son of Anchises advancing through the crowd of men to attack Achilles, she beckoned her friends to her side and said:

The gods agree not to intervene

'Poseidon and Athene, both of you now carefully consider what you should do next. Here comes Aeneas to attack Achilles, bronze armour glittering and backed by Phoebus Apollo. Come, let us send him straight back again. Or one of us could stand by Achilles and endow him with great strength. His courage must not be allowed to fail him. He must be made aware that the best of the immortals hold him dear and that those who, up till now, have saved the Trojans from defeat are of no account whatever. We all came down from Olympus to join in this battle so that Achilles should not suffer any harm at Trojan hands today, though later on he must endure what destiny spun for him with the first thread of life when his mother bore him. But if all this is not conveyed to him in a message from the immortals themselves, he will be terrified when he finds himself confronted by a god. The gods are difficult for any man to deal with, when they face him openly.'

Poseidon the earthshaker replied:

'Hera, don't be so unreasonably aggressive. There is no need. I, for one, am not anxious to set the gods at each other's throats. So let us move out of the way and sit down where we can watch from a convenient spot. War will be men's business. Of course, if Ares or Phoebus Apollo starts the fight or if they lay hands on Achilles to keep him out of the action, then we ourselves will immediately take them on in battle. But not for long, I think. Our enemies will soon have to break the battle off and go back to the other gods on Olympus, overwhelmed by our sheer strength.'

With these words the sable-haired god led the way to the high earthwork that the Trojans and Pallas Athene had made for godlike Heracles. Heracles had once vowed to get rid of a great sea-monster sent against the Trojans, and this was a place of refuge for him when it came up from the beach to attack him on dry land. There Poseidon and the other gods sat down and spread impenetrable mist round their shoulders. Their divine opponents also sat down on the brow of Callicolone on the other side, round you, Apollo, and Ares sacker of cities. Thus both parties settled down on opposite sides, plotting their next moves. Each of them hesitated to begin hostilities, though Zeus from his seat on high had told them to.

Meanwhile the plain was filled with human combatants and sparkled with the bronze of infantry and charioteers alike. The earth shook beneath their feet *Aeneas vs. Achilles* as the two forces charged towards each other. And now, in the intervening space, their two greatest champions, Aeneas son of Anchises and godlike Achilles, came together, determined to do battle. Aeneas was the first to step forward with a gesture of defiance. His massive helmet nodded on his head; he held his lively shield in front of him and brandished his bronze spear.

From the other side the son of Peleus sprang to meet him like a lion, a killer which a villageful of men have gathered together

in their determination to destroy. At first the lion goes its way and treats them with contempt, but when one of the bolder young men hits it with a spear, it snarls and crouches to spring; foam collects round its jaws, the brave spirit in its heart growls,
170 it lashes its ribs and flanks with its tail to work itself up into a fighting fury and, glaring fiercely, charges straight in, determined to kill a man or be killed itself in the forefront of the battle – so Achilles' proud spirit and determination drove him to confront great-hearted Aeneas.

When they had come within range of each other, swift-footed godlike Achilles spoke first:

'Aeneas, what has induced you to advance so far from the
180 ranks to meet me? Is it ambition that drives you to fight, hoping you will step into Priam's shoes and rule the horse-taming Trojans? But killing me will not make Priam abdicate for you. He has sons of his own; his health is sound; and he's not half-witted either.

Aeneas and Achilles exchange taunts

'Or perhaps the Trojans have sectioned off a piece of their best land with rich vineyards and cornfields for you to cultivate, if you succeed in killing me? Well, I think you will find it difficult. I seem to recollect that once before you ran from my spear. Or have you forgotten that time I caught you alone, cut you off from your cattle and sent you scuttling at speed down
190 the slopes of Mount Ida? You didn't even have time to look behind you! You then took refuge in Lyrnessus. But I followed up and sacked the place with the help of Athene and Father Zeus, carrying off into slavery the women I captured, though Zeus and the other gods protected you. But this time I don't think he is going to protect you, as you fondly imagine. So I do urge you to get back now, rejoin the ranks and not stand up to me, or you will suffer for it. Only a fool is wise after the event.'

Aeneas replied and said:
200 'Son of Peleus, don't imagine you're going to scare me with words, as though I were a little child. I too know perfectly well how to exchange insults and abuse. You and I know each other's ancestry and we know each other's parents, for though you have never set eyes on mine, nor I on yours, we have heard men celebrate them in song.

'They say you are a son of matchless Peleus and lovely-haired Thetis daughter of the Sea, while I can claim great-hearted Anchises as my father and Aphrodite as my mother. One or the other of these couples is going to mourn the loss of a beloved son today, since I am sure you and I will not settle our differences and leave the battlefield after a childish little chat. But if you really wish to learn who I am, I will tell you. Most people know my story already.

Aeneas' lineage

'Zeus who marshals the clouds began the line by fathering Dardanus. Dardanus founded Dardania at a time when the sacred town of Ilium had not yet been built as a town for men to inhabit, when the people there were still living under the foothills of well-watered Mount Ida. Dardanus had a son, lord Erichthonius, who was the richest man on earth. He had three thousand mares, feeding in the marshlands and rejoicing in their little foals. One day as they were grazing there, the North Wind fell for them and took the form of a black stallion to service them, and in due course they produced twelve foals. These in their frolics could run across a field of corn, brushing the highest ears, and never break one; and when they frolicked on the broad back of the sea, they skimmed the white foam on the crests of the waves.

'Erichthonius had a son called Tros who became lord of the Trojans; and Tros himself had three matchless sons, Ilus, Assaracus and godlike Ganymedes who grew up to be the most beautiful youth in the world, and because of his good looks was kidnapped by the gods to be the wine-steward of Zeus and live with the immortals for ever. Ilus was father to matchless Laomedon whose sons were Tithonus, Priam, Lampus, Clytius and Hicetaon ally of the War-god. But Assaracus was the father of Capys whose son Anchises is my father, whereas Hector is the son of Priam. That then is my family; that is the blood I claim as mine. As for prowess in war, that is a gift from Zeus who endows a man with it in greater or less measure, as he thinks fit. He is the most powerful god of all.

'Enough! No more standing here in the middle of the battle-field talking like little boys. We could sling plenty of insults at each other – enough to sink a ship. Man's tongue is glib. There

are words of all sorts at its command. They cover a wide range,
250 one way and another. You get the kind of answer you have
asked for. But there is no call for you and me to stand and insult
one another like women who have lost their tempers over some
festering dispute and come out into the middle of the street to
hurl insults at each other, so angry they will say anything, true
or false. I'm determined to fight, and no words of yours will put
me off till we have had it out with our spears. Enough now!
Let's taste each other's bronze!'

Aeneas spoke and launched his powerful spear at the other's
260 formidable, unearthly shield. The great shield bellowed with its
impact. Achilles in alarm thrust the shield well in front of him
with his mighty hand, thinking the long-shadowed spear of
great-hearted Aeneas was bound to pierce it – the fool. He had
forgotten that the renowned gifts of the gods are not liable to
crumple or yield to mortal assault. So the heavy spear of warlike
Aeneas did not break through the shield, but was stopped by
the gold that Hephaestus had put into his gift. It did succeed in
driving through two layers but there were three to come, since
270 the little lame god had put on five of them, two of bronze, two
on the inner side of tin and one of gold. It was in this gold layer
that the ash spear was held.

Aeneas comes   Achilles next threw his long-shadowed spear and
off worse   hit Aeneas' round shield on the outside of the rim,
                   where the bronze and the oxhide backing were
thinnest. The ash shaft from Mount Pelion burst right through
with a resounding crack. Aeneas ducked, thrusting his shield
above himself in terror; and the eager spear, breaking through
280 both layers of this all-enveloping shield, passed over his back
and hit the ground. The long shaft had not touched Aeneas, but
he froze, appalled by the closeness of the miss, and shock-waves
clouded his vision.

Achilles, drawing his sharp sword, charged furiously at him
with an intimidating yell. Aeneas then picked up a huge lump
of rock, a tremendous feat. Not even two men today could
manage it, but Aeneas tossed it about quite easily on his own.
And as Achilles came on, Aeneas would have struck him with
the boulder on the helmet or the shield (which had already saved

Achilles from an ugly end) and Achilles would have closed and   290
killed Aeneas with his sword, had it not been for the quick eye
of Poseidon the earthshaker. He immediately spoke his mind to
the gods:

'This will not do! I am very anxious about great-hearted
Aeneas. In a moment he will fall to Achilles and go down to
Hades because he took the Archer-god Apollo at his word –
the fool! As though Apollo would save him from an ugly end!
Why should this innocent man, who has always given the
most gratifying offerings to the gods who inhabit the broad
skies, suffer for his involvement in other people's troubles?
Let's take action and rescue him from death. Even Zeus might   300
be angry if Achilles kills Aeneas, who after all is destined to
survive and save the line of Dardanus from extinction. Zeus
loved Dardanus more than any other child he had by a mortal
mother, but now hates Priam's line. So mighty Aeneas shall
rule over Troy and be followed by his children's children in
the time to come.'

Ox-eyed lady Hera replied:

'Earthshaker, decide for yourself whether to rescue Aeneas or   310
abandon him. Pallas Athene and I have repeatedly sworn in the
presence of all the gods never to save the Trojans from their
doom, not even on the day when their whole town is consumed
by the devastating fires that will be lit there by the warlike
Greeks.'

When Poseidon the earthshaker heard this, he
plunged through the mayhem and the rain of spears,   POSEIDON
making for the spot where Aeneas and famous   *saves Aeneas*
Achilles were engaged. Once there, he spread a mist before   320
Achilles' eyes. Then he extracted the fine ash spear from great-
hearted Aeneas' shield, laid it at Achilles' feet and swept Aeneas
off the ground high into the air. Aeneas was propelled with such
force by the god's hand that he vaulted over all the intervening
lines of infantry and charioteers and came down on the very
edge of the battlefield, where the Caucones were arming for
battle. Poseidon the earthshaker approached him there and   330
spoke winged words:

'Aeneas, what is the meaning of this madness? Which of the

gods told you to fight proud Achilles, who is not only stronger than you but a greater favourite of the immortals? Whenever you come up against that man, retreat at once or you will find yourself in Hades' halls, in defiance of destiny. But when Achilles has met his fated end, you can return in full confidence to the front line, since no other Greek is going to kill you.'

340   With these words Poseidon left Aeneas there and immediately removed the divine mist from Achilles' eyes. Achilles looked around him hard and angrily reflected on the situation:

'Well, well, what an astonishing sight! My spear is lying here on the ground, but the man I meant to kill with it is no-where to be seen. It is clear that Aeneas is, after all, very close to the immortal gods, though *I* felt there was little truth in all that boasting of his. To hell with him. He will be so thankful to

350   have saved his skin this time that he won't be anxious to take me on again. Now I'll give the war-loving Greeks their orders and see what I can do against the other Trojans.'

He spoke, leapt back into the front ranks and exhorted every man:

'Godlike Greeks, don't stand there waiting for the Trojans, but each pick out your man and put your heart into the fight. I may be strong, but I can't deal with such a force on my own and take them all on. Even immortal gods like Ares or Athene could do little damage if they threw themselves into the jaws of

360   such a conflict. But whatever speed, skill and strength can do, I'll do it and without a moment's let-up. I am going straight through their lines and I don't think any Trojan is going to rejoice to find himself on the end of my spear.'

So Achilles spoke, inspiring his men. On the other side glorious Hector urged on the Trojans and talked of attacking Achilles:

'Proud Trojans, don't be frightened by the son of Peleus. I too could fight the gods themselves with words, but with a spear it's much more difficult: the gods are far too strong for us. Achilles

370   won't do all he says. He may succeed in some respects, but even he falls short in others. And I am going to meet him, though his hands are like fire, yes, though his hands are like fire and his courage like bright iron.'

So Hector spoke, inspiring them, and the Trojans
brought their spears to the ready. The two forces fell
upon each other, and the battle-cry went up. Then
Phoebus Apollo went up to Hector and said:

APOLLO
warns off
Hector

'Hector, whatever you do, don't advance to take on Achilles.
Stay with the troops and let him find you in the crowd. Other-
wise, he will hit you with his spear, or stab you at close range
with his sword.'

So he spoke, and Hector retreated back into the ranks in
alarm when he heard the god's voice.

But Achilles, clothed in martial valour, sprang at
the Trojans with an intimidating yell. First he killed
Iphition brave son of Otrynteus and leader of a large
contingent. His mother was a Naiad who had borne him to
Otrynteus, sacker of towns, below the snowy heights of Tmolus
in the rich land of Hyde. Godlike Achilles, as this man came on
against him, hurled his spear through the middle of his head,
splitting his skull in two. He thudded to the ground, and Achilles
triumphed over him:

Achilles kills
four *Trojans*

'Here you fall, son of Otrynteus, most impetuous of men.
This is where you die, though your birth was by lake Gygaea on
your father's estate by the eddying streams of Hermus and
Hyllus where the fish breed.'

So he boasted, and darkness engulfed Iphition's eyes. The
wheel-rims of the Greek chariots tore him to pieces at the front
of the fighting. Achilles then added Demoleon, one of Antenor's
sons, a brave man at repelling the enemy. He hit him on the
temple through his bronze-sided helmet. The bronze helmet
failed to hold the spear. The eager point went through, smashed
the bone and spattered the inside of the helmet with the man's
brains. That put a stop to Demoleon's assault.

Hippodamas was next. He had leapt from his chariot and
was running away when Achilles stabbed him with a spear
in the back. He choked out his life and bellowed as a bull
bellows when it is dragged round the altar of Poseidon lord
of Helice by young men, to the earthshaker's delight. Such was
the bellow that came from Hippodamas as the proud spirit left
his bones.

380

390

400

But Achilles was already after Priam's godlike son Polydorus
with his spear. Priam had forbidden him to fight because he was
410 his youngest child and his favourite; he beat everyone at racing.
But now in his innocence he was showing off his speed by
dashing about among the front-line men, until he met his death.
As he sprinted past, swift-footed godlike Achilles threw his spear
at the middle of his back where the golden buckles of his belt
were fastened and his body-armour overlapped. The spear-point
went right on through him and came out by his navel. He
dropped to his knees with a scream, the dark cloud of death
enveloped him and, as he sank, he clutched his innards to him
with his hands.

When Hector saw his brother Polydorus sink to the ground,
420 clutching his innards, his eyes were dimmed with tears. He could
no longer bear to remain detached, but made at Achilles like a
raging fire, brandishing his sharp spear. Directly Achilles saw
him, he leapt to meet him and spoke in triumph:

APOLLO
rescues *Hector*

'Here is the man who struck me the cruellest blow
of all when he killed my dearest friend! We have
done now with dodging one another down the
lines of battle.'

He spoke and, giving godlike Hector a black look, said:
'Come on, and the sooner your fate will be sealed.'
430 Unperturbed, Hector of the flashing helmet said:
'Son of Peleus, don't imagine you can frighten me with words,
as though I were a little child. I too know perfectly well how
to exchange insults and abuse. I know you are a great warrior,
and I am far inferior. But it surely lies in the lap of the gods
whether, inferior as I am, I kill you with a spear-throw. Before
now my spear has proved as sharp as any.'

He spoke, balanced his spear and launched it. But Athene
440 with a gentle puff of her breath turned the spear away from
illustrious Achilles, so that it flew back to godlike Hector and
fell at his feet. Achilles in his eagerness to kill charged with an
intimidating yell. But Apollo covered Hector in a dense mist
and snatched him away – as easily as a god can. Three times
swift-footed godlike Achilles charged in with his bronze spear,
three times he lunged at deep mist. But when he came on like

something superhuman for the fourth time, he gave a terrible shout and spoke winged words:

'You dog, once more you've saved your skin – but only just. Phoebus Apollo took care of you again: you must pray to him as the spears thud around you. But we shall meet once more and then I'll finish you off, if I too can find some god somewhere to help me. For the moment I'll attack anyone else I can find.'

With these words he stabbed Dryops with his spear in the middle of the neck. Dryops crashed at his feet. Achilles left him there and threw a spear at tall and handsome Demuchus. He hit him on the knee and stopped him in his tracks; then stabbed him with his long sword and took his life. Next he attacked Laogonus and Dardanus, sons of Bias, and knocked them both out of their chariot onto the ground, one with a spear-throw and the other at close quarters with his sword.

Achilles' massacre; Tros' plea

Tros son of Alastor was next. The man came up to clasp Achilles' knees in the hope that out of pity he would not kill one of his own age but merely take him prisoner and let him off with his life. The innocent – he had no idea his prayers were doomed to fail. Achilles was not sweet-tempered or tender-hearted, but a man of fierce passions; and when Tros, desperate to supplicate him, tried to touch his knees with his hands, Achilles struck him in the liver with his sword. The liver slithered out and drenched his lap with dark blood. Darkness enveloped his eyes as he lost his life.

Achilles then went up to Mulius and stabbed him in the ear with his spear, so hard that the bronze point came out through the other. Next he caught Echeclus full on the head with a stroke of his hilted sword, warming the whole blade with his blood. Inexorable destiny and purple death closed Echeclus' eyes. Deucalion next. Achilles pierced his forearm with the bronze point of his spear just where the sinews of the elbow are attached. Deucalion, waiting for him with his arm weighed down by the spear, looked death in the face. Achilles struck the man's neck with his sword and sent head and helmet flying off together. The marrow spurted out of his vertebrae and he lay there, stretched on the ground.

Achilles then went after matchless Rhigmus who had come from fertile Thrace. He threw at him and hit him in the middle. The bronze javelin stuck in his lung, and he crashed from his chariot. Areïthous, Rhigmus' attendant, immediately turned the horses round, but Achilles stabbed him in the back with his sharp spear and knocked him out of the chariot. The horses panicked.

490 As fire from the skies rages through deep gullies on a scorched mountain-side, a great forest is consumed and everywhere a driving wind sends the flames billowing, so Achilles ran amok with his spear like something superhuman, killing as he went, and the black earth ran with blood. As a farmer yokes a pair of broad-browed oxen to trample the white barley on a well-built threshing-floor, and the grain is shelled out under the hooves of the lowing animals, so the horses under great-hearted Achilles' command trampled dead men and shields alike. The whole axle
500 of the chariot and the rails that ran round it were sprayed with the blood thrown up by the horses' hooves and the wheel-rims. And the son of Peleus pressed on in search of glory, spattering his unconquerable hands with gore.

ACHILLES FIGHTS
THE RIVER

When the River Scamander speaks and acts, it does so as the River-god.

1–204: Achilles slaughters *Trojans* hiding in the River *Scamander*, including *Lycaon* and *Asteropaeus*.

205–382: The River-god of *SCAMANDER* tells Achilles to desist and pursues him with a massive flood. HERA, terrified for Achilles, tells HEPHAESTUS to turn his fire on the plain and burn up the River. *SCAMANDER* gives up.

383–513: The gods now take sides and fight each other. *ARES* takes on ATHENE and is flattened, as is *APHRODITE*. *APOLLO* refuses to fight POSEIDON over mere mortals. HERA boxes *ARTEMIS*' ears. HERMES refuses to fight *LETO*. *ARTEMIS* goes sobbing to ZEUS.

514–611: The gods return to Olympus, but *APOLLO* enters *Ilium* to protect it. *Priam* orders the gates to be opened. *APOLLO* in disguise leads Achilles away from the town while the relieved *Trojan* army floods back in.

When the Greeks reached the ford of the sweetly flowing river, eddying Scamander whose father is immortal Zeus, Achilles cut the Trojan force in two. One half he drove towards the town across the plain, where the Greeks had stampeded off in panic on the previous day when glorious Hector was creating havoc. Here the Trojans poured across the plain in flight; and to hamper their escape, Hera confronted them with a dense fog.

The rest were herded into deep-flowing Scamander with its
silvery eddies. They fell into the water with resounding splashes,
10   the rushing river roared and, as they swam about whirled
round in the eddies, the banks on either side threw
Trojans
back their cries. As a cloud of locusts lifts off to make
slaughtered
for a river because of a raging fire which has suddenly
in the river
sprung up and burns furiously, while the locusts
(18.336)
huddle in the water; so the echoing current of deep-
eddying Scamander was filled by Achilles with a medley of men
and horses.

But Olympian-born Achilles, leaving his spear propped
against a tamarisk bush on the bank and taking nothing but his
sword, leapt in like something superhuman, with murder in
20   his heart, and laid about him right and left. Hideous groans
went up from men being hacked to death by his sword, and
the water was reddened with their blood. As fish dart away in
terror before a huge dolphin and crowd into the corners of a
sheltered cove – where it consumes whatever it catches – so the
Trojans cowered under the overhanging banks of that terrible
river. When the work of slaughtering them had tired his arms,
Achilles selected twelve young men and took them alive from
the river to be a blood-price for Patroclus' death. He drove
them, bewildered like fawns, on to the bank and tied their
30   hands behind them with the well-cut leather belts with which
their strongly-woven tunics were equipped. Then he left them
for his followers to take down to the hollow ships and in his
eagerness for slaughter threw himself at the enemy again.

There he encountered Lycaon, one of Priam's sons, who was
making his escape from the river. He had met this man once
before in a night raid and taken him unwilling captive from
his father's orchard, where Lycaon was trimming the young
shoots of a fig-tree with a sharp knife to make chariot rails,
when godlike Achilles descended on him like a bolt from
40   the blue. On that occasion, Achilles had put him on board ship
and transported him for sale to well-built Lemnos – it was
Jason's son who bought him. From Lemnos he was ransomed
at a high price by a man whose hospitality he had once en-
joyed, Eëtion from Imbros, who sent him to bright Arisbe; but

Lycaon slipped away from his protectors there to return home
to Troy.

However, he enjoyed the company of his friends for no more
than eleven days after his return from Lemnos, since on the
twelfth the god landed him once more in the hands of Achilles,
who this time was going to send him on a journey he did not
wish to make – to the halls of Hades. Swift-footed godlike
Achilles recognized him easily, since he was quite unarmed, with
neither helmet, shield nor spear, having discarded his equip-   50
ment on the ground, limp and exhausted as he was after the
sweat and struggle of escaping from the river. Achilles angrily
reflected on the situation:

'Well, well, what an astonishing sight! I suppose I
shall have every Trojan I killed looming up at me   *Lycaon* suppli-
from under the western gloom, if this fellow is any-   cates Achilles
thing to go by: I sold him into slavery on sacred   (20.413)
Lemnos and now he has escaped that harsh fate and turned up
here again. The deep of the grey sea restrains many against their
will but it could not hold him. Well then, he can taste the point   60
of my spear. I want to satisfy myself and see whether he will
return as easily from that journey as well or whether the life-
giving earth, that holds down even the powerful, will hold him
too.'

As he paused and considered the matter, Lycaon approached
him and tried to seize his knees, bewildered and possessed by
one desire, to avoid dark destiny and escape a dreadful death.
Godlike Achilles raised his long spear to stab him, but Lycaon
ducked under the thrust, ran in and grasped his knees, and the
spear passed over his back to stick in the ground, still hungering   70
for human flesh. Laying one hand on Achilles' knees to suppli-
cate him and with the other gripping the sharp spear and refusing
to let go, Lycaon spoke winged words:

'Achilles, I am at your knees: respect me and have pity. I
already have the claims of a suppliant on you – and suppliants
command respect – because you were the first Greek whose
bread I tasted when you captured me in our well-built orchard,
carried me off from my father and friends and sold me on sacred
Lemnos. I fetched you a good price – a hundred cattle – but I

80   was ransomed for three times as much, and after many hard-
ships I returned to Ilium twelve days ago. Now deadly destiny
has brought me into your hands again.

'How Father Zeus must hate me, to have made me your
prisoner twice over! I am the short-lived son of Laothoe and
she is a daughter of old Altes, lord of the warlike Leleges,
who lives in the high fortress of Pedasus on the banks of the
River Satnioïs. Priam made this daughter of Altes one of his
many wives and she had two sons, both of whom you will
90   have butchered, since godlike Polydorus fell to you and your
sharp spear in the front line, and now an evil end awaits me
here. For I have little hope of escaping, now that a divinity has
delivered me into your hands. But I will tell you something else,
and you bear it in mind. I was not borne by the same mother
as Hector, who killed your brave and gentle companion. Don't
kill me.'

So the glorious son of Priam spoke in supplication. But there
was no mercy in the voice that answered him:

'You innocent, don't talk to me of ransom. Don't give me
100 your speeches. Before Patroclus met his destined end, I was not
disinclined to spare the Trojans; I took many alive and sold
them abroad. But now not a single man the god delivers into
my hands in front of Ilium is going to live; and that holds good
for all the Trojans, the sons of Priam above all.

'Yes, my friend, you die too. Why make such a song about it?
Even Patroclus died, who was a better man than you by far.
And look at me. Don't you see how big and handsome I am?
I am the son of a great man. A goddess was my mother. Yet
110 death and inexorable destiny are waiting for me as well. A
morning is coming, or maybe an evening or noon, when some-
one is going to kill me too in battle, with a throw of his spear
or an arrow from his bow.'

Death of
Lycaon

So he spoke, and then and there Lycaon's spirit
failed him, and he collapsed. Letting go of the spear,
he sank back, stretching out both his hands. But
Achilles drew his sharp sword and struck him on the collar bone
beside the neck. The two-edged blade was buried in his flesh; he
pitched forward headlong and lay there, stretched out on the

ground, and the dark blood ran out of him and drenched the earth. Achilles took him by the foot, hurled him into the river   120 to be carried away and in triumph spoke winged words:

'Now lie there among the fish, where they can lick clean the blood from your wound without a second thought. Your mother will not lay you on a bier and mourn you, but eddying Scamander will roll you out into the broad bosom of the sea, where many a fish will dart through the waves to the dark ripples on the top to eat Lycaon's white fat.

'Die, all of you, till we reach the citadel of sacred Ilium, you in rout, I killing from behind. Nothing shall save you, not even   130 sweetly flowing Scamander with its silver eddies, to whom for years you have been sacrificing bulls and into whose swirling pools you throw living horses. No: one by one you shall die an evil death, till you have all paid for the killing of Patroclus and the death of the Greeks you slaughtered down by their swift ships when I was away.'

So he spoke, and the River-god became extremely angry and began to consider ways of bringing Achilles' exploits to an end and saving the Trojans
Achilles kills
Asteropaeus
from disaster. Meanwhile the son of Peleus, bent on slaughter, hurled himself with his long-shadowed spear at Asteropaeus.   140 This man was the son of Pelegon, who was a love-child of Periboea and the broad River Axius with its swirling stream. When Achilles attacked him, Asteropaeus had just emerged from the river and stood facing him with two spears in his hands, emboldened by the River-god Scamander who resented the slaughter of the youths Achilles was mercilessly butchering up and down his stream. When they had come within range of each other, swift-footed godlike Achilles spoke first:

'Who on earth are you that dare to face me? And where do   150 you come from? Pity those fathers whose sons face me in my fury!'

The glorious son of Pelegon said:

'Great-hearted Achilles, why do you ask after my family? I come from distant, fertile Paeonia, which I left for Ilium eleven days ago at the head of my long-speared Paeonian troops. I am descended from broad-flowing River Axius, Axius, source of the loveliest water in the land. Axius was the father of the famous spearman Pelegon and I, they say, am Pelegon's son. 160 But enough now, glorious Achilles! Let us fight.'

So, defiantly, he spoke, and godlike Achilles raised his ash spear from Mount Pelion. But the warrior Asteropaeus, who was ambidextrous, threw both his spears at once. With one he hit Achilles' shield but failed to pierce it; the point was stopped by the gold that Hephaestus had put in as a gift. With the other he grazed Achilles' right elbow, causing the dark blood to flow; but the spear passed over him and stuck in the ground, still hungering for flesh.

Now Achilles hurled his straight-flying ash shaft at 170 Asteropaeus, determined to kill him. He missed his man and hit the high riverbank instead with such force that he buried half the length of the ash spear in it. Drawing his sharp sword from his side, the son of Peleus launched himself furiously at Asteropaeus, who was now trying in vain to wrestle the spear out of the bank with his great hand. Three times, in his desperation to retrieve the spear, he shifted it a little, three times he gave up the struggle. The fourth time he tried again to bend and break Peleus' ash shaft, but before he could do so Achilles was 180 on him and killed him with his sword. He hit him in the belly by the navel and all his innards gushed out on the ground. He lay there gasping, and darkness engulfed his eyes. Achilles, trampling on his chest, removed his armour and spoke in triumph:

'Lie there, and learn how difficult it is, even for children of a River-god, to fight the offspring of almighty Zeus. You said you were descended from a broad-flowing River, but I can trace my ancestry to Zeus himself. Peleus son of Aeacus, leader of many Myrmidons, is my father; Aeacus was a son of Zeus; and 190 a descendant of Zeus is greater than the son of a River by as much as Zeus himself is greater than all rivers that run murmuring down to the sea.

'Look at the River that is flowing past you now, Scamander. He is a mighty one, if that is any use to you. But there is no fighting against Zeus son of Cronus. Even Achelous lord of Rivers is no match for Zeus. Nor is the deep and potent Stream of Ocean, the source of all rivers, every sea and all the springs and deep wells that there are. Even Ocean is afraid of almighty Zeus' lightning-bolt and his terrible thunder when it peals from the skies.'

He spoke, pulled his bronze spear out of the bank and left the man he had killed lying where he was on the sand, lapped by the dark water and busily attended by the swarming eels and fish, who tore at his kidneys and devoured his fat.

Then Achilles went after the Paeonians in their plumed helmets, who had been left in a state of panic beside the swirling river when they saw their leader fall in the thick of the action to the sword and strength of the son of Peleus. He killed Thersilochus, Mydon and Astypylus, Mnesus, Thrasius, Aenius and Ophelestes. Indeed swift Achilles would have slaughtered even more Paeonians, had it not been for the eddying River-god Scamander, who in his anger took human form and addressed him, speaking from one of his deep pools:

The River-god's anger at the killings

'Achilles, you are supreme among men both in your strength and your outrageous deeds. And the gods themselves are always at your side. If Zeus really means you to kill all the Trojans, at least drive them away from me here and do your dirty work on the plain. My lovely channels are full of dead men's bodies. I am so choked with bodies that I cannot pour my waters into the bright sea, and you blindly kill on. Enough! Call a halt! I am appalled, commander.'

Swift-footed Achilles replied and said:

'Scamander, child of Zeus, your will shall be done. But I'm not going to stop killing these arrogant Trojans till I've penned them in their town and tested Hector face to face, whether he kills me or I him.'

With these words he fell on the Trojans like something superhuman. Then deep-eddying Scamander addressed Phoebus Apollo:

'For shame, god of the silver bow, son of Zeus! You have ignored the orders of Zeus, who has told you many times to stand by the Trojans and protect them till the evening sun falls and throw its shadows over the fruitful fields.'

He spoke, and the famous spearman Achilles leapt

from the bank and plunged into the middle of the
stream. The River-god Scamander rushed on him in
spate. He stirred up all his lovely streams, made them
rise and, roaring like a bull, flung up on dry land the many
bodies of Achilles' victims that had choked him, protecting
the survivors by hiding them in the large, deep pools along
240 his beautiful course. The waters rose terrifyingly and seethed
around Achilles; they beat down on his shield and overwhelmed
him. Unable to maintain his footing, he grabbed hold of a
full-grown elm. But the tree came out by the roots, brought the
whole bank away and fell into the river, which it dammed from
side to side, clogging the stream with a tangle of branches.
Achilles struggled out of the current and in his terror made a
dash to reach the plain as fast as he could.

But the great god had not done with him yet – he meant
250 to bring his exploits to an end and save the Trojans from dis-
aster. He rose over him in a darkening crest of water. The son
of Peleus fled, getting a spear-throw's start by swooping away
with the speed of the black eagle, that great hunter which is
both the strongest and the fastest thing on wings. That was how
he sprinted away, and his bronze armour rang frighteningly
on his shoulders. But as he slipped away from under the over-
hanging wave and made his escape, Scamander surged after
him in pursuit, roaring and rumbling. Like a gardener making
a channel in order to run water from a dark spring through
his garden and its plants; mattock in hand, he clears ob-
260 structions from the trench; as the water starts flowing, all the
pebbles are swept out of the way, and very soon it runs singing
down the slope, outstripping its guide – so the wave was always
catching up with Achilles, quick though he was. Gods are
stronger than men. Sometimes swift-footed godlike Achilles
tried to make a stand against it and find out whether every
god that inhabits the broad sky was chasing him. But when-
ever he stopped, a mighty wave from the sky-fed river came
crashing down on his shoulders. Exasperated, he would try to
270 jump clear. But the water, racing madly beneath him, would
unbalance him and eat the loose earth away from under any

foothold. The son of Peleus groaned aloud, looking up to the broad skies:

'O Father Zeus, to think that none of the gods promised to have compassion and save me from the River! I should welcome any other fate but this. Not that I blame the other Sky-gods so much as my own mother, whose false predictions deceived me. She said I should fall to Apollo and his flying weapons under the walls of the Trojan warriors. If only Hector could have killed me! He's the best warrior they have bred in Ilium, and the killer would have been as good as the killed. But now it seems I've been destined to die a wretched death, caught in a great river, like a boy in charge of pigs who is swept away by a mountain stream he has tried to cross in winter.' 280

So he spoke, and Poseidon and Athene immediately came and stood beside him. Adopting human form, they took his hands in theirs and uttered reassuring words. Poseidon began and spoke his mind:

ATHENE and POSEIDON reassure Achilles

'Achilles, don't be unduly afraid or alarmed when two such allies as myself and Pallas Athene have come down to help you, and with the approval of Zeus too. Believe me, you are not destined to be overcome by any river. This one will soon subside, as you will see for yourself. And here is some good advice from us, if you will take it. Do not desist from war the great leveller, till you have every Trojan who escapes you penned up inside the famous walls of Ilium. And do not go back to your ships till you have taken Hector's life. We guarantee you this triumph.' 290

With these words the two gods departed to rejoin the immortals while Achilles, greatly heartened by the gods' encouragement, went on across the plain. It was completely inundated and afloat with the fine armour and bodies of the butchered men. But stepping high, Achilles fought his way on against the current, and Athene so increased his strength that the spreading waters could not hold him back. Not that Scamander was relaxing his efforts either, but in a fresh onset of rage with Achilles he reared up his mighty wave in a curling crest and called aloud to the River Simoïs: 300

'Dear brother, let's unite to overpower this man or he will
310 soon be sacking lord Priam's great town without a Trojan
to stop him. Come quickly to my help! Fill your

*Scamander
asks River
Simoïs to help*

channels with water from the springs, replenish all
your mountain streams, lift up a great breaker and
send it down, seething with logs and boulders, so we
can stop this savage who is carrying all before him. He thinks
himself a match for the gods.

'But I say his strength and beauty will not save him now, nor
that splendid armour. It will lie deep in the slime beneath my
flood; and as for him, the sand will be his winding-sheet, with
320 shingle piled high above him. The Greeks will not know where
to find his bones, I will bury him so deep in silt. His burial-mound
will be ready-made for him and there will be no need to build
him another when the Greeks hold his funeral!'

He spoke and, boiling up, rushed upon Achilles with a tower-
ing surge, seething with foam, blood and bodies. A dark wave
from the sky-fed River hung high above the son of Peleus and
was threatening to engulf him, when Hera in her terror for
Achilles, whom she thought the great deep-eddying River was
about to sweep away, gave a scream of alarm and immediately
330 addressed her son Hephaestus:

*HEPH-
AESTUS
to dry River*

'Into action, little club-foot god, my child! It's you
we've been counting on to deal with Scamander in
this fight. Quick, to the rescue, and bring your flames
into action, while I go and rouse the west wind and
the bright south to blow up a fierce gale from the sea and spread
the blaze till the bodies and armour of the dead Trojans are
consumed. You burn the trees on Scamander' banks and set the
very river on fire. Don't let his gentle entreaties or threats put
340 you off and don't lessen your fury till you hear a shout from
me. Then you can let your inexhaustible fires die down.'

So she spoke, and Hephaestus produced a supernatural con-
flagration which started on the plain and consumed the bodies
of Achilles' many victims that were scattered there. The shim-
mering flood was stemmed, and the whole plain was dried up.
As the north wind dries up an irrigated orchard in autumn, and
the man who tills it is delighted, so the whole plain was dried

and the dead consumed. Hephaestus then turned his dazzling flames on the river. The elms, willows and tamarisks caught fire; and the lotus, reeds and galingale that grew in profusion by the lovely stream were burnt. In the very depths of the pools even the eels and fish were tormented by ingenious Hephaestus' torrid blasts and plunged about this way and that in agony along the lovely stream. The mighty river himself was scalded and spoke out: 350

'Hephaestus! You're more than a match for any god. I can't cope with this blazing fire of yours. The fight's off. Let godlike Achilles go straight in and drive the Trojans from their town. Why should I get mixed up in other people's quarrels?' 360

He spoke with the fire rising round him, and his lovely stream began to bubble up. As a cauldron is brought rapidly to the boil by a roaring fire and dry logs burning underneath, and melts down the fat of a well-fed pig while the fat spits up all round – so his lovely stream was consumed by fire and its waters boiled. Overcome by the blast delivered by the might of inventive Hephaestus, he lost heart and ceased to flow. He turned in supplication to Hera and spoke winged words:

'Hera, why has your son picked on my stream for persecution? Compared with all the others who are fighting on the Trojan side, I've done little to deserve it. However, if you tell me to, I will stop – but so must Hephaestus. I will do more: I will undertake on oath to make no attempt to save the Trojans from their doom, not even on the day when their whole town is consumed by the devastating fires that will be lit there by the warlike Greeks.' 370

The River gives up

When the goddess white-armed Hera heard this from Scamander, she immediately spoke to Hephaestus her dear son:

'Enough, Hephaestus, glorious child! It is not right to ill-treat a god like this merely to help mortals.' 380

So she spoke, and Hephaestus put out the supernatural fire and the river began to flow back again along his lovely course.

There was no more fighting between these two after Scamander's energies had been tamed. Hera, though still resentful, saw to that. But now the feud between the other gods, driven as they were by their loyalties into opposing camps, came to

The gods fight:
ATHENE
vs. ARES
(5.898)

a head in a momentous and painful conflict, and they fell on each other with a thunderous crash which made the great skies trumpet and the broad earth groan again.

390   Zeus, sitting on Olympus, heard the din. He laughed to himself in delight when he saw the immortals come to grips and hold back no longer. Ares piercer of shields began the fight by making for Athene, bronze spear in hand and shouting abuse as he came:

'You dog-flea, why have you set the gods at each other's throats again, you and your mad bravado? What have your obsessions pushed you into this time? Don't you remember when you encouraged Diomedes to stab me? You made no secret of it. You took his spear in your own hand; you drove it straight at me and cut my fine flesh. Now I'm going to make you pay for what you did to me then.'

400   With these words he stabbed at Athene's fringed aegis, the terrifying aegis that can withstand even the thunderbolt of Zeus. Here the murderous Ares lunged with his long spear. Athene drew back and with her great hand picked up a rock that was lying on the ground, a big, black, rough boulder which men of an earlier age had set up in the fields to mark a boundary. She threw this and struck wild Ares on the neck, bringing him down. There with a great clatter of armour he fell, covering seven acres, with his hair in the dust. Pallas Athene laughed and, triumphing over him, spoke winged words:

410   'You stupid food! It never occurred to you, before you matched yourself with me, to consider how much stronger I was. Think of yourself, then, as paying off the price of your mother Hera's curses: she has wished you ill ever since you angered her by deserting the Greeks to fight for the proud Trojans.'

With these words Athene turned her brilliant eyes away, and Aphrodite took Ares by the arm and led him from the battlefield. He had scarcely recovered his senses and was groaning all the time. But the goddess white-armed Hera noticed this move on Aphrodite's part and immediately spoke to Athene with winged words:

'Look sharp, Atrytone, child of Zeus who drives the storm- 420
cloud! There goes that dog-flea again, leading the butcher Ares
through the mayhem and away from the battlefield. After her,
quick!'

So she spoke, and Athene, delighted, sped after
Aphrodite, closed with her and struck her on the ATHENE *vs.*
breast with her fist. Then and there Aphrodite gave APHRODITE
up and collapsed. She and Ares lay together on the bountiful
earth, and Athene triumphing over them spoke winged words:

'May everyone who helps the Trojans in their fight against
the Greeks acquit themselves like these and show as much daring 430
and resolution as Aphrodite, when she ran to Ares' side and
found herself face to face with me in my fury! Then we should
soon have finished with this war and sacked the well-built town
of Ilium.'

So she spoke, and the goddess white-armed Hera smiled. And
now the lord earthshaker Poseidon addressed Apollo:

'Phoebus, why are we two standing apart? That is
not right when others have already begun. We ought POSEIDON
to be ashamed to go back to Olympus and Zeus' *vs. APOLLO*
bronze-floored palace without a fight. You begin. (*Laomedon*'s
You are my junior, and with my greater age and story)
experience, it would not be honourable for me to start. 440

'You fool, you must have lost your senses when you decided
to help the Trojans. You seem to have forgotten all the hard-
ships you and I endured at Ilium when we were segregated
from the gods and sent by Zeus to serve Troy's haughty lord
Laomedon for a year. We were on a fixed wage, and he gave the
orders. I built a wall for the Trojans round their town, a broad
and splendid one to make the place impregnable; while you,
Phoebus, herded the shambling cattle with their crooked horns
on the spurs of wooded Mount Ida with its many ridges.

'But when the joyful seasons brought round the time for 450
settlement, impetuous Laomedon refused outright to give us
anything and packed us off, threatening to tie our feet and hands
together and send us for sale to some distant island. He even
talked of lopping our ears off! So home we came in a rage,
furious with Laomedon about the offer he had promised and

withheld. That's the man whose people you are now so anxious
to oblige, instead of joining us and trying to ensure that these
460 insolent Trojans are utterly wiped out, together with their
children and honoured wives.'

The Archer-god lord Apollo replied:

'Earthshaker, you would credit me with very little sense if I
fought you for the sake of mortals, those wretched creatures
who, like the leaves, flourish in fiery brilliance for a little while
on the bounty of the earth, then in a moment droop and fade
away. No, let's call the battle off before it is too late, and leave
these mortals to do their own fighting.'

With these words Apollo turned and went. He thought it an
improper thing to come to blows with his uncle. But now his
470 sister Artemis, mistress of animals and lady of the wilds, insulted
him with biting words:

'So you are running away, Archer-god, after hand-
HERA   ing Poseidon a victory – and a pretty cheap one too!
attacks   What's the sense, you baby, in carrying a bow you
ARTEMIS   never use? Never let me hear you boast to the immor-
tal gods in our father's palace, as you used to, that you would
stand up to Poseidon.'

So she spoke, and the Archer-god Apollo made no reply. But
480 Hera, honoured wife of Zeus, was infuriated with Artemis and
hit back at her:

'Shameless bitch, how do you now propose, then, to stand up
to *me*? Even though you have got your bow, and Zeus set you
as a lioness against females, allowing you to destroy women
at your discretion, you would still find me a very dangerous
opponent. You would do better to slaughter beasts and wild
deer in the mountains than to fight your superiors. But since
you have thrown down the challenge, you might like to learn
about fighting and discover just how much stronger I am.'

She spoke, and with her left hand seized Artemis by both her
490 wrists, while with her right she removed the bow and arrows
from her shoulders. Then she boxed her round the ears with her
own weapons, smiling as her victim twisted and turned and the
arrows came tumbling out of the quiver. Artemis burst into
tears and fled from her like a pigeon that was not destined to be

caught, escaping in flight from a hawk into a cleft or hollow in a rock. So the goddess fled in tears, leaving her bow and arrows on the ground.

Hermes, the messenger and slayer of Argus, then spoke to Artemis' mother Leto:

'Leto, I am not about to fight you. People who come to blows with the lovers of Zeus who marshals the clouds have a hard time of it. No: you can boast to your heart's content and tell the gods that your brute strength got the better of me.'   500

So he spoke, and Leto gathered up the curved bow and arrows that had tumbled here and there in the swirling dust and retired with her daughter's weapons in her arms. Meanwhile Artemis had reached Zeus' bronze-floored palace on Olympus, where she sat down on her father's lap and sobbed, her immortal robe quivering with her agitation. The son of Cronus took his daughter in his arms and asked her with a kindly laugh:

'My darling child, which of the Sky-gods has treated you like this?'   510

The huntress with the lovely crown replied:

'Father, it was your own wife, white-armed Hera, who beat me. This quarrelling among the immortal gods is all her fault.'

While they were talking together in this way, Phoebus Apollo went into sacred Ilium. He was concerned about the walls of the well-built town, in case the Greeks sacked it that very day in defiance of destiny. But the rest of the everlasting gods, some angry, others triumphant, returned to Olympus and sat down with their father, god of the black cloud.   520

Meanwhile Achilles continued to destroy. Men and their horses fell to him alike. As smoke rises up to the broad sky from a blazing town, when the gods have directed their wrath against it and bring suffering to all and grief to many, so Achilles brought suffering and grief to the Trojans.

Old Priam stood on the tower Poseidon had built and saw awe-inspiring Achilles and the panic-stricken Trojans driven before him in confusion, all resistance gone. He gave a cry of alarm, and came down to give   530
urgent orders to the wall's tried and trusted gatekeepers:

Priam opens
Ilium's gates

'Hold the gates open, till our routed forces reach the town.

They have Achilles at their heels, and I fear a disaster. Directly they are safely inside the town getting their breath back, close the doors tight. I am appalled at the prospect of that savage leaping inside our defences.'

So he spoke, and the men unfastened the doors and thrust back the bars: safety beckoned through the open gates. Moreover, Apollo rushed out to meet them and avert disaster. They
540 were making straight for the town and the high wall, parched by thirst and covered with dust from their flight across the plain, while close at their heels came Achilles with his spear, intent on glory and still in the grip of the violent madness that had seized him.

Then the Trojans' town with its high gates would have fallen to the Greeks if Phoebus Apollo had not intervened and inspired Antenor's godlike son Agenor, a matchless and mighty man of war. The god breathed daring into his heart and, leaning against an oak-tree, stood by him in person, though hidden by a thick mist, to save him from the pitiless demons of death. In conse-
550 quence, when Agenor saw Achilles sacker of towns approaching, he stood his ground, his thoughts in turmoil as he awaited him. In anguish, he reflected on the situation:

Agenor takes on Achilles
'What shall I do? If I fly before godlike Achilles and join the others in their wild stampede, he will catch me all the same and slit my defenceless throat. On the other hand, if I leave the rest to be chased by him and use my speed to get away from the walls in the other direction, towards the Ilian Plain, till I reach the foothills of Mount Ida
560 and can hide in the woods . . . then in the evening I could bathe in the river, wash the sweat off my body and make my way back to Ilium . . .

'But why talk to myself like this? Achilles is bound to see me sneaking away from the town into the open country; he will come after me and with his speed he will catch me too. There'll be no escape from death and destiny: he's far too strong for anyone. But if I go to meet him here in front of the town . . . his flesh too is vulnerable to a sharp bronze spear . . . he has only
570 one life, and people say he's mortal, even if Zeus son of Cronus is granting him the glory . . .'

With these words Agenor braced himself and waited for Achilles. His courageous heart was determined to do battle and fight. As a leopardess steps out from her jungle lair to face the huntsman, fearless and immovable when she hears the baying of the hounds: if the hunter gets in first and hits her with a throw or stabs her, even with the spear stuck in her, her courage does not fail her, but she takes him on or dies in the attempt – so noble Agenor refused to run before he had put Achilles to the test. He held his circular shield in front of his body, brandished his spear at Achilles and shouted aloud: 580

'Glorious Achilles, no doubt you thought you were going to sack the proud Trojans' town this very day. You fool! It will survive to witness much suffering yet. There are plenty of us brave men to fight her battles under the eyes of our dear parents and wives and children. It is you that are rushing to your doom here, impetuous and self-confident a warrior that you are.'

He spoke and launched the sharp spear from his heavy hand. 590 He hit Achilles on the shin below the knee and did not miss, making the tin of the new shin-guard ring frighteningly on his leg. But the god's gift stood up to the blow, and the bronze point rebounded. It had hit but not wounded him.

Achilles in his turn attacked godlike Agenor. But Apollo did not let him win this encounter. Hiding Agenor in a thick mist, he swept him off and sent him quietly from the battlefield to return home. The *APOLLO diverts Achilles* Archer-god then used a trick to steer Achilles away from the rest of the Trojan army. Making himself look exactly like 600 Agenor, he presented himself in Achilles' path. Achilles started eagerly in pursuit and chased the god across the wheat-bearing plain, heading him off towards deep-eddying Scamander. Apollo kept a little way ahead, all the time cleverly encouraging Achilles into thinking he could overtake him.

Meanwhile the rest of the Trojans, fleeing in a jostling crowd, reached the town with grateful hearts and filled it as they crowded in. They did not even have the spirit to wait for each other outside the town walls in order to find out who had got away or who had fallen in battle. Instead, those whose speed of 610 foot had saved them poured eagerly inside.

THE DEATH OF HECTOR

So the Trojans, running for it like fawns, took refuge in the town. There they dried the sweat off their bodies, drank and slaked their thirst as they leant against the fine battlements, while the Greeks advanced on the wall, their shields at the slope on their shoulders. But deadly destiny shackled Hector where he was, outside Ilium in front of the Scaean gate.

Meanwhile Phoebus Apollo spoke to Achilles:

'Son of Peleus, why are you chasing me on those swift feet of yours? You are a man, and I an immortal god, as you might

have noticed, had you not been so preoccupied with your pur-   10
suit. But surely you must be neglecting your business with
the Trojans you put to flight. Look, they've shut themselves up
in the town, while you have been side-tracked all the way out
here. But you'll never kill *me*: I, naturally, am not marked out
for death.'

Furious, swift-footed Achilles replied:

'You've made a fool of me, Apollo, most malev-   Achilles rages at
olent of all the gods, by luring me out here away   *APOLLO*'s
from the walls. To think of all the Trojans who   trick
would otherwise have bitten the dust and not reached Ilium!
You have robbed me of a great victory by saving their lives, an
easy task for you, who have no retribution to fear. I would
certainly pay you back, if only I had the power.'   20

With these words Achilles made fearlessly for the town, racing
along like a prize-winning horse galloping effortlessly at speed
over the plain with its chariot. So lightly and easily Achilles
sprinted off.

Old Priam was the first to see him, shining like a star as he
sped across the plain – like the star that comes in autumn,
outshining all its fellows in the evening sky. They call it Orion's
Dog, and though it is the brightest of all stars, it heralds no   30
good, bringing much fever, as it does, to wretched mortals.
That was how the bronze gleamed on Achilles' chest as he ran.

The old man gave a groan. He lifted up his hands and beat
his head. With a great cry he shouted in supplication to his
beloved son Hector, who had taken his stand in front
of the gates, implacable in his determination to fight   *Hector* asked
it out with Achilles. Stretching out his arms, the old   not to fight
man piteously addressed him: (20.417,
                                                           21.117)
'Hector, I beg you, my dear son, don't stand up to
that man alone and without help. You are inviting defeat and
death at his hands. He is far stronger than you and quite ruthless.   40
The dogs and vultures would soon be feeding on his body (and
what a load that would lift from my heart!) if only the gods
loved him as little as I do – the man who has robbed me of so
many splendid sons, killed them or sold them off as slaves to
distant islands.

'There are still two of them I cannot find among the troops huddling in the town, Lycaon and Polydorus, children of mine by my mistress, lady Laothoe. If the enemy have taken them alive, we will ransom them presently with bronze and gold, of which there is plenty inside, since old Altes, Laothoe's famous father, gave his daughter a massive dowry. But if they are dead by now and in the halls of Hades, there will be one more sorrow for me and their mother who brought them into the world, even though the rest of Ilium will not mourn for them so long – unless you join them and also fall to Achilles. So come inside the walls, my son, to be the saviour of Trojan men and women; and do not throw away your own precious life to give a triumph to the son of Peleus.

'Have pity too on me, your poor father, while I still live my ill-fated existence, since Father Zeus has kept in store for my old age a hideous fate, innumerable horrors I shall have to see before I die – sons massacred, daughters raped, bedrooms pillaged, little babies hurled ruthlessly to the ground and killed, my sons' wives hauled away by murderous Greek hands.

'Last of all my turn will come after someone's spear or sword has removed the life from these limbs; and my dogs, turned savage, tear me to pieces at the entrance to my palace. The very dogs I have fed at table and trained to watch my gate will lie in front of my doors, restlessly lapping their master's blood. It looks well enough for a young man killed in battle to lie there mutilated by a sharp spear: death can find nothing to expose in him that is not beautiful. But when an old man's dogs defile his grey head, his grey beard and his genitals, wretched mortals plumb the depths of human misery.'

The old man spoke and tore at his grey locks and pulled the hair from his head; but he did not shake Hector's resolve. And now his mother Hecabe in her turn began to lament and weep. Drawing open the folds of her dress, she held up her breast in her hand and, with the tears running down her cheeks, spoke winged words:

'Hector, my son, have some respect for this and pity me, if ever I gave you this breast to soothe away your troubles! Remember those days, dear child. Deal with your enemy from here inside the walls and do not go out to meet that man in single combat. He is ruthless; and if he kills you, I shall never lay you out on a bier and weep for you, dear child of my flesh, nor will your wife, however rich her dowry; but far away from both of us beside the Greek ships the swift dogs will consume you.'

So they spoke in tears to their dear son. But all their entreaties   90
did not shake Hector's resolve: he stayed where he was, awaiting the approach of awe-inspiring Achilles. As a mountain snake waits for a man beside its hole: it has swallowed poisonous herbs, its anger is dreadful and it stares intimidatingly at him, wreathing its coils round its lair – so Hector, his determination unquenchable, refused to retreat. He leaned his glittering shield against the project- ing tower and, deeply troubled, reflected on the situation:

Hector refuses to retreat (18.266)

'What am I to do? If I retire behind the gate and the wall, Polydamas will be the first to point the finger of blame at me   100
that, on this last accursed night when godlike Achilles rose up again, I did not take his advice and order a withdrawal into the town. It would have been much better if I had. As it is, having sacrificed the army to my own reckless stupidity, I would feel nothing but shame before the Trojan men and the Trojan women in their trailing gowns. I could not bear to hear some second- rater say: "Hector trusted in his own right arm and lost an army." But it *will* be said, and then it would be far better for me to stand up to Achilles and either kill him and come home alive, or be killed by him gloriously in front of Ilium.   110

'If I put down my bossed shield and heavy helmet, prop my spear against the wall and approach matchless Achilles myself . . . if I promise to return Helen and all her property with her . . . everything in fact that Paris brought away with him to Troy in his hollow ships, which was how this war started . . . to give it all to Agamemnon and Menelaus to take away, and to divide up everything else with the Greeks as well, everything the town possesses . . . and then if I take an oath with the elders in council on behalf of the Trojans not to hide anything but to divide it all   120
up equally, all the property our lovely town contains . . .

'But why talk to myself like this? If I approach Achilles as a suppliant, he'll show me no pity, no respect. He'll kill me out of hand, exposed as I will be when I take off my armour, like a woman. I can't somehow see Achilles and myself engaging in intimacies "from an oak or a rock", as a girl and boy do, a girl and boy, just the two, with their intimacies. No: better to waste no time and come to grips. Let's find out to which of us the Olympian intends to hand the victory.'

As Hector paused and considered the matter, Achilles came on at him, looking like the god of war, the warrior with the nodding helmet. Over his right shoulder he was brandishing the formidable ash spear from Mount Pelion, and his bronze armour glowed like a blazing fire or the rising sun. Hector saw him and shook. He could not stand his ground; he left the gate and ran in panic. But the son of Peleus, counting on his speed, was after him. Like a mountain hawk, the fastest thing on wings, when it effortlessly swoops after a timid dove; under and away the dove dives off, and the hawk, shrieking close behind, strikes at it again and again in its determination to make a kill – so Achilles started off in hot pursuit, and Hector fled in terror before him under the walls of Ilium, fast as his feet would go.

Passing the lookout-post and the windswept fig-tree and always keeping some way from the wall, they sped along the waggon-track and came to the two sweet-flowing springs that are the sources of Scamander's eddying stream. In one of these the water comes up hot; steam rises from it like smoke from a blazing fire. But the other, even in summer, gushes up like hail or freezing snow or water that has turned to ice. Close beside them, wide and beautiful, stand the stone washing-places where the wives and lovely daughters of the Trojans used to wash their shining clothes in earlier days, when there was peace, before the coming of the Greeks.

Here the two raced past, Hector in flight and Achilles after him – a fine man in front but a far stronger one at his heels. And the pace was furious. They were not running for the usual prize at a foot-race, a sacrificial beast or leather shield: they were competing for the life of horse-taming Hector. As powerful

Achilles charges;
Hector runs

prize-winning race-horses corner at speed round a turning-post: a great prize has been set up, a tripod or a woman, in honour of a warrior who has died – so the pair of them circled three times round Priam's town, feet flying.

All the gods were looking on. The Father of men and gods then began and spoke his mind:

'This is an unhappy business! I have a warm place in my heart for this man who is being chased before my eyes round the walls of Ilium. I grieve for Hector. He has burnt the thighs of many 170 oxen in my honour, on the heights of Mount Ida with its many ridges and on the lofty citadel of Ilium. But now godlike Achilles is pursuing him at full speed round Priam's town. Consider, gods, and help me to decide whether we shall save his life, or let a good man fall this day to Achilles son of Peleus.'

ZEUS decides not to save Hector

The goddess grey-eyed Athene replied:

'Father, lord of the vivid lightning, god of the dark cloud, what are you talking about? Are you proposing to reprieve from the pains of death a mortal man whose destiny has long been 180 settled? Do what you like, then; but not all the rest of us gods will approve.'

Zeus who marshals the clouds replied and said:

'Have no fear, Triton-born Athene, dear child. I was not in earnest and do not mean to be unkind to you. Act as you see fit, and act at once.'

So he spoke, and encouraged Athene, who had already set her heart on action, and she came swooping down from the heights of Olympus.

Meanwhile swift Achilles continued his relentless pursuit of Hector. As a hound starts a fawn from its mountain covert and pursues it through the glens and valleys: even when it takes 190 cover in a thicket, the dog continues to track it until it finds it – so Hector could not shake off swift-footed Achilles. More than once, Hector made a move towards the Dardanian gate, hoping to get close enough under the well-built towers for those above to protect him with their missiles; but Achilles, hugging the inside path, intercepted him every time and headed him off towards the plain.

Like a chase in a nightmare when no one, pursuer or pursued,
200   can move a limb, so Achilles could not catch up Hector, nor
Hector shake off Achilles. How could Hector have escaped the
demons of death, had not Apollo come to him for the last time
and given him new drive and fresh speed? Achilles too had been
signalling to his men with his head not to shoot at Hector, in
case someone else hit him and won the glory, and he came
second.

But when they reached the springs for the fourth time, the
210   Father held out his golden scales and, putting death that lays
APOLLO   men low in either pan, on one side for Achilles, on
deserts *Hector*   the other for horse-taming Hector, raised the balance
                           by the middle of the beam. The beam came down on
Hector's side, spelling his doom. He was on his way to Hades.
Phoebus Apollo deserted him; and the goddess grey-eyed Athene
came up to Achilles and, standing beside him, spoke winged
words:

'Now, glorious Achilles dear to Zeus, our chance has come
to go back to the ships with a great victory for the Greeks.
Hector is hungry for battle, but you and I are going to kill
him. There is no escape for him from us now, however much
220   humiliation the Archer-god Apollo endures, grovelling abjectly
at the feet of his Father Zeus who drives the storm-cloud. You
stay here now and recover your breath, while I go to Hector
and persuade him to fight you.'

So spoke Athene, and Achilles was delighted and did as she
told him. He stood there, leaning on his bronze-barbed spear,
while Athene went across from him to godlike Hector,
borrowing the appearance and tireless voice of his brother
Deiphobus. She came up to Hector and spoke winged words:

'My dear brother, swift Achilles has certainly been pressing
230   you hard, chasing you at that speed round the town. Let's make
a stand and keep him off together.'

Great Hector of the flashing helmet replied to her:

'Deiphobus, you were always by far the closest of all the
brothers Hecabe and Priam gave me. But now I shall think even
better of you, since you had the courage, when you saw the

situation, to come outside the walls and help me, while all the rest stayed inside.'

The goddess grey-eyed Athene replied:

'Dear brother, our father and lady mother took my knees   240 and, one after the other, entreated me to stay where I was. My men were there and did the same – they are all in such terror of Achilles. But I was tormented by anxiety on your behalf. Now let's make a determined attack, straight at him, and no restraint with the spears! We'll soon find out   ATHENE whether Achilles is to kill the pair of us and go off   tricks *Hector* with our bloodstained armour to the hollow ships,   into fighting or himself be conquered by your spear.'

With these words Athene treacherously led him forward. When Hector and Achilles came within range of each other, great Hector of the flashing helmet spoke first:

'Achilles, I'm not going to run from you any more. I have   250 already been chased by you three times round Priam's great town without daring to stop and let you come near. But now I have made up my mind to fight you man to man and kill you or be killed.

'But let us call on the gods to witness an agreement: no compact could have better guarantors. If Zeus grants me staying-power and I kill you, I will not violently maltreat you. All I shall do, Achilles, is to strip you of your famous armour. Then I will give up your body to the Greeks. You do the same.'

Swift-footed Achilles gave him a black look and replied: 260

'Hector, I'm never going to forgive you. So don't talk to me about agreements. Lions don't come to   Achilles rejects terms with men, the wolf doesn't see eye to eye with   agreements the lamb – they are enemies to the end. It's the same   (7.76) with you and me. Friendship between us is impossible, and there will be no truce of any kind till one of us has fallen and glutted the shield-bearing god of battles with his blood.

'So summon up all the courage you possess. This is the time to show your bravery and ability as a fighter. Not that anything   270 is going to save you now, when Pallas Athene is waiting to bring you down with my spear. This moment you are going to pay the full price for all the sufferings of my companions you killed on your rampage with your spear.'

He spoke, balanced his long-shadowed spear and hurled it. But glorious Hector was on the lookout and avoided the bronze spear. He crouched, his eye on the weapon, and it flew over him and stuck in the ground. But Pallas Athene snatched it up and brought it back to Achilles without Hector shepherd of the people noticing. Hector spoke to the matchless son of Peleus:

280   'You missed! So, godlike Achilles, Zeus gave you the wrong date for my death after all! You thought you knew everything. But then you're so glib, so clever with your tongue – trying to frighten me and undermine my determination and courage. But you won't make me run and then hit me in the back with your spear. Drive it through my chest as I charge – if the god lets you. But first you will have to avoid this one of mine. May the whole length of it find a home in your body! This war would be an easier business for the Trojans if you, their greatest scourge, were dead.'

He spoke, balanced his long-shadowed spear and hurled it.
290   He hit the centre of Achilles' shield and did not miss, but the spear rebounded from it. Hector was frustrated that the swift spear had left his hand to no purpose and stood there dismayed, since he had no other one. He shouted aloud to Deiphobus of the white shield, asking him for a long spear. But Deiphobus was nowhere near him. Hector realized what had happened and said:

'It's over. So the gods did, after all, summon me to my death. I thought the warrior Deiphobus was at my side. But he is behind
300   the wall, and Athene has deceived me. Evil death is no longer

Hector understands ATHENE's trick

far away; it is staring me in the face and there is no escape. Zeus and his Archer son must long have been resolved on this, for all their earlier goodwill and help.

'So now my destiny confronts me. Let me at least sell my life dearly and not without glory, after some great deed for future generations to hear of.'

With these words Hector drew the sharp, long, heavy sword

hanging down at his side. He gathered himself and swooped like a high-flying eagle that drops to earth through black clouds to pounce on a tender lamb or cowering hare. So Hector   310 swooped, brandishing his sharp sword.

Achilles sprang to meet him, his heart filled with savage determination. He kept his chest covered with his fine, ornate shield; his glittering helmet with its four plates nodded, and above it danced the lovely plumes that Hephaestus had lavished on the crest. Like a star moving with others through the night, Hesperus, the loveliest star set in the skies – such was the gleam from his spear's sharp point as he weighed it in his right hand   320 with murder in his heart for godlike Hector, searching that handsome body for its most vulnerable spot.

Hector's body was completely covered by the fine bronze armour he had taken from great Patroclus when he killed him, except for the flesh that could be seen at the windpipe, where the collar bones hold the neck from the shoulders, the easiest place to kill a man. As Hector charged him, godlike Achilles drove at this spot with his spear, and the point went right through Hector's soft neck, though the heavy bronze head did not cut his windpipe and left him still able to speak. Hector crashed in the dust, and godlike   330 Achilles triumphed over him:

Achilles kills Hector (16.852)

'Hector, no doubt you imagined, as you stripped Patroclus, that you would be safe. You never thought of me: I was too far away. You innocent. Down by the hollow ships a man much better than Patroclus had been left behind. It was I, and I have brought you down. So now the dogs and birds of prey are going to mangle you foully, while we Greeks will give Patroclus full burial honours.'

Fading fast, Hector of the flashing helmet replied:

'I entreat you, by your knees, by your own life, and by your parents, do not throw my body to the dogs by the Greek ships but take a ransom for me. My father and my lady mother will   340 give you bronze and gold in plenty. Give up my body to be brought home, so that the Trojans and their wives can cremate it properly.'

Swift-footed Achilles gave him a black look and replied:

'You dog, don't entreat me by my knees or my parents. I only wish I could summon up the will to carve and eat you raw myself, for what you have done to me. But this at least is certain: nobody is going to keep the dogs off your head, not even if the Trojans bring here and weigh out a ransom ten or twenty times

350 your worth, and promise more besides; not even if Dardanian Priam tells them to offer your weight in gold – not even so shall your lady mother lay you on a bier to mourn the son she bore, but the dogs and birds of prey will divide you up, leaving nothing.'

Dying, Hector of the flashing helmet said:

'How well I know you and see you for what you are! Your heart is hard as iron. I have been wasting my breath. But reflect now before you act, in case angry gods remember how you treated me, on the day Paris and Phoebus Apollo bring you

360 down in all your greatness at the Scaean gate.'

As he spoke, the end that is death enveloped him. Life left his limbs and took wing for the house of Hades, bewailing its lot and the youth and the manhood it had left behind. But godlike Achilles spoke to him again, though he was gone:

'Die! As for my death, I will welcome it when Zeus and the other immortal gods wish it to be.'

He spoke, withdrew his bronze spear from the body and put it on one side. As he removed the bloodstained arms from Hector's shoulders, other Greeks came running up and gathered

370 round. They gazed in wonder at the stature and marvellous good looks of Hector. As each went in and stabbed the body, they looked at each other and said as one man:

'Well, well! Hector's certainly softer to handle now than when he set the ships on fire!'

So they spoke, as they stood by, stabbing him. After stripping Hector, swift-footed godlike Achilles stood up among the Greeks and spoke winged words:

Achilles drags Hector back to the city

'My friends, rulers and leaders of the Greeks, now that the gods have let us get the better of this man,

380 who did more damage than all the rest together, let's make a circuit of the town under arms and find out what the Trojans mean to do next, whether they will abandon their town now

that Hector is fallen, or make up their minds to hold it without his help . . .

'But why talk to myself like this? Lying by my ships is a dead man, unburied, unwept – Patroclus, whom I shall never forget as long as I am among the living and can walk the earth, my own dear comrade, whom I shall still remember even though 390 the dead forget their dead, even in Hades' halls. So come now, young Greeks, let us go back to the hollow ships carrying this body and singing a song of triumph. We have won great glory. We have killed godlike Hector, who was treated like a god in Ilium.'

He spoke and foully maltreated godlike Hector. He sliced into the tendons at the back of both his feet between the heel and ankle, inserted leather straps and tied them to his chariot, leaving the head to drag. Then he lifted his famous armour into the chariot, got in himself, and lashed the horses with the whip 400 to get them moving. The willing pair flew off. Dust rose from the body they dragged behind them; Hector's sable hair streamed out on either side and his whole head, so graceful once, lay in the dirt. Zeus now let his enemies disfigure him in the very own land of his fathers.

So his whole head was enveloped in the dust. When his mother saw her son, she tore her hair, hurled her bright head-dress far away and screamed aloud. His father groaned piteously, the people round them took up the cry of grief and the whole town gave itself up to despair. It was as if the whole of 410 frowning Ilium were smouldering from top to bottom. The stricken old man made for the Dardanian gate, determined on going out, and when the people only just managed to stop him, he grovelled in the dung and implored them all, calling on each man by name:

'Friends, hold off. I know your concern for me, but let me go out of the town alone to the Greek ships. I want to supplicate this inhuman monster, who may perhaps feel respect for my years and pity my old age. After all, he too has a father of the same age as 420 myself, Peleus, who gave him life and brought him up to be the scourge of all Trojans, though none of them has suffered at his

Priam and *Hecabe* lament

hands so much as I, the father of so many sons butchered by him in their prime.

'And yet, though I weep for them all, there is one I mourn still more with a bitter sorrow that will bring me to the grave – Hector. If only he could have died in my arms! Then we could have wept and lamented for him to our hearts' content, I and the mother who brought him, to her sorrow, into the world.'

So he spoke in tears, and the people took up the cry. Now
430   Hecabe led the Trojan women in a shrill lament:

'My child! Ah, misery me! Why should I live and suffer now you are dead? Night and day in Ilium you were the answer to my prayers, and to every man and woman in the town a dream come true, a man they greeted like a god. You were their greatest glory while you lived. Now death and destiny have claimed you.'

So Hecabe spoke in tears. But Hector's wife Andromache had not yet heard the news. No reliable messenger had in fact gone
440   to tell her that her husband had remained outside the gates. She
Andromache was at work in a corner of her lofty house on a web
senses Hec- of purple cloth to be folded double, and weaving
tor's death flowers into it. She had just called to the lovely-haired
waiting-women in her house to put a large cauldron
on the fire so that Hector could have a hot bath when he came home from the battle – the innocent. She never dreamed that, far away from any baths, grey-eyed Athene had killed him at Achilles' hands.

But now the grief and lamentation at the battlements reached her ears. A tremor went through her and she dropped the shuttle on the floor. She called again to her waiting-women:
450   'Come with me, two of you: I must see what has happened. That was my husband's mother I heard, and she is a reticent woman. My heart is in my mouth: I am paralysed with fear. Some disaster is threatening the house of Priam. May I never hear such news, but I am terrified that godlike Achilles has caught my daring Hector by himself outside the town and chased him out over the plain; indeed, that he has already put an end to that fatal overconfidence of his. Because Hector would never

hang back with the crowd – he always advanced far ahead of the rest, second to none in his courage.'

With these words Andromache, with palpitating heart, rushed   460
out of the house like a mad woman, and her waiting-women went with her. When she came to the tower where the men had gathered in a crowd, she stood on the wall, searched the plain and saw her husband being dragged off in front of the town and the swift horses hauling him unceremoniously away towards the Greek ships.

Black night came down and engulfed Andro-   *Andromache*'s
mache's eyes. She crashed backwards, fainting. The   lament
bright head-dress flew far from her head, with the   (6.407 ff.)
headband, the cap, the woven braids and headscarf
that golden Aphrodite had given her on the day when Hector of   470
the flashing helmet, after giving an untold bride-price, came to fetch her from her father Eëtion's house. Her husband's sisters and his brothers' wives crowded round and supported her between them; she was distraught to the point of death. When at length she recovered and came to herself, she burst out sobbing and said to the Trojan women:

'Hector, what unhappiness is mine! So you and I were born under the same star, you here in Priam's house and I in Thebe under the woods of Mount Placus in the house of Eëtion, who   480
brought me up from childhood, the ill-fated father of a more ill-fated child. He should never have fathered me! For you are on your way to Hades under the depths of the earth, leaving me behind in hateful misery, a widow in your house. And your son is no more than a baby, the son we got between us, we unhappy parents. You will be no joy to him, Hector, now you are dead, nor he to you.

'Even if he survives this war with all its tears, nothing remains for him but hardship and distress. Others will take over his lands. An orphaned child is cut off from his friends. He goes   490
about with downcast eyes and tear-stained cheeks. Need drives him to his father's acquaintances, and he tugs a cloak here and a tunic there till someone out of pity holds up a wine-cup briefly to his mouth, just enough to wet his lips but not to drink. Then comes another boy, with both his parents living, who drives him

from the feast, punching him and jeering at him: "Go on, get out! You've got no father dining here!" So the child runs off in tears to his widowed mother – the little Astyanax, who used to sit on his father's knees and eat nothing but marrow and mutton fat and, when he was drowsy and tired of play, slept in his bed, softly cradled in his nurse's arms, heart full of contentment. But now with his father gone, suffering will be the lot of Astyanax, "Town-lord", as the Trojans called him, seeing in you, Hector, the one defence of their long walls and gates.

'And you, by the beaked ships, far from your parents, naked, will be eaten by the wriggling worms when the dogs have had their fill. Yet delicate and lovely clothing made by women's hands is still stored at home. I am going to burn it all in the consuming fire. It is of no use to you: you will never even be buried in it. But the men and women of Troy will do that for you as their last mark of honour.'

So she spoke in tears, and the women took up the cry.

23

THE FUNERAL AND
THE GAMES

1–108: The Greeks withdraw to their ships. Patroclus is mourned, and his ghost visits Achilles in his sleep [night before 28th day].

109–257: [28th day] Firewood is collected, and Patroclus' body taken in funeral procession. Achilles dedicates a lock of his own hair, and the pyre is lit. *APHRODITE* and *APOLLO* preserve *Hector*'s body. Winds are summoned to prevent the pyre going out, and [29th day] Patroclus' bones are gathered and placed temporarily in a golden vessel, awaiting Achilles' death.

257–652: Achilles seats the army in readiness for Patroclus' funeral games. The chariot race is first up: Nestor exhorts his son Antilochus 262–361, the race includes Eumelus' crash and Antilochus' sharp manoeuvre against Menelaus 362–447, Diomedes' victory and the dispute between Antilochus and Menelaus 499–652.

653–99: The boxing: Epeius knocks out Euryalus.

700–39: The wrestling: Ajax son of Telamon and Odysseus fight a draw.

740–97: The foot-race: *ATHENE* helps Odysseus beat Ajax son of Oïleus.

798–825: Armed combat: Ajax son of Telamon and Diomedes fight a draw.

826–97: Throwing the lump of metal; archery; and spear, in which Achilles gives the prize uncontested to Agamemnon.

While the Trojans took up the cry across the town, the Greeks withdrew to their ships by the Hellespont and then dispersed, each man to his own ship. The Myrmidons alone were not dismissed. Achilles kept his war-loving companions with him and addressed them:

'Myrmidons with your swift horses, faithful companions, we will not unyoke our horses from their chariots yet but, mounted as we are, will drive them past Patroclus and mourn for him. That is the honour due to the dead. Then, when we have drawn some comfort from our bitter tears, we will unyoke the horses and eat together here.'

[Night 27]
Funeral feast
for Patroclus

So he spoke, and the Myrmidons all broke into lamentation together. Achilles led them, and three times, in tears, they drove their lovely-maned horses round the dead, while Thetis stirred in them all the desire to weep. The sands were wet with tears, their armour was wet with tears: so great a master of the rout had they lost. Now the son of Peleus, laying his man-slaying hands on his companion's chest, led them in the loud dirge:

'Farewell and rejoice, Patroclus, even in the halls of Hades. I am now keeping all the promises I made you: I have dragged Hector's body here for the dogs to eat raw; and at your pyre I am going to cut the throats of a dozen splendid sons of Troy to vent my anger at your death.'

He spoke and foully maltreated godlike Hector, flinging him down on his face in the dust by Patroclus' bier. His warriors then took off their gleaming bronze armour, unyoked their proud, snorting horses and sat down in their multitudes by the ship of swift-footed Achilles, who had provided for them a magnificent funeral feast. Many a white ox fell bellowing to the iron knife, many a sheep and bleating goat was slaughtered and many a fine fat hog with gleaming tusks was stretched across the flames to have its bristles singed. Blood in cupfuls was poured all around the body.

Meanwhile lord Achilles, swift-footed son of Peleus, was taken by the Greek leaders to godlike Agamemnon, though it had been hard to persuade him, still enraged as he was for his companion. When they reached Agamemnon's hut, they told the clear-voiced heralds to stand a great three-legged cauldron over the fire in the hope of inducing Achilles to wash the congealed blood from his body. But he blankly refused and swore a great oath as well:

'By Zeus highest and best of the gods, never shall I permit any water to come near me till I have cremated Patroclus, made him a grave-mound and shorn my hair, since however long I live I shall never suffer again as I am suffering now.

'But for the moment, though I hate the thought of food, we have to eat. And at dawn, Agamemnon lord of men, order wood 50
to be collected and everything to be provided that a dead man ought to have with him when he travels under the western gloom, so that Patroclus can be consumed by the unflagging fire as soon as possible and the men return to their duties when he is gone.'

So he spoke, and they heard and complied. They hurriedly prepared the food and ate it, and no one went without a fair share. Their hunger and thirst satisfied, they returned, each to his hut, to sleep. But the son of Peleus, groaning heavily, lay 60
down on the shore of the sounding sea among his many Myrmidons, in an open space where the waves were surging on to the beach. His splendid limbs were exhausted from chasing Hector towards windswept Ilium; but no sooner had he fallen into sleep's sweet embrace, resolving all his cares, than he was visited by the ghost of poor Patroclus, looking and talking exactly like the man himself, with the same stature, the same lovely eyes and the same clothes as those he used to wear. It stood over his head and said:

'You are asleep: you have forgotten me, Achilles. You did not 70
neglect me in life; you do in death. Bury me as quickly as possible and let me pass the gates of Hades. I am *Patroclus in*
kept out by the spirits, the images of the dead, who *Achilles'*
refuse to let me cross the river and join them, but *dream*
leave me to wander forlornly up and down on this side of Hades' halls with its wide gates. And give me your hand, I beg you; for once you have passed me through the flames, I shall never come back again from Hades. Never again in life will you and I sit down together out of earshot of our men to scheme our schemes. For I have been swallowed up by the dreadful doom that must

80   have been my lot from birth; and it is your destiny too, godlike
     Achilles, to perish under the rich Trojans' walls.

     'Something else now, one more request. Do not let them bury
     my bones apart from yours, Achilles. Let them lie together, just
     as you and I grew up together in your house, after my father
     Menoetius brought me there as a child from Opous because of
     the disastrous homicide I committed when I killed Amphidamas'
     son by accident in a childish quarrel over a game of knuckle-
     bones. The charioteer Peleus welcomed me to his palace,
90   brought me up with loving care and appointed me to be your
     attendant. So let the one container, the golden two-handled
     vessel your lady mother gave you, hold our bones.'

     Swift-footed Achilles replied to him and said:

     'Dearest Patroclus, why did you come and make these requests
     of me? Of course I will see to everything and do exactly as you
     command. But come nearer to me now, so that we can hold
     each other in our arms, if only for a moment, and draw some
     comfort from our bitter tears.'

     With these words he held out his arms, but embraced nothing.
100 Like smoke the spirit vanished underground, gibbering. Achilles
     was amazed and sprang to his feet. He beat his hands together
     and in his desolation cried:

     'So it is true! Something of us does survive in Hades' halls,
     some spirit and image of a man, but without real existence, since
     all night long the spirit of poor Patroclus has been standing at
     my side, weeping and wailing. It told me what to do and looked
     marvellously like him.'

     So he spoke and stirred in them all the desire to weep; and
     rosy-fingered Dawn found them still in tears around the pitiable
     dead.

110   Meanwhile Lord Agamemnon sent mules and men from
                         every part of the camp to fetch wood. Noble
     [Day 28]   Meriones, amiable Idomeneus' attendant, took
     Wood is   charge. The men carried woodsmen's axes in their
     gathered   hands together with well-woven ropes, and the mules
     walked ahead of them. Uphill and downhill, crossing and zig-
     zagging, they came at last to the spurs of Mount Ida with its
     many springs. There they set to work with a will, felling the tall

oaks with their long-bladed axes, and trees came crashing down.   120
The Greeks split the logs and then roped them to the mules,
which furrowed up the ground with their hooves in their eager-
ness to get down to the plain through the tangled undergrowth.
The woodcutters too all carried logs, by orders of Meriones,
amiable Idomeneus' attendant. When they reached the shore,
they laid them down in rows at the spot where Achilles planned
to build a great grave-mound for Patroclus – and himself.

Having stacked this huge supply of wood all round the site,
they sat down and waited there all together. Achilles then gave
orders for his war-loving Myrmidons to put on their bronze
armour and every charioteer to yoke his horses. They hurried   130
off and got into their armour, and the fighting men and chario-
teers mounted their chariots. The charioteers led off and after
them came a cloud of infantry one could not count. In the middle
of the procession Patroclus was carried by his companions,
clothing his body with the locks of their hair that they cut off
and placed on it. Behind them godlike Achilles supported the
head, grieving. He was dispatching his matchless companion to
Hades' halls.

When they reached the place appointed for them by Achilles,
they put Patroclus down and quickly built up a sufficient quan-
tity of wood. But then swift-footed godlike Achilles had an   140
idea. Stepping back from the pyre, he cut from his
head an auburn lock he had allowed to grow ever   Preparing the
since its dedication to the River Spercheus back at   pyre (18.336,
home. Angrily he spoke, looking out over the wine-   21.27)
dark sea:

'Spercheus, there was no point in my father Peleus praying to
you and promising that, on my home-coming from Troy, I
should cut off this lock for you and make you a holy offering of
fifty rams, sacrificed by your very waters where you have a
precinct and smoking altar. That was my old father's prayer;
but you have denied him what he prayed for. So now, since I
shall never see the dear land of my fathers again, I will give this   150
lock to the warrior Patroclus to take with him instead.'

With these words he placed the lock in the hands of his
beloved companion and stirred in them all the desire to weep.

Sunset would have found them still lamenting, if Achilles had not quickly gone up to Agamemnon and said:

'Agamemnon son of Atreus, you are the man the troops will listen to. Of course they can mourn as much as they wish; but for the moment, dismiss the men from the pyre and tell them to prepare food. We who are the chief mourners will see
160 to everything here, but I should like the Greek commanders to remain.'

When Agamemnon lord of men heard this, he dismissed the troops to their ships; but the mourners stayed where they were and piled up the wood. They made a pyre thirty metres in length and breadth and with sorrowful hearts laid the body on top. At the foot of the pyre they skinned and prepared many fat sheep and shambling cattle with crooked horns. Great-hearted Achilles, taking fat from all of them, covered Patroclus' body with it from head to foot and then piled up the flayed carcasses round the body.

170 Then, to accompany the spirit on its journey, he added two-handled jars filled with honey and oil, propping them up against the bier; and impetuously threw four high-necked horses on to the pyre, groaning aloud as he did so. Lord Patroclus had kept nine dogs as pets. Achilles slit the throats of two of these and threw them on the pyre as well. He carried out his murderous plan for the twelve noble sons of great-hearted Trojans and put them to the sword, and then unleashed fire's pitiless might to devour everything. This done, he gave a groan and called on his beloved companion:

'Farewell and rejoice, Patroclus, even in the halls of Hades. I
180 am now keeping all the promises I made you. Twelve noble sons of great-hearted Trojans will be consumed by the same fire as you. For Hector son of Priam I have other plans – I will not give him to the flames: I will throw him to the dogs to eat.'

So, defiantly, he spoke, but the dogs never did swarm round Hector's corpse. Day and night Zeus' daughter Aphrodite kept them off; and she anointed the body with ambrosial oil of roses, so that Achilles should not lacerate it when he dragged Hector up and down. Moreover, Phoebus Apollo caused a dark cloud
190 to sink from the sky and settle on the body, covering the whole

area in which it lay, so that the heat of the sun should not wither the skin on his sinews and limbs too soon.

Patroclus' pyre then refused to catch. But swift-footed godlike Achilles had an idea. Standing clear of the pyre, he prayed and promised magnificent sacrifices to the two winds, Boreas from the north and Zephyr from the west. He poured many a libation from a golden cup and implored them to come, so that the wood might start to burn and the bodies quickly be cremated. Iris heard his prayers and sped off to convey his message to the winds, who were all feasting together at a banquet in Zephyr's draughty house. Iris came running up and stood on their stone threshold. When they saw her, they all leapt to their feet and each invited her to come and sit beside him. But she refused their offers and said:

Achilles summons the winds

200

'I have no time to sit down. I must get back to Ocean's Streams and the Ethiopians' land, where they are entertaining the immortals at a sacrificial banquet I am anxious not to miss. But Achilles is praying to you, Boreas and roaring Zephyr, and promising you magnificent sacrifices if you will come and light the pyre under the body of Patroclus, for whom the whole Greek army is mourning.'

210

With these words Iris left, and the two winds rose with a terrifying roar, driving the clouds before them. In a moment they were out at sea, blowing hard and raising the waves with their shrill blasts. When they came to the fertile land of Troy, they fell upon the funeral pyre, and the fire blazed up with a terrific roar. Howling round the pyre, they helped each other all night long to fan the flames; and all night long swift Achilles, using a two-handled cup with which he drew wine off from a golden mixing-bowl, poured out libations, drenched the earth with wine and called on the spirit of poor Patroclus. As a father weeps when he is burning the bones of a son who has died newly married and left his poor parents inconsolable, so Achilles wept as he burned his companion's bones, dragging himself around the pyre with many a deep groan.

220

At the time when the morning star comes up to herald a new day on earth and saffron-robed Dawn spreads over the sea, then the fire sank low, the flames expired and the winds set out for

230   home across the Thracian sea, whipping up its waves and making
it roar. Achilles was exhausted. Turning from the pyre
he sank to the ground and sweet sleep overwhelmed
him. But the other commanders under lord Agamem-
non now gathered round him. Woken by their voices
and footsteps, he sat up, got to his feet and spoke his mind:

[Day 29]
Patroclus'
bones saved

'Agamemnon and you other leaders of the Greeks forces, first
use sparkling wine to put out whatever is still burning. Then we
240   must collect Patroclus' bones, being careful to distinguish them,
though that will not be difficult: he was placed in the centre of
the pyre, separate from the rest, who were burnt round the edge
of it, horses and men together. Then we must wrap the bones in
a fold of fat for protection and put them in a golden vase against
the time when I myself shall have vanished to the world below.
As for his grave-mound, I ask you not to construct a very large
one, but just something moderate. Later you can build a great,
tall one, you Greeks that are left in your many-benched ships,
when I am gone.'

So he spoke, and they did as Achilles had directed. First they
250   put out with sparkling wine whatever was still burning, and the
deep ash fell in. Then, weeping, they collected the white bones
of their gentle companion in a golden vessel and wrapped them
in a fold of fat, laid the vessel in his hut and covered it with a
fine linen cloth. For his grave mound they drew a circle round
the pyre and set round it a base of stones. Then they fetched
earth and piled it up over it.

When the troops had built the monument, they
prepared to leave. But Achilles stopped them and
made the whole assembly sit down for Patroclus'
funeral games. For these he brought out prizes from
the ships – cauldrons and tripods; horses, mules and
260   fine head of cattle; grey iron and well-girdled women.

Funeral games
for Patroclus:
chariot-race
(5.265, 323)

The first event was a chariot-race, for which he laid out the
following splendid prizes: for the winner, a woman skilled in
arts and crafts and a tripod with handles holding twenty-two
measures; for the runner-up, a mare six years old and not broken
in, with a little mule in her womb; for third, a fine cauldron

holding four measures, untarnished by the flames and still as bright as ever; for fourth, two talents of gold; and for fifth, a two-handled pan as yet untouched by fire. Achilles stood up and addressed the Greeks:

'Agamemnon and you other Greek men-at-arms, these are the prizes that await the charioteers in this contest. Of course, if we Greeks were competing in honour of some other man, I would walk off to my hut with the first prize: you don't need me to tell you how vastly superior my horses are, being immortal and a present from Poseidon to my father Peleus who passed them on to me. But I and my horses will not compete: they have lost so great and glorious a charioteer. How kind Patroclus was to them, always washing them down with clean water and grooming their manes with olive-oil! No wonder they stand there and grieve for him. Their manes trail on the ground and in their sorrow they refuse to move. However, any other Greek in the whole army who believes in his horses and finely built chariot should come forward.'

So spoke Achilles son of Peleus, and the swift charioteers quickly formed a group. The first to spring to his feet was Admetus' son Eumelus lord of men, who was an excellent horseman. Next, mighty Diomedes son of Tydeus, who yoked the horses of the breed of Tros that he had taken earlier from Aeneas on the occasion when Apollo saved Aeneas' life. Then auburn-haired Olympian-born Menelaus son of Atreus, who yoked a fast pair, Aethe a mare of Agamemnon's and his own horse Podargus. Aethe had been presented to Agamemnon by Echepolus son of Anchises, on condition that he need not go with him to windswept Ilium but could stay at home in comfort – Zeus had given him great wealth, and he lived in spacious Sicyon. This was the mare that Menelaus yoked – she was champing to be off. The fourth man to harness his lovely-maned horses was Antilochus. He was the glorious son of great-hearted lord Nestor son of Neleus, and his chariot-horses had been bred at home in Pylos. His father Nestor now went up to him and spoke to him with the very best of intentions, though Antilochus knew his business well enough himself:

'Antilochus, young as you are, Zeus and Poseidon

are on your side and they have taught you all the
skills of driving horses. So there is no great need for
me to teach you any more. But expert as you are at cornering

310 round the turning-post, your horses are very slow, and therefore
I expect the worst. Yet even if the other pairs are faster, their
drivers do not have the judgement that you do. So you must
rely, my dear son, on the judgement you can bring to bear, if
you do not wish to say goodbye to the prizes. It is judgement
rather than muscle that makes the best wood-cutter. Judgement,
again, enables a steersman to keep a straight course over the
wine-dark sea when his ship is being buffeted by the wind. And
it is by judgement that one charioteer beats another. The man
who stupidly leaves too much to his chariot and pair does not

320 take the correct line at the turn; his horses wander, and he does
not keep them tucked in. But the intelligent charioteer, though
behind a slower pair, always has his eye on the post and turns
tightly round it; he knows the right time to use the oxhide reins
and give his horses their head; he keeps them firmly in hand and
watches the man in front.

'Now let me tell you something to look out for. It is obvious
enough; you cannot miss it. There is a dead tree-stump, an oak
or pine, standing nearly two metres high. It has not rotted in the
rain and is flanked by two white stones. The track narrows at

330 this point, but the going is good on either side of this monument,
which either marks an ancient burial or must have been put up
as a turning-post by people of an earlier age. In any case, it
is the mark swift-footed godlike Achilles has chosen as the
turning-post for this race. As you drive round it, keep your team
close to it and lean in your chariot just a little to the left yourself.
Call on your outside horse, touch him with the whip and give
him rein; but make the inside horse hug the post close enough

340 almost to scrape it with the hub of your wheel. But avoid
touching the stone, or you may injure the horses and wreck the
chariot, which would delight the rest but not stand to your
credit.

'So use your wits, my dear son, and be on the alert; for if you

could overtake them at the turning-post, no one could catch
you up or pass you with a sudden burst, not even if he were
coming up behind you with Adrestus' swift horse, the divine
Arion who was sired by a god, or the horses of Laomedon, the
best that Troy has bred.'

With these words Nestor son of Neleus went back to his seat
after he had explained the essential points to his son.   350

Meriones was the fifth to get his lovely-maned horses ready.
And now they all mounted their chariots and threw their lots
into a helmet, which Achilles shook. The first lot to jump out
was that of Antilochus son of Nestor; then came that of lord
Eumelus, followed by that of Atreus' son the great spearman
Menelaus. Meriones drew the fourth starting-place, and the last
fell to Diomedes, the best charioteer of them all. They drew up
side by side and Achilles pointed out the turning-post, far away
on level ground. He had posted godlike Phoenix, his father's   360
attendant, as the umpire there, to keep an eye on the running
and report what happened.

At one and the same moment they all gave their horses the
whip, shook the reins on their backs and set them going with a
sharp word of command. The horses raced at speed across the
plain and soon left the ships behind. The dust that rose from
underneath their chests hung in the air like a storm-cloud or a
fog, and their manes streamed back in the wind. At one moment
the chariots were in contact with the bountiful earth and at the
next bounding high in the air. The drivers stood up in their   370
chariots, and every man's heart was pounding with desire for
victory. They each yelled at their horses, who flew along in a
cloud of dust.

But it was not till their speedy teams were on the
final stretch heading back to the grey sea that each
man showed his true ability and forced the pace.
The fast mares of Eumelus now surged ahead, but
Diomedes' stallions of the breed of Tros stayed close
behind, and there was very little in it. They looked as though at
any moment they might leap into Eumelus' chariot. They were   380
flying along with their heads just over him, warming his back

ATHENE
helps Diomedes
and wrecks
Eumelus

and broad shoulders with their breath. In fact, Diomedes would
have overhauled Eumelus then and there or made it a dead heat,
if Phoebus Apollo, who was still angry with Tydeus' son, had not
knocked the shining whip out of his hand. Tears of frustration
poured down Diomedes' face as he saw Eumelus' mares pulling
away and his own horses slowing down in the absence of the
whip.

But Apollo did not get away with it: Athene spotted him
foiling Diomedes. She sped after that shepherd of the people,
390 gave him back his whip and put fresh spirit in his horses. In her
fury she chased after Eumelus too and used her powers as a
goddess to smash the yoke of his chariot, with the result that
his mares ran free, off on their own, and the shaft slipped to the
ground, while Eumelus himself was flung out of the chariot and
came down by the wheel. The skin was ripped off his elbows,
mouth and nose; his forehead was bruised; his eyes filled with
tears and any words stuck in his throat. Meanwhile Diomedes
swept round the wreckage with his horses, having left the others
400 well behind. Athene filled his pair with strength and ensured his
victory.

Next after Diomedes came auburn-haired Menelaus, Atreus'
son; and next again Antilochus, who was shouting at his father's
horses:

'Run on, you two! Give it everything, now! I'm not asking
you to catch that pair ahead, warlike Diomedes' horses. Athene
has just given them a new turn of speed and won him the glory.
But catch Menelaus' pair and don't get left behind by them.
Quick! Or the horse Aethe will pour scorn all over you – and
she a mare! Why are you hanging back, my fine horses? I tell
410 you bluntly and I mean it – no more of Nestor's tender loving
care for you! He'll slit your throats without a moment's hesita-
tion if you take it easy and leave us with a smaller prize. So get
after them! Come on! Flat out! Trust me to find some way of
slipping past Menelaus where the track is narrow. I shan't miss
my chance.'

So he spoke, and his horses, taking their master's threat to
heart, put on speed for a while.

Very soon, warlike Antilochus saw a place where the sunken track grew narrow. It ran through a gully: water piled up by the winter rains had carried part of it away and deepened the whole pass. Menelaus was picking a course through it, making it difficult for anyone to come alongside. But Antilochus steered off the track altogether and gave chase along a slight diversion. Menelaus was alarmed and shouted at him:

Antilochus 'carves up' Menelaus

'Antilochus, this is stupid driving! Slow down! The track's narrow here. There will soon be more room to pass. Watch out you don't hit my chariot and wreck us both.'

So he spoke, but Antilochus, pretending he had not heard him, laid it on with the whip and drove faster than ever. They both ran on for about the distance a discus will carry when a young man releases it with a swing of the arm to test his strength. Then Menelaus' pair gave way and fell back. He eased the pace himself on purpose, fearing the horses might collide on the track and tip over the light chariots, in which case their masters, through their eagerness to win, would find themselves rolling about in the dust. Auburn-haired Menelaus shouted abuse at him and said:

'Antilochus, you're the most appalling driver in the world! Go to hell! We Greeks were mistaken to think you had any sense. You won't carry off the prize till you've answered on oath for this affair.'

With these words Menelaus called out to his horses:

'No holding back! Don't stand there feeling sorry for yourselves! That pair ahead of you will tire in the leg far sooner than you. They are neither of them as young as they were.'

So he spoke, and his horses, taking their master's orders to heart, ran on more strongly and soon closed the gap on the other pair.

Meanwhile from their positions in the crowd the Greeks were looking out for the horses as they flew along in a cloud of dust. Idomeneus leader of the Cretans was the first to see them. He was sitting well above the rest on high ground outside the crowd, and when he heard a charioteer urging on his horses in the distance, he knew the voice even from there. He also recognized one of the leading horses, which showed up well, being chestnut all over except for a round white patch like the full moon which it had on its forehead. Idomeneus stood up and called to the Greeks:

'My friends, rulers and leaders of the Greeks, am I the only one who can see the horses, or do you see them too? It seems to me a new pair are leading and the driver also looks different. Eumelus' mares, who were ahead on the outward lap, must
460 have come to grief out there on the plain: I certainly saw them leading at the turning-post and now I can't see them anywhere, though I've searched the whole Trojan plain. Perhaps Eumelus dropped his reins, could not hold his horses round the post and failed to complete the turn. Yes, that's where he must have taken a fall and crashed his chariot, while his mares swerved off the track, panicked and bolted. But do get up and have a look for your-
470 selves. I can't be quite sure, but the leading man looks like an Aetolian to me, yes, one of our Greek leaders, the son of horse-taming Tydeus, mighty Diomedes!'

Idomeneus and Ajax argue about the leader

Swift Ajax son of Oïleus contradicted him rudely:

'Idomeneus, why have you always been such a loud-mouth? Those high-stepping mares out there have a long way to go yet. And you aren't by any means the youngest man among us and you don't have the sharpest pair of eyes in your head either. Yet there you are, mouthing off as usual. There is absolutely no need for it. There are many better men here. That pair in front
480 is the same that led before, Eumelus' mares. And there's Eumelus in the chariot, reins in his hands.'

The leader of the Cretans was furious and replied:

'Ajax, master of the insult and so stupid, you've no equal in the army for sheer pig-headedness. Come on, let's have a bet – a tripod or a cauldron – about the leading pair, and make Agamemnon our referee. You'll learn the truth when you pay up.'

So he spoke, and swift Ajax son of Oïleus rose in fury to
490 retaliate with abuse. And the quarrel would have gone further still, if Achilles himself had not leapt to his feet and spoken:

'Ajax and Idomeneus, stop quarrelling and exchanging these disgraceful insults. It's not right. You would be the first to condemn anyone else who did it. Sit down in the crowd and keep your eyes on the horses. They'll soon be coming along, flat out for victory. Then each of you can recognize them for himself, and who's first and second.'

So he spoke, and Diomedes was by now very close. He was driving with the whip, swinging his arm right back for every lash. His horses stepped high, speeding over the ground. Showers of dust fell on the driver all the time and, as the fast pair flew over the ground, the gold- and tin-plated chariot came spinning after them and scarcely left a tyre-mark on the fine dust behind.

Diomedes drew up in the middle of the gathering, sweat pouring to the ground from his horses' necks and chests. He leapt down from his glittering chariot and leant his whip against the yoke. Mighty Sthenelus his attendant did not stand on ceremony but promptly took possession of the prizes, giving the tripod with the handles to his exultant men and telling them to lead the woman off. Then he unyoked the horses.

As he did so, Antilochus son of Nestor came in next. He had beaten Menelaus not by any turn of speed but by his clever manoeuvre. Yet even so Menelaus and his horses came in close behind. Picture the space that separates a horse from the wheel of a chariot when it is straining at the yoke and pulling its master over the plain; the tip of its tail keeps brushing the wheel-rim and as the wheel spins there is hardly any gap between them, however far the horse runs over the flat. There was no more than that between Menelaus and matchless Antilochus. It is true that, at the time of the incident, Menelaus had been left as much as a discus-throw behind. But he quickly made up the ground: Aethe – she was Agamemnon's lovely mare – had begun to show what she was made of, and in a longer race Menelaus would have overtaken Antilochus. There would have been no dispute about it.

Meriones, Idomeneus' brave attendant, came in a spear-throw behind famous Menelaus. His lovely-maned horses were the slowest pair in the race and he himself the least able driver. The

500

Diomedes wins, Antilochus second

510

520

530

last of them all to arrive was Admetus' son Eumelus. He was
dragging his handsome chariot himself and driving his horses
on in front of him. When he saw this, swift-footed godlike
Achilles was sorry for the man. He stood up among the Greeks
and spoke winged words:

'The best driver of the lot has come in last! Let's give him a
prize, as he deserves. Make it second, since Diomedes, of course,
takes first.'

So he spoke, and everyone applauded the idea. Then Achilles,
540 encouraged by the Greeks' applause, would have given the mare
to Eumelus, if Antilochus son of great-hearted Nestor had not
leapt up in front of him with an objection:

Second prize:
the dispute
(21.183)

'Achilles, I shall be extremely angry if you do as
you suggest. You are proposing to rob me of my prize
because Eumelus' chariot and horses came to grief –
as did Eumelus himself, excellent charioteer though
he is. The fact is that he ought to have prayed to the immortal
gods; then he would never have come in last in the race.

'However, if you are sorry for the man and sympathetic to
him, there is plenty of gold in your hut, and bronze and sheep,
550 and you have female slaves too and horses. Choose something
out of these later on and give him an even larger prize than
mine. Or hand it to him here and now and hear the troops
applaud you. But I will not give up this mare. Anyone who
wants to try can come and fight me for her with his fists.'

So he spoke, and swift-footed godlike Achilles smiled. He had
always liked his comrade-in-arms Antilochus and was delighted
with him now. He replied and spoke winged words:

'Antilochus, if you are telling me to find an extra prize from
my store for Eumelus, I will do so. I will give him the body-
560 armour I took from Asteropaeus. It is made of bronze, decorated
with a bright tin overlay all round. It will be worth a great deal
to him.'

He spoke and told his companion Automedon to fetch the
body-armour from his hut. Automedon went and brought it to
him; and Achilles handed it to Eumelus, who was delighted to
have it.

Now Menelaus got to his feet. He had by no means forgiven

Antilochus and was in an ugly mood. A herald handed him the speaker's staff and called for silence. Then Menelaus, a godlike man, spoke up:

'Antilochus, you used to be a very sensible fellow. Now see what you have done. By cutting in across me with your much slower pair, you have humiliated me and everything I stand for, and robbed my horses of a win. Rulers and leaders of the Greeks, come, judge between the two of us impartially, without favour to either side, so that none of our warriors will be able to say: "It was only by lying that Menelaus beat Antilochus and walked off with the mare. His horses really were much slower. It's his rank and power that bring him out on top."

'No, on second thoughts, I will settle the matter myself. And I am not afraid any Greek will criticize me for it: it will be a straight deal. Olympian-born Antilochus, come forward here, as convention dictates; stand in front of your chariot and pair, holding the slender whip you earlier drove with; touch your horses; and swear in the name of Poseidon, the earthshaker who encircles the world, that you did not obstruct my chariot with a deliberate foul.'

Sensible Antilochus replied:

'Hold on, now! I am a much younger man than you, lord Menelaus, and you, my elder and better, know well enough how a young man can go too far. He thinks faster, but his judgement is not so sound. So bear with me. I myself will give you the mare I won. Moreover, should you ask for something better from my store, I would rather give it to you at once than for ever fall out of your favour, Olympian-born Menelaus, and be at fault in the eyes of the gods.'

Great-hearted Nestor's son spoke, led the mare over and handed her to Menelaus, whose heart was warmed like the dew that hangs on ears of corn when the fields bristle with a ripening crop. So, Menelaus, was your heart warmed. Menelaus addressed him and spoke winged words:

'Antilochus, it is my turn to yield: I cannot be angry with you now. You have never been impulsive or foolish before, though this was certainly a case where the high spirits of youth got the

570

580

Agreement is reached

590

600

better of discretion. But another time be careful not to play
tricks on your betters. No other Greek would have found me so
easy to placate. But you have endured a lot and worked hard on
my behalf, and so have your excellent father and your brother
Thrasymedes. I therefore accept your apology. And not only
that, I will give you the mare, though she is mine, to show our
countrymen here I'm not arrogant or inflexible.'

He spoke and handed over the mare to Noemon, one of
Antilochus' men, to lead away, and himself took the gleaming
cauldron. Meriones, who had come in fourth, took the two
talents of gold. The fifth prize, the two-handled pan, remained
unclaimed. Achilles gave this to Nestor. He carried it across the
gathering to him, stood by him and said:

'Here, venerable sir, is a keepsake for yourself. Let it remind
you of Patroclus' funeral, for you will not see the man himself
among us any more. I am giving you the prize just like that,
since you will not be boxing or wrestling or entering for the
foot-race or javelin. Your years sit too heavily on you for that.'

With these words Achilles put the prize in Nestor's
hands. Nestor was delighted to receive it and
addressed him and spoke winged words:

'Yes, my boy, you are quite right in all you say.
My knees are gone, I am not so steady on my feet, dear friend,
and I cannot throw rights and lefts as quickly as I used to.

'Ah, if only I were still as young, and with all my powers
intact, as I was when the Eleans buried lord Amarynceus at
Buprasion, and his sons held funeral games in his honour. There
was not a man to match me there, from Elis, Pylos or proud
Aetolia. In the boxing I beat Clytomedes son of Enops, and in
the wrestling Ancaeus from Pleuron. Over distance, I defeated
Iphiclus, who was a fine athlete; and in the javelin I out-threw
Phyleus and Polydorus too. It was only in the chariot-race I
was beaten, by the two Moliones who used their two-to-one
advantage to get in front. They begrudged me the victory,
because the biggest prizes were reserved for this contest. They
were twins, you see. All the way from start to finish, yes, all the
way, one of them did the driving and the other wielded the
whip.

Prize-winner
Nestor tells a
story

'That's the kind of man I was. But now I must leave this sort of thing to younger men and take the painful lessons of old age to heart. But at that time I stood in a class by myself. Well, get on with honouring your companion in these funeral games. Meanwhile I accept your gift with pleasure. I am delighted you always realize how well disposed I am to you, and never pass up the chance of paying me the respect I am rightly owed among the Greeks. May the gods reward you fully for what you have done.' 650

So he spoke, and after he had heard all that Nestor had to say by way of thanks, Achilles made his way through the great gathering of Greeks and brought out the prizes for the boxing, a dangerous sport. For the victor he fetched and tethered in the crowd a hard-working mule, a female six years old and broken in – which is a hard job in the case of such animals. For the loser there was a two-handled cup. Achilles stood up and addressed the Greeks:

'Agamemnon and you other Greek men-at-arms, these are the prizes for which we now invite our two best men to square up to each other and box to a finish. The man blessed with endurance by Apollo and who comes off best in everyone's opinion here can take this hard-working mule back to his hut. The loser will receive this two-handled cup.'

Boxing:
Epeius beats
Euryalus
660

So he spoke, and immediately Epeius son of Panopeus rose up, a fine, tall man and superb fighter. He put his hand on the hard-working mule and said:

'Step forward, the man who wants to carry off the two-handled cup. I tell you, the mule is mine, and nobody is going to knock me out and take her: I am the greatest. True, I'm not 670 so good on the battlefield – no one can be a winner at everything – but isn't that enough? But I tell you bluntly and I mean it. I'm going to tear his flesh to ribbons and smash his bones. His family mourners had better be standing by to take him away when I've finished with him.'

So he spoke and was received in complete silence by them all. The only man who dared to take it up was Euryalus, a godlike man, the son of lord Mecisteus whose father was Talaus. After

Oedipus had fallen, Mecisteus went to Thebes for the funeral
680 games and there beat all the Thebans. His cousin the great
spearman Diomedes bustled round Euryalus and gave him the
warmest encouragement, because he very much wanted to see
him win. First he helped him on with his loin-cloth and then
bound on his hands the well-cut oxhide thongs.

When the two men had kitted themselves out, they stepped
into the middle of the gathering, put up their massive fists and
fell on each other. Heavy blows were exchanged; cheek-bones
cracked fearfully; and the sweat began to pour off them. Then,
as Euryalus was looking for an opening, godlike Epeius, leaping
690 in, caught him on the cheek. Euryalus remained upright no
longer, and his whole body sagged. As a fish leaps up from the
weed-covered shallows and falls back into the dark waves when
the north wind ripples the waters, so the blow lifted Euryalus
off the ground. Great-hearted Epeius gave him a hand and set
him on his legs. His companions gathered round and led him
off through the gathering on trailing feet, spitting clots of blood,
with his head lolling to one side. He was still groggy when they
put him down among his own people. They had to go and fetch
the two-handled cup themselves.

700 Achilles son of Peleus immediately laid out and displayed
before the Greeks the prizes for the third event, the
wrestling, a dangerous sport. For the winner there
was a big three-legged cauldron to stand over a fire
– it was worth a dozen oxen by the Greeks' reckoning
– and for the loser he brought forward a woman thoroughly
trained in domestic work whom they valued at four oxen.
Achilles rose and addressed the Greeks:

'Come forward two men to compete for this prize.'

So he spoke, and great Ajax son of Telamon rose at once, and
so did quick-thinking Odysseus, who knew all the tricks. The
710 two girded themselves up, stepped into the middle of the gather-
ing and gripped each other's arms with their powerful hands,
like the sloping gable-rafters that an expert builder locks
together in the roof of a high house to resist the wind. Their
backs creaked under the massive pressure exerted by their great
arms; the sweat streamed down them; and blood-red weals

*Wrestling:
Odysseus ties
with Ajax*

sprang up all along their sides and shoulders. And still they struggled on for victory and the fine cauldron. But Odysseus was no more able to trip his man and bring him to ground than Ajax could master Odysseus' great strength. After some time, 720 when they began to bore the troops, great Ajax son of Telamon said:

'Olympian-born son of Laertes, resourceful Odysseus, either you lift me or I'll lift you. We'll leave the rest to Zeus.'

With these words he lifted Odysseus off the ground. But Odysseus' craft did not desert him. He caught Ajax with a kick from behind in the hollow of the knee, unbalanced him and dumped him on his back, himself falling on Ajax's chest. The gathering looked on in astonishment. Now all-daring godlike Odysseus had to try a lift. He shifted Ajax just a little off the 730 ground but could not raise him. So he crooked a leg round Ajax's knee, and they both fell down side by side and were smothered in dust. They jumped up and would have tried for a third time, if Achilles himself had not risen to his feet and interposed:

'End the fight and don't wear yourselves out with your exertions. You have both won. Share out the prizes equally and withdraw, so that other Greeks can compete.'

So he spoke, and they heard and agreed. After wiping off the dust, they put on their tunics.

Achilles son of Peleus went on at once to lay out the prizes 740 for the foot-race, a silver mixing-bowl of fine work-manship, holding six measures. It was the loveliest thing in the world, a masterpiece of craftsmanship which had been shipped across the misty seas from Sidon by Phoenician traders and presented as a gift to lord Thoas when they put in at his port. Then Euneus son of Jason had given it to the warrior Patroclus in return for Lycaon, Priam's son; and now Achilles laid it out as a prize in honour of his dead companion to the man who should come in first in the foot-race. He offered the runner-up a large, well-fattened ox; and the third, half a talent of gold. Achilles rose and addressed the 750 Greeks:

The foot-race
(21.40)

'Come forward the men to compete for this prize.'

So he spoke, and swift-footed Ajax son of Oïleus immediately rose; so too did quick-thinking Odysseus and Nestor's son Antilochus, who was the fastest of the younger men. The three of them lined up side by side, and Achilles pointed out the turning-post.

760 They went flat out from the start. Ajax son of Oïleus soon shot ahead but godlike Odysseus stuck close behind, like the rod near the breast of a girdled weaving-woman: she carefully draws it along with her hands to get the spool out past the warp and brings it right up to her breast. So close was Odysseus behind Ajax, his feet falling in Ajax's tracks before the dust had settled down again; and he kept up so well that his breath fanned Ajax's head. He was desperate to win, and all the Greeks cheered him on, shouting encouragement to a man who was doing all he could already. As they drew near the finish, Odysseus offered up a silent prayer to grey-eyed Athene:

770 'Hear me, goddess, be kind and help me. Come and speed my feet.'

ATHENE ensures Odysseus wins

So he spoke in prayer, and Pallas Athene heard him and lightened his feet, arms and all his limbs. The runners had the prize almost in their grasp when Ajax at full stretch slipped and fell. Athene had put him out of action, and it happened where the ground was littered with dung from the lowing cattle that were slaughtered by swift-footed Achilles for Patroclus' funeral. So Ajax had his mouth and nostrils filled with cattle-dung, while all-daring godlike Odysseus, having caught him up and finished, carried off the silver bowl. Illustrious Ajax took possession of the farmyard 780 ox. He stood there with his hands on one of the animal's horns and, as he spat out dung, said to the Greeks:

'Damn it! It was the goddess tripped me up – the one who always dances attendance on Odysseus, like a mother.'

So he spoke, and they all laughed delightedly at him. And now Antilochus came in. He took the last prize with a smile and said to the Greeks:

'Friends, I'll tell you all something you know already. The gods still favour the older man; for though Ajax is only a little

older than myself, Odysseus over there is the product of an   790
earlier generation, a positive throwback. But, as they say, there's
life in the old dog yet; and it's a hard job to beat him in a race –
for any of us but Achilles.'

So he spoke, and complimented swift-footed Achilles. Achilles
replied to him and said:

'Antilochus, I cannot allow your tribute to go unrewarded.
You've won a half-talent of gold already; here's another.'

With these words he handed the gold to Antilochus, who
received it with delight.

Achilles son of Peleus now produced and laid out in the
gathering a long-shadowed spear, a shield and a helmet, the
arms that Patroclus had taken from Sarpedon. He rose and   800
addressed the Greeks:

'We now invite our two best men to fight each
other for these prizes before the assembled troops.   Combat: Ajax
They must put on their armour and use naked   ties with Dio-
weapons. To the one who first hits the other's fine   medes (16.663)
flesh, I will give this lovely silver-riveted Thracian sword which
I took from Asteropaeus. The armour here will be shared
between the combatants, and I will also give them a magnificent   810
feast in my hut.'

So he spoke, and great Ajax son of Telamon rose up, as did
Tydeus' son mighty Diomedes. Each armed himself on his own
side of the gathering, and the pair advanced on each other in
the centre, in fighting mood and glaring daggers, and all the
Greeks looked on, spellbound. When they had come within
range of each other, they charged three times, and when they
had tried three lunges at each other, Ajax succeeded in pierc-
ing Diomedes' rounded shield. But the spear failed to reach
his flesh: he was saved by the body-armour underneath. It was
now Diomedes' turn. Thrusting repeatedly above the rim of   820
Ajax's large shield, he tried to hit him on the neck with his
glittering spear-point. The Greeks were so terrified for Ajax that
they called on the combatants to stop and share the prizes.
However, Achilles awarded Diomedes the great sword, which
he handed to him with its sheath and well-cut shoulder-strap.

Then Achilles son of Peleus laid out a lump of cast
iron, which powerful Eëtion used to throw and which
had been carried off on board ship with his other
possessions by swift-footed godlike Achilles after he
830   had killed him. Achilles rose and addressed the Greeks:

'Come forward the men to compete for this prize. This lump
is big enough to keep the winner in iron for five years or more,
even if his farm is out in the wilds. It will not be lack of iron
that sends his shepherd or his ploughman in to town. It will
provide all his needs.'

So he spoke, and resolute Polypoetes rose, as did godlike,
powerful Leonteus, Ajax son of Telamon and godlike Epeius.
They stood in a row, and godlike Epeius picked up the weight,
840   whirled it round and let it fly. But all the Greeks only laughed
at his effort. Leonteus ally of the War-god was the next to throw.
Then great Ajax son of Telamon hurled it from his mighty hand
and passed the marks of all the others. But when it came to
resolute Polypoetes' turn, he overshot the whole field by the
distance a herdsman can hurl his throwing-stick when he sends
it spinning among a herd of cows. The crowd erupted, and
mighty Polypoetes' men got up and carried off their master's
prize to the hollow ships.

850   Then Achilles laid out grey iron as a prize for archery – ten
double-headed and ten single-headed axes. He set up the mast
of a blue-prowed ship a long way off in the sands; and he had a
timid dove tied to it by the foot with a thin cord. He instructed
them to make this their target:

'The man who hits the timid dove can take the
whole set of double-headed axes home with him. If
anyone hits the string and not the bird, he won't have
done so well but he can have the single axes.'

So he spoke, and mighty lord Teucer rose, as did Meriones,
860   Idomeneus' brave attendant, and shook lots in a bronze helmet.
It fell to Teucer to shoot first and he quickly let fly an arrow
with tremendous force. But he had forgotten to promise lord
Apollo an impressive offering of first-born lambs and failed to
hit the bird – Apollo grudged him that success. Yet he did strike
the cord by which the bird was tethered near its foot. The sharp

*Throwing the
lump of metal
(6.414)*

*Archery:
Meriones wins*

arrow severed the string, and the dove shot up into the sky,
leaving the string dangling down. The Greeks roared. But Mer-
iones, who had been holding an arrow ready while Teucer   870
aimed, immediately snatched the bow from Teucer's hands and
promptly vowed an impressive offering of first-born lambs to
the Archer-god Apollo. He saw the timid dove fluttering high
overhead beneath the clouds and as it circled there he hit it from
below, plumb in the wing. His arrow went clean through and
fell back to stick in the earth in front of his feet, while the bird
managed to settle on the mast of the blue-prowed ship, with
wings drooping and head down. In a moment it was dead and   880
fell all the way to the ground from the mast-head. The spectators
looked on in astonishment. Meriones carried off the set of ten
double axes, and Teucer took the single axes to the hollow
ships.

Finally Achilles son of Peleus brought into the
gathering and laid out a long-shadowed spear and   Spear: Aga-
an unused cauldron embossed with flowers, worth   memnon wins
an ox. The spear-throwers rose to compete, and wide-ruling
Agamemnon, Atreus' son, and Meriones, Idomeneus' brave
attendant, stood up. But swift-footed godlike Achilles spoke to
them:

'Lord Agamemnon, we know by how much you excel the rest   890
of us, and that in throwing the spear no one can compete with
your prowess. Accept this prize and take it with you to the
hollow ships. If you are agreeable, let us give Meriones the
spear. That is what I propose.'

So he spoke, and Agamemnon lord of men complied, gave
Meriones the bronze spear and then handed his own beautiful
prize to his herald Talthybius.

24

PRIAM AND ACHILLES

1–21: Achilles cannot sleep for thinking about Patroclus. He drags *Hector*'s body round Patroclus' tomb, but *APOLLO* protects it from disfigurement.

[Eleven days of Hector's mistreatment, which began from the day of his death, cf. 24.107–8].

22–142: [39th day] The other gods pity *Hector*, but HERA, ATHENE and POSEIDON remain hostile. *APOLLO* pleads *Hector*'s case, and ZEUS instructs THETIS to tell Achilles he must return the body. Achilles agrees.

143–87: ZEUS tells the mourning *Priam* to take gifts to Achilles and ransom *Hector*.

188–321: *Priam*, after rounding on his sons, sets off, with an omen from ZEUS.

322–469: [Night before 40th day] HERMES in disguise accompanies *Priam* safely to Achilles' quarters.

469–571: *Priam*'s supplication of Achilles succeeds. They both weep, and Achilles compares *Priam*'s fate with that of his own father, Peleus.

572–691: *Priam*'s gifts are unloaded, and *Hector*'s body placed on the waggon. Achilles and *Priam* eat together. By night HERMES leads *Priam* secretly away.

691–784: [40th day] *Cassandra* sees *Priam* approaching. *Andromache*, *Hecabe* and Helen utter laments. Wood is collected.

[Nine days to build Hector's pyre].

785–804: [49th day] *Hector* is cremated and [50th day] buried, and a grave-mound set up. A funeral feast is held in *Priam*'s palace.

The gathering broke up, and the warriors scattered to their several ships; they were thinking of the pleasures of food and sweet sleep. But Achilles began to weep for his dear companion whom he could not banish from his mind, and all-conquering sleep refused to visit him. He tossed and turned from side to side, always thinking of his loss, of Patroclus' manliness and spirit, of all they had been through together and the hardships they had endured, of battles against the enemy and dangers at sea. As memories crowded in, the warm tears poured down his cheeks. Sometimes he lay on his side, sometimes on his back and then again on his face. Then he would get up and roam agitatedly along the salt-sea beach.

Dawn after dawn as it lit up the sea and coastline never failed to find him there. He would yoke his swift horses to his chariot, tie Hector's body loosely to the back of it and, when he had hauled it three times round Patroclus' grave-mound, go back and rest in his hut, leaving the body stretched face downward in the dust. But dead though Hector was, Apollo still felt pity for the man and protected his flesh from all disfigurement. Moreover, he wrapped him in his golden aegis, so that Achilles should not tear his flesh when he was dragging him along.

Achilles mutilates Hector's body

So Achilles in his fury disfigured godlike Hector. The blessed gods looked on and took pity on him. They even urged Hermes, sharp-eyed slayer of Argus, to steal the body, but while this found favour with the rest, it had no appeal for Hera, Poseidon or grey-eyed Athene. These hated sacred Ilium and Priam and his people just as much now as when Paris first committed that act of blind folly at the judgement in his shepherd's hut, when he humiliated Hera and Athene by preferring Aphrodite – whose reward was his fatal lust for women.

Eleven days went by, and at dawn on the twelfth Phoebus Apollo spoke out to the immortals:

'You are hard-hearted, you gods – monsters of cruelty. Did Hector never burn for you the thighs of oxen and of unblemished goats? Yet now you will not even go so far as to save his body for his wife, mother and child to see, and for his father Priam and

[Day 39] APOLLO and HERA quarrel over Achilles

his people to cremate and honour with funeral rites. No, it's the
40   murderous Achilles you gods choose to support, Achilles, who
has no decent feelings in him and remains utterly relentless, like
a lion that, when it wants its food, looks to nothing but its own
great strength and arrogant appetites and pounces on shepherds'
flocks. Achilles, like the lion, has destroyed pity; he has no
respect for others.

'Many a man, I presume, is likely to have lost an even dearer
one than he has, a brother borne by the same mother, or maybe
a son. He weeps and laments for him, and that is the end of it,
since the fates have endowed men with an enduring heart. But
50   Achilles first robs godlike Hector of his life and then ties him
to his chariot and drags him round the tomb of his beloved
companion. As though that will do him honour or credit! He
had better beware of our anger, great man though he is. All he
is doing in his fury is disfiguring dumb clay.'

Angrily, white-armed Hera replied:

'There would be something in what you say, lord of the silver
bow, if you gods had it in mind to honour Hector as you do
Achilles. But Hector is a mere mortal, who was suckled at a
woman's breast; while Achilles is the son of Thetis, a goddess,
60   whom I myself brought up and took under my wing and gave
in marriage to a man, to Peleus, the greatest favourite we had.
All you gods came to the wedding. And so did *you*, Apollo, and
sat down at the wedding feast, lyre in hand. But then you always
were two-faced, you and your crooked friends.'

Zeus who marshals the clouds replied and said:

'Hera, stop losing your temper with the gods.
ZEUS orders   There is no question of putting the two men on the
return of   same footing. But the fact remains that Hector was
Hector   our favourite out of everyone in Ilium. He certainly
was mine: he never failed to give me what I like. My altar never
lacked its share of generous offerings, libations of wine and the
70   fat from burnt sacrifice, the honour gods have been granted as
our right. But we must abandon this idea of secretly stealing
Hector's body. In any case it is not feasible, since Achilles'
mother stays beside him night and day. However, let one of the
gods tell Thetis to come here to me. I have a carefully considered

solution to suggest, to make Achilles accept a ransom from
Priam and release Hector.'

So he spoke, and Iris, quick as the wind, sped off on her
mission. Halfway between Samothrace and rugged Imbros she
dived into the dark sea, and the waters boomed and echoed. She
sank to the bottom like the piece of lead that an angler attaches   80
to his ox-horn lure to bring death to the greedy fish. She found
Thetis in her vaulted cavern, surrounded by a gathering of other
salt-sea Nymphs; she was in the middle, bewailing the lot of her
matchless son, destined, as she knew, to be killed in fertile Troy
far from the land of his fathers. Swift-footed Iris came up to her
and spoke:

'Come, Thetis. Zeus in his infinite wisdom calls you to his
side.'

The goddess silver-footed Thetis replied:

'What does the great god want me for? I am so overwhelmed   90
with sorrow that I shrink from mixing with the gods. However,
I will come – Zeus' words will not be idle.'

With these words the goddess took a dark-blue shawl – there
was nothing blacker she could wear – and set out on her journey,
preceded by swift Iris, quick as the wind. The waters of the sea
made way for them, and they came out on the shore and sped
up to the skies where they found far-thundering Zeus with all
the other blessed everlasting gods seated round him. Thetis sat
down by Father Zeus – Athene let her have her chair – and   100
Hera, with a warm word of welcome, passed her a lovely golden
cup which Thetis returned to her when she had drunk from it.
The Father of men and gods began and spoke his mind:

'So, goddess Thetis, you have come to Olympus in spite of
your troubles. You are distraught with grief – I know that as
well as you. Nevertheless I must tell you why I called you here.
For nine days the gods have been quarrelling over Hector's body
and Achilles sacker of cities. They have even urged Hermes, the
sharp-eyed slayer of Argus, to steal the body. But I intend to
grant Achilles glory and in that way preserve your future respect   110
and goodwill.

'Go at once to the camp and convey my orders to your son.
Tell him the gods are displeased with him and that I am the

angriest of them all, because in his senseless fury he refuses to
part with Hector's body and has kept it by his beaked ships. If
he will somehow fear me and release Hector, I will send Iris to
great-hearted Priam to suggest that he should ransom his son
by going to the Greek ships with gifts for Achilles that will warm
his heart.'

120   So he spoke, and the goddess silver-footed Thetis complied.
She came swooping down from the heights of Olympus and
reached her son's hut. There she found him, groaning
incessantly, while his comrades bustled around him
in busy preparation of a meal, for which a large fleecy
sheep was being slaughtered. Achilles' lady mother
sat down close beside him, stroked him with her hand and spoke
to him:

THETIS
persuades
Achilles

'My child, how much longer are you going to eat your heart
out in lamentation and misery, forgetful even of food and bed?
130   It must be a good thing to make love to a woman – you have so
short a time to live and already stand in the shadow of death
and inexorable destiny.

'Listen to me now and understand I come from Zeus, who
wishes you to know the gods are displeased with you and that
he himself is the angriest of them all, because in your senseless
fury you refuse to part with Hector's body and have kept it by
your beaked ships. Come now, give it back and accept a ransom
for the dead.'

Swift-footed Achilles replied and said:
140   'If the Olympian is in earnest and himself commands me,
then bring in the man who would offer a ransom and take
the body away.'

While mother and son exchanged many a winged word with
each other down there among the ships, Zeus dispatched Iris to
sacred Ilium:

IRIS' mission
to *Priam*

'Off with you, swift Iris. Leave your Olympian
home and take a message to great-hearted Priam in
Ilium. Tell him to ransom his son by going to the
Greek ships with gifts for Achilles that will warm his heart. He
must go alone, without a single Trojan to escort him, except
150   maybe one of the older heralds who could drive the mules and

smooth-running waggon and bring back to Ilium the body of the man godlike Achilles killed. Tell him not to think of death and to have no fears whatever. We will send him the best of escorts, Hermes slayer of Argus, who will remain in charge till he has brought him into Achilles' presence. Once he is inside his hut, no one is going to kill him, neither Achilles himself nor anybody else. Achilles will see to that. He is not foolish, thoughtless or wicked. On the contrary, he will spare his suppliant and show him every kindness.'

So he spoke, and Iris, quick as the wind, sped off on her mission. She came to Priam's palace where sounds of lamentation met her. In the courtyard Priam's sons were sitting round their father, drenching their clothes with tears, and there in the middle sat the old man wrapped up in his cloak, showing just the outline of his body, with his head and neck plastered with the dung he had gathered in his hands as he grovelled on the ground. His daughters and his sons' wives were wailing through the house, remembering the many fine men who had lost their lives at Greek hands and now lay dead.

The messenger of Zeus stood by Priam and addressed him. She spoke in a low voice, but his limbs began at once to tremble: 170

'Courage, Dardanian Priam! Compose yourself and have no fears. I come here not as a messenger of evil, but of hope. And I am the messenger of Zeus who, far off as he is, is much concerned on your behalf and pities you. The Olympian orders you to ransom godlike Hector with gifts for Achilles that will warm his heart. You must go alone without a single Trojan to escort you, except maybe one of the older heralds who could drive the mules and smooth-running waggon and bring 180 back to Ilium the body of the man godlike Achilles killed. Do not think of death and have no fears whatever. The best of escorts, Hermes slayer of Argus, will remain in charge till he has brought you into Achilles' presence. Once you are inside his hut, no one is going to kill you, neither Achilles himself nor anybody else. Achilles will see to that. He is not foolish, thoughtless or wicked. On the contrary, he will spare his suppliant and show you every kindness.'

With these words swift-footed Iris disappeared. Priam told

190 his sons to get ready a smooth-running mule-waggon with a wicker basket lashed on top. Then he went down to his high-roofed, scented store-room which was built of cedar-wood and was full of treasures. He called out to Hecabe his wife and said:

'My dear, an Olympian messenger has come to me from Zeus and told me to ransom Hector's body by going to the Greek ships with gifts for Achilles that will warm his heart. Tell me, what do you make of that? My own feelings impel me to go down to the ships and pay this visit to the broad Greek camp.'

200 So he spoke, and his wife shrieked aloud and replied:

Hecabe fails to stop *Priam*

'Are you mad? Where is the wisdom which people from abroad and your own subjects used to praise in you? How can you think of going by yourself to the Greek ships into the presence of a man who has killed so many of your fine sons? You must have a heart of iron. Once you are in his power, once he sets his eyes on you – that flesh-eating, faithless savage – he will show you no mercy at all nor the slightest respect.

'No: all we can do now is sit at home and weep for our son from here. This must be the end that inexorable destiny spun
210 for him with the first thread of life when I brought him into the world – to glut the swift dogs, far from his parents, in the clutches of a monster whose very liver I would sink my teeth into and devour. That would pay him back for what he has done to my son, who was not playing the coward when Achilles killed him, but fighting, without any thought of flight or cover, in defence of the sons and full-girdled daughters of Troy.'

Venerable godlike Priam replied:

'I am determined to go. Do not keep me back or turn into a bird of ill-omen in our palace – you will not dissuade me. If
220 any human being, a prophet or a priest, had made me this suggestion, I would have said it was a lie and disregarded it. But I personally heard the goddess' voice: I saw her there in front of me. So I am going and the goddess' words will not be idle. If I am destined to die by the ships of the bronze-armoured Greeks, then I choose death. Achilles can kill me then and there, once I have taken my son in my arms and wept my fill.'

He spoke and lifted the lovely lids of the storage-
chests. From these he took out twelve beautiful robes,
twelve single cloaks, as many sheets, as many white
mantles and as many tunics to go with them. He also weighed
and took ten talents of gold; and he took two shining tripods,
four cauldrons and a very lovely cup which the Thracians had
given him when he went there on a mission. It was a fabulous
present, but so great was his desire to ransom his beloved son
that the old man did not hesitate to part with it also.

Priam gathers
the ransom

230

There were a number of Trojans hanging around the portico.
Priam drove them all off with a stream of abuse:

'Get out of here, you despicable, worthless wretches! Haven't
you enough to weep about in your own homes without intrud-
ing on my grief as well? Or wasn't it enough for you that Zeus
son of Cronus has afflicted me with the loss of the best of sons?
If so, you will soon learn better. The Greeks will find you still
easier to deal with now Hector is dead. As for me, I only hope I
go down to Hades' halls before I see the town plundered and
laid waste.'

240

He spoke and drove them off with his staff, and they fled
from the quick-tempered old man. Next he shouted angrily
at his sons, abusing Helenus, Paris and godlike Agathon;
Pammon and Antiphonus and Polites master of the battle-cry;
Deiphobus, Hippothous and noble Dius. He shouted at all nine
of them and told them what to do:

250

'Move, you miserable, cowardly children of mine! I wish you
had all been killed beside the swift ships instead of Hector. Ah,
how calamity has dogged my life! I had the best sons in the
broad realm of Troy. Now all of them are gone – godlike Mestor,
Troilus the charioteer and Hector, a god among mortals, who
looked more like a god's son than a man's. The War-god has
taken them and left me this disgraceful crew – swindlers and
show-offs every one of you, stars of the song-and-dance routine,
when you aren't looting your own people of their sheep and
kids. Now won't you be so *kind* as to get my waggon ready at
once and put in everything I need to see me on my way?'

260

So he spoke, and his sons were terrified by their father's
fulminations and quickly fetched a fine new smooth-running

mule-waggon and lashed a wicker basket on it. They took down
from its peg a yoke of box-wood for the mules, with a knob in
the middle and the proper guides for the reins; and with the
270   yoke they brought out a yoke-binding four metres long. They
laid the yoke carefully on to the polished shaft, in the notch
at the front end of it, slipped the ring over the pin, tied the
yoke-binding round the knob with three turns either way, then
wound it closely round the shaft and tucked the loose end in
under the hook.

This done, they went to the store-room, fetched the immense
ransom that was to buy back Hector's body and packed it in
the polished waggon. Then they yoked the sturdy mules who
were trained to work in harness and had been a splendid gift
to Priam from the Mysian people. Finally, they brought out
Priam's chariot and yoked to it the horses that the old man
280   kept for his own use and fed at the polished manger.

As Priam and the herald, with much to occupy
their thoughts, organized the yoking of the mules
and horses in the high palace, they were approached
by Hecabe in great distress, carrying a golden cup of delicious
wine in her right hand for them to make a drink-offering before
they left. She came up to the chariot and spoke to Priam:

Libation and omen

'Here, make a libation to Father Zeus and pray for your safe
return from the enemy's hands, since you are set on going to the
ships. You go against my will, but if go you must, address your
290   prayer to Zeus son of Cronus who darkens the clouds, god of
Mount Ida, who sees the whole region of Troy spread out
beneath him. Ask for a bird of omen, a swift ambassador from
him. And let it be his favourite prophetic bird, the strongest
thing on wings, flying on your right so that you can see it with
your own eyes and put your trust in it as you go down to the
ships of the Greeks with their swift horses. But if far-thundering
Zeus refuses to send you his messenger, I should advise you not
to go down to the Greek ships, however much you may have set
your heart on it.'

Godlike Priam replied and said:

300   'My dear, I will surely do as you suggest. It is a good thing to
lift up one's hands to Zeus and ask him to have pity.'

The old man spoke and told his housekeeper to pour pure water over his hands. She brought a jug and basin and attended on him. When he had washed his hands, he took the cup from his wife, went to the middle of the forecourt to pray, looked up into the sky as he poured out the wine and said:

'Father Zeus, you that rule from Mount Ida, greatest and most glorious! Grant that Achilles receives me with kindness and mercy; and send me a bird of omen, your swift ambassador, 310 your favourite prophetic bird, the strongest thing on wings, flying on my right, so I can see it with my own eyes and put my trust in it as I go down to the ships of the Greeks with their swift horses.'

So he spoke in prayer, and Zeus wise in counsel heard him and instantly sent out an eagle, the most perfect of prophetic birds, the dusky hunter they call the golden eagle, whose spread wings would span the width of a well-bolted door of the lofty chamber in a rich man's house. They saw it flying on their right 320 across the town and were overjoyed at the sight. It warmed the hearts of everyone.

The old man quickly mounted his chariot and drove out by the gateway and its echoing colonnade. He was preceded by the four-wheeled waggon, drawn by the mules and driven by wise Idaeus. Then came Priam's chariot. The old man used his whip and drove it quickly through the town; yet even so his whole family kept up with him, lamenting incessantly as though he were going to his death. But when they had made their way down through the streets and reached the plain, the people, his 330 sons and sons-in-law, turned back into Ilium and went home.

Far-thundering Zeus saw the two men strike out across the plain. He felt pity for the old man and immediately said to his son Hermes:

'Hermes, escorting men is your greatest pleasure, and you listen to the requests of those you favour. *[Night 39]* So off you go now and conduct lord Priam to the HERMES Greeks' hollow ships in such a way that not a single accompanies Greek sees and recognizes him till he reaches Achilles.' *Priam*

So he spoke, and the guide and slayer of Argus complied, and bound under his feet his lovely sandals, golden and imperishable, 340 that carried him with the speed of the wind over the water and the boundless earth; and he picked up the wand which he can use at will to cast a spell on men's eyes or wake them from sleep. With this wand in his hand the mighty slayer of Argus made his flight and soon reached Troy and the Hellespont. There he proceeded on foot, looking like a young lord at that most charming age when the beard first starts to grow.

Meanwhile the two men had driven past the great grave-mound of Ilus and stopped their mules and horses for a drink at the river. Night was coming on by now. When Hermes was quite close to them, the herald Idaeus looked up and saw him, and said to Priam:

'Look out, Priam. We must be very careful. I can see someone. I think we're going to be butchered. Quick, let's make our escape in the chariot, or if not that, fall at his knees and beg him for mercy.'

So he spoke, and the old man was completely bewildered and filled with terror; the hairs stood up on his bent limbs; he stood there, paralysed. But Hermes the runner went straight up to Priam, took him by the hand, questioned him and said:

HERMES wins *Priam*'s trust

'Father, where are you driving to with those horses and mules through the immortal night when everyone else is asleep? Aren't you afraid of the Greeks, breathing courage, those deadly enemies of yours, so close at hand? If any one of them saw you coming through the black night with such a valuable load, what could you do? You are not young enough to cope with anyone that might assault you; and your companion is an old man too. However, I certainly do not mean you harm. In fact, I am going to see that no one else molests you; for you remind me of my own father.'

The old man godlike Priam replied:

'Our plight, dear child, is very much as you describe. But even so some god must have extended a protecting hand over me when he let me fall in with a traveller like you, who come as a godsend, so distinguished are your looks and bearing, as well as your good sense. Your parents must be blessed.'

The guide and slayer of Argus replied:

'Sir, everything you have said is right. Now answer my questions and tell me exactly. Are you sending a splendid haul of treasure to some place of safety in a foreign land? Or has the time come when you are all deserting sacred Ilium in panic at the loss of your greatest warrior, your own son, who never let anyone down in battle against the enemy?'

The old man godlike Priam replied:

'Who are you, good sir? Who are your parents? How wonderfully you speak to me of the fate of my unhappy son.'

The guide and slayer of Argus replied:

'You're testing me, venerable sir, and trying to discover what I know about godlike Hector. Well, I have seen him with my own eyes – and seen him often – in battle where men win glory. And what's more, I saw him drive back the Greeks on to their own ships and mow them down with his sharp spear, while we Myrmidons stood by and marvelled, since Achilles would not let us fight, having quarrelled with lord Agamemnon. 390

'I am the attendant of Achilles and came here in the same good ship as he. I am a Myrmidon, and my father is Polyctor, a rich man and about as old as yourself. He has seven sons, of whom I am the youngest; and when we drew lots, it fell to me to join the expedition here. Tonight I left the ships and came out on to the plain because at daybreak the dark-eyed Greeks are intending to assault the town. They are tired of just sitting there and so eager for a fight that the Greek leaders cannot hold them back.' 400

The old man godlike Priam replied:

'If you really are an attendant of Peleus' son Achilles, come, tell me the whole truth: is my son still by the ships, or has Achilles already cut him up and thrown him piecemeal to his dogs?'

The guide and slayer of Argus replied: 410

'So far, venerable sir, neither the dogs nor birds of prey have eaten him. His body is intact and lies there in Achilles' hut beside his ship, just as it was. And though he has been there for eleven days, his flesh has not decayed at all nor has it been attacked by the worms that devour the bodies of men killed in battle. It is true that every day when bright Dawn appears Achilles drags him mercilessly round the grave-mound of his beloved

companion; but that does not defile him. If you went into his
hut yourself, you would be astonished to see him lying there
as fresh as dew, the blood all washed away and not a mark on
420 him. His wounds too have healed, every wound he had; and
there were many men who stabbed him with their spears. This
shows what care the blessed gods are taking of your son, dead
though he is, because he was very dear to them.'

So he spoke, and the old man rejoiced and said:

'My child, what an excellent thing it is to give the gods their
proper offerings! I am thinking of my son – if ever he was my
son – and how he never neglected the gods of Olympus in our
home. That is why they are repaying him like this, even though
he has met his destiny and died. But here, accept this beautiful
430 cup from me, keep me safe and, under the protecting hand of
the gods, escort me till I reach Achilles' hut.'

The guide and slayer of Argus replied:

'You are an old man, sir, and I am young, and you are testing
me. But you will not persuade me when you tell me to take a
bribe behind Achilles' back. I fear and respect my master too
deeply to defraud him: the consequences for myself might be
severe. However, I am ready to serve you as escort all the way
to my home in famous Thessaly in Greece and to assist you
loyally on board ship or on foot. No one would attack you
through underestimating your guard.'

440 Hermes the runner spoke and leapt into the chariot, seized
the whip and reins in his hands and put fresh heart into the
horses and mules. When they came to the ditch and the wall
round the ships, they found the sentries just beginning to prepare
a meal. But the guide and slayer of Argus put them all to sleep,
unfastened the gates, thrust back the bars and ushered Priam in
with his waggon-load of precious gifts.

They went on to the lofty hut of Peleus' son Achilles. The
450 Myrmidons had built it for their master with planks of deal cut
by themselves and roofed it over with a rough thatch of reeds
gathered in the meadows. It stood in the large enclosure they
made for their master surrounded by a close-set fence, and the
gate was fastened by a single pine-wood bar. It took three men
to drive this mighty bolt home and three to draw it back; three

ordinary men, of course – Achilles could work it by himself.
Now Hermes the runner opened it up for the old man, drove in
with the splendid presents for swift-footed Achilles, dismounted
from the chariot and said to Priam:

'Venerable sir, an immortal god has been accompanying   460
you. I am Hermes and my father sent me as your escort. But I
shall leave you now, as I do not intend to enter into Achilles'
presence. It would be reprehensible for mortals to entertain an
immortal god face to face in that way. But go inside
yourself, clasp Achilles' knees and, as you suppli-   *Priam* left in
cate him, invoke his father and his lovely-haired   Achilles' hut
mother and his son, if you want your words to go straight to his
heart.'

With these words Hermes went off to high Olympus. Priam
leapt from his chariot to the ground and, leaving Idaeus there   470
to look after the horses and mules, walked straight into the hut
where Achilles dear to Zeus usually sat. He found him inside.
Most of his men were sitting some way off, but two of them,
the warrior Automedon and Alcimedon ally of the War-god,
were waiting on him busily, as he had just finished eating and
drinking and the table had not yet been removed. Great Priam
came in unobserved by them, went up to Achilles, grasped his
knees and kissed his hands, those terrible, man-slaying hands
that had killed so many of his sons. As a thick cloud of delusion   480
possesses a man who, after murdering someone in his own
country, seeks refuge abroad in the home of a wealthy man, and
the onlookers are astounded, so Achilles was astounded when
he saw godlike Priam. The others were astounded too and
exchanged glances.

Supplicating Achilles, Priam addressed him:

'Remember your own father, godlike Achilles,   *Priam* supplic-
who is the same age as I am and on the threshold of   ates Achilles
miserable old age. No doubt his neighbours are tormenting him
and there is nobody to protect him from the harm and damage
they cause. Yet, while he knows you are still alive, he can rejoice   490
in spirit and look forward day by day to seeing his beloved son
come back from Troy.

'But my life has been dogged by calamity. I had the best sons in the whole of this broad realm and now not one, not one I say, is left. There were fifty when the Greek army arrived. Nineteen of them were borne by one mother and the rest to other women in my palace. Most of them have fallen in action, and the only one I could still count on, the mainstay of Ilium

500 and its inhabitants – you killed him a short while ago, fighting for his native land. Hector. It is to get him back from you that I have now come to the Greek ships, bringing an immense ransom with me.

'Achilles, respect the gods and have pity on me, remembering your own father. I am even more entitled to pity, since I have brought myself to do something no one else on earth has done – I have raised to my lips the hands of the man who killed my sons.'

With these words he awoke in Achilles a longing to weep for his own father. Taking the old man's hand, Achilles gently put him from him, and they were both overcome by their

510 memories: Priam, huddled at Achilles' feet, wept aloud for man-slaying Hector, and Achilles wept for his father, and then again for Patroclus. The house was filled with the sounds of their lamentation. But when godlike Achilles had had enough of tears and the longing had ebbed from mind and body, he leapt at once from his chair and in compassion for the old man's grey head and grey beard took him by the arm and raised him. Then he spoke winged words:

'Unhappy man of sorrows, you have indeed suf-
Achilles coun- fered much. How could you bring yourself to come
sels Priam alone to the Greek ships into the presence of a man

520 who had killed so many of your fine sons? You must have a heart of iron. Here now, be seated on this chair and, for all our grief, let us leave our sorrows locked up in our hearts, for weeping is cold comfort and does little good. We men are wretched creatures and the gods have woven grief into our lives: but they themselves are free from care.

'Zeus who delights in thunder has two jars standing on the floor of his palace in which he keeps his gifts, evils in one and blessings in the other. People who receive from him a mixture of

530 the two enjoy varying fortunes, sometimes good and sometimes

bad. But when Zeus serves a man from the jar of evil only, he debases him; ruinous hunger drives him over the bright earth and he goes his way respected by no one, god or man.

'Look at my father Peleus. From the moment he was born, the gods showered splendid gifts on him, fortune and wealth unparalleled among men, lordship over the Myrmidons and, though he was a man, a goddess for his wife. But the god also gave him his share of evil – no children in his palace to follow in his steps, only a single son and he destined for an   540 untimely death. What is more, even though he is growing old, he gets no care from me because I am sitting around here in Troy far from the land of my fathers, seeing to you and your children.

'Now we have heard, venerable sir, there was a time when fortune smiled on you. They say there was no one to compare with you for wealth and sons in all the lands that are enclosed between Lesbos out to sea where Macar reigned, Phrygia inland and the vast Hellespont. But ever since the Sky-gods brought me here to be your scourge, there has been nothing but warfare and carnage round your city.

'Endure and do not mourn without end. Lamenting for your   550 son will do no good at all. You will not bring him back to life before you are dead yourself.'

The old man godlike Priam replied:

'Do not ask me to sit down, Olympian-born Achilles, while Hector lies neglected in your huts, but give him back to me without delay and let me set my eyes on him. Accept the great ransom I bring. May you enjoy it and return safely to the land of your fathers, since from the very first you spared my life.'

Looking blackly at him swift-footed Achilles replied:

'Now don't push me too far, venerable sir. I have made my   560 mind up without your help to give Hector back to you. A messenger from Zeus came to me – my very own mother that bore me, daughter of the Old Man of the Sea. What's more, I know all about you, Priam; you cannot hide the fact that some god brought you to the Greek ships. Nobody, not even a young man, would venture by himself into our camp. For one thing,

he would never get past the sentries; and if he did, he would find it hard to shift the bar across the gate. So don't provoke my grief-stricken heart any more, sir, or I may break the commands
570 of Zeus and, suppliant though you are in my huts, fail to spare your life.'

So he spoke, and the old man was afraid and did as he was told. Then, like a lion, Achilles leapt out of doors, taking with him two of his attendants, the warrior Automedon and Alcimedon, the men closest to him after the dead Patroclus. They unyoked the horses and the mules, brought in the herald, old Priam's crier, and sat him down. Then they took out of the polished waggon the immense ransom for Hector's body. But
580 they left a couple of white mantles and a well-woven tunic in which Achilles could wrap the body when he gave it to Priam to take home.

Hector's body is returned

Achilles then called out some waiting-women and told them to wash and anoint the body but in another part of his quarters, so that Priam should not see his son. Achilles was afraid that Priam, if he saw him, might in the bitterness of his grief be unable to control his anger; and then his own feelings would be provoked into killing the old man and breaking the commands of Zeus. When the waiting-women had washed and anointed the body with olive-oil and wrapped it in the fine mantle and tunic, Achilles lifted it with his own
590 hands on to a bier, and his comrades helped him to put it in the well-polished waggon. Then he gave a groan and called on his dear companion by name:

'Patroclus, do not be indignant with me if you learn, down in the halls of Hades, that I let his father have godlike Hector back. The ransom he paid me was a worthy one and I will see that you receive your proper share of it.'

Godlike Achilles spoke and returned to his hut, sat down on the inlaid chair he had left – it was on the wall opposite Priam – and said:

'Your demands are granted, venerable sir: your son has been
600 released. He is lying on the bier and at daybreak you will see him for yourself as you take him away. Now let us turn our thoughts to food.

'Even lovely-haired Niobe remembered to eat – and that was after she had seen her twelve children done to death in her own house, six daughters and six sons in their prime. Artemis who delights in arrows had killed the daughters; and Apollo with his silver bow shot down the sons. He was furious with Niobe for seeing herself as the equal of their own mother, lovely-cheeked Leto, and contrasting the many children she had produced with the two that Leto bore. Yet that pair, though they were only two, killed all of hers; and for nine days the children lay in pools of blood, as there was no one to bury them, Zeus son of Cronus having turned the people into stone. But on the tenth day the Sky-gods buried them, and Niobe, exhausted by her tears, made up her mind to take some food. And now, turned to stone, she stands among the crags in the lonely hills of Sipylus – where people say the Nymphs, when they have been dancing on the banks of River Achelous, lay themselves down to sleep. There Niobe broods on the desolation the gods dealt her.

Achilles and Priam eat (Niobe's story)

610

'So now, venerable lord, let us two also think of food. Later, you can weep once more for your son, when you take him into Ilium. He will indeed be much mourned.'

620

Swift Achilles spoke, leapt up and slaughtered a white sheep which his men skinned and carefully prepared in the usual manner. They deftly chopped it up into small pieces, pierced the pieces on spits, roasted them carefully and then withdrew them from the fire. Automedon fetched some bread and set it out on the table in handsome baskets; Achilles divided the meat into portions; and they helped themselves to the good things spread before them.

Their hunger and thirst satisfied, Dardanian Priam let his eyes dwell on Achilles and saw with admiration how large and handsome he was, the very image of the gods. And Achilles dwelt with equal admiration on the noble looks and utterance of Dardanian Priam. When they had had their fill of gazing on each other, the old man godlike Priam spoke first:

630

'Send me to bed now, Olympian-bred Achilles, so that Idaeus and I can get our fill of sweet sleep. My eyelids have not closed over my eyes since the moment my son lost his life at

your hands. Ever since then, I have been lamenting and brood-
640 ing over my countless sorrows, grovelling in the dung in my
stable-yard. Now at last I have tasted some food and poured
sparkling wine down my throat; but before that I had tasted
nothing.'

He spoke, and Achilles instructed his men and waiting-women
to put beds in the portico and cover them with fine purple rugs,
spread blankets over these and add some thick cloaks on top
for covering. Torches in hand, the women left the room and set
to work preparing the two beds. Now swift-footed Achilles
spoke to Priam, causing him some agitation:

650 'Sleep out of doors, old friend, in case some Greek counsellor
pays me a visit. They always come here to discuss tactics with
me – it is our custom. If one of them were to see you here at
dead of night, he would at once tell Agamemnon shepherd of
the people, and your recovery of the body would be delayed.
Now answer my question and tell me exactly how
A truce agreed   many days you propose to devote to godlike Hector's
funeral, so that I myself refrain from fighting and ensure the
army does too for that space of time.'

The old man godlike Priam replied:

660 'If you really wish me to give godlike Hector a proper funeral,
you would do me a kindness, Achilles, by acting as follows. You
know how we are cooped up in the town; it is a long journey to
the mountains to fetch wood, and the Trojans are afraid of
making it. We would be nine days mourning Hector in our
homes. On the tenth we would bury him and hold the funeral
feast, and on the eleventh build him a grave-mound. On the
twelfth we will fight, if we really have to.'

Swift-footed godlike Achilles replied:

'Venerable Priam, everything shall be as you require. I will
670 hold up the fighting for the time you have demanded.'

With these words he took the old man by the wrist of his right
hand to banish all fear from his heart. So Priam and the herald
settled down for the night there in the forecourt of the building,
with much to occupy their thoughts. But Achilles slept in a
corner of his well-made hut; and fair-cheeked Briseis slept beside
him.

The other gods and fighting men slept through
the night, conquered by soft sleep. But Hermes the
runner kept wondering how he was going to bring
lord Priam away from the ships without the guards noticing;
and he could not get to sleep. So he went and stood over Priam's
head and said:

HERMES
escorts *Priam*

680

'Venerable sir, since Achilles spared you, you seem to have
no misgivings left, to judge by how soundly you sleep among
your enemies. Just now you ransomed your son's body at a great
price: your sons that are left would have to give three times as
much to ransom you alive, if Agamemnon son of Atreus and
the whole Greek army got to know you were here.'

So he spoke, and the old man was afraid and woke up his
herald. Hermes then yoked the mules and horses for them and
drove them quickly through the camp himself; they passed
unrecognized. As saffron-robed Dawn spread over the world,
they reached the ford of the sweetly flowing river, eddying
Scamander whose father is immortal Zeus. There Hermes set
out for high Olympus; and the two men, groaning and
lamenting, drove the horses on towards the town while the
mules came along with the body.

690

Cassandra, who looked like golden Aphrodite, was the first
among the men and women of Troy to recognize them as
they came. She had climbed to the top of Pergamus and from
that point she saw her dear father standing in the
chariot with the herald, his town-crier. Then she saw
him too, lying on the bier in the mule-waggon. She
gave a scream and shouted aloud for all the town to
hear:

700

[*Day 40*]
Priam returns
to *Ilium*

'Trojans and women of Troy, if ever in the past you welcomed
Hector back when he came home safe from battle – a moment
for everyone in the town to rejoice – come out and see him now!'

So she spoke, and the whole town was plunged into inconsol-
able grief. Soon there was not a man or woman left in Ilium.
They met Priam with Hector's body at no great distance from
the gates. His dear wife and lady mother threw themselves on
the smooth-running waggon, to be the first to tear their hair in
mourning for him and touch his head. They were surrounded

710

by a weeping throng. Indeed, they would have stayed there by the gates and wept for Hector all day long till sunset, if the old man had not spoken out from his chariot:

'Let me through with the mules. You can mourn for Hector to your hearts' content when I have got him home.'

So he spoke, and they fell back on either side and made a passage for the waggon. When the family had brought Hector into the palace, they laid him on an elaborate bed and set beside him dirge-singers to lead the laments and chant their melancholy songs, while the women took up the cry. White-armed Andromache, holding the head of man-slaying Hector between her hands, began her dirge:

Andromache's lament (22.477) 'Husband, you were too young to die and leave me widowed in our home. Your son, the boy we luckless parents brought into the world, is but a little baby. And I have no hope that he will grow to manhood: Ilium will come tumbling to the ground before that can ever be. For you, her guardian, have perished, you that watched over her, you that kept her cherished wives and little babies safe. They will be carried off soon in the hollow ships, and I with them.

'And you, my child, will go with me to labour somewhere at degrading tasks under the eye of a merciless master; or some Greek will seize you by the arm and hurl you from the walls to an ugly death, venting his fury on you because Hector perhaps killed a brother of his, maybe, or else a father, or a son. Yes, at Hector's hands many a Greek bit the dust of the broad earth; for your father was no gentle soul in the cruelty of battle.

'And that is why everyone in Ilium now laments him. Ah, Hector, you have brought untold tears and misery to your parents. But my grief is cruellest of all, because you did not die reaching out from our bed to me with your arms, or utter some memorable word I might have treasured night and day through my tears.'

So she spoke in tears, and the women took up the cry. Hecabe now led the women in a shrill lament:

'Hector, dearest to me of all my sons, you were dear to the gods too while you were with me in the world; and even now you have met your destiny and died, it turns out they still care for you. Swift-footed Achilles took other sons of mine and sent them over the murmuring seas for sale in Samothrace or in Imbros or in misty Lemnos. And he took your life with his long spear; but though he dragged you many times round the grave-mound of Patroclus, the companion of his you killed, that did not bring Patroclus back to life. But you have come home to me fresh as the dew and lie in the palace like one whom Apollo lord of the silver bow has visited and put to death with his gentle shafts.' *Hecabe's lament*

So she spoke in tears, and aroused unbridled grief. Helen then led them in a third lament: 760

'Hector, dearest to me of all my Trojan brothers, godlike Paris brought me here to Troy and married me – I wish I had perished first – but in all the nineteen years since I came away and left the land of my fathers, I never heard a single harsh or spiteful word from you. Others in the palace insulted me – your brothers, your sisters, your brothers' well-robed wives and your mother, though your father was the soul of kindness. But you calmed them down every time and stopped them out of the gentleness of your heart, with your gentle words. So these tears of sorrow I shed are both for you and for my luckless self. No one else is left in the wide realm of Troy to treat me kindly and befriend me. They all shudder at me.' *Helen's lament* 770

So she spoke in tears, and the vast multitude took up the cry. Now the old man Priam spoke to the people:

'Trojans, bring firewood to the town and do not be afraid of a Greek ambush. Achilles assured me, when he let me leave the black ships, that they would do us no harm till the dawn of the twelfth day from then.' 780

So he spoke, and they yoked mules and bullocks to their waggons and assembled speedily outside the town. Over nine days they gathered a huge supply of wood. When the dawn of the tenth day brought light to the world, they carried out daring Hector, weeping, laid his body on top of the pyre and lit it. *[Day 49 and 50] Cremation; burial*

But when early-born, rosy-fingered Dawn appeared, the

people flocked together round glorious Hector's pyre. When
790 everyone had assembled and the gathering was complete, they
first put out with sparkling wine whatever was still burning.
Then Hector's brothers and comrades-in-arms collected his
white bones, lamenting and with many a tear running down
their cheeks. They took the bones, wrapped them in soft purple
clothing and put them in the golden coffin. This coffin they
immediately lowered into a hollow grave which they covered
with a close-set layer of large stones. They hurriedly piled up
earth over it to mark the grave-mound, posting guards all round
800 in case the Greeks launched a premature attack. When they had
piled up the mound, they returned into the city and reassembled
for a magnificent funeral feast in the palace of Priam their
Olympian-bred ruler.

Such were the funeral rites of horse-taming Hector.

Appendix 1: A Brief Glossary

For specific epithets applied to gods and the major heroes, see *The Main Characters*.

aegis: a sort of divine cloak which, when a god shakes it in the face of the enemy, causes panic. It is also used to protect *Hector*'s body. But it also means 'storm-cloud', which ZEUS is said to drive.

attendant: like the ancient 'squire', someone sent to accompany and help a warrior, often as his charioteer.

blood-price: murder and homicide could be settled if compensation was accepted by relatives. Otherwise, blood could be satisfied only by further blood.

body-armour: *thôrêx*, the cuirass or corselet protecting the body.

booty: booty gathered from raids was divided up by agreement among the whole army, the leader getting the lion's share.

DELUSION/BLIND FOLLY: see Index under 'DELUSION', and 'personification' below.

Enyo: a personified deity of strife.

guest-friendship: a bond of friendship created between families, involving obligations and often sealed with an exchange of gifts.

herald: one who keeps order at meetings, makes announcements, acts as escort, carries messages, runs errands and serves at feasts and sacrifices.

honour: the Greek word (*timê*) means basically 'evaluation', the way you are assessed by those around you. Honour is commonly associated with material rewards.

incest: the children of URANUS, CRONUS and ZEUS, the first divine rulers of the world, intermarried at will. After all, the world of gods had to be populated somehow.

marriage: Homer talks sometimes of the bride-price – gifts from the suitor to the father – and sometimes of the dowry, a gift going with the bride to the husband.

personification: Greeks were in the habit of taking a common idea or thing and giving it human or even divine qualities. Thus a spear could 'hunger' to hit human flesh, a rock could be 'shameless'. Likewise, powerful human forces like 'panic', 'confusion', 'force' and 'delusion', and natural features like 'night', 'sleep' and 'rivers', could be turned into gods.

sceptre: symbol of authority and power. The speaker in assembly holds it.

sickle-wielding: ZEUS' father CRONUS came to power by slicing off the genitals of *his* father, URANUS, with a sickle.

Styx: river of the underworld by which gods swore.

supplication/entreaty: the act of pleading for help often involving kneeling before a person and touching their knees and/ or chin. There was a strong moral pressure on the person supplicated to accede to the request. In the real-time story of the *Iliad*, no human accedes to a human supplication until Achilles accedes to *Priam* in the last Book.

Tartarus: an even lower region of the underworld than Hades.

value: there is no money in the Homeric world. Values are usually determined in terms of number of oxen or females.

Some general epithets

beaked: (of ships): ships had high, curved prows with a 'beak' at the top.

girdled: refers to the belt round a woman's robe, which could hang over the belt to form a sort of pocket ('full-girdled').

horse-taming: horses are aristocratic animals, very expensive to keep.

long-haired: a sign of aristocracy.

master of the battle-cry: a healthy yell is very off-putting to opponents.

of the good ash spear: flexible ash was the best material for making spears.

See also under individual names, pp. lxvi ff.

Appendix 2: Omitted Fathers' Names

See Notes on this Revision, 7.

Acamas son of *Eussorus*
Agelaus son of *Phradmon*
Alcimedon son of Laerces
Alcmaon son of Thestor
Amphimachus son of Cteatus
Amphius son of *Selagius*
Amyntor son of Ormenus
Aphareus son of Caletor
Apisaon son of *Hippasus*
Apisaon son of *Phausius*
Archelochus son of *Antenor*
Archeptolemus son of *Iphitus*
Ascanius son of *Hippotion*
Asius son of *Hyrtacus*
Astynous son of *Protiaon*
Axylus son of *Teuthras*
Bathycles son of Chalcon
Caletor son of *Clytius*
Cleitus son of *Peisenor*
Dardanus son of *Bias*
Demuchus son of *Philetor*
Diomede daughter of Phorbas
Diores son of Amarinceus
Echeclus son of *Agenor*
Echepolus son of *Thalysius*
Elephenor son of Chalcodon

Eniopeus son of *Thebaeus*
Epeigeus son of Agacles
Euryalus son of Mecisteus
Eurypylus son of Euaemon
Hippomachus son of *Antimachus*
Hypsenor son of *Dolopion*
Hyrtius son of *Gyrtias*
Iphinous son of Dexius
Itymoneus son of Hypeirochus
Laodamas son of *Antenor*
Laodocus son of *Antenor*
Laogonus son of *Bias*
Laogonus son of *Onetor*
Leiocritus son of Arisbas
Leitus son of Alectryon
Lycomedes son of Creon
Lycophron son of Mastor
Maeon son of Haemon
Mecisteus son of Echius
Meges son of Phyleus
Melanippus son of *Hicetaon*
Menestheus son of Peteos
Menoetius son of Actor
Morys son of *Hippotion*

Mydon son of *Atymnius*
Peiros son of *Imbrasus*
Peisander son of Maemalus
Periboea daughter of
   Acessamenus
Perimus son of *Megas*
Periphas son of *Epytus*
Periphas son of Ochesius
Phaenops son of *Asius*
Phaestus son of *Borus*
Phorcys son of *Phaenops*
Podes son of *Eëtion*
Polymelus son of *Argeas*
Polyphontes son of
   Autophonus

Promachus son of Alegenor
Prothoenor son of Areilycus
Ptolemy son of Peiraeus
Rhesus son of *Eloneus*
Rhigmus son of *Peiros*
Scamandrius son of
   Strophius
Schedius son of Iphitus
Schedius son of Perimedes
Sphelus son of Bucolus
Sthenelaus son of
   Ithaemenes
Thestor son of *Enops*
Tlepolemus son of *Damastor*
Tros son of *Alastor*

Index

This is a select index, concentrating on the main characters, and themes. References are to Book and line number.

protects what is his 1.300; rejects food 19.210, 306, cf. 23.44 (fed by ATHENE 19.352, cf. 24.129); son 19.326; speed 13.325; strength 1.280; touchy 11.649; unyielding 16.33, 204; used to take captives alive for ransom 6.427, 11.104, 21.35, 101, 22.45, 24.751; value to Greeks 1.283, 5.788, 6.99, 18.268, 19.61.

Death: accepts own death 18.90, 98, 115, 332, 19.329, 337, 421, 21.110, 22.365, 23.150, 244, 24.540; death predicted 1.352, 416, 505, 9.410 (cf. 20.337), 17.197, 21.275, 23.80, 24.85, 131; double fate 9.410; to be buried with Patroclus 23.91, 126, 244.

Gifts: accepts gifts 19.140, 172, 278; feels cheated of rightful rewards 1.161, 9.316, 332, 367, 16.56, 18.444; hates Agamemnon's gifts 9.378, 679; importance of gifts 9.515, 602, 19.140, 172; right to be angry before gifts offered 9.523.

Hector: feared *Hector* 7.230; *Hector* feared him 9.352; mutilates *Hector* 22.395, 23.24, 24.15, 51, 416; rejects burial conditions 22.261, 335, 348 (cf. 6.417); vows revenge on *Hector* 18.114, 336, 20.425, 452, 21.225, 22.271, 23.21, 181.

Honour: feels keenly about honour 1.353, 16.84, 90; determined to win glory 18.121, 20.502, 21.543, 22.393, cf. 24.110 (by returning *Hector*'s body).

Parents: ancestry 21.187; appeals to THETIS to intercede with ZEUS 1.393, 407; as baby 9.485; divine mother 1.280, 20.206, 21.109, 24.59; kept informed by THETIS 16.37, 17.409, 18.9, 24.562; Peleus' advice 9.253, 438, 11.784; pity for Peleus 18.331, 19.322, 24.538.

Patroclus: accepts responsibility for Patroclus' death 18.82, 100; asks forgiveness from Patroclus 24.592; blood-price for Patroclus 21.28, 23.22; cannot forget Patroclus 22.390, 23.4, 24.1; cuts hair for Patroclus 23.144; does not want Patroclus to outshine him 16.90; fears for Patroclus' safety 16.247, 18.6; ignorant of Patroclus' death 17.402, 641; visited by spirit of Patroclus 23.65.

Priam: admires *Priam* 24.629; counsels *Priam* 24.518; pities *Priam* 24.516.

Walk-out: embassy 9.112, 11.609, 16.84, 18.448; leaves the fighting 1.306; return foretold 2.694, 8.474, cf. 9.702, 15.68; stays out of fighting 1.489, 2.688, 772, 4.512, 7.229, 10.106, 13.746 (cf. 14.139), 14.367; watches fighting 11.599, 16.255; will return home 1.169, 9.356.

Aeneas

Battlefield: attacks Diomedes 5.225, Idomeneus 13.500, Achilles 20.160; his troops

2.819; kills his man 5.541,
13.541, 15.332, 17.343; runs
from Menelaus and Antilochus
5.571; saved by *APHRODITE*
from Diomedes 5.311; saved by
APOLLO 5.344; saved by
POSEIDON 20.325; urges
Pandarus to take on Diomedes
5.171; urged on by *APOLLO*
17.323, 20.79.

Other: anger at *Priam* 13.460;
as good as *Hector* 5.467, 6.78;
escaped from Achilles earlier
20.90, 191; parentage 5.247,
313, 20.208; view of human
speech 20.244.

Agamemnon

Achilles and his men:
acknowledged by Achilles
23.890; acknowledges mistakes
in dealing with Achilles 2.377,
9.115, 515, 19.90 (see also
DELUSION); dishonours
Achilles and others 1.356, 412,
507, 9.111, 647, 13.113,
16.274, 18.445; fondness for
Menelaus 4.169, 10.124,
11.139; insults Odysseus 4.338,
Diomedes 4.370.

Battlefield: arms 11.16;
encouraged by POSEIDON
14.143; feat of arms 11.91; kills
his man 5.38, 533, 6.33, 64,
11.92, 93, 101, 122, 246, 260;
praises Teucer 8.281; prevents
Menelaus challenging *Hector*
7.109; retreats 8.78, 11.273;
reviews troops 4.223; storms
weak points of *Ilium* 6.435; tells
Menelaus to take no prisoners
6.55; tests Greeks 2.73; troops

2.569; volunteers to challenge
Hector 7.162; wounded
11.252.

Capacities, feelings: authority
(or lack of it) 1.231, 281, 9.38,
98; bullies the weak 1.11, 32,
106, 379; commands the most
troops 1.281, 2.577; coward
1.225, 9.42; deceived by dream
2.36; demands compensation
1.118, 135, *Briseis* 1.184,
obedience 1.185, 286, 9.158;
described by Helen 3.178;
gloomy about expedition/
recommends flight 2.114, 8.236,
9.17, 10.9, 91, 14.44, 75; greed
1.122, 2.226; mad 1.342;
outrageous behaviour 1.203,
205, 214; outstanding 2.476,
578, 23.890; prefers *Chryseis* to
Clytaemnestra 1.113; threatens
others 1.138, 145, 2.391; yields
to criticism 14.104.

Criticized: by Achilles 9.308,
Diomedes 9.32, Nestor 9.105,
Odysseus 14.83, POSEIDON
13.108, Thersites 2.225 (see also
under Achilles).

Deluded by BLIND FOLLY:
1.412, 2.111, 8.237, 9.18, 115,
119, 16.274, 19.88, 136, 270.

Ajax, son of Oïleus (from Locris, The Lesser)

argues with Idomeneus over
horse-race 23.450; foot-race
23.754, 774; inspired by
POSEIDON 13.6; kills his man
14.442, 520, 16.332; not as
good as Ajax son of Telamon
2.529; retreats 8.79; rallies
Greeks 12.268; stays close to

gods 11.80, 13.8; forbids intervention 8.7; kind to ATHENE 8.39, 22.183; laughs at gods fighting 21.389; lets gods fight it out 20.24; older and wiser than POSEIDON 13.355; stronger than POSEIDON 15.162 (cf. 13.355); superior power 1.581, 4.56, 8.18, 211, 450, 15.23, 107, 132, 16.688, 17.176, 21.193; tells APHRODITE to forget warfare 5.428; threatened with binding 1.399.

Omens, signs: eagle omen 8.247, 24.315; sends bloody shower 11.53, 16.459, false dream 2.6, lightning 2.353, 8.76, 17.595, storm 12.252; shakes aegis 17.593; signals victory for Trojans 8.170, 9.236; signs 4.381; snake omen 2.308; spreads darkness 16.567; thunders 7.479, 8.75, 15.377, 17.595, 20.56; unleashes lightning bolt 8.133; see also Omens.

Other: changes mind 17.546; deceitful 2.114; holds the scales of fate 8.69, 16.658, 19.223, 22.209; honours rulers 1.175, 279, 2.197; ignores the fighting 13.3; laments Sarpedon 16.433, Hector 22.168; oversees agreements 3.276, 4.160, 235, 7.76, 411 cf. 22.254; plots the future 8.470, 11.191, 13.347, 15.61, 232, 599, 16.249, 644, 17.201, 443, 21.230, 24.110, 145; power over human affairs 2.118, 3.65, 8.143, 16.688, 17.176, 18.328, 20.242; previous lovers 14.315; rejects prayers 2.419, 3.302; respect for Trojans 4.48, cf. 13.633; saves Sarpedon 5.662, 12.402; supports Trojans/Hector 11.163, 200, 12.174, 252, 437, 13.55, 15.231, 461, 594, 612, 694, 17.331, 627 cf. hates Trojans 20.306; urn of good and evil 24.527; watches the fighting 8.51, 11.82, 16.644, 20.23; will/purpose 1.5, cf. 19.273.

PENGUIN ⟨𝐏⟩ CLASSICS

The Classics Publisher

'Penguin Classics, one of the world's greatest series.' JOHN KEEGAN

'I have never been disappointed with the Penguin Classics. All I have read is a model of academic seriousness and provides the essential information to fully enjoy the master works that appear in its catalogue.' MARIO VARGAS LLOSA

'Penguin and Classics are words that go together like horse and carriage or Mercedes and Benz. When I was a university teacher I always prescribed Penguin editions of classic novels for my courses: they have the best introductions, the most reliable notes, and the most carefully edited texts.' DAVID LODGE

'Growing up in Bombay, expensive hardback books were beyond my means, but I could indulge my passion for reading at the roadside bookstalls that were well stocked with all the Penguin paperbacks ... Sometimes I would choose a book just because I was attracted by the cover, but so reliable was the Penguin imprimatur that I was never once disappointed by the contents.

Such access certainly broadened the scope of my reading, and perhaps it's no coincidence that so many Merchant Ivory films have been adapted from great novels, or that those novels are published by Penguin.' ISMAIL MERCHANT

'You can't write, read, or live fully in the present without knowing the literature of the past. Penguin Classics opens the door to a treasure house of pure pleasure, books that have never been bettered, which are read again and again with increased delight.' JOHN MORTIMER

CLICK ON A CLASSIC
www.penguinclassics.com

The world's greatest literature at your fingertips

Constantly updated information on over 1600 titles, from
Icelandic sagas to ancient Indian epics, Russian drama to
Italian romance, American greats to African masterpieces

•

The latest news on recent additions to the list, updated
editions and specially commissioned translations

•

Original scholarly essays by leading writers: Elaine Showalter
on Zola, Laurie R King on Arthur Conan Doyle, Frank
Kermode on Shakespeare, Lisa Appignanesi on Tolstoy

•

A wealth of background material, including biographies
of every classic author from Aristotle to Zamyatin, plot
synopses, readers' and teachers' guides, useful web links

•

Online desk and examination copy assistance for academics

•

Trivia quizzes, competitions, giveaways, news on
forthcoming screen adaptations

•

eBooks available to download

READ MORE IN PENGUIN

In every corner of the world, on every subject under the sun, Penguin represents quality and variety – the very best in publishing today.

For complete information about books availabale from Penguin – including Puffins, Penguin Classics and Arkana – and how to order them, write to us at the appropriate address below. Please note that for copyright reasons the selection of books varies from country to country.

In the United Kingdom: *Please write to* Dept EP, Penguin Books Ltd, Bath Road, Harmondsworth, West Drayton, Middlesex UB7 0DA

In the United States: *Please write to* Consumer Services, Penguin Putnam Inc., 405 Murray Hill Parkway, East Rutherford, New Jersey 07073-2136. *VISA and MasterCard holders call 1-800-631-8571 to order Penguin titles*

In Canada: *Please write to* Penguin Books Canada Ltd, 10 Alcorn Avenue, Suite 300, Toronto, Ontario M4V 3B2

In Australia: *Please write to* Penguin Books Australia Ltd, 487 Maroondah Highway, Ringwood, Victoria 3134

In New Zealand: *Please write to* Penguin Books (NZ) Ltd, Private Bag 102902, North Shore Mail Centre, Auckland 10

In India: *Please write to* Penguin Books India Pvt Ltd, 11 Community Centre, Panchsheel Park, New Delhi 110017

In the Netherlands: *Please write to* Penguin Books Netherlands bv, Postbus 3507, NL-1001 AH Amsterdam

In Germany: *Please write to* Penguin Books Deutschland GmbH, Metzlerstrasse 26, 60594 Frankfurt am Main

In Spain: *Please write to* Penguin Books S. A., Bravo Murillo 19, 1°B, 28015 Madrid

In Italy: *Please write to* Penguin Italia s.r.l., Via Vittoria Emanuele 451a, 20094 Corsico, Milano

In France: *Please write to* Penguin France, 12, Rue Prosper Ferradou, 31700 Blagnac

In Japan: *Please write to* Penguin Books Japan Ltd, Iidabashi KM-Bldg, 2-23-9 Koraku, Bunkyo-Ku, Tokyo 112-0004

In South Africa: *Please write to* Penguin Books South Africa (Pty) Ltd, P.O. Box 751093, Gardenview, 2047 Johannesburg

VIRGIL

The Aeneid

'I sing of arms and of the man'

After a century of civil strife in Rome and Italy, Virgil wrote *The Aeneid* to honour the emperor Augustus by praising Aeneas – Augustus' legendary ancestor. As a patriotic epic imitating Homer, *The Aeneid* also provided Rome with a literature equal to that of Greece. It tells of Aeneas, survivor of the sack of Troy, and of his seven-year journey: to Carthage, falling tragically in love with Queen Dido; then to the underworld, in the company of the Sibyl of Cumae; and finally to Italy, where he founded Rome. It is a story of defeat and exile, of love and war, hailed by Tennyson as 'the stateliest measure ever moulded by the lips of man'.

David West's acclaimed prose translation is accompanied by his revised introduction and individual prefaces to the twelve books of *The Aeneid*.

'The most truthful translation ever, conveying as many nuances and whispers as are possible from the original' *The Times*

'Sweet prose, clear and clean and dancing like a mountain stream, as here ... West opens the window and the winds bring life into Virgil's body' *Wall Street Journal*

Translated with an introduction by DAVID WEST

HOMER

The Odyssey

*'I long to reach my home and see the day of my
return. It is my never-failing wish'*

The epic tale of Odysseus and his ten-year journey home after
the Trojan War forms one of the earliest and greatest works of
Western literature. Confronted by natural and supernatural
threats – shipwrecks, battles, monsters and the implacable
enmity of the sea-god Poseidon – Odysseus must test his bravery
and native cunning to the full if he is to reach his homeland
safely and overcome the obstacles that, even there, await him.

E. V. Rieu's translation of *The Odyssey* was the very first
Penguin Classic to be published, and has itself achieved classic
status. For this edition, Rieu's text has been sensitively revised
and a new introduction added to complement his original
introduction.

**'One of the world's most vital tales ... The Odyssey remains
central to literature' MALCOLM BRADBURY**

Translated by E. V. RIEU
Revised translation by D. C. H. RIEU
With an introduction by PETER JONES

BAMBA SUSO
AND BANNA KANUTE
Sunjata

Famous across West Africa from Guinea to the Gambia, through Mali and into Burkina Faso, the heroic exploits of Sunjata – based on events in the early thirteenth century – are still constantly being reinterpreted in many different media.

Sunjata started life as a gluttonous and slow-witted child, but went on to become a celebrated warrior, who defeated the Susu overlords and founded the great Mali empire, which lasted two centuries. Equally crucial was the role of his sister Nene Faamaga, who seduced his arch-enemy Sumanguru into revealing the secret magical powers which made him invulnerable.

These stories remain central to the culture of the Mande-speaking peoples. This book brings together translations of live performances by two leading Gambian *Jalis* (or bards). Where Banna Kanute's exciting version is all about violent action, supernatural forces and the struggle for mastery, Bamba Suso uses far more dialogue to reveal his insight into human relationships. A map, notes and lists of characters (many of whom have several names) help non-specialists gain access to one of the major epic traditions of Africa.

Translated and annotated by GORDON INNES
Edited with an introduction and additional notes by
LUCY DURÁN *and* GRAHAM FURNISS

ARISTOPHANES
Lysistrata and Other Plays

'We women have the salvation of Greece in our hands'

Writing at a time of political and social crisis in Athens, Aristophanes (*c.* 447–*c.* 385 BC) was an eloquent, yet bawdy, challenger to the demagogue and the sophist. In *Lysistrata* and *The Acharnians*, two pleas for an end to the long war between Athens and Sparta, a band of women and a lone peasant respectively defeat the political establishment. The darker comedy of *The Clouds* satirizes Athenian philosophers, Socrates in particular, and reflects the uncertainties of a generation in which all traditional religious and ethical beliefs were being challenged.

For this edition Alan Sommerstein has completely revised his translation of the three plays, bringing out the full nuances of Aristophanes' ribald humour and intricate word play, with a new introduction explaining the historical and cultural background to the plays.

Translated with an introduction and notes by
ALAN H. SOMMERSTEIN

PLATO

The Republic

'We are concerned with the most important of issues, the choice between a good and an evil life'

Plato's *Republic* is widely acknowledged as the cornerstone of Western philosophy. Presented in the form of a dialogue between Socrates and three different interlocutors, it is an inquiry into the notion of a perfect community and the ideal individual within it. During the conversation other questions are raised: what is goodness; what is reality; what is knowledge? *The Republic* also addresses the purpose of education and the roles of both women and men as 'guardians' of the people. With remarkable lucidity and deft use of allegory, Plato arrives at a depiction of a state bound by harmony and ruled by 'philosopher kings'.

Desmond Lee's translation of *The Republic* has come to be regarded as a classic in its own right. His introduction discusses contextual themes such as Plato's disillusionment with Athenian politics and the trial of Socrates. This new edition also features a revised bibliography.

Translated with an introduction by DESMOND LEE